CADOGAN GUIDES

"Cadogan Guides are mini-encyclopaedic ... they give the explorer, the intellectual or culture buff—indeed, any visitor—all they need to know to get the best from their visit ... a good read too by the many inveterate armchair travellers.'
—The Book Journal

"The quality of writing in this British series is exceptional ... From practical facts to history, customs, sightseeing, food and lodging, the Cadogan Series can be counted on for interesting detail and informed recommendations."
—Going Places (US)

"Standouts these days are the Cadogan Guides ... sophisticated, beautifully written books."

—American Bookseller Magazine

"Entertaining companions, with sharp insights, local gossip and far more of a feeling of a living author ... The series has received plaudits worldwide for intelligence, originality and a slightly irreverent sense of fun."
—The Daily Telegraph

D0822401

Other titles in the Cadogan Guides s

AUSTRALIA
BALI
BERLIN
THE CARIBBEAN
ECUADOR,
   THE GALÁPAGOS
   & COLOMBIA
GREEK ISLANDS
INDIA
IRELAND
ITALIAN ISLANDS
ITALY
MOROCCO
NEW YORK
NORTHEAST ITALY
NORTHWEST ITALY
PORTUGAL
PRAGUE

ROM
SCOTLAND
SOUTH ITALY
SOUTHERN SPAIN
SPAIN
THAILAND & BURMA (Myanmar)
TUNISIA
TURKEY
TUSCANY, UMBRIA &
   THE MARCHES
VENICE

Forthcoming:

AMSTERDAM
CENTRAL AMERICA
GERMANY
PARIS
SOUTH OF FRANCE

To Helen
With love

ABOUT THE AUTHORS

Katharine and Charlotte Thompson grew up on a hill farm in Perthshire, Scotland.
After studying English and Italian at Edinburgh University, Katharine alternated
between living in Italy and working in publishing. Charlotte studied English and
American Literature and Film at the University of East Anglia and then joined a
six-month archaeological expedition to remote parts of Mexico and Guatemala.

To research a country the size of Mexico required ingenuity, fortitude and a sense of
humour. The Thompsons travelled in light aircraft, on the back of vegetable lorries, by
train, in a battered VW Beetle, even on horseback. They wrote the final text in the
relative calm of a Suffolk farmhouse.

Despite living in each other's pockets, the Thompson sisters remain good friends. As a
direct result of their love of Mexico and their skill in portraying it in this book, they have
returned to Mexico as co-editors of its most respected travel and historical magazine.

PLEASE NOTE

Every effort has been made to ensure the accuracy of the information in this book at the time of going to
press. However, practical details such as opening hours, travel information, standards in hotels and
restaurants and, in particular, prices are liable to change.

We will be delighted to receive any corrections and suggestions for improvement which can be
incorporated into the next edition, but cannot accept any responsibility for consequences arising from the
use of this guide.

We intend to keep this book as up-to-date as possible in the coming years, so **please do write** to us.
Writers of the best letters will receive a free copy of the Cadogan Guide of their choice.

CADOGAN GUIDES

MEXICO

KATHARINE and CHARLOTTE THOMPSON

CADOGAN BOOKS
London

THE GLOBE PEQUOT PRESS
Chester, Connecticut

Cadogan Books plc
London House, Parkgate Road, London, SW11 4NQ

The Globe Pequot Press
6 Business Park Road, PO Box 833, Old Saybrook, Connecticut 06475 - 0833

Cover design by Keith Pointing
Cover illustration by Povl Webb
Maps © Cadogan Books plc
Index by Valerie Elliston

Editor: Lorna Horsefield
Series Editors: Rachel Fielding and Paula Levey

First published 1991
Reprinted 1996

British Library Cataloguing in Publication Data

Thompson, Katharine
  Mexico.—(Cadogan guides).
  1. Mexico
  I. Title   II. Thompson, Charlotte
  917.204834

ISBN 0–947754 18–0

Library of Congress Cataloging-in-Publication Data

Thompson, Katharine
  Mexico / Katharine and Charlotte Thompson: illustrations by Lucy Milne.
    p.   cm.—(Cadogan guides)
  Includes bibliographical references and index.
  ISBN 0–87106–151–1
  1. Mexico—Description and travel—1981-   —Guide-books.
I. Thompson, Charlotte, 1966–   II. Title.   III. Series.
F1209.T46   1991   91–14547
917.204'834—dc20   CIP

Printed in Great Britain by Redwood Books Ltd

CONTENTS

Acknowledgements *Page ix*

Introduction *Page xii*

The Best of Mexico *Pages xiii–xiv*

Part I: General Information *Pages 1–28*

Part II: Mexican Culture *Pages 29–50*

THE CENTRE
Part III: Mexico City and the State of Mexico *Pages 51–105*

CONTENTS

vi

THE NORTH
Part IX: Querétaro, Guanajuato, Aguascalientes and Zacatecas Pages 253-91

Part X: The Northwest Pages 292-350

Part XI: San Luis Potosí and the Northeast Pages 351-81

THE SOUTH
Part XII: Oaxaca Pages 382-419

Part XIII: Tabasco and Chiapas *Pages 420–54*

Part XIV: The Yucatán Peninsula *Pages 455–517*

Glossary of Architectural Terms *Page 518*

Language *Pages 519–23*

Further Reading *Pages 524–25*

Index *Pages 526–38*

LIST OF MAPS

ACKNOWLEDGEMENTS

More than anyone else we would like to thank John and Sarah Wiseman for their unfailing support and good humour throughout our many visits to Mexico and Ian Graham who introduced us to Mexico and generously lent us his house while we wrote the book.

The Mexican Departments of Tourism helped us immeasurably: in particular Victor Hugo Vidal of Mexico City, Nini in San Luis Potosí, Adalberto Goena in Mazatlán, Licenciada Victoria Barron and Memo Suárez in Chihuahua, Abel Ramírez in Oaxaca and Don William Sosa in Mérida. We are indebted to Raul Ortiz y Ortiz for all his help with the language section.

A big thanks to all those who helped along the road: first and foremost all the mechanics of Mexico who kept us on it, Antonio and Cristina Galvez, Colinette Gallienne and, of course, our parents, Ann and Christopher Thompson.

Last but not least, many thanks to Paula Levey for throwing us headlong into the book and to Lorna Horsfield, our invisible editor, for fishing us out.

Tijuana

Agua Prieta
Ciudad Juárez

①

②
Nogales

②
Casas
Grandes

BAJA CALIFORNIA

⑮ SONORA
Hermosillo

Chihuahua

Cd. Acuña

CHIHUAHUA
Guaymas

BAJA CALIFORNIA

①

Hidalgo del Parral

⑮

COAHUILA

⑮

Pacific Ocean

Loreto

BAJA CALIFORNIA SUR

3

SINALOA

⑰

⑲ Torreón
Saltill

La Paz

DURANGO

ZACATECA

ESCALA GRAFICA
0 80 160 240
Kilómetros

⑮ Durango

Mazatlán

Zacatecas

Los Cabos

Cities
1 Distrito Federal
2 Villahermosa
3 Los Mochis
4 Cd. Victoria
5 Cuernavaca

NAYARIT
Tepic →

⑥

⑤⑤

⑥

⑤④

⑤⑤

Guadalajara

GU

Puerto Vallarta

JALISCO

N

States
6 AGUASCALIENTES
7 MEXICO STATE
8 MORELOS
9 QUERETARO
10 TABASCO
11 TLAXCALA

⑳⑳

⑪⑩

COLIMA

MICHC

Zihuatanejo

Pacific

MEXICO

INTRODUCTION

Mexico is a subtle country which is keen to play up to others' preconceptions. It still has the cactus landscape of countless Sunday afternoon westerns where sombrero-clad horsemen fade into the sunset, miles of sultry tropical beaches where film stars flirted in the fifties and the crumbling Aztec pyramids of children's adventure books. But Mexico is much more.

Vividly full of life, pulsing to the music of the *mariachi, son, cumbias, salsa* and *merengue*, it is the canvas for Diego Rivera's monumental murals, home of intellectuals such as Octavio Paz and Carlos Fuentes and adoptive home of Gabriel García Márquez. It is also the land of revolutionaries such as Pancho Villa and Emiliano Zapata and the one-time refuge of León Trotsky, André Breton and Luis Buñuel.

The Tropic of Cancer cuts across it and the Sierra Madre mountains form its spine, running down to the threatened jungle in the south. Its heaving cities have recently leapt from the 19th to 21st centuries, leaving great parts of rural Mexico far behind. Its coast is generous, with thousands of miles of coastline hiding secret bays lapped by translucent waters, where exotic fish swim about the coral reefs like pouting debutantes.

Arrive expecting appointments to be met (sharp time-keeping is laughingly referred to as *hora inglés*) and the languid Latin *mañana* will bring a nervous tic to the eye. Time is a floating concept and appointments rarely keep to a schedule. Lunches begin at 4 o'clock in the afternoon and last till the next day, fiestas in villages go on all week and tomorrow rarely exists. Mexico is mischievous. Any question will be answered in the affirmative, not least because of a desire to please. Rhetorical questions are disastrous. If a confused tourist, searching a timetable, asks, 'The train leaves in an hour, doesn't it?', the answer will always be 'Yes', even if the train is at that moment steaming out of the station. At the same time, the Mexican is equally perplexed by foreign visitors, smiling with incomprehension at white-kneed tourists rushing from pyramid to pyramid.

The people of Mexico fit no mould. It is a nation that has been conquered more than once and few but the very upper echelons of society or inhabitants of remote villages can claim blood which is not a blend of European and native American. Spanish influence continues in many towns. Braided girls still peep from behind colonial shutters and massive wooden doors open onto wide courtyards with flowering lime trees. Dignified and gentle, the Mexicans will accept the discerning traveller with graciousness but their past, strewn with wars, revolutions and invasions, has taught them to take nothing at face value. And that nothing includes traffic lights, death, politics and love. None of these fits a rule—rules after all are only made to be broken.

The Best of Mexico

This is admittedly subjective and only touches on the best of Mexico, but it should at least provide argument and incentive.

Artisania: the states of Oaxaca, Michoacán and Chiapas.

Beaches: the Caribbean coast, especially south of Tulum ruins (Quintana Roo).

Books: *Distant Neighbours* by Alan Riding (sold in Britain as *Inside the Volcano*); *Labyrinth of Solitude* by Octavio Paz.

Bookshop: El Parnaso, Coyoacán, Mexico City.

Colonial cities: Puebla (Puebla), San Miguel de Allende (Guanajuato), Morelia (Michoacán), Oaxaca (Oaxaca).

Dancing in the streets: the port of Veracruz (Veracruz), Sta Eulalia (Chihuahua).

Diving: Cozumel (Quintana Roo) and the Caribbean.

Ex-mining villages: Real de Catorce (San Luis Potosí) and Alamos (Sonora).

Festivals: the Day of the Dead in Michoacán (2 November), Good Friday in San Juan Chamula and Zinacantán (Chiapas), and Easter in Taxco (Guerrero).

Film: *María Candelaria* (1943) directed by Emilio Fernández, with Dolores del Río and Pedro Armendáriz.

Fruit: pithaya (see Yucatán).

Heroes: Cuauhtémoc, Hidalgo, Zapata and Cárdenas.

Hill towns: San Cristóbal de las Casas (Chiapas), Guanajuato (Guanajuato), Taxco (Guerrero).

Hill villages: Tapalpa (Jalisco) and Cuetzalán (Puebla).

Hotels:

Expensive: Stouffer Presidente in Oaxaca.

Moderate: several in Mérida (Yucatán); Posada de la Fuente, Tapalpa (Jalisco); Osho, Tulum (Quintana Roo); Hacienda, Uxmal (Yucatán).

Dirt cheap: Casa de Huéspedes, Mérida (Yucatán) or Room 6, Posada Jackelin, Cuetzalán (Puebla).

Lake: Pátzcuaro (Michoacán).

Markets: Villages around San Cristóbal de las Casas (Chiapas); Tancanhuitz on Sunday (San Luis Potosí); Cuetzalán on Thursday or Sunday (Puebla); and, for food, San Juan (Mexico City).

Monasteries: the Franciscans' in the Sierra Gorda (Querétaro).

Month of the Year: October.

Mountain road: the drive from Mazatlán to Durango.

Murals:

Pre-Hispanic: Bonampak (Chiapas), Cacaxtla (Tlaxcala).

20th-century: Diego Rivera's series in the SEP building (Mexico City) and Orozco's in Guadalajara (Jalisco).

Museums: the Museum of Anthropology (Mexico City); Regional Museum, Tepic (Nayarit); Museum of Science and Technology, Monterrey (Nuevo León).

Pre-Hispanic ruins: Palenque (Chiapas), Mitla (Oaxaca), Uxmal (Yucatán.)

Railway: Chihuahua–Pacífico across the Sierra Madre (Chihuahua).

Resorts:
  Expensive: Puerto Vallarta (Jalisco), Huatulco (Oaxaca).
  Moderate: Puerto Escondido (Oaxaca).
  Cheap: Playa del Carmen (Quintana Roo).
Restaurant: Willy's in Mazatlán (Colima).
Tequila: Siete Leguas, Real Hacienda, Herradura.
Whale-watching: Los Cabos in January (Baja California).

Part I

GENERAL INFORMATION

Chac-Mool, Toltec messenger of the gods

Before You Go

Getting to Mexico

By Air

There is a plethora of flights from the USA and Canada to various destinations in Mexico. Europe is just beginning to wake up to Mexico and an increasing number of charter flights are flying into the two big holiday resorts, Acapulco and Cancún. Distances in Mexico are so huge that it may be worthwhile flying in and out from different cities. It is quite easy to fly into Mexico City and out from Mérida, for example, thereby saving two or three days' travelling time.

SCHEDULED FLIGHTS FROM EUROPE

Air France, KLM and Lufthansa fly to Mexico from Paris, Amsterdam and Frankfurt respectively (with connecting flights from London), all with stop-overs in the USA. Continental, American Airlines and PanAm have connecting flights from London, and KLM also fly from Glasgow, Edinburgh and Manchester. Northwest Airlines operate a direct flight from Glasgow to Boston. The cheapest way is to buy a discount flight from Europe to Miami, and pick up a ticket down to Mexico from there. Flights may already be full at Christmas and Easter. The main airports for transatlantic flights are Mexico City, Mérida, Cancún and Acapulco.

1

SCHEDULED FLIGHTS FROM NORTH AMERICA

Airlines such as Aeroméxico, Mexicana, PanAm, Continental and Delta run daily flights to Mexico City and regional centres, from all major cities in the United States and Canada.

Flights are generally cheaper from Monday to Thursday. An 'open-jaw' ticket will enable you to fly into one city and return from another (eg fly into Mexico City and return from Mérida).

CHARTER FLIGHTS

Mexican resorts are rapidly becoming package destinations, even from as far afield as Europe. Look in newspapers and listings magazines for details of flights, which are getting cheaper every year. Consider buying a package to Acapulco for the cheap flight alone. There is an enormous number of package deals and cheap flights to Mexico from the USA and Canada: it is worth shopping around travel agents for competitive prices.

UK TRAVEL AGENTS

Whilst flights from Europe are becoming more frequent and therefore cheaper, few travel agents specialize in flights to Mexico. Of those that do, the ever-resourceful Trailfinders (42–50 Earl's Court Rd, London W8 6EJ, tel 071 938 3366) have a large and flexible selection of cheap flights, as do Journey Latin America (14–16 Devonshire Rd, London W4 2HD, tel 081 747 3108) (see below). South American Experience (Garden Studios, 11–15 Betterton St, Covent Garden, London WC2H 9BP, tel 071 379 0344) is another specialist company.

STUDENTS

The Student Travel Centre in London (tel 071 434 1306) and STA Travel (74 Old Brompton Road, London SW7, tel 071 937 9962) can both arrange flights to Mexico, as do student travel agencies throughout the country. To qualify for a student flight, you will need a valid matriculation or international student card.

TOURS

Although this book is designed for independent travellers, small tours, such as those mentioned below, can take the strain out of a first visit. In the UK, Journey Latin America (14–16 Devonshire Rd, London W4 2HD, tel 081 747 3108) specialize in tours focused on seeing the real Mexico. Always friendly and reliable, they are also particularly good at recommending cheap flights and routes in and out of the country. Encounter Overland (267 Old Brompton Rd, London SW5 9JA, tel 071 370 6845) arrange 'adventure tours'. More upmarket, Serenissima Travel (21 Dorset Sq, London NW1, tel 071 730 9841) arrange tours of the Maya ruins, through both Mexico and Guatemala.

In the USA, Pacific Adventure Tours (PO Box 5041, Riverside, Calif 92517, tel 714 684 1227) run outdoor tours specializing in horse-back riding, kayaking, scuba diving and sailing. Mayan Adventure Tours (PO Box 15204, Wedgewood Station, Seattle, Washington 98115–15204, tel 206 523 5309) specialize in trips to smaller Maya sites which aren't generally visited. They confine numbers to nine or ten per group.

The Mexican Tourist office can send lists and brochures of all tours available.

By Bus and Car

There are 24 border crossings between Mexico and the USA. The main entry points, from west to east, are Tijuana, Mexicali, Ciudad Juárez, Piedras Negras, Nuevo Laredo, Reynosa and Matamoros. Border controls have recently been relaxed to allow buses to continue from the USA to destinations in Mexico.

Bear in mind the long distances to be covered before deciding to come by car. Road surfaces aren't good and motorways are a rich and rare treat. Mexico City is a long, two-day drive from the US border. There are three main routes down: via Highway 15 on the west coast, Highway 45 through the centre or Highway 57 on the east coast. Petrol is cheap but a two-week holiday may get eaten up behind the wheel.

On the other hand, car hire within Mexico is very expensive. Look out for fly/drive offers, or try to agree a rate with a big international company like Hertz or Budget before arriving.

By Train

The Mexican Ferrocarril del Pacífico runs down the Pacific Coast, from Tijuana on the northern border (south of San Diego) to Mexico City. There are also border rail links at Agua Prieta, Ciudad Juárez, Nuevo Laredo and Matamoros. This may be the cheapest way to travel down, but it is also the most time-consuming and frustrating. Trains are invariably hot and subject to long delays: save the experience for a shorter journey.

Formalities

Passports and Visas

The Mexicans are happy to welcome to Mexico anyone in possession of a valid passport. Every visitor will be given a **tourist card** (FMT) to fill in: this is then stamped by the immigration officials and should be retained at all times. Tourist cards are available at borders, Mexican consulates, Mexican Tourist Offices and on incoming aeroplanes. They are valid for 30 days but can be extended for up to six months at any immigration office. In Mexico City, these extensions can be applied for at the Dirección General de Servicios Migratorios, Calle Albañiles (tel 795 6685). Business visitors need a business card which should be applied for, well in advance, from a Mexican Consulate. In theory, tourists should show a ticket out of the country and sufficient funds to maintain themselves during their stay, but in practice these formalities are usually waived.

As most aeroplanes from Europe stop in the United States, European travellers will normally require a **US visa**. Check with the airline. Visa Shop Ltd in London (tel 071 379 0419) can arrange rapid processing of visas.

Happy to welcome you, the Mexicans get their pound of flesh as you leave, when an airport tax of at least $12.00 is charged. No-one can leave without paying.

Insurance

Possessions have as good a chance of going missing in Mexico as anywhere and health even more so. Insurance is not only advisable but essential. Choose an insurance company with a 24-hour emergency number and one that will speak your own language if your Spanish isn't up to a crisis. Many credit card companies, such as Access/Master-card, automatically issue a form of travel insurance, whereas American Express offer Centurion Assistance, an excellent policy for card holders. Endsleigh Insurance (tel 0242 223300 or 071 436 4451 in UK; 213 937 5714 or 212 986 9470 in USA; 416 977 3703 in Canada) have the most efficient policy for longer stays and will reimburse claims in Mexico City.

Foreigners are not eligible for state medical care in Mexico, and have to go to private hospitals, which are expensive. All doctors automatically up their bills on hearing a foreign vowel and full health cover is a wise precaution.

Car insurance is not a legal requirement (and most Mexicans don't bother) but police can slap unsuspecting tourists into jail unless they can prove their innocence and their ability to pay for damages in an accident. The only recognized insurance is Mexican insurance and this can be bought at all towns on the US/Mexican border.

Inoculations
Go to see a doctor at least six weeks before leaving to have any necessary inoculations. Those recommended for Mexico are typhoid (two injections a month apart), tetanus, polio (drops) and hepatitis (a blood test will be done first to see whether you are immune). Mexican doctors insist that there is no malaria in Mexico, but if you are likely to be going to the southern border region or over into Guatemala, it is worth packing some Chloroquine pills, at least. (Alternatively, you can buy malaria pills over the counter at chemists in Mexico: ask local advice.) Foreign embassies and consulates can supply lists of English-speaking doctors. (See also Health, On Arrival.)

Geography

It is a proposition of Mexican geographical logic that the nearest way
between two points is by a distant third.
—Sybille Bedford, *A Visit to Don Otavio*

Eight times the size of Great Britain or the state of Oregon and four times the size of Spain or France, Mexico is a vast, tropical country of high plateaux and mountain ranges, bordered to east and west by over 8000 km of coastline. From the desert plains in the north to the shrinking rain forests in the south, the spiny back of the long, high Sierra Madre bisects the country, making 50 per cent of the land too steep for farming. During Mexico's stormy past, volcanoes and earthquakes pushed up silver, copper, mercury and lead, providing rich mining land for modern technology. Gold and silver poured out for the Spanish, as oil does for the modern age.

Shaped like a hunting horn, Mexico is the buffer state between the jungle lands of Central America to the south and the developed lands of the United States in the north. The narrow Isthmus of Tehuantepec was once submerged, representing a literal split between the two continents. Mexico's geography has had to cope with this split ever since. Creases and folds of mountains and gorges rip across the country, making the terrain a complicated morass which comprises an isthmus, a continental mass and two large peninsulas.

4

Northern Mexico

Although northern Mexico makes up 40 per cent of the country, its arid lands are inhabited by under 20 per cent of the people. The long 3326-km northern border with the United States is on the same latitude as Shanghai and Jerusalem, stretching from the Pacific coast at Tijuana across to the Gulf of Mexico in the east. Mexican territory once included California and Texas: now the frontier marks a sharp, uneven division between the high technology of the US and the underdevelopment of its southern neighbour.

In the extreme west, the long, barren peninsula of Baja California is the closest wilderness to southern California. Its beaches, national parks and desert lands, so unconducive to farming, are now drawing in tourists attracted by their isolated rawness. On the mainland, the northwest is largely desert land, softening out along the banks of the Río Sonora. The ancient volcanic rocks which make up the Sierra Madre Occidental separate the coast from the inner plateau of semi-desert lands. On the east side, the limestone Sierra Madre Oriental is a far less divisive mountain chain. A wide corridor passes through the vast industrial city of Monterrey to the savanna lands of the northeast and the Gulf of Mexico.

Central Mexico

Central Mexico has had to contend with the mountains and the volcanoes which brace it like an over-tight belt. From the gentle, orchard-clad slopes of Veracruz in the east, the land climbs up through Hidalgo's agave-covered hills to the Valley of Mexico and Michoacán's volcanic peaks, before meeting the mountains of the west coast which drop sharply into the Pacific ocean. The great central Mexican cities are like islands within this mountainous belt. Veracruz sits on the coast, Fortín de las Flores on the lower slopes of the Sierra Madre Oriental and Mexico City, Toluca and Querétaro on the high central plateau, the **Valley of Mexico**. Some 125 km by 80 km, this valley was formed by volcanic eruptions: at the time of the Aztecs, its floor was covered by five lakes, which were drained by the Spanish. The capital city built on top has been gently subsiding into the soft lake bed ever since.

In central Mexico, **volcanoes** blowing their tops are as much the stuff of fact as legend. The 19th parallel has been the worst hit. In 1943, a crater erupted at the feet of a farmer in Michoacán and swallowed the village of Paricutín, drowning all but the spire of the church in a flood of lava which lasted for ten years. Just as it died down, a second volcano erupted in a tiny Mexican island in the Pacific. Today, it is said that every major city in central Mexico has a volcano outside its window. The tongue-twisting list goes back to the Aztecs: Popocatépetl, Iztaccíhuatl, Malinche and Citlaltépetl. The Colima Volcano, on the Colima–Jalisco border, erupted in April 1991 and still lets off occasional puffs of smoke, accompanied by little deposits of lava flowing down the mountainside.

Southern Mexico

From the central plateau, the Panamerican Highway inches its way south through Oaxaca's mountain passes to the **Isthmus of Tehuantepec** (Mexico's narrowest point) and then curves through oil ports and jungle to the Guatemalan border at Tapachula. From the capital, the direct route to the **Gulf of Mexico** bisects the state of Veracruz, with its fertile, tropical slopes of coffee and banana plantations, orchids, dahlias and gardenias, leading down to the Gulf Coast lowlands. These, flooded again and again by

5

the sea, were left rich deposits of animal and vegetable matter in recompense. Given millions of years to mature, the fossil fuels are now mined as oil, bringing huge wealth and controversy to one of the richest areas in Mexico.

The concave land bordering the Gulf of Mexico forms part of a great coastal plain which starts at Long Island in the US and gently slopes all the way round, through Veracruz and Tabasco to the **Yucatán peninsula**. This flat limestone shelf in the south of the country is out on its own. The dry, thorny land of the north gives way to the rain forest of Guatemala and Belize, Mexico's southern neighbours, bordered on its eastern shores by the opalescent waters of the Caribbean.

When to Go

The Tropic of Cancer cuts through the middle of the country, making October to May, when it is generally dry and warm, the best time of year to visit. The tourist season is from Christmas to Easter, when North Americans and Europeans escape their long winters in the temperate, tropical climate of Mexico. Outside the beach resorts and the well-trodden Cuernavaca–Taxco route, the 'season' as such makes little difference (except for the mad rush of Christmas week and Easter week), but in the resorts, prices of hotel rooms often double.

The wettest months are from June to October. The rains come in the afternoon, in violent two-to-three-hour downpours. Although these wash out roads and refill the dried-out river beds, there is never enough to cover all the needs of farming, industry and the cities. The rainy season is not a bad time to visit for anyone used to, or prepared to put up with, the vagaries of the climate. Teachers, families or students often have no choice. Besides, the weather is warm and the rains make a good excuse for a long siesta.

Hurricanes are considerably less predictable. These huge balls of saturated air hit the Gulf of Mexico and Baja California in September, knocking over buildings and trees like skittles, leaving behind untold damage and flooding.

Climate

The climate depends as much on altitude as latitude. South of the Tropic of Cancer and below 1000 metres, the average annual temperature is 22.5°C, but north of the Tropic and above 1000 metres the average is below 15°C. There are, in effect, two climates: one for the *tierra caliente* or hot land, and one for the *tierra fría* or cold land. Between these two extremes, the *tierra templada*, above the low-lying plains but below the mountain ranges, is where most of the population (and most of the profitable agriculture) is to be found.

Average Annual Temperatures in °C

Acapulco	27	Mérida	26
Cancún	28	Monterrey	29
Chihuahua	18	Morelia	17
Cuernavaca	19	Oaxaca	18
Guadalajara	18	Puerto Vallarta	27
Guanajuato	18	Tijuana	19
Mazatlán	24	Veracruz	24

Time

Most of Mexico is on US Central Standard Time which is between 6 and 7 hours behind Greenwich Mean Time. Exceptions to this are the states of Sonora, Sinaloa and Southern Baja California which are on Mountain Standard Time (an hour behind the rest of the country), and Northern Baja California, which is on Pacific Standard Time (an hour behind MST).

What to Pack

Unless you plan to travel entirely by car, be prepared to carry whatever you bring. A row with the only taxi driver in town or a succession of packed buses flying past may leave you with no option but to struggle on in the hot sun.

Mexico City and the big towns remain formal, and buttock-revealing shorts are looked at somewhat askance. Any location is likely to be baking hot during the day but often quite cool at night, particularly in higher altitudes, and it is worth bringing a sweater or jacket. At night, socks are an invaluable protection against mosquito bites to the ankles. In the summer (from May to October), torrential rain pours down for a couple of hours every afternoon. Either bring a raincoat or be prepared to sit inside and wait for it to stop.

Chemists in all the big towns are well stocked with ordinary toiletries such as soap and shampoo. Less easy to find outside the big cities are tampons, contraceptives and contact-lens solution. Useful but not essential are an alarm clock (buses can leave at horribly early hours), a torch (electricity supplies can cut out during storms or fits of temper), a one-size bath plug (there never seems to be one), a pocket knife, insect repellent and post-bite cream, and playing cards. Photographs or postcards of home always go down well, conveying a sense of exoticism which may be far removed from the truth.

Quetzal bird, one of the rarest and most beautiful in Central America

Tourist Information

Maps, brochures, lists of hotels and travel timetables are available on request from Mexican tourist offices in Europe and North America. If you know where you want to go, ask for information on specific states. Some of their offices are:

Trafalgar Sq, **London**, England (tel 071 734 1058)
Via Barberini 3. 00187 **Roma**, Italy (tel 06 474 2986)
Wiesenhuettenplatz 26, D600 **Frankfurt** 1, Germany (tel 49 69 25 3413)
405 Park Avenue, Suite 1002, **New York**, NY 10022, USA (tel 212 755 7261)
10100 Santa Monica Blvd, Suite 2204, **Los Angeles**, Calif 90067, USA (tel 213 203 8151)
181 University Avenue, Suite 112, **Toronto**, Ontario M5H 3 M9, Canada (tel 416 364 2455)

and in Mexico City the main office is:
DDF, Amberes/Londres, Zona Rosa, Mexico DF (tel 514 0946, 207 5241).

On Arrival

Money and Credit Cards

Mexican pesos are the official currency. Notes begin in ludicrously large denominations and only get bigger: the smallest note is 2000 pesos. It is advisable to order some Mexican pesos from your bank before leaving home (they usually require at least a week's notice): only the more jaded tourist resorts will accept dollars for everything. Larger amounts are best taken in the form of US dollars or dollar traveller's cheques. European currencies are rarely seen in Mexico, and even major banks will often refuse to change them.

All the well-known **credit cards** are accepted, especially in the capital and larger towns. American Express has 15 offices nationwide, which will hold mail or cash traveller's cheques (or reimburse stolen cheques) on the spot. Access, Mastercard or Visa are better for use in shops and restaurants.

Emergency numbers in Mexico city are:
American Express: (5) 578 7122 or (5) 598 8133 (weekends)
Visa: (5) 658 2188
Diners Club: (5) 543 7020.

Although the cost of living is still far less than in the USA or any European country, Mexico is no longer the very cheap country it once was. Variations in the exchange rate and inflation combine to make accurate pricing no more than a hit and miss affair. For an inevitably approximate guide to the costs of food and accommodation, see Where to Stay and Eating Out.

Getting Around

Getting around is an adventure in itself. Somehow, any seemingly straightforward journey from A to B is never quite as predictable as it might appear. The Mexican bus

8

network, with over 800 separate companies, provides the easiest, cheapest, and most regular method of travelling, although the trains have been much improved and the domestic airlines offer the advantage of speed.

By Air

Domestic air fares are reasonably priced, ten times more expensive than a first-class bus but ten times quicker. Mexico is a huge country and flying from one end to another in a few hours can save several days' travelling. For long-distance hauls, between the US border and Mexico City, or between Mexico City and Chiapas (Tuxtla Gutiérrez) or the Yucatán (Mérida or Cancún), it is nearly always worth paying the extra cost of the flight.

Mexicana (tel in Mexico City 680 4444 or in the US (800) 531 7921) and **Aeroméxico** (tel in Mexico City 207 8233 or in the US (1 800) AEROMEX) have connections to all major US and Mexican cities. There is little to choose between the two. Reservations are not normally essential, outside of the busy holiday seasons (Christmas and Easter). They can be made by telephone easily enough, however, and do not have to be confirmed or paid for until three days before the flight.

Private companies have recently opened up new routes across the country. **Small aeroplanes** are often used to get to isolated areas such as jungle sites or mountain villages. Whilst the safety record is eyebrow-raising, there is usually little alternative.

All airports are linked to cities by minibuses and taxis.

By Bus

First-class buses (Pullman) are rapid and direct, while second-class are unhurried and low-slung. Seats can be reserved on first-class buses, and most have nominal air-conditioning and tachograph meters which limit speeds to 95 km/h. Second-class buses have no reserved seats, stop often and are likely to be used for house-moving. Every bus, whether first- or second-class, will have a Virgin of Guadalupe hanging from the driver's mirror or embossed on the head of the gear stick, and will play raunchy ranchera or woeful mariachi music. The best seats are directly behind the steering wheel (though not for back-seat drivers).

Whenever a bus stops, people clamber on selling peanuts, tacos, corn and ices. Often a hard-selling missionary or polemicist will pass around leaflets or gewgaws and then deliver a speech. At the end he'll come round for donations for the gewgaw you didn't want: return it and you won't be asked for anything more.

Holidays, particularly Christmas and Easter, can be bedlam, and tickets should be booked at least a week in advance. Picking up buses midway along a route can also be difficult, as reservations are made only from the principal cities and bus after bus may sail past without any room for extra passengers.

There is no national bus company. The companies all congregate under one roof in the central bus station, known as the 'Central Camionera'. Once right in the centre of cities, these are increasingly being pushed to the outskirts, linked to the main squares by buses and taxis.

By Train

Not so long ago, a journey by train had to include a power cut, a cow on the line, or inexplicable delays in a carriage where the heating was stuck at full blast, the windows didn't work and it was 45°C outside. Things have changed dramatically. Although there are relatively few first-class services, those that exist have been overhauled and are now comfortable, modern and extremely cheap. It is, however, necessary to book as long as possible in advance, either at the station or through a travel agent. Ask for the reserved *Primera Especial* or *Numerada*.

Few people, other than Paul Theroux, have travelled the length of Mexico by train and fewer still would want to, but for one unmissable, unforgettable ride, take the 13-hour Chihuahua–Pacífico through the Sierra Madre mountains, over the Barranca del Cobre and a myriad of narrow passes, twists and bends.

For information on rail services in general, write to the Departamento de Tráfico de Pasajeros, Gran Estación Central de Buenavista, Av Insurgentes Norte, 06358 México DF (tel (5) 547 8972; in the US, AT and T users can dial direct, 011 525 547 8972). For the Chihuahua–Pacífico train, write to PO Box 46, Chihuahua (tel (141) 22284 or 23867).

By Car

Car permits are required for driving anywhere in Mexico except in Baja California. These permits can act as tourist cards and are available at border crossings on production of a driver's licence, passport and proof of ownership of the vehicle. They are valid for 90 days, and the owner must leave the country with the car. (If it has been written off, the nearest embassy or consulate can help with the official forms.) Non-Mexican **insurance** is not valid anywhere in Mexico. Mexican car insurance is not mandatory, but any driver involved in an accident, whether guilty or not, may be imprisoned until proof of ability to pay damages can be shown.

Driving is definitely the best way to see the country, despite the attendant traumas. There are roads to every corner. Some of these are just hard-packed tracks, known as *caminos blancos*, but most are good well-surfaced highways. Hard shoulders, however, are seen as gilding the lily and rarely exist. *Topes* are the Mexican equivalent of speed bumps or sleeping policemen. Often unmarked, or only signposted as you're flying over them with four wheels up in the air, they are unpredictable, as high as Everest and can wreak untold damage on an unsuspecting car. They are usually sited at the outskirts of villages and towns. The north has fewer than the south, with Chiapas winning the booby prize for the most. Avoid driving at night: not least of the hazards are the *topes* and stray animals on the road.

Petrol (*gasolina*) is extremely cheap, and is sold by the state-owned Pemex company. It is plentiful along the highways, but on lesser roads fill up as often as you see an orange Pemex station. The fuel in Mexico is of a lower octane rating than in the US (excellent for Rolls-Royces and not too bad for any other car). Unleaded fuel ('Extra') is a legal requirement at any garage. It is common practice to check that the dials are at zero to avoid being undersold.

Green Angels (*Angeles Verdes*) monitor the main roads every few hours, looking out for cars in distress (flat tyres, no petrol, lost, or overheating engines) and sort out what they can. For more information on this excellent free service, tel (5) 250 0123.

Mechanics (*mecánicos*) in Mexico are extremely resourceful and cheap. They don't believe in buying expensive new parts until anything that can be soldered back in place, hung up by string or given an extra bolt has been tried first.

10

Car hire is just as expensive as in the US or Europe. The main companies are the usual international brigade of Hertz, Avis and Budget Rent-A-Car. Local firms may be cheaper but will probably not accept credit cards. Requirements are generally a valid licence, a passport and a driver over 25. Picking up a car in one city and dropping it off in another involves a large surcharge. The most common hire car is the VW beetle, usually in pristine condition.

By Taxi

Every village has a taxi—essential for the odd fiesta or foreigner. They are generally yellow, with a lighted taxi sign on the roof. Individual operators also wheel their private cars out at the weekend or in the evening and tout for some extra income. Prices are very cheap, but should nevertheless be negotiated before setting off, which provides the unscrupulous with a chance to see what they can get away with. Some of the cheapest rides of all are in Mexico City, while the most expensive are undoubtedly in Mérida and Tijuana.

Combis, *Colectivos* and *Peseros*

In any town, VW vans whizz from one place to another. Known alternatively as combis, *colectivos* or *peseros*, these nippy taxi-buses are a tenth of the price of a taxi and only slightly more than the heavy urban buses. They are often pale green on the outside (though new white micro-buses are now being introduced), while inside the seats will have been ripped out and replaced by planks, to get as many people in as possible. Even so, there will usually be a couple of passengers hanging out of the side door. The driver will have a crucifix hanging off the dashboard and a large sign propped up inside the windscreen displaying his route plan. He has to cope with the traffic whilst sorting out the fares—squashed though the vans are, money is passed from back to front and the change returned.

To hail a combi, flag it down or look for the nearest combi stop. To get off, pay the driver a few blocks in advance (give the exact amount if possible) and pull the bell-string at your stop.

By Thumb

Hitching (known as *un ride* or *aventón*) isn't exactly advised but it can be a fun, quick and direct way to get from A to B. In the south, where ruins and waterfalls are often off the main roads or serviced by only one bus a day, hitching is an accepted practice. Offer to pay a small amount at the end of the journey, particularly for routes which are not covered by buses, even though it will usually be refused. In general, hitching is safer the further south you are. However, it should always be done in twos, with minimum luggage and at least a smattering of Spanish. The states of Sinaloa, Guerrero and Michoacán are not suitable for hitching. Beware too in Baja California, where there are fewer cars on the roads, little shade, only a sprinkling of houses and scorching sun.

Maps

The Mexican tourist office will send a tourist road map (1:350,000) on request. It gives a good overview of Mexico's main roads, airports and railway lines. Better still is the Pemex map, which can be bought in Mexico at large petrol stations and in bookshops.

11

Sorting Things Out

Tourist Offices

There are three tourist information departments in Mexico: federal, state and local. Each is at loggerheads with the others and all complain of lack of finance. The state offices are more accustomed to dealing with foreign tourists and are generally the best. They will produce maps and leaflets, and information on hotels, transport and restaurants, but are unable to stretch much beyond their own state.

Compliments, queries and complaints should be addressed to the federal SECTUR offices, either in the individual states or better still in Mexico City (Av Mazarik 172). A reverse-charge **emergency** telephone number—(5) 658 1111— can be used from any part of the country for any problem, however large or small.

In the beach resorts it is harder to avoid tourist information than to find it. Pamphlets and leaflets are thrust into any beach-clad passer-by's hand and the world is your oyster if you'll just sign your name on the dotted line. Don't! There is no such thing as a free lunch, drink, boat trip or disco. Each offer comes with strings attached, including video presentations and three-hour breakfasts. The young sales people recite their hard sell on time-sharing condominiums until figures fly and any price seems worth it just to get away.

Embassies and Consulates

All the embassies are in Mexico City, on and around the Paseo de la Reforma. Newspapers from home arrive here spasmodically. Embassy staff can renew passports, advise on English-speaking doctors and help with legal difficulties.

Australia: Paseo de la Reforma 195 (tel 556 3055)
Canada: Schiller 529, Polanco 11580 (tel 254 3288)
UK: Río Lerma 71 (tel 511 4880)
USA: Paseo de la Reforma 305 (tel 211 0042).

Post Offices

Nearly every town in Mexico has a post office or *oficina de correos*. Generally on or close to the main square, they are open 09.00–13.00 and 15.00–18.00 on weekdays and 09.00–12.00 on Saturdays. Post boxes or *buzónes* are very common, and are often sited in hotels and shops.

Once mail is in the box, there is no guaranteee of a speedy and safe arrival. Letters often go missing and sending anything important is not recommended. Turning up at a hotel to find that your carefully worded letter of reservation never arrived is a standard complaint. Only a foreigner would send money by post in an unregistered envelope and expect it to arrive. Registered (*registrado*) mail costs double, and comes with a receipt (*recibo*). Always write your own name and address on the back left-hand corner of the envelope and add *por avión* for airmail.

To receive letters en route, make sure they are marked *Lista de Correos* or *Poste Restante*. Post offices will hold *Lista de Correos* mail for up to 10 days, and compile a daily list. *Poste Restante* mail is held for up to a month but a list of what has been sent is kept only rarely (and has to be asked for specifically). If staying in one place for more than a month, it may be worth paying the small fee for a PO box number (known as *apartado postal*). Identification must be provided when picking any mail up.

Banks
Banks are open 09.00–13.00, Monday–Friday. They require an infinite amount of patience and good humour: even the simplest of transactions involves a long queue and reams of paperwork. Queueing becomes a form of Russian roulette. No matter how many people you've asked, there is a fair chance that when you finally reach the counter you will have spent 30 minutes in the wrong queue and will have to begin again. Ask the *gerente* (manager) who will usually take the time to point you in the right direction.

For foreigners of any nationality, the most readily acceptable currency is the US dollar or dollar traveller's cheques. Banks will also cash money from Access, American Express, Mastercard and Visa credit cards for a small charge: this is the most convenient way of getting money if you take a passport for identification. The two main banks are Bancomer and Banamex, the latter usually housed in an elegant colonial building. Bancomer accept Visa and Banamex accept Access and Mastercard.

Telephones
If banks don't finish you off, the telephone system will. Avoid it wherever possible. The system is antiquated and erratic and as local calls are free, numbers are usually engaged. Long-distance telephoning is expensive, especially from hotels which charge such exorbitant surcharges that they often pin notices by the telephone to warn guests. If possible, try to ring direct from a *larga distancia* (long-distance telephone booth).

Mexicans answer the telephone with '*bueno*' or more formally '*a sus ordenes*'. Some useful numbers are 03 for the time, 02 to make national reverse charges (*por cobrar*), 09 for international reverse charges and 06 for emergencies. The prefix for all long-distance calls within Mexico is 91.

Voltage
The current is 110 volts (the same as in the United States and Canada), and plugs are the flat, two-pronged type.

Lavatories
Bars, restaurants, hotel lobbies, and petrol, train and bus stations all have lavatories, of varying degrees of comfort. Ask for *servicios* or *baños*. Men are marked as *Señores, Hombres* or *Caballeros* and women as *Señoras* or *Damas*. A roll of paper can be invaluable. To buy one, ask for *papel sanitario* or one of the brand names like *Pétalo*.

Health and Other Concerns

Health
Anyone can get sick anywhere and Mexico is no exception to the rule. The change of bacteria upsets most foreigners and attacks of diarrhoea are common. The only way to reduce the risk is to avoid lettuce, uncooked vegetables, fruit that cannot be peeled, and ice, and to drink bottled water, soft drinks or beer. Some people bring water-purifying tablets, but they are hard work, make the water taste even worse and are usually thrown

out along with the first paperback. Common Mexican preventatives are lime, papaya, garlic and coca-cola. (There are so many chemicals in the latter that they knock internal parasites for six.) Lime can be squeezed over food and is often served with meals. If it doesn't appear, ask for it (*'¿No hay limón?'*).

If, and when, an attack does occur, try to avoid block-up pills such as Lomotil which only delay the attack. Drink as much as possible and stick to plain food like rice and bananas, avoiding coffee, chilli and alcohol. Lomotil does come into its own on long bus trips, and may make the journey pass in a pleasant drowse.

Most towns have a 24-hour chemist (*farmacia*), which can deal with minor illnesses. *Amoebas* is a cover-all term for griping stomach upsets (known coyly amongst tour operators as Moctezuma's Revenge). Most medicines have the price written on the side of the packet.

Mosquitoes are another scourge. Try rubbing lime over exposed flesh to ward off attack. It also soothes and sterilizes bites, to some extent.

Police Business

Although tourists are unlikely to encounter violent crime, Mexico has its fair share of petty crime. Cameras, purses and jewellery left lying around are considered fair game, and anyone walking around with an expensive Nikon around his neck or a wallet bulging with dollars sticking out of a back pocket is a target. Many hotels have safes where money and valuables can be stored. Theft from and of cars is common. Always park a car in a garage or in a well-lit street and never leave anything valuable inside.

With the US mounting a big anti-drugs campaign, Mexican police are cracking down on drug use in any form. It would be unwise to travel with even small quantities for personal use.

Opportunities are equal on the beat and strong women standing guard outside banks, wielding huge rifles, are a daunting sight. Sexual stereotyping, however, means that these fierce Amazons temper their aggression with beautifully painted lips and long mascara-laden lashes.

Tipping

Service charges are rarely added to bills in Mexico and tipping is always expected. The rate varies from 10 to 15 per cent, depending on individual generosity and the smartness of the surroundings. Maids and bellboys depend on tips to survive and it is customary to leave small change behind in a hotel room. The only people who don't expect tips are taxi drivers.

Allied to the tip is the infamous *mordida* or bite, which many petty officials and police expect to help an enquiry along or to expiate a traffic sin. Foreigners, particularly women, will rarely be expected to cough up, although no Mexican thinks twice about paying a small bribe to avoid lengthy and costly police charges. The regular traffic-fine performance begins when a policeman stops a driver who has cut a red light. The plaintiff will first of all explain that he is rushing to see his mother, who is seriously ill in hospital, and doesn't have the time to go down to the police station to pay the charge. The policeman will look sympathetic but perplexed and will exclaim, '*¿Como nos arreglamos?*'. This key phrase is the cue for the plaintiff to scratch his chin and suggest that he settles on the

14

spot. The policeman mentions a sum, the plaintiff balks, clapping his pockets and exclaiming that he has mistakenly left his wallet behind, and so on. Eventually, a small sum is fixed on, honour satisfied on both sides, and the matter closed. Strangely no record of the case ever reaches the police station.

Begging

There will be a strong temptation to hand out a few meagre pesos to the many hands waiting desperately for them. Many visitors are appalled or embarrassed by the street children and the street families who pour into the large cities from the country, looking for jobs. Others find it easy to dismiss them as daylight beggars and night-time affluents. The Mexicans themselves have adopted the philosophy of 'There but for the grace of God go I.' However rich or poor, they will always have some change ready, and most restaurants or cafés will only hustle people out of the door when they have been given some tortillas.

Begging is never obtrusive but unpersistent and resigned—an outstretched hand or a pleading face. In the grasping Zona Rosa hotel area of Mexico City, barefoot women, with children slung on their backs, beg on every street corner and it is impossible not to get jaded. On the other hand, children selling packs of chewing gum at the traffic lights, or coming past the bars with last week's roses, are patently trying to rise above the assumed dishonour of asking outright for money.

Photography

Mexico is a most photogenic country. Light and colour are superb, and there are always more shots demanding to be taken than film for the camera. Although few customs officers bother to check, the official limit is 12 rolls of film and one camera. A wide-angle lens and a polarizing filter to cut down glare are both useful. Don't buy or develop film in Mexico if it can be avoided. It is not only expensive, but often out of date and of poor quality.

As in many other countries, great sensitivity is needed before shooting rolls of film of people. They are not animals in a zoo and despise being treated as such. In Chiapas particularly, there is much local animosity to photographers, especially during the festivals, as they believe that the camera robs the soul. Children may be more obliging, but their parents should always be asked first. They may expect or even directly ask for a tip, though only in areas where trigger-happy photographers are thought to exploit local dress and colour.

Travelling with Children

Parenthood is considered to be a very serious and sacred institution. Mexicans are used to dealing with families, whether travelling with a single child or a batch of ten, and are always willing to help. Hotels will put another bed in a double room for little extra cost. In such a large country, with great distances to be travelled, children can become restless and bored. Books, maps, puzzles and a corner to sleep in will keep them more occupied than the unchanging scenery of desert plains. Food can be a problem. Chillies and hot sauces weren't made for palates reared on fish fingers and baked beans, but there are much simpler alternatives like grilled chicken, rice, fruits and vegetables.

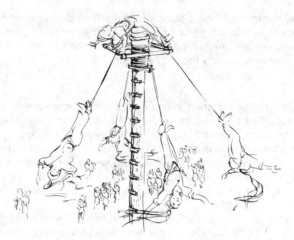

Voladores at Papantla, paying homage to Tonatiuh, the Sun God

Women

One of the most unattractive sides of machismo is its presumption about women. If you aren't the Virgin Mary, somebody's mother or wife, then you are everyone's prize. Foreign women, with fair hair and blue eyes, have become synonymous with easy sex and fallen virtue. This is due in part to beach resorts where young girls come on holiday, ready to have a good time in a place where nobody knows them—the sort of good time they'd never consider having back home. The bark is worse than the bite. Constant hassle can be wearing on the nerves and protestations of undying love may be tediously boring, but it shouldn't go beyond this unless feelings are obviously reciprocated. The flip side of machismo is chivalry: men are exaggeratedly polite to the weaker sex, devoted to their sainted mothers and fiercely protective of their ever-virginal sisters. Any hassle stopped with us as soon as it was discovered that we were sisters and therefore 'family' and sacrosanct.

Ordinary friendship between the sexes is far rarer in Mexico than it is in the States or Europe. Girls have their brothers around them until they are 15 or so and then a suitable *novio* (a boyfriend with a view to marriage) until they marry (as soon as they have finished their studies). After that, there is no time between babies for friendships and few husbands would countenance it anyway. For better or worse, this is the way Mexican society operates. Unfortunately, 'leading someone on' begins with a smile of thanks. The only word a potential suitor expects and the only one he will understand is 'No': anything else is tantamount to 'Yes'.

This should not make any woman intending to travel alone in Mexico rush back to the travel agent to cash in her ticket. It is a serious subject but one that can be largely avoided by a mental attitude displayed like a shield. Single women will always be given a seat on the bus, often invited back to people's homes, and generally looked after in a way that may even become claustrophobic.

Businesswomen in Mexico will find the exaggerated chivalry both a help and a hindrance. Treated as curiosity pieces, they will find doors opening and invitations given on the strength of their sex alone. However, if travelling with male colleagues, they will

16

soon notice how deference is paid to the men over their perhaps more capable female heads. The still rare Mexican businesswoman is unlikely to be sympathetic: many Mexican women understandably resent the freedom that foreign women seem to exude when they have had to battle so hard for respect at work or at home.

Marriage

Should the need arise, it is easy to get married in Mexico if both partners are foreigners. The only documents required are tourist cards and either birth certificates or passports. A divorce or death certificate must be shown for a second marriage, and parental consent is needed for anyone under 18 (minimum ages are 14 for women and 16 for men). Marrying a Mexican is only slightly harder, and requires a lawyer. Despite rampant Catholicism, the marriage ceremony is civil and the law is based on the Napoleonic Code (the one that presumes guilt until innocence is proven).

Entertainment, Shopping and Sport

Fiestas

Mexicans take their festivals seriously, both national and local. The church and state provide numerous excuses for fiestas. In addition, every town and village has at least one saint and will stop at nothing to celebrate its day, garlanding the streets with colour and noise. The fiesta is an intensely Mexican phenomenon, a whirlwind of passion which is not intended for tourists. Consequently, it can often be more fun to happen upon, rather than to plan a trip around, fiestas.

National holidays are also celebrated with gusto, when the Mexican flair for colour, laughter and exuberance comes into its own. It helps to be in the right place at the right time. Suggestions for a newcomer to Mexico are to celebrate Carnival at the beginning of Lent in either **Mazatlán** or **Veracruz**, and Easter in **Taxco**, with its gruesome procession of silence. **Aguascalientes** has a big fair to celebrate San Marcos at the end of April and **Oaxaca** hosts a festival of regional dances, the Guelaguetza, at the end of July. **Guanajuato** holds Mexico's biggest arts festival, the Cervantino, in October, **Guadalajara's** is in November and the film festival in **Mexico City** runs through November. The afterlife is celebrated with sugared skulls and marigold-bedecked graves at the beginning of November during the joyful Day of the Dead, particularly in Pátzcuaro, **Michoacán** and in hill villages in **Puebla**. For Christmas, **Mexico City** is as festive as anywhere in the 12 days leading up to 25 December. Markets are full of poinsettias and *posadas* (clay jars filled with presents and wrapped in resplendent twirls of bright crepe).

Public Holidays

Public holidays are treated like Sundays and banks and public buildings close.

1 January:	New Year's Day
6 January:	Epiphany
5 February:	Constitution Day
21 March:	Birthday of Juárez
Easter week (*Semana Santa*)	
1 May:	Labour Day
5 May:	Battle of Puebla

17

1 September:	Opening of Congress
16 September:	Independence Day
12 October:	*Día de la Raza* (Columbus Day)
1–2 November:	All Souls' Day, Day of the Dead
20 November:	Anniversary of the Revolution
12 December:	Virgin of Guadalupe
25 December:	Christmas

Newspapers and Magazines

For Spanish speakers there is a wide variety of national and regional newspapers, the majority of which tout the official government line. *La Jornada* is considered to be the best non-establishment, left-of-centre national paper and *Excélsior* is the most widely read.

The *Mexico City Daily News* is an English-language paper whose staff is largely North American, reporting on Mexican and international events as well as church bazaars and jumble sales. The **Daily Bulletin** is a meagre little paper, printed daily and distributed free to all the hotels and Sanborns department stores in Mexico City. The same useful but basic information is endlessly repeated in English, with a column inch or two for international news. For a weekly list of what's going on in the capital, **Tiempo Libre** can't be bettered. Various other towns, particularly in Baja California, produce English papers as vehicles for advertising, incorporating useful lists of what's going on where and when. *Time* and *Newsweek* are on sale at news stands and Sanborns shops. *México Desconocido* is an excellent magazine focusing on unknown places, people and customs in Mexico, produced monthly with an English-language translation.

Comics have a wider circulation than any other form of print. Lewd, bodice-ripping covers are swapped from one taxi driver to another and children fight for the latest Batman. They are produced as book-sized paperbacks and the long soap-opera serials run and run.

Cinema

Every small town has a cheap cinema (*cine*), usually showing execrable US imports such as *Rambo V*—in English with Spanish sub-titles. For something with more meat and less blood, try the Casa de la Cultura in any town and, in Mexico City, the Cineteca Nacional in Coyoacán.

Mexico was once no more than Hollywood's back yard for Westerns. In the 1930s, Sergei Eisenstein came to give it a better treatment, lured from the restrictions of working for Paramount by Diego Rivera. In *¡Qué Viva Mexico!*, he filmed the stark beauty of post-revolutionary Mexico, but his original was never shown.

Luis Buñuel moved to Mexico and made some of his most famous films here, including *Los Olvidados*. However, it was Dolores del Río who brought Mexican cinema its greatest fame. She was first discovered internationally at the 1946 Cannes Film Festival, in the leading part of *María Candelaria*, directed by Emilio Fernández. Wet afternoons in hotel lobbies are taken up with TV re-runs of her films and the madcap antics of Mexico's Charlie Chaplin, Cantinflas. Recently, Mexico's low production costs have attracted films such as Jane Fonda's *The Old Gringo*—filmed in Zacatecas, the James Bond team, *Rojo Amanecer* (Red Dawn)—about the student massacre in Mexico

18

City in 1968, and the controversial *Santa Sangre* which used the Mexican landscape for its backdrops.

Opening Hours

As a general rule all museums are open (as a minimum) from 09.00 to 14.00, from Tuesday to Sunday; most are also open for a couple of hours in the afternoon. All state museums are shut on Mondays but most sites stay open all week. Archaeological sites have recently been classified according to price and importance. None are expensive (the most expensive, Class A, is currently $5.00). Entrance is free for those under 13 and over 60 (with identification), and half-price for students (with international identification). Few museums charge more than a nominal fee, worth as much as the paper it is printed on.

Shops shut on Sundays and open during the week from 09.00 to 14.00 and 17.00 to 20.00. All large shops stay open throughout the day.

Market Shopping

Shopping can become a chronic disease in Mexico. Forget department stores, chichi boutiques and designer labels: Mexico's shopping is far more grass roots than that. It begins with the weekly outdoor markets (*mercados*) or *tianguis*, which are usually fruit and vegetable markets, with piles of plastic buckets on sale next to the mangoes and the suckling pigs. These integral parts of Mexican life explode with riotous colour and the conflicting aromas of sweet-smelling herbs, cheap cooking oil, unwashed bodies, flowers and fruits. At festival time and in specialized daily or weekly markets, ceramics, weavings, tapestries and other crafts all share their place on the plaza floor. The best states for markets are San Luis Potosí, Michoacán, Jalisco, Chiapas and Oaxaca. Mexico City itself has several large markets, all over the city, while Toluca, an hour away, also has a vast open-air Friday *tianguis* (only worthwhile for those who don't have time to get any further).

Bargaining is mainly concerned with satisfying both buyer's and seller's honour. Many prices are standard: ask several stall holders to get an idea and never hesitate to walk away and come back a few minutes later to clinch the deal. No-one needs more than 10 fingers to count with and '*¿Cuanto?*' ('How much?') to get started. Then the intricacies begin. A clever ploy is for the seller to ask the buyer how much he or she is willing to give, knowing the price will be impossibly low (unless the buyer is completely green). Gradually, both give a little ground, and a mutually acceptable price can be agreed.

It is very tempting to buy far too much. Practical considerations, such as weight and money, are often forgotten in the heat of the moment, and suddenly that spangled sombrero you only glanced at for a moment is yours. Almost impossible to carry onto the plane, it will inevitably lose its dubious appeal back home. It's a good idea to check out any Mexican craft shops in your own area before you leave for Mexico. More and more Mexican goods are now being imported, and it's not worth breaking your back to get things through customs (and paying a heavy surcharge) only to find the same stuff is in the Mexicana shop up the road. Remember, too, that the gaudy colours which work so well against the parched landscape of Mexico can seem just tacky back home (unless you're prepared to repaint your whole house to accommodate them).

Some of the most lasting and successful buys are the shawls and weaves from the south. San Cristobál de las Casas in the Chiapan highlands has the most beautifully embroidered work, on shawls, shirts and jackets. Much of it is brought in from Guatemala, the rest from the villages around. *Sarapes*, blanket-like shawls, come in a hundred shapes and forms, bought when the weather turns cold by those who forget to bring a jersey. The cold also brings on longings for thick, pungent, rich, dark, hot chocolate, which can be bought in tablets with an idiosyncratic whisk. In Pátzcuaro, the week leading up to the Day of the Dead festival (2 November) sees an ever-expanding market spread out over the plaza, when the work of many months is brought down from the villages to be sold. Ceramics are almost irresistible and many agencies can now ship goods home. Michoacán, Oaxaca and Jalisco are the states to begin looking in. With hammocks and panama hats from the Yucatán, masks from Guerrero, tequila from Jalisco, silver from Taxco, leather from the northwest, you'll find that each region has something worthwhile to offer. Good small presents include purses and black bead necklaces from Oaxaca, or hammocks which pack surprisingly small and light.

Sport

Swimming is possible at any time of year, although the more exposed Pacific coast can have a dangerous undertow and the Gulf of Mexico can be polluted. Which leaves the Caribbean. This stretch of the coastline has been hyped up by countless tourist brochures and travel agents but still lives up to its reputation. The world's second-longest coral reef provides superb **snorkelling** and **scuba diving** in the clearest of waters. Inland, several natural **hot springs** are dotted over Hidalgo, Querétaro, Guanajuato and the appropriately named Aguascalientes.

Despite what aficionados may tell you, **bullfighting** is not a pan-Mexican sport by any means. Introduced by the Spanish, it is largely confined to the colonial belt of the centre. Aguascalientes, Zacatecas, Guanajuato and Jalisco are all centres for bull breeding and fighting. Mexico City also has packed Sunday *corridas*. Ironically, as fewer and fewer Mexicans are enamoured of it, more and more tourists coming down to Cancún expect it. As a result, the bullring there has more *corridas* than almost any other place in Mexico. Few tourists understand what is going on and fewer still can stomach the whole show.

Rodeo-like **charreadas** are events of skill and horsemanship, featuring competitions between opposing teams, usually held on Sunday afternoons at the local *Lienzo Charro*. Breaking in young cattle and horses, lassoing or bringing down cattle with an ankle around the tail at full gallop, passing from one horse to another in the *paso de muerto* are all part of the performance. It is accompanied by a band playing in the stands, a constant hawking of beer and peanuts, and an interval display by the *scaramouche*, the female equivalent of the *charro*, wearing long, flowing skirts and wide-brimmed sombreros.

Football (soccer), **basketball** and **baseball** are national passions. Having hosted two football World Cups (in 1970 and in 1986 when Diego 'Hand of God' Maradona and his Argentinian team won), the Mexicans were somewhat surprised to be thrown out of the 1990 Cup for allegedly cheating. Apparently they sent some bearded old men down to play Guatemala in an under-18 league and their credibility slipped beyond the pale. The unofficial and highly scurrilous line is that they were disqualified only so that the US could pitch a team in World Cup football before hosting the competition in 1994.

Football is, to say the least, a volatile subject. The Mexicans are justly proud of their great international, Hugo Sanchez, who has brought many new fans to the game.

Horse and dog racing is not a big craze outside Tijuana and Mexico City, but anything that can be betted on, including gruesome **cock fighting**, will be, especially if it is illegal. **Jai Alai**, a Basque game introduced by the Spanish, is as popular for the endless betting possibilities as it is for the technique. It is played on a long squash court, where the two or four players whack a ball off a long curved basket-bat (*cesta*) to the end wall of the court, in a game of 30 points. Gamblers bet on everything: the next point, the game and the winnning margin. The two main centres for it are Mexico City (Plaza de la República) and Tijuana.

Golf is usually played in exclusive country clubs on the edges of major cities. Foreigners are welcomed on a day-membership basis. Many hotels have **tennis** courts and will hire out rackets. **Horse riding** on big western saddles is fun when you get the chance—across mountains or jungle, or along beaches.

Where to Stay

Even before modern tourist Babels sprouted up in the beach resorts, Mexicans themselves were inveterate travellers. This has created a market for accommodation ranging from a few thousand pesos for a hammock on the beach to a king's ransom for the suite where Bo Derek languished in the film *10*. The flip side of increased tourism is manifested in the dearth of modest family-run hotels in some popular spots.

Mexico has several national and international **hotel chains**, from the reliable Sheraton to the home-grown Camino Real group. The Secretaría de Turismo produces a fat annual bible of the nation's best to worst places. **Sanborn's** shops in Mexico City and other large towns stock copies, as should the various regional offices of SECTUR (or write directly to Av Mazarik 172, tel (5) 250 0151).

Star Ratings

Within the text we have given the star (*) ratings used by the Secretaría de Turismo. These run in descending order from *Grand Turismo* (GT) (which includes every possible comfort) down through the five stars to *Clase Económico* (CE) at the bottom of the scale (where there is often just one communal bathroom for the whole establishment). All hotels listed in this book have private bathrooms except where specified.

Star ratings judge a hotel by the services it offers—whether it has a restaurant, garage, air conditioning, TV or swimming pool, etc. Since it reflects nothing of the aesthetics, it is more a guide to the price and standard than a seal of approval. We have very occasionally seen fit to disagree with the current rating and added or subtracted a star. All hotels are required by law to display their star rating and current price list in reception. Ninety per cent automatically do so: if not, they will usually, on being asked, shamefacedly produce a quickly dusted-down copy from a drawer.

Prices

Prices vary from state to state, but should be uniform within each state. The north is considerably more expensive than the south. In popular resorts the rate for rooms can vary by as much as 50 per cent, depending on the time of year. High season runs from Christmas to Easter.

Inflation and variations in the rates of exchange make any comprehensive attempt at accurate pricing impossible in a guide of this nature. The table below lists current (1991) prices for a double room, for hotels in Mexico City (which are not subject to seasonal fluctuation).

Price for a double room in Mexico City (in US dollars):

One star:	US$10	Four star:	US$60
Two star:	US$20	Five star:	US$90
Three star:	US$40	GT:	US$120

A tax (IVA) of 15 per cent is included in the given price.

A single room is up to two-thirds the price of a double; putting in an extra bed adds 10 per cent to the cost. A room with a double bed is a *cama matrimonial*, one with two beds is a *doble*, and one with a single bed is a *sencillo*. For three beds in a room, ask for a *triple*, and for four a *quadruple*.

Reservations

Booking hotels ahead of time can become a nightmare. It is only strictly necessary in the best-known (and correspondingly easiest-booked) hotels and at the busiest times of year (when it will happily be unacknowledged anyway). Several hotels now have telex and fax machines (numbers are included in the text) but the vast majority of bookings are made by phone. A booking made by post will probably arrive too late, unless sent literally months in advance. When making a reservation, specify any special requests, such as an *interior* (inside) room if you are sensitive to noise, or a sea view (which may add to the standard price).

Expensive

Truly expensive accommodation is confined to very small pockets of Mexico, usually those areas that survive off dollar tourism or rely entirely on businessmen. In tourist resorts like Acapulco and Cancún, expect prices to be at least twice as much as in country towns and bargains few and far between. On the other hand, the converted sugar cane haciendas of Morelos, the excellent Quinta Real chain, the Villas Arquéologicas group and the beautiful convent of Santa Catalina in Oaxaca are expensive by Mexican standards but a fraction of home prices, and blessed with incomparable settings.

Moderate

In Mexico the division between travel as a necessary evil for many or a purely sybaritic pleasure for a few has led to a paucity of friendly family-run hotels. **Four-star (****) hotels** are of a high standard. They tend to be well established and well run, with swimming pools, cable TV, safe parking, air conditioning and something more (such as colonial architecture or an enviable position) which raises them above the ordinary. Some of the best are close to the archaeological sites of the Yucatán and in Chiapas.

Three-star (***) hotels are middle-of-the-road, and would be given two stars in Europe. Inexpensive and popular, and often centrally located, they may well be the smartest on offer in the smaller towns, with the only restaurant worth going to. As a general rule, the older hotels have the most character and the most potential (not always lived up to). Modern, motel-inspired places, with smoked-glass doorways and orange carpets, usually provide little atmosphere but may be more comfortable. Most three-star hotels provide safe parking (which, in older hotels, may be right in the courtyard). We have recommended the best buys in each town: comfort and character are prerequisites, although one may have been sacrificed to the other.

Cheap

Mexico still has plenty of cheap accommodation. Any Mexico pro shudders in horror at the price hikes of the last few years and it is certainly not a pauper's paradise. Yet, since many thousand Mexicans travel within the country every year—on business, to see their family, to look for work or for a hundred other reasons—there are many hotels which cost very little. Travelling with children should cause no problem. Another bed or two will be brought into the room and an additional charge added to the bill.

The two-star (**) and one-star (*) hotels deliberately keep their prices down to keep business up. They can normally be found near bus or train stations, although there will invariably be a couple in the centre as well. Taxi or bus drivers may try to steer you to the place of their choice, but everyone understands *económico*. The best of the two-star hotels are no worse than three-star, the real difference being no telephone in the room (which is no great hardship). One star typically ensures a basic, no-frills-attached comfort, with a scrawny towel, a bare lightbulb, a hole in the mosquito netting and an insistently whirring fan that looks as if it going to fall out of its socket. In both categories, places advertised as *familiar* are insistently not 'houses of ill repute'. Around bus stations, some of the busier places obviously will be. Although the manager will probably be delighted, if a little surprised, to rent a room for the night to foreigners, cleanliness is further from godliness and doors bang all night long. Single women will definitely be considered competition.

Cheaper still are the *casa de huéspedes* (generally for long-term guests) and the *Clase Económico*, where bathrooms are shared between rooms. These are fine, especially in the older, high-ceilinged, tall-windowed Spanish mansions, with interior courtyards and slatted blinds. Nothing will have been done to them for generations: a bare bed in an unfurnished room is considered more than enough. Look out for them particularly in the older cities, including Guadalajara, Mérida, Campeche, Jalapa, Oaxaca and, of course, Mexico City.

Camping

Camping in Mexico is a fairly recent idea. Camper vans and off-the-road vehicles have taken over Baja California and the Pacific coast as far as Mazatlán, in organized camping grounds or on isolated beaches. The rest of the country is still wide-eyed at the winter invasion of these so-called 'snow birds', which sometimes come for months at a time, laden with all manner of equipment including the kitchen sink.

At the other end of the scale, the simplest of accommodation, known as a *cabaña*, is available at some of the beaches on the Caribbean and the Pacific. These beach-front, palm-roofed huts with sand floors are ideal for hanging a hammock in and cost next to nothing.

No camper should even think of leaving home without the excellent and endlessly amusing tome, *The People's Guide to Camping in Mexico* by Carl Franz (available from specialist bookshops or direct from John Muir Publications, PO Box 613, Santa Fe, New Mexico 87504, USA).

Eating Out

Corn has been the staff of life for 4000 years. Once given its own god, it is still held in great reverence and flat, pancake, corn **tortillas**—the Mexican bread—come warm with every dish. The corn is soaked and ground with water and lime, and then patted into shape. Savour your first tortillas with great care and find out what they do to you: acquiring a taste for them will be a great advantage. Some consider them to be a meal in themselves, others only a bland apology for bread. Those who don't get to grips with the corn tortilla often find they prefer the wider wheat tortilla from the north. When rolled around anything from chicken or salad to fish or beans, tortillas become **tacos**; when covered in sauce, they are **enchiladas**, and when rolled into a fat round, stuffed with meat and steamed, they are **tamales**.

The other two staples of the Mexican diet are **chillies**, packed with vitamin C, and **beans**, filled with protein. **Tropical fruits** abound, including *tuna* (prickly pear), mango, papaya, pineapple, *pithaya* (cactus fruit), bananas and plantains.

Meat, although *de rigeur* on all tourist menus, is often left out of the Mexican diet because of its expense. Apart from chicken (*pollo*), the most common is *bistec*, a beefsteak that is rarely beef (*res*) but more likely to be pork (*lomo* or *puerco*).

Fish can be exquisite. Grilled or fried, served with chunks of lime and washed down with beer, it is a great Sunday special, eaten in *marisquerias*. Lunch might start with *ceviche* (a cocktail of raw marinaded fish mixed with tomatoes and chilli), followed by *huachinango a la veracruzana* (whole red snapper in a tomato, caper, chilli and onion sauce).

Non-meat eaters will find most large towns have a vegetarian restaurant with a daily set menu. In many restaurants, the concept of vegetarianism hasn't quite filtered through. A diet without meat is understood, but only out of necessity and never out of choice, and the waiter will helpfully try to convince you that a little bit of ham with your eggs isn't really meat at all. A safe way out is to order *quesadillas* (tortillas stuffed with cheese and lightly fried) or cheese-stuffed chillies (*chile relleno de queso*).

The New World and the Old did a brisk trade. The Spanish brought domestic animals, sugar and cheese, and discovered avocadoes, vanilla, cacao, turkey, peanuts and potatoes, as well as exotic fruits. The traditional *metate*, a stone grinding slab, has now been generally replaced by mechanical mills. The grinding bowl (*molcajete*), like a pestle and mortar, must have been the negative inspiration for electrical mixers: sauces with 30 ingredients, like *mole poblano*, now take only hours to prepare, rather than days.

The use of local ingredients still ensures considerable variation between the food of different regions. In the north, steaks and beef figure more highly on the menu, whilst in the deep south fried bananas and tropical fruits take over from chillies and spices. Menus are also seasonally affected, particularly with regard to fruits and vegetables: just as you learn all about crushed pithaya fruit with ice and lemon, the short season has been and gone.

Breakfast (*desayuno*) can either be a coffee and *pan dulce* (sweet roll) or a hefty meal. It may start with a plate of fruit or a glass of freshly squeezed orange juice, followed by eggs. These come in several ways, usually with tortillas and beans and often cooked with chillies (if you prefer them without, ask for *sin chile*). *Rancheros* are fried eggs on tortillas, covered with tomato sauce mixed with garlic, chilli and onion. *Chilaquiles* are another unlikely favourite—a mush of left-over tortillas, eggs, chilli and chicken.

Lunch (*comida*), as in Mediterranean countries, is the big meal of the day. Business grinds to a halt between 13.00 and 16.00 as negotiations move to the dining rooms. The more important a bureaucrat, the longer his lunch. A common, cheap lunch is the **comida corrida** served throughout the country. For a paltry sum, dish after dish is presented, sometimes running to six courses. It might begin with fruit or soup (often dry or *seca*, which means it is a plate of rice), and progress through tacos, enchiladas or a meat dish with chocolate *mole* to vegetables, ending with a predictable *flan* (crème caramel).

Dinner (*cena*) is altogether lighter: a bowl of vegetable soup, some eggs (for those who can resist them at breakfast) or filled French rolls (*bolillos*).

Places to eat range from market stalls to studiously elegant dining rooms. Outside the home, one can still find good home cooking. Look for restaurants that specialize in Mexican rather than international dishes. Some of the bigger towns now boast the full range of Italian, Chinese, Japanese, German, French and Spanish restaurants. In addition, more and more US-style fast-food joints are springing up (with ubiquitous orange plastic seats), offering brisk service and large platefuls of Tex-Mex enchiladas.

Prices vary considerably throughout the country, and are affected significantly by the restaurant's location on or off the tourist track. The table below gives an approximate price range for the categories used in this book.

Approx price range for a main meal for two people (in US dollars):

Cheap:	US$5–20	Expensive:	US$60–100
Moderate:	US$20–60		

Drinking

This is a serious business, and one that starts with the **water**. Some rare travellers can drink the water out of any tap or stream and come back smiling. Others only have to look at a cool glass of iced water before they are rushing cross-legged to the lavatory. It is best to be careful: drink bottled water (making sure that the seal hasn't been broken) and avoid ice that hasn't been made out of purified water.

Alternatively, stick to the sweet, sugar-soused fizzy drinks that come in as many brands as days of the year. Fizzy water in bottles is usually called by the brand-name of 'Tehuacán': to get rid of the fizz, drop a few grains of uncooked rice into the bottom of the bottle. Freshly squeezed fruit and vegetable juices, known as *jugos*, are available everywhere. In the early morning, vendors appear on street corners, preparing glassfuls for breakfast. As well as orange juice, there is carrot, alfalfa, beetroot, mango, papaya and the fruit of the cactus plant, *tuna*. Shakes, known as *licuados*, come in as many varieties: the fruit or vegetable is added whole to a glass of milk or water and then crushed with ice in a liquidizer. *Aguas frescas* are often included as part of a set lunch, served from big jugs on the counter, and are merely fruit and sugar crushed together and mixed with water. The most common are lime (*limón*) and the bright red hibiscus flower (*jamaica*).

Although **coffee** is grown in Mexico, freshly ground coffee is often hard to find. Massive exports of the crop leave the average bar serving Nescafé (the cover-all for any instant coffee), often already sweetened. For the real stuff, ask for *café americano*. **Tea** (*té*) comes in bags, either ordinary (*negro*) or camomile (*de manzanillo*).

Mexican Beer

Beer (*cerveza*) was first introduced by German immigrants but now it is the Mexicans who are reintroducing designer-name beers back to Berlin. Bottled Corona and canned Tecate are already well known in the United States. The light Sol and the richer Bohemia are now also being exported to the US and Europe. Of the 20-odd other brands, the Pacífico of Mazatlán and the Montejo of Mérida are smooth, light, local favourites. The Guinness substitute, Negro Modelo, is a far darker alternative. When drinking in a bar, expect the empty bottles to be left on the table as a record how many have been drunk, so that only one bill needs to be made.

Wine

Although Mexico isn't renowned for its wines, the proximity of California's vineyards has given them a certain amount of reflected, and not always merited, kudos. When the Spanish conquered the New World, the monks brought wine with them: Hernán Cortés ordered that 1000 vine shoots should be planted for every 100 indigenous people under their care. Towards the end of the 16th century, Mexican wines started to compete seriously with the Spanish ones, whereupon Philip II expeditiously prohibited the cultivation of vineyards in Mexico.

Wine production began again at the turn of this century. Although the quality control is not very rigid, it's worth trying the red and white Los Reyes produced by the prestigious Pedro Domecq, the dry white Calafia, and the local wines of Hidalgo, Aguascalientes and Baja California.

Mezcal, Tequila and Pulque

Produced from the maguey plant, these are the hard boys of Mexican drink. **Tequila**, drunk in shots with a lick of salt and a suck of lime, or watered down with ice, grenadine and lime in a **margarita**, is as much a part of Mexico's image as the sombrero. Patriots, and others out to get blind drunk, drink their tequilas in imitation of the national flag, laying out a row of three glasses: the fiery white tequila, the sharp green lime and the blood-red sangria to wash it down. Of the many brands of tequila, Sauza is the most popular but the more expensive Herradura and Siete Leguas are considerably better. The darker-coloured *añejo* or *reposado* have been given time to mature: although they cost more, they have the superiority of malt whisky over the ordinary. **Mescal** is a rougher version of the same, often to be found with a *gusano de maguey* or worm in the bottom of the bottle. **Pulque**, although alcoholic, is far milder than the other two, and often given to children because it is so full of vitamins and minerals. It was drunk by the Aztecs, and is made from the fermented sap of the maguey plant. It has never been successfully bottled and so hasn't reached the socially acceptable heights of tequila. Instead, it is drunk by country people at home and sold in *pulquerías* in towns. For more on all three, read Malcolm Lowry's *Under the Volcano*, written on their combined strengths.

Women are scarcely ever seen behind saloon doors, although it is no longer legal to ban them. Foreigners are even more rare.

Itineraries

Where does one start? For North Americans who can make several trips in one lifetime, there is a possibility of beginning to know Mexico, but for the hard-pressed European, who may only have one chance, the itinerary is a tall order.

Mérida—Playa del Carmen—Akumal—Tulum—Villahermosa—Palenque—San Cristóbal

This is the standard tour for the imaginative (about three weeks), and a very good one it is too. It covers the Yucatán peninsula and its Maya sites, together with the hauntingly beautiful jungle ruins of Palenque and the excellent museums of Villahermosa. (It may also be stretched to take in Guatemala.) For a more leisurely tour of the same area, ditch some of the ruins and allow a few days on the outrageously clear Caribbean coast (Mexico's undoubted best), having made a special effort to get up to the hill town of San Cristóbal in the highlands of Chiapas (a rough bus ride from Palenque).

Mexico City—Cuernavaca—Taxco—Acapulco

The most hackneyed one-week tour is undoubtedly from Mexico City to Acapulco, with obligatory, lightning stops in Taxco and Cuernavaca. Were it not for the other tour buses hammering down the single highway, it wouldn't be half so bad. As it stands, however, it represents crass overkill—for those who really wished they'd never left the comfort of their own homes.

The routes below all fit easily into a ten-day to three-week itinerary.

Baja California and Chihuahua

Anyone coming from the southern states of America could try the northwest, possibly travelling the length of the Baja California peninsula (north to south) and crossing by ferry from La Paz to Los Mochis, from where the Chihuahua–Pacífico train sets out across the Sierra Madre mountains. Keep the south and Mexico City for another time. This is a good trip for a second or third visit and includes lots of beach in Baja.

Mexico City and the West

An alternative for a second visit is to explore colonial Morelia and buy ceramics from Pátzcuaro in Michoacán, perhaps continuing to Guadalajara, beginning or ending in Mexico City. The best time to visit these rural states is in the autumn, particularly around the Day of the Dead (2 November). This is a good itinerary for fans of Mexican artisania.

The Bajío

Another inland journey might include the rich, colonial silver cities of the centre—Querétaro, San Miguel de Allende, Zacatecas and heavenly Guanajuato. There will be no sea, but plenty of sun, lots of culture and a taste of the everyday life of Mexico.

Oaxaca–Huatulco–Puerto Escondido

The southern state of Oaxaca is another popular choice for a varied holiday, visiting ruins or shopping for native art in the markets around the city itself, and relaxing in the low-key resorts on the Pacific coast.

27

San Luis Potosí
For those who know Mexico well, San Luis Potosí is one of the loveliest and most underrated states, with its rich, green Huasteca region full of Sunday markets and waterfalls, and the ghosts of old mining towns like Real de Catorce. This itinerary will appeal to those who like to explore off the beaten track.

Veracruz
Tropical Veracruz is another place to visit and revisit but is often overlooked by tourists in a hurry to reach better-known sites. Its steamy port is home to an exuberant mix of nationalities, whilst the state includes the excellent museums of Jalapa, the Totonac site of El Tajín, the multicoloured porticoes of Tlacotalpan, and Lake Catemaco. This itinerary will work for those who like to sit and watch the world go by, but want a bit of culture and sea thrown in too.

Nayarit, Colima and Jalisco
This southwest corner of the country, buffeted by the Pacific Ocean, is virtually unknown to Mexicans and tourists alike. Its dusty museums are filled with pre-Hispanic artefacts, whilst its countryside represents rural Mexico at its furthest from the 20th century. Guadalajara, the regional capital, is filled with murals and *charros* in wide sombreros. This is an excellent itinerary for old-timers seeking the soul of Mexico.

Mexico City
Since international flights stop in Cancún and Mérida on the Yucatán peninsula, and several other cities besides, there is no need even to set foot in Mexico City. On the other hand, this, the most polluted city in the world, is also one of the most fascinating. For just a taste of what it has to offer, plan at least three days at the beginning or end of a trip (although a week would be by no means too long).

Part II

MEXICAN CULTURE

Maya head from the Museum of Anthropology, Mexico City

History

Mexican history is abruptly split into two parts: before and after the Spanish conquest. The fantastical, semi-mythical world of jungle kingdoms, emperors, human sacrifice and exotic cultures, exemplified by the Aztecs and the Maya, was finally extinguished by the Spanish conquest in 1519, and for the next 300 years, Spanish ascendancy was on the up and up. Unlike the Anglo-Saxons in New England, however, the Spanish intermarried with the indigenous people, and a new race, the Mexicans, grew up out of this cultural mélange. This mix, often referred to as *'mestizaje'*, was never easy. Even after a lengthy war of independence, several civil wars and a revolution, Mexico is still far from settled with its own past.

Pre-History

Mexico's story begins in the Pleistocene Ice Age, 50,000 years ago, when nomadic people first crossed a land bridge connecting Siberia to Alaska. As the ice gradually melted, this bridge was flooded (to become the Bering Straits), ending any further migration from Asia and bringing about the complete isolation of American man, until the arrival of the European Spanish in the 15th century. Man gradually pushed south in search of food, across the wide, open plains of Canada and North America, the vast expanses of northern Mexico and the volcanic peaks of the Sierra Madre, and eventually as far south as the tip of South America.

29

The earliest sign of humans in Mexico is probably a spearhead found near Durango in the northwest, which has been dated to the 12th millennium BC. Their descendants continued to live as nomads for the next 9000 years, a lifestyle that changed only with the planting of the first corn kernel in the 3rd millennium BC and the later cultivation of the other great staples, beans and chillies.

The Olmecs (1200 BC–AD 100)

Hunters and gatherers, supplementing their diet with fish and meat, settled in the central highlands, but it was the Olmecs of the Gulf coast who emerged as the first civilization— the great 'Mother Culture' of Mesoamerica. From c 1350 BC, the Olmecs settled in the low-lying alluvial plains of Veracruz and Tabasco. With a developed agricultural system for feeding the populace, they had time, resources and imagination left over to create exquisite pottery figurines, delicately carved jades, and monumental basalt heads and sculptures of the human form. These leave us with some idea of their physical appearance: faces were round and chubby, eyes slit, lips fully rounded, noses broad and stature stocky. Teeth were filed, heads shaved, and the cranium was deformed from birth, leaving a long sloping forehead.

It was the Olmecs who first fashioned a ball out of rubber and laid down the rudimentary guide lines for the famous *pelota* or ball game, which was to continue long after the Olmecs were no more than a legendary memory. They too were the first to build temples and permanent constructions. Lacking stone, they built mainly with clay, painted in bright colours, but at La Venta they surrounded the central courtyard with huge basalt columns—brought in by an ingenious rolling log raft all the way from the Tuxtla mountains, 100 km away, supported and maintained by a vast army of slaves. Although the great majority of the population of 350,000 still continued to live in perishable palm-thatched huts, the priestly and ruling classes used enforced labour to construct great temples at the ceremonial centres of Tres Zapotes and La Venta (which supported a population of 18,000).

The Olmecs also created the first entire, complicated pantheon of gods. As with all subsequent Mesoamerican cultures, the Olmecs were polytheistic, taking their gods from nature and necessity, often merging man with animals, particularly the jaguar. The nobility of nature was contrasted with its deformities. Depictions of hunchbacks, pustulating corpses and dwarfs began an artistic tradition which continues today. Although no written records have survived, their legacies, such as the first Mesoamerican calendar and system of writing, were to influence every contemporary and subsequent Mesoamerican civilization.

The Classic Period (AD 100–900)

In part through Olmec influence and in part through a common progression, several cultures in different regions of Mexico reached a peak at much the same time—the Teotihuacános in the Valley of Mexico, the Maya in the jungles of Guatemala and the Yucatán peninsula (see History, Part XIV), the Zapotecs in the the Oaxaca valleys, and the Huasteca in Veracruz. These 600 years, often considered the Golden Age of Mesoamerica, saw the establishment of a complex social, mercantile and religious system. Today the vast pyramids and temples of Monte Albán, Teotihuacán, Palenque and El Tajín testify to their magnificence. Incredibly, all these buildings were constructed without the use of metal, beasts of burden or the wheel. The intricate carving on the stone stelae, the profoundly complex calendrical and astronomical systems, and the rigidly hierarchical religious codes were all developed without any of these basic tools of other great civilizations. Yet their calendar was fractionally more accurate than the Gregorian and they grasped the concept of zero before the Hindus in the 5th century and long before the Europeans in the 12th.

Society

Connections between the various cultures were largely pacific, under the auspices of trade and not bellicose expansion, and in time religious tenets overlapped from one place to another. Religion became an art as crop rotation and harvests made the people dependent on nature's never too dependable bounty. Figurines, sculptures, murals and stelae were created in the gods' image, to be importuned in times of drought, flooding or fear. With far too much for one harassed god to cope with, they invoked hundreds of gods and goddesses—for fire, volcanoes, childbirth, the New Year, harvest, bees, corn and rain. The growing sophistication of the pantheon soon created space for abstract gods of learning, wisdom and warfare. Ever more powerful and stylized, the gods dictated to man through their priestly vassals on earth. Priests were rulers, born to high and noble families, despotic and dynastically secure, given a sinecure on their position for as long as their family could support them. The carved figures on stone monuments, at which the Maya excelled, often refer to families and dynasties, as with the jaguars in Palenque. Society was almost exclusively male-dominated: women were the child-bearers and field labourers, only occasionally allowed power as an important wife or mother of a local ruler.

Whilst each great civilization had its own language, customs, pantheon, trade and rulers, several concepts were held in common. The Maya Rain God, Chac, corresponded to the Teotihuacán and Toltec Rain God, Tlaloc. Everywhere there was a common obsession with death and dying. The **ceremonial ball game** was played at every major site in Mesoamerica. Highly complex and ritualized, its outcome was never decided with a shake of the hand but could instead end with the sacrifice of the players to the gods. It was played with a rubber ball hit off the hips, elbows, knees or heels, but never touched by the hand or kicked with the foot. The ball had to be aimed through a narrow stone hoop placed halfway up one of the two sloping walls which made up the sides of the court. Great pads, later stylized in sculpted forms, were used to protect the players (usually seven on each side), who were hero worshipped as much as our modern football and baseball equivalents. Whole fortunes were won or lost on the game: occasionally, one-to-one games were held to settle dynastic successions or points of honour.

Teotihuacán

Of all the great cultures which emerged during this period, Teotihuacán in the fertile, well-irrigated Valley of Mexico was the greatest, with the most long-ranging and profound effect on the rest of Mesoamerica. The city developed gradually, supporting a population of 50,000 by the 1st century AD. It attracted people from nearby villages and small population centres to its markets, so extending its power and influence beyond its confines, out as far as the Zapotecs in the Oaxaca valleys, the Huastecs along the Gulf coast and the Maya in the deep south. Teotihuacán became a true urban centre, with a north–south axis (like La Venta before it) and monumental pyramids to the Sun and the Moon gracing the long, broad Avenue of the Dead. By AD 600, its population of 200,000 made it the largest city in the world, ten times the size of Constantinople.

The most extended of all city-states, it was the first to overstretch itself. Temples were constructed at great speed, in a frenzy of piety, as if to atone for the greed of man. It was to no avail: as the city expanded, so the countryside around was depleted. Dues were exacted from neighbouring peoples, forests cut and lakes dried out to satisfy the demand for water. Around AD 650, a horde came down from the north, possibly enraged by taxes or by the encroachments of the city, and Teotihuacán was sacked and burnt. These northern semi-nomadic people were quickly designated *chichimecs* or barbarians. They continued to live in the city for several years but the boom had burst: the city collapsed and its greatness eventually resided only in the memory of a much-lauded past.

The Toltecs in the post-Classic Era (AD 900–1200)

To fill the void left by the fall of Teotihuacán, lesser powers in Xochicalco and Cholula rose to the fore. A lack of cohesion, however, and the absence of a central, authoritarian city-state, prevented the emergence of any single great empire until the beginning of the 10th century, when the Toltecs, led by Mixcóatl, came down to the Valley of Mexico from Zacatecas.

Mixcóatl was viciously assassinated by his brother, but his pregnant wife escaped to a small village near Xochicalco. Here she gave birth to Ce Acatl Topiltzin, who was to become one of the most famous of all rulers. As a young man, Topiltzin was educated in the priestly rites of the great god, Quetzalcoátl, adding his name to his own. Avenging his father's death, he killed his uncle and in 879 moved the capital from Tollancingo (in the present-day state of Hidalgo) to Tula (north of Mexico City), which went on to dominate central Mexico for several generations. A warlike faction within the Toltecs subsequently engineered the disgrace of their young, deified ruler, and in 987 he was expelled. He fled to the south, vowing to return one day. Cortés later made use of this myth, convincing Moctezuma that he was the returning god. (See Tula, Hidalgo.)

Shortly afterwards, Toltec influence could be seen in the Maya cities of the Yucatán (see Chichén-Itzá). The remaining Toltecs at Tula took to war and human sacrifice with a vengeance, overpowering neighbouring states and constructing gigantic stone warriors to adorn their temples. At the end of the 11th century, drought and famine combined to cause the fall of their city.

The End of the Classic Era (AD 900–1200)

Libraries of books have been written posing the one question: why did these fabulous civilizations disintegrate? Ignoring the cycle of civilizations the world over, historians and archaeologists have debated this issue with passion: the reasons for their demise have provoked far greater enthusiasm and incredulity than their phenomenal rise.

It was once thought that their collapse was sudden, cataclysmic and revolutionary, but this apocalyptic vision has little substance. There may have been palace revolutions against despotic rulers, and internal struggles as discontented populaces fought for a more equitable system. What is certain is that the system of 'slash and burn' agriculture used up a great deal of land for poor return, and proved unable to meet the needs of a large population. As population centres grew, so fertile lands were lost. Forests were pulled down to create cities, and devastated jungle canopies could no longer absorb the rain. Drought and famine followed; rivalries became wars, and nations collapsed. It is also conceivable that European diseases, brought over by shipwrecked Spanish sailors, ravaged the unsuspecting people.

Different civilizations came to an end at different times. During the 13th century, established settlements all over the central plateau were disintegrating or being overrun by nomadic barbarians who had come down to the valleys to exploit the fall of Tula, whilst in the far south the Maya moved from the Guatemalan highlands and the jungle of the Petén to the flat lands of the Yucatán peninsula. The jungle covered over abandoned sites in the south and the great imperial city of Teotihuacán had long since burned to the ground. The Zapotecs at Monte Albán had seen their temples and necropolises taken over by the Mixtecs, and the Huastec lands were invaded by the Totonacs. It was the coming of the Aztecs, however, which created the greatest shock waves throughout Mesoamerica.

The Aztecs (AD 1168–1519)

Together with the Incas of the Peruvian Andes, the Aztecs of Mexico are the most famous of all the indigenous civilizations of the Americas. Largely because they were both conquered so emphatically by the Spanish in the 16th century, their fame has lived on through history books, adventurers' tales and popular mythology. It matters little to most people where they came from, or how they lived: the image of a gold-bedecked warrior with a great plumed headdress is enough. Sumptuous as the mythic picture is, the reality must have exceeded it many times.

When the Spanish conquerors, led by Hernán Cortés, first saw Tenochtitlán, the monumental capital city of the Aztecs, they were at a loss to describe it. Seville, the largest city in contemporary Spain, was a fraction of its size. Tenochtitlán was the culminating glory of a people who only 200 hundred years before had been despised as *chichimec* barbarians from the wild lands of the north. No people has ever risen from such humble beginnings to so great a power in such a short time, only to see it destroyed at its apogee.

Founding a City
The mythic Aztec place of origin continues to be disputed today. It might have been the fabled Aztlán in the mangrove swamps of Nayarit (see Mexcaltitan), southern Zacatecas or the legendary seven cities of the north. The Aztecs themselves were assiduous in fudging the issue, archly linking their ancestry to the Toltecs, the Teotihuacános and even to their great God of Creation, Huitzilopochtli. Branded as uncouth *chichimecs*, they roared into the Valley of Mexico around 1168 and roamed from one place to another as

33

bellicose mercenaries for 200 years. While the Toltecs wielded power in Tula, the Aztecs had little credibility without land or lineage.

In 1323, whilst working for the Lords of Culhuacán on the shores of Lake Xochimilco, their leader Nopaltzín asked for a royal bride to lend him nobility. The request was granted and the girl's father was invited to join them in inaugurating a new deity. To his horror, he found not his daughter but her flayed skin: worn by a priest, it had become the object of worship and the first Aztec goddess.

Roundly expelled, the Aztecs followed the advice of their god, Huitzilopochtli, and searched for an eagle devouring a serpent on a nopal cactus (today the emblem of the Mexican Republic), designating the site where they were to build a city. The prophecy was finally fulfilled in 1345, on an island in a snake-infested marsh on the shores of Lake Texcoco. The great island-city of Tenochtitlán, doomed to last under 200 years, had been auspiciously founded.

The Aztec Empire

The Aztecs continued to support themselves as mercenaries and allies until 1427 when, under their fourth leader, Itzcóatl, they rebelled against their bosses, the Tepanec Lords. Two years later they formed a triple alliance with the nearby cities of Tlacopan and Texcoco (both now swallowed up by Mexico City's great tendrils). The Aztecs soon dominated the alliance, whose influence expanded to the furthest reaches of the known world. They controlled their surrounding city states in a loose confederation, tolerating local autonomy and local gods provided that taxes were paid to Tenochtitlán and their Sun God, Huitzilopochtli, was recognized as the supreme god. This fluidity of government and religion set the way for the Spaniards, whose Catholicism with its economical one god could easily be incorporated into a cosmos shared by several thousand others.

Aztec society became extremely stratified. The highest position was held by the supreme Speaker or *tlatoani*, who was advised by four counsellors and supported by a vast and complex clergy. The incumbents of each of these posts, including the Speaker, had to be elected. In effect, however, the ruling elite established themselves as hereditary office-holders, passing appointments on within the family. The Speaker took on divine significance—Moctezuma II ate his daily 100 dishes of food behind a screen, to prevent his subjects suspecting such a mortal need.

Through battle or the priesthood, any man was able to rise up to a position of honour, but equally a transgressing lord had to expect to fall from grace. On one occasion, the unfaithful wife of one Speaker (and daughter of another) was executed in public, along with three of her lovers. In this puritanical society, a woman's faithfulness was held to be inviolable, although a man of high social standing might have hundreds of wives—Moctezuma II was said to have had 150 of his wives pregnant at the same time. Schooling was compulsory and drunkenness prohibited (a capital offence at its most extreme), but the use of hallucinogenic drugs was common practice, at least amongst the leisured classes. Taxes and tributes and the selling of slaves were all part of Aztec daily life.

The power of the military was equal to that of the priests, under the patronage of the belligerent War God, Tezcatlipoca. An extraordinary voluntary agreement between the powerful Aztecs and their proud but outnumbered Tlaxcalan neighbours resulted in a series of grisly wars, waged with the single purpose of appeasing the increasingly voracious demands of such gods. Conquest was not the aim: they were fought in order to win prisoners, who were then sacrificed in gladiatorial contests and fed to the gods.

The Beginning of the End

As the population of Tenochtitlán increased to 200,000, it was fed by a series of *chinampas*, or floating gardens, on which crops could be grown. Even so, there was not enough at hand to feed and support a city of such magnitude. Merchants, known as *pochteca*, went as far as Central America, travelling in long caravans. They played a unique double role in Aztec society, supplying the city with rare, exotic goods and with vital intelligence from distant lands. They traded with the unconquered Maya and also tried to discover the secret of the metal weapons used by the independent Purépecha of Michoacán.

It was the merchants who first brought back news of ominous change. In the first years of the 16th century, reports of sightings of white men around the Yucatán coast filtered back up to the Speaker Moctezuma II, in his capital of Tenochtitlán. These ominously fulfilled the Toltec omen, adopted by the Aztecs, that the great God, Quetzalcóatl, would one day return from the east to exact revenge. At the same time, in all parts of the overextended empire, local rulers, who had been given great powers of autonomy, began to rebel against the taxes and injustices levied on their people. In the capital, a labyrinthine bureaucracy strangled diplomacy and negotiation. The tiny state of Taxcala was clawing back after years of military setbacks in the sacrificial wars, ripe for an alliance with a foreign power in order to defeat its Aztec enemies.

Cortés, little did he know it, could not have come at a better time. The Aztec Empire, which may well have survived for hundreds of years in other circumstances, was at a moment of acute crisis, with doubts both within and without the leadership. Cortés played his cards masterfully, making both disaffection and the religious prophecy of the return of Quetzalcóatl act to his advantage. The scene was set for a mighty debacle but no-one could have foreseen that 500 Spaniards could vanquish a city of 300,000 people in a campaign that lasted less than two years.

The Spanish Conquest (1519–21)

The truth is that the history of Mexico is a history in the image of its geography: abrupt and tortuous. Each historical period is like a plateau surrounded by tall mountains and separated from the other plateaus by precipices and divides. The Conquest was the great chasm, the dividing line that split our history in half.

—Octavio Paz, Nobel prize winner

Hernán Cortés

Although he never reached Mexico, Columbus' arrival in the Americas (which he mistakenly supposed to be India) instigated the beginning of the Spanish Empire. Twenty-seven years later, in 1519, Hernán Cortés, a headstrong adventurer from the impoverished province of Extremadura in Spain, left Cuba in search of fortune in the still uncharted territories to the west. With an extraordinary mixture of luck, bravado and diplomacy, he went on to conquer an empire the size of Italy with no more than 550 men,

Typical church in the Catholic, colonial and conservative city of Puebla

11 small ships, some cannons and a handful of horses, claiming for the Spanish crown what was to become the richest of all Spanish domains in the so-called 'New World'.

Cortés' ships first touched Mexico off the Yucatán coast, on the Caribbean island of Cozumel. Here they heard reports of two white men who had survived a shipwreck in 1511 and landed on the same shores. One of them, Padre Jerónimo de Aguilar, joined his compatriots. The other, Gonzalo Guerrero, had settled, marrying a chieftain's daughter and tattooing his body. He made it clear that he had no intention of being rescued, and was later killed in a battle against the Spaniards.

Cortés continued around the Gulf of Mexico to the site of present-day Veracruz, where he founded the city of Villa Rica, claiming the title of Captain-General for himself. Here he gradually learnt of the all-powerful Aztec leader, Moctezuma, from disaffected vassals forced to pay huge tributes to Tenochtitlán. To show his strength, Cortés staged a mock battle on the beach, flaunting his stampeding horses and blazing cannons. The natives presumed that man and horse comprised one terrifying monster, sent by the gods, and the fire-breathing cannons which blew holes in the earth only confirmed their fears. Reports of these four-legged, fire-breathing gods were relayed to Moctezuma, confirming his suspicions that this was indeed the prophesied return of the God-King Quetzalcóatl.

Paralysed with indecision, Moctezuma sent lavish offerings to Cortés, trying to forestall his advance whilst he consulted his gods. Meanwhile, Cortés gathered support from the political enemies of the Aztecs. Most significantly, he managed to win over the Tlaxcalans, thereby gaining the advantage of a vast, bellicose army. In all his negotiations, he was aided immeasurably by Jerónimo de Aguilar, who was fluent in the Maya tongue, and by the infamous La Malinche, fluent in both Maya and Nahuatl (the language of the Aztecs), who became Cortés' lover and interpreter.

Aware of divisions and plots within his own ranks, Cortés scuppered his ships to prevent a mutiny: with no escape route, his men were forced to fight to survive. En route to the Aztec capital of Tenochtitlán, they stayed in Cholula, an Aztec vassal-state. There, La Malinche told them that they had been lured into an ambush of 30,000 men.

Pre-empting defeat, the Spanish attacked first, killing over 6000 men, women and children and razing the city.

This massacre was the turning point for Moctezuma. He was now convinced of the Spaniards' supernatural powers, and allowed them to enter his capital of Tenochtitlán—built on an island in the middle of a lake and linked to the shore by a series of waterways (the site of present-day Mexico City). The Spanish were overawed by Tenochtitlán's gleaming walls and maze of canals, but horrifed by the evidence of human sacrifice (the unwashed hair of the priests was matted with the blood of victims). To prevent an uprising, Cortés took Moctezuma hostage: with no-one to lead them, the Aztecs passively put up with the intruders for six months. Then, Cortés heard of the arrival of a second Spanish fleet in Zempoala, led by Pánfilo de Narváez, who had been sent from Cuba to take over his mission. Leaving half his force in Tenochtitlán, under the command of the headstrong Pedro de Alvarado, Cortés marched to Zempoala. The ensuing battle between the two rival Spanish forces eventually ended in compromise: Cortés managed to persuade most of Narváez' men to join his own expedition, promising them gold and land in return.

The Sad Night
On his return to Tenochtitlán, Cortés found a riot. During a bloody Aztec festival, Alvarado had attacked and killed 200 Aztec nobles. Some 4000 Aztecs died in the subsequent battle, and Alvarado's men found themselves besieged in Moctezuma's palace. The Aztecs waited until Cortés and his troops had joined them before beginning their counterattack. In an effort to quell the riot, Cortés had Moctezuma hauled up onto the roof to address his people: thoroughly disillusioned, they refused to be pacified. Moctezuma was mortally wounded—it is said that someone in the crowd shot him down with a stone—and the Spanish had no option but to escape. Weighted down with gold, they fled across the waterways in an undignified stampede, dropping solid gold ingots into the murky waters of the lake, and leaving for dead 450 Spaniards and 4000 Tlaxcalans. The night was known thereafter as the *noche triste* or sad night.

Cuauhtémoc
Moctezuma was succeeded first by his nephew, who died shortly after—an early victim of Spanish diseases, and then by his son-in-law, the 20-year-old Cuauhtémoc. It was he who masterminded the Aztecs' final counterattack, and he is still revered by Mexicans today as a symbol of valour.

The fleeing Spaniards found a safe haven in Tlaxacala. After 5 months' recuperation, they laid their final siege to the island-capital, sealing off every exit. With no fresh water or food, the city that had seemed so perfectly defensive, surrounded by water on all sides, proved to be just as easily besieged. In August 1521, in a valiant final attempt to fight back, Cuauhtémoc was captured, and months later tortured to death. With him died the empire of the Aztecs.

Consolidating the Conquest (1519—1615)

From Conquistadors to Bureaucrats
The conquered lands, which comprised an area over 40 times the size of Spain, were given the name of New Spain. Although there were, and still are today, over 36 distinct

peoples and languages, the indigenous people of the Americas were lumpenly called Indians, a misnomer which originated with Columbus' discovery of the land he thought was India, whose people he assumed to be Indians.

Control gradually slipped out of the hands of the conquistadors. A handful enriched themselves, but many erstwhile carpenters, blacksmiths and wainwrights returned to the trades from which they had hoped to escape. Instead, the balance of power shifted to more conventional representatives of God and the King, in whose name the colonies had been won—royal agents and Catholic missionaries.

The first royal appointee, Nuño de Guzmán, was undoubtedly the worst. Appointed the leader of Mexico's first *audiencia* in 1527, he was responsible for the bloodiest of all conquests, in western Mexico, before finally being brought to trial in Spain. In 1535, the first viceroy, Antonio de Mendoza, arrived in Mexico City to begin almost 300 years of rule by the Catholic kings of Spain.

Lawyer-bureaucrats from the lower echelons of the minor nobility flocked out from Spain, lured by the prospect of making a fortune, by fair means or foul. As a result, a web of regulations soon came to dominate every aspect of colonial life, extending even to the layouts of the towns, in a mandatory grid-like pattern. Inexorably, during the remaining years of the 16th century, the conquest was consolidated: Spanish bureaucracy was superimposed over the Aztec empire, churches built on the razed 'infidel' temples and the indigenous people enslaved to their new masters.

The End of Cortés

Cortés was one of the few of the original conquerors to escape an untimely end, lending credence to the native belief in his divinity. His first, despised, wife died of a dubious asthma attack a few months after her unwelcome arrival in Mexico, while many of his various political enemies died in mysterious circumstances shortly after crossing his path. Whether due to bad luck or Machiavellian machinations, these deaths proved grist to the mill of his detractors. By 1528 his reputation was thoroughly tarnished and he was hauled back to Spain. Although he was treated with great respect by Charles I, and given huge land-holdings and titles, he never regained political clout in the empire he had conquered for the Spanish crown.

Through the medium of one of his close friends and fellow conquistadors, Bernal Diáz del Castillo, Cortés was able, like all conquerors, to rewrite his history during his lifetime and to erase much of what came before, especially when it disagreed with his chosen view. Yet, however much he might have manufactured his account of the conquest, he was undoubtedly a heroic man.

European Diseases—the Deadly Conquerors

That the conquest was successful at all was largely due to the decimating diseases unwittingly introduced by the Spanish. The commmon cold, diarrhoea, mumps, measles, typhus, pleurisy and smallpox—the most deadly of all—ravaged the native population, far more than any act of war. The first diseases may well have arrived with shipwrecked Spanish sailors, long before Cortés, paving his way by weakening resistance. By 1600 there had been 19 major epidemics, and the native population had shrunk from between 15 and 25 million to less than 1½ million.

The Spanish, in their turn, had to combat New World diseases. With one possible exception, none of these proved to be so deadly. Although there is no mention of its symptoms in any historic document, it is thought that syphilis may have existed in the Americas before it came to Europe. On the other hand, Diego Rivera, the 20th-century muralist, was convinced that none other than Cortés introduced it to Mexico, portraying him as a syphilitic hunchback.

The Spiritual Conquest

Life before the Spanish should not be seen through rose-tinted glasses. The military conquest merely preserved the original hierarchy of slaves and chiefs that had existed long before Cortés. The first Catholic missionaries were treated with suspicion when they suggested that the indigenous people deserved to be treated as humans and not as a minor subspecies of the human race.

Although the missionaries were originally full of Utopian ideals, educating in the vernacular so that the Christian message could be spread by indigenous priests, they later suffered from the conservative backlash brought over from the Spain of Philip II, which had been challenged by Lutheranism and Protestantism, and so reverted to entrenched Catholicism.

Franciscan, Dominican, Augustinian and Jesuit missionaries organized the construction of great cathedrals, using the forced labour of the indigenous people who decorated them with with their own interpretation of the tenets of Christianity. The Franciscans were the first to arrive in 1524, dominating central Mexico, Michoacán, the Huasteca and the Yucatán with their fortress-style monasteries. The Dominicans arrived four years later, setting themselves up in the Mixtec and Zapotec regions of Oaxaca. The late-coming Augustinians (1533) had to take what was left—parts of Puebla and Michoacán.

Some 40 years later, the Jesuits came out to the New World to set up the first universities and seminaries. Their predominantly creole students were encouraged to question the status quo, and taught to 'look for truth, thoroughly investigate everything, unravel mysteries, distinguish between what is certain and what is questionable.' These teachings proved so unsettling to the Spanish authorities that the Jesuits were expelled by Charles III in 1767. By then, however, their legacy was assured. Their spirit of intellectual liberalism had been disseminated by colleges throughout the country, and when the wars of independence finally erupted in the 19th century, they were led by a Jesuit-educated priest.

The 18th Century: the Seeds of Discontent

For some the Age of the Enlightenment, for most the 18th century merely witnessed the consolidation of Spain's hold on the economy. Mining soon became the economic backbone of the colony. At its late 17th-century peak, the silver production of Mexico equalled that of the rest of the world combined, yet all the gold and silver was sent to Spain, coins and ingots departing annually with the royal armada, heavily protected against Dutch and English pirates. There was no international market: Spain insisted that all imports and exports to and from the colonies had to pass through Seville and later Cadiz. This policy was later extended to any native product that might interfere with

Spanish monopolies. Two industries introduced by the missionaries—the manufacture of silk and wine—were subsequently prohibited, to avoid any direct competition with Spain's interests in Europe.

From the start, the Spanish-born *peninsulares* or *gachupines* fought to keep control of the economy from the native-born creoles. All governmental posts were reserved for *peninsulares*, while inheritance regulations stipulated that a younger son, born in Spain, could take precedence over an older son born on the property in Mexico. Two other distinct castes occupied the lowliest positions in colonial Mexican society: the mestizos, with mixed indigenous and Spanish blood, and those indigenous people who had never interbred with the Spanish. Many of these marginalized people worked deep down in the mines—responsible for creating the fabulous wealth of the colony, but never allowed to receive any benefit from it.

During the 18th century Mexico increased its territory, population and wealth. New towns sprang up around the lucrative mines, Texas and Tamaulipas were conquered in the north and the huge California region was settled by Jesuit and Franciscan missionaries. The population rose as Spaniards flocked over to make their fortunes. Originally from the impoverished areas of Andalucia, these new colonists now came from every region of Spain, including the northern provinces of Asturias, Galicia and the Basque country. Although 60 per cent of the population was still indigenous, the urban middle classes burgeoned. Among them, a new middle class of educated creoles nurtured the seeds for separation from Spain.

The Movement towards Independence

Whilst Spain maintained itself as a world power, its prestige in the colonies was only privately challenged. Towards the end of the 18th century, the Spanish king, Charles III, initiated a policy of benign despotism in the colonies, introducing more local governors to take the place of Spanish appointees. This small step forward only increased awareness of greater inequalities, voiced by the Bishop of Valladolid who described Mexico as a country divided into two groups—'those who have nothing and those who have everything'. The American War of Independence, the French Revolution, and a famine in Mexico in the late 1780s all encouraged the development of liberal societies whose members dared to question the role of Spain in the Mexican economy. In 1796, war with Great Britain forced Spain to suspend the export of manufactured goods to Mexico, thereby opening up the home market for many local industries. Independence was increasingly seen as less of an ideal and more of a possibility.

Spanish influence in Mexico was on the wane throughout the reign of the last Hapsburg, Charles IV. Under Napoleon's malign influence and incompetent French command, the Spanish fleet was destroyed at the Battle of Trafalgar in 1805. Three years later, Napoleon forced the abdication of Charles IV, replacing him with his brother Joseph Bonaparte, and unleashed the Peninsular War. While Spain was distracted, Mexico began to think seriously about governing itself. The middle-class creoles refused to accept the authority of Napoleon, using this as an excuse in their increasingly vociferous campaign to win more power and freedom from the thrall of Spain. Although the independence movement began with them, they were, nevertheless, horrified to see it take off and become, in the heat of the moment, a popular uprising, led by a parish priest and armed by peasants with slings and sickles.

The Turbulent Century (1810–1910)

Hidalgo's 'Grito'

On 15 September 1810, the Jesuit-educated parish priest, Miguel Hidalgo y Costilla, delivered his famous 'grito' to his parishioners in the small Guanajuato town of Dolores: '¡Mexicanos! ¡Viva Mexico! ¡Viva la Independencia!' His cry for independence was met by immediate and uncontrollable popular support. Armed with scythes, machetes, rakes and a few blunderbusses, the crowd turned into a mob and soon took over the state. Sympathy movements erupted in surrounding states, and it seemed as if independence was a fait accompli. Hidalgo was not a military man, however. Failing to make the most of his one chance to take over the capital, perhaps through horror at the violence he had unleashed, he was captured within months and executed for treason. In Mexican history he lives on as one of the few untainted heroes of the independence movement, and 15 September, the day of his 'grito', is the most revered of national holidays.

The Shadow of Iturbide: from Colony to Republic to Empire

Meanwhile, a new liberal Spanish government had emerged from the fight against Napoleon. In 1811, Mexican delegates were invited to a conference in Cadiz which declared a a liberal constitution, including greater rights for creoles. It was, however, too little and too late. The ultra-conservative Spanish and the wealthy creoles were horrified by the increasing pace of liberalism, and the constitution was overruled in Mexico. In an uneasy truce, the Spanish hold on Mexico limped on through the next decade, against a background of sporadic guerrilla fighting. By 1820, a liberal revolution in Spain forced the re-establishment of the 1811 constitution. Anxious to keep their comfortable status quo, the peninsulares and the creoles agreed to support separation from Spain in an attempt to avoid any such reform in Mexico.

On their express orders, and with the support of the Catholic Church, the creole Colonel Agustín de Iturbide (1783–1824) made a deal with Vicente Guerrero, the most successful of the guerrilla leaders, and signed the treaty of 'Three Guarantees'. This treaty, however, went a great deal further than Iturbide's conservative backers had expected. Realizing that the conservatives had had their day, Iturbide had changed horses mid-stream: the treaty guaranteed equality before the law for all Mexicans, an independent Mexico ruled by a European monarch and the separation of church and state.

Hoist by its own petard, the Spanish government was forced to recognize this radical new constitution and Mexico was finally ratified as an independent country. Ideals, however, came to little for the average Mexican who had hoped for land and liberty. After 1820, the Spanish in Spain may no longer have held the balance of power but their descendants in Mexico certainly did.

After a decade of civil discontent, the nascent republic was ripe for a dictatorship. Iturbide persuaded those who mattered that he was the obvious candidate, and induced Congress to elect him as emperor in 1823. He then proceeded, with an extraordinary amount of pomp and circumstance, to bestow titles on every member of his large family. His airs and graces so infuriated his former allies that he was forced to abdicate. Iturbide wisely doffed his crown and left the country for Europe; less wisely, he returned a year later and was shot on the spot.

41

The Comings and Goings of Santa Ana

In the 30 years from 1821 to 1850, government in Mexico was in a constant state of turmoil, dogged by economic disaster, chopping and changing from liberal to conservative with monotonous irregularity. There were more than 50 governments in this one period, 11 of which were presided over by one man, the quixotic General Antonio López de Santa Ana (1794–1876). A leader in the fight both against Spain and Iturbide, and consequently regarded as a dashing romantic hero, Santa Ana was first elected president in the early 1830s and for the next two decades had the leading role in the anarchic production of Mexican history. Yet, with an uncharacteristic show of restraint, he ruled in name rather than actuality, leaving the day-to-day business of government to his deputies, preferring cock fighting to constitution making.

Although ostensibly liberal, Santa Ana was, privately, a staunch conservative, quick to defend the interests of his ruling class whenever the reforming liberals in his various governments appeared to be making some headway. Always quick to take to arms, it was he who led the infamous massacre of Anglo-Saxon settlers during the battle of the Alamo in 1836. These unfortunates had proposed that their state of Texas (then a part of Mexico) should join the United States, with whom they had more in common. Santa Ana was captured shortly afterwards and forced to recognize Texas' independence, in exchange for his life.

Out of favour for his hot-headed incompetence, he retired to the wings for three years until, amongst a plethora of rebellions, liberal reforms and growing foreign debt, the French turned up to reclaim money owed to a French pastry cook. Called back to centre stage, Santa Ana valiantly fought the French, in the so-called 'French Pastry Wars',losing his left leg in the process. In honour of the leg and the man, he was reinstated to the presidency, subsequently renouncing it, reclaiming it, being expelled, exiled and then restored by popular demand.

In the midst of all of this, in 1845, Mexico declared war on the United States when the US army crossed the Río Grande, the border between Texas and Mexico. The country was in domestic turmoil, lacking both the funds and the infrastructure to cope with such an invasion. In a pincer movement, US troops swarmed through the northwestern states while General Zachary Taylor swept down to Veracruz, defeated Santa Ana and took Mexico City, whose defence had been left to the fresh-faced 15-year-old cadets of the military college (the famous niños héroes of innumerable street names). These boys wrapped themselves in the national flag and jumped off the battlements of Chapultepec Castle rather than surrender. It was all to no avail: at one of the most ignominious moments in Mexican history, the US flag was raised over the capital. The crippled Mexican government was forced to cede half its land, which then included Arizona, California and New Mexico, for the risible price of $15 million.

European Invasions

Whilst the liberals were stymied by debt, the conservatives were wily enough to seek European help. England, Spain and France, Mexico's three greatest creditors, agreed to intervene in the hope of collecting some of their debts by force. In 1861—when the US was still in the throes of its own civil war and unable to help the Mexican liberals—a joint European task force arrived off the coast of Veracruz. England and Spain were quickly bought off by an interim payment. France, however, was determined to create a monarchical, Latin and Catholic barrier against the US, in order to prevent any further expansion of its territory. Aided and abetted by the conservatives, the French took Mexico City, forced the resignation of Benito Juárez' liberal government, and invited a hapless Austrian archduke, Maximilian of Hapsburg (1832–67), to come over to rule the country. In June 1864, Maximilian and his wife, the Belgian princess Charlotte (who changed her name to Carlota in sympathy with her new country) moved into Chapultepec Castle.

Maximilian and Carlota

Poor Maximilian! A puppet of the French, he proved to be both vacillating and incompetent—a regal farce, and not at all what the French had hoped for. He had insisted on a referendum amongst the Mexican people, to assure himself of his welcome, but was all too easily persuaded when the French responded with a forged document. In essence a decent but weak liberal, he soon disconcerted his conservative hosts by supporting reform and decreeing religious tolerance. His decrees were never passed. Within a matter of months, the French, under Napoleon III, were convinced of their mistake and ready to pull out to fight their own war against the Prussians.

With the end of the civil war in the United States, the liberal anti-monarchists, headed by Juárez, suddenly found their cause supported by the North Americans. The last rat in a sinking ship, Maximilian implored the French army for support, offering to hand over everything in his fast-dwindling coffers. It was to no avail. He was forced to surrender, and only three years and one week after his triumphant arrival in the city of Mexico, he was shot by a Mexican firing squad in the city of Querétaro. Carlota, mad with grief, lived on for another 60 years, locked up in European castles, insisting to the end that she was the lawful Empress of Mexico.

Benito Juárez

A Zapotec liberal from the Oaxacan mountains, imbued with the spirit of the Enlightenment, Benito Juárez (1806–72) was the first indigenous Mexican to rise to the rank of president. As a young lawyer, he often worked for nothing, appalled by the fantastical fees charged for the registration of marriages, births and deaths (which meant that only one couple in ten was legally married). Elected governor of Oaxaca in 1848, he embarked on a radical programme, building rural schools and cutting back on the mismanagement of state bureaucracy. He had his critics and in 1953 was exiled to New Orleans, where he was reduced to selling cigarettes on the streets.

Juárez was first elected president in 1858. Ousted by the French four years later, he was re-elected in 1867 after the surrender of Maximilian. Although he was magnanimous to his political enemies, he showed no such generosity to Maximilian, signing his death warrant despite international clamour and the pleas of Victor Hugo.

With the re-establishment of the republic, Mexico became firmly liberal in outlook. Juárez had always argued fiercely against the excessive power of the Church, and now attempted to curb it by forcing the sale of its huge landholdings. These radical reforms backfired, however. Communal lands came under review and were sold off to the highest bidder—usually a local landowner and rarely the tiller of the soil. Yet Juárez's courage and honesty in a confused age, which ran roughshod over contemporary opinion, have made him one of the most popular of all presidents, and no village in Mexico is complete without its Plaza, Calle or Avenida Juárez.

Porfirio Díaz
On the other hand, Porfirio Diáz (1830–1915) has only a mocking epithet coined after him—*Díazpotism*. With a smattering of education, Díaz came to power through the army, rising to the rank of brigadier-general at the age of 32. Initially a liberal supporter of Juárez, he became inceasingly right wing, standing as his opponent in two presidential elections, but only achieving the presidency four years after Juárez's death in 1872. His motto, 'little politics, much administration', effectively meant that the republic was reduced to a dictatorship. Even his family had to bow to pressure: when his nephew, Félix Díaz, attempted to stand as governor of Oaxaca against his uncle's wishes, he was rerouted to a minor diplomatic role in Chile.

During Díaz' dictatorship, foreign capital was courted to boost the economy, earning him the ironic title of 'the mother of foreigners and the stepmother of Mexicans'. Although he certainly stabilized the country and prepared it for the modern age, under his administration the economy became entirely business-based—providing little for those who had little to give. By 1910, the country had had enough.

The 1910 Revolution

Francisco Madero
After years of one-man rule that had proved highly beneficial to the ruling elite and scandalously unjust for the bulk of the population, the Revolution seemed not so much surprising as long overdue. In 1908, Porfirio Díaz told a North American journalist that Mexico was ready for democracy and that an opposition party might be tolerated. Although most Mexicans disbelieved him, one man—Francisco Madero (1873–1913)—took him seriously.

Madero was born in Coahuila in 1873, the son of a wealthy landowner who had earned his fortune in mining, banking and cattle. Educated at Berkeley, California and finished off in Paris, he returned home to manage some of his father's estates. Here he was to experience the gross inequalities of the Díaz system first-hand, through his daily contacts with peasants tied to the land by constant debt and derisory wages.

In the spring of 1908, he published his inflammatory *The Presidential Succession of 1910*, offering himself as a possible opposition candidate. (Diáz' age made it unlikely that he would see through another term of office.) It was a protest rather than an outright bid for election, but the country shared his sentiments and Díaz was forced to imprison Madero in order to secure a favourable outcome for himself. Madero had opened a can of worms, which culminated in the uprising of 1910. Díaz was forced into exile in Europe, and Madero was declared president. His victory was short-lived, however: he was murdered by the ambitious General Huerta, and his revolution passed into the hands of others.

The Revolutionary Decade
The Revolution lasted for 10 bloody years. Pancho Villa led his troops from the north, Emiliano Zapata the peasants from the south, and various rival factions fought over the

middle. During this period there were 11 presidencies (including one which lasted for 45 minutes). By 1920, nearly all the soldiers and politicians who had been in the forefront of the fight had been killed by political opponents. The fighting finally stopped on 30 November 1920, when Alvaro Obregón (1880—1928), from the northern state of Sonora, was elected president.

Post-revolutionary Mexico (from 1920)

Under Obregón began the slow process of unification and reform, of a country torn apart by a decade of civil war. Governmental positions were no longer automatically denied to union leaders, and the vexed question of land distribution was aired once more. Although slow and notoriously incomplete, these reforms were nevertheless so radical that no-one was surprised when Obregón was assassinated in 1928.

Cristeros

The Revolution came down hard on the Catholic Church. All church property was nationalized, and the wearing of cassocks was prohibited in public places. In 1926, to the cry of '¡Viva Cristo Rey!' ('Long live Christ the King'), the more conservative and Catholic parts of the country, in particular Guanajuato and Jalisco, rose up in rebellion. The Cristero movement was firmly suppressed by the government, under the presidency of Obregón's hand-picked successor, Plutarco Elías Calles (1877—1942). Priests were executed, churches razed, and the power of the Catholic Church in affairs of state was finally destroyed.

Before the 1980s, no pope visited or even acknowledged the Mexican government. Yet, ironically, despite its ostensibly secular status, the country remains 90 per cent Catholic, and it is a thoughtless politician who doesn't let it slip that he is a regular Mass-goer.

Lázaro Cárdenas

In 1934 Lázaro Cárdenas was elected president on the platform of radical social reform. After so many promises and so little substance, few people expected this mild-mannered ex-governor of Michoacán to have the strength to pull the country together. Yet he did more than any other president, before or since, to address the land issue, restoring over 46 million acres of private land to the communal *ejidos* introduced by Juárez. Ignored abroad, he suddenly made headlines in 1938 when he expropriated foreign holdings and nationalized oil. (He also offered asylum to León Trotsky, who was murdered by Stalinists two years later in Mexico City.) In retaliation, the US led a world boycott of Mexican oil exports. It seemed as if Cárdenas and his government would be swamped by high inflation and a plummeting economy, when the outbreak of World War II saved the nation from collapse.

Post-war Mexico

The war created a watershed in Mexican politics, dragging the country from an agricultural to an industrial revolution within a matter of years, in response to the urgent foreign demand for the raw materials, such as oil, corn, meat and minerals, that Mexico could provide. Although the socialist ideals of the Revolution were still touted, the corridors of power were taken over by university-educated middle-class bureaucrats, who raced ahead with plans for industrialization. Once again, the social problems of the urban and rural poor were relegated to the back-burner.

In 1968, Mexico City was chosen to host the Olympic Games, a sure sign of the republic's standing in the international economic community. Throughout that summer, however, the city was torn by a series of riots, sparked by student unrest which erupted into a mass protest movement. Middle-class students and the working class joined in protest against the authoritarian stance of the one-party state, and on 1 September, 300,000 people marched on the Zócalo. This highly publicized protest was enough to get government deputies talking with student leaders, but a month later, a second, much smaller march ended in a massacre. In a desperate attempt to hush it up, before the imminent opening of the games, the government blamed it on ill-advised and nervous police officers, claiming that only 32 had been killed. More open-minded estimates put the figure at between 200 and 500.

Modern Mexico

Since the 1910 Revolution, the Mexican people have taken an increasing pride in their Mexican (as opposed to Spanish) roots. However, this is still far more evident in bombastic presidential addresses, avid collecting of suddenly valuable pre-Hispanic artefacts and gloriously up-lifting nationalistic murals than it is in the lives of the ever-marginalized 'Indians'. Still branded with Columbus' absurd misnomer, the Maya, Nahua, Zapotec and Mixtec people remain emphatically at the bottom of the economic pyramid, with a long way to climb before they reach the heights attained by their few role models—the 19th-century Zapotec president, Benito Juárez, or the 20th-century revolutionary, the *campesino* Emiliano Zapata. After almost 500 years, Don Quixote look-alikes—the Wasps of New Spain, born in Mexico but without a drop of non-European blood—continue to control most of the political and economic power.

Identity is not a constant in Mexican history. Where once the split was between Spaniard, mestizo and the so-called Indian, today it is exemplified by the growing hold of Mexico's northern neighbour and big brother, the United States of America. The infamous quotation attributed to Porfirio Díaz, 'Poor Mexico, so far from God and so close to the United States', has continuing relevance. Mexican immigrants make Los Angeles the second-largest Mexican city in the world, and the pros and cons of a free-market economy between the two countries are endlessly and avidly discussed. The north today represents the wealthiest, most industrialized section of the country, reluctantly paying its taxes and accepting the law imposed by the government bureaucracy of Mexico City—the all-powerful and ever-expanding megalopolis, which is far further from most people than is the promised land of California and Texas.

Politics have become as institutionalized as the name of the party which has governed Mexico without interruption for the last 50 years—the PRI, the party of institutionalized revolution! Opposition there is, increasingly more vociferous from both the right (PAN) and the left (PRD), but the custom whereby the outgoing president chooses his successor, who is then nominally elected, shows no sign of changing. With rare exceptions, presidents have been notoriously corrupt. The current president, Carlos Salinas de Gortari, elected in 1988, has, so far, a clean slate, successfully attempting to pull Mexico

46

out of its escalating spiral of inflation and foreign debt by a stringent policy of price control and a sharp lesson in free-market economics (translated as foreign investment in Mexican commodities).

Although military coups and dictatorships may have rocked Mexico in the 19th century, it is now a proud and stable country. With the economy under control, the doors of goverment being prised open to free elections, and the army no more than a silent force in the background, it occupies a buoyant position, and one which compares favourably to that of all its Central and South American neighbours.

Topics

Colour and Form

Anglo-Saxons 'know' that red and purple should be kept at a decorous distance; Mexicans think that such rules and restrictions are only made to be broken. Cornflower blue, burnt sienna, bitter orange, mustard yellow, terra-cotta red and Schiaperelli pinks are all thrown together, and that is just where Mexicans begin. Colour is everywhere, from riotous tumbles of hot pink bougainvillea to heaped piles of market fruits—the brown skin of the *mamey* acting as a foil to its delicate pink flesh, the proclamatory puce and psychedelic green of the *pithaya*, the reds, greens, yellows, browns and blacks of chilli peppers. A green cactus-leaf salad is thrown into relief by strips of bright red chilli, sprinkled with white cheese. The dark, rich chocolate brown of the *mole* sauce doesn't just happen to be that colour but is the product of 32 ingredients and hours of careful combination. Parched landscapes are brightened by the sharp splash of a flame tree or the soft lavender of jacaranda.

The Mexican has an innate, audacious sense of colour, form and texture. Natural, bright dyes from pomegranate seeds, marigold flowers and cochineal are used to colour wool and woven together into elaborate shawls and textiles, worn by all the indigenous Mexicans who haven't yet been seduced by fluorescents. The white Maya dresses in the south are brightened by embroidered flowers; in Chiapas, all the villagers in Zinacantán dress in shocking pinks, whilst their neighbours in San Juan Chamula wear bright turquoises. From fiestas to buses, Mexico is coloured through and through.

Life and Death

Cultures that view birth as a beginning and death as an end can have no sense of a living past. For Mexicans, neither birth nor death is seen to interrupt the continuity of life and neither is considered overtly important.

—Alan Riding, *Distant Neighbours*

The concept of death as celebration is unfamiliar to Anglo-Saxons. In Mexico, however, the most important festival of the year is during the first couple of days of November (loosely aligned to All Souls' Day), when the dead are brought back to life through memory, and honoured through flowers, food and drink. There is nothing macabre about this preoccupation with death. As good Catholics, Mexicans believe that the life hereafter is a luxury worth waiting for. And so, being Mexican, they use it as an excuse for a fiesta. Sugared skulls with the names of the living iced on to the forehead, tissue-paper cutouts of fancy cadavers, papier mâché skeletons and cardboard coffins fill the markets and children queue to buy as many as possible. Death is brought out into the open, celebrated and laughed with, and not hidden behind circumspect veils of silence.

This dates from long before the arrival of the Catholic Spanish. Pre-Hispanic cultures also saw death as a great honour, particularly on the battlefield or in childbirth, and warriors or ball-game players who died in action were often deified. Even today, the pragmatic Mexicans have a furious energy to live for the moment. Fatal car accidents are not uncommon, given the rough state of many roads and the idiosyncratic driving skills of Mexicans. In rural communities the infant mortality rate is high. Amidst this anarchy which is daily life, worries are consigned to a *mañana* which may never arrive.

History on the Streets

> The hero's tomb is the cradle of the people.
> —Octavio Paz

Mexicans are proud of their heroes and keen to commemorate them with murals, statues and street names. The tradition of mural painting has a long history in Mexico, from the walls of Maya and Aztec temples to the lavish interiors of the Spanish missionaries' churches and monasteries, where the life of Christ was graphically depicted in order to convert illiterate non-Christians. In the 1930s, the radical government of Lázaro Cárdenas encouraged mural painting as a swift method of mass education, at a time when education for the masses scarcely existed, using these public blackboards to instil a sense of national unity in a country riven by different factions and class distinction. Mexicans were encouraged to feel proud of their pre-Hispanic past (Cárdenas himself liked to draw attention to the fact that he had Purépechan blood). On the walls of government buildings, Diego Rivera and others painted huge frescoes of an idyllic pre-Hispanic way of life and of heroes such as Hidalgo, who freed Mexico from the yoke of Spain.

No city, town or village is ever complete without the names of streets, boulevards and alleyways commemorating presidents such as Juárez, the first indigenous president and the founder of the republic, battles such as Cinco de Mayo, Independencia or Revolución, or heroes such as Cuauhtémoc, nephew of Moctezuma, or the *Niños Heroes*, the five boys who died unsuccessfully defending Chapultepec Castle from the US army. These heroes become instantly recognizable through endless repetition. Just as remarkable is the absence of the anti-heroes of the Mexican past. Search in vain for statues or street names commemorating Hernán Cortés, the original Spanish conqueror, Porfirio Díaz whose dictatorship spawned the Revolution, or Santa Ana, president eleven times during the 19th century who was also responsible for the loss of Texas.

At times this zeal for didactic street names has gone from the sublime to the ridiculous, following the caprices of one urban planner or another. Names like Effective Suffrage or No Re-election echo the political message of the ruling party, whilst others honour artists as remote from Mexico as Watteau or Bosch, or authors such as Daniel Ortega or George Eliot.

Lovers

The Catholic Church asks for fidelity (so do the women) but the men are proud to say that it is biologically impossible, leaving fatherless families littered all over the country and the mothers working long hours as maids to support their several children.

History hasn't set much of a precedent. The first Spanish conqueror, Hernan Cortés, left his Spanish wife behind when he first came to Mexico and took instead the native-born La Malinche as his interpreter, lover, and the mother of his child. When his wife turned up some months later, with little prior warning, she found herself housed next door to La Malinche: within a horribly short time, she died under still mysterious circumstances. The pragmatic La Malinche knew the ways of her *macho méxicano*, however, and when her charms began to wane, moved on to marry one of Cortés closest friends and soldiers. Cortés showed his approval of the deal with a wedding present of several thousand acres in Querétaro. Seen by many as a Mexican Eve who betrayed her people to feather her own nest, La Malinche lives on in the term '*malinchismo*', a disparaging reference to those who look abroad for inspiration and turn their backs on Mexico.

No better role models were the Austrian puppet emperor Maximilian and his young wife, the Belgian princess Carlota, sent to rule Mexico by Napoleon III of France. Pleasure lovers both, they soon moved from the capital to Cuernavaca, where he spent all of his time with his mistress, the '*India Bonita*', for whom he built a little cottage on one side of town. Carlota ignored him and busied herself flirting with cavalry officers. Less than three years later, when Maximilian was fighting for his empire and his life, Carlota forgot Cuernavaca and became his staunchest supporter. She raced around Europe in an unsuccessful attempt to drum up support amongst the monarchy, breaking down in an interview with the Pope. When Maximilian was finally shot in Querétaro, she was driven insane, ending her days in a strait-jacket in Belgium.

Perhaps the most famous of all Mexican lovers are Diego Rivera, the muralist, and his painter wife and fellow communist, Frida Kahlo. She fell in love with him when she was 13, and married him at 19, after a bad accident in a bus crash had left her with severe spinal injuries. She was unable to have the children she so wanted and her health deteriorated throughout their marriage. She and Diego painted each other, loved each other, left each other and came back together again. He had numerous affairs (including one with her sister), as did she (both with her nurse and with Trotsky). During her last illness, when she was in excruciating pain after her left foot had been amputated, he stayed in the hospital with her every night for over a year and was there when she died.

Machismo

Machismo is the backbone of Mexican society. A knee-jerk reaction to any situation, this form of male arrogance is practised the length and breadth of the country with an assiduity that is breathtaking. Although as much of a cliché as the Sicilian Mafia, it has just as much relevance. Tourists don't escape it, neither men nor women. Try arguing with a bank clerk, after he has left you for 20 minutes to coo down the telephone to his girlfriend, and see his hackles rise in an instinctive macho response of aggressive defence. Mexicans don't like direct confrontation: on the other hand, requests for help are rarely refused. Apologetic references to a desperately ill wife/mother who needs to be rushed to hospital are a far more tactful (and standard) method of getting the clerk off the telephone.

Women will find that they can use sexism to their advantage. A double-headed serpent, machismo is sinuously attractive when its not unappreciable powers are turned full on. Chivalry goes hand in hand with peacock pride and exaggerated manners are as much a facet of machismo as gross one-upmanship. It is no use arguing about splitting bills or finding your own way home. A Mexican has an instinctive courtesy which no amount of explanation of women's independence is going to shift, so enjoy it whilst it lasts (which is rarely beyond courtship).

Drinking and driving both exacerbate the condition (and the two often go hand in hand). When behind the wheel or with a tequila or two too many inside them, macho men will suddenly remember all the wrongs that have ever been done to them and the women responsible. Jokes and jibes are interpreted as masculinity-threatening challenges, which have to be dealt with at once. In the old days, pistol shots would fly; today, fists are bared (though rarely used). Whilst fierce gesturing is all part of the act, most of these machos are keen to be dragged back from the fray, honour satisfied, before they lurch drunkenly home. In cars, the horn takes over from the pistol and towns resound with the constant pumping of overworked claxons. Bewildered tourists shouldn't feel they are the victims of a personal vendetta: other motorists simply feel obliged to join in the general cacophony.

Masks

> The Mexican whether young or old, *criollo* or *mestizo*, general or labourer
> or lawyer, seems to me to be a person who shuts himself away to protect
> himself: his face is a mask and so is his smile.
>
> —Octavio Paz, *The Labyrinth of Solitude*

Invaded and conquered many times over the years, Mexico is wary of exposing its inner self to the gaze of outsiders, preferring a mask of bland indifference or even unctuous servility. The Mexicans love theatre, show and colour. The Maya, Toltecs and Aztecs dressed up their priests and put on bloody shows to enthral their peoples. The Spanish arrived with befrocked bishops and lacy gallants, bedazzling the eye of the beholder and belying the weakling underneath. So, today, street heroes use disguise to draw the crowds. Painted clowns juggle at traffic lights, worthy citizens cover their heads at Easter and go on long processions of self-flagellation, while in the villages the elders put on masks of animals and birds to recreate the dances of their forefathers during religious festivals.

The *lucha libre* is a purely Mexican tradition. Every neighbourhood has its ring where masked wrestlers go on stage to enact predestined fights of good against evil. Everyone in the audience knows who is going to win but the stadium will ring with whoops of enthusiasm time after time as the bad guy goes down. Winners become national heroes. Superbarrio, a former *lucha libre* victor, has gone on to champion human rights, exhorting his numerous supporters to use condoms to prevent the spread of Aids and campaigning against pollution. These Robin Hood figures symbolize all the hopes and aspirations of the people, which they themselves prefer not to voice for fear of disappointment.

Part III

MEXICO CITY AND THE STATE OF MEXICO

Packed VW combi van (used as taxis all over the country)

MEXICO CITY

I have never felt so thoroughly bad-tempered as during the week we spent in Mexico City.

—Aldous Huxley

Fifty years on, Aldous Huxley wouldn't have changed his mind. Mexico City is confusing, contaminated and crowded—and these are just some of the more common adjectives flung in the megalopolis' direction. It shares the joint dishonour of being both the most populated and the most polluted city in the world, having doubled in size in the last two decades and covered itself with an umbrella of dense smog. However, despite these considerable and often repeated drawbacks, it would be unforgivable to avoid it.

Avoiding Mexico City would also mean avoiding the world's most outstanding murals, the country's greatest collections of pre-Hispanic, colonial and contemporary art, and, just as important, its nerve centre and political base. As in every large city, its architecture reflects its past: every conquering power has left behind images in its memory, from the Paseo de la Reforma of the French to the colonial palaces of the Spanish, from modern

51

American skyscrapers to—most enduring of all—the street plan and foundations of the ancient Aztec empire, overthrown by the Spanish 500 years ago.

Anyone visiting the city for the first time will be able to see the main sites and museums within four packed days, but give Mexico City a chance, and it will prove itself again and again.

Time Well Spent

To make the writhing octopus of Mexico City and its surrounding state as manageable as possible, the city has been divided into areas and the state presented as a series of one-day trips for those who have a little more time. The most important thing to remember is that nearly all the museums are shut on Mondays. The hard-pressed traveller with little time could see each section of the city at breakneck speed in one day, but no-one, however hard-pressed, should miss the murals around the main square, the Zócalo, the pre-Hispanic art in the Museum of Anthropology (Chapultepec Park) or the Rivera-Kahlo memorabilia in the south of the city.

Monday: since all the museums and archaeological sites are closed on Mondays, this is the best day to wander around the Zócalo and the old centre of the city which never closes. Alternatively, shop: the markets are especially lively on Mondays (see Markets).

Tuesday: the Museum of Anthropology really deserves at least two visits. It is free on Sundays, but horribly crowded throughout the weekend: weekdays (Tues–Fri) are far better.

Wednesday: this is a good day for a visit outside the city, northeast to the pyramids at Teotihuacán, the modern basilica of Guadalupe and the Augustinian convent at Acolman (see The State of Mexico). All three will be more rewarding after a visit to the Museum of Anthropology.

Thursday: the university, deep in the south, is an entire city within a city. As the murals are on the outside, it matters little whether it is visited by day or night or at the weeekend, but it tends to be more fun during the week (and during term time). To feel the pulse of the city, spend the afternoon at the races (see Racing).

Friday: Friday morning is the traditional time to visit the open-air *tianguis* in Toluca (1 hr from the city). Continue to the Aztec site of Malinalco or, alternatively, make a weekend of it and head west to Valle de Bravo. (See The State of Mexico.)

Saturday: Coyoacán and San Angel, in the south of the city, are both weekend places. The Bazar Sabado in San Angel's Plaza San Jacinto is the place to spend the morning (but don't rush: it doesn't think of beginning until 10.00). After a late lunch in Coyoacán, and at least half an hour in the main square, spend the rest of the afternoon in Frida Kahlo's and Léon Trotsky's houses (also in Coyoacán). Saturday is a good night for dancing. For the best venues see Nightlife.

Sunday: a month of Sundays in Mexico City wouldn't be enough. It is the great family day, when the city overspills with children and grandmothers. Some of the most popular places, filled with makeshift stalls, candyfloss sellers, buskers and ice-cream carts, are: the floating gardens of Xochimilco (see South of the City), the Alameda, Chapultepec Park, the main plaza in Coyoacán, and the mariachi square of the Plaza Garibaldi. All the museums are free on Sundays (they cost very little anyway) and so tend to be busier than usual.

History

A SHORT SYNOPSIS

Mexico City sits sunk in a plateau 2240 m above sea level, hemmed in by overtowering volcanic mountains. Fifty million years ago, volcanic activity caused these mountains to rise out of the sea and break the back of the earth. Over the next 30 million years, the plateau which today forms the Valley of Mexico evolved into its present oval shape (109 km north–south by 80 km east–west).

The threat of earthquakes is, and always has been, part of the consciousness of the valley. As recently as 1985, a huge earthquake, registering 8 on the Richter scale, killed thousands of people and flattened whole districts of the city. Add to earthquakes the lack of ventilation caused by the encircling mountains and the absence of surface water or rivers, and some of the manifold problems of the city become apparent.

After the Second World War, these geophysical problems were compounded by massive overpopulation. Industrialization attracted the impoverished rural poor, who moved into the city in droves in an attempt to improve their lot. Mexico City is already the largest metropolis in the world, yet this immigration shows no sign of abating. As the city swells, so the countryside is depleted.

Yet, ever since the first inhabitants of the Valley of Mexico began to make a precarious living around 10,000 BC, it has been the political and economic centre of the country.

TEOTIHUACAN

The nomadic hunters who moved into the valley from 10,000 BC onwards, continued ever southwards. Even by 1000 BC, the valley had a population of no more then 10,000. The first city was built 40 km north of present-day Mexico City by farmers who had discovered underground water, which they used to grow their staple crop, maize. Set in the midst of farmers' fields, this city had 20,000 inhabitants by AD 1, encompassing temples and a huge Pyramid of the Sun, and divided up into well-planned zones. By AD 500 its population had grown to 100,000, making it larger than imperial Rome. Yet its fall was to be as rapid as its rise, because of the old story—as the population grew, so the natural resources of water and wood were depleted. Teotihuacán literally burnt itself out and the city was razed to the ground.

THE AZTECS

After the fall of Teotihuacán, the valley was left without a single centralized power and attention was turned to Xochimilco in the south and Tula in the north. It was only with the coming of the Aztecs in 1325 that the site of present-day Mexico City, then a series of several islands in Lake Texcoco, was first developed. Within a generation, the Aztecs dominated the surrounding city-states and set themselves up as the masters of the valley. Their city was not left to grow haphazardly. Every street, square, area and house had its place, all interconnected by a series of canals which made the Spaniards liken it to Venice. It was divided into five sacred zones, four representing the compass points and the fifth the ceremonial heart of the city. From the centre, four great causeways made of lime and stone—so broad that the horses brought by the Spanish could be ridden 12 abreast—led out to the mainland, protected by drawbridges. In the heart of the city, the Aztecs built temples to their many gods. Of these, Huitzilopochtli, the Sun God and God of War, was the most important of all. (His myth relates that his mother, Coatlicue, was decapitated by her other children whilst pregnant with him, whereupon he emerged fully grown and armed to redeem her.)

Under the first emperor Moctezuma (ruled 1440–8), a series of natural disasters during a time of great growth and stretching of resources led the priests to initiate human sacrifices, to maintain the Sun God in his course and prevent him from falling from the sky. Moctezuma was followed by the three brothers, Caxayácatl, Tízoc and Ahuitzotl. Whereas the first two merely kept the empire running, Ahuitzotl (ruled 1486–1501) extended it as far south as Oaxaca, Guatemala and El Salvador. His son, Moctezuma II, assumed command of an overextended population of 200,000, who lived on the tribute brought in from the furthest reaches of the swollen empire.

THE SPANISH

In his polemic, *The Decline and Fall of Western Civilization*, Oswald Spengler wrote of the Aztecs: 'This is the only culture that died a violent death. It did not die of decay, nor was it hindered or repressed in its development. It was murdered at the height of its evolution, cut down like the flower lopped off by a stroller's walking stick.'

Hernán Cortés was the stroller who entered the city on 8 November 1519, with his army of native Tlaxcalan allies and 300-odd Spanish soldiers. For several months, the Spaniards were suffered as unwanted guests of Moctezuma II, until an Aztec uprising resulted in the death of Moctezuma, the routing of the Spaniards (30 June 1521) and the bitter Spanish siege of the city, which finally starved the Aztec population, under the brave leadership of Moctezuma's nephew Cuauhtémoc, into a reluctant submission. The marketplace of Tlatelolco was the last place to fall. Today, in this calm square, flanked by new department blocks, ancient Aztec ruins and a colonial church, a plaque poignantly describes the fall of one nation and the creation of another: 'On August 13, 1521, heroically defended by Cuauhtémoc, Tlatelolco fell into the hands of Hernán Cortés. It was neither a triumph nor a defeat: it was the painful birth of the mestizo nation that is Mexico today.'

Cortés looked no further for a capital. He simply razed the Aztec temples and palaces and build his new city on top, using the available stone and an enslaved workforce. The canals were filled in with the debris, the lakes gradually dredged and the valley transformed into a damp, swampy hole. Over the centuries, the cathedral has sunk into the ground on which it was built, slipping further and further into the still subsiding bog.

Later Spanish viceroys formalized the urban plan, straightening out the grid system around the Zócalo. Maximilian laid out the great sweep of the Paseo de la Reforma in the 1860s, effectively joining the old centre to the new along an east–west axis. French elegance and *savoir faire* were added during the dictatorship of the Francophile Porfirio Díaz. Many buildings such as the landmark Bellas Artes date from this period. Post-revolutionary Mexico added the final touches. A new confidence was born and Mexican architects were encouraged to give the city a modern but distinctly Mexican feel. The city finally came of age only to discover the perils of maturity: most of its efforts are now directed at ridding itself of the taint of contamination.

GETTING TO AND FROM MEXICO CITY

By Air: The international airport, Benito Juárez, is 6½ km east of the city centre in Blvd Puerto Aereo (tel 571 3600). The main carriers for domestic flights are Mexicana de

Aviación (Xola 535, tel 660 4443) and Aeroméxico (Paseo de la Reforma, tel 207 8233). Between them, these two airlines fly daily to all the state capitals. Few flights within the republic take over 3 hrs, the longest being Chetumal and Tijuana at 3½ hrs each.

Taxis provide the easiest connections between the airport and the city centre: it is a long walk from the airport to the bus stop on Blvd Puerto Aereo. To avoid confusion, an excellent system has been established to standardize taxi tariffs, and tokens are on sale at official booths (bilingual English/Spanish) in the arrival lounge.

The journey by **metro** is not as easy as it looks on the map. Officially, large suitcases are not allowed onto trains, and this rule is strictly enforced during rush hours (08.00–10.00 and 18.00–20.00). The nearest stop for the airport is *not* Aeropuerto, which is in fact about 1 km away. Instead, use the **Terminal Aerea** stop on yellow line 5.

Ticket Offices:

Aeroflot (for Cuba):	Insurgentes Sur 569 (tel 523 8729)
Aeroméxico:	Paseo Reforma 445 (tel 207 8233, 553 1577, 762 4022)
Air Canada:	Hamburgo 108 (tel 511 2094)
Air France:	Paseo de la Reforma 404 (tel 511 3990, 566 0066)
American Airlines:	Paseo de la Reforma 300 (tel 533 5446)
British Airways:	Mariano Escobedo 752 (tel 525 9133) or Paseo de la Reforma 332 (tel 525 9133)
Continental:	Andrés Bello 45 (tel 545 0185, 203 1143)
Delta:	Paseo de la Reforma 381 (tel 533 2000, 207 4013)
Iberia:	Paseo de la Reforma 24 (tel 566 4011)
	Airport (tel 762 5844)
	Reservations (tel 592 2988)
KLM:	Av de las Palmas 735–7 (tel 202 4444, 571 3246, 596 8088)
Mexicana:	Xola 535 (tel 660 4443) or Paseo de la Reforma and Amberes (tel 511 3660)
	Airport (tel 784 5399)
	Reservations (tel 660 4444)
Pan Am:	Blvd Amila Camacho 1 (tel 395 0077, 557 8722)

Any travel agent can also book tickets.

By Bus: There are four main bus stations, each loosely covering a cardinal point. Taxis wait at the arrival gates, and each station is close to a metro station.

North: Terminal Central del Norte (Av de los 100 Metros 4907; tel 587 5967; metro Autobuses del Norte, line 5): this is the largest station, for buses to and from Teotihuacán (1 hr), Pachuca (2 hrs), Papantla (8 hrs), Tuxpan (8 hrs), Guadalajara (7 hrs) and all of northern Mexico. It has a large left-luggage office.

South: Terminal Central del Sur (Tasqueña 1320; tel 544 2101; metro Tasqueña, line 2): this is the station for buses to and from the Pacific coast—between Acapulco (6 hrs) and Ixtapa (10 hrs), Taxco (4 hrs) and Cuernavaca (1 hr).

East: Terminal de Autobuses de Pasajeros del Oriente (TAPO) (Czda Ignacio Zaragoza; tel 702 5977; metro San Lázaro, line 1): use this terminal for buses to and from southeast Mexico—Puebla (2 hrs), southern Veracruz, Chiapas, Oaxaca and the Yucatán peninsula.

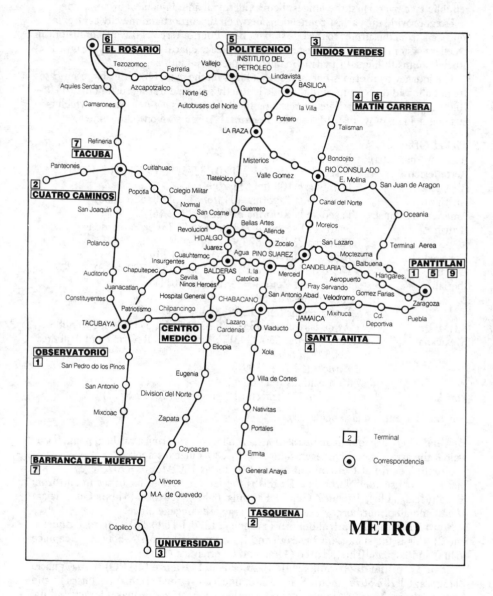

West: Terminal de Autobuses del Poniente (Río Tacubaya 102; tel 516 4857; metro Observatorio, line 1): this is the smallest of the bus stations, used principally by buses going to and from Toluca (1 hr), Morelia (4 hrs) and Guadalajara (7 hrs).

By Car: The city centre ('Centro Histórico') is signposted well in advance on all main roads into the city. **Insurgentes**, the longest avenue in the world, cuts the city north–south. Travelling its length is best avoided, as it is slow and congested, lined with shops and passing through residential areas. The **Periférico**, a three-lane ring road, links the north and south, avoiding the main city: this is the best route between Cuernavaca, Taxco and Acapulco in the south, and Querétaro and the north. All the main north–south roads eventually hit the Paseo de la Reforma, the city's central avenue, and the main east–west route. The **Viaducto** leads east from the Periférico to the airport. (See also Getting Around in Town).

By Train: The central railway station (Ferrocarriles Nacionales de México) is on Av Insurgentes Norte at the junction of Alzate and Mosqueta (tel 547 9060/1084/1097; metro Revolución, line 3).

There are surprisingly few trains a day and all need to be booked in advance (best done by visiting the station). The most popular journeys are to and from Oaxaca (8 hrs), Veracruz (6 hrs) and Morelia (9 hrs).

GETTING AROUND IN TOWN

Unless or until you become a a fully fledged capital city resident, the quickest and least complicated way of negotiating the city is to stick to the metro and taxis. Buses are cheap and efficient but slower and more complicated.

By Bus: The most popular and useful route for tourists is 'Ruta 100', which runs all along Reforma, passing the Zona Rosa, Chapultepec Park and the Alameda. Another easy, uncomplicated bus journey is along the length of Insurgentes (several numbers), from its junction with the Paseo de la Reforma to San Angel and the university in the south.

By Combi: VW vans, known as combis, and newer microbuses (both generally white) run along fixed routes, displayed on the windshields. They can be flagged down at any point. The central pick-up point for combis going to any part of the city is Chapultepec metro station, at the entrance to the park on Reforma.

By Car: The key to driving in Mexico City is to assume that there are no rules: a red light is merely a decoration, one-way streets were invented to practise reversing in and a road with more than one lane was designed as a Grand Prix course. Police, however, see the matter differently: although they are inclined not to tussle with foreigners, because it wastes too much time, they have a whole book of rules which the average driver breaks 20 times a day.

One rule is universally respected. One day a week, every car in the city has to 'rest' and may not be driven. Introduced late in 1989 to cut down on pollution and overcrowding, it is seen to be modestly working. The fine for driving on a 'rest' day is steep and few people try it. Every rented car bears a coloured sticker, and these are the days to avoid:

Monday:	yellow	Thursday:	green
Tuesday:	pink	Friday:	light blue
Wednesday:	red		

Anyone intending to drive in Mexico City should buy a city guide (*Guia Roji*), available from any book shop. Badly bound, it will come apart within hours, but it is an invaluable key to the labyrinth, with an index of streets and 100 maps.

The two principal streets in the city are Insurgentes which runs north–south, and the Paseo de la Reforma which runs east–west. Insurgentes Sur runs through San Angel and past the university in the south, and Insurgentes Norte leads to the pyramids at Teotihuacán in the north.

Car hire is available at all the main hotels, the airport and at travel agents.

By Metro: The metro system is quick, fast, clean and efficient. Built on the lines of the Paris metro, it is a thousand times more pleasant than the ancient and overloaded systems in London and New York, although it is still far from complete.

Several lines crisscross the city and the connecting stations between one line and another are called *correspondencias*. Signs indicate the direction of the trains, displaying the first and last stop on the line. Yellow tickets costing next to nothing should be bought at the beginning of the journey (most people buy ten at a time). These are then fed into a machine and never seen again.

Bag-snatchers and pickpockets undoubtedly haunt the metro. Anxious foreigners counting out their traveller's cheques are an obvious target. Regular commuters, or those who look as if they know their destination, are rarely bothered.

By Taxi: Now that all taxis (other than the black bruisers outside the hotels) are legally required to display a meter, taxis have once again become an affordable and pleasant method of travel. The only obvious disadvantage is that the driver may well be moonlighting and not have a clue as to the geography of the city (and, as a passenger, you might not either).

Yellow taxis are cheap and numerous. Orange taxis (*sitio*) are more reliable, consequently more expensive, and operate from a fixed rank. Hotels generally know the number of the nearest *sitio*. The most expensive taxis of all are the black saloons which hover around the doors of tourist hotels. Their drivers normally speak English, however, and are thus a safe bet for the desperate.

GENERAL INFORMATION

American Express
The main American Express office is halfway down Reforma (Paseo de la Reforma 234, tel 533 0380). It is an efficient and consequently crowded place in which to buy or cash traveller's cheques or exchange money. It also provides a mail-holding service.

Bookshops
One whole street in the centre (Cinco de Mayo) is devoted to bookshops, the best with small cafés attached. Otherwise try the **Parnaso** in Coyoacán's main square, the **Librería Gandhi** (Calle Miguel Ángel de Quevedo, Coyoacán), or the **Librería Británica** (Av de la Paz 23, San Angel). For the best in art books, try both the bookshops in the Anthropology Museum and the Centro Cultural Contemporáneo (Campos Elíseos, Polanco, behind the Nikko Hotel and Reforma).

Cinemas
There are hundreds of cinemas all over the city, and the best guide to them is the weekly magazine, *Tiempo Libre*. The largest centre is the **Cineteca Nacional** in Coyoacán, near

the Coyoacán metro (line 3) at Av México–Coyoacán 389, Prol Av Cuauhtémoc. Its four screens show foreign, Mexican and art films, with numerous retrospectives, and it also plays host to the international film festival in November. Paseo de la Reforma has three or four cinemas usually showing the latest Hollywood releases.

Embassies

The **British Embassy** (tel 207 2233, 207 2089, tlx 001773093) is at Río Lerma 71, one block north of the Paseo de la Reforma and one block east of the **US Embassy** (tel 211 0042) on Río Lerma and Paseo de la Reforma 305, to one side of the María Isabel Sheraton Hotel. The **Canadian Embassy** is in the Colonia Chapultepec at Schiller 529.

Fonart Shops

These excellent state-run craft shops display and sell artisania from all over the country. The five main centres are:

Av Juárez 89 (by the Alameda)
Av Patriotismo 691
Insurgentes Sur 1630
Londres 136, Zona Rosa
Av de la Paz 37, San Angel.

Markets

There are markets of every type for every day of the week. The most interesting, for visitors without a kitchen, must include the vast craft **Bazar Sabado** in the Plaza San Jacinto, San Angel, on Saturday (10.00–18.00). The restaurants buy their food in the **San Juan Market** (three blocks south of the Alameda). Fish comes from **La Viga** (Czda La Viga) and flowers from the **Jamaica** market (Czda de la Viga and Av Morelos). The biggest of the lot is **La Merced**: the metro of the same name comes out right in the middle of it. Toys and witches' brews are on sale at the more traditional **Mercado de Sonora** (metro Fray Servando). On Sundays, the flea market **La Lagunilla** (in the centre, on Calle Comonfort near the Plaza Garibaldi) is at its busiest and Sullivan Park becomes one large open-air market.

Newspapers

Tiempo Libre lists all events such as theatre, cinema and sports and comes out every Thursday. *The News* is a North American publication, in English, which is short on analytical comment but good for English-language film listings. Less pretentious and more useful, the slight *Daily Bulletin* is given away free in the lobbies of all tourist hotels. It is a good guide for the first-time visitor, full of tips about what is on where, together with a list of hotels and their current prices. The *Excelsior* is perhaps *The Times* of Mexico, while *La Jornada* is a humourless version of the *Guardian*. Cars, houses and dogs are bought and sold through the pages of the *Universal*.

Nightlife

Tiempo Libre includes listings of all current films, exhibitions and shows. To hear **mariachi** music, drop in on the Plaza Garibaldi (particularly on Sundays), where strolling musicians in tight black spangled trousers and wide-brimmed sombreros play until dawn. For popular Mexican **theatre**, there is nowhere better than the Teatro de la Ciudad (Donceles, in the Centro Histórico).

For **dancing**, there are two places on top of each other on the corner of Reforma and Nisa. Above is **Rockstock**, predominantly rock but with live Mexican music from 24.00 to 01.30. Underneath is **Tropicoso** with live *salsa* until 03.00. On Insurgentes, the smaller **Rockotitlan** restaurant has the best Mexican rock groups playing live. More offbeat are the **Bar León**, on Brazil just north of the Zócalo, or the **Grand León and Antillanos** in the Colonia Roma. The Bar León looks like a scruffy café but in reality is one of the best places for dancing to Latin American music, always packed by those in the know. Antillanos plays uplifting dance music from the French-speaking Caribbean. In Coyoacán, **El Habito** (Calle Madrid 13, between Centenario and Aldama, tel 524 2481) is a wonderfully decadent nightclub, run by the theatrical Jesusa Rodríguez. If you want to dine, drink and listen to music, but not to dance, try the **New Orleans Jazz Club** in San Angel (on the corner of Revolución and Altavista).

The city's best and biggest **concert hall** is the **Auditorio Nacional**, on Paseo de la Reforma in the middle of Chapultepec Park. It hosts an eclectic mix of performances, from classical music and international opera to Latin American rock.

There is one indispensable magazine for **gay nightlife**. *Macho Tips* comes out fortnightly and is sold at newsagents and kiosks, with full lists of events, bars and nightclubs. Two men-only bars are in the Zona Rosa—**El Taller** (Calle Florencia 37) and **El Nueve** (Calle Londres 56). For women there is **El Don II** in Colonia Roma (Tonalá 79 on the corner of Av Obregón), and for both the disco **Queen's Palace** (Pensador Mexicano II, Col Guerrero).

Police Business

Many complaints can be dealt with by the Secretaría de Turismo (Mazarik 172, tel 250 0123, 250 0151), which also operates a 24-hour **emergency** telephone number (tel 658 1111). For lost, stolen or extended **tourist cards**, go to the Secretaría de Gobernación (Calle Albañiles in Col Penitenciaría—better known as Lecumberri ex-prison; metro San Lázaro; tel 795 6166, 795 6685; open 09.00–13.00). The immigration department at the airport can help with emergency **exit visas** (Mezzanine 78, tel 571 3600).

It is only worth reporting anything **lost or stolen** for insurance purposes. Go to the police station on the corner of Calle Aldama and Mina, in Colonia Cuauhtémoc, and ask to '*poner un acto de robo*'. They are very used to filling out the requisite form with the minimum fuss.

Post Offices

There is no shortage of post offices (*correos*). The fabulous, main post office, designed by an Italian, faces onto Bellas Artes and the Eje Central, by the Alameda.

Racing

One of the cheapest forms of entertainment (not including the betting) in Mexico City is a day at the races. The **Hipodromo**, one of only four race tracks in the country, was built during the Second World War when the US tracks were closed down. It is a beautiful, full $7\frac{1}{2}$-furlong track, its infield landscaped with fountains and ponds. Races are held from 15.00 on Tuesdays, Thursdays, Fridays, Saturdays, Sundays and holidays, only closing for Easter week and the last two weeks of the year.

The Hipodromo is only 10 minutes from Reforma. To get there by car, take the Periférico Norte, exit at Legaria and turn left at the first traffic lights. Alternatively, take the metro to Tacuba (line 7) or a combi marked 'Hipodromo' or 'Defensa Nacional'.

Sanborns
This chain of restaurants, soda fountains and department stores provides an indispensable capsule of nostalgia for homesick foreigners who want to be cosseted. Although the soda fountains serve food which is heavily Mexican, they are modelled on and a successful repeat of their US counterparts. They sell English-language books and magazines and are attached to Sanborns department stores. The most attractive of all is the Casa de los Azulejos in the centre (see Eating Out).

Tourist Offices
The main tourist office in Mexico City is in the Zona Rosa, on the corner of Amberes and Londres (tel 523 9380; open 09.00–15.00 and 17.00–21.00, Mon–Sat). For 24-hour assistance, ring the Locatel number: 658 1111.

WHAT TO SEE

Centro Histórico

The historic centre of the city covers the site of the ancient Aztec capital of Tenochtitlán, on whose ruins the colonial city was built, in part with the very stones razed from the pyramids. Although no longer the administrative or residential base of the city, as it was during the 300 years of Spanish rule, it remains the historical heart. Its attractions are by no means confined to museums and historical sites: it is still the place to see Mexican street life in full force 24 hours a day, in the open-air park, the Alameda, and in the markets and countless theatres.

Mariachi players in the Plaza Garibaldi

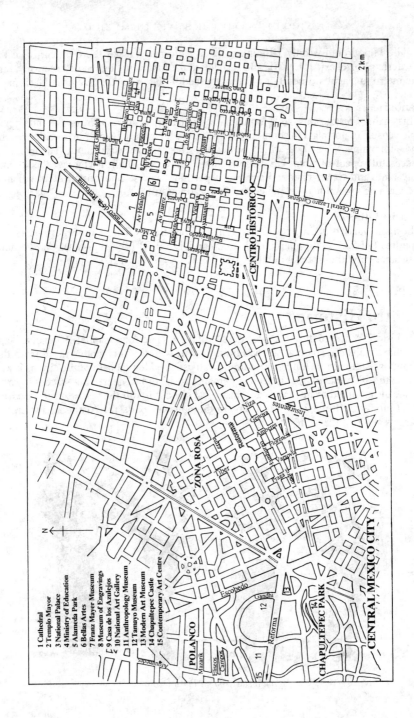

CENTRAL MEXICO CITY

1 Cathedral
2 Templo Mayor
3 National Palace
4 Ministry of Education
5 Alameda Park
6 Bellas Artes
7 Franz Mayer Museum
8 Museum of Engravings
9 Casa de los Azulejos
10 National Art Gallery
11 Anthropology Museum
12 Tamayo Museum
13 Modern Art Museum
14 Chapultepec Castle
15 Contemporary Art Centre

POLANCO

ZONA ROSA

CHAPULTEPEC PARK

CENTRO HISTÓRICO

GETTING AROUND

By Bus: The Centro Histórico is a traffic trap, which makes it difficult to get right down to the Zócalo by bus. Buses from the south run along Eje Central, skirting the square. From the west (Reforma, Zona Rosa etc), take a 'Ruta 100' bus to the Alameda and walk six blocks east, along Madero, Cinco de Mayo or Tacuba.

By Foot: The Zócalo is in the east of the city, ten blocks from the Hidalgo metro station on Reforma and six from Bellas Artes and the Alameda. Walking is the best way to get around. Three streets run in parallel, east–west between the Zócalo and the Alameda: Cinco de Mayo, Madero and 16 de Septiembre.

By Metro: To arrive bang in the middle of it all, take line 2 to the Zócalo and emerge on the square itself.

Zócalo

Ever since the Aztecs built their ceremonial centre here in the 14th century, Mexico City's Zócalo has been the largest and most important square in the country. Once it was a great market, shaded by tall trees, but during the Revolution the trees were torn down and the market paved over to allow for interminable processions and parades. The national flag is still raised with great pomp and circumstance every morning and lowered in the evening. Vast and impersonal on a quiet weekday, at weekends and on holidays, particularly Independence Day (15 September) and Labour Day (1 May), it fills to the brim with holiday makers and candyfloss sellers.

The National Palace

Facing onto the east side of the Zócalo, the National Palace is a hybrid construction housing the government offices and archives. Begun by Cortés on the ashes of Moctezuma's palace, it was originally a fortress: subsequent fires, riots and earthquakes all played a part in determining its present, still-evolving form. Above the central doorway hangs a small insignificant-looking bell, rung by the independence leader and parish priest, Miguel Hidalgo, on 15 September 1805, to rouse the people to insurrection.

The reason to visit the palace, however, is to see **Diego Rivera**'s monumental murals around the stairwell and first floor. Rivera (1886—1957) followed the dictates of Mayakovski, who believed that art should instruct the people. His murals portray five centuries of Mexican history, from the Aztecs through the conquest to independence and revolution, weaving the past with the present and hopes for the future.

Around the **main stairway**, Rivera painted a vast triptych on the walls. On the central panel, epochs and movements are layered on top of each other, with the pre-Hispanic at the bottom: almost every character who ever walked across the stage of Mexican history is introduced into the action, from Cortés (in the thick of battle), to the priests Las Casas, Sahagún and Vasco de Quiroga, and the revolutionary hero, Emiliano Zapata, portrayed in the semicircular central arch with his banner proclaiming '*Tierra y Libertad*' ('Land and Freedom').

On the left wall of the stairway is *The Struggle of the Classes*—a direct result of Rivera's 1927 visit to the nascent Soviet Union. He included both his wife, the surrealist artist Frida Kahlo, and her sister, Cristina (with whom Rivera had an affair), wearing a red shirt and holding an open book. On the right-hand wall is *The Legend of Quetzalcóatl* with a reversed sun, the fifth and last in Aztec mythology, falling out of the sky in the face of the Spanish conquest.

Around the **first floor**, panels illustrate scenes from each part of the pre-Hispanic world. The first is *La Gran Tenochtitlán* (1945), the Aztec capital with its market at Tlatelolco. The temples of Tenochtitlán stand in the background, framed by volcanoes. On the far right a prostitute, representing the Goddess of Love and tattooed from head to foot, has the face of Rivera's wife, Frida Kahlo. The second panel (1947) represents the Tarascan/Purépechan civilization from Michoacán, with Lake Pátzcuaro in the background and natural inks for dying cloth in the foreground. A priest unravels the religious calendar for a young mother whose child was unlucky enough to have been born on a 'Rabbit' day, the sign of drunkenness. The third panel (1947) concentrates on the Zapotec culture of Oaxaca, famed for its feathers and metalworks. In the fourth panel (1950), Totonacs from Veracruz are forced to pay taxes to the Aztecs, dominated by the Pyramid of the Niches. Next to this, the fifth panel portrays the Huastecs from the west, with the volcano of Orizaba in the far distance and the corn plant in pride of place. On either side of a doorway on the east wall, the two main indigenous Mexican products are being cultivated: the cacao bean and the century plant. In the latter panel, the woman on the extreme left, making paper from the bark, is Ruth, Rivera's daughter. The final mural (1951) shows the arrival of Hernán Cortés on Mexican soil. Rivera maintained that Cortés' remains were syphilitic and accordingly painted him as a disease-ridden hunchback. In the top left corner, Cortés' lover, La Malinche, openly rules from behind the scenes. The natives, tied, branded and enslaved, form a chain gang, while in the bottom left corner are black slaves, who were later shipped in to do the work. In the centre foreground a native woman follows her Spanish lover (or ravisher), carrying a blue-eyed baby on her back, the first example of mixed blood. All around are the domestic animals that the Spanish first introduced to the Americas.

Metropolitan Cathedral

Built on a lake bed which is still drying out, Mexico City has severe problems with water—both too much and too little. The 57-m high, 3000-ton marble and granite cathedral has gradually sunk 3 m into its watery grave. A smaller cathedral, laid out on an east–west axis, was demolished in 1626 when the present cathedral (begun in 1572) was well under way. On the north side of the Zócalo, it was built over some 55 Aztec temples, but only consecrated in 1677 and finally finished in 1813, two and a half centuries after the first stone was laid. So many Spanish architects had a hand in its construction that is difficult to separate the workmanship. In 1787 Damian Ortiz de Castro was commissioned to finish the towers but died before he completed the portals. In 1793 the work was handed over to Manuel Tolsá, who created the dome, the central portion of the facade, the balustrades and the torch holders in the stone balustrades of the nave.

The cathedral forms a massive cruciform with five naves. The central one is the highest, decorated with barrel vaults. The side aisles, with groin vaulting, diminish in height from the middle to the outer walls to let more light in. Seven chapels lead off the side aisles. A chapel in the west aisle is dedicated to the Mexican saint, San Felipe, who went to Japan and was murdered in Nagasaki—two Samurai swords diagonally pincer his body. The most impressive of all the chapels is the **Capilla de los Reyes**, directly behind the main altar, which is decorated with a labryinth of wood carving superimposed with painted and gilded angels.

The main churrigueresque altar, known as the **Altar de los Reyes**, dominates the apse, built for the Spanish kings who never came. Designed by the Sevillian Jerónimo de Balbás between 1718 and 1725, it is studded on four levels with kings of saintly renown, the champions of Christianity. They include the English Queen Margaret (bottom left), Elizabeth of Hungary (two along) and above them Henry, Edward and Casimir. Further above them are Louis of France and Spain's own Ferdinand III of Castile.

In the centre of the cathedral sits the choir. The metalwork came entirely from Macau. Disaster struck in 1967 when an electrical fire started here, burning much of the gold-leaf woodwork, paintings and statues. There are still two massive organs with over 3500 pipes each (the one on the right was imported from Spain in the 17th century, and the one on the left is an almost exact 18th-century Mexican copy).

Below the cathedral, the **crypts** (open 09.00–13.00) house the ashes of 10,000 cremated bodies—including some of the wealthiest Spaniards in Mexican history—and still have room for another 6000.

El Sagrario

Adjoining the cathedral, the 18th-century parish church of El Sagrario was built as a glorified storeroom for all the consecrated relics and chalices of the archbishop. It has a finely proportioned churrigueresque facade, begun by Lorenzo Rodríguez in 1749, with exuberant sculpted figures severely upstaging the sober, mixed-up cathedral. It lurches lopsidedly, having survived numerous earthquakes. Within, it follows the plan of a Greek cross, lit up by a confection of gilt panelling.

Calle Moneda

Along the east wall of the National Palace, Calle Moneda slopes gently downhill, following the contours of the temple it was built over. It is a street of firsts: the first university was built here (in 1551), the first archbishop's palace and the first mint. Begun in 1731 at No 13, the mint is now an uninspired **Museum of World Cultures**, with an early Rufino Tamayo mural (1938).

The Templo Mayor and Museum

(Parallel with the cathedral, on the northeast corner of the Zócalo; open 10.00–18.00, Tues–Sun.)

The present-day Zócalo covers much of the original Aztec city. After the conquest, the Spanish spared no blushes and simply razed it to the ground, using the labour of its cowed inhabitants. When the metro was being built, the authorities discovered more and more pre-Hispanic pieces. Today, the main archaeological excavations concentrate on the site of the Aztec Templo Mayor or **Teocalli**.

Every 52 years, new temples were built over old to greet the new calendar round (similar to our century). Excavations are currently down to the fourth of seven impositions. For an idea of the days of glory, look at the huge maquette of the main square of

Tenochtitlán as it was 500 years ago, facing onto the site. There is another inside the museum.

On the edge of the site, a colonial mansion was converted into a museum by the contemporary architect, Pedro Ramírez Vásquez (who designed the Anthropology Museum), to house the treasures found. Built on four floors, it is divided into two sections, representing the traditional division of the original temple: half was dedicated to the Sun God, Huitzilopochtli, and half to Tlaloc, the Rain God. From the top floor there is an excellent aerial view of a replica of the vast 8-tonne stone disc displayed in the Museum of Anthropology. This portrays the Moon Goddess, Coyolxauhqui, decapitated and limbless: when her mother, Coatlicue, the giver of life and death, became pregnant for the 402nd time, Coyolxauhqui conspired with her 400 brothers and sisters to kill her. As the knives were being sharpened, out of her womb sprang the fully grown and armed Huitzilopochtli, who revenged his mother by dismembering Coyolxauqhui, throwing her down a mountain and driving his other brothers and sisters into the sky, where they still glow as stars.

National Pawn Shop

(West corner of the Zócalo, at Av Cinco de Mayo.)
The National Pawn Shop stands on the site of an Aztec and subsequently a viceregal palace. Still very much a going concern, it was founded in 1775 by José Romero del Monte, the Conde de Regla, who owned the Real del Monte silver mines in the state of Hidalgo and was one of the richest men in Mexico's history.

North of the Zócalo

The best murals in the city are within easy walking distance, just north of the Zócalo.

National Preparatory School

(San Idelfonso 33, two blocks north of the Templo Mayo.)
The Escuela Nacional Preparatoria occupies the site of an early 16th-century school, established to groom Jesuit novices for posts in the colonial government. So successful was it that a new seminary (the present building) had to be built in its place. In 1767 the Jesuits were thrown out of the king of Spain's dominions and it was briefly converted into a barracks for the Flemish regiment, before being returned to clerical orders for a few years. In 1833 the leaders of the independence movement turned it into a jurisprudence college. Within 30 years it had been turned back over to the Jesuits, but was then wrested from them and given to the French as a barracks. It was Juárez who finally stabilized the flux and founded the preparatory school in the 1860s.

In 1923, the forward-looking Minister of Education, José Vasconcelos, commissioned the young muralists to decorate the walls with instructive, revolutionary, idealistic murals. His aim was to educate a largely illiterate population through a very traditional Mexican medium—painting walls. Diego Rivera, David Alfaro Siqueiros, Jean Charlot, Fermín Revueltas and Fernando Leal all painted murals on the first floor of the building, but it is **José Clemente Orozco**'s work around the staircase and upper floors that really stands out. Orozco's cynicism about modern Mexico is almost as acute as his disillusionment with the past. Subjects such as *The Strike*, *The Aristocrats*, *Maternity* and *The Old Order*, all painted between 1922 and 1925, express the human tragedy of the Revolution's prostituted ideals and the gap between words and actions.

Ministry of Public Education (SEP)

(Argentina 28, three blocks north of the Templo Mayor.)
Once the old Convent of the Incarnation, founded in 1594, this building became the headquarters of the education ministry in 1922. José Vasconcelos commissioned Diego Rivera to decorate the corridors of the building with frescoes between 1923 and 1928. The outstanding result makes up the greatest body of Rivera's work in the world, with 239 panels covering 1585 square metres.

The first patio concentrates on work scenes (ground floor), the sciences (first floor), and the arts (second floor). The second patio is dedicated to festivals, the states of the republic (painted by Rivera's helpers) and markets: the landless peasant, enslaved by the Spanish, gains his freedom with the Revolution (the 1920s were still years of optimism). One of Rivera's most beautiful murals, by the lifts, is of women washing their clothes— *Las Mujeres de Tehuantepec* (*The Women of Tehuantepec*). The west floor of the second patio was the last to be completed, after Rivera's 1928 trip to the Soviet Union. Here he paints an idealistic anthem to peace through revolution, with portraits of Frida Kahlo and David Alfaro Siqueiros as well as peasants and labourers.

Santo Domingo Plaza and Church

Continuing north from the SEP building, Av Argentina opens into the Plaza Sto Domingo where *evangelistas* (professional letter writers) wait in their confessional boxes on the west side of the square, writing letters for the illiterate and the lovesick, and also helping with complex tax forms. The 18th-century **Customs House**, on the southeast corner of the square, was built in a record six months in 1731. This century it was decorated with some fine Siqueiros murals, full of the empty promises of the Revolution, as heroes are ploughed down by the onslaught of capitalism.

The **Palace of the Holy Office of the Inquisition** is on the northeast corner of the square. In its day, from 1481 to 1808, the Holy Office was responsible for burning 35,000 people and imprisoning another 300,000, and was only closed when it charged a sterile woman with having laid an egg. The Dominicans established it in Mexico in 1571, to prosecute the crimes of sorcery, heresy and polygamy: the indigenous Mexicans were exempted, as they were 'too young' to know the right path.

Santo Domingo church was once the headquarters of the Dominican Order in the New World. The present church is 18th century, replacing two earlier constructions, and is built of *tezontle*, a volcanic stone used because of its porous qualities. When part of the monastery was demolished in 1861, 12 mummies were found, including that of the monk, Fray Servando Teresa de Mier, which was sold to an Italian impresario and carted around from circus to circus. Within, a series of side chapels (including one, on the right-hand side, dedicated to the Saint of the Blind, who is offered a plateful of eyes) leads down to a disarmingly simple Tolsá altar, overwhelmed by the baroque splendour all around. Before leaving, note the chapel to the right of the entrance, which contains a gory Christ with bloody ankles. When the Spanish arrived, they had to avoid such graphic depictions because they implied that Christians also practised human sacrifice.

67

South of the Zócalo

Supreme Court

Due south of the National Palace, at Pino Suárez 2, the 1935 Supreme Court is an uninspired building, decorated with three angry 1940 José Clemente Orozco murals parodying the institution itself. Using black, red and grey, he painted Justice asleep on the job, while a masked Liberty flees the ransacked court with various rich burghers.

Museo de la Ciudad

(Pino Suárez 30 and Salvador, three blocks south of the Zócalo.)
This museum traces the history of the city, from the first sign of man in the valley, through the arrival of the Spanish, colonial rule, independence and the urban explosion since the 1910 Revolution. The house itself is more interesting than the museum. It stands on one of the main roads that led to Tenochtitlán and dates from the 18th century, when it was the home of the Conde de Santiago de Calimaya. His shield, resting on four clawed feet like a piece of Chippendale, is set into the facade. On the corner of the building is a carved serpent's head, taken from the Templo Mayor and embedded into the wall.

Templo de Jesús Nazaro

At right angles to the museum, in Salvador, is the hospital founded by Cortés in 1524, on the site of his first meeting with Moctezuma. The outside promises little but the interior is made up of a series of light, airy patios. Many people believe that Cortés was buried in the chapel attached to the hospital. The church was founded in 1601, and took 67 years to complete. Between 1942 and 1944 José Clemente Orozco was commissioned to paint the cupola and the choir wall with representations of God and the Devil, time and eternity: since their completion, there has been no money to light them properly.

West of the Zócalo towards the Alameda

Three streets run from the Zócalo to the Alameda: **Cinco de Mayo**, filled with bars and bookshops, which leads off from the northwest corner of the Zócalo and the cathedral; the seven-block-long **Madero** which runs from the Majestic hotel on the Zócalo to the Casa de los Azulejos; and **Av 16 de Septiembre** which begins at the Gran Hotel de la Ciudad de México.

GETTING AROUND

This is definitely walking territory. Either walk west from the Zócalo metro (line 2), or do it in reverse order and walk east from the Bellas Artes metro (also on line 2).

Calle Madero

Two blocks from the Zócalo is **La Profesa Church** (on the corner of Isabel la Católica), with a fine baroque exterior and an exquisite mudéjar carved wooden screen. At the corner of Calle Bolívar stands the impressive building that was once the modest town house of the fabulously wealthy silver miner, José de la Borda.

At 17 Madero, further down on the left-hand side, is **Iturbide's Palace**—one of the city's most exquisite structures both within and without. It was completed in 1784, for the Marquis Jaral de Berio, known as the Conde San Mateo de Valparaíso. In order to to prevent his fortune falling into the hands of his daughter's suitor, he had the original building demolished, and ordered the present house to be built by the architect Antonio de Guerrero y Torres, for the exact cost of her dowry. In 1821 it was offered to the presumptious president of the republic, Agustín Iturbide, as his presidential palace. It subsequently fell into decline, being used both as a hotel and as government offices, but was marvellously restored this century by the Banco Nacional de México, which regularly holds exhibitions of its art collection in the patio. In front of the palace is the most extravagant of pastry shops, **L'Ideal**, with 10-tiered cakes precariously assembled in the windows.

A block further west, the church of **San Francisco** was founded in 1524, on top of Moctezuma's zoo. Cortés personally funded the original building, which was given to the Franciscans as their headquarters. The present church dates from 1716 and occupies less than a quarter of the former site—in the 19th century much of it, including the original church, was given to the Chiarini Circus and used as stables and warehouses. Directly in front is the **Casa de los Azulejos** (see Eating Out), one of the finest examples of mudéjar architecture in the country. The facade is completely overlaid with blue and white Pueblan *azulejos* or tiles, dating from 1750 but covering a much earlier construction. On the same corner, the **Torre-Latino Americana** towers 44 floors above the city, overlooking the Alameda. The restaurant-observatory at the top gives an appalling view over the city, sealed in by its thick, black cloud of smog.

Alameda

This manicured public park was named after the poplars that once grew there. It was built in the 16th century as a defensive plot of land on a drained marsh, but immediately became a promenade for the wealthy and the site of dawn duels. It was closed to the general public throughout the colonial period, but since 1810 it has become one of the most popular meeting places, particularly on Sunday afternoons. It is also an important starting point for demonstrations and sit-ins. The large, grandiose monument to Benito Juárez, made entirely of white marble, was built in 1910, when Díz's ostentatious government was at its peak, just before it fell in the Revolution of the same year.

GETTING AROUND

Again, this is an area to walk around. 'Ruta 100' buses from the Zona Rosa pass the Alameda, as do numerous minibuses and taxis. Alternatively, take the metro to Bellas Artes (line 2) on the eastern end of the park, or to Hidalgo (line 3) on its western end.

Palacio de Bellas Artes

This mouth-gaping Palace of Fine Arts was designed by Adamo Boari, of Carrara marble and to the Italian style. Construction began in 1900 but was not completed until 1934, and it has since sunk several metres into the soggy subsoil. The palace houses government offices, a theatre—and a powerful set of murals on the third floor.

Any commission given to Rivera seemed doomed to controversy. The Rockefellers asked him to paint a mural entitled *Man at the Crossing of the Ways* for the Rockefeller Center in New York: as soon as they became aware of its Marxist leanings, they ordered it to be destroyed. He recreated it here. At the other end of the same corridor, he recreated another unaccepted work, *The Carnival of Mexican Life*. This was commissioned for the grand opening of the Hotel Reforma in 1936 but rejected by the hotelier because of its unsympathetic depiction of tourists. The palace also houses works by Siqueiros (*The New Democracy*, painted with a spray gun), Orozco, Juan O'Gorman and Rufino Tamayo (on the stairways).

Every week, the palace's theatre hosts excellent performances by the **Ballet Folklórico** (daily at 21.00 and also at 09.00 on Sundays). Although the audience is almost entirely composed of tourists, the performances are nonetheless spectacular and colourful, including dances from the Yaquis in the north, the Tehuanas of the Tehuantepec peninsula, the '*son*' of Veracruz and the Caribbean-influenced south. If you have no time to see them, try to sneak into the theatre to see its main curtain—a huge metal screen embossed with opalescent crystals, created by the Tiffany Studios of New York from a drawing by Dr Atl.

Correo Mayor
(Lázaro Cárdenas and Tacuba.)
This impressive quarrystone construction was designed as the central post office by the Italian architect, Adamo Boari, and opened in 1907. Its facade combines Venetian, gothic and plateresque styles, complete with bronze fittings. Inside is the **National Stamp Collection**, which begins with the first stamp ever issued in Mexico—an 1856 effigy of Miguel Hidalgo.

The post office was built on the site of the house of Moctezuma's daughter, Tecuichpo. When the Spanish arrived, she was hurriedly baptized a Catholic, and found herself married in turn to Cuitláhuac, Moctezuma's successor Cuauhtémoc and then a series of Cortés' closest friends: Alonso de Grado, Pedro Galego, Juan Cano and, finally, Juan Andrade (although public opinion always linked her to Cortés himself).

Museo Nacional de Arte
(Calle Tacuba 8; the opening hours are erratic due to lack of staff: officially the first floor (20th century) is open 09.00–19.00, on Sun, Wed and Fri; and the top floor (16th–19th centuries) 09.00–19.00, on Tues, Thurs and Sat.)
A Jesuit seminary originally occupied the site. After they were expelled in the 1760s, it became a hospice for syphilitics. In 1867 the non-syphilitic body of the Emperor Maximilian was taken here to be embalmed, a process which took all of 70 hours. The building was razed in 1904 and the present palace (designed by Silvio Contrio) inaugurated in 1911.

The collection is endless and inexhaustible yet few foreign visitors explore beyond the marvellous, baroque, marble staircase of the entrance hall. Colonial Mexican art is often dismissed as derivative, adding nothing to the tenets of its European masters, yet it takes only a few minutes to see where rules were broken and new standards set.

ROOM I
The first painters to arrive from Spain were Sebastián Pereyns and Andrés de la Concha. Their art, and that of their disciples, was strictly confined to religious subjects. As the Reformation swept across Europe, the Catholic Church opened up old dogmas in a

fierce backlash against Protestantism. No hint of Mexico enters the paintings but Italian, Flemish and, particularly, Spanish influences are strong.

ROOM II

The 18th century was dominated by two events: the founding of the Mexican Academy of Arts in 1754 and the shock of the indigenous artist Miguel Cabrera's study, *Maraviglia Americana*, with its dark-skinned Virgin of Guadalupe. Throughout the century, art remained firmly religious in content but varied considerably in form. Although the artists remain largely anonymous, the patrons are well known: *El Ministerio de San José* is dominated by a flourishing epistle testifying to the subject's nobility and generosity. At a more humble level, the tradition of *ex-votos* began to take hold. These ranged from full-scale oils such as the 1711 *Ex-voto de Alférez de la Parra* to small painted tin plates, offered in thanks to a saint who had interceded with a miracle. Traditional customs were often portrayed: *Cuadro de la Casta* shows a public *auto-da-fé*, in which Spanish nobles sit in judgement over heretics, distinguished by their conical hats, while dark-skinned Mexicans hover on the outskirts.

ROOMS III AND IV

Room III concentrates on the varied history of the Academy of Arts, from its foundation as a firmly neoclassical influence, to its dispersal to the provinces after independence. Tresguerras moved to the Bajío and José Manzo to Puebla, and both subsequently started to paint landscapes and scenes of small-town life. Room IV is no more than a small corridor, hung with the intimate works of José María Estrada (1810–65). His oil portraits of dignitaries of church and state show an acute awareness of the temporality of power (most particularly in his striking 1852 deathbed scene, the *Ex-voto of Bernardino Marueño*).

ROOM V

In 1843, the impossible president Santa Ana passed two ingenious laws. With the first, he reopened the Academy but allowed it no money; with the second, he bequeathed it the proceeds of the National Lottery. With this injection of cash the Academy could afford to import European masters, such as the sculptor Manuelvilar, the painter Pelegrín Clavé, and the architect Javier Cavallari. Conservatism remained rampant but metaphorical reworkings of old themes slipped into many works, such as Joauín Ramírez's *El Interior del Arca*, showing the calm after the storm as Mexico became a republic. For the first time, academicians began to represent historical people. Outstanding is Manuelvilar's (1812–60) colossal sculpture of the Tlaxcaltecan warrior, Tlalhuicole (1851). One section is devoted to the much-acclaimed, arrogant and demanding Juan Cordero (1824–84). Apart from a sycophantic painting of president Santa Ana's child-bride, Doña Dolores Tosta (1855), his works are all, predictably, self-portraits.

ROOM VI

This room is devoted to late 19th-century landscapes, in which Mexico's vibrant colours and textures finally come into their own. José María Velasco was the undoubted master of his genre. Born to a large family of embroiderers in Temaxcalcingo, Mexico State, he learnt the art of his fathers and translated the intricacy of thread and yarn onto his

71

canvases. His *Evolution of the Plants* in the centre of the room is Ruskin-like in its detailed study of rocks, clouds, plants and leaves. He painted the Valley of Mexico in a guise that can only be dreamt of now: transparently clear skies, snow-capped volcanoes and wide fields and plains, imbued with the pinks and blues of half-light, and studded with the dark green hues of the cactuses and the reds of the raw baked rocks. *Lumen en Coelo* (1892) is a romantic pastoral of a shepherd and his flock, wending their way home in the dusk.

Other paintings on this floor represent a move to the provinces, bringing the 19th century to a close. Popular and regional drawings find their place, as nationalism became set in its way under the dictatorship of Porfirio Díaz.

FIRST FLOOR

The 20th century begins with turn-of-the-century decadence, the precursor for the muralists, typified by the engraver José Guadalupe Posada. Surrealism found its feet early in Mexico—look no further than the fantastic oils and engravings of Julio Ruelas and Roberto Montenegro (1886–1968). When the great master of the art, André Breton, came to Mexico in 1938 (inspired by Rivera, Julio Castellanos (1905–67) and Trotsky), he found there was nothing left to teach Mexicans about surrealism.

The 1910 Revolution turned artists into navel-watchers, as nationalism reared its ugly bombastic head, but still managed to produce Mexico's most remarkable, sweeping statement to the world: mural painting. Dr Atl (1875–1946) and Joaquin Clausell (1866–1935) led the way. An early death prevented Saturnino Herran (1887–1918) from embracing the movement: in *La Ofrenda*, he represented the three ages of man on a Xochimilco barge filled with flowers. Angel Zarraga (1887–1946) brought the populace into art with his thin, gaunt people. Painting moved beyond Mexico's borders to include other revolutionary heroes, from Simón Bolívar to Napoleon. Painters turned to film: Alfredo Ramos Martínez captured the movie star Dolores del Río looking petulantly expectant at the precocious age of 12. And they turned to the urban environment, reflecting the contradictions between euphoria at apparent progress and nostalgia for lost traditions.

The Alameda Museums
(Open 10.00–18.00, Tues–Sun.)
Several museums face onto the Alameda. None are worth spending too long in, but all are fascinating in their own right.

Leaning precariously side by side, on the north side of the Alameda, the excellent **Museo de Franz Mayer** houses the private collection of an eclectic German patron of the arts, while the **Museo de la Estampa** next door is the repository for the most extensive collection of Mexican prints in the country. On the south side of the park, the **Museo de Artes Populares y Industrias** is a large hall filled with folk art from all over the country—every piece is on sale.

At the southwest corner, the **Museo de la Alameda** is given over to Diego Rivera's mural, *Sunday Afternoon in the Alameda*. This frozen moment of a fantastical yet typical Sunday day out in the park is surreal in its disjunctions. Familiar faces appear from the surging crowd, including Diego Rivera himself as a young boy, Frida Kahlo with her hand on his shoulder, a vapid Maximilian with his wife, Carlota, Sor Juana Inés de la

Cruz and, in the heart of the march of humanity, a skeletal figure dressed in all her finery, clutching the hand of the boy Rivera. The mural was painted in 1947–8 for the Hotel del Prado, which was damaged in the 1985 earthquake. The original version excited huge controversy in the press, because it included the words '*Dios no existe*' ('God doesn't exist'). These had to be removed, after Catholic uproar, much to communist Rivera's disgust.

Paseo de la Reforma

This, the Champs Élysées of Mexico, runs past the Alameda on the east side of the city, right through the modern centre, flanked on one side by colonial mansions and on the other by high-tech, glass-fronted offices. The broad, straight, tree-lined avenue was laid out in the 1860s by the ill-fated Maximilian, so that his wife could watch the daily progress of his carriage from Chapultepec Castle to the National Palace in the Zócalo.

Bronze statues down its length commemorate Aztec heroes—Cuauhtémoc, Tetlepanquetzal, Coanoch and Quetzalcóatl. The golden Angel of Independence marks the halfway stage between the Alameda and Chapultepec Park. This park, the biggest in Mexico, is also one of the most popular, particularly on Sundays. Called, longingly, the 'lungs of Mexico', it includes museums, a zoo and both the present and the former presidential palaces. In the far western third of the park, a vast fun fair has one of the few remaining *wooden* roller-coasters in the world.

Paseo de la Reforma bisects the park, passing, on the right, the Rufino Tamayo Museum and the Museum of Anthropology and, on the left, the Museum of Modern Art and the Auditorium. Further west it swings past the Monument to the Petrol Workers and up into the exclusive, expensive district known as Las Lomas, where embassy families feel safe behind tightly locked doors patrolled by gun-toting policemen.

GETTING AROUND

By Bus and Combi: Large 'Ruta 100' buses run the length of Reforma, from the Alameda, past the park and up into Las Lomas. Once famed for the clouds of black smoke which emerged from their exhausts, they are now painted with romanticized pictures of lakes and mountains to emphasize that they have gone green and changed to lead-free fuel. Combis marked 'Chapultepec' and 'Centro' also run up and down Reforma. For Chapultepec, get off at the entrance to the park, where the six-columned monument to the *Niños Héroes* towers above the trees.

By Metro: Insurgentes is the metro for the Zona Rosa, emerging in Calle Liverpool near the tourist office. Chapultepec metro station (line 1) is near the entrance to the park. Auditorio (line 7) is closer to the Museum of Anthropology: come out onto Reforma, cross it, and the museum is a 5-minute walk to the right.

Zona Rosa

(Metro Insurgentes, line 1.)

Wistfully referred to as the 'international' area, the Zona Rosa is filled with tourist hotels, restaurants and shops. Its heyday, if it ever had one, is long since past, although the increasingly tacky hotels and restaurants still flaunt their status. A small area between the

Angel Monument and Av Insurgentes, it is no more than eight streets deep, from Paseo de la Reforma to Av Chapultepec. Each street echoes old Europe with names such as Viena, Londres, Hamburgo, Sevilla, Florencia, Genova, Havre, Liverpool and Niza.

Although its attractions are often extolled (and the tourist office has made an effort by closing the area to traffic and creating small gardens everywhere), the Zona Rosa has little more to offer than various pedestrian streets lined with open-air restaurants, a craft-filled market on Londres, and genteel, relaxing tea shops along Hamburgo (one street nearer Reforma). Its reputation as an affluent area means that there are women patiently begging on every street corner, accompanied by insistently tugging children and, occasionally, a man playing the accordion for any pesos that might come their way. The shoe-shiners are also on every corner. The client is seated like a Wimbledon umpire, while his shoes are shined and polished with assiduous zeal. Women are rarely seen in the chair: they are expected to hand their shoes in discreetly and come back for them in 10 minutes.

Independence Monument
Better known as the Angel, this occupies a huge roundabout on Reforma, marking the Zona Rosa. Built in 1910, its single column is topped by a sculpted female form representing independence from the Spanish. At its base a vault holds the remains of various heroes of the independence movement, including an Irishman known as Gillén de Lampart: convicted by the Inquisition in the 1640s, he was imprisoned for 17 years and then burnt alive for writing inflammatory independence messages on ripped-up sheets, with an ink made of chocolate and ashes.

Museo de la Cera
(Londres 6; open 11.00–19.00; closed Mon; adm.)
Further east on Londres is an extraordinary **Wax Works Museum** (with a ludicrously high entrance charge), proudly displaying hopeful models of Ronald Reagan looking half his age. A sign at the entrance warns the emotionally unstable to take care—as indeed any fervent royalist must, on seeing the caricatures of Charles and Diana.

Chapultepec Park

Chapultepec Park is the Hyde Park or Central Park of Mexico. Once home to Moctezuma's pre-Hispanic zoo, it is now the great Sunday-with-the wife-and-kids park, dotted with museums, including the Museum of Anthropology.

Chapultepec Castle
(Open 09.00–17.00, Tues–Sun; adm.)
The park entrance off the Paseo de la Reforma is dominated by a monument composed of six standing columns, dedicated to the memory of six 15-year-old cadets—the *Niños Héroes*—who preferred to jump to their deaths off the balcony of the castle rather than give themselves up to the US troops in the war of 1847. Beyond this begins the steep drive up to the 18th-century Chapultepec Castle, begun in 1783 by the Spanish viceroy on a site that had been used as a summer retreat since the time of the Aztecs. It became a military academy in the 1840s but was converted 20 years later into a private retreat for

the emperor Maximilian. After the restitution of the republic, the castle became the presidential palace, and in 1940 it was converted into the **National History Museum**.

The two floors of the castle offer a run-through of Mexican history from the Spanish to the Revolution. There are murals by O'Gorman, Orozco and Siqueiros, and Maximilian and Carlota's apartments are on display, including a marvellously ostentatious marble bathtub.

The Gallery of History

Known as the *'caracol'* for its snail-like design, this gallery perches like a wart on the side of Chapultepec hill, just below the castle. The exhibits provide a whistle-stop tour through the key moments, people and places of modern Mexican history, from the last days of the viceroys to the Revolution, leading inexorably to a specially constructed alcove housing the 1917 Constitution. A bombastic and didactic commentary explains the dioramas, models, maps and paintings.

Museum of Modern Art

(On the edge of the park, at Ghandi and Reforma; open 10.00–18.00; closed Mon.)

This museum has one hall for temporary exhibitions and two halls for its permanent collection. The exhibits range from the earliest works of the great muralists in the 1920s to examples of the most up-to-date movements in contemporary Latin American art. Without any great walls to work on, the muralists are reduced to portrait-sized oils and etchings. As well as the three big names of Orozco, Rivera and Siqueiros (note particularly Siqueiros' placid, calm portrait of *Blanca Antebi*), the often overlooked women are also represented—including Frida Kahlo, María Izquierdo and Remedios Varo—who played a highly influential role in post-war Mexican art. The museum has a good art bookshop and a sculpture garden in the grounds.

Rufino Tamayo Museum

(Open 10.00–18.00, Tues–Sun.)

On the other side of Reforma, this museum houses the private collection of Rufino Tamayo, one of the foremost painters of this century. Born in Oaxaca in 1899, he spent most of his life in Mexico City. His collection is by no means exclusively Mexican, including works by Andy Warhol, Francis Bacon, De Kooning, Rothko, Moore and Picasso. One room is devoted to the works of Tamayo himself.

Museum of Anthropology

(Paseo de la Reforma and Ghandhi; open 09.00–19.00, Tues–Sun.)

Many visitors come to Mexico City specifically to see the Museum of Anthropology, requiring no other reason for their visit. Quite apart from its pre-Hispanic exhibits, the museum itself is superlative, designed by Pedro Ramírez Vázquez with such forethought that it has no equal in the country and few in the world.

The airy, large entrance hall has an excellent bookshop. In its basement, an **Orientation Room** gives a 15-minute introduction to the collection, with models rising up from the floor and popping out of the walls, all explained by a sepulchral voice in Spanish (occasionally English). From there, the museum spreads back to an open patio with 12 rooms, on two floors, each covering a culture or epoch in the 35,000 years of Mexico's history. The ground-floor rooms open onto a large courtyard dominated by a vast mushroom-shaped column, designed by José Chávez Morado and sculpted by his brother, Tomás. The column has two faces, one to the east, whence came the Spanish, and one to the west and the Orient, whence came the first peoples to cross over into the Americas.

It would be impossible to appreciate the entire collection in one visit—and exhausting too. As each room represents a distinct culture, it is better to concentrate on one or two at a time. Begin with the rooms on the right and work around counterclockwise. Sadly, the museum's policy is to use only Spanish labelling. ('If the Louvre and the Metropolitan don't have Spanish, why should we have their language?' is the simple reasoning.)

ROOMS I–III

The first three rooms are devoted to a general overview of world anthropology and the beginnings of culture in Mexico, including various exhibits from Egypt, the Arctic and the Americas.

ROOMS IV AND V: TEOTIHUACAN

This, the first great civilization in Central Mexico, came into its own between AD 100 and 600, when the vast, monumental pyramids were built in the valley of Teotihuacán. The Teotihuacános were the first to create a known pantheon of gods: both the Toltecs and the Aztecs later inherited many of these divinities. The vast pyramids of the Sun and the Moon were probably dedicated to the much represented Water God, Tlaloc, and his Goddess, Chalchiutlicue, though the Aztecs named them after the sun and moon. Other gods such as Huehuetéotl, the old Fire God with a brazier on his stooped head, Xipe Totec, the God of New Life dressed in the flayed skin of the young victim sacrificed for his regeneration, and Mictlantecuhtli, the God of Death, are all represented in elaborate, highly symbolistic forms. In a city so far from the sea, water took on mystical qualities, and snails and shells (associated with fertility) were highly prized. One of the most outstanding exhibits in this room is a reproduction of the mural in the Temple of Quetzalcóatl, in its original bright colours, vivid proof that wall paintings have been used as instruction throughout history.

ROOM VI: THE TOLTECS

After the fall of Teotihuacán, there was a power vacuum in the Valley of Mexico, filled in turn by the Maya-influenced trading and astronomical centre of **Xochicalco** in the south and the Toltec capital of **Tula** in the north. The fiercely competitive ball game was developed into an elaborate ceremony, and the feathered serpent deity, Quetzalcóatl, ritualized into a fetish. Writhing snakes with plumed headdresses appear in every form and shape. The two great Toltec symbols of the Atlantean column, towering above the other exhibits, and the sphinx-like Chac-Mool, his hands ready to accept the still palpitating hearts of sacrificial victims, are lasting testimonies to this bellicose and omnipotent civilization.

ROOM VII: THE AZTECS

The Aztecs, more correctly known as the Mexica (the derivation of the name of Mexico), dominate this, the most superlative of all the rooms. If there is no time for more, come here first.

By the time the Aztecs were established in Tenochtitlán (the site of present-day Mexico City) in the 13th century, a central Mexican pantheon of gods was well established. The Aztecs merely added their own modifications. Their influence stretched down into Central America and over into western Mexico, and the great market places of the city attracted traders from every corner of the known world. The exhibits range from massive basalt sculptures to small, delicate wooden instruments. Almost all seem stamped with a preoccupation with death, sacrifice and honour. One of the most remarkable pieces is the jaguar at the entrance, its hollowed-out back ready to accept human hearts. The most extraordinary of all, however, is the huge, round **Calendar Stone**, which encompassed the whole of the Aztec world in its intricate patterns and schemes, its centre dominated by the ever-hungry Sun God, Tonatiuh, who was fed on human hearts to keep him in the sky. The stone was found by the Spanish, who buried it in horror. It was dug up again in 1790, propped up against the cathedral, reburied, and rediscovered this century.

ROOM VIII: OAXACA

Oaxaca is Mexico's most mountainous state, encompassing hundreds of separate communities which have been isolated from each other throughout history. The two great Oaxacan cultures both came from the central valleys. The **Zapotecs** were the most monumental, building their ceremonial centres on mountain tops and burying their dead with great show and magnificence. Their tombs were later taken over by the Mixtecs, who replaced Zapotec bodies with their own. The main exhibits in this hall are recreations of two such tombs from Monte Albán. Tomb 105 is decorated with polychrome murals, in which three of the five figures are women. The entrance to Tomb 104 is set deliberately low, forcing the visitor to stoop down (out of respect for the dead). There are also reproductions of the *Danzante* figures fromn Monte Albán, mutilated and naked in simple relief. Although known as 'dancers', they probably portrayed ill or wounded warrriors. Beautiful ceramic masks depict the Bat God of the Underworld, and the two other principal gods—Cocijo, the God of Water, and Pitao Cozobi, the Corn God.

The Zapotecs were followed and superseded by the **Mixtecs**, who adopted and elaborated on many of their traditions but also left behind two great legacies: codice writing on the bark of wild fig trees, and exquisite metalwork. Their intricate carving extended to engraving ivory and even hard rock crystals. Exhibits also include examples of their multicoloured pottery (like the hummingbird bowl) and reconstructions of their palaces.

ROOM IX: THE GULF COAST

Far to the south of the central highlands, in flat lowland plains, the Gulf of Mexico spawned what is commonly acknowledged to be the first, great civilization of the Americas—the Mother Culture—in the 2nd millennium BC. The **Olmecs** introduced many of the basics of Mesoamerican culture, including the cult of the jaguar, monumental basalt heads and the rudiments of the ball game. Exhibits in this hall include floor mosaics, tombs of basalt columns, examples of stone drainage systems, and one wonderful figure, like a wrestler, poised in a dynamic twist.

When the Olmec lands were flooded, the people dispersed throughout Mexico (c 100 BC) and the Gulf momentarily lost its importance. The Huastecs later settled in the area north of Veracruz and east of San Luis Potosí. Part of their culture is represented by a single, solitary sculpture potraying Quetzalcóatl, in the form of a totem pole, decorated on all sides. Another sculpture from Tamuín in San Luis Potosí shows a young adolescent with huge ear holes and tattoos down his right-hand side, back and arms— possibly a young priest in the Quetzalcóatl cult. Pieces at the far end of the room represent the Totonacs, a proud people who inhabited the area when the Spanish first arrived in Mexico in 1519.

ROOM X: THE MAYA

At the entrance to this room, a large relief map illustrates the diversity and extent of Maya territory, stretching from southern Mexico into Guatemala and on south to El Salvador and Honduras. The Maya represent the greatest of Mexico's indigenous cultures. Whilst the hierarchy of their advanced civilization had collapsed before the arrival of the Spanish, the people themselves survived, albeit at a subsistence level, and today they still maintain their language and customs. Ruins of their ancient cities, dating from the post-Classic period (AD 750–1100), still cover the Yucatán peninsula, many hidden by overgrown jungle.

Their murals and sculptures, jade masks and stelae all attest to their artistic sensitivity. Outstanding amongst the exhibits is the jade Pacal mask from Palenque, which was stolen in a sensational robbery and recovered in 1989. Examples abound of their percussion and wind instruments (including tambourines, shells and flutes), and of their intricate knowledge of astronomy and medicine, which was as advanced as that of any contemporary Western culture. One sculpture shows a man with a tumour in his left eye and another an old man dying in a young flower. There are also reproductions of the Bonampak murals and the original tablets from the Temple of the Cross in Palenque.

ROOMS XI AND XII: THE WEST AND NORTHWEST

Unforgivably lumped together, the various cultures of the west and northwest represent the most geographically isolated and the most historically overlooked part of the country. Lacking the materials or the need for self-publicity, these nomadic peoples produced artefacts of an everyday, homely simplicity, which tended to be pushed to the sidelines of archaeological research, until collectors such as Diego Rivera and Carlos Pellicer brought them back into the spotlight. The maquettes of daily scenes which were buried with the dead give a revealing glimpse into the domestic life of a pre-Hispanic culture, showing women breast-feeding, dogs playing and lovers embracing.

THE SECOND FLOOR

Ten more rooms, on the second floor, are devoted to ethnography and to the indigenous cultures which still survive in every part of the country. The scope is wide, with linguistic and anthropological exhibits as well as examples of weaving, textiles, clothing and farming. In the second room a clever photomontage attempts to pin down the elusive Mexican face, at once so obvious and so difficult to define.

Centro Cultural de Arte Contemporáneo

On the same side of Reforma as the museum, opposite the **Auditorio Nacional** (National Auditorium), this cultural centre mounts ever-changing exhibitions (including, recently, 'Dali's Dalis' and 'Women Artists in Mexico'). Its excellent shop is filled with art books and imaginative, well-thought-out presents.

Polanco
(Metro Polanco or Auditorio, both line 7.)
North of Chapultepec Park is the affluent area known as Polanco, where the streets are named after writers such as Homero, Lord Byron, Poe and Julio Verne. It is renowned as an enclave of rich foreigners, whose tastes are catered for by numerous restaurants offering take-away sushi, sauerkraut or kosher tacos. Polanco's only **museum** is the house and studio of **David Alfaro Siqueiros** (Calle Tres Picos 29), one of the three great muralists and painters of the 20th century and also the attempted murderer of León Trotsky (see Trotsky's house). It is difficult to make a spontaneous visit, as appointments should be made with the caretaker (tel 531 3394). However, he may let you in if you arrive at the door between 10.00 and 14.00 (closed Sun).

South of the City

The longest avenue in the world, Insurgentes, crosses Reforma and leads south, past San Angel to the west and Coyoacán to the east. It continues south past the university, before finally joining the main ring road (for routes south towards Cuernavaca).

GETTING AROUND
Insurgentes' 20-km-plus length is far too long to walk: instead, take a bus, combi or metro, which all leave from the Glorieta Insurgentes in the Zona Rosa.

To make the most of the south of the city, visit the university on a weekday, Coyoacán during the weekend, and San Angel on Saturday for the market (10.00–18.00) in the Bazar Sabado.

Avenida Insurgentes

Polyforo Siqueiros
(Insurgentes and Calle Filadelfia.)
The Polyforum is the most outstanding work of David Alfaro Siqueiros in the city. Designed by the artist, it is a complicated piece of modern architecture, built in an octagonal shape on an elliptical base. On the top floor, the walls and ceiling are covered by Siqueiros' 2400-square-metre mural, *The March of Humanity*. Stand anywhere in the vast room, and you will find yourself beneath a vast pair of outstretched hands. Wet walls and paint weren't enough for the modernist Siqueiros: here he used panels of asbestos-cement, overlaid with metal appliqué and acrylic paint. The outside walls of the building are also covered by 12 panels of murals, painted and sculpted in his raw, enraged colours and forms.

The Polyforum is, however, more than just an artwork. It incorporates a theatre in the round, workshops, galleries and some extraordinarily out-of-place collections, such as a set of miniatures of US presidents (in the basement).

Behind the Polyforum languishes the never-to-be-completed **Hotel de México**, begun in the 1970s, which now lies exposed to the elements, because the money ran out.

Teatro Insurgentes
(Av Insurgentes Sur 1587.)
This well-known theatre was one of the first public buildings to be decorated with a mosaic mural on the outside, representing a breakthrough in the combination of architecture and painting. No one liked the result of Diego Rivera's work back in 1953, and few like it now. The mural portrays the history of theatre and dance (the mask and the female hands represent the dramatic arts). The centre figure is the popular folk-hero, Cantinflas (Mexico's Charlie Chaplin), who gives to the poor what he receives from the rich.

San Angel

Less than 30 years ago, San Angel could still claim to be outside Mexico City, separated by fields and surrounded by maguey cactuses, with clear views of the volcanoes. Today, it is buried in the south of the city. Its pretty cobbled streets and attractive plazas turn into open-air markets at the weekends (see Markets) and its old colonial mansions have been bought up by those who can afford the increasingly high prices.

GETTING AROUND
Buses and combis along Insurgentes will drop passengers off either at the San Angel market or on the corner of Av de la Paz (the eastern edge of San Angel). There is no easy metro: the best are Miguel Angel de Quevedo (line 3) or Barranca del Muerto (line 7).

Museo Carrillo Gil
(Alta Vista and Av Revolución 1608.)
On the northern outskirts of San Angel proper, this museum of modern art was named after the Yucatecan doctor, Alvar Carrillo Gil (1899–1974), who was a friend of Orozco, Siqueiros and Rivera. It represents one of the earliest and most complete collections of works by the three great muralists (including examples from Rivera's cubist phase). In the 1960s, before modern art became so prohibitively expensive, Carrillo Gil travelled to Europe and Japan, buying paintings by Klee, Kandinsky, Picasso and the Japanese Murata. He also bought Maya pieces from the island of Jaina and engravings by Rouault and Cuevas, establishing the greatest private collection of his generation. The museum was opened in 1974, a few weeks before his death.

El Carmen Church and Museum
(Revolución and La Paz.)
A monument to the last days of the viceroys in the 19th century, this has always been one of the more conservative churches in the city. With its golden dome, tiled in blue and yellow, and its painted walls and ceilings, it is a perfect repository for a permanent collection of colonial and religious art, tiles and altarpieces. Its patrons were military men and colonial governors, some of whom were buried in the low-ceilinged crypt, in glass-topped coffins revealing their mummified bodies, with tattered black habits still in place.

Museo Estudio Diego Rivera

(Alta Vista at the San Angel Inn (see Eating Out); open 10.00–18.00; closed Mon.)

Diego Rivera and Frida Kahlo lived in Coyoacán but worked in these double studios. They were built to their commission in 1930, like two colourful building blocks, by their old friend, the architect Juan O'Gorman. The connected but separated houses are now a museum. Kahlo's has become administrative offices and Rivera's has been opened to the public. It is disappointing initially, with unimaginative exhibitions on the ground floor, but the journey is made worthwhile when one climbs up the narrow stairs to Rivera's studio space, still filled with his personal clutter.

Coyoacán

Condescendingly described as 'a quiet, leafy suburb' or 'the Bohemian quarter', Coyoácan is, in fact, one of the few villages left within the city's tentacles. Although an affluent neighbourhood, wedged between two inner-city ring roads, it has kept its charm by default. The default is the smog. Although there are few factories on this side of the city, air currents drive the pollution to the south, where it becomes trapped by the mountains and falls back on itself. Coyoacán, therefore, is one of the most contaminated parts of the city and many people who would like to live there, choose not to.

It is, however, one of the liveliest areas. The main double plaza, which becomes a moveable feast on Sundays, is one of the oldest in the city. Cortés built his palace here (on the main square and Aguayo) and brought his Mexican lover, La Malinche, to live beside him (on the corner of Higuera and Vallarta). Affairs and intrigues weave Coyoacán's history. Cortés' first wife died here under very suspicious circumstances, and in the 1940s and 1950s Diego Rivera and Frida Kahlo turned their house into a work of art, filled with mementos of both their lives. A few streets away, Kahlo's one-time lover, the much-hounded León Trotsky, spent the last years of his life, feeding his pet rabbits in his fortress-home.

GETTING AROUND

Coyoacán is not one of the easiest places to get to. 'Ruta 116a' buses connect the district with San Angel, and there are also three metro stations, although none are close to the main plaza.

Coyoacán (line 3) is the best station for the Kahlo museum: from there, walk down Av México to Londres and then follow the signs. Trotsky's house is a 5-minute walk from the museum: walk two blocks to the left along Londres and turn left into Gómez Farías; his house is just to the right, where Farías hits the main Río Churubusco road.

The other two metros (also on line 3) are Viveros—on the San Angel side of Coyoacán, and Miguel Angel de Quevedo—on its southern side. Both are some 12 blocks from the main square. To make the most of the walk to the square, through cobbled streets and past colonial mansions, get off at the Miguel Angel de Quevedo station: walk along Av Universidad Norte to the prettiest street of them all, Francisco Sosa (which has a small church at the intersection) and follow that right down to the plaza.

Museo Frida Kahlo

(Londres 47, on the corner of Allende.)

This beautiful house, painted a deep cornflower blue, was the lifelong home of Frida Kahlo, the painter, who was married, divorced and then remarried to Diego Rivera. Today it stands as a paean to Kahlo herself and to her passionate love for Diego Rivera. Even though every room is gaily painted in the strong colours of Mexico and decorated with folk art from around the country, the house, with its decaying garden, is mournfully sad. Frida Kahlo's life was plagued by a combination of physical disability and internal anguish. Permanently injured in a crash when she was still a teenager, she was unable to have Rivera's child (a passionate desire since she was 13) and died in a wheelchair at the age of 47.

In the gateway, a giant papier-mâché figure, known as *judas* and burned on Good Friday, wears the heavy denim dungarees Rivera always painted in. The house is filled with Kahlo's paintings of herself and her family—including some excruciatingly analytical self-portraits, and with works by Rivera and their group of friends. The kitchen is covered with vast Mexican ceramics, including both their names over the stove. Their bedroom is decorated with her self-portrait over the bed, Stalin's bust, her diminutive shoes and Rivera's vast dungarees. On the floor above are their library-studio and the bedroom she died in. Stairs lead down into the neglected garden.

Casa Trotsky

More of a shrine than a museum, this house has been freeze-framed ever since Trotsky was murdered here on 20 August 1940. His desk remains as it was, and *British Trade Unionism Today* lies open at the page he was reading. After seven years in Turkey and Norway, in flight from Stalinist Russia, Trotsky was finally shipped to Mexico in an oil tanker in 1937, and given asylum by President Lázaro Cárdenas. In the same year he had a brief but intense affair with Frida Kahlo, meeting often in her sister's house (the same sister who was, ironically, having an affair with Diego Rivera).

The house, modest and middle-class, was quickly transformed into a fortress with steel doors, electrified wire, gun holes on the roof and a dozen Mexican soldiers on permanent guard against Stalinist agents. It was no good. The first attack came within three years, when 30 men, including the Stalinist muralist David Alfaro Siqueiros, bombarded the house and indiscriminately shot 200 bullets through the walls and windows. Trotsky was in the patio, and was unharmed. Within three months, however, a second attack by a former friend and Catalan Stalinist caught him off guard, while he was feeding his pet rabbits in the garden. The Catalan plunged an ice pick into his head. His ashes remain in the garden, under a monolithic memorial stone, etched with the hammer and sickle.

In 1990, to commemorate the 50th anniversary of his death, the next-door house was bought and the museum turned into a true example of *perestroika* and free-market economics. The entrance fee is now the most expensive of any museum in Mexico (still precious little), but with it come the display cases filled with the minutiae of his daily, personal and political life.

Ciudad Universitaria

(Insurgentes Sur, 19 km from the Insurgentes roundabout.)
In the 1940s, the government made the decision to move the university from the crowded historic centre down to the very south of the city. Building began in 1950 on the vast lava fields south of San Angel, on a site comprising over 7 million square metres.

GETTING AROUND

Although there is a Universidad stop on the metro, Copilco (line 3) is closer to the central buildings. Buses marked 'Ciudad Universitaria' run the length of Insurgentes, stopping outside the main complex.

The Murals

Many Mexican muralists and artists had a hand in the various buildings, creating between them the most avant-garde university in the Americas. One outstanding construction is the **Rectory Tower**. Its mosaic mural by David Alfaro Siqueiros represents three key years in Mexican history: the coming of the Spanish in 1519, independence in 1820 and the founding of the republic in 1857; a date for the future is left open. Diego Rivera studded the outside wall of the 100,000 seat **Stadium** with a stone mosaic in high relief, representing the god Quetzalcóatl. The four walls of the 12-storey **Central Library** are covered with a colourful mosaic by Juan O'Gorman, while the auditorium of the Science Buildings is decorated in glazed mosaic by José Chávez Morado.

The Far South

Further south still are the little visited Museo Anahuacalli, with some wonderful pieces from the west of Mexico, and the floating gardens of Xochimilco, a traditional Sunday excursion for many Mexican families.

GETTING AROUND

For both the Anahuacalli museum and Xochimilco, take the metro to Tasqueña (line 2). From there, take the light railway (*tren ligero*), bus or a taxi. The Anahuacalli is best reached by taxi from Tasqueña, as the train station and bus stop (Xotepingo) is eight blocks from the museum, five of which are uphill. The museum is well signposted but it is an uncomfortable walk in the middle of the day.

Museo Anahuacalli

(Calle del Museo 150, near División del Norte; pesero 'Ruta 29'; open 10.00–18.00, Tues–Sun; adm.)
Out of the way of all the other museums, the Museo Anahuacalli was designed and built by Diego Rivera to house his collection of pre-Hispanic art. Constructed from volcanic stone, on a lava bed, it was designed to resemble a pre-Hispanic pyramid (which means that the interior lighting is awful). Most of the pieces are from the western states of Colima, Nayarit and Jalisco—the most naive, charming and immediate of all. Rivera also used it as a studio. On the second floor are studies for some of his later murals, and the unfinished painting he was working on when he died.

Xochimilco

The suburb of Xochimilco is 24 km from the centre. Its name means 'the place of flowers' and, indeed, it still has the best flower market in the city, as well as several nurseries. The fertile land is made up of *chinampas* or rafts of mud and reeds, firmly rooted to the bottom by plants and by *ahuehuete* trees, which reinforce the walls. These ingenious rafts are of pre-Hispanic origin, first used when Xochimilco was an independent kingdom, and subsequently when it became a vassal state of the Aztecs in the 13th century.

On Sunday, innumerable boats are punted along the canals and waterways which connect one part to another. Marimba players moor alongside and play their songs, while food boats float by offering ice creams, tacos and drinks. At night, the boatmen light candles and the whole area feels like a film set (the film *María Candelaria* was shot here). Although most Sunday visitors merely take a boat out for an hour's gentle float, the canals in fact extend for 189 km, stretching down into the state of Morelos. The older boatmen, who know them well, can disappear for days.

There are eight embarkation points around Xochimilco, all signposted from the main square ('Embarcaderos'). Prices are all fixed (per boat and not per person) and notice boards list current charges at every pier.

Xochimilco is surrounded by little villages, all trying not to be submerged in the suburbs, whose *viveros* or nurseries supply all the saplings for the entire city. Eucalyptus, a former favourite, needs more air than most other trees and has virtually died out because of the smog.

WHERE TO STAY   (area code 5)

There are hotels in every part of the city, and choosing the right one can be time-consuming. The most elegant, efficient and expensive hotels are in Chapultepec Park. The Zona Rosa has less style than its reputation might suggest, but for bland modernity and medium-to-expensive hotels, it will do. For a combination of character and good prices, however, nothing beats the area around the Zócalo. If price is more important than character, stick to the hotels around the railway station on the north side of Reforma.

Around the Zócalo

The oldest and most original hotels are in the heart of the city. So too are the cheapest and tackiest. Beware of elegant entrances which belie the squalor of the rooms, and look for the word *familiar* which, if it means what it says, designates a hotel which does not rent rooms for use by the hour. Always ask to see your room and check different sides of the building to see which is the noisiest.

Originally a department store, the entrance of the ******Gran Hotel** (on the Zócalo, 16 de Septiembre 82, tel 5104040, tlx 01773069) is a vast expanse of Art Nouveau, where parrots hang in huge golden cages and wrought-iron lifts are operated by buttoned bell boys. The rooms are less grandiose than the hall, however: it's better to come for a drink than to spend the night. Also on the Zócalo itself, the ******Majestic** (Av Madero 73, tel 521 8600, tlx 01772770) is a wonderful hotel, serving the best Sunday brunches in Mexico from its seventh-floor balcony hanging over the square. Each room comes with an in-built alarm clock, provided by the military pipes and drums which play early every morning as the flag is raised in the Zócalo. Its entrance hall is filled with glazed Pueblan tiles and is often used in film sets. (See Eating Out.) Not right on the square but within spitting distance, the ****Ritz (Av Madero 30, tel 518 1340, tlx 01772770) is another comfortable hotel which has managed to retain a lot of character, despite being part of the Best Western chain.

All the other hotels around the centre are inexpensive. One of the best is the ***Monte Carlo, a 2-minute walk from the Zócalo (Uruguay 69, tel 521 2559 or 510 0081), with a garage—a distinct advantage in the centre, and big rooms. Often full, the mustard-yellow **Isabel (Isabel La Católica 63, tel 518 1213) is a good, cheap hotel filled with international backpackers who have forced the reluctant staff to learn a smattering of German, English and French. Money has reportedly been stolen from the rooms but this hasn't dinted its popularity. Another safe bet, providing clean, simple, modern rooms, is the **Canada (Av 5 de Mayo 47, tel 518 2106). Right behind the cathedral, the appropriately named **Catedral (Donceles 95, tel 512 8581, 512 8141) is long-established and reassuring. Alternatively, try the amazingly low-priced **Fleming, one block from Juárez (Revillagigedo 35, tel 510 4530). Also worth trying are the **Washington (Av 5 de Mayo 54, tel 512 3502, 521 1143), the Galicia (Honduras 11, tel 529 7791) or the **Lafayette (Motolinía 40 and 16 de Septiembre, tel 521 9640). At the bottom end of the scale, the *Roble (Uruguay 109, tel 522 7830) is not particularly cheerful, with glaringly orange walls, but consistently popular with young travellers.

The North Side of Reforma

The north side of Reforma is less fashionable and consequently cheaper than the Zona Rosa opposite. Just off the Alameda, near the Franz Mayer museum, the small burnt-ochre ****Cortés is set in a glorious Mexican baroque building which was once a shelter and hospice for passing Augustinian friars. It was converted in 1943 and has long enjoyed a reputation as one of the most characteristic of Mexican hotels. In Río Lerma, near the British and US embassies, the ****María Cristina (Río Lerma 31, tel 546 9880, fax 566 9194) occupies another colonial building, once the home of the Anglo-Mexican Rule family who came from Cornwall to mine silver. Today it is an attractive and comfortable hotel, although its restaurant wouldn't win any prizes. Round the corner, the ***Jardín Amazonas (Río Amazonas 73, tel 533 5950, tlx 01774418) comprises rather shabby motel suites, which are constantly being remodelled. Family suites with two double beds and two sofa beds justify the claim to charge 'very reasonable prices', and the complex includes a swimming pool and parking facilities. Close by, the modern ****Bristol (Plaza Nacaxa 17, 533 6060) is popular with visiting business people who don't enjoy an unlimited expense account. The ****Reforma (Paseo de la Reforma and Paris, tel 546 9680, tlx 1772115) clings onto a very glitzy 1930s Hollywood past—in spirit if not in fact.

For far cheaper hotels, head further east, always parallel with Reforma. The **Edison (Edison 106, tel 566 0933) is popular with long-stay tourists for its reasonable rates. The ***Mayaland (Antonio Caso 23, tel 566 6066) attracts visiting archaeologists amongst others and is well placed, its rooms adequate if somewhat dull. Other hotels worth trying in this range are the tastelessly redecorated but once elegant 1940s-style **Oxford, two blocks northeast of the Revolution Monument (Plaza Buenavista, Ignacio Mariscal 67, tel 566 0500) and the **Carlton, across the plaza from the Oxford

(Ignacio Mariscal 32, tel 566 2911). Further west, near Av Hidalgo, the plain, cheap **Managua** (Plaza de San Fernando 11, tel 521 4961, 521 5581) is set off another pleasant square, with a small café downstairs—the best of a dingy bunch, in this area of super-cheap hotels.

South of Reforma: the Zona Rosa
In and around the expensive Zona Rosa area, the hotels have the advantage of being in the centre of things. Both the Zócalo and Chapultepec, as well as the main tourist shops, are within walking or easy taxi distance. The *****Holiday Inn Crowne Plaza** on Reforma (no 80, tel 566 7777, tlx 1762092, fax 7051313) buzzes with foreign journalists, businessmen and local beauty queens and is an efficient, comfortable hotel for anyone on an expense account. It comes complete with a well equipped gym, a variety of restaurants, a rooftop swimming pool and all mod cons. The elegant and attractive ****Calinda Geneve** (Londres 130, tel 211 0071) is the only hotel worth staying in in the Zona Rosa. Colonial-style and recently modernized, with big bright rooms, its heart is still in the right place, although it is patronized by tour groups.

Just west of the Zona Rosa, near the French Embassy, the ***Internacional Havre** (Havre 21, 211 0082, tlx 1761462) is an offbeat choice: set in a cultural time warp, its large rooms are decorated with reproduction French furniture. Close by, the ***Vasco de Quiroga** (Londres 15, west of Insurgentes, tel 546 2614) is a small, well-run hotel with the atmosphere of a family home. Downstairs, bookcases, sofas and tables to write on are set around a big fireplace. The ***Marlowe** (Independencia 17, tel 521 9540) is cheaper with less character, but a safe bet nonetheless.

Chapultepec
The Zona Rosa was once *the* place to stay, but now the top hotels are further down Reforma, overlooking Chapultepec Park.

The high-rise **Nikko**, just opposite Chapultepec Park and the Auditorium (Campos Elíseos 204, tel 203 4800, tlx 1763523, fax 255 5586) has ousted its rivals and become the top hotel for businessmen. The Japanese use it all the time, enjoying the special Japanese rooms, although it also includes regular western bedrooms. Now overshadowed by the Nikko, the *****Stouffer Presidente** (Campos Elíseos 218, tel 250 7700) is still a comfortable second-best. The elegant **GT Camino Real** (Mariano Escobedo 700, tel 203 2121) is spread over 3 hectares of land beside Chapultepec Park and is considered by many to be the best hotel in the city, particularly because of its restaurant, Fouquet's of Paris. The busy *****María Isabel Sheraton**, next to the US Embassy and overlooking the Angel (Paseo de la Reforma 325, tel 211 0001, tlx 1773936) is always super-comfortable, with plenty of choice in its seven restaurants. An alternative to these is the very de luxe *****Clarion**, half a block west of the Angel (Paseo de la Reforma 373, tel 525 9184, tlx 1772028, free call 91 800 90000). Its luxurious suites are designed for business people, and it provides secretarial services, fax and telex machines, and saunas and jacuzzis in each suite.

EATING OUT
In a city the size of Mexico City, there are any number of restaurants. This is by no means a comprehensive guide but rather a list of some personal favourites. Breakfast and lunch

are the main meals of the day. Evenings are quieter: indeed, many restaurants are closed by 18.00.

Centro Histórico

The centre abounds with small cheap cafés on every street corner, for breakfasts, *pan dulce* and endless coffee. At night, when the theatres and nightclubs come alive, many people go to eat at one of the numerous turn-of-the-century bars, with their starched waiters and unconvincing formality. Far cheaper than the bars in the Zona Rosa or Polanco, they are also far more charming.

The wonderful *belle époque* **Bar Opera** (5 de Mayo and Filomeno Mata) once hosted the revolutionary Pancho Villa: there are still bullet holes in the walls to commemorate the occasion. Its white-clothed tables are set back in discreet carved wooden niches. The menu includes plates of Portuguese sardines heaped with mashed potato, fried squid and thick steaks. Moderate. In the parallel street one block behind, the reassuring **Café de Tacuba** (Tacuba 28, opposite Allende metro, tel 518 4950) is another well-established meeting-place, founded in 1912 in an ex-convent. A whole generation of students congregated here after classes, before the university moved to the south of the city. The walls of the long, thin restaurant are covered in tiles, and its menu includes all the Mexican standards: the *Cuatro Cositas* is a selection of four favourites. Cheap.

Opposite Bellas Artes, the **Casa de los Azulejos** (Madero) belongs to the famous Sanborns chain. These restaurants are scattered all over the city—you don't find them: they find you—and are famed for traditional Mexican breakfasts, served by long-skirted waitresses in starched white aprons. Most have a bookshop attached, filled with magazines, and often a full department store as well. The Casa de los Azulejos is a 16th-century mudéjar-style building, covered in blue tiles (*azulejos*) from China and Puebla, once the home of the Counts of Orizaba. The story goes that a wastrel son was told by his father that he would never have a house of tiles, a symbol of great wealth. Piqued, the son duly married a rich heiress and shortly afterwards covered the mansion with tiles from top to toe. The main restaurant is in a courtyard with a flowing fountain. Halfway up the stairs there is an enormous Orozco mural. Cheap.

The most famous of all the restaurants in the centre is **Prendes** (Av 16 de Septiembre 10, tel 521 1878). It was founded in 1892 and soon became *the* place to be seen in. Latterly, it has begun to live on its reputation, though it still commands the faithful, who return day after day to the faded elegance of its interior, filled with murals and paintings. Its reliable if somewhat overpriced menu includes fresh oysters, *jamón tipo español* (Parma ham) and a huge paella on Sundays. León Trotsky was a regular and ate his last supper here. Moderately expensive.

Overlooking the Zócalo, the rooftop restaurant of the hotel **Majestic** is a *sine qua non* for long lazy Sunday breakfasts, prepared as a special buffet. One can sit for hours watching bands marching down below in the Zócalo. Moderate.

To the east of the Zócalo, the **Fonda Don Chon** (Regina 159, tel 522 2170) specializes in authentic pre-Hispanic dishes, from wild boar in a mango sauce to pheasant, quail, *escamoles* (ants' eggs), *chapulines* (tiny grasshoppers) and *gusanos de maguey* (the worm from the mezcal cactus). Vegetarians needn't despair, however, as they also prepare *tacos de huitlacoche* (a mature corn which tastes of mushroom) and *flor de* *calabaza* (fried courgette flowers). To all intents and purposes a scruffy café, it is easy to miss: attention has been lavished on the food rather than the decor. Moderate.

Three streets north of Tacuba, **Hostería de Santo Domingo** (Domínguez 72, tel 510 1434) is divided into two floors. This lively restaurant is filled with Mexicana, from cut-out paper *grecas* to photographs of Jorge Negrete. The cuisine matches the decor, offering good home-cooked *puchero de gallina* (a thick chicken soup), *ensalada de nopale* (cactus salad) and thick cuts of beef. At weekends there are often queues waiting to get in. Moderate.

South of the Alameda, **Lincoln** (Revillagigedo 24, tel 510 1468) has an expensive-looking green and white facade, while inside dining booths are lined in dark wood, deliberately reminiscent of a gentleman's club. Meals begin with large bowls of fresh cucumber, carrots and radishes, together with delicious pickled heads of garlic. Fish is the speciality and dishes include mountain oysters in a hot sauce, *jaibas rellenas jarocha* (stuffed crab) and an excellent version of *huachinango a la veracruzana* (red snapper cooked with tomatoes and olives). Moderately expensive.

Zona Rosa

The Zona Rosa is packed with restaurants which fill with businessmen (rarely women) for lunch and tourists for dinner. As there is a high demand, the food is always of excellent quality and the prices correspond. Calle Copenhagen, off Londres, is devoted entirely to restaurants.

The **Champs Élysées** (Amberes 1, tel 514 0450, closed weekends) provides classic French cuisine, disdaining any of that fancy *nouvelle* stuff. Vegetables are always cooked *au point* and the wine list is excellent. It specializes in home-cured charcuterie and pâtés as well as the best cuts of meat. The *coquille de pescados gratinados* and the popular bouillabaisse are both excellent. The restaurant caters for those who really know and care about food and is patronized by government politicians. Downstairs is the place to see and be seen, though there is also a pleasant terrace upstairs. Expensive.

The small, discreet **Estoril** (Hamburgo 87, tel 511 2679) has a consistently excellent menu which includes a mouthwatering *perejil al Estoril* (fried parsley), rich creamy avocado soup and smoked oyster mousse, as well as prawns lightly poached in Chablis, quail cooked with pepper and mushrooms, and sea bass in coriander sauce. Expensive. On the north side of Reforma, facing the Zona Rosa, **Les Moustaches** (Río Sena 88) is a studiously elegant, highly pretentious restaurant: moustaches are compulsory for all the waiters, including the owner, and jackets and tie for all the guests. However, it does serve exquisite abalone and, in September, the best *chiles en nogada* covered in a pomegranate sauce. Expensive.

Bellinghausen (London 95, tel 511 9035) is another institution, a sister restaurant to Prendes (see Centro Histórico). It has a pleasant garden courtyard at the back of the restaurant, which is more lively than the interior. Its waiters are all old-timers, with a full sense of their own importance. Tried and tested standards are *sopa de hongos* (a specially good mushroom soup), paella and roast lamb. Expensive. The **Trucha Vagabunda** (Londres 104, tel 533 3178) is a glass-fronted seafood restaurant, popular and cheerfully efficient, looking out onto one of the busiest shopping streets in the Zona Rosa. Its menu includes giant prawns in a *chipotle* sauce, red snapper *a la veracruzana* and spinach and walnut salads. Moderately expensive.

Italian food is almost always disappointing in Mexico City, pasta in particular. The altitude makes it hard to keep water boiling at the right intensity, and pasta tends to be cooked for hours in tepid water. **La Góndola** (Génova 21, tel 511 6908) is better than most, providing excellent seafood risottos. Moderate.

For cheap tacos, few places beat **Beatriz** (Varsovia 24, tel 511 6054)). It specializes in chicken soup laced with coriander, followed by tacos filled with tomato and avocado and a choice of chicken, cheese and meat fillings.

Vegetarian: The biggest vegetarian restaurant is **La Fuente**, opposite the Zona Rosa (near the Sheraton on the corner of Río Tiber and Pánuco). It is relatively expensive but offers a wide selection of dishes. An excellent vegetarian restaurant in the Zona Rosa itself, where lunchtime queues persist until after 2 o'clock, is the **Yug** (Varsovia 3, tel 452917). Its huge four-course comida corrida includes good rich soups and salads. Cheap. Alternatively, just south of the Zona Rosa is a small, macrobiotic café, the **Tao** (Cozumel with Sonora), which serves well-prepared standard lunches with lots of rice, tofu, vegetables and corn cakes for a very low price.

Tea Shops in the Zona Rosa: Tea and coffee shops are not Mexican institutions but the Zona Rosa, catering for tourists, has given them somewhere to put their feet up. For breakfasts or cups of tea and coffee throughout the day, try the Danish **Konditori** (Génova 61, tel 5144828). Cheap. In Hamburgo, the **Auseba** and the **Duca de Este** both serve delicious pastries. Cheap.

Japanese: The Daikoku chain deserves a special mention as its restaurants are some of the best in Mexico City. Of these, the best of all is in Michoacán 25, in the Colonia Condesa, just south of the Zona Rosa (tel 584 8557). Try *ume*, a variety of raw fish served on rice balls with a horseradish sauce, or the rolls of avocado wrapped round rice with a prawn centre. More filling are noodles with fish, meat or vegetables (known as *fideos*). Go through the café-style front of the restaurant to the slightly smarter suchi bar and tables at the back. The other branches, which for some reason are never quite as good, are at Genova 44 (Col Juárez, Zona Rosa, tel 533 4953) and Pánuco 170 (Col Cuauhtémoc, on the opposite side of Reforma to the Zona Rosa, tel 514 8257). All are moderately priced.

Chapultepec

Feeling more like a private house than a restaurant, the international **Isla Victoria** (Monte Kamerún 120, Lomas de Chapultepec, tel 520 5597) is small and exclusive. Its set menu includes unusual dishes such as *ensalada Miguel Angelo*, with French lettuce, fresh orange, walnuts and goat's cheese topped with a piping hot orange sauce. Moderately expensive. The light and airy **Mediteranée** (Av de las Palmas 210, Lomas de Chapultepec, tel 520 8244) is where Las Lomas housewives breakfast on tropical fruits and yoghurts. It specializes in seafood, such as *sopa de camarón* (seafood soup) or paella. Moderately expensive.

For something more modest, there are a number of well-known *taquerias* and cantinas. In the third section of Chapultepec, the **Mirador** (13 Septiembre and Av Chapultepec) is a spit-and-sawdust cantina on one side (for men only) and a white-tableclothed restaurant (for both) on the other. Its many seafood dishes include large paellas for two people. Cheap. **Los Panchos** near the Chapultepec metro is also good for tacos. Cheap.

Polanco

Many Europeans live in Polanco and over the years a number of excellent European restaurants have opened up around them. Of these the small **El Buen Comer** (Edgar Allen Poe 50, tel 203 5337 and 545 8057) used to be particularly recommended for superlatively good French food, though lately standards have dropped with the arrival of a new and less diligent chef. The French owner converted his garage and front yard, stretching an awning across the patio. It is always full and only open for lunch: reservations are essential. Temptations include *cèpes* (wild mushrooms which grow on oak trees) *à la bordelaise*, Norwegian smoked salmon, quenelles of fish in a seafood sauce, and house pâtés of which the duck is particularly recommended. Moderate.

La Petite France (Mazarik 360, tel 250 4470 and 548 3918) is set in a shopping arcade, its white wrought-iron chairs tumbling out onto the street under a stretched canopy. It is strong on grilled fish with imaginative light sauces, and roulades of salmon or lobster in basil. Alternatively, try the duck in a pear and blackcurrant sauce or steaks bathed in artichoke. Moderate.

For more seafood, the outwardly unprepossessing Catalonian restaurant **Costa Dorada** (Av Ejército Nacional 648, tel 545 3086 and 531 1277) is well worth a visit. It specializes in a mouth-wateringly tender *pescado a la sal* (a whole fish baked in sea salt). Starters include abalone, squid and shellfish, with particularly good *pipirrana* (shrimps mixed with cucumber and green peppers). Moderately expensive.

For good Italian home cooking, **Capri** (Júlio Verne 83, tel 545 7856 and 531 2688) is a safe bet. The pasta and the pesto sauce are all home made. Try the ravioli stuffed with spinach or the *risotto con funghi* (mushroom risotto). Moderate. Another excellent Italian restaurant is the more modern **La Botiglia** (Edgar Allen Poe with Campos Elíseos, tel 520 6033), simply decorated with unglazed wood and dried flowers. The chef, Elena Pizzaoli, comes from Pisa and dishes such as *zuppa dei funghi* (mushroom soup) and *filete de trucha al pesto* (trout in a basil sauce) have an authentic touch. Moderate.

The beautiful **ex-Hacienda de los Morales** (Vázquez de Mella 525, tel 540 3235) has been converted into a restaurant serving Mexican cuisine at its best. Try the cold walnut soup or have a fish cooked in front of you in exactly the way you want. The chicken is corn-fed and especially delicious, though the partridge casserole is also a strong contender. Expensive. A cheaper restaurant specializing in Mexican food is **El Kino** (Campos Elíseos 363 A, as it crosses Goldsmith, tel 540 5970) which combines a small café-style restaurant with a shop and recreates old dishes with a new twist: try the *sopa de flor de calabaza* (courgette-flower soup). Moderately cheap.

Insurgentes

Down the southern end of Insurgentes, towards Coyoacán and San Angel, the **Fonda del Factor** (Mercaderes 21, off Insurgentes, tel 563 4607) serves amazingly cheap Mexican breakfasts. The especially good scrambled eggs come with *nopale* (a cactus tasting a bit like French beans), dark rich black beans and a spicy *mole* sauce. The restaurant is large, with photo-clad walls, and fills with Mexican families for Sunday lunch. Moderate. Pope John Paul II orders specialities from the Polish **Mazurka** (New York 150, tel 523 8811) when he comes to Mexico. Its main attraction for the lay eater will be the frozen vodka, which can be consumed in vast quantities. Aficionados of heavy

Polish food will find borscht and goulash, as well as goose in a variety of forms, all accompanied by thick, rich sauces. Moderately expensive.

Coyoacán

In the south of the city, Coyoacán buzzes with life over the weekend, when its main square fills with hawkers, dancers, idlers and small children. **Café Parnaso**, on the main square, is the place to sit and watch it all, over capuchinos, carrot juice, rolls and cakes. It is usually full of people reading *La Jornada* (a left-of-centre newspaper) or examining copies of books bought in the shop attached (one of the best in Mexico). Cheap. For breakfast or lunch, **Los Geranios** nearby (where Francisco Sosa meets the main square; open 09.00–17.00) serves fresh pasta with basil, big salads, *crepas de huitlacoche* (pancakes filled with a mushroom-like corn) and *crepas de flor de calabaza* (pancakes filled with courgette flower). Moderate. Further up Francisco Sosa, in the lovely Jardín Sta Catarina, the **Hostería Sta Catarina** (Jardín Sta Catarina 6, tel 554 0513) is a small unpretentious restaurant, attached to a tiny theatre, serving heaped plates of *chiles rellenos* (big green chillies stuffed with cheese or tuna and covered in a rich tomato sauce), enchiladas and chilaquiles. Cheap.

San Angel

There are a number of good, lively restaurants in San Angel, in the south of the city. Most people visit the area on a Saturday, to go to its market and wander around its cobbled streets. The **San Angel Inn** (Calle Palmas 50, tel 548 4514; closed Sat) occupies a beautifully preserved hacienda, as much of a tourist attraction as many of the museums. Special margaritas are served in chilled glasses, poured from small flasks, and the food is of a very high quality, ranging from *crepas de huitlacoche* and tortilla soup to excellent cuts of beef and duck served in a blackberry sauce. The only drawbacks are the obnoxious waiters and the dress rules, which prohibit women in trousers and men in jeans or without a tie. Expensive.

La Casona del Elefante (Plaza de San Jacinto 9, tel 548 5238 and 548 2289), next door to the Bazar Sabado, is a richly decorated Indian restaurant which also has tables outside. It offers an extensive and varied menu. Particularly recommended are the large mixed platters—vegetarian, fish or a mixture of everything. Across Revolución, **Le Petit Cluny** (Av La Paz, between Revolución and Insurgentes, opposite the Fonart shop) is a small, informal and always crowded Italian restaurant which is deservedly popular for its pastas. Moderate. The bakery next door sells the best baguettes and *pan chocolat* in town. Opposite is its sister restaurant, the **Cluny**, which specializes in crêpes. Moderate. On the east side of Insurgentes, **El Rincón de la Lechuza** (Miguel Angel de Quevedo 34; open 12.00–01.00) is a small, steamy, noisy taco restaurant, where the tortillas are freshly made in front of the tables and served with strips of chillies, beef, melted cheese or courgette flowers, washed down with bottles of beer. Cheap.

Desierto de los Leónes

High above the smog, amongst the pines of the Desierto de los Leónes park, is a French bistro in an old convent, which is well worth the 40-minute drive or taxi ride (30 km west of San Angel: take Camino al Desierto west from Insurgentes). Go for a walk in the pines first and then come back for breakfast or lunch in **Del Convento** (Desierto de los

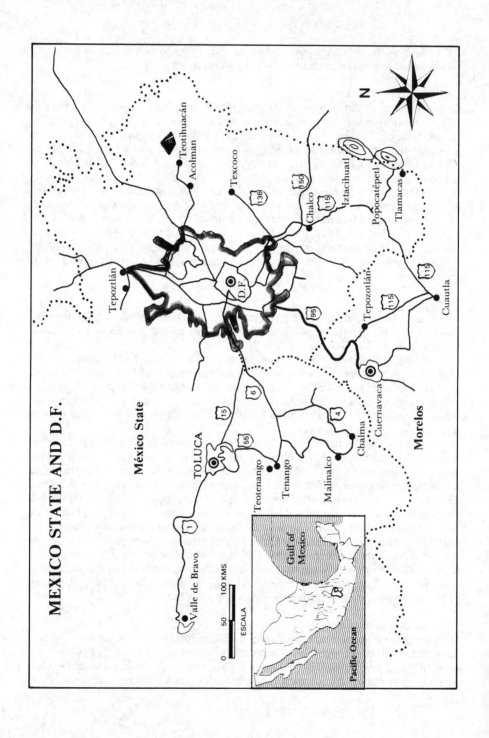

MEXICO STATE AND D.F.

Leones, tel 570 3158; closed Mon). The French chef uses organically grown vegetables and fruits, and his original menu includes locally grown morel mushrooms, home-cured hams, home-made sausages and enormous fruit pies.

The State of Mexico

Confusingly given the same name as both the capital city and the country, the Estado de México encircles the sprawling city in a giant bear hug. The state contains more than its fair share of large industrial cities, with Toluca, the highest city in Mexico, as its capital. Around these industrial centres, the national parks around the volcanoes of Ixtaccíhuatl and Popocatépetl on the state's eastern border with Puebla, the Nevado de Toluca volcano on its western reaches, markets and villages, all provide a breath of fresh air for asphyxiating city folk at weekends. Few tourists make the most of these simple pleasures, only venturing beyond the city's limits to visit the world-famous pyramids at Teotihuacán or the huge Friday market in Toluca.

All the places described in this section can be visited as an easy day trip from Mexico City—except for Valle de Bravo, which is further afield and deserves a couple of nights.

Northeast to Teotihuacán

Northeast of Mexico City, the modern basilica of Guadalupe, the pre-Hispanic pyramids of Teotihuacán and the colonial monastery of Acolman can all be visited within a day. Anyone dependent on public transport, or with little time, would be better advised to confine the trip to the easily accessible pyramids.

GETTING AROUND
By Car: The **basilica** is on Cerrito de Tepeyac, on the outskirts of the city suburbs: take Insurgentes Norte, turning east down Av Montevideo for ½ km.

The pyramids of **Teotihuacán** are 48 km north of the city centre: continue on Insurgentes Norte and follow signs for Pachuca (Highway 85-D); turn east down Highway 132 (signposted to Tulancingo). Highway 85-D passes through the *cinturónes de miseria*, some of the poorest areas of the city.

For the monastery of **Acolman**, follow the route for Teotihuacán, taking Highway 132 for 20 km. The monastery is signed to the left, about 11 km before Teotihuacán.
By Public Transport: For the **basilica**, take the metro to the Basilica stop (line 3) and walk ½ km east down Av Montiel.

For **Teotihuacán** and **Acolman**, take a metro to Autobuses del Norte (line 5; direction Politécnico). Kiosk 8, on the left side of the bus station, sells tickets for buses to San Juan Teotihuacán ('*las pirámides*'). Buses leave every 30 minutes from platform 8, dropping passengers off either at Acolman or at the entrance to the site (it opens at 08.00, and it is worth getting there early to avoid both the sun and the other tourists).
Tours: There are any number of tours to Teotihuacán, most of which take in Acolman and the basilica as well. No travel agent will be without one and all the big hotels arrange

special trips (the Camino Real is the best of these). Taking a tour is by far the easiest way of seeing all three places in one day.

Basilica de Guadalupe

Gaudy, gold, glitzy and some might even say grotesque, the Basilica de Guadalupe is a Mexican Mecca, revered throughout Mexico as its most important place of pilgrimage.

The story goes that one Quauhtlatohua, renamed Juan Diego by the Spaniards who pronounced his name as Guadalupe, had a vision of the Virgin on Tepeyac hill. She commanded him in his native tongue to build a church on the spot. He rushed to the local bishop who dismissed the vision as the effects of too much pulque. However, she appeared before him again, and ordered him to pick some of the red roses with which she had covered the hillside. These he was to present to the bishop as proof (roses had never been known to grow in the area). Quauhtlatohua filled his cloak full of roses and rushed back to the bishop. When he opened it, he found that they had been replaced by a beautiful painted image of a dark-skinned Virgin. Convinced at last, the bishop ordered a shrine built in her honour, and the cult began. Conveniently for the Catholic conquest, the Aztecs had previously worshipped the Goddess Tonantzin (mother of the gods) on Tepeyac hill, and so religious observances were able to coincide.

The Virgin of Guadalupe was recognized by papal bull in 1754, whereupon she became the patron saint of Mexico. Unlike other saints, she was portrayed not as a white European, but like an Aztec princess, with dark skin, to endear her yet further to the people. In what is officially a secular country, the cult of the Virgin of Guadalupe is the single most important factor in uniting Mexicans. The main plaza is constantly filled with exhausted-looking penitents, who come on their knees from far afield, bearing the white lilies which are her symbol.

The original 18th-century baroque basilica started to sink into its foundations and is now disused, totally overshadowed by its modern counterpart, built in 1971 and designed by the much-esteemed architect Pedro Ramírez Vázquez (who built the Museum of Anthropology). Inside, pilgrims and onlookers pass by Quauhtlatohua's cloak on a moving walkway, which gives the whole thing the feel of Disneyland. Nonetheless, it is a deeply moving experience for most visitors and an eye-opener for any non-Catholic. On 12 December, the feast day of the Virgin of Guadalupe, celebrations go on all night.

Teotihuacán

One of the most imposing and monumental as well as the earliest site in pre-Hispanic Mexico, Teotihuacán was also the site of the first city, revered throughout pre-Hispanic history as the birthplace of the gods—the Olympus of Mexico.

History

Teotihuacán was the most highly urbanized centre of its time in the Americas. It flourished and declined at about the same time as imperial Rome, between c 500 BC and AD 500, and supported an even greater population. Even after the city was burned to the ground, the Aztecs continued to use it as a ceremonial centre, burying their rulers there.

Its influence extended as far as Guatemala in the south and Sinaloa in the north of Mexico.

The grandiose nature of Teotihuacán's pyramids testify to its early importance as a religious centre. During its apogee (200 BC– AD 700), it extended to 25 sq km, with a population of over 200,000, and controlled the religious, political and economic affairs of hundreds of thousands of people living in Mesoamerica. Its original name is unknown: the ruined city was called Teotihuacán (meaning 'Place of the Gods') by the Aztecs, who used the site for religious ceremonies only. Because it had been abandoned some 800 years before the conquest, it was not built on by the Spanish—unlike almost every other religious centre they discovered.

Little is known about the original inhabitants of Teotihuacán, as no written documents have survived. Human bones have been found in cooking pots, indicating that their society was cannibalistic (although this did not deter the vast number of pilgrims who visited the city). Frescoes and masks suggest that they were slim and of medium height, with sharp, filed teeth and flattened foreheads (boards were fixed to the heads of babies, to aid this cranial deformation). Heads were partially shaved and feathered headresses were an important indication of social rank.

Set in a fertile valley, next to a lake and with large obsidian mines nearby, Teotihuacán dominated the natural trading corridor between the highlands and the eastern and southern lowlands. Like any large metropolis today, it attracted a large number of outsiders, including merchants and itinerant workers, who settled in ghettoes around the city centre. The remains of many public and domestic buildings show that while some of these districts were devoted to particular trades, such as pottery making, others were distinctly regional, such as the Oaxaca district. Arts and crafts flourished, sustained by a huge ready market of visiting pilgrims (*plus ça change*).

Teotihuacán's control of the important obsidian trade gave it enormous clout (equivalent to control of the oil industry today), which it maintained right up until around AD 700, when the mines dried up. There are signs that the city then began to disintegrate, the victim of economic decline and dwindling natural resources, exacerbated by deforestation. No one is entirely sure why, but around AD 700 Teotihuacán was entirely abandoned. Archaeologists presume that there was a great fire, which may have been accidental or the result of an invasion. The city was never inhabited again.

TOURIST INFORMATION

The site is open from 08.00 to 17.00, closed Mondays and free on Sundays. A *Son et Lumière* perfomance takes place every night except Monday, between October and May—at 19.00 in English and at 20.15 in Spanish. Bring a hat and sun cream, and try to get to the site as early as possible.

The ceremonial centre around the pyramids can be seen in a couple of hours. However, clambering up and down the pyramids is tiring, and it is a good idea to pace it—ideally, allow a day and explore some of the outlying ruins as well. A dust track runs around the main site. More temples, with murals, are to the west of the track, opposite the Pyramid of the Sun.

There is a **restaurant** at the main entrance (moderate) and drinks are on sale throughout the site—the vendors' favourite pitches are at the top of pyramids, where they can charge exorbitant prices to the desperately panting few who reach the top. Numerous hawkers also sell bits of obsidian and the haunting *saltero* flutes.

VISITING THE SITE

ENTRANCE

It is not worth spending much time in the small museum at the entrance (and it is currently undergoing repairs), as all the best pieces have been removed to the Museum of Anthropology in Mexico City. This was the site of a vast marketplace.

CIUDADELA AND TEMPLO DE QUETZALCOATL

Opposite the entrance, at the south end of the main throroughfare (Calle de los Muertos), the enormous sunken quadrangle of the **Citadel** would have been used for important ceremonies. The **Temple of Quetzalcóatl** is at its far end, dedicated to the feathered serpent who was also the God of the Air. When compared with the precise lines employed elsewhere in the city, this temple seems almost baroque, adorned with 366 enormous heads of Quetzal in the form of plumed serpents as well as the boggle-eyed Tlaloc, God of Water and Rain. Well preserved, they still pack a punch today. Recent excavations show that human sacrifices took place within the temple, implying that the city was governed by despotic rulers and not just by a pacific priestly society as was originally believed. The temple is an important example of the *talud* (sloping wall) and *tablero* (vertical wall) style of architecture, which is an unmistakeable feature of Teotihuacán's constructions.

CALLE DE LOS MUERTOS

The **Street of the Dead** was originally a broad causeway which formed the main axis of the ceremonial centre, running for 4 km north–south. Pilgrims regularly walked its length to worship at the pyramids. 'Street of the Dead' is a misnomer, given by the Aztecs who presumed that rulers were buried in the low flat palaces along its length. In fact, these, like the pyramids, were the bases for temples whose exact use is still unknown. The centre was once paved entirely in volcanic stone and all the buildings off this main causeway were plastered and painted in red and white.

PIRAMIDES DEL SOL Y DE LA LUNA

Halfway up Calle de los Muertos is the **Pyramid of the Sun**, one of the biggest known pyramids in Mexico today. It was one of the first main structures to be built in the city, c AD 100, and became the focal point for religious ceremonies. Its base is almost the same size as that wonder of the ancient world, the Cheops pyramid in Egypt. However, unlike their Egyptian counterparts, Mexican pyramids served as monumental bases for tiny temples which perched on top and not as elaborate mausoleums for great rulers.

A cave originally traversed by a running stream was discovered directly underneath the centre of the Pyramid of the Sun, reached by a natural tunnel running from west to east and bearing the remains of man-made adaptations. In Mexico, caves have always been endowed with religious significance, while water is an all-important life-giving force. Thus it is probable that the cave was a place of worship (a small primitive altar was discovered within it), and that the pyramid was built to embellish it.

Originally, the Pyramid of the Sun had only four storeys. The archaeologist Leopoldo Batres, who worked on the site from 1905 to 1910, was so keen to find treasure buried underneath that he blasted the south side to pieces, later reconstructing it with considerable artistic licence.

On the right, towards the northern end of the Calle de los Muertos, a colourful, well-preserved mural, **Mural del Puma**, gives some idea of what the city must have looked like when all its walls were covered in brightly painted stucco.

The **Pyramid of the Moon** is at the far end of the Calle de los Muertos. A smaller, more elegant structure, it was built later than the Pyramid of the Sun and stands at right angles to it, under its shadow, closing off the Calle de los Muertos.

PALACIO DE QUETZALPAPALOTL

To the left (west) of the Pyramid of the Moon, the **Palace of the Quetzal Butterfly** housed the priests who were associated with the Pyramid of the Moon. Its walls were adorned with butterflies (*papálotl*), a symbol of male fertility. Priests were political leaders, considered to be of divine origin, particularly when they donned gods' clothing. Many murals show priests dressed in the image of Tlaloc, God of Rain, or as butterflies, birds or jaguars. The pillars of the palace are carved with owls and butterflies. Rings were once attached to the inner sides of the pillars, used to tie back the curtains which took the place of windows and doors.

OTHER PLACES OF INTEREST

The Pyramid of the Moon was once surrounded by over 2000 one-storey residential houses. Rooms were arranged around Roman-type atriums, separated by curtains to allow air to circulate in the heat. Each house contained an altar, underlining the importance of religion in this society. The chief priest and his colleagues would have lived closest to the centre, the courtiers and nobles in a circle around them, and so on through lesser dignitaries to merchants and artisans. The **Palacio de los Jaguares** (next to the Palace of Quetzalpapálotl) and the **Templo de las Conchas** (under the Palace of Quetzalpapálotl) are the most intact examples of priestly homes to have survived.

West of the Pyramid of the Sun (a 10-minute walk) are the residential quarters of **Tepantitla**, with the remains of a mural representing the paradise of the Teotihuacános. This paradise is unmistakably tropical, filled with water, flowers and butterflies— particularly inviting to the inhabitants of an arid plain. Nearby are the well-preserved murals of **Tenitla**, depicting Quetzal with his masked head and long painted finger nails, in red cochineal dye.

San Agustín Acolman

The 16th-century Augustinian monastery of Acolman is one of the finest in Mexico. Built as much as a fortress as a place of worship, it occupies the site of an earlier Aztec temple. The spiked merlons on its roof and the double arched windows of its upper rooms and cells give it a distinctly Moorish look. It is fronted by a wide atrium, where the Otomí would gather to listen to Mass (being too suspicious to enter the church). The balcony above the main door served as an open pulpit from which sermons were preached; to the right are the portals under which pilgrims would rest.

The monastery is famed for the restrained elegance of its plateresque facade, which would originally have been painted. The interior of the church is covered in 16th-century murals of early Augustinians and swirling golden *retablos*, and also contains a charming, fragile wooden altar. The portals of the cloister, which surround an orange grove, are decorated with black and white friezes whose letters represent the seven sacraments.

Northwest to Tepotzotlán

Another rewarding day trip from Mexico City, worth it for lunch alone, is to the small colonial town of Tepotzotlán. Many consider Tepotzotlán's Jesuit monastery to be the most magnificent example of highly decorative churrigueresque architecture in the world. Today it also houses an excellent collection of colonial art, furniture and costumes.

GETTING AROUND
By Car: From Mexico City, take Highway 57 (the Querétaro road) and turn off at the first toll (signposted Tepotzotlán). The town is to the left of the highway, 43 km from the city centre (50 mins).
By Public Transport: Take the metro to Tacuba (lines 2 and 7) from where local buses go to Tepotzotlán. Alternatively, take a Tula bus or a second-class Querétaro bus from the Autobuses del Norte bus station, and get off at the first toll booth on the highway. From here it is a 20-minute walk (2 km) to the centre of the town.

WHAT TO SEE
The Monastery of San Francisco Javier
(Museum open 11.00–18.00, Wed–Sun; adm; free Sun.)
This baroque and opulent monastery was founded by the Jesuits in 1584 and embellished throughout the next couple of centuries as a testament to their power and influence within the country. Both the facade and tower of the church are spectacular, decorated with elaborate carvings.

The interior of the church is an Ali Baba's cave of dripping gold. Huge *retablos* hang from the wall, their rich golden hue enhanced by mirrors and by the alabaster which surrounds the windows. Yet more elaborate is the **Camarín del Virgen**, an octagonal chapel whose every inch was carved and curlicued by native craftsmen, with naive interpretations of fruit, flowers and angels.

Inside the main entrance to the monastery, a cloister leads past a sunken well, surrounded by illustrations of the life of Ignacio Loyola, the founder of the order. The rooms opening off this cloister form part of the **museum**: the **Ofrebreria** filled with silver reliquaries, chalices and crucifixes, the **Armoury**, and the **Botica** or pharmacy with its bottles and jars of potions. Upstairs are the treasures gained through trading with the East, particularly porcelain and precious metals. The **Capilla Domestica** is a swirl of rococo, all gilded mirrors and plaster angels.

Downstairs a smaller cloister is filled with citrus trees and large wooden statues. Outside, the walled garden has been restored to its former glory—an earthly paradise of medicinal herbs, exotic vegetables, scented flowers and leafy trees.

WHERE TO STAY AND EAT
There are a couple of two-star hotels in the main square, of which the ****Posada Pepe** is the better.

Some of the best regional food in Mexico is available at the **Hostería del Convento** within the monastery itself. Try the *chile en nogada* (chilli stuffed and covered in cream and red pomegranate seeds) or the *enchiladas poblanas* (tortillas filled with chicken and covered liberally in a thick spicy sauce). Moderate. A couple of cheaper restaurants are in the square—the **Virrey** and the **Monte Carlo**, both adequate if unexciting.

Pastorelas (nativity plays) are performed in the main square at Christmas, when the whole town is booked up months in advance.

East to Popocatépetl and Ixtaccíhuatl

Not so many millennia ago, the whole Valley of Mexico was convulsed in a series of volcanic upheavals, and the area is still pockmarked by craters. One of the oldest settlements in the valley, Cuicuilco, was drowned in a great outpouring of lava in 100 BC. By the time the Spanish arrived, the volcanoes were dormant and Cortés was able to march his men over the saddle between Popocatépetl and Ixtaccíhuatl down into the great city of Tenochtitlán below. Now deforested and overpopulated, the valley was then covered in trees, bordering the lakes on which the Aztec empire was founded.

These two snow-clad volcanoes are all but hidden from view in the city itself, by the thick layer of smog that hangs over the valley. It is only for those arriving by plane, circling high above the smog, that the twin peaks seem to tower over the city. Most of the time they are an absent presence, causing great excitement on the few days when the smog lifts and their icy peaks peep over the skyline.

GETTING AROUND

Leave Mexico City on the Puebla toll road, Highway 150-D. Turn south on Highway 115 to Chalco and Cuautla, and then follow signs to Amecameca (approx 70 km, 1½ hrs). Buses for Amecameca leave every hour (1½ hrs) from the eastern TAPO terminal.

From Amecameca, a road winds steadily uphill for another 21 km to Tlamacas, on the tree line and the site of the hostel and visitor's centre. It is accessible by car, taxi or hitching (the latter is easy at weekends but more risky during the week).

WHAT TO SEE

At weekends, hundreds of cars leave the capital and head up to the hills. A visitor's centre, including a surprisingly good restaurant and hostel, is sited at **Tlamacas** (3950 m), the end of the road. Popocatépetl (5465 m) is the main attraction for hikers, who set out for the freezing, windy snow line, armed with axes and crampons. Ixtaccíhuatl (5230 m), the triple-peaked sister volcano, may be yet more beautiful but is certainly a tougher proposition to tackle. Only experienced hikers, with proper equipment, should attempt the ascent of either: advice is available from the Club de Exploraciónes de México (tel 578 5730).

Most people prefer a more leisurely walk around the lower reaches of the volcanoes, through pine forests carpeted with wild flowers and sweet with resinous pine. Huddled on the side of the road, Nahuatl women, hunched up under *sarapes*, cater for tired climbers and mountain-braced appetites, keeping *café de olla* warm over a *comal* or charcoal griddle, and frying up tacos, corn-dough *gorditas* and *sopes*. A jar of pulque or firewater is normally hidden beneath their voluminous skirts.

The small, ancient town of **Amecameca**, at the foot of the volcanoes, is in itself well worth a visit. On Sunday mornings, a large market spills out from the Zócalo, its stalls crammed with chilli peppers in 30 different shapes, sizes and colours, black, blue, brown and speckled beans, tropical and mountain fruits, wooden toys, shawls, ceramics and bead necklaces. In the covered section, strips of beef are hammered into slithers and fried on makeshift grills, and fillets of white fish are dipped in oil and drowned in batter.

West to Toluca

Toluca is the capital of the state of Mexico and, at 2680 m, the highest capital city in the country. It was one of the first cities to accommodate the overspill from the cramped living conditions of Mexico City. Most people visit it for its Friday market, a relic of earlier days when the town's chief industry revolved around cream, cheese and butter. Today, Toluca is a vast industrial centre, its dairies replaced by assembly plants for Japanese cars and computer components.

GETTING AROUND
By Bus: Buses for Toluca and all points west leave from Mexico City's **Terminal de Autobuses de Poniente** (tel 271 0578; take bus 76 west along Reforma or the metro to Observatorio). Buses operated by Turismos y Autobuses Mexico–Toluca (tel 271 1433) leave every 7 minutes for the hour-long journey to Toluca, arriving in Calle Felipe de Beriosabal. Flecha Roja buses continue to Morelia (4 hrs) or Valle de Bravo (1½ hrs).
By Car: Toluca is only an hour's drive from Mexico City along the fast dual-carriageway toll road, Highway 15, which continues west to Morelia and Guadalajara.
In Town: The market surrounds the bus station. Red buses or light blue taxis head for the centre. Combis marked 'Centro Cultural' go to the museums south of the city and second-class buses to the surrounding villages.

TOURIST INFORMATION
Most visitors come only to see the market and so never make it to the centre or the tourist office (opposite the Cosmovitral, on Mercado 16 de Septiembre).

MARKET
Toluca's famous and endless Friday market spills out in every direction around the bus station. It begins before dawn and goes on all day, beneath awnings strung up to give some feeble protection from the glaring sun. Everything is on sale: the prize pig, freshly cut herbs, bunches of flowers, yesterday's bread, pots, plates and cheap tack. Otomís, Mazahuas and Matlatzincas come in from their villages and mingle with the crowd, splashes of colour amidst the uniform grey.

The market is so vast that it is probably not worth trying to fight your way around it, unless it represents your only chance to see a proper *tianguis* or outdoor market in Mexico. Those of Oaxaca, Michoacán or Chiapas are infinitely preferable: more traditional, more manageable and less commercial.

Alternatively, visit **Casart**, a government-sponsored craft shop at Paseo Tollocan 7000 (the road to Valle de Bravo). It offers a wide range of crafts—the best shawls from Tenancingo, textiles from Almoloya, and ceramics from Metepec (where there is a Monday market), with more artisania sold out in the streets.

WHAT TO SEE

In Town

Toluca was conquered by Cortés in the 1520s and the Zócalo remains indomitably Spanish. The unremarkable cathedral, its roof studded with statues, and the surrounding government offices of red volcanic stone lend some elegance to a city which has forgotten its centre to concentrate on its suburbs. At right angles to the cathedral, on the Plaza España, is the Art Nouveau **Cosmovitral conservatory**, built between 1909 and 1933. Its stained-glass windows, added in 1978 and designed by Leopoldo Flores, provide light for over 1000 plants species inside.

Toluca's vast **Centro Cultural Mexiquense** is 8 km from the centre, along Vía Venustiano Carranza. Museums and concert halls lie side by side with halls and libraries. The first building on the left is the **Museum of Modern Art**, originally conceived as a planetarium, with a small collection of secondary works, including paintings by the Morelian Alfredo Zalce and the well-established Carlos Mérida (whose work most tourists see only in the departure lounge of Mexico City's airport). After the muddle and confusion of the market, the **Museum of Popular Art**, the second building on the right, is a sanitized and romanticized version of the same, where quality and order are imposed on fast-dying traditions.

The Ruins of Calixtlahuaca

These ruins are only 14 km northwest of Toluca. By car, leave the city on Highway 55 to Querétaro, turn left after 12 km, and park on the left after a further 2 km. Second-class buses leave Toluca's bus station every hour (30 mins): the ruins are a 10-minute walk from the last stop, through the quiet village of Calixtlahuaca.

The ruins of Calixtlahuaca were the scene of some of the bloodiest battles between the resident Matlatzincas and the invading Aztecs. In 1475, the Aztecs won a great battle here, taking over 11,000 prisoners for sacrifice to their restless war gods. Of the 17 remaining monuments, three have been restored, among them the foundations of a **calmecac** or training college, set around a large quadrangle. Moctezuma II burned it in 1510, as a final reprisal against his still belligerent vassals. The cruciform structure decorated with death's heads and hooks was the **tzompantli**, or skull rack, where the heads of prisoners were left to fester. The circular **Temple of Quetzalcóatl** is up the slope, on the right. Built originally of volcanic stone, it was remodelled four times and would have been covered over with stucco. It was dedicated to the Wind God, Ehecatl, who came into the Aztec pantheon from the Huasteca.

Nevado de Toluca Volcano

The Nevado de Toluca is a popular weekend excursion from Toluca (44 km), accessible only by car—public transport is non-existent. Take Highway 134 southwest of Toluca, turning left after 18 km for Sultepec-Nevado (signed). After 8 km, turn left again, following 18 km of unpaved road to the top.

The 4690-m-high crater is surrounded by a natural wall, affording magnificent views. To the east, the twin peaks of Popocatépetl and Ixtaccíhuatl rise out of the Sierra Nevada mountains. To the south, the valley of Toluca falls away, bordered by the mountains of Guerrero. Down in the crater itself are the bottomless dark blue waters of the two lakes, the Sun and the Moon. At weekends families arrive with dogs, kites, children and picnics. During a cold winter it is even possible to ski on the slopes. Lodging is available in the **Albergue** (chalets), 5 km from the entrance.

West to Valle de Bravo

Valle is sufficiently far from Mexico City to have preserved its own character. The town is set around the eastern shore of a large artificial dam, whose waters reflect the greens and blues of pine-clad hills and a clear sky, softened by suspended pockets of mist. At weekends, water-skiers, windsurfers and kayakers take to the lake, but during the week Valle de Bravo reverts to calm village life. Glibly compared to Switzerland, the region may possess the self-conscious charm of the Alps, but it has nothing of their manicured order.

GETTING AROUND
Buses to Valle de Bravo leave every 2 hours from Mexico City's Terminal de Autobuses de Poniente (3 hrs; tel 271 0578) and from the bus station in Toluca (1½ hrs). By car, take the fast toll road, Highway 15, to Toluca and then follow the clear signs to Valle de Bravo (2½ hrs). West of Toluca, the road cuts through pine forests, across the trail of the monarch butterflies, which come down from Canada in December to breed. The trees are covered in a great blanket of electric orange and yellow wings, and signs are put up by the roadside: 'TAKE CARE, BUTTERFLIES CROSSING'.

VILLAGE LIFE
Valle de Bravo is a world away from the vast agglomerations of Toluca and Mexico City. A fat woman sells *pozole* in the square, watched by Otomí, Mazahua and ancient Nahuatl women. Steep, cobbled streets wind away from the water's edge, up to red-tiled houses where well-heeled *capitalinos* have built their weekend retreats. Up above the highest house, hang-gliders poise in the sky like giant butterflies. The walks around the lake are a delight: bright sunlight falls on the edges of corn fields, and the paths are strewn with wild flowers and crossed by little streams.

WHERE TO STAY   (area code 726)
Most of Valle's visitors own weekend houses in the village or in nearby Avandaro, where dinky German chalets try to recreate the Black Forest. It can be difficult to find a room on Friday, when hoteliers wait to see whether weekend reservations will be taken up. During the week, there are hardly any visitors, and large discounts are readily available. Rooms are almost impossible to find at the end of May, when the town hosts an excellent fireworks display.
    Near the Zócalo, ***Los Arcos** (Fco González Bocanegra 310, tel 20042) has 24 large, simple rooms with painted wooden furniture. Of the resort hotels, the pleasant ***Loto Azul**, on the road in from Toluca, is surrounded by a tranquil garden, with

views over the lake. The cheapest in town is the **Mary, on the main square, with 15 low-ceilinged rooms.

EATING OUT

El Vegetariano (Fco González Bocanegra and the Zócalo, opposite the billiards cantina) seats its customers in director's chairs shaded by umbrellas, in a pretty fountain patio. It is open for breakfasts of fresh fruit and orange juice, sandwich lunches of alfalfa and avocado, and more elaborate evening meals extending, somewhat anomalously, to grilled meats. Moderate. **La Taberna del León** (evenings only) is set in a Hansel and Gretel house overlooking the lake (the owners talk of moving back to Mexico City). It offers superb *nouvelle cuisine*, including tagliatelle with artichoke hearts or quails' eggs with duck-liver pâté. Moderately expensive. The delicatessan shop attached is a place to die happy. **Balzaretti** (Joaquin A Pragaza 106, no tel) is owned by an Italian and specializes in *saltimbocca alla romana*, lake trout and pasta with wild mushrooms. Moderate.

From either of these, people move on to the **Bar de los Artistas** (Bocanegra 303) for margaritas in front of the open fire in the early evening, and occasional exhibition openings. A livelier crowd takes over later on. Coffee and drinks are also served in several bars around the lake side. One of the best is the **Oasis**, with an attractive balcony, offering Mexican music and simple food such as *quesadillas* and *spaghetti a la marinera*. Moderate.

South to Malinalco and Guerrero

From Toluca, Highway 55 leads south to Taxco in the state of Guerrero (140 km), through farming country, hills, valleys and villages. Some 49 km south of Toluca, **Tenancingo** is a growing village famed for its *rebozos* (shawls made of cotton, silk or rayon) and its 16th-century Carmelite monastery. Here there is a choice of route: south on Highway 55 to the thermal springs of Ixtapan de la Sal and from there to Taxco, or east to the Aztec ruins of Malinalco. From Malinalco, the lovely La Marquesa road winds slowly north through pastureland and pine-clad hills back to the main Mexico City–Toluca highway (about 70 km) or south to Chalma and a longer route to Taxco. Buses from the **Observatorio** terminal in Mexico City go direct to Chalma every two hours and local buses make the journey from Ixtapan and Tenancingo every hour.

Ixtapan de la Sal

The flower-filled spa town of Ixtapan is 73 km south of Toluca on Highway 55. Here wealthy Mexicans lounge in the foul-smelling sulphurous pools of the smart hotels, whilst the less well-off use the public pools (*balnearios publicos*). The waters are reputed to assuage rheumatism as well as many other bodily malfunctions. The drive from Ixtapan to Taxco, via the Cacahuamilpa caves, takes under an hour (67 km).

Malinalco

Malinalco must be one of the most dramatic of all Aztec sites. Its temples, hewn into the rock, loom above the present-day village.

GETTING AROUND
Malinalco is 15 km east of Tenancingo. A signpost in Tenancingo boldly announces this fact, pointing to a paved road. This soon comes to an abrupt halt, hanging over the broad sweep of the fertile Valley of Malinalco. However, what looks to be a treacherous and impassable dirt track is in fact just navigable, even in a Volkswagen Beetle, winding down past smallholdings and tattered churches into the village of Malinalco.

WHAT TO SEE
Malinalco is a rural backwater which few would bother to visit were it not for the ruins. Chickens scratch as men idly clip the grass in what's left of the atrium of the convent. This stalwart early 16th-century Augustinian church, noted for its simplicity, dominates the Zócalo. The stones used for the foundations were taken from the Aztec temples, and the sober facade and solid walls were built to last rather than to adorn. Inside, the walls are decorated with traces of black and white frescoes, symbols and intricacies of the Augustinian order, including a very grim reaper whose skeletal form glares at a penitent monk from the back of an alcoved confessional.

VISITING THE SITE
The Aztec site, one of the few to have been left more or less intact by the Spanish, is on the hill opposite the church. Ask in the Zócalo for '*las ruinas*'. It's a long climb up 473 steps cut into the hillside. From halfway up you can see the ruins of temples and caves to the left. The Matlatzincas, a branch of the Otomí, who originally inhabited the site, worshipped Oxtoctéotl, Lord of Caves.

The real excitement comes right at the top. The Aztecs conquered the area in 1426 and began marking their territory by building temples in an adventurous new style, only to be interrupted by the arrival of the Spanish in 1521. The **main temple** is a monolithic structure carved into the protruding rock, incorporating a flight of stairs flanked by two jaguars, which were once painted yellow with black spots. In the middle, a sculpted human figure would originally have borne standards. These stairs (now officially closed to the public) lead up to a round temple dedicated to the ordination of the most bellicose of all warriors—the Eagles (Cuauhtli) and the Jaguars (Ocelotl). At the top is a relief of a serpent, whose hugely yawning mouth spews out a tongue which carpets the entrance to the temple. Inside, representations of jaguars and eagles surround a small hole, in which the still throbbing hearts of victims would have been placed.

Nearer the village, the round temple on the left is known as the **Tzincacalli**. Here the bodies of warriors killed in combat or sacrificed by enemies were brought for ritual cremation: the Aztecs believed that they would then be transformed into stars for their heroism. Next door is the **Temple of the Sun**, where the end of every religous Aztec year (260 days) was celebrated.

WHERE TO STAY
There are two modest hotels in the village: the **(CE) Sta Mónica**, on the way to the site, offers no more than a bed for the night, while the smarter ****Cabañas** (3 blocks north of the Zócalo) has two rooms each with a bathroom.

Chalma

The La Marquesa road south of Malinalco passes through Chalma (11 km), a slip of a village at the foot of a deep gorge. Here an enormous church, belonging by rights to a Hans Christian Andersen fairy tale, straddles the banks of a tiny stream. It is the centre of devout pilgrimage, its walls hung with touching offerings and letters of thanks. Pilgrims crawl on their knees past vendors of religious artefacts up to the main altar. It is busiest on Sundays and during the main Catholic festivals, such as Easter.

Near the church is a large cave, where the God of Caves was originally worshipped. The Augustinians, anxious to divert this paganism, built the church next to the site in 1683. Nonetheless, weary pilgrims still retire there to bathe in its salutary waters.

Taxco is 110 km south of Chalma (1½ hrs).

Part IV

MORELOS AND GUERRERO

View from the Valley of Mexico

These two states have always been a southern getaway from Mexico City. The large city of Cuernavaca and the pretty town of Taxco are inundated daily by tourists, brought in by tour bus to see picture-postcard Mexico on their way to their final resort destinations of Acapulco and Ixtapa–Zihuatanejo on the Pacific coast. Were it not for this touristic overkill, these two states would be far more attractive. Indeed, this journey is often referred to as the Poster Route, because it passes so many bougainvillea-covered patios and tiled roofs of colonial houses, endlessly photographed and used for tourist brochures. Although the towns of Taxco and Cuernavaca have too much life of their own to be dragged down to the lowest common tourist denominator, the unimaginative tour groups keep on trying.

The State of Morelos

This is certainly one of the most beautiful lands in the world, and if it were not for the great heat it would be another Garden of Eden. There are delightful springs, wide rivers full of fish, the freshest of woods, and orchards of many kinds of fruits.
—Fray Diego Durán, 16th-century chronicler

Morelos is closed off from the Valley of Mexico by the peaks of the Sierra Ajusco, which soften down into the valleys and hills of this green and opulent state. Its fruits—mameys,

106

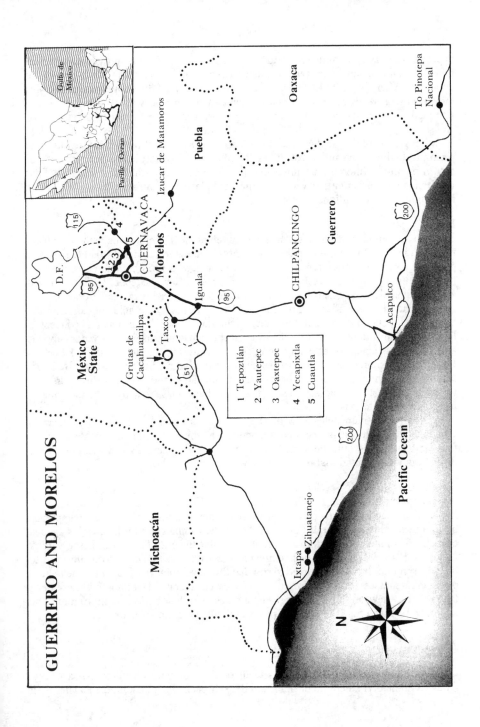

GUERRERO AND MORELOS

1 Tepoztlán
2 Yautepec
3 Oaxtepec
4 Yecapixtla
5 Cuautla

papayas, bananas and chimoyas—and its sugar cane have given it an easy passage, but this very wealth has also attracted the attention of wistful outsiders who want a slice of the good life. After the terrible Mexico City earthquake of 1985, thousands of families moved out in all directions. Morelos' capital, Cuernavaca, with its gentle climate, attracted all those who could afford its high prices, turning the former town into a large city.

Although one of the smallest states in Mexico, Morelos' stature is great thanks to its proximity to the capital and its role in the Revolution of 1910, which earned it the title of *patria chica* (little fatherland). Named after José María Morelos, the finest tactician of the independence movement, it was later the birthplace of Emiliano Zapata, the most revolutionary of revolutionary heroes.

History

The native Tlahuicas, a Nahuatl-speaking branch of the Toltecs, came to the area from the north in the 12th century. In the 15th century the Aztecs, under Itzcóatl (1428–40), put Cuernavaca under fiefdom. The first Moctezuma, whose mother was a Cuernavacan princess, built a great palace for himself near present-day Oaxtepec. Cortés followed suit, building his own palace 80 years later. He also introduced sugar cane from the West Indies. The vast haciendas of Cocoyoc and Vista Hermosa, the fields of cane and the black slaves shipped in to cut it, transformed the state. The Tlahuica had no concept of land ownership and pleaded powerlessly against encroachments on their water supplies and communal lands. Almost four centuries later, during the dictatorship of Porfirio Díaz, the government continued to sell common land to private landowners. By 1908, just 17 men owned 30 per cent of the state's cultivable land. Villages shrank in size, remaining only as service stations to the local haciendas, tied by debt to modern, mechanized plantations.

In 1903, a 25-man delegation of villagers went to plead with President Díaz in Chapultepec Castle. He patted them avuncularly on the back and told them dismissively that land disputes would be sorted out in the end. Emiliano Zapata was one of the delegation who decided that the end had better come quickly.

EMILIANO ZAPATA

It was Zapata who wouldn't let the Revolution die. When Díaz was overthrown in 1910, Zapata demanded not just a cosmetic change of administration but a radical reappraisal of land ownership in general. For a full decade he campaigned for land rights against every head of state from Madero to Carranza, earning the title of the 'Attila of the South'. In March 1919, 16 years after he had first pleaded with Díaz for land reform, he wrote to the government: 'It never occurred to you that the Revolution was fought for the benefit of the great masses, for the legions of the oppressed ... the old landholdings have been taken over by new landlords and the people mocked in their hopes.' Within a month he had been betrayed for 100,000 gold pesos and killed at point-blank range.

Cuernavaca

Cuernavaca, for its sins or its virtues, is an all too easy hour and a half from Mexico City. Away from the permanent lid of smog and densely packed population, the journey is an

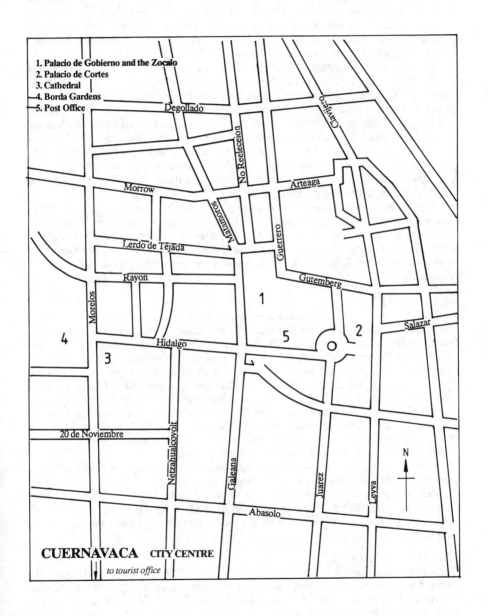

1. Palacio de Gobierno and the Zocalo
2. Palacio de Cortes
3. Cathedral
4. Borda Gardens
5. Post Office

Degollado

No Reeleccion

Calleja

Arteaga

Morrow

Matamoros

Guerrero

Lerdo de Tejada

Gutemberg

Rayon

Salazar

1

5

2

Morelos

Hidalgo

4

3

20 de Noviembre

Netzahualcoyolt

Galeana

Juarez

Leyva

N

Abasolo

CUERNAVACA CITY CENTRE

to tourist office

invigorating roll down the hill into flame trees, lavender-blue jacarandas, orchids, and coral and fuchsia bougainvilleas. The delight of being in the tropics, at an altitude of 1500 m, ablaze with colour and gentle warmth, has attracted people as diverse as Moctezuma and Hernán Cortés, José de la Borda, the Emperor Maximilian, Malcolm Lowry and, more recently, retired but not retiring North Americans.

Few of them would come today. The town now embraces a population of over a million, a huge industrial sector, daily tour buses and, worst of all, relentless weekend pilgrimages by capital-city escapees. The double main plazas are a constant nightmare of hawkers, tourists and hassle. By Saturday night the town is filled with cars with DF number plates, the restaurants bulge, and the discos steam. The pace calms by Sunday night, when the cars file back to another week of work. The museums close for Monday's recuperation and there is a general exhalation of breath, until the daily buses begin their grind again. A Cuernavaca weekend in a private house is a Mexican middle-class institution—one that would be impossible to replicate without darling Fernanda's house just dripping with those divine flame trees.

It's better to come mid-week, avoiding the crowds and the main squares, and hunting out the far more interesting alternatives such as Maximilian's amorous hide-away, the house where the muralist Siqueiros lived and the solid majesty of the pyramids of Teopanzolco, all right in the city itself. Spend another day at the ruins of Xochicalco, or in the calmer, more solicitous Tepotzlán, under the jagged heights of the Sierra de Tepozteco.

GETTING AROUND

By Bus: The Mexico City–Cuernavaca–Taxco–Acapulco run is a piece of cake. Buses leave every few minutes from the Terminal Central de Autobuses del Sur in Mexico City (on the metro: Tasqueña, Line 2). The better companies are Flecha Roja (Av Morelos 255, tel 125797) or Pullman de Morelos (Abasolo and Netzahualcóyotl, tel 143650), because their terminals are in the centre of Cuernavaca, close to the main squares. These two companies also run buses from Cuernavaca to the caves of Cacahuamilpa every 2 hours (see under Taxco, Guerrero). Long-distance Estrella de Oro buses (Av Morelos 255, tel 123055) skirt the centre, 1½ km to the south at the Las Palmas Circle.

There are 20 numbered **minibus** routes within the city. Each minibus displays a notice on its windscreen, giving the beginning and the end of the route. No 8 goes to the pyramids of Teopanzolco and No 6 to Maximilian's house.

By Car: If coming down from the capital, take the super-highway 95-D (85 km). Extremely swift (sometimes 8 lanes wide) and extremely beautiful, it climbs 3000 m up the side of the Valley of Mexico to crest in pine forests, before crossing the Tres Cumbres pass and falling down into the Valley of Morelos. Continuing south, it's 95-D all the way to Acapulco (326 km). The old road, Highway 95, passes through Taxco (100 km).

TOURIST INFORMATION

The Cuernavaca office is at Morelos Sur 802 (tel 14 39 27), southwest of the Plaza de Armas where there is also a small booth. The staff are generous with their leaflets, and also have information on the many language schools (although this is not the best city to study in, being expensive, unintimate and full of English speakers). Cuautla has a booth at the railway station (tel 2 52 21).

WHAT TO SEE

Cuauhnáhuac Museum and Cortés' Palace
(Blvd Juárez; open 09.30–19.00, closed Mon; adm.)
Cortés built a palace retreat here in 1522, on the razed foundations of the Aztec pyramid of Tlahuica. Despite a worthy two floors of exhibits outlining the state's progress and development, most visitors come only to see the wonderful 1930 Diego Rivera mural on the second-floor terrace. He was commissioned by the American ambassador, Dwight Morrow, a great fan both of Rivera and Cuernavaca (he even had a street in the city named after him). From floor to ceiling, right to left, Rivera has traced an enslaved history of the state. Iniquities scream from the walls: the backs of the conquered are bent double under their loads, whilst the white colonialists recline in their hammocks. Cortés is there, as is Emiliano Zapata and Morelos, the independence hero after whom the state was named. Morelos was in fact painted as a self-portrait of Rivera, with whom he shared the same jowly jaw-line and frog-like eyes. On the final wall is Zapata's marvellous white horse, Golden Ace—Rivera's homage to the famous horse rumps of Paolo Uccello.

The Cathedral
(Hidalgo 23, on the corner with Av Morelos.)
The Franciscans came quickly to Cuernavaca. They began building the present cathedral in 1529 and finished the first phase in 1574, following the plans of Francisco Becerra, the Spaniard who later moved to Peru. The view from the gateway reveals all the main features of his design: the merlon battlements at the top, the stocky tower, the open atrium and the flying buttress lending a shoulder to the church walls. The open chapel was for the unbaptized, who were banned from the cathedral itself. Much was restored in the 1980s, some of it rather oblique, such as the seven hanging lamps which, one is told, are a minimalist reinterpretation of the seven sacraments. Recently uncovered murals, once concealed beneath layers of paint, commemorate the 16th-century Mexican friars who crossed the Pacific on a mission to bring God to the Japanese. The happily heathen Japanese warlords summarily crucified the 24 friars. On Sunday mornings the 11.00 Mass is accompanied by mariachi musicians.

The Borda Gardens
(Facing the cathedral: the entrance is on Av Morelos at the corner with Hidalgo.)
In 1908, Charles Macomb Flandrau wrote, 'Even if it were not one of the most beautiful of tangled, neglected, ruined old gardens anywhere, it would be lovable for the manner in which it tried so hard to be a French garden and failed.'

It is still trying and still failing, clinging to the steep hillside. The Frenchman, Joseph de la Borde (who was known universally as José de la Borda), made a mint in the 18th century from silver mining. He spent a million pesos building Santa Prisca in Taxco and another million on these gardens. Now tawdrier than ever, they are remembered chiefly as the poor man's Versailles of the Emperor Maximilian and his young wife Charlotte (who also Mexicanized her name to Carlota). Some tell tall tales about the tunnels he had built from here to his palace, so tall he could ride a horse through them for his illicit meetings with his lover, the 'india bonita'. Not to be outdone, Carlota was meanwhile flirting under the flame trees with the officers of the Imperial Guard. During the first week of May, a superbly colourful **flower festival** is held here. Av Morelos was originally part of the *camino real* between Taxco and Mexico City. The caravans and muleteers would camp out in the gardens before embarking on the final stretch to the capital.

David Alfaro Siqueiros' Workshop
(Calle Venus 7; open 09.00–14.00; closed Mon; adm.)

Cuernavaca abounds in fascinating places that no-one ever bothers to go to and which most residents don't even know about, such as the house where Siqueiros worked and died. One of Mexico's three great muralists (alongside Rivera and Orozco) and a staunch Stalinist, he once masterminded an unsuccessful attempt to assassinate Trotsky. For such an uncompromising painter, whose works ring out with garish, bold, psychedelic colours, this house seems too tame. A small exhibition illustrates his life with photos and lithographs.

Maximilian's House/the Museum of Traditional Medicine
(Matamoros 200, in Colonia Acapatzingo; garden open 09.00–17.00; house/museum open 09.00–14.00; both closed Mon.)

From the market, 'Ruta 6' minibuses go to within a block of the museum, which is opposite the church (ask the driver for directions). The alternative is a taxi.

This is not the easiest place to get to, but it was never meant to be. In 1866, Emperor Maximilian designed the little house and big, 4-hectare garden as a love nest (from which his Empress was excluded). The poor man probably never stayed there himself: within a year he had been shot by a firing squad in Querétaro. Today there is a small botanical garden, and a museum detailing 101 natural cures for Moctezuma's revenge (including camomile), verrucas (figs) or acne (poinsettias). It must be the calmest spot in Cuernavaca and makes a delightful refuge for an afternoon.

Museo Brady
(Calle Netzahualcóyotl 4, tel 12 11 36; by appointment only, 10.00–14.00 and 16.00–18.00 Thurs and Fri, and 10.00–14.00 Sat.)

This house-museum was formerly known as the *Casa de la Torre*, or Tower House and part of the bishop's cloister which dates back to the 16th century. In 1961 the Iowan-born artist, Robert Brady, bought it and built up a large art collection, including African tribal art, Nepalese gods, and paintings by Paul Klee, Graham Sutherland and the Mexican group of Rufino Tamayo, Miguel Covarrubias, Frida Kahlo and Tamara de Lempicka. Noteworthy amongst the exhibits are the large rugs designed by Brady and woven, under his supervision, in Chiconcuac. Not a blank wall remains: every inch is covered, including the arch leading into his bedroom which is decorated with crucifixes of every shape and size. After his death in 1986, he was buried, alongside his dogs, in the main patio, and the house became a museum. He bequeathed it as it stood, complete with 17th-century altarpieces and pre-Hispanic gods. For those with the time to prearrange a visit, the house and collection are a fabulous example of the gilded life which goes on behind the massive doors of so many houses in Cuernavaca.

The Pyramids of Teopanzolco
(Calle Río Balsas in the Colonia Vista Hermosa, 3 km from the town centre; open 09.00–14.00; closed Mon.)

Although not outstanding, these monuments are mournfully beautiful. Sadly, they live up to their Nahua name, 'in the abandoned temple'. Once the most important ceremonial centre of the Lords of Cuauhnáhuac, Teopanzolco has now been absorbed into the mass of Cuernavaca and is seldom visited, except by immaculate crocodiles of neatly pressed school-children. The grounds, mown and mown again to the smoothness of a billiard table, look as if they are waiting for a state visit.

In AD 1450, the site was an important Aztec outpost. Seventy years later, it was still a marvel to be wondered over by the early Spanish chroniclers. It was built on top of basalt rock, which was levelled to form a platform for the 14 monuments, once covered in a layer of red volcanic stone mortar. Over time, they became hidden by layers of earth. During the Revolution, one of the covered mounds was used by government forces attacking the city: a great blast shot the place to pieces and revealed the temple underneath. This, the most important temple, has a double stairway, each flight leading up to a shrine on the top. As in the Aztec capital of Tenochtitlán, this would have been dedicated to Tlaloc, the God of Rain, and Huitzilopochtli, the God of Fire and War, and was built over an older temple.

FESTIVALS
Traditional festivals are held during the 12 days leading up to Christmas and at Easter, and are both good times to be in the area. However, the liveliest of all is the week-long carnival held at the beginning of Lent (see also Tepoztlán).

MARKET
The market is five blocks north of the main square, along Guerrero, on the right. It is chiefly a food and household market but has an abundance of the large, woven, Ali Baba baskets, painted with splashes of fuchsia, yellow and green, that are sold all over Taxco and Cuernavaca.

WHERE TO STAY AND EATING OUT   (area code 731)
If you can afford to play Cuernavaca at its own game of gilding the lily, there are several opulent sugar-cane hacienda hotels both in the city and around the state. Lesser mortals take what's left. Always book at weekends.

Expensive
The most spoiling hotel of all is the *****Ex-Hacienda de Cortés (Atlacomulco, tel 160867; 20 mins' drive from the town centre), one of three of his sugar-cane haciendas to have been turned into a hotel. This was supposedly to have been his retirement home. The 22 suites have each been decorated by the present owner and his wife, quite distinct one from the other. The colours are defiantly Mexican—electric blues, bright yellows and soft pinks. The furniture is well weathered, looking as if it was brought over with the first Spaniards. The gardens are deeply peaceful and the restaurant, with vines and branches trailing down from the roof, very romantic. Its location means that this is more a place of retreat than a base for seeing Cuernavaca.

(GT) Las Mañanitas (Ricardo Liñares 107, off Av Morelos North, tel 12 46 46) is the most prestigious hotel of the lot. Not far from the centre, it is admired more than anything for its restaurant. The daily menu is brought to guests in the garden on large blackboards. Peacocks and African crowned cranes, toucans and macaws strut past as guests deliberate between sea bass Roquefort, *fettuccine al pomodoro* or calves' brains in black butter.

In the north of the city, the *****Cuernavaca Racquet Club** (Fco Villa 100, tel 136122) is, as the name implies, a serious tennis club, but more as well. The rooms are continuously luxurious with beds the size of football pitches, white fluffy towels and fireplaces. The gardens stretch for hectares, and the food is beautifully presented: strawberries and cream beside the tennis courts, Tampiqueña steak with avocados or garlicked red snapper in the restaurant, or fresh fruit and yoghurt breakfasts brought to the rooms.

The ****Posada Xochiquetzal** (one block down from the Palacio de Cortés in Francisco Leyva 200, tel 120220) slopes up steeply to a large palapa-covered restaurant and swimming pool. The 14 rooms are furnished in the dark colonial style, with elegant tiled bathrooms. The ****Casino de la Selva** (Calle Leonardo Valle 1001, tel 124700) is one of the oldest of the resort hotels, once the city's casino. In its earlier days, Siqueiros decorated the chapel with a vast fresco. The hotel lends itself to the knees-up-Mother-Brown mentality, but it is worth dropping in to see the mural.

Inexpensive

The more modest hotels are in the centre. From the Pullman de Morelos bus terminal, turn left into Calle Netzahualcóyotl and first right into Calle Motolinía to find the cheerful **Papagayo** (tel 141924). It has lots of rooms, lots of parking, and a swimming pool, and the low price includes breakfast. The **Mesón las Hortensias** (Hidalgo 22, tel 126152) is a well-run hotel for students of the language schools. Homesick students clock up exorbitant bills on its long-distance telephone (a rare commodity). The **Peñalba** (Matamoros 304, tel 124166) also mothers students, although the cruelly caged birds in the patio prefer to mimic their struggling Spanish. The hotel has a 'What's On' list and the price for a room includes breakfast.

Outside Cuernavaca

Outside the town are two more of Cortés' sugar-cane haciendas, smartly renovated into hotels. Some 35 km along the Cuautla road, just short of Oaxtepec, is the ****Hacienda de Cocoyoc** (tel 22000, tlx 1772042; to reserve from Mexico City, tel 550 44 22). The grounds are enormous, with horse riding, golf and tennis (on floodlit courts). The aqueduct crosses the swimming pool in arches, tumbling into a waterfall on the other side. The hotel itself goes on and on, with 300 rooms, five bars, a disco and nightclubs. It is said to have been built by Cortés for the Christianized daughter of Moctezuma, Isabel Cortés Moctezuma, with whom he was passionately (but only momentarily) in love.

Five minutes from the crater-lake of Tequesquitengo (43 km south of Cuernavaca) is the ****Hacienda de Vistahermosa**. To get there, leave Cuernavaca on the south-bound toll road, coming off at the Morelos toll booth, the turn-off for Alpuyeca Tequesquitengo. The hotel is 7 km on the left, 2 km from the lake (tel 734 70492; for reservations from Mexico City, tel 546 4540, tlx 277541). The hacienda belonged in turn to Cortés, his son, grandson and great grandson, until it was sold in 1621. For lack of wood and iron, Cortés had it built as a solid brick fortress. Within its walls, the effect is softened. The aqueduct has become a swimming pool, the stables bedrooms, and the warehouses a restaurant. Within the endless grounds are a *lienzo charro* (a charro/rodeo ring), tennis, squash and badminton courts, and an adorable chapel. Although full at weekends, it is calm during the week. American plan is encouraged.

East of Cuernavaca: the Convent Route

The state of Morelos is one of the smallest in Mexico, but the concentration of monasteries in its northern half is more dense than in any other part of the country. In colonial times there would have been one convent in each of the 32 municipalities. Only a handful are still occupied today, but many have been well maintained. It is possible to see several of them and return to Cuernavaca or Tepoztlán the same day.

GETTING AROUND

The convent villages of Yecapixtla, Ocuituco and Tetela del Volcán are all on the same road. Take Highway 115 north of Cuautla and after 12 km turn right, following a blue sign to the *conventos*. The land is flat and agricultural at first but then climbs up through fields of figs and peaches towards the always distant peak of Popocatépetl. Recently, a 'scenic railway' has been opened between Cuautla and Yecapixtla. It makes a 5-hour round trip on Thursdays, Saturdays and Sundays, including a guided tour of the convent (tel 73 143860).

Yecapixtla

The church is in Calle No Reelección (the state of Morelos enjoys taking politics to the streets: one in Cuernavaca is called Effective Suffrage). The Franciscans first came here in 1525 but it was the Augustinian design of 1540 that made it more fortress than House of God. Like the fortified convents of Castile, the church resembles a keep, enclosed within battlement walls, and with four oratories in the four corners of the atrium. The plateresque facade, alive with flowers and cherubs, is set off by the spiky merlons and the lookout towers on the roof above. With its jaunty rose window, the facade is the exception to the military style of this otherwise austere monastery. On one side of the doorway is a shield emblazoned with St Francis' five wounds and, on the left, the familiar heart pierced by three arrows. The construction of the church was ordered by Fray Jorge de Avilar, who had a portrait of himself slipped into the facade, on the bottom left-hand corner, parallel with the lowest step. Hernán Cortés matches him on the right. Within, the single high nave retains the original polychrome colouring. The rose-tone pulpit and choir were built with stone from the nearby village of Jantetelco.

The largest of the villages and the largest of the monasteries, Yecapixtla also has one of the most traditional Day of the Dead ceremonies, on 1 and 2 November.

Ocuituco

The very simple village of Ocuituco is 17 km further on. Its 16th-century monastery was the first to be completed by the Augustinians in New Spain. It is still just inhabited, although its bougainvillea-filled atrium is more given over to local dog fights than to religious meditation. The cloisters are as peaceful as can be, with a pretty fountain (a replica of one in the Alhambra) on which lions that might as well be frogs stoop to drink. The cloisters are being turned into town offices and the lawyer has already moved in.

The church itself has been repainted inside. It has two oval paintings of San Agustín and his woeful mother, Sta Monica.

Tetela del Volcán

As the road climbs up to Tetela del Volcán (7 km), the air becomes clearer and sharper, the mountains seem to be within touching distance and Popocatépetl is more than just a glint in the distance. The Augustinian monastery was founded in 1580 but handed over to the Dominicans almost immediately. It was altered in the second half of the 17th century and then changed hands once again, becoming a Carmelite convent. Carmelite nuns still live here. The red, black and white murals around the cloister were painted before the 17th-century alterations, but have been little cared for since.

The area around Tetela de Volcán is wonderful walking country and the state government has converted an old house into a modest **Posada Turistica** for those who want to stay (contact the tourist office in Cuernavaca, tel 14 39 27).

Tepoztlán

Less than half an hour from Cuernavaca (21 km), Tepoztlán has certainly been tainted by it but proved remarkably resilient. Protected by the Tolkien-inspiring crags of the Sierra de Tepozteco, the Tlahuica people (who still speak Nahua) have withstood several invasions—first by the Aztecs at the beginning of the 15th century, then by the Spanish in 1521, and 30 years later by the Dominicans. The monks proselytized with great vigour and for a while mass baptisms in the forecourt of the monastery were commonplace (especially during the Easter Week celebrations, when traditional Tlahuica dances became melded with tales of Christ and Judas).

Sunday, market day, is the only busy day of the week in Tepoztlán, when weekenders flock in to enjoy its clear air, visit the fine Dominican monastery and the market and, if sound of limb, make the hike up the Cerro del Tepozteco, 600 m above the village.

GETTING AROUND

The bus station is on Av Cinco de Mayo. Buses to Tepoztlán and Amatlán run every 20 minutes from the Abasolo terminal in Cuernavaca. There is an hourly service (until 19.00) between Tepoztlán and Mexico City's Terminal del Sur.

WHAT TO SEE

The Dominican Convent

Domingo de L'Anunciación, who evangelized the area between 1551 and 1559, kept his missions close to, or directly on top of, the ruined temples of conquered idols. Accordingly, this church, begun in 1559 by the Dominican friar Francisco de Becerra, came to represent more than the worship of God: it was there to reinforce the strength of the Spanish in Mexico. The front is extremely sober, its doorway decorated simply with the seals of the order of Saint Dominic. The triangular tympanum above is dedicated to the Virgin of the Immaculate Conception (unusually, already holding a child), with Catherine of Siena on her left and Dominic on her right. The convent is now a museum (adm), with some ecclesiastical exhibits. The views from the loggia are superb, stretching across to the mountains and the shrine of Tepozteco high above.

Behind the church, in Calle González, is a small archaeological museum (closed Mon) with surprisingly good figures and pottery donated from the collection of the archaeologist, Carlos Pellicer.

The Cerro del Tepozteco

High above the village, this pyramid shrine to the pre-Hispanic god of *pulque* (a crude alcoholic drink) commands views over the entire valley of Morelos. It isn't, however, a quick stroll along smooth ground but a strenuous calf-straining hour or more straight up a steep-sided canyon. Take Av Tepozteco, northeast of the marketplace, as far as it goes and then follow the well-trodden rocky path. The site closes at 16.30 sharp: no matter how red your face, it will remain closed until 09.00 the next day.

The temple was built over an earlier one at the very end of the 15th century, when the district was occupied by the Aztec king Ahuitzotl. The gruelling climb, rewarded by a hot, sticky lemonade, increases one's appreciation of the craggy landscape. The same rocks that make up the path have taken millennia to form. They are a combination of volcanic eruptions and sediment from various prehistoric floods, which have twisted together into these tortured formations. There are spectacular views of the valley stretching out below, and of the village directly beneath the shrine, full of the pinks and purples of the cherry and jacaranda trees.

Amatlán

This small adobe village, a 20-minute drive or bus journey northwest of Tepoztlán, is planted with plum, lemon, lime and yellow *amate* trees, nestling among the foothills of the extraordinary dreamscape formations of the Tepozteco hills. It was the birthplace, in AD 843, of the historical figure, now made legendary, Ce Acatl Topiltzin, better known as the good and wise God-King Quetzalcóatl. The young boy was brought up in Amatlán by his grand-parents, until he went to study in Xochicalco at the age of seven. In 879 he left to regain his father's throne in Tollancingo (now Tulancingo, in Hidalgo), which had been usurped by his uncle. He was instated as high priest and king and went on to preside over a renaissance in Toltec history, until political enemies turned his people against him. He fled to the east but promised to return some day. This was a prophecy that Cortés used to great advantage when he arrived from the east some 650 years later.

FESTIVALS

Tepozteco and other pre-Hispanic gods are celebrated on the night of 7 September. The party begins on the hill-top, and then comes down to the village for mock battles between the king of Tepoztlán and those of Cuernavaca and Oaxtepec. A similar festival with dances and music is celebrated during carnival—the three days leading up to Ash Wednesday. Tepoztlán also has its own festival for Saint Catherine on 16 January, again celebrated with wonderful dances.

MARKET

The market is held on Sundays. Once a village affair, it has opened up to tourism and now features crafts from all over the country and beyond, including Guatemalan textiles, Oaxacan ceramics and wooden masks.

117

Every sort of Mexican food is on offer in the *fondas* around the market stalls—*tamales*, *corundas*, tortillas and a hundred variations on the theme of maize, as well as *mole* and chillies.

WHERE TO STAY   (area code 738)
Tepoztlán has two hotels, each with a restaurant, swimming pool, and fabulous views. The elegant, colonial ***Posada del Tepozteco (tel 50323) is on the hillside at Calle del Paraíso 3 and the unattractive ***Tepoztlán (tel 50522) is in Calle de la Industrias.

EATING OUT
On Sundays most people eat in the market. Recently, some colonial houses have opened their patios up as restaurants, often with trios playing on Sunday mornings. Two of the best are on Av Revolución: **La Luna Mextli** (tel 50800) and **La Sandía Azul**.

Xochicalco

The hill-top acropolis of Xochicalco looks out over the Valley of Cuernavaca. Between AD 750 and 900, at the end of the Classic period and after the fall of its powerful neighbours in Teotihuacán, it emerged as a great trading city and centre of scientific and astronomical studies. At a crossroads between the Balsas River and the central Mexican plateau, it was an important trading post for cotton, cacao, feathers and obsidian.

GETTING AROUND
Although Xochicalco is only 42 km south of Cuernavaca, buses are hard to come by. Two buses a day leave at 08.00 and 09.00 from the central terminal. Later buses pass by the turn-off to the site, leaving would-be visitors to walk back 4 km in what can be torrid, unshaded heat. By car, it is much simpler: take the Taxco road, Highway 95, and turn off for the site at the signpost.

VISITING THE SITE
Carlos Fuentes wrote, 'From the air Xochicalco must look like a sand castle after the tide has washed and smoothed it', but there is nothing so impermanent about the hard, granite grey rock used in all the buildings, nor in the decoration which looks as if it has been incised with the aid of a firm stick.
   Xochicalco was built on three mountains and includes three **ball courts**. The largest of these, at the heart of the site, is similar to the ball court in the Maya site at Copán, in far-off Honduras. Xochicalco had strong trading and cultural links with the Maya: on the **Temple of the Feathered Serpent**, figures in Maya dress, adopting Maya postures, are intertwined in the great undulations of a feathered serpent. Other influences from Veracruz, Oaxaca and the Valley of Mexico make it one of the most cosmopolitan of all pre-Hispanic cities.
   Like a modern conference town, Xochicalco was used by various groups of mathematicians as a meeting place, for agreeing minute readjustments to the current calendar. On

the east side of the site, a tunnel leads down to the underground **observatory** where, at midday on 14 May, the rays of the sun pass directly over a small hole in the roof, illuminating the whole of the interior.

The State of Guerrero

This small southern state, crisscrossed by the still impossible barrier of the Sierra Madre del Sur, has as its most prized possession that perennial starlet, Acapulco. Like an ageing swinger still there long after the party has moved on, Acapulco has never acknowledged that it is long past it. And as long as the escaping capital-city crowd flock down to it, it never will. More enduring and more endearing, the steep, hilly town of Taxco has far more to offer than over-hyping tourist brochures imply. The state's capital, Chilpancingo and its second largest city, Iguala, are not worth stopping in. The coast is the aim, with Acapulco a dead straight line south of Mexico City. For less congested sea, sun and sand, keep on going northwest along the Pacific to the one-time fishing village of Zihuatanejo and the glitzy resort of Ixtapa. Outside of these secure tourist areas, Guerrero is a beautiful but inaccessible, impoverished and dissatisfied state, which has seen little of the great wealth engendered by Acapulco.

It is named more out of shame than pride after General Vicente Guerrero, one of the greatest and most respected architects of the 19th-century independence movement. Guerrero roamed the four mountain ranges of the state during years of guerrilla war. Finally inaugurated as president, he proved too ardent a nationalist for the hesistant, early reformers. He was betrayed by an Italian friend, the captain of a ship moored in Acapulco, for 30 bits of silver. He was first imprisoned and then shot by a firing squad on St Valentine's Day 1831, as new reforms swept across the country.

Taxco

Taxco is one of those enchanting hillside towns draped in bougainvillea, jacaranda and jamaica trees, with red tiled roofs on white houses and narrow, cobbled streets, clinging precariously to sheer slopes like a mountaineer to Everest. Described lovingly as 'undiscovered' and 'sleepy', it is neither, but still remains charming. As it is on the route to Acapulco, tourists come and go in droves, pasty white on their way south and blotchily red on the way home, but few of them linger. Resident Americans are the ones the bus left behind. Aldous Huxley found them in the early 1930s: 'Taxco is largely inhabited by artists and by those camp-followers of the arts whose main contribution to the cause of Intellectual Beauty consists in being partially or completely drunk for several hours each day.'

Try to stay one night at least, as the early morning and the late afternoon are utterly calm. A gentle walk around the Zócalo, some music from the band and a drink in one of the eagles'-nest bars is the liveliest entertainment Taxco will offer, outside weekends or festivals.

History

As early as 1521, Cortés sent his engineers down to the lush hills of Tlachco, inspired by reports that the Tlahuica had paid the previous conqueror, Moctezuma, in blocks of solid gold. None emerged, but silver deposits and tin were found in quantities. The road in from the north passes under the aqueduct of the Hacienda del Charillo, a silver foundry built by Cortés in 1534. The 18th century was boom time. José de la Borda heard tales of the region's wealth and came in pursuit. One day his horse slipped and dislodged a stone, gleaming with traces of silver. His fortune was made, and the church of Santa Prisca was begun, on the premise that since God gave to Borda, Borda should give to God. Following the slump in the 19th century, it took the enterprise of the Canadian William Spratling to revive the flagging industry in 1929 and the town has thrived ever since, selling genuine and not so genuine silver to visitors ever since.

GETTING AROUND

No parapets dull the sensations of the passengers; char-a-bancs and limousines still race each other down the pass round hairpin bends, swiping the two-seaters off the track, and meet head-on with lorries.
—Sybille Bedford, 1953

Arriving has always been an adventure. Taxco is 35 km off the fast toll road between Mexico City and Acapulco, on the old Carretera Nacional 95. **Buses** make the detour every 2 hours from Mexico City (200 km), Cuernavaca (122 km) and Acapulco (250 km). The first-class bus terminal, Estrella de Oro, is south of town on the main road: it virtually closes at 18.00, after the last bus north to Mexico and the last south to Acapulco and on to Zihuatanejo have passed through. The second-class terminal, Flecha Roja, is at Calle Becerra and the main Av John F Kennedy, with services to Toluca, Cuernavaca and the nearby caves of Cacahuamilpa.

Taxis are fast, nippy and unimpressed by dollars. The streets are narrow, twisted and steep—always choked with traffic, and with nowhere to park.

TOURIST INFORMATION

There is a disorganized office at the north end of town, at Av John F Kennedy 28 (tel 21525), by the aqueduct. The central office at Plazuela de Bernal 2 (tel 21705), below the Zócalo, is better. The post office is at Juárez 6 (open 08.00–19.00).

WHAT TO SEE

Santa Prisca

This parish church must surely be the most remarkable present ever given a newly ordained priest. José de la Borda, the silver-mining magnate, had it built for his son, Manuel. The bottomless wealth of the Borda mines ensured that it was built in a record time of only 10 years (1748–58), under the direction of Diego Durán. As a result, it possesses great symmetry of aim and execution, from the perfectly balanced soft-pink baroque facade to the two sober projecting towers. Isaac Rogers, the Big Ben clock-maker, is credited with Santa Prisca's clock, which is still chimed by hand every hour of the day. To contemplate the weaving and winding of the facade, where saints and cherubs fight for an inch of space with pomegranates, shells and vegetables, sit back in one of the bars (Bar Berta is the closest and least predictable) and digest it slowly, like a rich fruit cake.

Within, the dark interior is lit by fabulously ostentatious gold-leaf churrigueresque altarpieces. Those of the apse and transept veer out of control, swirling and foaming over the edges. There can be nothing more superbly over the top than the high altar. With a childlike fascination for detail, it portrays the first 32 popes hidden amongst the horns of plenty, surrounded by shells and biblical figures.

Miguel Cabrera, the untrained Zapotec (1696–1768), restores some calm. He painted 56 works in the church, sacristy, and Chapel of the Indians. Above the chapel's doorway is his interpretation of the 13-year-old martyr, Sta Prisca, who was fed to the lions on the orders of Claudius in AD 270. The sensitive lions turned her down but Claudius promptly had her beheaded. Cabrera often took an unorthodoxly frank line in interpreting the Gospel (his Virgin on the right side of the altar is rather too obviously pregnant), and he had to keep one city ahead of the Inquisition throughout his life.

Casa de Figueroa
(Guadalupe 2, above Santa Prisca and the Zócalo; open 09.00–13.00 and 15.00–19.00; closed Mon.)
A fine mansion from bygone days, the Casa Figueroa was once the mint, protectively built with only one door and two windows. It was constructed in 1767 by the Count de la Cadena, using the labour of Tlahuica men who couldn't pay their taxes. Today, it has a few more windows and houses a display of viceregal memorabilia.

Museo William Spratling
(Porfirio Delgado, behind Santa Prisca; open 10.00–17.00; closed Mon; adm.)
Born in 1900, William Spratling lived over 40 years of his life in Mexico, dying in a car crash in 1967. Like Rivera, Tamayo and Covarrubias, he was an avid collector of pre-Hispanic art, fascinated by the Olmecs and the civilizations of the southwest. These great collectors provided the passionate impetus behind the re-evaluation of early Mexican art. Here, his own pieces are contrasted with reproductions from other cultures, such as Picasso's portrait of Gertrude Stein and Egyptian hieroglyphs. The ground floor concentrates on the man himself and his two other passions—silver and Taxco.

Casa de Humboldt/Casa de Artesanías
(Calle Ruíz de Alarcón: turn right and right again from the Spratling Museum; open 09.00–13.00 and 15.00–19.00.)
The house's namesake, Baron Friedrich Heinrich Alexander Von Humboldt, the German naturalist, in fact spent only one night in this old staging inn, in April 1803. It was one of the earliest mansions to be built during Taxco's golden 18th century, and its facade is interlaced with Moorish weavings and rosettes. Inside is a small regional museum. Once upon a time, they say, there were mirrors inside which wiped out any physical defects in those who gazed upon them. Too good to be true, they were 'lost' in the last century.

The Caves of Cacahuamilpa

These caves are 31 km northeast of Taxco. If driving, leave on Highway 95 north, turning left after 22 km towards Toluca; 9 km further along, turn right at the sign. Alternatively, take a Toluca bus at 11.00 or 13.00 from Taxco and ask the driver for tongue-twisting Cacahuamilpa ('*las grutas*', meaning 'the caves', is just as good).

The inexplicable lure of caves is particularly inexplicable in Mexico, where endless caves, such as these at Cacahuamilpa, have become mandatory stops on every tourist route. Tours leave every hour to walk 2 km deep into the 20 enormous caverns. Imagination knows no bounds as guides regale their captive audience with colourful interpretations of ordinary-looking stalagmites as champagne bottles (would that they were!) and suspended stalactites as cathedral organs.

FESTIVALS

Taxco seems to have more holidays than work days and on Palm Sunday and throughout Easter Week they reach a crescendo. On Maundy Thursday the Zócalo becomes the garden of Gethsemane and Christ's capture is replayed. Candlelit processions of hooded, masked, gowned and often self-flagellating penitents attract visitors from around the world. At midnight on Good Friday, there is an eerily breath-holding Procession of Silence. In surrounding villages, such as Xalitla, Maxela and Ahuelicán, the celebrations are less notorious but just as colourful. The owner of the mask shop, **Arnoldo's** (Plazuela de los Gallos 2, tel 21272), will take visitors to some of the least visited of all.

In the third week of May, the annual cultural festival, Jornadas Alarconians, honours the Taxco-born playwright, Juan Ruíz de Alarcón, with plays and recitals. For more information, ask at the Palacio Municipal (a single-storied building on the north side of the Zócalo, which has three storeys on the other side because of the slope of the street).

MARKET

The market straddles the gulleys of the town. Steps lead down from the left side of the Zócalo, like the entrance to a mine. Stalls, with fruits, flowers, ceramics and baskets, are layered in tiers wherever there is a metre of flat ground. It's busiest at weekends but never quiet.

SILVER SHOPPING

Taxco is literally built on silver and there are opportunities to buy it everywhere. As any non-Taxco taxi driver will tell you, it is cheaper in the markets of Mexico City, but the choice is larger here. Alloys are sometimes sold masquerading as the real thing, particularly 'alpaca', an amalgam of copper and zinc: always check the hallmark of sterling silver (.925) before buying. The **Silver Museum** (open 09.00–18.00) is to the left of Santa Prisca, in a cavernous maze of restaurants and shops. Although small, it exhibits the work of local masters, including Antonio Pineda's arresting chess set representing the battle between the conquerors and the Aztecs. The Pineda brothers' shop is directly to the left of the church. **Los Castillos**, in Casa Borda, is another beautiful and reliable shop, with its own workshop. Bargain hunters are in the hands of the hawkers.

WHERE TO STAY   (area code 732)

Taxco isn't exorbitant. It has a few expensive weekend retreats, but far more modest little hotels cluster around the corkscrew streets leading off the Zócalo.

The *****Monte Taxco (tel 21300, tlx 173900) is cut off, high above the town, reached only by a tortuous road or cable car. It wears its five rather garish stars loudly and proudly, offering horses, mariachi, tennis, golf, a large pool and smug views of the town straggling far below. Anyone can use the cable car (open 08.00–19.00): the views are spectacular in the rainy season, when everywhere is green and water cascades down the cliffs. The ****Posada de la Misión (Av John F Kennedy 32, tel 20063, tlx 173903) is a soothing hotel with its own theatre, a 10-minute walk from the Zócalo along cobbled streets. It's worth taking the time to go for a drink there, in order to see Juan O'Gorman's mosaic mural of the Aztec hero, Cuauhtémoc, which acts as the backdrop to the swimming pool.

The ***Rancho Taxco Victoria (Calle Nibbi 5, tel 20010) sits resplendently surrounded by bougainvillea and jacaranda trees, facing the church. The ***Santa Prisca (Cena Obscura 1, by the Plazuela San Juan, tel 20080) is quiet and central, with two sunny courtyards. Just below the Zócalo, the **Posada de los Castillo (Calle Juan Ruíz de Alarcón 3, tel 21395) is definitely underrated, with 15 charming and well-decorated rooms. Opposite, ***Los Arcos (tel 21836) is just as pretty, with beams, antique furniture, and a restaurant, pool and lovely terrace. When these are full, try the **Melendez (50 m from the Zócalo at Cuauhtémoc 6, tel 20006). On the second floor above a cinema, the very cheap *Casa Grande (Plazuela San Juan 7, tel 20123) has clean but basic rooms.

EATING OUT

Apart from the hotels, the town's main restaurants are around the Zócalo. Closest to the church, Bar Berta is bestrewn with bullfighting posters and old-time characters. To have one of Berta's cocktails may be seen as a misfortune; two looks like carelessness. Cielito Lindo (tel 20603), next door, offers an antidote with generous platefuls of guacamole, enchiladas in chocolate *mole* and lots of fish and shrimps. Moderate. Above the road to Acapulco, La Pagaduria del Rey (tel 23467) is a small posada and restaurant, providing the best view in Taxco as well as the best *chile relleno* (stuffed chilli peppers). Moderate. Down the left-hand side of the church, the Bodega del Duende (Calle Veracruz) is a cellar restaurant with classical music. It serves grilled red snapper and Chateaubriand steaks, either inside or on its large terrace (which sometimes doubles as a theatre). Moderate. The Santa Fe (Hidalgo 2, by Plazuela San Juan, tel 21170) provides good breakfasts of *rancheros* eggs and Mexican staples throughout the day, to a packed house. Cheap. Along an alleyway leading off the Plazuela San Juan, by the Presbyterian church, the vegetarian restaurant, Sasha 100% Natural, serves sandwiches, salads and fruit juices. Cheap.

The Guerrero Coast

Emerging from a tangle of untamed jungle, and sheltered by the mountains of the Sierra Madre del Sur, Guerrero's coastline offers a stark choice between two extremes: overdeveloped resort, or underdeveloped wilderness with only palms to string a hammock on. It has suffered for its proximity to Mexico City. The temptation to carve huge resorts out of its quiet bays proved too much for successive governments whose budgets were severely in the red. Acapulco, the country's biggest resort, was built in the 1940s. The newer resort of Ixtapa, up the coast, followed in the 1970s, designer built and overpowering its neighbouring village of Zihuatanejo. The closest beaches to the capital (although Acapulco is still a winding 5 hours' drive away), they are often besieged by those anxious to escape the fumes of urban life. All three are consequently expensive: the best deals can be arranged through tour operators, before leaving home.

Acapulco

Ask anyone to name somewhere in Mexico, and more often than not, Acapulco will spring to mind. Set around a sheltered bay where the spurs of the Sierra Madre finally plunge deep into the sea, Acapulco once gloried as the epicentre of Mexico's China trade. Today it reaps rich rewards from the gaggle of groups who come from all over the world to jostle for a place along its shores. Whilst the sound of its exotic Aztec name conjures up visions of swaying palms and indolent days, its literal translation, 'destroyed place', is the more accurate. When the trade route to Manila was opened, one galleon a year set sail from the port, to return piled high with silks, spices, incense and jade. Despite harbouring such precious cargoes, Acapulco was a feverish spot, ridden with plague and diseases brought in by sailors from around the world. One Spanish official plaintively described his placement there as a sentence in hell.

President Miguel Alemán, drawing a line from Mexico City on a map, chose it as the site of Mexico's first tourist resort in the 1940s. (Veracruz was nearer but the discovery of oil had already made it lucrative.) He carefully bought up huge tracts of land himself, before building a runway and a fast new road to connect it with Mexico City. The glamour world was courted and came. Acapulco thrived on the publicity it gleaned from international stars such as Hede Lamar, who lay on its sands drinking rum cocktails and Starlight Swizzles. Johnny Weismuller, fresh off the Tarzan set, was so enthused that he even bought a hotel. By the time Elvis Presley and Ursula Andress filmed *Fun in Acapulco* there, it was firmly on the tourist map. Old-timers still reminisce fondly of ice-cold margaritas sipped as the sun set over the bleached sand of the Bay of Acapulco. This reputation lingers on. Over-exposure has turned sour, however. The more up-to-date will linger less fondly either over memories of swimming pools packed with inveterate fun seekers out to get blind drunk by noon, or over the endless battle to save the shirt being ripped off their sunburnt backs by dollar-hungry tourist vultures.

GETTING AROUND
By Air: Acapulco is one of the easiest places to fly to in Mexico. The surge in package tourism has resulted in direct, daily international flights to and from North America and Europe, as well as connections with all airports in Mexico. The airport is 22 km to the south of town. Combis wait to take arrivals into the centre (marked 'Centro').
By Bus: Buses leave every half-hour to and from Mexico City. Buses going up and down the coast are almost as regular. The first-class bus station is in Av Cuauhtémoc at 158, and the second-class in the same street at 97.

By Car: Highway 95-D, a swift, mainly two-lane toll road, connects Mexico City with Acapulco. It bypasses Cuernavaca before starting to twist and turn on its switchback route across the Sierra Madre range. It staightens out for the last stretch, which finally slopes down into the Bay of Acapulco. The trip usually takes 5 hours (411 km). Long, flat Highway 200 runs up and down the coast, connecting Acapulco to Zihuatanejo (311 km) and Pinotepa Nacional (259 km). Beware of its surface: it varies greatly and pot holes often loom unexpectedly around corners.

In Town: Combis connect the centre with both stations and the airport, and there are always fleets of taxis waiting outside every hotel. The old town sits to the west, under the shadow of the promontory of La Quebrada. To the east, the glittering towers of the new resort hotels rise up from the sands of the shore. Buses go up and down the 15 km of La Costera, the road which connects the old to the new. Taxis can be hideously expensive: fares should always be settled firmly in advance.

TOURIST INFORMATION
Unofficial hawkers of information are everywhere. The official office is at La Costera 54 (tel 41014).

WHAT TO SEE

Divers
One of Acapulco's most famous tourist attractions is to watch young boys dive from the heights of the La Quebrada cliffs, into the waves which crash upon the rocks of a narrow channel below. This was originally an innocent sport: boys would dive just for the thrill of it. Then the jet set came to watch and dollar signs started to flicker in people's eyes. A hotel and nightclub emerged and the boys formed a union, diving only when paid to do so. The skill lies in timing the wave to the split second, so that there is water and not just bare rock below. The boys clamber up the meagre footholds on the cliff face: at the top, they hyperventilate, brace themselves, flaunt, kiss the statue of the Virgin and finally arch themselves into a perfect dive. They can be seen from the hotel El Mirador (see below) and also from the road opposite the cliffs. The spectacle starts every evening at 19.30, finishing at around 22.00. It takes 20 minutes to walk up Calle Quebrada from the Zócalo of the old town.

Centro Cultural
(Costera 4834, in the old town; open 09.00–14.00 and 18.00–20.00; closed Mon.)
The cultural centre organizes dance classes, yoga lessons and concerts. It also houses a small archaeological museum, filled with funeral urns, deformed skulls and other pre-Hispanic artefacts which have been found in the state.

BEACHES
The Bay of Acapulco is notoriously polluted. Attacks of typhoid are fairly common and, unfortunately, it is wiser to stick to hotel swimming pools. **Condesa** is the most crowded of the beaches, running along the main hotel strip in the centre of town. Quieter, outside weekends, is **Puerto Marqués**, on the road south to the airport, set in a small hidden bay. Further south, the Princess hotel has a long strip of isolated beach fringed with palm

which is one of the least spoilt. **Caleta** and **Caletilla** are two small sheltered bays near the old town, patronized more by Mexicans than by foreigners.

SPORTS

Water skiing, windsurfing, parasailing and scuba diving can all be arranged, either through the hotels or directly on one of the beaches.

WHERE TO STAY   (area code 748)

There are of course any number of hotels in Acapulco, with the cheapest around the bus station and the most expensive towards the east on Costera Miguel Alemán, but there aren't any finds. Forty years on, Mexico's first resort has grown weary and lost its sparkle. Many hotels have grown slap-happy, anxious only to herd as many guests as possible in and out, without paying too much attention to the worn carpets and well-oiled bedcovers. No small hotel has been able to keep a toe in on the main beaches, where money talks and five-star hotels have a monopoly. The medium-range hotels tend to emulate the big prices of top-range hotels, without the service to accompany them.

Of the top hotels, two preserve a haughty isolation from the hordes around and fight to retain the glamour of old Acapulco. The **(GT) Princess** (on Revolcadero Beach, tel 43100), far out to the east of the town, is built like an Aztec temple in a 195-hectare garden, with its own long stretch of sand. Guests can lie under palm trees, or horse ride, surf, parasail, snorkel or even play golf on one of the 18-hole golf courses. **(GT) Las Brisas** (Carr Esénica 5255, tel 41650) is most renowned for the jeeps it gives its guests to drive around in. The hotel's 300 cottages, each with its own swimming pool, are balanced precariously on the hillside, which slopes up 350 m from the shore. Health clubs and tennis courts punctuate the carefully manicured gardens.

Down the scale, the *****Caleta (tel 48739), to the south of the old town, looks out onto the yacht harbour. The rooms are large and light with wicker rocking chairs on the balconies. Its kidney-shaped swimming pool is built high up on the rocks above Caleta Beach. This same bay has two smaller and much more modest hotels, of which the **Nao is the better. On the beach, the **Marinera** restaurant serves fish from a palapa-covered balcony.

One of the most original hotels is *****El Mirador (tel 31155), at the far west of town by La Quebrada, where divers fling themselves from the cliffs. One can go for dinner, a drink or to spend the night. The restaurant is covered from floor to ceiling with autographs, from Errol Flynn to Joan Collins. Just behind the Mirador there is a much cheaper and smaller alternative, the **Raul and Tony**, which has a palapa restaurant attached.

EATING OUT

Restaurants which are in one night are out the next, and they change hands just as fast. Breakfast and lunch are usually eaten in the hotels and on the beaches and many restaurants only open for dinner. Anything and everything goes: Japanese, German, French and Italian restaurants add variety to the Mexican diet. A few old-timers can be relied on, with prices which match the length of their reputation. **Normandie** (on the corner of Malaspina and Costera, tel 51916) has a well-deserved reputation for really good French food. It closes from June to October. Expensive. **Coyuca 22** (tel 35030) is both the name and the address of a restaurant which sits on top of a hill overlooking old Acapulco. It is quiet and exclusive, with a Mexican menu. Expensive.

Cocula, the terraced restaurant next to Bancomer on the Costera, is popular for steaks, with tables set outside under palm trees. Moderate. The best and cheapest seafood is served simply from palapas on beaches such as Caleta and Angosta, in the old town. Alternatively, **Beto's** on Playa Condesa, which has been going since the 1950s, serves unusual fish dishes like *quesadillas de cazón* (tortillas filled with baby shark). Moderate. The main drag of La Costera is crammed full of fast-food joints mostly catering for North Americans.

Zihuatanejo and Ixtapa

A small fishing village set in a sheltered bay, **Zihuatanejo** owes its name (from the Nahuatl, 'land of women') to the pre-Hispanic colony of women which once ran its affairs. The surrounding hills are dotted with mango, papaya, lemon and tamarind trees. It's a peaceful antidote to the gaudy bright lights of Acapulco, though it lost its innocence when it was grafted onto the nearby resort of Ixtapa. Nowadays, it tempers an indolent lack of concern with a rather half-hearted attempt to cash in on the tourist boom. Street signs have been put up and the roads haphazardly cobbled to entice visitors.

Five km to the north, **Ixtapa** is a dignified if soulless resort built along 3½ km of beach. Computer planned like Cancún, it has learnt from the former's mistakes and has not gone in for the same orgy of overdevelopment.

GETTING AROUND
By Air: The international airport is on the Acapulco road, 17 km southeast of Zihuatanejo, with direct flights to and from the major cities in the western United States as well as Guadalajara, Mexico City and Puerto Vallarta. Minibuses connect the airport with both town centres.

By Bus: Both bus stations are in Zihuatanejo: the first-class is in Paseo del Palmar and the second-class in Paseo Zihuatanejo, the main road leading into town. Regular first- and second-class buses link the town with Lázaro Cárdenas and points northwest, and with Acapulco and Mexico City.

By Car: Zihuatanejo is 237 km northwest of Acapulco on Highway 200, which cuts through coconut groves and mangrove swamps before continuing erratically all the way up to Puerto Vallarta. The quickest route from Mexico City is via Acapulco, on Highways 95-D and 200, and takes 9 hours.

In Town: A regular microbus links the two towns, leaving whenever it is full. In Zihuatanejo, it leaves from Av Morelos at 5 de Mayo.

TOURIST INFORMATION
The office in Ixtapa is opposite the Hotel Stouffer Presidente (tel 31967; open 9.30–18.00). The office in Zihuatanejo, on the waterfront in Paseo del Pescador, is less helpful and often closed, though officially open the same hours.

BEACHES
In **Zihuatanejo**, three stretches of beach lead south from town. **La Madera**, near the main square, and the long white sands of **La Ropa** (named after a cargo of fine clothes,

'*ropa*', washed onto its shore when a Chinese ship was wrecked nearby) are a quick walk from the centre. The secluded **Las Gatas**, where Purépecha queens swam in the pale green waters of the sheltered cove, is further afield and consequently less crowded. There are organized trips to Las Gatas beach but the local fisherman to be found on the pier will always negotiate to ferry individuals who prefer to escape the crowd. An alternative is to take an hour's horse ride from La Ropa beach, through jungle and rocky terrain (horses can be hired on the beach). It's easy to snorkel out from Las Gatas to the reef which encircles the bay.

In **Ixtapa**, a handful of exclusive hotels huddle in a corner of **Palmar Bay**. The beach is long and wide, making it easy to escape the crowds. The small promontory of **Punta Ixtapa** is a 10-minute walk south of Ixtapa. Here boatmen have formed a cooperative to take passengers to the surrounding rocky islets, to swim in peace amongst the pelicans.

WHERE TO STAY
(area code 743)

In Zihuatanejo
During the winter, the package-holiday market fills the hotels in Zihuatanejo. However, in the summer, when Mexican families come down, prices are often halved and it's easy to find a room.

*******Villas del Sol** (Playa La Ropa, tel 42239) are so popular that they are often booked for a year in advance. Originally there were only seven or eight beautifully furnished *cabañas*, each with a large living room and an upstairs loft to sleep in. Now there are at least 30, but the service is still excellent. This is one of the loveliest hotels in Mexico, owned by a Swiss and run with exemplary efficiency by a German. The ******Sotavento** (Playa La Ropa, tel 42032, tlx 16208) is another lovely hotel which sprawls down a hill, looking out onto its own bay to the south of the town. Hammocks are strung on the long balconies outside each room and it is all to easy to while away an evening sipping tequilas and swinging languorously. The rooms vary in price according to size with better deals to be had on the lower floors. The food in the restaurant is uninspiring, except for breakfast. The adjoining ******Catalina** (same address and rates as for the Sotavento) was once a barracks (which it has never quite forgotten) and has a funicular to lift its guests from the beach to the varying levels of the hotel. *****Bungalows Allec** on Playa Madera have long had a reputation for pleasant rooms at reasonable prices. Whilst showing its age, this German-run hotel, with pastel blue and pink cottages set in a garden of palms, is still good value. *******Villas Miramar** (tel 42106) opposite have large rooms and a small secluded pool.

On the street which winds above sits *****Irma** (tel 42025), a family hotel with ocean views over the bay. The modest ***Casa Aurora** (Nicolás Bravo 27, no tel) has well-kept white-washed rooms, though hot water is only available on the second floor. Inexpensive alternatives amongst the jumbled streets of the centre are ****Avilar** (Playa Principal), ****Raul 3 Marías** (Noria 4), **Imelda** (Catalina González 11, tel 43199), or the youth hostel **(CE) CREA** (Paseo Zihuatanejo).

In Ixtapa
Of the plethora of big-name hotels which fill Ixtapa, the *******Sheraton** (tel 43184) stands head and shoulders above, with its consistently excellent service. Glass lifts swoop guests up and down. The large rooms have boldly tiled bathrooms, balconies for

breakfast and strangely compulsive 24-hour American television channels. The best rates can be had by booking direct in Britain or the United States. Other safe bets are the *****Stouffer Presidente (tel 42013), or the *****Camino Real (tel 43300), set on its own beach with an unprepossessing entrance resembling the central bus station.

EATING OUT

Ixtapa has little to offer other than standard resort restaurants in the hotels and a variety of international restaurants in its shopping mall. There are some surprisingly good finds, however, in Zihuatanejo. The long-established restaurant Coconuts (Agustín Ramírez 1, tel 42518) has a smart inside dining room as well as tables outside in the garden, where lobster bisque, black bean soup and gazpacho are served. Moderately expensive. The Captain's Table (Nicolás Bravo 18, tel 42027) has an upstairs bar built into the hull of an old ship. Downstairs it specializes in seafood, accompanied by a rich 'thousand spice' sauce. Moderately expensive.

Zihuatanejo is filled with *pastelerías* selling pastries and bread. The best is El Buen Gusto (in Guerrero by Ramírez). To counterbalance this, 100% Natural (Av Catalina González and Cuauhtémoc) serves wholewheat sandwiches filled with toasted cheese, avocado, spinach and tuna, to be washed down with an eclectic selection of drinks such as the *engergetic*—a mixture of beetroot, spinach, celery and orange. Palapa huts on La Ropa serve *ceviche* (raw fish cocktails marinaded with chilli, lime and lemon), red snapper and *sopes* (small thick tortillas filled with refried beans and topped with cheese).

For long, drawn-out lunches, the village of Barra de Potosí, south of Zihuatanejo off the Acapulco road, offers grilled fish or grilled fish. Eaten on rickety tables, it is washed down with the Mexican Guinness, Negro Modelo. The restaurants are no more than palm-roofed huts, with fishing tackle and lobster pots as decoration and someone's borrowed music machine for ambience, but the seafood needs no apologies.

Part V

PUEBLA, TLAXCALA AND HIDALGO

Nahua woman in Cuetzalán

The Mexican Republic holds more within its boundaries than anyone could begin to see in a couple of weeks, and the states bordering Mexico City tend to be overlooked in favour of more conventional tourist destinations. The huge state of Puebla is renowned for its traditional capital and its outstanding food. More fascinating than the city are the hill villages and their markets in the Sierra Norte de Puebla, a world and 500 years away. Tlaxcala is a miniscule state which nonetheless manages to pack into its territory pre-Hispanic ruins, Maya murals, a gentle state capital, a volcano, mountains and plains. The little-known state of Hidalgo, to the northeast of Mexico City, is not on anyone's route to anywhere. Its capital, Pachuca, is only 1½ hours from Mexico City, surrounded by silver-mining hills which enclose a national park providing an ideal retreat for city dwellers

Each of these states has an important pre-Hispanic ruin: in Puebla it is the great honeycombed pyramid near Cholula; in Tlaxcala it is Cacaxtla with its vivid murals; and in Hidalgo it is the Toltec capital of Tula with its Atlantean statues. It would be a pity not to see any of these, but more of a pity not to explore further. For those who want to leave the big cities behind, and rest in small villages with no more than a weekly market and a couple of hotels on the main square, where Spanish is treated as a foreign language, then the villages of the Sierra Madre in Puebla and Hidalgo have it all.

The State of Puebla

The large state of Puebla is divided from Mexico City and the smog-covered Valley of Mexico by the chain of mountains which includes the guardian volcanoes, Popocatépetl and Ixtaccíhuatl. The only city of great size is Puebla, the country's fourth-largest and the world centre for production of the Volkswagen Beetle. The rest of the state is made up of good agricultural land, riven by the spine of the Sierra Madre which spends its time trying to decide whether to be tropical or alpine. The heights are covered in pine forests, the valleys in mamey, bananas and mangoes, and the slopes in coffee.

PUEBLA

Catholic and conservative, Puebla manages to combine these famous traits with an outrageous sense of the baroque. As one of the first cities to be built by the Spanish on virgin land, it was planned out on paper, set around a main square dominated by a church, with a town hall, a house for the governor, and various impressive mansions for the original settlers to either side of it. It was designed to be a noble and staunchly guarded city, acting as midway point between the premier port of Veracruz and Mexico City, the capital of New Spain. Later, the French came, adding a touch of radical chic to the conservative stronghold and leaving behind a legacy of delicious pastries.

Even today, over 400 hundred years after its conception, the core of this large city retains its colonial stamp, with stately houses and a wealthy cathedral in its Zócalo. Considered the Rome of Mexico, and renowned for its Catholicism, it still has over 60 churches and convents within its precincts.

The sobriety of the Spanish grid plan is set off by gaudiness in everything else. Sybille Bedford visited the city in the 1950s and described the interiors of the churches as

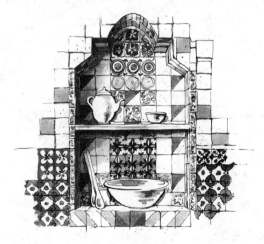

Pueblan tiled kitchen

131

HIDALGO, PUEBLA AND TLAXCALA

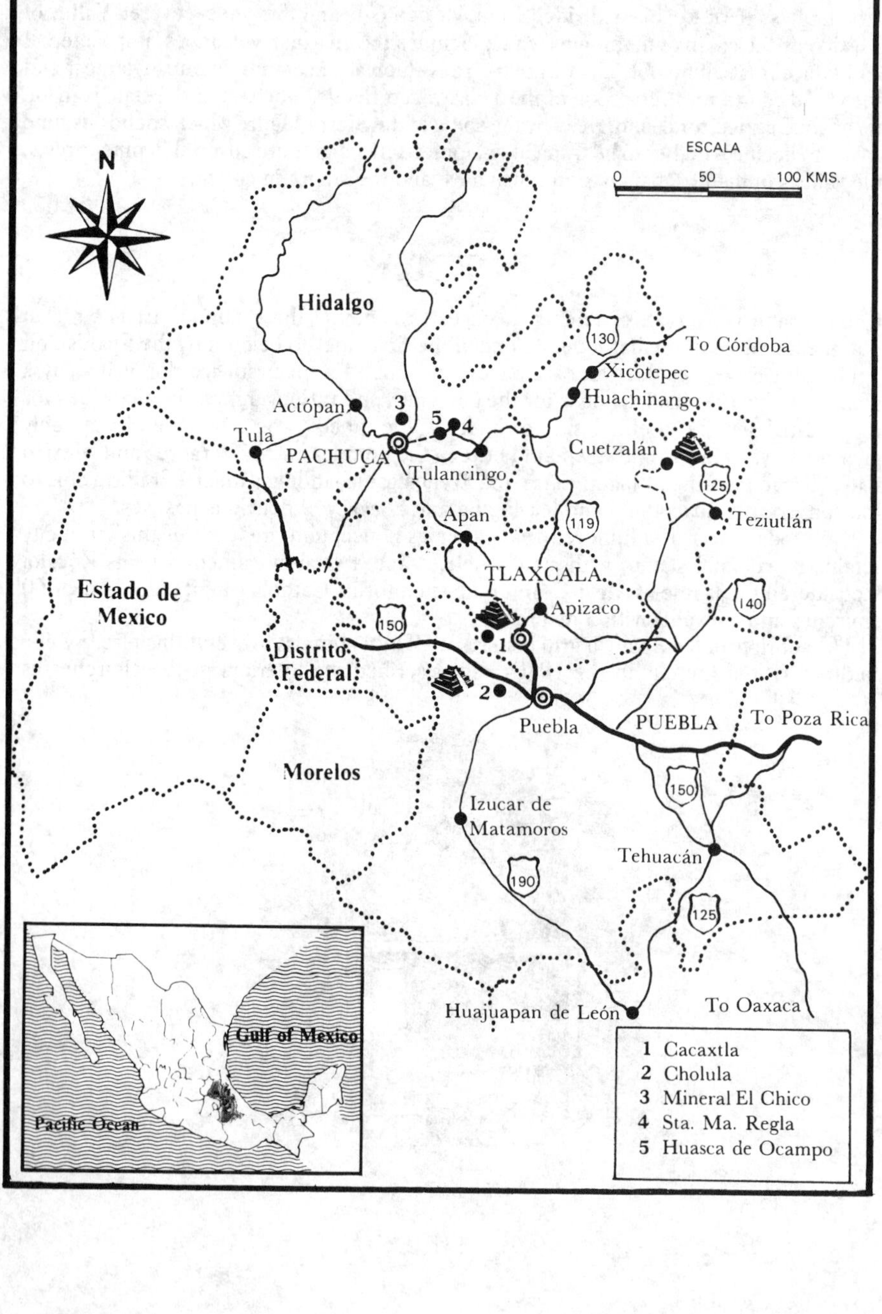

ESCALA

0   50   100 KMS.

N

Hidalgo

To Córdoba

(130)

Xicotepec

Actópan   3   Huachinango

Tula   5   4   Cuetzalán

PACHUCA

Tulancingo   (125)

Apan   Teziutlán

(119)

Estado de
Mexico

TLAXCALA

Apizaco   (140)

Distrito   (150)

Federal   1

2

Puebla   PUEBLA   To Poza Rica

Morelos

(150)

Izucar de
Matamoros

Tehuacán

(190)

(125)

To Oaxaca

Huajuapan de León

Gulf of Mexico

Pacific Ocean

1	Cacaxtla
2	Cholula
3	Mineral El Chico
4	Sta. Ma. Regla
5	Huasca de Ocampo

'blazing forests of gold and exotic statuary'. On 'all the fronts of all the buildings', she saw:

> a glaze of every period, shape and colour of mudéjar tiles, while cornices and casements are moulded—not reticently—in white stucco ... on the whole an arty job for modern taste but delicately managed, and the momentary effect quite charming. The tiling is not solid like so many mosques and baths, but panels are set in varying proportions in a brick facade, and this is a redeeming feature. Not much brick shows but the occasional base or edging gives a rest and starting point to the eye.

Puebla is famed throughout the republic for its tiles and pottery. Dating from the 17th century, the tiles are found in every nook and cranny of the city, including many of Arabic design. The highly valued pottery, known as *talavera* (after a town in Spain), is decorated by a hand-painted glaze: once it was considered only good enough to be used as kitchen ware.

A rapidly growing city, choked with cars and people, Puebla is not particularly conducive to a long stay (and as it is within 1½ hours of Mexico City, it could be seen from there in a rushed day). However, taken together with the mountain villages dotted all over the state and the ruins of Cholula close by, it has a great deal to offer.

GETTING AROUND

By Air: The small airport of Huejotzingo, west of Cholula, is used only for flights to and from Guadalajara. It was built for emergencies, after the 1985 earthquake in Mexico City, but grass now grows on the little-used runway.

By Bus: Puebla's modern bus station, known as CAPU, is north of the city, on the crossroads of 11 Nte and Blvd Nte. ADO buses run every 15 minutes to and from Mexico City's TAPO terminal (2 hrs). Other buses run regular services to and from Tlaxcala (40 mins), Oaxaca (7 hrs), Veracruz (4 hrs), and Pachuca (5 hrs). There are daily buses to Cuernavaca (second-class, 3½ hrs), Villahermosa (8 hrs), Mérida (15 hrs) and San Cristóbal de las Casas (15 hrs). Combis marked 'Centro' or 'Central Camionera' run between the bus station and the centre (stopping at 10 Pte and 2 Nte, as they are not allowed into the Zócalo).

By Car: Puebla is well connected. A swift toll road (150-D) runs from Mexico City (125 km), continuing through Puebla to Córdoba and then on to Veracruz (301 km). The old, free Highway 150 runs south from Puebla through Tehuacán to Oaxaca (363 km). The quickest route from Puebla to Pachuca is to return to Mexico City and take Highway 85 north, although the winding back roads via Tlaxcala and Apizaco are lovely.

In Town: The fast toll road (150-D) from Mexico City to Veracruz bypasses the city itself, so that loaded lorries avoid the centre. The Spanish grid system has kept the old city rigidly in shape, making orientation easy. The pivotal streets are 5 de Mayo/16 de Septiembre which runs north–south through the Zócalo and Av Reforma/Camacho which runs east–west. All other streets are numbered. Streets running east–west are called *avenidas* and those running north–south are *calles*.

The best way to get around is on foot, as nowhere is far from the Zócalo. There are two types of **taxi**: the yellow ones are authorized and the black aren't.

TOURIST INFORMATION

The tourist office is in the ex-archbishop's palace to the right of the cathedral, at 5 Ote No 3 with 16 Septiembre (tel 461285; open 08.00–20.00, Mon–Fri; 09.00–14.00,

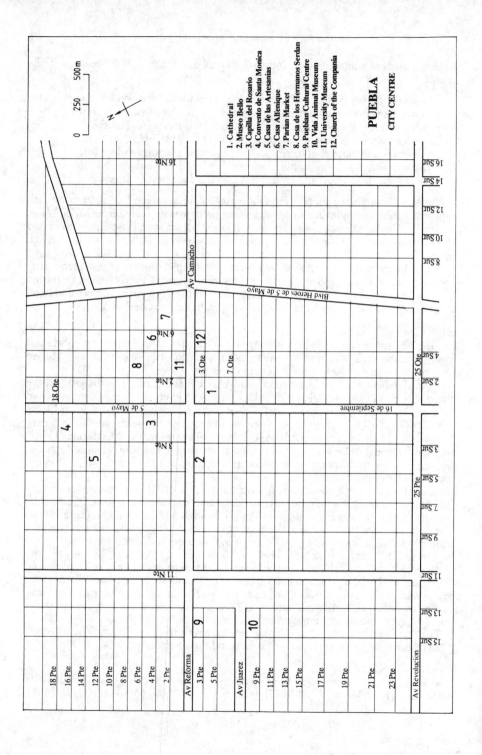

PUEBLA

CITY CENTRE

1. Cathedral
2. Museo Bello
3. Capilla del Rosario
4. Convento de Santa Monica
5. Casa de las Artesanías
6. Casa Alfenique
7. Parian Market
8. Casa de los Hermanos Serdan
9. Pueblan Cultural Centre
10. Vida Animal Museum
11. University Museum
12. Church of the Compania

0   250   500 m

Sat–Sun). The staff are generous with maps and information on cultural events in the city.

WHAT TO SEE
Around the Zócalo

The tree-shaded Zócalo makes a good base for planning an itinerary, with plenty of cafés beneath the portals of the colonial houses.

The Cathedral

The cathedral dominates the Zócalo, with 70-m towers. Begun in 1575 and finished 100 years later, before Mexico City's, it is a fine example of well-proportioned early baroque. It was founded by the Jesuit Bishop Juan de Palafox, who devoted most of his life to raising funds to build it: however, he is given no more than a small plaque, having been kicked out of Mexico along with all the other Jesuits and sent back to Spain.

The atrium is surrounded by a high iron fence decorated with angels (the symbol of Puebla) and keys, bishops' hats and shepherds' crooks (symbols of the papacy). The entrance to the cathedral is via two huge, original, hingeless wooden doors, which are rarely opened together. When they are (as during the pope's visit), there is a general amnesty: queues form to pass through and receive forgiveness. A relief on the portals illustrates the mystical marriage vows of Sta Rosa of Lima, the first American saint, who was canonized in 1668 and played a crucial role in the Catholic faith of Latin Americans. The north facade is sculpted with high reliefs of the four kings during whose reigns the cathedral was constructed—Charles I, and Philip II, III and IV. Spanish coats of arms were quickly plastered over during the fight for independence, but easily uncovered in later years.

The vases of lilies which decorate the interior five aisles of the cathedral symbolize the Immaculate Conception, to which it is dedicated. The magnificent choir is decorated with inlaid woods and topped by a monumental 12-m-high organ. The main altar was designed by Manuel Tolsá and depicts the kings and queens of Europe (Edward of England, Ferdinand and Isabella of Spain, Louis of France and Margaret of Scotland). The pulpit beside it is made entirely of onyx. The dome is made of pumice, covered in local glazed tiles—a replica of St Peter's in Rome. The priest on duty can grant permission to enter the sacristy, and will also give a guided tour of the 17th-century oil paintings.

Biblioteca Palafoxiana

(Corner of Av 5 Ote and 16 de Septiembre.)
Opposite the cathedral, in the same block as the tourist office, the Archbishop's Palace now comprises the Casa de la Cultura and, on its second floor, the library built by Juan de Palafox y Mendoza in the 17th century. At that time, it was considered to be the finest in the New World. He donated 5000 of his own books in Creole, Hebrew, Latin, Sanskrit and Spanish, as well as many works by his great mentor, St Thomas Aquinas. The collection now stands at 43,000 books, stored on glorious hand-carved cedar-wood shelves, hung with water flasks in case of fire. The desks, etched with autographs, are marble topped and the floor exquisitely tiled.

Callejón de los Sapos
(Calle 4 Nte and Blvd Héroes del 5 de Mayo.)
This narrow, traffic-free alleyway behind the cathedral is full of antique shops, known collectively as *bazars*, where antique furniture in the Spanish colonial style is sold alongside collections of kitsch postcards, scratched records from the 1940s, religious calendars, modern reconstructions of antiques, gilded saints and much more. Although most are open throughout the week, Sunday is the best time for browsing. Stalls are set up all around the little central plaza and sellers congregate from all over the state.

Museo Amparo
(Calle 2 Sur; open 09.00 to 17.00; closed Tues.)
This, the newest of Puebla's museums, holds the pre-Hispanic and smaller colonial collections of the Fundación Amparo on the two floors and around the patios of an elegant colonial mansion (formerly a school). The hallway is dominated by a vast Diego Rivera portrait of Amparo Espinoza Iglesias, after whom the museum and collection were named by her widower. The collection itself is fabulous, beautifully laid out by the museographers of the Museum of Anthropology in Mexico City and clearly explained by a tape-recorded guide, available in four languages, which can be rented at the entrance.

Museo Bello
(West of the Zócalo, at 3 Pte No 302; open 10.00–14.00; closed Mon.)
The house of José Luis Bello is filled with artefacts from all over the world. Extraordinarily, he himself never travelled, relying instead on friends and relations to bring him back bits and pieces from Europe and other parts of Mexico. An only child, whose own offspring died in infancy, he amassed a huge collection, which he left to the state, ranging from Pueblan *talavera* to Flemish paintings and Chippendale chairs. An admirer of Napoleon, he had his own bedroom decorated in Empire style, complete with a replica of Napoleon's own bed and busts of Napoleon and his second wife, Marie Louise of Austria. The museum also includes a large selection of miniatures, glass paperweights and fans.

North of the Zócalo

Santo Domingo
(North of the Zócalo, on Av 5 de Mayo where it crosses 4 Pte.)
The most opulent church in a town of opulent churches, lavishly decorated with tiles, Sto Domingo (1611) is a shining example of the Pueblans' Catholic enthusiasm. Enamelled angels sit on pediments above each of the dome's windows, notable both for their golden locks and for the risqué sashes draped around them (their only clothing) in this most circumspect of cities. The stone arch was too big for the door and so a double frame was built around it.

The **Capilla de Rosario** (1690) within is dedicated to the sailors' Virgin, who protected travellers on this trade route to the ocean. Built in the form of a Latin cross with a half-barrel vault, it is a baroque flourish in which no inch is left uncovered, as tiles jostle for space with gold-leaf, polychrome, sculpted figures and carvings. A constant light is shed from the many candles lit by hushed pilgrims.

Just beyond Sto Domingo, at 5 de Mayo and 6 Oriente, is the **Mercado de la Victoria**, a tall green Porfirian building which used to be the main market. It is now slowly being turned into a cultural centre and shopping mall.

Casa de los Serdán

(Northeast of the Zócalo at Av 6 Ote No 206; open 10.00–17.00; closed Mon.)
Officially known as the Regional Museum of the Mexican Revolution, this modest town house was the home of the Serdáns, a hardened and enlightened family of revolutionaries. Aquiles Serdán was to become one of the first martyrs to the cause. On the express orders of Porfirio Díaz, he was shot here on 18 November 1910, the day which marked the end of Díaz' long dictatorship and the start of the 10-year Revolution.

Aquiles, his brother Máximo and his sister Carmen all belonged to the Anti-Reelection party which opposed Díaz. Persecuted by their political opponents, they fled to Texas to plan the Revolution, returning to Puebla in November 1910 to turn their house into an armoury, ready for action. The police were informed and stormed the house, and Aquiles was killed in the ensuing shoot-out. The house is now as it was on that night in 1910: the bullet holes which riddled its facade are prize exhibits.

Av 4 Oriente

Northeast of the Zócalo, 4 Oriente houses the 18th-century **Teatro Principal**, which is the oldest in the country and claims to be the oldest in the Americas. It still hosts occasional performances. Next door, the **Barrio del Artista** was originally the artists' quarter: today, paintings are on sale to tourists. Beyond this is the **Mercado Parián**, where the onyx for which Puebla is famed is sold in vast quantities, together with inferior but cheap examples of Pueblan *talavera*.

Casa de Alfeñique

(4 Ote, no 416 with 6 Nte; open 10.00–17.00; closed Mon.)
Puebla is a city to walk around with your nose in the air, because many of the most splendid houses are at their best from the first floor up. This house is decorated like an almond cake, with bright blue and white tiles set off against a background of red tiles. It is now the state museum, with historical artefacts from all over the state.

Casa de los Muñecos

(Av Camacho and 2 Nte.)
Northeast of the Zócalo, this other famous Pueblan facade is carved with doll-like figures showing the twelve labours of Hercules. Inside, the university has mounted an exhibition of scientific apparatus.

Convento de Santa Mónica

(18 Pte 103 and 5 de Mayo; closed Mon.)
When the anticlerical reform laws were passed in 1857, the convent of Sta Mónica was closed, the premises sold, and it was believed that the nuns had returned to the bosoms of

their families. In 1935 a shocked Puebla discovered that they had continued to live there secretly (bang opposite the police station), with the aid of false panels, double-bottomed sideboards and revolving bookcases. It had always been a cloistered order, and several generations of nuns had merely retreated from all contact with the outside world. Many of the most important families in Puebla were involved, providing food, disposing of the dead and even bringing novices. The nuns had almost doubled in number when they were discovered.

The convent was founded in 1606 as a safe lodging place for noblewomen whose husbands didn't trust them to live alone whilst they themselves went off on journeys. These women understandably kicked up a fuss, and the institution foundered after a couple of years. It then became an enforced refuge for prostitutes, before being turned into a convent for young novices, who had to be of noble birth. It is believed that many of these had strayed from the path of virtue and were incarcerated for nine months by horrified families, who let it be known that they were travelling to Europe. In the ossuary are the skeletons of their young babies.

It is a gruesome place today, with a foreboding, claustrophobic atmosphere, seeped in repression and deprivation which was ostensibly self-imposed and divinely inspired. The present entrance was once the living quarters of a family, thus providing a normal front to the convent. Behind there is a small, tiled garden courtyard, off which lead the museum, chapel and cloisters, and a beautiful Pueblan tiled kitchen. The museum is filled with religious relics, including chains for self-flagellation, while the wooden planks of the beds in the cells are wrapped around with barbed wire. Between 1857 and 1935, the convent 'door' was a small opening disguised as a cupboard in the dining room.

From the second floor, dark passages hung with crosses, crowns of thorns and paintings lead to the Mother Superior's office, decorated with miniatures which the nuns used to sell in order to buy food. A secret door leads to the concealed Courtyard of the Novitiate: the round grid was used for confession, to a priest from the outside world. Above this cloister, the nuns could look down into the church from behind a one-way mirror in the choirstalls. From here a spiral staircase leads down to a small room where a secret door opened out onto the street. Further down is the crypt where the bones of babies were found.

Next to the Sta Mónica Convent there is an excellent, small tile factory, **Casa Rugerio** (18 Pte 111, tel 413843). Family run, it keeps going on a wing and a prayer. The sole potter is already past retiring age but still sits behind his wheel, calmly throwing pots. They sell all the old patterns of tile here and will also send packages abroad (pay half up front and the rest on delivery).

Sta Rosa Convent
(Calle 3 Nte, no 1203, and 14 Pte.)

This, the largest convent in the city, was formerly a Dominican stronghold. It has now been turned into the **Museum of Popular Arts**, whose prize exhibit is a restored kitchen, complete with tiled walls, huge earthenware cauldrons and chocolate beaters. Legend claims that it was here that the nuns first invented the famous *mole poblano*. Although the convent is now full of light and airy patios, during the backlash against

Catholicism its cloisters were turned into a neighbourhood tenement and asylum for the insane, which have been only recently restored.

San Francisco
(Blvd Héroes del 5 de Mayo and Av 12 Ote.)
This handsome church has one of the finest facades in Puebla, dating from the 18th century and made up of a folding screen of tiles and bricks along its entire length. The basic structure was completed by 1585, and is characteristic of the 16th century, with its single nave, ribbed vaulting and side chapels. It stands back from the ring-road in its own large atrium, where children congregate during the weekend to play on the fairground toys while their parents buy crafts from the Centro Artesanal.

Centro Cívico Cinco de Mayo
(Above the town, 2 km northeast of the Zócalo; a cheap taxi ride, or take a bus from outside San Fransisco.)
The battle that took place between a small Mexican force under Ignacio Zaragoza and a large, invading Napoleonic French army, on 5 May 1862, gave rise not just to this collection of museums on the site of the battle, but to countless street names and, most important of all, a national holiday. The Mexicans, of course, won this battle. However, the following year the French returned, besieged the city for two months, and finally captured it shortly after the 5 de Mayo anniversary. Puebla was then more or less controlled by the French (who were there to protect the puppet-emperor Maximilian) for four years, until a third, bitter battle left the city and the much-damaged forts in Mexican hands.

This historic site now houses a collection of monuments and museums, the latter including natural history, anthropology, a chronicle of the French intervention and a planetarium. However, its distance from the Zócalo means that it will appeal only to enthusiasts, the French or long-term visitors.

WHERE TO STAY
(area code 22)

Puebla's smartest hotel is the quiet *****Mesón del Angel (Av Hermanos Serdán 807, tel 482100, fax 487935), a 10-minute taxi ride north of the centre, on the Puebla–Mexico City road. It is set in tropical gardens, which include a swimming pool, health centre and tennis court. Despite its colonial exterior, the ****Astra (Reforma and Cinco de Mayo) has large, modern bedrooms and is well situated in the centre of town. Also in the heart of Puebla is the characterless but comfortable ****Posada San Pedro (2 Oriente 202, tel 465077), with a small garden equipped with swings and slides for children, a swimming pool, and cable TV.

The charming ***Colonial (4 Sur 105, on the corner with 3 Ote, tel 464199, 464709 or 464612) used to be a hostelry for Jesuit fathers and pilgrims. It's the best moderate hotel in Puebla, with large rooms and *talavera*-tiled bathrooms leading off a central courtyard. Old writing desks overlook the restaurant and its white-jacketed waiters. The ***Palacio San Leonardo (2 Ote 211, tel 460555) was built in a French turn-of-the-century style, with a stained-glass ceiling and a sweeping Art Nouveau staircase. The rooms are modern, leading out onto balconies; the best are on the top floor (710 to 700), with impressive views over to the La Malinche volcano. There is a small swimming pool. On the Zócalo, ***Royalty Centro (Portal Hidalgo 8, tel 420202) has a faded gentility, with ranchero-style bedrooms equipped with heavy wooden furniture and tiled bathrooms. There is a 'Ladies' Bar' downstairs where women are allowed to go for a drink, which speaks volumes about its 'traditional' attitude. If the other hotels in this category are full, the ***Del Portal (Portal Morelos and Avila Camacho 205, tel 460211) is a functional and central alternative, much used by Mexican business travellers and families.

Puebla doesn't think much of travellers on a budget and most of the cheap hotels are dives. Some of these are a cut above the rest. **Imperial (4 Ote 212, tel 424980) is clean and very simple. Downstairs an attempt has been made to recreate an English pub, complete with Union Jacks on the ceiling and pumps for drawing beer. It also has a small restaurant. *Halconeros (Reforma 141, tel 427456) has an elaborate tiled entrance, friendly staff, and cheap if rather dingy rooms, with new windowless bathrooms. Cheaper still, *Teresita (Av 3 Pte 309, tel 417072) has small but clean rooms and is always popular with Mexican workers.

EATING OUT

Puebla is renowned for the richness of its food—in particular, for its *mole poblano*, a thick rich, spicy, chocolate sauce poured over chicken. The city is also famous for its pastries and sweets (such as *camotes*, made of sweet potato and coloured with a vegetable dye). The sweet factories lining Av 6 Ote are the best place to buy these. Other local favourites are *chalupas*, small pasties filled with meat or vegetables.

To try Pueblan food at its best, the popular and long-established **Fonda Sta Clara** is the place to go for chicken in a *mole* sauce or *romeritos*, or the pumpkin-seed sauce of the *pipián verde* or *rojo*, as well as *chalupas*, *molotes* and tacos. Seasonal specialities are offered every month. There are two branches: 3 Poniente no 920 (tel 461919; closed Tues) and 3 Poniente no 307, in front of the Museo Bello (tel 422659; closed Mon). Moderate. A less traditional but just as popular regional restaurant, particularly on Sundays, is the **María Bonita** (31 Ote, 2 Sur, tel 409877), which has a patio restaurant and bar. Its specialities are *chiles rellenos* and *pollo en pipián*. Moderate.

Several restaurants are near the big US-style shopping centre, Plaza Dorada. **La Garita** (Blvd Díaz Ordaz, tel 370814) serves excellent pasta dishes as well as steaks and Mexican favourites. **El Vaquero Andaluz** (2 Sur 3905 with Blvd 5 de Mayo, behind the Parque Juárez, tel 409579) offers a good selection of steaks, all delicious and imported from Argentina. It specializes in a rich sherry sauce. Moderate. The **Bodegas del Molino** (San José del Puente, Puente de México, tel 490651 and 490399) is housed in a 16th-century converted mill: the food does not match the setting, but the restaurant does offer a very elegant ambience and an attractive bar for those who want to see the mill but not necessarily to eat. Expensive.

Puebla even has its own successful Japanese restuarant, the **Royal Kyoto** (Plaza Express), where the mushroom soup and *tepanyaki* combination are particularly recommended.

For something more simple and less expensive, try **Juliu's Pizzas** (13 Sur 1302 with 13 Poniente, tel 435122), which will also deliver to any address in town. For tacos, the *tacos arabes* of **Tacostito** (various locations including the Zócalo) are unbeatable. Cheap. For simple, everyday vegetarian food, try the **Zanahoria Esmeralda** in Av Juárez in the Zona Esmeralda.

Cholula

> Cholula is a monument to human thoroughness. The Spanish as a matter of general policy razed every native temple in conquered territory and built a Christian church on its site.
> —Sybille Bedford, *A Visit to Don Otavio*, 1955

The small colonial town of Cholula, with its pleasant porticoed Zócalo, is famed for its mass of churches and towering pyramid.

The city of Cholula flourished at the same time as Teotihuacán, by which it was strongly influenced. When the Spanish arrived, the great ceremonial centres had fallen into disuse but the city still included 400 temples and over 40,000 houses. As a centre for the worship of Quetzalcóatl, it attracted pilgrims from all over the country. Merchants, too, used it has a stopping point on the north–south trade route and its pottery was highly prized. The Cholulans proffered friendship to Hernán Cortés but ambushed him on his departure from the city. Incensed by this betrayal, the Spanish embarked upon a massacre, in which 6000 Cholulans were killed and the city was ravaged. Cholula later suffered further for its temerity: Cortés swore that one church for each day of the year would be built over its ruins. Although this was not achieved, Cholula does have a disproportionately large number of churches for its size. The mustard-coloured **San Gabriel Monastery** alone, to the east of the Zócalo, has three churches within its precincts. The most interesting is the 16th-century Capilla Real, topped with 49 Arabic domes.

GETTING AROUND

Cholula is 12 km west of Puebla. Many of the second-class buses between Puebla and Mexico City stop in Cholula. Alternatively, take a red and white bus marked 'Cholula' from the Puebla terminal on the corner of Av 8 Pte and Calle 7 Nte. These stop in Cholula's Zócalo, which is only a 300-m walk from the pyramid.

Buses for the villages of Tonantzintla and Acatepec leave Cholula from the corner of Av 6 Pte and Calle 3 Nte. It is quickest to walk between the two villages, which are only 1½ km apart.

WHAT TO SEE

Great Pyramid of Tepanapa

Now looking like a grassy mound, with a church on its summit, the Great Pyramid is presumed to have been the largest ever built in the world, with a volume of 3 million cubic metres. Like many other pyramids, it attained this hefty size during a lengthy process, in which one pyramid was superimposed above another every 50 years or so. A 50-m mural was discovered inside, portraying local men indulging in an orgy of pulque drinking—part of a rite associated with the worship of Quetzalcóatl. The church of N S de los Remedios, built by the Spanish, occupies a defiant position at the summit of the pyramid. From here there are wonderful views of surrounding churches, but it is a long, hot climb. The less energetic can explore the tunnels which thread underneath the pyramid for over 8 km. They were dug during excavations and not all are open to the public. Badly lit and musty, they open out into the most recent excavations on the east side. There is a small museum on the north side of the pyramid.

The Churches of Tlaxcalancingo, Tonantzintla and Acatepec

These three beautiful and very Mexican churches are set in a triangle between Puebla and Cholula (on the back road, Highway 190, to Atlixco).

Tlaxcalancingo is 12½ km from Puebla. The facade of this church is an example of talaveresque baroque—a combination of red brick and tiles placed together on a background of white plaster.

Some 1½ km further south is the church of **San Francisco Acatepec**. Its extravagant churrigueresque facade is built like a folding screen, entirely covered in multicoloured tiles, whilst its exquisite interior is filled with gilt carvings and polychrome plaster. The native craftsmen sneaked their own representations of Christianity into their work, most notably in the face of the sun—set into the roof above the aisle—which has thick eyebrows, full lips and an aquiline nose.

Some 1½ km further along (4 km south of Cholula), the plain tiled facade of the church of Santa María in **Tonantzintla** gives no indication of the splendours within. Every inch of the dome is filled with a dazzle of colour, carved entirely by indigenous craftsmen, on the site of a former temple to the Earth Goddess, Tonantzin. Distinctly Cholulan-looking angels, dressed in short skirts, are adorned with roses, chillies and grapes, painted in crimsons, magentas and azure blues. Its naive enthusiasm makes it one of the loveliest interiors in Mexico. On 15 August the village celebrates the Assumption, and comes alive with a series of dances.

WHERE TO STAY AND EAT   (area code 22)
Given its vicinity to Puebla, there is little need to stay in Cholula. One of the five well-run hacienda-style ****Villas Arqueológicas** (tel 471960, fax 471508) is 10 minutes from the site; like the others in the group, it has an excellent library and restaurant. For something less elaborate, try the ***Calli Quetzalcóatl** (in the Zócalo, tel 471555), with pleasant rooms set around a courtyard. The **Los Portales** café on the Zócalo is a popular place for coffees and breakfasts. Cheap. The **Tío Nico** nearby serves snazzier international dishes. Moderate.

The Sierra Norte de Puebla

Mexico's mountains have formed important political and geographical boundaries throughout its history, but few present-day visitors put them at the top of their lists, preferring the warm coast. The Sierra Norte de Puebla, however, is close enough to the capital to warrant a long weekend visit for those with a little more time, imagination or love of nature. Lost in pockets of mist, and living off bananas, coffee, mangoes, mameys and little else, these villages are quite without equal in Mexico, offering a very different but far more realistic view of the pulse of life than that provided by colonial cities and international resorts. Here, life is raw: nature may be bountiful, but the living isn't easy. If the coffee harvest is a disaster (and in 1990, one unexpected night of frost destroyed the whole crop), then the next year will be one of great poverty and hardship. If the coffee comes through, and the fruits, bean and corn grow as they always do, then the simple daily pattern of life will carry on for another year.

The population of these villages is made up of Nahuas, Totonacs and Otomís, as well as Mexicans of Spanish descent. Although the latter are always the shop owners, landowners and government representatives, they are as foreign to most of the villagers as the odd European who comes their way. Visitors are rare. Festivals, however, are frequent, and anyone thinking of visiting the area during Easter week or for a village festival should be prepared to book one of the small hotels in advance or to sleep out in the church.

GETTING AROUND
There are two routes into the sierra from Puebla. For **Cuetzalán**, take eastbound Highway 150-D to the first toll booth at Acatzingo. From there, a straight side road (Highway 140) leads north to Oriental (79 km), where it joins Highway 129. At Zaragoza, 52 km further north, there is a left-hand turn just before a petrol station, signposted to the Wednesday market town of Zacapoaxtla (17 km). Now all pretence at flat plains is left behind as the road climbs up to La Cumbre, a narrow shelf between two gorges where wave after wave of mountains recede into the mist, and then veers down for the last and longest 36 km into the village of Cuetzalán. By car, the journey takes 2½ hours from Puebla (173 km) and 5 hours (316 km) from Mexico City; allow at least an hour longer for the twice-daily bus.

For the **Western Sierra Norte**, leave Puebla on the toll road to Tlaxcala. Then head north on Highway 119 until it hits the east–west Poza Rica–Mexico City road (Highway 130), just south of Huachinango (186 km from Puebla). There are regular buses from Puebla to Tlaxcala, but only four second-class buses a day continue north.

When coming directly from Mexico City, it is quicker to take Highway 45/85 to Pachuca in the state of Hidalgo, and then take Highway 130 east; either turn off whilst still in Hidalgo, at the signpost to Honey and Pahuatlán, or continue to Huachinango and Xicotepec de Juárez.

There are no trains or planes.

Cuetzalán

Of all the villages in the Sierra Norte de Puebla, this is the most appealing, largely because it is at the end of the paved road, with nothing but tracks between it and the Gulf of Mexico, 90 km away. Set in a tropical temperate zone, at 1200 m, Cuetzalán is the nerve centre for the outlying villages: during the rainy months (from June to October) nothing except four-wheel-drive trucks can get any further.

Vertical streets rise perpendicularly from the plaza, squeezed narrowly between teetering houses which seem to lack any solid foundation. Yet, at the turn of the century enough money was found to build a sky-scraping church, an icing-sugar-white Palacio Municipal, a bandstand and some of the larger houses perched on the square. One of these houses is now a café, which still keeps up its blackboard list of debtors (the professor is always at the top of the list, followed by the doctor and the lawyer). Outside one of its doors, a woman squeezes fresh orange juice every morning, while tacos, gorditas, enchiladas and stuffed chillies are fried up outside the other, on a flat griddle known as a *comal*.

WHAT TO SEE

The Market

Cuetzalán is famous for its Sunday market (there is a smaller one on Thursday). In this area, market day is called *día de plaza*, while a small market is a *mini-plaza*. The name makes sense when you see the stalls start to take over the terraced plaza on Saturday afternoon, as the first sellers walk in from their villages (which may be as far as 40 km away). The plaza continues to fill up with barefoot Nahuas and Totonacs dressed in embroidered shirts and *quechquémitls*, who come to buy, sell and discuss. It is not a market for outsiders but a very local affair. Oranges, beans and coffee come far higher on the list than textiles and weavings (although the women can sniff out potential buyers of hand weavings from a mile away: once found, they won't let them go). Anything goes—a popular delicacy is *pata de res*, the skin and hoof of a cow. Sandals, called *huaraches*, are made to size on the spot: feet are measured against a length of old car tyre, which is then cut to shape and strung up with a leather strap.

White is the colour of the day in all its deteriorating shades. The women selling weavings wear long, white skirts and embroidered shirts, tied with a single length of red material wound round and round the waist like a cummerbund. The older women still weave thick strands of purple and green wool into the hair piled on top of their heads, whilst the majority of the men wear patched-together white cotton trousers and loose shirts.

Excursions Around Cuetzalán

There are some impressive ruins 8 km north of Cuetzalán, known as Yohuallichán, reached by a rough dirt track. They include several mounds and a niched pyramid similar to the more famous pyramid at El Tajín in the state of Veracruz (only 50 km northwest as the crow flies, but a long, long journey from Cuetzalán).

To the east of Cuetzalán, a long, pot-holed track drops slowly down to the valley floor, past fields of coffee and through tiny villages. There are several waterfalls on or just off this bumpy road, the best of which is, needless to say, the hardest to reach. The 15-km journey to **Las Hamacas** takes all of 2 hours, and can only be attempted in a four-wheel-drive vehicle. (It is easy to negotiate a daily fee with a driver from Cuetzalán, on any day but market day.) Alternatively, the journey can be walked—in only double the driving time. However, the temperature climbs considerably the lower one goes, and it is a long, strenuous walk back uphill.

As it tumbles down towards the valley floor, the river crashes into a series of boulders, forming pools along the way, before finally cascading down a sheer rock face. Although as cold and fierce as a Scottish burn, it is surrounded by absurdly tropical fruits, including mamey, mango and orange trees. It is wonderful to swim here—but it can be dangerous. People have been killed, carried away by the undercurrents or losing their grip on the slippery rocks.

144

WHERE TO STAY (area code 233)

Cuetzalán has several small hotels, though none are very luxurious. Book ahead for Christmas, Easter and the festivals on 15 July, 4 October and 30 November.

For a simple cornflower-blue, wooden-ceilinged room with stunning views over the plaza and the sierra, head straight for Room 6 of the *Posada Jackelin (no tel), above the plaza and near the church. The hotel itself is light and charming, although utterly basic. The ***Posada Cuetzalán (Zaragoza 12, tel 10295) is smarter, verging on the chichi, with a decent restaurant and parking. It also runs to a Saturday night disco (a mistake) and a swimming pool. Another simple but adequate hotel is the *Rivello, around the corner from the Jackelin, also just off the square.

The Western Sierra Norte de Puebla

There is no connection between Cuetzálan and the villages on the western side of the Sierra Norte, apart from long tortuous dirt roads and tracks. They really have to be two different journeys (see Getting Around). The villages and towns in this northwestern corner of Puebla are on or close to Highway 130, which runs from Pachuca to Poza Rica in Veracruz.

Huachinango is the largest settlement. It was created a city in 1861, having nobly defended itself during the French occupation. Its population is made up of four indigenous groups—the Totonacs, Otomís, Nahuas and Tepehuas—who use it as the commercial and market base for the region. Saturday is market day (it begins early), when azaleas, camellias and gardenias are brought in from all over the region to be sold alongside daily necessities such as mangoes, oranges, corn and beans. The main festival takes place around Easter.

Continuing eastwards from Huachinango, in the direction of Veracruz, the road drops down towards **Nuevo Necaxa**, a town developed at the end of the last century by dam-building Canadian engineers, who wanted to make the most of the rainfall. It then climbs back up to **Xicotepec de Juárez**, the last town of any size before the state of Veracruz.

The most interesting villages in this part of the state are north of the main Highway 130: the entry point is west of Huachinango, actually in the state of Hidalgo (signposted Honey and Pahuatlán). The twin villages of **Pahuatlán** (inhabited by Nahuas) and **San Pablito** (Otomí) are on opposite sides of a valley. Both are famous for their continuing use of *papel amate*—bark paper which is beaten into thin sheets and then written and painted on. The ancient pre-Hispanic codices were produced in exactly the same way. Pahuatlán is the most accessible village, with a couple of small but comfortable hotels and a Sunday market. San Pablito, 25 km further on down an increasingly deteriorating track, resounds to the sound of the *amate* paper being beaten into shape. It has no hotels, no shops and only the occasional combi linking it to Pahuatlán. Between the two villages, as the road hits the valley floor, there is a fast-flowing river, ideal for swimming in. On the way to or from these villages, drop into the fast-dying village of **Honey**, close to the main Highway 130. It was founded and mined by an Englishman, Mr Honey, who built his own railway station and hacienda. Today it is an unkempt scatter of houses, famed only for its fighting cocks.

145

The State of Tlaxcala

The tiny, mountainous state of Tlaxcala is tucked in between the states of Hidalgo and Puebla. Its pleasant, well-preserved colonial capital and the ruins of the city of Cacaxtla, with its vivid pre-Hispanic murals, can both be visited on a day trip from Mexico City or Puebla. On the border between Puebla and Tlaxcala, surrounded by pine forests, La Malinche volcano dominates the landscape, with cabins to stay in for a weekend of fresh air.

History

The tiny state of Tlaxcala has played a disproportionately large role in the history of Mexico. Without the Tlaxcalans, the Spanish could never have conquered Mexico. When Hernán Cortés arrived in 1519, Tlaxcala was a small, independent, warlike nation, isolated within the Aztec empire, to which it had never submitted. After a few skirmishes with the Spanish, the Tlaxcalans decided to join forces against their bitterest enemies—Moctezuma and the Aztecs. When Cortés first attacked Tenochtitlán, three-quarters of his army was made up of Tlaxcalan warriors. He later used Tlaxcala as a base for his operations, building a fleet of ships which the Tlaxcalans subsequently carried over the mountains for the final assault on Lake Texcoco. As a reward for their loyalty, the Tlaxcalans were exempted from the exorbitant taxes extracted by the Spanish, and the city of Tlaxcala became a cradle of Catholicism.

After the conquest, Cortés sent Tlaxcalan fighting forces to subdue other peoples all over the country, and gave them incentives to settle. Even today, residual Tlaxcalan colonies can still be found in cities as far removed as Saltillo in Coahuila and San Cristóbal in Chiapas. The Tlaxcalans later sided with the Spanish during the fight for independence, and this long history of collaboration has meant that the rest of the country looks at Tlaxcala somewhat askance. Today, the state remains an isolated enclave, embracing traditional colonial values.

Tlaxcala

All roads into Tlaxcala lead to its pretty, porticoed Zócalo, dominated by fine colonial palaces. The smaller Plaza Xicoténcatl is filled with bookshops and student cafés, and leads up to the exquisite Monastery of San Francisco. To the west of the city, the Museo de Artesanía is a living museum, where local artisans explain their work as they weave or knit.

GETTING AROUND

By Bus: The bus station is 1 km west of the centre (tel 20217), connected by regular combis. Buses to and from Puebla (45 mins) leave every 30 minutes, and there are five a day to and from Mexico City's TAPO terminal (2 hrs). Buses for the village of Sta Ana leave from the corner of Plaza Xicoténcatl.

By Car: Tlaxcala is 113 km east of Mexico City and 30 km north of Puebla. From Mexico City, take the toll road, Highway 150-D, to San Martín Texmelucan, and then bear left for Tlaxcala down Highway 117 (a further 25 km). Highway 119 from Puebla is swift and direct.

TOURIST INFORMATION
The tourist office is on Primero de Mayo, which leads off the south side of the Zócalo (tel 20027; open 09.00–17.00 weekdays; closed at weekends).

WHAT TO SEE AND DO
Zócalo
One whole side of the Zócalo is taken up by the **Palacio de Gobierno**, whose patterned brick facade incorporates much of the original building constructed by the Spanish when they first arrived. Inside are some garishly restored murals by local artist Desiderio Hernández Xochitiotzin, originally painted in the psychedelic 1960s. These graphically illustrate the history of the Tlaxcalans and their intimate involvement with the Spanish. The **Palacio Municipal**, which also overlooks the Zócalo, was once a grain store. Its heavy romanesque front is relieved by the richly decorated Moorish windows on the second floor.

Museo de Artesanía
(Five blocks west of the Zócalo in Blvd Sánchez.)
This is an unusual museum where local artisans work *in situ*, so that visitors can watch and ask questions. Tlaxcala is famed throughout the country for its weaving and the local council is anxious that these traditions should be preserved. Everything that is made is for sale, from thick woollen jerseys, embroidered *rebozos* (shawls) and tablecloths, to masks, belts and rugs. The displays embody the philosophy of the living museum, including glowing clay ovens which are used like saunas in mountain villages, and dripping stone jars used to filter water.

Monastery of San Francisco
A sloping cobbled street leads off Plaza Xicoténcatl and up to this monastery, which was one of the first to be built by the victorious Spanish. It benefited from their enthusiasm to impress the Mexicans with aesthetic beauty, with exquisitely carved cedar beams, an inlaid tiled floor and an organ loft laced with intricate Moorish inlaid *lacería* woodwork. A smaller chapel contains the large font where the Tlaxcalan King Xicoténcatl was baptized. Wrapped around one of the cloisters is the **Museo Regional**, housing a dusty jumble of local artefacts.

Ocotlán Sanctuary
(One km east of the Zócalo; walk three blocks north up Juárez, turning right onto Zitlalpopoca, or take an Ocotlán bus from the station.)
A swirl of white plaster overlooks the town from a hill to the east. The sanctuary of Ocotlán is renowned for its florid baroque carvings and sweeping churrigueresque forms, finished off with plain red tiles, which decorate the facade. Inside, the 18th-century local artist Francisco Miguel spent 25 years of his life painstakingly carving fanciful wooden figures, which have been gilded and polished into a frenzy of adoration for the Virgin. Legend has it that the Virgin appeared to a pious Tlaxcalan in 1521, after

seven years of drought, and made water flow from this very spot. Ever keen to use natural occurrences to major effect, the Spanish quickly whipped up a sanctuary in her honour. The best time to visit is the third Monday in May, when an image of the Virgin is carried round in a colourful festival.

Santa Ana
A couple of km east of Tlaxcala, the town of Santa Ana is a thriving centre selling the woven woollen goods for which the state is famed. The weavers have been increasingly seduced by mass-marketing, but there is still a wide selection of jerseys, rugs and blankets for sale.

Tizatlán
The remains of King Xicoténcatl's palace lie 4 km north of Tlaxcala, next to the village of San Estéban Tizatlán. The site (closed Mon) includes some faded frescoes and the crumbled ruins of palaces, but its main attraction is its situation, overlooked by the volcanoes of Popocatépetl, Malinche and Iztaccíhuatl.

WHERE TO STAY AND EAT
Tlaxcala's hotels are nothing to write home about. The most comfortable is the *****Jeroc** (Revolución 4, on the way to Santa Ana, tel 21577). ****Albergue de la Loma** is more homely, set on a small hill above the town (Guerrero and 20 Noviembre, tel 20424). In the centre, the ****Mansión Xicoténcatl** (Juárez 18, tel 21900) is family run, with large dark rooms.

The best place to eat is the restaurant of the **Casa de Artesanías**, which specializes in local cooking and pre-Hispanic recipes. Try the stone-ground blue tortillas filled with *flor de calabaza* (courgette flowers) and the juices crushed from local fruits. Moderate. On the corner of Plaza Xicoténcatl, **Méson Taurino** (tel 24366) serves standard meat and fish dishes. Moderate. The same plaza is filled with small cafés for coffee or snacks.

Cacaxtla

The site of Cacaxtla was discovered in 1975 and has puzzled archaeologists ever since. The beautiful murals which cover its walls betray a marked Maya influence—an anomaly here, in the heart of Mexica country. Dating from AD 750, around the time when the great city of Teotihuacán was in decline, they bear witness to a struggle for power between the centre and the south of Mexico. Cacaxtla itself was subject to the nearby city of Cholula, which dominated the whole of the Puebla–Tlaxcala region. It was also on the main trade route between the centre and the south, which may explain the Maya influence in the murals.

GETTING AROUND
By Bus: Buses leave every hour from Tlaxcala to San Miguel Milagro, from where it is a short walk to the site (1 km).
By Car: Cacaxtla is 20 km southwest of Tlaxcala and 35 km northwest of Puebla, just beyond the village of San Miguel Milagro. From Tlaxcala, take the Tetlatlahuca road

south, turning right (west) in Tetlatlahuca to San Miguel Milagro. From Puebla take Highway 119 via Zacatelco. From Mexico City, turn off the Puebla toll road at San Martin Texmelucan and follow signs to Tepetitla and Xochitecatitla, from where Cacaxtla is signed (it is half an hour from the toll road).

VISITING THE SITE
(Open 10.00–17.00; closed Mon; adm.)
The main part of the site, the **Gran Basamento**, is covered by an enormous, protective, modern roof. Climb the stairs to see the foundations of the palaces where priests and bureaucrats lived. The famous murals are on the right-hand side of this building (to make the most of the light, try to arrive before 13.00). A small museum and a good restaurant are by the entrance.

THE MURALS
On first impression, the murals seem to be of purely Maya composition. The faces of the figures have the foreheads and rounded noses so distinctive of the Maya, while the costumes of the rulers, with headdresses in the shape of mythical animals, are undoubtedly Maya. On further inspection, however, the influence of Teotihuacán asserts itself, as in the symbols for water, including Tlaloc the Rain God, and the famous symbol of a reptile's eye.

Structure A contains the most famous of the murals. Its doorway is flanked by two stelae representing painted portraits of Maya warrior lords. One, painted black, wears the costume of a bird (later to become the symbol of Aztec eagle warriors) and has the clawed feet of an eagle. The other wears the Maya symbols of a jaguar lord. The borders which decorate these portraits are influenced by the art of Teotihuacán. A legend told to the Spanish at the time of the conquest explained how, at the beginning of time, the deity Tezcatlipoca (identified with the jaguar) defeated Quetzalcóatl (identified with the bird).

Round the corner from Structure A, the **Battle Mural** portrays central Mexican warriors in jaguar costumes, bearing symbols of Tlaloc, God of Rain, defeating, disemboweling and dismembering bird warriors with Maya features. The battle is depicted in mid-fray, including realistic scenes of wounded warriors slumped in despair, and fierce spear thrusts. The jaguar warriors are obviously victorious. This may indicate that the Maya ventured north in an unsuccessful attempt to extend their territory.

La Malinche

Named after Cortés' infamous lover, La Malinche towers above the plains of Tlaxcala and Puebla. Its often snow-covered peak (4461 m) is visible for miles around, and is easily accessible by foot.

GETTING AROUND
From Tlaxcala, take the Apizaco road north (17 km) and then turn right (east) on the Huamantla road, Highway 136. After 16 km, the government-run IMSS Centro Recreacional Malinche is signposted on the right.

WHAT TO DO

A small tarmacked road winds its way up for 15 km, past fields of maize and into pine forests, before emerging at the foot of the volcano. Here there are simple **cabañas**, sleeping six, equipped with log fires and basic kitchen facilities.

A dirt track continues up the mountainside for 3 km (just manageable in a VW Beetle). After that, there is a path through the forest leading to the summit. From the cabañas there are other less strenuous walks through the countryside, with the omnipresent volcano always on the horizon.

The State of Hidalgo

Hidalgo was named after Miguel Hidalgo y Costilla, the great priest who catalysed the Mexican independence movement. The state that took his noble name, however, had nothing to do with him. He never even set foot in it.

Ironically, Hidalgo never did as well after the withdrawal of the silver-mining Spanish as it did with them. Before the Spaniards came, the area was inhabited by the Otomí, and before them by the Toltecs, the ancestors of and inspiration for many of the great central Mexican civilizations, including the Aztecs. Today, Hidalgo's most visited site remains the great Toltec capital of Tula, on its western edge. Few people venture further into its uncharted, often mountainous regions, dotted with monasteries and mining villages.

Pachuca

Cold and windswept, Pachuca does a disarmingly good impression of a Cornish mining town in mid-winter. An 1859 replica of Big Ben stands in the main square, the Episcopalian church is out in force, and the town delicacy is a *pastee* stuffed with mince, potatoes and carrots. This is not merely coincidence. The Spanish discovered silver in the hills surrounding the town in 1534, perhaps following Aztec leads, but it was not until the 18th century that mines such as the Real del Monte became really successful. To exploit the wealth of this and other mines nearby, 250 families were brought in from Cornwall, and today Pachuca can boast Cornish names, an entire Cornish cemetery, the ubiquitous *pastee* and football, introduced by Cornish miners. Pachuca was the first place in Mexico in which football was played, but the home team now languishes in the second division.

It is a pleasant, self-assured town, with a laid-back atmosphere. There is really no reason to come out of the way to visit it, although it does make a natural stopping-off point on the way to the El Chico Park.

GETTING AROUND

Pachuca is not a crossroads, and although transport is good between it and the capital city, it is to all intents and purposes directly on the road to nowhere.

By Bus: Hourly buses ply between Pachuca's Central Camionera in the southwest of the city and Mexico City's TAN terminal (1½ hrs). There are regular first-class services between Pachuca and Puebla (5 hrs), Tula (2 hrs) and Tulancingo (1 hr), but for most other destinations it is quicker to return to the capital and go from there.

To get to the bus station, take one of the abundant, cheap taxis or a minibus from the Plaza de la Independencia.

By Car: Pachuca is linked to Mexico City (88 km, 1½ hrs) by a fast four-lane toll road, Highway 85, which leaves the capital from Insurgentes Norte. Highway 45 leads slowly west to Tula and the Toltec site (88 km), but it is quicker to go from the capital.

By Train: The train provides an efficient twice-daily link between the capital and Pachuca, taking 2 hours (longer than by bus). It leaves Mexico City at 06.00 and 15.45, and Pachuca at 10.00 and 16.45. The station is in the south of town, close to the bus station, linked to the Plaza de la Independencia by minibuses.

TOURIST INFORMATION

The well-equipped and central tourist office is close to the main square at Allende 406, on the first floor (tel 23253 and 23276).

WHAT TO SEE

Within Pachuca itself, there is only one place worth lingering over: the Photography Museum. Just north of town, hills and mining villages provide an ideal weekend retreat away from the capital (see Around El Chico National Park).

The Plaza de Independencia

This main square is the centre of the city. Beside the mock Big Ben clock is a renovated bandstand, where music is played on Sunday evenings. From the Bancomer building, Calle Bravo leads west past the **Foro Cultural** arts centre (open 10.00–14.00) which shows local and national exhibitions. The same street opens out in front of the old university (the new one has been moved out to the suburbs).

Centro Cultural de Hidalgo

(A 15-minute walk from the Plaza de Independencia (signposted), along the *acueducto* and Arista.)

For something a little more lively, head for Hidalgo's cultural centre, set in the former 17th-century monastery of San Francisco. People who know nothing about Pachuca may well have heard of its **Photography Museum**, which includes the archives of Tina Modotti amongst its 1.8 million photos. A permanent exhibition is devoted to the history of photography in Mexico from 1873, including the earliest photographs taken in the country. The centre also includes a regional museum, cinema and theatre—and a triptych mural by Roberto Cueva del Río, who popped Diego Rivera into the corner in an attempt to improve a mediocre work.

WHERE TO STAY   (area code 771)

The most comfortable hotel is undoubtedly the modern, low-slung ****Calinda Pachuca, a 20-minute drive south of town, on the Mexico City road. It has an imaginative restaurant, light, large rooms and a swimming pool, but its distance from the centre makes it more popular with businessmen than with casual tourists.

The other hotels in Pachuca are far more modest, all set around the main square. Of these, the gaudy, red ***Emily** (tel 56122) is the modern alternative, usually preferred to the older, pink-fronted ****Los Baños** (tel 30700) or the ***Grenfell**.

Around El Chico National Park

The hills and villages north of Pachuca, in and around the national park of El Chico, provide endless opportunities fo walking, riding, fishing, or just relaxing. The area has become a haven for people who want to get away from the capital at weekends.

GETTING AROUND
Highway 105 from Pachuca passes the El Chico park and continues north to Huejutla (214 km) on the northern edge of the state, and on to Tampico in Veracruz. Second-class buses leave Pachuca's Central Camionera at least once an hour, stopping at all the villages mentioned.

WHAT TO SEE
The National Park of El Chico
Highway 105 skirts the Centro Cultural de Minería, with its display of redundant mine workings, both inside and out. It then climbs up into the hills of Loreto, past San Juan Pachuca—one of three working mines, which might be Ebbw Vale transported to sunnier climes. Hairpin bends weave through coniferous woods carpeted with wild mountain flowers such as the yellow *silvestre*, opening up into glades where campers set up their tents on mountain-climbing weekends. Horses can be hired for treks through the park, and there is also a government-run hostel, the **Albergue Miguel Hidalgo** (book through the tourist office in Pachuca, tel 771 23253 or 23276). Only 9 km from the outskirts of Pachuca, the air is sharp, clear and pure, and the town left far behind.

At the end of a side road leading off Highway 105, at km 9, is the tiny village of **Mineral El Chico** (29 km from Pachuca). Its outsize church is simply whitewashed, decorated only with a profusion of wild flowers around the altar. One old, stalwart house is being converted into a hotel. The houses set around the square open irregularly to serve good country food, such as tortillas filled with cheese and nopal cactus, or rabbit and bean stews.

Mineral del Monte
This once-prosperous mining village, 7 km north of Pachuca off Highway 105, still boasts several outsize mansions, a Cornish cemetery, a still-working mine and a super-abundance of *pastees*, although there is not a single Cornishman to be found.

Huasca de Ocampo
Some 18 km further along Highway 105 (25 km from Pachuca), a right-hand turning leads to the attractive, small hill village of Huasca, imbued with the atmosphere of Tuscany in the 1950s. There is a market on Mondays, but stalls sell ceramic pots and jugs every day of the week. The road continues for 3 km to the village of **San Miguel Regla**, set around a former mining hacienda (see Where To Stay). From here tracks lead

off in all directions, principally to the yet more impressive hacienda of **Santa María Regla** and to the trout-fishing lake at **Las Truchas**.

WHERE TO STAY

The two ex-mining haciendas of San Miguel Regla and Sta María Regla have both been turned into four-star hotels, conversions which would have made their one-time owner, Romero de Terreros, Conde de Sta María de Regla, turn in his grave. ******Sta María Regla**, the elder of the two, is further off the road, down a dusty track from Huasca lined with the finger-like organ cactus. It is dramatically situated, facing the *Prismas Basálticas*, which look like petrified organ pipes etched into the rock, drenched by the San Antonio waterfall. A myriad of underground tunnels, pools, halls and ovens is all that remains of the hacienda's former industry. The little chapel, with its unusual black Virgin of Loreto, has been repainted in a jaunty pink and white. Many of the buildings remain as they were: there is still a corral for the horses, a charro ring and a fronton court.

Large cabins with tiled floors, wooden-beamed ceilings and fireplaces are set in the gardens of the ******San Miguel Regla** (3 km from Huasca; reservations in Mexico City, tel 379 4668). It is very popular at weekends, as a perfectly relaxing retreat, but quiet during the week. Unfortunately, the restaurant is badly managed, providing set menus and set meal times, for registered guests only.

The tourist office in Pachuca (tel 771 23253 or 23276) will give advice about camping or staying in the government-sponsored hostels. In addition, there is a small, very cheap hotel in Huasca, ***Las Palmas**, which can be recommended only for the village it finds itself in.

Tula

Tula, the site of the Atlanteans and the home of the wise Toltecs, is one of the greatest sites in the Valley of Mexico, in size and splendour second only to Teotihuacán.

History

The Toltec city of Tula has its origins in a semi-mythic past: even the Aztecs, who followed hot on the heels of the Toltecs, invested them with almost divine attributes. They have gone down in history as sensitive creators (their very name signifies 'makers' or 'artificers'), although their highly stylized art and architecture screams of war and human sacrifice.

When the first Spaniards asked the Aztec chroniclers to write their history, they were surprised and intrigued by their references to the mythologized Toltec city of Tollán, to the north of the Aztec capital. The origins of the Toltecs themselves are confused: it is thought that in the late 9th century, several disparate, northern nomadic tribes united because of their common Nahuatl tongue. They founded the cities of Tollán (present-day Tulancingo, in the far east of Hidalgo), and then Colhuacán, before finally settling on the defensive limestone plain of Tula. Their first leader was Mixcóatl (Cloud Serpent), who has been described as 'an Indian Genghis Khan'. He was later deified as the God of Hunting. More significantly, divine status was also awarded to his son, Topiltzin, who during his lifetime became synonymous with Quetzalcótl, the Feathered Serpent God, who recurs again and again throughout Mesoamerican history and legend.

Topiltzin was born in the 930s and brought up by his grandparents in the present-day state of Morelos: his mother died in childbirth and his father was viciously assassinated by his own brother. It was Topiltzin who moved the Toltec's capital to Tula, having avenged his father's death and retaken command. He led the Toltec empire through its first great age of splendour—the age of construction, architecture, art and music. There was dissent, however, within the city and in AD 987 a warrior faction, followers of the belligerent god Tezcatlipoca (Smoking Mirror), engineered Topiltzin's fall from power. He was forced to leave the city he had founded. Some legends say that he set himself on fire and ascended to the sky as the Morning Star. Others claim that he set sail for the south, where his cult was adopted by the Itzá Maya of Chichén, or that he disappeared out to sea, vowing to return from the east and reconquer his land. (This latter prophecy rang in Moctezuma's ears when Cortés landed in the east, in Veracruz, and claimed divinity.)

The unusually precise date given for Quetzalcóatl's fall from grace, AD 987, comes from the haunting Nauhuatl poetry which recorded the event even whilst the opposing Tezcatlipoca faction held the balance of power in Tula. They expanded the Toltec empire to its greatest limits, but by the late 12th century the city was ravaged by a civil war which ultimately destroyed it. Half the population remained in Tula, but the rest followed the last ruler, Huémac, to the hill known as Chapultepec, then on the western bank of Lake Texcoco, now in the heart of Mexico City. Paul Gendrop claims that Huémac's name, which translates as 'Big Hand', was given to him because of his preference for women who measured at least four hands across the hips. He obviously didn't find what he was looking for: he committed suicide, and with him died the once omnipotent Toltec empire.

GETTING AROUND
Although Tula is in the state of Hidalgo, it is reached most easily from Mexico City (1½ hrs). The ruins are about 3 km outside the nondescript town of Tula de Allende.
By Bus: Autotransportes Valle del Mezquital runs a regular service between Tula and the Terminal Central de Autobuses del Norte in Mexico City, leaving every 20 minutes (1½ hrs). The buses arrive in the centre of Tula (Calle Xicoténcatl), from where it is a 3-km walk or short taxi ride to the ruins. Buses between Tula and Pachuca, operated by the same company, also run every 20 minutes (1½ hrs).
By Car: Tula is 75 km north of Mexico City and 88 km west of Pachuca. From Mexico City, take the Periférico and Highway 57 (towards Querétaro). The turning north for Tula is signposted 'Tula–Tepeji del Río'. It is 32 km from the toll-road exit. From Pachuca, take the Actopan road which cuts east–west across the state and takes under 2 hours.
By Train: Two daily trains to and from the capital stop at Tula's railway station, at 08.00 and 18.00. However, this is a slow and ponderous way to get to the ruins: the train invariably takes more than the scheduled 1½ hours, and the station is some distance from the site.

VISITING THE SITE
(Site open daily 09.00–17.00; museum closed Mon; adm.)
The visitor's centre at the entrance to the site includes an excellent introductory **museum**. The excavated site is but a fraction of the whole, and the long walk in from the

car park gives some idea of the extent of the city and of the urban grid pattern on which it was planned. As well as being artisans and creators, the Toltecs were extremely practical and scientific, devising a complicated drainage system and building a central reservoir to catch all the rain water.

The main path leads in past the ball court and around the back of the most impressive monument, Pyramid B, more romantically known as the **Templo de Tlahuizcal-pantecuhtli** (Morning Star). This north side is decorated with a free-standing wall, known as the **Coatepantli**, whose 40-m length is decorated with a geometric step motif and rattle snakes devouring human skeletons. The rear wall of the pyramid has a single frieze made up of jaguars (one spitting out a Tlahuizcalpantecuhtli mask from his jaws), pairs of eagles eating human hearts, and coyotes.

On its way round to the south and front side of this same Pyramid B, the path passes on the right a three-patioed structure known as the **Palacio Quemada**, which was burnt by barbarians in AD 1168. Here various Chac-Mool figures were discovered in the mid-19th century by the French pioneer archaeologist, Désiré Charnay. He also explored extensively in the Yucatán, where he found similar Chac-Mools. This extraordinary discovery of identical architectural finds convinced Charnay of the connection between Tula and Chichén. The Chac-Mool is a free-standing sculpture of a warrior, half reclining on his back, with his legs bent at the knee: on his chest he bears a receptacle, supposedly for sacrificial offerings.

The path continues towards the main plaza of Tula, passing on the left the front side and steps of Pyramid B. This southern side supports a colonnade with a bench still partly covered with a frieze of warriors. On top of the tiered pyramid stand the four towering **Atlantes**, 4.6-m tall, and composed of four basalt drums fitted together. These sculpted figures represent warriors dressed for battle and standing rigidly to attention, armed with an *atlatl* (spear thrower) in the right hand, and a spear in the left, wearing a spread-eagle breastplate and plumed headdress. They were originally painted in red, blue, black and white, their eyes studded with obsidian and shell. These vast columns once provided the supports for a roofed construction. When the city was sacked by barbarians towards the end of the 12th century, they were hurled off the top of the pyramid and ritually buried: they were only rediscovered this century.

Actopan

This Otomí town is 56 km east of Tula de Allende and 36 km west of Pachuca, on the main bus and car route between the two towns.

In the centre of Otomí territory, Actopan was chosen by the Augustinians as the site for a powerful fortress-monastery, built in the 1540s. Designed by the architect friar Andrés de Mate, it harmoniously combines a variety of styles, ranging from its Moorish tower and medieval battlements on the walls and roof, to the gothic patios and cloisters and the austere plateresque facade. The town has two market days, on Sunday and Wednesday.

Part VI

VERACRUZ

Pyramid of the Niches, El Tajín

Curving sinuously around the Gulf of Mexico, this long slip of a state was well favoured when the gods were handing out gifts. The birthplace of the most ancient of pre-Hispanic cultures, the Olmecs, and home of the later Totonacs, contemporary Veracruz is an aristocrat by right but isn't afraid to dirty its hands to profit from the huge deposits of oil in the Gulf. The ruins of ancient Totonac cities gaze wistfully over their successful modern petrol-producing replacements. Natural assets range from subtropical forest to the highest peak in Mexico, the 5700-m Citlaltépetl or Pico di Orizaba, which rises from the tree-covered mountains of the eastern Sierra Madre. On lower slopes cane, coffee and fruit plantations are surrounded by fields of exotic flowers. Down below, the fertile coastal plains are rich in crops and well-fed cattle graze on lush pasture.

Veracruz has produced two great anti-heroes—La Malinche, who betrayed her people and became Cortés' lover, and General Santa Ana, who stomped through history on his wooden leg, changing sides as often as he got the chance. The chequered history of the state is dominated by the turbulent past of its port, which has been endlessly invaded and fought over. As Mexico's gateway to the outside world, control of the port was essential for any would-be government. In the latter half of the 20th century, the invasion has been commercial. Cruise ships and oil tankers have replaced battleships in the Gulf. The scars of the state's youthful past have faded as comfortable, middle-aged Veracruz begins to rest on the wealth of its oil and rich agricultural land. It plays an active political role and is a keen supporter of the ruling PRI party, which keeps its oil revenues flowing in return.

Mexicans love a disaster. Veracruz has had its fair share, and it remains the most popular of states. Its exuberance and natural beauty are added attractions. Mention

Veracruz to any Mexican and a smile will spread from cheek to cheek, accompanied perhaps by a verse from 'La Bamba', the most infamous of its many ribald songs. The people's hero has emerged from its troubles with a carefree smile and an urgency to live for today, accompanied everywhere by music and dancing. The heady dance music has a strong Afro-Caribbean beat, a heritage from African slaves brought by way of Cuba.

The town of Veracruz is a hoary old sailor who winks, leers and charms despite a crumbling frame. As a port it's had a multicultural upbringing and the faces in the streets reflect a jumbled mixture of races. Beside this sassy cosmopolitanism, the capital Jalapa, in the northwest, prefers to keep out of the limelight. It's more of a quiet academic, with a mass of small cafés and gardens to sit in and a superb museum dominated by huge Olmec heads. Set high in the hills, it towers above the fertile plains of Fortín de las Flores and Córdoba. Further north still, the ancient city of El Tajín, with its distinctive niched architecture, sits in grandiose state beside the sprawling oil-rich town of Poza Rica. To the south the volcanoes, lakes and waterfalls of the Tuxtlas balance these industrial riches with a fey natural beauty.

History

PRE-HISPANIC HISTORY

Mexico's earliest recorded civilization, the Olmecs, flourished in southern Veracruz as far back as 800 BC. Little is known about the origins of this mysterious people, who left behind colossal carved stone heads with striking negroid facial features. Their huge sculptures are nearly 3 m high with broad noses, wide lips and what appear to be close-fitting helmets. Smaller pieces have the pudgy bodies of infants. They worshipped the jaguar, whose cult was identified with rain and fertility. Olmec carvings show were-jaguars (half-jaguar, half-man) and even jaguars in sexual union with women. Human forms are often sculpted with down-turned, snarling jaguar mouths.

In the classic period, after the fall of Teotihuacán (about AD 650), the ceremonial centre of El Tajín rose to prominence and dominated the east coast. Here the ball game, *ollama*, developed into an obsession and matches were followed with an eager intensity. So serious were the contests that losing captains could find themselves on the sacrificial block.

THE ARRIVAL OF CORTES

A later civilization, the Totonacs, were on the coast of Veracruz when Cortés sailed his brigantines up from the Yucatán. He landed at San Juan de Ulúa (by the present-day port) on Good Friday 1519, to be greeted with astonishment. He described the Totonacs in a letter back to Spain:

> some pierce their ears and put very large and ugly objects into them;
> others pierce their nostrils down to the lip and put in them large round
> stones which look like mirrors; and others still split their lower lips as far
> as the gums and hang there some large round stones or gold ornaments
> so heavy that they drag the lips down, giving a most deformed
> appearance.

The stone used was obsidian. The women wore elaborately embroidered skirts and the men were just as elegant, wearing trinkets and jewellery.

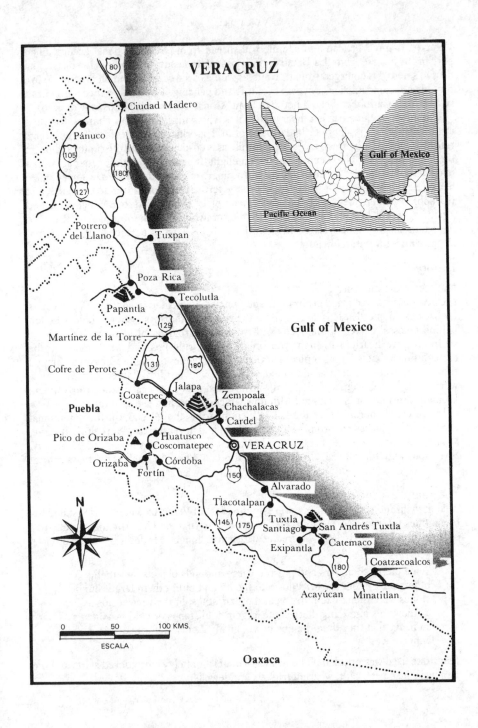

Cortés' men returned palefaced from expeditions, reporting 'stones on which sacrifices had been made, and the flint with which their breasts had been opened to tear out their hearts'. They went on to describe dismembered bodies whose limbs had been carried off to be eaten. This had so terrified many of the Spanish that plots were hatched to desert Cortés and return as swiftly as possible to Cuba. Only too aware of this, Cortés waited until his troops were in neighbouring Zempoala (see Zempoala) before ordering his pilots to strip and scupper his ships, using the flimsy excuse that they were unseaworthy. It was an audacious move which horrified his men but forced them into a loyalty born of necessity.

Cortés received invaluable advice in planning his campaign from his mistress, La Malinche. The daughter of a chieftain from Veracruz, she was fluent in a number of languages, and often acted as his interpreter. Realizing that reports of his presence would reach Emperor Moctezuma, Cortés staged a mock battle to impress him, firing cannons and having horses stampede. The bewildered Totonacs, who had never seen a horse before, were terrified by the steaming, rearing creatures. Then he conned the inhabitants of the nearby Totonac settlement of Zempoala. As the tribes on the east coast were subject to Aztec dominion and forced to pay tribute, Cortés found them willing to ally with him in an attempt to oust Moctezuma. Many tribes were persuaded to throw in their lot and Cortés finally marched inland towards Tenochtitlán at the head of a sizeable army.

The museum in Jalapa has an excellent collection of replica Olmec heads and figurines as well as many Totonac and Huastec pieces.

VERACRUZ

Like all good books, Veracruz should not be judged by its cover. Bizarre rather than beautiful, the indisputable charms of the irascible old port have been known to escape visitors on first arrival. Fanny Calderon de la Barca, Scottish wife of the Spanish ambassador, wrote in 1839: 'the scene may resemble the ruins of Jerusalem, though without its sublimity'. Although she found it horrifyingly dilapidated, she couldn't help but like the warmth and openness of its people. Paul Theroux, more recently, found himself intrigued, too, despite initially seeing only a 'faded seaport, with slums and tacky modernity crowding the quaintly ruined buildings at its heart'. Caught up in the wonderful improbability of it all, he watched a priest solemnly bless eight new pick-up trucks with holy water as the military band struck up vigorous marches in the middle of the square.

As the main door to the rest of the world, Veracruz is imbued with an anything-goes cosmopolitanism, unusual in the rest of Mexico. There's a marked Cuban influence in the strong dark coffee drunk in the cafés, the slurred dropped 's' of the lazy accent and the wide smiles of Afro-Iberian faces. The cliché of Veracruz is constantly self-fulfilling: outstanding kindness, hospitality and bold disregard for solemnity. The people are proud to call themselves *jarochos* (meaning 'shockingly rude'). Renowned throughout Mexico for their outrageously bad language, little old women use paint-stripping obscenities whilst weighing out kilos of oranges, without batting an eyelid.

Though the centre has been largely destroyed and modern shops line the main streets, colonial buildings still hang over the neon-lit shop fronts. The clothes shop, *La Galatea* on Independencia, has a full-blown art-nouveau facade above its display of female underwear. The pier (*malecón*) stretches out beyond the harbour, opening up the town to the fresh airs of the Gulf. Here the citizens of Veracruz perambulate by night, side by side with Nordic sailors in beards and sawn-off shorts, before returning to the main square to sit, drink and dance.

History

The history of Veracruz began in earnest when Hernán Cortés landed on a large, rocky reef opposite what is now the island of San Juan de Ulúa and, after some delay, founded the city of Villa Rica de la Veracruz. Landing on Good Friday and anxious to establish the religious nature of his mission, Cortés chose an appropriate name (meaning 'the true cross') for the city, driving in a symbolic cross to mark the spot. The Spanish were met by Emperor Moctezuma's envoys and given rich presents, including lavish turquoise masks, in case they should turn out to be divinities. Lured by the prospect of more treasure, Cortés and his men soon gathered allies and began the long march inland towards Tenochtitlán.

Although for many years Veracruz was the only port which imperial Spain allowed to operate, in its infancy it was scarcely more than a port of call. Ships were anxious to depart the unhealthy airs and it remained little more than a collection of timbered shacks until the 18th century. Adventurers, including the English privateers John Hawkins and Francis Drake, menaced its harbour. They kept a weather eye on the provisions which a loaded galleon brought from Spain once a year and unofficially bartered stolen African slaves from nearby Cuba. Dutch and French buccaneers weren't slow on the uptake and throughout the 17th century the port was plagued by attack.

Santa Ana, Mexico's most famous anti-hero, was born in Jalapa, Veracruz in the late 18th century. After fighting to help Mexico win independence from Spain, Santa Ana

Traditional dancers from Veracruz

fell foul of his erstwhile colleague, the conservative Agustín Iturbide, self-styled Emperor Agustín I. In a fit of pique Santa Ana swapped sides and joined the liberals and anti-monarchists in Veracruz. In 1822 he rode through the streets at the head of 400 troops: the ensuing revolt forced Iturbide to resign and flee the country.

In 1847, fresh from winning most of northeast Mexico from Santa Ana, the US was anxious to annex California and New Mexico as well. The offensive shifted to Veracruz, Mexico's major port. American General Scott surrounded the city with troops, bombarded it for 48 hours and refused to allow women and children to flee or to countenance a truce. The town was forced to surrender on 27 March 1847. Sixty-seven Americans were killed or wounded whilst dead Mexicans numbered almost 1500, mostly civilians. Scott stormed on to Mexico City, which he took, and forced a treaty whereby California, New Mexico and Texas were officially ceded to the US.

Veracruz had its fair share of invasions. After the French and the US, the combined might of the British, French and Spanish arrived in 1861, to reclaim the debts owed to them by the Mexican government. The French stayed on to install Napoleon III's puppet, Emperor Maximilian, in 1864. Punch-drunk with foreign intrusion, liberal Veracruz was so reluctant to accept this redundant monarch that it shuttered up its doors and windows. The royal couple were given such a cold shoulder that Maximilian's wife, Empress Carlota, was in floods of tears by the time she reached the station. It wasn't just the lack of a magnificent reception (the tawdry welcoming committee arrived late), but the buzzards which circled over the humid malaria-infested town and the flies which covered its dirty streets. It was all a far cry from the civilized Austrian court she had left behind. Brought up in Europe, the couple hadn't the faintest notion of what was in store for them, or any idea that public opinion was strongly against them.

Veracruz dominated national news again, during the Porfiriato, when industrial dissent was beginning to have a fragile voice. A strike at the Río Blanco textile mills in 1906 was a precursor to the later Revolution. Paid less than a subsistence wage, the desperate workers formed a secret union, the *Gran Círculo*, thereby risking immediate dismissal. They took their complaints to President Díaz in person, and his glib dismissal sparked off the strike. Troops were called in: firing point-blank, they killed many women and children, while families who returned in the evening to collect and bury their dead were also shot. Though reports of the event were strictly censored, word spread throughout the nation and the Revolution wasn't long in following.

During the Revolution, the US refused to recognize the undemocratic dictatorship of General Huerta (who had murdered the previous president, Madero), and decided to intervene. Relations were tense when, in 1914, the US consul in Veracruz signalled that a German ship was about to dock, filled with arms for Huerta. The North Americans occupied the harbour, killing over a hundred Mexicans, including many women and children. The Mexican congress was outraged and even its opponents expressed their horror. Nonetheless, the US continued to blockade the port, stopping all revenues. With pressure from Pancho Villa in the north and Zapata in the south, Huerta realized that his time was up and resigned on 8 July.

The insecurity of the open port and the insalubrious climate didn't encourage people to settle and build permanent homes. The houses were originally built with timbers from Cortés' ships: apart from the hospital and the fort, the first stone wasn't laid until the 18th century. Grass grew in the streets after the wars of independence, when whole

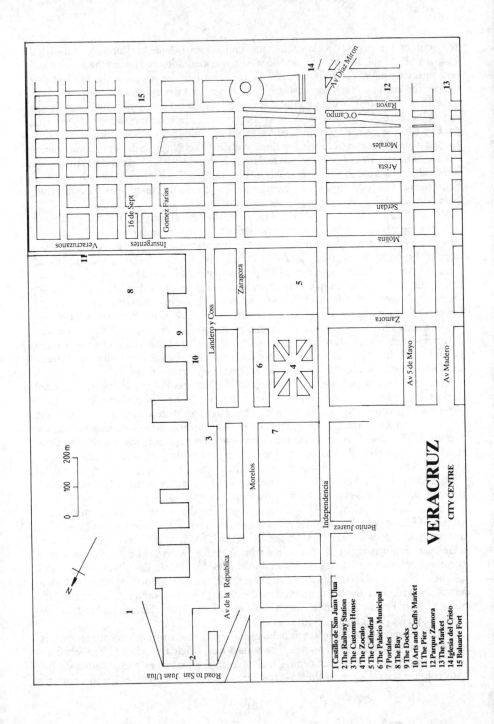

VERACRUZ
CITY CENTRE

1 Castillo de San Juan Ulua
2 The Railway Station
3 The Customs House
4 The Zocalo
5 The Cathedral
6 The Palacio Municipal
7 Portales
8 The Bay
9 The Docks
10 Arts and Crafts Market
11 The Pier
12 Parque Zamora
13 The Market
14 Iglesia del Cristo
15 Baluarte Fort

families evacuated the town for safety. By the mid-19th century, the central government wanted to abandon the port as the docks were in such disrepair. They couldn't find a suitable alternative, however, and so it soldiered on. As a result, Veracruz, the first city to be founded by the Spaniards, tumbled into the 20th century with remarkably few of its original features.

GETTING AROUND

By Air: The airport (tel 370417) is 12 km southwest of town, off Highway 140. Combis and taxis meet every flight. Mexicana and Aeroméxico run six flights daily to and from Mexico City.

By Bus: The first- (tel 376790) and second-class (tel 372376) bus stations are back to back in the south of town on Diáz Mirón. Buses from Iglesia del Cristo at the western end of Independencia go down Diáz Mirón and drop passengers at the bus stations.

Long-distance buses connect Veracruz with all parts of the country. There are frequent daily services to and from Mexico City (7 hrs), Poza Rica (4 hrs), Villahermosa (8 hrs), Jalapa (3 hrs), the Tuxtlas (4 hrs) and Mérida (18 hrs). (Buses to Veracruz from Mexico City leave from the TAPO terminal: San Lazaro metro on the pink line).

Local buses leave the centre (Zaragoza and Serdán) every half-hour for a hot ride past the faded pastels of clapboard houses to the Villa del Mar beach and on to Mocambo and Boca del Río (20 mins).

By Car: Highway 150 from Mexico City (433 km) and Puebla (301 km) joins the main coastal Highway 180, south of Veracruz. Along the coast, Poza Rica is 255 km northwest and Villahermosa 480 km southeast. Oaxaca is 383 km due south (Highways 175/180).

Taxis have a cheap fixed tariff, one price for anywhere in town (tel 346299). Check with the tourist office for the going rate. For **car hire**, Budget, 5 de Mayo and Lerdo (tel 312769), is as fiendishly expensive as everywhere else.

By Train: The railway station is north of the Zócalo on Plaza de la República. Trains between Mexico City and Veracruz run twice daily in both directions and take 10 hours. Overnight sleepers are comfortable and inexpensive, leaving both cities at 21.30. All journeys should be booked at least a week in advance by going to the railway station and buying a ticket.

Local trains make daily trips to Jalapa, Fortín de las Flores and Córdoba.

TOURIST INFORMATION

The office is in the Palacio Municipal on the main square (tel 329942). They claim plaintively that they spent all their money 'helping' elect the current president, and are thus unwilling to let go of maps, but they are good on travel timetables.

WHAT TO DO

Head straight for **La Parroquia** café, off the main square in Independencia, where you should forget the idea of sightseeing altogether. Here, in the heady confusion under spasmodically whirring fans, the exuberant atmosphere makes eating an optional extra. Between 8 and 9 in the morning, businessmen and politicians uniformly dressed in *guayabera* shirts have impassioned discussions over glasses of coffee. The tiled walls, mosaic floor and wickerwork wooden seats resound to the tinkle of glasses being tapped to attract the attention of flurried waiters. Finally a steaming kettle arrives and frothy milk is poured from a great height into an inch of coffee in the glass below. All around shoes are being cleaned and lottery tickets sold to old-timers sitting at regular tables reading *Dictamen*—the local paper and the oldest in the republic. Outside, military bands and marimba players compete to drown with sound.

In the main square itself is the modest cathedral, also known as **La Parroquia** (meaning parish church). Considerably less famous than the café which bears its name, it contains little of note and watches resignedly as the square gets more and more *louche* by night. The portals opposite are filled with tables where sea-weary sailors swill beers cheek by jowl with exquisitely made-up transvestites. Russians converse in faltering Spanish with Swedes. At least ten different bands play at the same time and all around Mexican couples burst into spontaneous hip-swings of dance.

With so much happening in the streets, museums aren't Veracruz's strongest point. The main archaeology and history museum is the **Museo Cultural** (Zaragoza and Morales, open 10.00–14.00 and 16.00–18.00). It's user-friendly with lots to look at but not much to digest, from the Olmecs and Toltecs through Santa Ana to blown-up photographs of the multiracial faces which can be seen in the streets today. The colour of the carnival is recreated in a room filled with larger-than-life papier mâché models of costumed participants.

Continuing down Zaragoza, take one block left into Coss for the **Casa de la Cultura** (open all day), where an old convent and hospital has been painted cornflower blue and filled with temporary exhibitions. At the back there's a large garden where regional music known as *son* is scratched on fiddles and scraped on the jawbones of cattle. Well-known bands like *Siquisiri* and *Mono Blanco* often come to play dance rhythms in the evenings.

San Juan de Ulúa

One km northeast of town, the fort of San Juan de Ulúa is built on an island resting on a coral reef, joined to the mainland by a causeway (open Tues–Sun 10.00–17.00; adm). Buses marked San Juan de Ulúa pass the western edge of the Zócalo on Zaragoza every 15 minutes.

This was the last piece of Mexican land that Spain surrendered in 1825 when giving Mexico her independence. It was also one of the first pieces of territory that a Spaniard touched, over 300 years earlier, when Cortés landed. Once entirely made of white coral, it has now been bolstered up by red brick and stucco but the contorted shapes of the coral plant still make up most of the walls. San Juan de Ulúa was the customs house for every bit of trading with Spain throughout the colonial era and was expanded into a fort in the 18th century to defend Veracruz from British pirate attacks. Two 19th-century presidents, Juárez and Santa Ana, were imprisoned here: Juárez later returned, using it briefly as his presidential palace. It was renowned for the filth of its dungeons under the Porfiriato, and President Venustiano Carranza finally closed it in 1915. Since then it has become a favourite haunt of film crews: the *Count of Monte Cristo* used it as a backdrop and the crew of *Romancing the Stone* left behind the thick wooden doors at the entrance to the fort.

Boca del Río

Twelve km south of town, where a confluence of rivers finally meets the sea, the suburb of Boca del Río devotes itself to the preparation of an endless variety of seafood. Shrimps from Alvarado and stuffed crabs (*jaiba rellenos*) are served in waterfront cafés or in large breezy restaurants. Quintets play whilst a young couple dance to *La Bamba*, tapping out the steps on a tiled floor. Groups of singers perform *decimos* (ten-line poems) made up on the spot about whomever they are singing to. **Pardino**, in the centre, is the best restaurant and always popular. Moderate. Cafés on the waterfront at the far end of town are cheaper and quieter.

BEACHES
For proper stretches of beach, see Chachalacas (under North to La Antigua and Zempoala). The straggles of sand around town are better for dipping in a toe whilst sipping a beer. The bay in town is taken up by a large pier and sweating international tankers. Three km further south, the **Villa del Mar** beach is popular with families and frisbee players. Seven km further on, **Mocambo** has been better organized with municipal swimming pools and sunshades.

CARNIVAL
Four days before Lent, the streets fill with floats, fireworks and fancifully dressed transvestites. A hectic jumble of humanity takes over the squares and the party winds itself up to a frenzy before fizzling out, exhausted, on Ash Wednesday. Get to a table in the main square by midday for a ringside seat.

DANCING IN THE STREET
On Sunday evenings the Parque Ciriaco Vasques, southwest of the main square, fills with *jarochos* of every age, who have come to dance like strutting peacocks until the small hours of the morning. The regional dance of Veracruz, *danzón*, arrived from Andalucia and Africa via Cuba getting faster and headier en route. It's serious stuff. Older men wearing crisp, white *guayabera* shirts, pressed linen trousers and shiny patent-leather shoes lead out women clothed in bright Sunday best. A master of ceremonies masterminds the almost continuous music and the dancing begins. Couples look solemn enough to be attending a funeral, though under a frozen torso and poker face, legs and hips gyrate frantically to the furious beat. The music stops and the men look bored, whilst women fan themselves nonchalantly. Only the novice hints at exertion or enjoyment. The dance is all the more passionate for this icy repression. Foreigners are tolerated and even danced with, providing they observe the greatest of solemnity. It's hard to keep the flicker of a smile off one's face whilst surrounded by such an orgy of rhythm, but it's an evening which shouldn't be missed. The same people gather to dance in the busier main square on Friday evenings. Alternatives on a Sunday are: the Villa del Mar beach, where there are performances of salsa and cumbia all through the afternoon and evening, and Parque Zamora, at the end of Independencia off Rayón, where there's more *danzón* from 18.00 to 21.00.

WHERE TO STAY (area code 29)
Veracruz has a superabundance of hotels for the sailors, cruise-ship passengers, oil magnates and tourists who all want beds for the night. There are a number of hotels in the main square for those who want a slice of the action. The birds start singing when the marimba players stop, so it's better for night owls. More peaceful rooms can be found off centre and down on the beaches.

On the Square

The smartest hotel is the peaceful *****Veracruz in Independencia (tel 312233, tlx 151812) with seven floors of modern rooms, a soothing sauna and a swimming pool. The dilapidated ***Gran Hotel Diligencias dominates the main square in Independencia (tel 322967). It claims to be the oldest hotel in Mexico, but they've modernized the rooms and whitewashed over most of its original character. The ***Colonial (Lerdo 117 on the main square, tel 320193) has a smart tiled lobby with cheerful mosaic walls and is done up in 1980s colonial. The ***Prendes (Independencia 1064, tel 311741) has a hopeful smart lobby but very variable rooms upstairs. Those looking onto the square have been remodelled with big bathrooms and given four stars. The others are more modest and cost less.

The best of the worst is the (CE) Rex in an ex-Franciscan convent, reputedly undermined by tunnels which the monks used for escape during religious persecution. It is in Morelos, opposite the Customs House and a Porfirian twinset of buildings—the Telegrafos and Correos. The rooms are huge and basic and there is only one shared bathroom. Women on their own may be considered competition by the local prostitutes. The *Imperial (Lerdo 153, on the main square, tel 311741) gives itself a fictitious two stars though the rooms reached by a dangerous open lift are small and poky. Don't be fooled by the charming if peeling courtyard: it should only be used as a last resort.

Off Centre

The best is ***Hotel Baluarte (Canal 265 and 16 de Septiembre, tel 360844), a good economical family hotel by the port and only a 5-minute walk from the centre. *Hotel Ulisses (no tel) behind the bus station is wonderfully cheap and clean and an easy bus or taxi ride away from the centre. For the price you'll be given a scraggy towel, a quiet fan and a bathroom with hot water. Locals play dominoes and eat squid in the restaurant Rogue below.

On the boulevard leading south to Mocambo there is a mass of more expensive beach-front hotels, of which the ****Hostal de Cortés (Avila Camacho and Bartolomé de las Casas, tel 320065) is the most functional. Further down on Mocambo beach is the traditional *****Mocambo (Ruíz Cortínes, tel 371661). Its ageing process has been speeded up by the salty Veracruz air but it has matured gracefully. The rooms are large and light and the terrace is lined with rocking chairs overlooking the Gulf. There is an unintimidating pot-holed tennis court and a large swimming pool. This is where the British consul and other minor dignitaries home in. The Boca del Río bus drops passengers off at the door.

WHERE TO EAT

Veracruz consumes quantities of seafood and exotic tropical fruit. *Guanábana, chirimoya,* mamey and *chico zapote* are all used for preparing ices and defy description: taste and see. The good coffee for which it's famed comes from Oaxtepec and the delicate chocolate and vanilla sweets from Papantla. Tamales are another regional speciality (tortilla dough cooked in banana leaves and flavoured with an anise-like leaf called *hoja santa*). In Veracruz they are often filled with fish. The sauce made from tomato, olives, capers and chillies is known all over Mexico as *a la veracruzana*. Influences from Africa, Spain and France have also blown in with successive invasions. Try the *chilpachole de jaiba* (crab soup cooked up with garlic and chilli), and *mondongo de frutas* (mangoes, mamey, pineapple or whatever fruit the kitchen has to hand, often capped by iced sorbet).

Breakfasts of long coffees and omelettes or *pan dulce* are best had in **La Parroquia** (see above), either by the cathedral or in the new expansive branch by the pier (Insurgentes 340, tel 322584) which is only open in the afternoon onwards and is always filled to the brim with everyone and anyone. The **Café la Rueda** under the Hotel Diligencias is good for seafood, especially *pulpo con salsa marinera* (squid fried in garlic and olives). Graham Greene got blind drunk here before embarking on what subsequently became the worst journey of his life in a tub to Villahermosa (see *The Lawless Roads*). Inexpensive. The **Prendes** is renowned for its good daily comida corrida and its *filete relleno* (fish filled with seafood). Moderate. Under the portals opposite the cathedral a mass of small cafés wrestle for space. Here people sip coffees, beers and tequilas 24 hours a day. This area is liveliest at night and is renowned for the prostitutes of both sexes who perambulate past to solicit clients. *Chicote* (Lerdo 71, tel 322174) specializes in steaming frying pans of traditionally cooked paella. Inexpensive. *Samborcito* (16 de Septiembre), near the Hotel Baluarte, specializes in simple regional food like *gordas* (beans and maize rolled together and fried in oil) or *picadas* (tortillas filled with fresh cheese and covered in a spicy tomato sauce). Inexpensive.

Further out, **El Gaucho** (Bernal Diáz del Castillo 187, tel 350411) in Colón off Blvd Camacho, just past Viajes Olymar, is the bourgeoisie's evening version of La Parroquia. Here families, courting couples and businessmen come for Argentinian cookery. It's done up in modern colonial, with bullfights constantly shown on television. The waiters are run off their feet serving up jugs of *jerico*, a sangria drink. The menu concentrates on grilled meats and Hereford ribs but also does a weighty *tortilla de espinaca con camarón* (an enormous omelette of cheese, fresh-water shrimps and Popeye spinach). The Italian influence in Argentina means big bowls of pesto on the tables and dishes like *ravioles de ricotta con nuez* (ravioli filled with cheese and nuts). Moderate. There's a vegetarian restaurant, **El Profeta**, in the Parque Ciriaco Vasques, where the dancing takes place on Sunday evenings.

North to La Antigua and Zempoala

The sleepy hamlet of La Antigua, where Cortés' built his first house, and Zempoala, the little-visited remains of a Totonac city where he and his troops were reluctantly entertained, are both a pleasant day trip from Veracruz. As an antidote to these historical sites, there are wide swathes of empty beach at **Chachalacas** to relax on.

GETTING AROUND

Highway 180 leads north from Veracruz and the turn-off for La Antigua (20 km) is marked just before the beginning of the toll road. The road continues to Cardel (12 km) where there are signs to the right for Chachalacas. Continuing from Cardel, Zempoala is a further 15 km north. There are regular second-class buses to Zempoala from Veracruz via Antigua and Cardel and also from Jalapa. Ancient buses are always waiting in Cardel (a big junction) to take passengers to Chachalacas.

La Antigua

This small village of whitewashed houses straddles the banks of the River Antigua. Its streets are cobbled and overhung with mamey, mango and zapote fruit trees. During the week there's nothing going on but the odd scratching hen or grandmother patting tortillas. People come up from Veracruz for long lunches of seafood in one of the cafés which spill onto the street, under the shade of the leafy trees. Cortés founded the original Veracruz here, but later abandoned it for the beaches of the present port. A gnarled silk-cotton tree leans precariously by the river and locals swear blind that Cortés tied one of his boats to it.

Chachalacas

The toll road continues to Cardel, where buses wait to take passengers on to Chachalacas (10 km). Bear right and follow signs to the isolated Barra de Chachalacas or La Playita for an endless stretch of Gulf beach and enormous sand dunes (which can be explored by dune buggies rented out by the hotels). A number of small hotels cater for escapees from Veracruz. The best is the ***Chachalacas (tel 296 20241) with good big rooms and, their pride, 13 swimming pools (more like paddling pools).

Zempoala

The village of Zempoala (also spelt Cempoala) is signed to the left, 4 km off Highway 180. Buses and taxis wait at the road end. The once-glorious Totonac city of Zempoala has fallen into a sad state of disrepair. Present-day villagers are happy to ignore the site and play baseball in and around the ruins. These aren't signed: a track to the right, just before the village, leads to a small white building which serves as both ticket office and cupboard-sized museum.

History

During the post-Classic era (AD 900–1500), a number of rich Totonac cities sprang up in the Gulf region, of which the largest was Zempoala. Shortly after the Spaniards landed on the beach facing the island of San Juan de Ulúa, the site of modern Veracruz, they were invited by Quatlachana, chief of Zempoala, to visit his city. When they first arrived, they mistakenly thought the gleaming white-washed walls were made of silver. Cortés finally persuaded Quatlachana to become his first ally against the Aztecs, of whom the Totonacs were reluctant vassals. Quatlachana had used his obesity as an excuse for being unable to travel to meet Cortés and was immortalized by Cortés' companion Bernal Díaz as the 'fat cacique'. To make up for this slight he gave Cortés a couple of Totonac princesses as wives. One of these, his niece, was as unattractive as her uncle, though Cortés tactically 'received her with a show of pleasure'.

Anxious to appear to be colonizing the New World in the name of Christianity rather than out of lust for gold, Cortés ordered every sacred Totonac idol to be pulled down and destroyed. The bewildered Totonacs, for fear of both the Aztecs and the Spaniards, could only stand by and watch. Then, to add insult to injury, Cortés persuaded the terrified chief to imprison five Aztec tax gatherers who arrived to exact a heavy tribute. The wily Cortés secretly released two of them under cover of night and sent them back to Moctezuma with his best wishes, disclaiming any responsibilty for their incarceration.

When the Zempoalans discovered the escape of the two tax collectors, they were terrified of Aztec vengeance. It was at this point that they agreed to join Cortés against the Aztecs, feeling that they now had little to lose.

Their patience was tried further when, the next year, rival Spanish troops led by Pánfilo de Narváez arrived from Cuba to challenge Cortés' dominion. They met him in Zempoala and the ensuing battle wreaked havoc on the foundations of the city. The opposing Spanish forces then decided to cut their losses and unite to march on the Aztecs. The Totonacs loyally stuck to their alliance, but the city had had its day. The damage caused by the warring Spanish, epidemics and exploitation by conquistadors, who enslaved most of the population, meant that it was abandoned to the jungle by the 17th century.

VISITING THE SITE

Zempoala was a late developer and didn't rise to prominence until about AD 1200. It was built for defence, with large walls surrounding its ceremonial centre. The main temple (Templo Mayor), opposite the entrance, has a double staircase leading up to a crenel-lated terrace surrounded by battlements. Cortés entrenched himself here when fighting Pánfilo de Narváez. To the right, the Temple of Chimneys (Templo de las Chimeneas), where Cortés and his troops stayed, has a square altar outside. Beyond this, across the fields, a construction with an open stairway used to be ornamented inside and out with rows of clay skulls—hence its name, Temple of the Little Faces (Templo de las Caritas). It still has the fading remains of paintings representing the sun, moon and evening star. Back past Templo Mayor and the baseball pitch, the remains of the round Temple of Ehecatl, God of Wind, are attached to a five-tiered rectangular base. The small circular buildings in front of the temples were altars and pools for ceremonial ablutions. Every building is coordinated by the use of stepped merlons on top.

WHERE TO STAY AND EAT

The village has nothing more than a couple of cafés and a modest hotel, the **Principal** (Av Hidalgo 48, tel 34).

The Northern Gulf Coast

From the port of Veracruz to the state's northern border with Tamaulipas, there is only a thin slither of land between the Sierra Madre Oriental and the Gulf of Mexico. Rainfall is high as the mountains meet the plains. Rivers run down from the hills and fall into the sea, irrigating the rich agricultural land along the way. Between Veracruz and Poza Rica, Highway 180 clings to the coast with lagoons and sand dunes the only barrier to the Gulf.

Some 260 km from Veracruz is the ancient and rarely visited site of El Tajín with its unique Pyramid of Niches, surrounded by vanilla and banana plantations. The nearby village of Papantla, the centre for the dance of the flying men, makes a good place to stop. Oil refineries have blighted Poza Rica and much of the rest of the coast, with cataclysmic effect upon the environment but enormous benefit to the Mexican economy.

Papantla

Papantla is the closest town to El Tajín. A Totonac centre for vanilla and coffee growing, it is an excellent base for visiting the ruins. In the Zócalo, grey, black and brown squirrels race from branch to branch, overlooked by the cathedral on one side and the small Hidalgo market on the other. The Totonacs wear loose shirts over white cotton trousers, tapering in at the ankle, with black high-heeled ankle boots underneath. The larger market on Juárez sells these cool, cotton clothes alongside the vanilla pods for which the town is renowned. *Vanilla planifolia*, which grows all around Papantla, is a member of the orchid family. The actual flavouring, called vanillin, is a crystallized substance which forms on the pendulous bunches of green fruit and provides the base of vanilla essence.

GETTING AROUND

Papantla slopes uphill from Highway 180, 230 km (3 hrs) north of Veracruz and 16 km (20 mins) south of Poza Rica.

The ADO bus station is on Juárez 207 (tel 202018), on the far side of Highway 180. To reach the Zócalo from here, cross the highway, walk up Juárez to Enríquez, and turn right.

First-class ADO buses run daily services to and from Veracruz (4 hrs, 4 daily), Villahermosa (9 hrs, 1 daily), Poza Rica (20 mins, 10 daily), and Jalapa (4 hrs, 8 daily).

When leaving Papantla by bus, it's best to book in advance. (If the bus is full when it arrives, it won't stop.) Alternatively, leave from the station in Poza Rica which carries more clout.

Local buses for El Tajín or Tecolutla use a separate station nearer the centre of town, one block below the Zócalo on 20 de Noviembre.

THE DANCE OF THE VOLADORES

The town is famous for the dance of the *voladores* or flying men: of all the dances in Mexico, it is the most haunting, the most agonizing and the most beautiful. It is performed for Tonatiuh, God of the Sun in the Totonac pantheon, the source of energy and creation.

The dancers dress in white shirts, red trousers and conical hats decorated with round mirrors (to reflect the rays of the sun) and long, coloured ribbons. Five men climb up a pole, about 30 m tall, pulling themselves up by ropes to rest on a narrow platform. One man stands to play a haunting flute-song, the 'Song of Forgiveness', on five-tone reeds, turning to each cardinal point to make obeisance to the sun. Meanwhile, the other four dancers tie long ropes around their waists, secure them to their ankles and hurl themselves headfirst from the platform, spiralling in ever-increasing circles around the pole, towards the ground. Just as they are about to reach the earth, they flip themselves upright and land on their feet.

FESTIVAL

The town's main festival, with performances by the *voladores*, is Corpus Christi in May.

WHERE TO STAY
(area code 784)

There are only three small hotels in town and during Corpus Christi week there are no spare beds to be had for love or money. The best of these is the ****Tajín** (to the left of the church, Nuñez y Dominguez 104, tel 20121), with lovely views over the square and the countryside beyond, and a good restaurant. Its 1940 exterior is painted a swimming-pool blue. The tacky **Totonacapan (20 de Noviembre, tel 21220), by the main road, has a relentless disco attached. The *Papantla (Enríquez 103, tel 20080), on the Zócalo, has big, bare rooms with old hospital beds and high ceilings.

If these are full, it may be worth driving 35 km south to the tiny resort of Tecolutla. Turn off Highway 180 at Gutiérrez Zamora and follow the pitted road east. The Balneario Tecolutla (Matamoros, tel 27) is a large spa hotel on the beach, with rocking chairs set out along the terrace and around the swimming pool. There are a few more hotels in Tecolutla and various seafood cafés, of which the Cabaña del Pescador is the best.

EATING OUT
The choice isn't large. The Tajín's restaurant serves big platefuls of *carne a la tampiqueña* (steak with beans, fried bananas, avocado and cheese). Moderate. Underneath the cinema, Las Canastas offers wild rabbit grilled with garlic (a regional favourite). Inexpensive. Evening dances are sometimes held in the Zócalo and a good place to watch them from is the terrace café Terrazza, by the town hall (the entrance is through the door on the Zócalo marked 'Foto Felipe'). For breakfast, the Tajín café and bakery (Calle Nuñoz, leading off the Zócalo) provides freshly baked sweet breads that automatically come with a tall glass of frothy coffee.

El Tajín

> These stones are alive and dancing ... El Tajín is neither petrified
> motion nor time suspended. It is geometry dancing; undulation; rhythm
> ... midway between Teotihuacán severity and Maya opulence.

So wrote Octavio Paz, the Mexican Nobel Prize-winning poet, about this unique, out-of-the-way site with its extraordinary niched pyramid, like a six-layered wedding cake or monumental beehive. Light plays with shadow as the sun hits it from different angles throughout the day, dancing from inverted niches to protruding cornices, and giving the whole mass a wave-like movement. Few tourists visit distant El Tajín and it preserves an air of eerie mystery, as if it is still waiting to be discovered by the modern world.

GETTING AROUND
El Tajín is 12 km west of Papantla—a 30-minute journey via two local buses, along bumpy back roads. The blue Jaloapan bus drops passengers off at the El Chote junction (8 km) and a Poza Rica bus covers the 4 km to the Coca-Cola sign outside the site. It is easy to hitch from El Chote.

History
In a lush tropical valley, dotted with hillocks and banana trees, El Tajín has been shrouded in the mysteries of its invisibility, hidden under thick forest until a Spanish

official, searching for illegal tobacco plantations, stumbled over it in 1785. Once the city stretched over hundreds of acres, but only the core has been uncovered since work began in 1934.

The Olmecs introduced the complicated ceremonial ball game to El Tajín, as in the Gulf plains further south. At the height of its power, the city may well have been a centre for these games, equivalent to Olympia in Greece. The site had at least 11 ball courts, and intricately carved stone yokes, axes and *palmas* (all associated with the game) were found in quantities. El Tajín was completed by AD 600 and was certainly occupied throughout the Classic period (AD 300–900), although by whom is not clear: there were Huastecs and Otomí in the area at the time, its style was influenced by the Maya in the southeast and Teotihuacán in the southwest, and the Totonacs were there at the time of the Spanish conquest. However, there is no evidence that any of these groups actually masterminded the building. The Totonacs have the strongest association with the place today because they live in large numbers all around and perform their sacred dance at the ruins during the Corpus Christi festival. They also named it El Tajín, after their God of Thunder, Lightning and Rain.

VISITING THE SITE
(Open daily 09.00–18.00; adm.)

MUSEUM
The museum is no more than a shed, with several fine friezes along the wall and a lugubrious collection of pickled snakes found in the ruins. Its one glory is a stone slab from the Classic period, intertwined with serpents decorated with quetzal plumes which coil around ball-court markers. On each side two noblemen and their servants stand to attention.

SOUTH BALL COURT
The entrance to the site, south of the partly excavated Plaza del Arroyo, leads north into the Lower Plaza where there are several low rectangular structures, once painted red and blue. On the left is the southern ball court (measuring 60 m by 10 m). Of the 11 ball courts, this is the best preserved. The six exquisite bas-relief panels on the walls tell a story of gladiatorial combat, gambling and sacrifice. The first two panels show, on the left, a young warrior being initiated into the rites of the game, counterpointed, on the right, by a human sacrifice, overlooked by expectant death gods. The two central panels are lighter in subject, dominated by pulque-induced states of intoxication, a common theme with the Huastecs, often expressed in the smiling or ecstatically grinning faces of their sculptures. (Pulque is a raw, alcoholic drink, distilled from the maguey cactus and given no time to be refined.) The furthest two panels also depict initiation or conse-cration ceremonies. On the left, a young warrior stretched out on a bench is instilled with the power of the sunbird who hovers over him with his wings outspread. Opposite, another warrior addresses a group of priests or gods.

PYRAMID OF THE NICHES
The northern wall of the ball court doubles up as the southern wall of Monument V, a temple surmounting a platform guarded by a chiselled statue of a god. Behind it is the

unmistakable Pyramid of the Niches. It is built on six tiers, which surround a central solid core. The tiers are hollow, and each is studded around its four sides with once-crimson window-like openings. Originally, the pyramid was stuccoed over in peacock-blue, to add depth and contrast to the recessed red niches. When it was complete, there were 365 niches—one for each day of the pre-Hispanic calendar (more accurate than the Gregorian calendar used in Europe). A wide staircase with a balustrade on either side leads to the top but, for conservation reasons, no-one is allowed to clamber up.

EL TAJIN CHICO
North of the Pyramid of the Niches, away from the entrance, is a smaller ball court also decorated with bas-relief panels on the walls. One shows an animal midway between an armadillo and a tortoise, in a sacrifice scene. Above this, on an artificially raised platform, stands a series of palace-like buildings, constructed in the late-Classic period. The northernmost building in the group, Structure A, is rectangular with a corbelled (flat arched) doorway, characteristic of the Maya. All the buildings are decorated with geometrical motifs and key patterns in a stepped fret design. Above the complex, at the end of an overgrown path that leads uphill to the northwest, is the **Building of the Columns**. The remaining drums of the columns, decorated with processions of warriors and noblemen, would once have made up a gallery running along the front of the building. Other drums have been laid out beside the car park, awaiting reconstruction.

The Oil Coast

Poza Rica
Sixteen km (20 mins) north of El Tajín, Poza Rica is a hideous sprawl of unplanned growth, awake 24 hours a day with juggernauts charging up and down the pot-holed streets and balls of fire from gas burn-offs lighting up the sky. In their hurry to put up oil works, the developers left no room for a centre and what life there is pustulates around the ADO bus station and market on Av Ruíz Córtines. The hotels are all commercial, abused and bruised from the constant stream of would-be oil magnates checking in and out in a hurry. The bus station is a useful and important junction for bus routes running inland or north–south along the coast, but don't expect any more from Poza Rica.

Tuxpan
It gets no better further north. Once charming, Tuxpan (70 km north of El Tajín and 190 km south of Tampico) has recently had a power station constructed on its long beach and no longer rates a visit. Originally a Huastec settlement and later used by the conquering Aztecs as a garrison, it is now suffering a more popular invasion—the oil boom.

Jalapa and the West

Western Veracruz is dominated by the jagged spine of the Sierra Madre Oriental. Pico de Orizaba or Citlaltépetl, Mexico's highest volcanic mountain (5700 m), lies almost due west of the port, and its sharp peak, covered in snow, can be seen for miles. The rolling green foothills below are covered in coffee plantations and fields of flowers, the two local staples. The old towns of Jalapa, Fortín de las Flores, Orizaba and Córdoba were once the domain of rich coffee merchants and continue to prosper quietly.

Jalapa

Known as the Athens of Mexico, this unassuming state capital is set high up in the hills of the Cerro de Macuiltépec, to the northwest of Veracruz. In the centre its paved streets wind around slopes revealing quick glimpses of the ice-capped Citlaltépetl. The cooler contemplative air encourages academia, theatre and the arts in general. It's famed for its free-thinking university and its anthropology museum. Gone is the vivid street life of the coast and in its place are steamy cafés filled with students and bearded lecturers in John Lennon glasses. Dance companies on tour often explode into impromptu performances in the central squares. Even Swedes and Germans, enrolled at one of the many language schools, cautiously throw off their native *froideur* and become more Latin every day. Everywhere unruly flowers escape from the gardens of elegant colonial houses.

GETTING AROUND

By Bus: The first-class bus station is northwest of the centre on the main road in from Mexico City, under the Hotel Jalapa (Camacho 84). Buses run to and from Veracruz every half-hour (2½ hrs), and to and from Mexico City every hour (4½ hrs). Regular buses also go to Coatepec, Orizaba, Fortín de las Flores, Poza Rica, Puebla, Córdoba, Villahermosa and the Tuxtlas.

By Car: Jalapa is 99 km northwest of Veracruz on Highway 140, which continues westwards for Puebla and Mexico City. A much more circuitous but beautiful route between Jalapa and Veracruz leads south through the mountains via Córdoba (see South of Jalapa).

TOURIST INFORMATION

The tourist office is by the Hotel Salmones on Zaragoza (tel 73030). The staff speak good English as they're used to language students. It is closed at weekends.

WHAT TO SEE

In the heart of town, next to the carefully kept gardens of Parque Juárez, the **cathedral**, built in 1772, clings to the land, with an unusual slope uphill to the altar. Its gothic arches and stained-glass windows betray an Anglo-Saxon influence. Jalapa came into its own in the 18th century as the site of the only annual fair held to barter goods from galleons newly arrived from Spain. This attracted merchants from all over the country and the cathedral was built to celebrate its new-found importance. Just below the prim Parque Juárez is the long stretch of **Parque Paseo de los Lagos**, where lavender jacaranda trees surround a small lake. Here a **Casa de Artesanías** sells uninspired local work like bamboo furniture and gaudily embroidered dresses, but is redeemed by a good selection of work from all over Mexico, including ceramics from Oaxaca and purses from San Cristóbal.

The Anthropology Museum
(Av Jalapa and 1 Mayo; open 09.00–17.00; adm.)
Jalapa's modern Anthropology Museum is deservedly the pride of the state, providing an outstanding introduction to the civilizations of the Gulf coast, from the northeast of the state to Tabasco. The Tesoreria bus from the centre heads north to Av Jalapa, taking at least a quarter of an hour. (Make sure to keep mouthing 'Museo de Antropologia' at the driver as it is easy to miss).

The museum has 29,000 pieces but shows only 3000. Colossal Olmec heads sit sagely in the entrance and from here the museum is arranged on a gradually descending series of levels, devoted to the Olmec, the Huastec and the Totonac civilizations.

The Olmecs were the Greeks of Mesoamerica. By 1800 BC, they were fashioning sculptures and carving jade, building temples and incising the enigmatic basalt heads for which they are best remembered. Their influence and style can be traced through every subsequent culture. Each of the enormous Olmec heads is quite distinct, but all share the same negroid nose, wide lips, round head, slow slanting eyes and tightly fitting cap.

At the beginning of the second level is the famous jade sculpture of **the Priest of Lima**—once stolen but finally traced and retrieved from the lobby of a hotel in Texas. The dignified priest has a typically feline Olmec mouth. He sits cross-legged, carefully holding a child who wears a diadem with a symbol of the Sun God.

The third and fourth levels are devoted to the Classic period (AD 300–800) of the central Gulf plains, including finds from the northern site of El Tajín. The collection concentrates on ceramics, in particular terra-cotta figures with ecstatic smiling faces, grinning like Cheshire cats, their heads supported only by a tiny dancing body underneath. Associated with dancing, music and the sun, they seem intoxicated and intoxicating.

The post-Classic Huastec collection is on the last level, where a mass of squashed skulls provides grim evidence of cranial and dental deformation. One of the most important pieces is that of **Xipe Totec**, God of Fertility, who wears the flayed skin of a sacrificial victim. An elaborate ceremony was held every year at which an unfortunate youth was given the honour of wearing this flayed skin until it rotted off. His young body would then emerge like new corn from an old husk. The collection also includes several *ixquintles*, ceramic representations of the dogs who crossed the River of Death with the Huastecs.

Each level leads out into a small botanical garden, filled with sculpture and suffused with peace, scent and colour, providing plenty of space to sit and think. The guides are usually anthropologists and a full tour takes 2 hours. The tour is free though a voluntary contribution is always appreciated (and expected).

The Hacienda of El Lencero
(Open Tues–Sun, 10.00–17.00; adm.)
One of the best-preserved haciendas in Mexico, El Lencero is a 5-minute journey by local bus or taxi along flower-lined Highway 140, east of Jalapa. The turn-off to the right is marked by a white signpost.

The country retreat of Santa Ana (1794–1876), it is the only remaining monument to this most ambivalent of all Mexican anti-heroes. Despite being president on eleven occasions, and responsible for saving the country from several foreign invasions, he nevertheless managed to lose Texas, Arizona and New Mexico to the US and to be exiled almost as many times as he was president. Mexico's answer to Napoleon, he was the most extravagant of all 19th-century figures, whose real pleasures were cock fighting and horse riding.

In the chapel here he married his second wife, the 15-year-old Dolores Tosta, who rarely returned to the tropical hacienda. The gardens are full of fig trees, bougainvillea, jacarandas and ancient laurel trees. The house is beautifully restored, with canopy beds (including Santa Ana's own, emblazoned with an eagle on the headboard), parquet floors and elegant treasures from Spain and France. So few of Mexico's haciendas have survived its wars and revolutions that El Lencero is unusual—restored and yet not a hotel.

Coatepec

A pungent smell of coffee fills the air in Coatepec, a small village with cobbled streets, 15 km (20 mins) south of Jalapa. In the heart of the coffee-growing region, it is well worth a visit, to buy or even just taste some of its freshly ground coffee. **Café Andreade** (Juárez 54, tel 62539), behind the main square, serves coffee on Lilliput-sized tables and sawn-off barrels. In the same street, **Casa Bonilla** is a simple restaurant with rickety tables haphazardly strung over an airy courtyard. The fish is delicious. The village is full of weekenders but empty during the week.

WHERE TO STAY   (area code 281)
The ******Xalapa** (on Victoria above the ADO station, tel 82222), high up with a good view of the volcano, is government-owned, modern and efficient, with a swimming pool. Its inexpensive café boasts an award-winning chef who produces dishes like *codorniz* (quail) cooked with *huitlacoche* (an indescribably delicious matured corn with a taste of mushroom). *****Salmones** (Zaragoza, one block behind the cathedral) is an older colonial-style hotel with its own modest restaurant, central and pleasantly run. The ****México** on the main square (Dr Lucio, no tel) has good, modest rooms and a pretty tiled café where Jalapans prefer to eat.

EATING OUT
Apart from the hotels, there are two excellent up-market restaurants. **La Casa de Mama** (down the hill from the Hotel Xalapa, tel 73144) is small and cosy with a log fire in the winter and an open terrace in the summer. It's filled with antiques, pictures and people (advance booking is wise). Try the chicken covered in avocado or one of the various prawn dishes, from simply 'fried in garlic' to the more elaborate 'soused in whisky'. Moderate. Its rival is the up-and-coming **La Pergola** (Lomas del Estadio, tel 74414, overlooking the stadium in the university), which has been in the same family for a generation and has recently been taken over by the youngest son, Arturo Murillo. At lunch-time it's filled with lawyers from tribunal courts and the nearby faculty of law. It's open from breakfast until late and specializes in cuts of the best meat and *camarones Gabardine* (fresh river prawns marinaded in beer). Moderate.

The combination of tight student budget and bracing mountain air accounts for a superabundance of cake and coffee shops all over the main square and along Enríquez, the road leading up to it. **Café de Chino** and **Enrico's** next door pile cakes in their window and dare to be refused. Another packed café is **La Casona del Beaterio** (Zaragoza, running parallel to Enríquez one block south, tel 82119). The walls are decorated with sepia photographs of turn-of-the-century Jalapa. It's in the garden of an old colonial building and offers yoghurt and fruit as well as more traditional staples like tacos, tostados and chilaquiles. Notice boards list local events and cinema and theatre programmes. Inexpensive. **Gondolesas**, three doors up, is good for hearty breakfasts of fried eggs on toast with spinach and potatoes. Inexpensive.

South of Jalapa

South of Jalapa, the road between Coatepec and Fortín de las Flores bumps and bends over potholes through scenes from the last century. Men on horseback gallop through fields of Friesian cattle. Coffee pickers sit in the shade, exuding an air of efficiency whilst doing as little as possible. The road spirals on southwards, through the Totonac villages of Huatusco and Coscomatepec (with a Monday market) and down into the small town of Fortín de las Flores. In the early morning, the approach to Fortín is dominated by the coned summit of the Pico de Orizaba, which clouds over later in the day. This road can be taken as a more leisurely route back to Veracruz, picking up Highway 150 in Fortín.

Fortín de las Flores

Fortín de las Flores basks in the fame of its orchids, bougainvillea and other botanical splendours and has little to offer but a peaceful stop. ****Fortín de las Flores** (Av 2, tel 271 30055) is a lovely old family hotel. Its entrance hall is filled with the scent of gardenias and its pool with their petals. The orchids in the gardens come out in May. Two modest posadas, ***Virginia** and ***La Marina**, are on the main square, together with the restaurant **Jardín** which does good imaginative comida corridas like chicken in a thick peanut sauce, for next to nothing.

Córdoba

The sturdy colonial town of Córdoba is much earthier than Fortín. It is a thriving commercial centre, with its feet firmly on the ground. There are good unfancy hotels and a bus station connecting east to west and north to south. Once a major stopping point on the road from Veracruz to Mexico City, it's now usually passed through at speed. Its greatest moment came in 1821 when the last viceroy, Juan O'Donojú, signed away Spain's right to rule Mexico in the Hotel Zevallos in the Zócalo. The treaty was never formally recognized by Ferdinand VII, though the Spanish knew they were beaten.

Everything happens in the spacious Zócalo fringed with porticos. In the middle there's a faded green neoclassical cathedral, with three naves and a resplendent 24-carat gold altar. In the cafés under the arches, merchants rue the fall in the price of coffee and sugar cane over lemon ices or snail cocktails.

GETTING AROUND

Córdoba is 7 km east of Fortín on Highway 150, which continues east and then north to Veracruz (a 2-hr drive). The bus station is two blocks west of the Zócalo, with connections to Veracruz, Mexico City, Puebla, Jalapa and local villages.

TOURIST INFORMATION
There is a tourist office in Calle 5 (tel 28177), behind the Hotel Virreynal.

WHERE TO STAY AND EAT
There are good unfancy hotels in Córdoba. Next to the cathedral, the ***Virreynal (tel 22377) has a hallway and stairs which remain as they always have been, tiled in Pueblan blue. The rooms upstairs have been modernized. Next door, the ***Mansur (tel 26000) is an elegant building of dark volcanic stone with open terraces overlooking the square. The rooms have a clumsy modernity to them but the location more than compensates.

Of the many cafés, **Victoria** is best for the evening and the **Córdoba** for morning coffees.

The Coast Road South

South of Veracruz, the sultry heat of the Tropics takes over. Just beyond Alvarado, a great bridge spans the River Papaloapán as it finally gasps into the sea. Swollen watermelons grow lazily in the fields like beached whales. Cows chew lilies and round pigs graze indolently, secure in the knowledge of a plentiful supply. The wide, wide banks of the river are lined with coconut palms and flame trees. Further south still, the volcanic hills around the Tuxtlas are studded with tobacco plantations, lakes and waterfalls.

GETTING AROUND
Highway 180 follows the coast south from Veracruz to Alvarado and across the Alvarado lagoon. It is then forced inland by the Tuxtla volcanoes, rejoining the coast at Coat-zacoalcos and continuing east to Villahermosa in Tabasco. Highway 175 forks right, south of Alvarado, bound for the Sierra Madre del Sur and Oaxaca. Buses go along both highways to Oaxaca and Villahermosa.

Alvarado
On a narrow spit of land surrounded by a lagoon, the small fishing town of Alvarado is slowly losing its grip as the heat pounds down. Once it was a thriving port, but now boats rot in the harbour. The stuccoed fronts of the colonial houses, painted jaunty colours in more prosperous times, have faded away. No-one's too bothered. Carts wind up the main street bearing ice to the harbour, where awnings shade small cafés that sell fish to sleepy clients. Stop for a drink and petrol rather than the night.

Tlacotalpan
The colonial village of Tlacotalpan lies beside the River Papaloapán, off Highway 175, 26 km after the 175/180 junction (1½ hrs from Veracruz). Renowned circumspectly in guides for the beauty of its pastel-coloured houses, it has more fame in the state for the high percentage of gay men it produces and for its fair at the end of January. As in Pamplona, bulls rampage through the streets. The Virgin is ferried across the river with great pomp, and celebrations go on for a week. For the rest of the year Tlacotalpan slumbers, disturbed only by the occasional photographer or weekend visitor.

The charm of this village that time forgot comes from the mass of porticos which line each street. Underneath these arches, houses are painted in different shades of pastel, from candy pink to egg-shell blue. In an old pharmacy, the chemist still dispenses from wooden shelves filled with apothecary jars. A small museum details Tlacotalpan's brief moment in the 19th century, when 1200-ton ships were built here and it gloried in a nautical college. An apology of a Casa de Artesanías has the odd chair for sale, while the Casa de la Cultura has nothing inside (though the house it stands in is a fine remnant of a more dignified past).

The main hotel is the ***Posada Doña Lala** overlooking the pier (Carranza 11, tel 288 42580). The dining room specializes in langoustine and rice with almonds. Behind this there's the simpler **Reforma**, with small rooms around a courtyard. Most people come for a lunch of river prawns and then leave, making the town a quiet (too quiet for the Mexicans) stop for those who spend the night.

The Tuxtlas and Catemaco

From the plains of southern Veracruz rises the range of Los Tuxtlas, an imposing cluster of volcanoes forming a gigantic bowl of rich dark earth blanketed with tropical vegetation, criss-crossed by rushing rivers and studded with waterfalls and calm volcanic lakes.

So wrote Miguel Covarrubias, the author and artist, in the 1940s, and nothing much has changed. Southeast of Alvarado and ugly industrial Lerdo, the flat seascape gives way to a fairy-tale land of mushrooming hills and roundles of conifers, where horses plough furrows in the rich red soil. Cortés was so taken with the Tuxtlas that he made sure he kept the title deeds. He had huge sugar mills here, whilst the Germans later secured a monopoly on the coffee industry. Alexander von Humboldt compared the area to Switzerland, with its 14 lakes in about as many kilometres squared. This is proudly reiterated by locals, although the presumption that Switzerland is a land of tropical overgrowth and searing heat might raise an eyebrow in the Alps. Coffee and tobacco grow abundantly, but it's the discreet marijuana plantations which provide a living for many.

GETTING AROUND

The Tuxtlas and Catemaco are all on Highway 180. Santiago Tuxtla is 140 km from Veracruz, San Andrés Tuxtla 154 km, and Catemaco 166 km. Villahermosa is 312 km from Catemaco. Long-distance buses connect the towns with Veracruz and Villahermosa as well as Puebla, Mexico City and Oaxaca.

The bus station in San Andrés is the main departure point for local buses around the area. It's a block behind the main square in Calle Rascón. Autotransportes Tepango (tel 21462) leave every half-hour for Catemaco and Santiago. Seven buses a day leave for Tres Zapotes, from 5.30 to 16.30 (1½ hrs). Autotransportes las Tuxtlas run frequent buses to Catemaco and around the lake (although 4 km of road are still missing from a complete circuit). Buses for the Exipantla waterfall leave every hour.

The bus station in Catemaco is one block behind the church.

Santiago Tuxtla

Highway 180 curves in and out of lowlands ploughed by yoked oxen and grazed by Brahmin cattle before arriving at Santiago Tuxtla. This pretty colonial village was founded by Cortés himself. The main square prefers to remember its pre-Hispanic past and is dominated by a huge Olmec head from Tres Zapotes, its eyes unusually closed in an attitude of serene contemplation. In the square the one-roomed **Museo Tuxteco** (open erratically and closed Mon; adm) has a few local Olmec finds and the painted cloth lizard and jaguar costumes used for the festival on 24 June. The garden at the back is filled with amorphous sculptures found in the region. Live crabs are often sold in the small market.

San Andrés Tuxtla

Fourteen km south, San Andrés has more of a commercial buzz, with supermarkets, banks, hotels and a big bus station. It's the most important town in the Tuxtlas and useful as a base, though it lacks the charisma of Catemaco.

Out on the road to Catemaco, a big white building houses Tabacos San Andrés (Blvd 5 de Febrero 10, tel 21200)—a Dickensian workhouse of a cigar factory. A rich smell emanates from the premises, enough to tempt even the most hardened non-smoker. Banks of leather-aproned workers bend over dried leaves, their expert hands painstakingly fashioning them into Churchillian rolls. For this they earn no more than a couple of tourist beers a day. Unofficial visits are tolerated during working hours (9.00–13.00 and 16.00– 19.00) and boxes of cigars are sold at factory prices.

Salto de Exipantla

A stupendous 40-m stretch of waterfall, fed by the effluence of Lake Catemaco, cascades down just outside San Andrés. Take the Catemaco road, past corrugated-iron sheds thatched with palm and filled with tobacco. After 4 km a dusty red dirt track, signed 'Salto de Exipantla', leads off to the right, meandering past maize fields and women washing clothes in the many streams. Some 6 km down the track, a couple of palapa cafés indicate where the 244 fragile cement steps begin their surreal descent to the foot of the fall. It's not a place for city-slicker shoes as the steps have an unnerving tendency to stop mid-air, where the cement has cracked. At the bottom a gentle spray of water permeates the air and there are big pools to swim in, surrounded by overhanging trees. During the week the only people around are a scramble of children anxious to guide.

Tres Zapotes

Some 23 km west of Santiago (take the bus from San Andrés) are the impoverished remains of Tres Zapotes, a late Olmec ceremonial centre which flourished after the fall of La Venta in 400 BC. It is famed for a stela dated 291 BC which was found here, and which gave the earliest positive proof of the use of zero in the Americas. Today only grass-covered mounds remain of what were some of the oldest temples in the country. A colossal head and some stelae are in the museum 1 km away, although the best finds were carted off to the Museum of Anthropology in Mexico City. As there is little to see at the site, a visit is recommended only for keen archaeologists.

Catemaco

The village of Catemaco sits on the western shores of a deep lake, often swathed in the mists from its waters. It has long been famed for its witches and nowadays the small town encourages tales of the supernatural to keep visitors coming. During the week no-one does much and children pounce on any lone car that enters, anxious to wash even the most gleaming of bodyworks for a negotiable fee. Wizened women in the market sell herbs promising to restore anything from a wayward lover to an abundant mass of hair. The elaborately painted church in the Zócalo looks a hundred but is in fact an ornate replica built in the 1950s.

The main attraction of the village is its 16-km-wide lake, which was formed from a giant crater. Boats line up on the pier, ready to take parties out on the lake. They operate a fixed tariff, and as they are hired by the boat rather than by the passenger, it is cheapest to inveigle as many people as possible onto a trip.

Lake Catemaco deserves and rewards exploration. It is filled with lotuses, lilies, egrets and islands where nonchalant cattle graze. The best beaches to swim off are on the opposite side of the lake to the village—the others are overused and dirty. On the eastern shore is a shrine to the Virgin del Carmen whose festival is celebrated on 17 July with a big fiesta.

On the biggest of the islands the University of Veracruz has established a colony of spider monkeys. They were imported from Vietnam so that scientists could study their habits in this similar tropical climate. It's a terrifying parody of the human world in microcosm. Males rut, strut and fight, waving their swollen red bottoms in the appalled red faces of their human counterparts. The university is anxious to stop boat-loads of tourists feeding them and disrupting their natural environment.

WHERE TO STAY AND EAT

There is a small haven of a hotel in **Santiago Tuxtla**. The ***Castellanos** (5 de Mayo, tel 294 70200) is built in the round, six floors high with a welcoming swimming pool overhung with tropical vegetation. The restaurant serves cheerful home-cooked food.

The hotels in **San Andrés** are the cheapest and least interesting. Try the main square where the terraced café of the ***Hotel del Parque** (Madero 5, tel 294 20198) spills out into the street. The ***de los Pérez** (round the corner in Calle Rascón 2) is small and pristinely clean.

Catemaco has the distinct advantage of its lake to look at and this is reflected in its prices. The ****Bertangel** (on the main square, tel 294 30007) has air-conditioned rooms and is well run by the Rosio family. The television in the hall attracts a wide audience. Lured by black-and-white 1940s Pedro Infante films, they come to chat or just eat ice creams. The small café looks out onto the boys chasing tourists around the main square. ******Catemaco** (tel 294 30045) is on the same square. Although it looks more up-market, the rooms are much the same. On the other hand, the bare white, stone-floored rooms of hotel and restaurant ***Julieta** (down on the waterfront, no tel) are refreshingly plain at a no-nonsense price. The kitchen serves *mojarra* (sun fish), straight from the lake, drowned in cloves of garlic. Inexpensive. The ***Playa** (tel 294 30001) is 2 km out of town, on the eastern shore of the lake, with its own pool and pier. It feeds guests rather better views than food.

Catemaco was once renowned for its monkey meat (*changocon*). However, with their natural habitat disappearing fast, local monkeys are almost extinct and this is now illegal. Where it's purportedly served, it is usually goat meat. Another speciality is *tegogolo*, a snail found at the bottom of the lake and usually served in a spicy tomato sauce. The restaurants down by the waterfront are best for these. There is fierce competition between **La Luna** and **La Ola** and both are worth a visit. The town's most up-market restaurant is **Casona del Recuerdo** (on the main square). Behind the wooden terrace and white porticos, there is a jungle of a garden where people crowd to eat plates of seafood. Moderate.

Part VII

JALISCO, COLIMA AND NAYARIT

A Huichol man in traditional dress

The western states of Jalisco, Colima and Nayarit are furiously, frantically fertile. The parched plains and deserts of northern Mexico finally give way to the exuberant overgrowth of the Tropics. Even in the mountains, citrus fruits grow side by side with coffee. Luscious jungle borders the Pacific, revealing untouched beaches, occasional fishing villages and the odd burgeoning resort.

Jalisco encompasses the big-city rumbustiousness of Guadalajara and the bright lights of the resort of Puerto Vallarta, as well as unspoilt hill villages. Foreign visitors are few and far between in Colima, a tiny state of great natural beauty and rural calm. Nayarit is another little-visited state, with long stretches of unspoilt coast, deep lagoons, volcanoes and the isolated communities of the Cora and Huichol peoples hidden within its mountains.

History

Western Mexico developed apart, isolated from the sophisticated centre of the country by the barrier of the Sierra Madre and a deep ravine cut by the torrid waters of the River Santiago. Inward looking, it never started any great reform movements though generally acquiesced when news of them filtered through.

PRE-HISPANIC
Whilst elaborate civilizations such as the Olmec and the Maya rose and fell in the east, no dominant group emerged to lead the west. Simple nomadic peoples, who had migrated

183

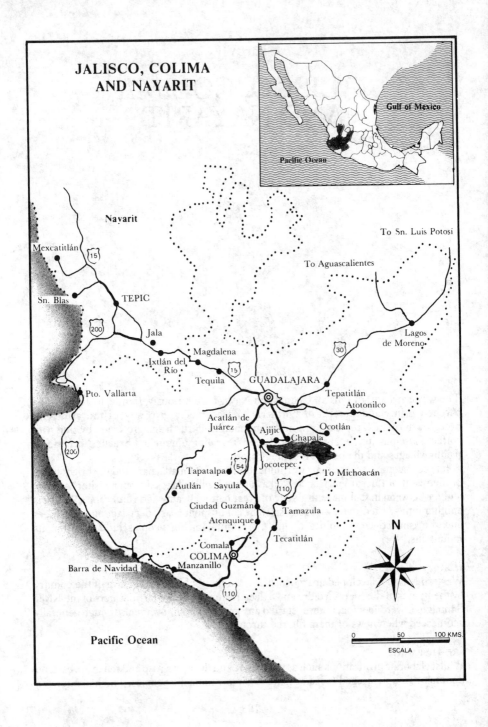

JALISCO, COLIMA
AND NAYARIT

Gulf of Mexico

Pacific Ocean

Nayarit

To Sn. Luis Potosi

Mexcatitlán

15

To Aguascalientes

Sn. Blas

TEPIC

200

Jala

Ixtlán del
Río

Magdalena

Lagos
de Moreno

30

Tequila

15

GUADALAJARA

Pto. Vallarta

Tepatitlán

Atotonilco

200

Acatlán de
Juárez

Ajijic

Ocotlán

Chapala

54

Jocotepec

Tapatalpa

To Michoacán

Autlán

Sayula

110

Ciudad Guzmán

Atenquique

Tamazula

Tecatitlán

Comala

COLIMA

Barra de Navidad

Manzanillo

110

N

Pacific Ocean

0   50   100 KMS.

ESCALA

in straggles from the north as early as 1500 BC, retained their village cultures for over 2000 years. The Santiago River, the largest in the country, runs through a great canyon in eastern Jalisco that for centuries formed a natural barrier in Mesoamerica. To the east were the agricultural peoples of Mexico and Michoacán, and to the west the nomadic hunters and gatherers whose greatest legacy was their ingenuity and talent for producing delightful and lively ceramics.

It wasn't until the collapse of the Toltec empire at the end of the 11th century that the west finally came into contact with the centre. The Toltecs, who had dominated central Mexico, dispersed as far afield as Jalisco and Colima in search of new land. They introduced concepts of gods and war. Temples started to appear, as in Ixtlán del Río, as well as moustachioed figurines worshipping Tlaloc, the God of Rain.

In the 15th century, the west allied under the protection of the central Aztec empire against the muscle-flexing Purépecha in neighbouring Michoacán. Yet there was little time for the effect of this alliance to influence society, as within 50 years a greater threat had appeared on the scene—the Spanish.

NUNO DE GUZMAN

In 1527, Charles I of Spain appointed a court of justice purportedly to control the excesses of the original conquistadors. Nuño de Guzmán, a lawyer of noble family, was sent from Spain as president. Within two years, he had made Hernán Cortés look like a choirboy. He enslaved 21 ship-loads of natives from the province of Panuco, selling them off to work to death in mines. His ferocious slave raids in other states made him feared and loathed throughout the land. Any correspondence criticizing his regime was intercepted before it reached Spain. It was only when Bishop Zumárraga, a humane Franciscan, travelled in person to Veracruz and managed to smuggle a letter out, that a horrified Spain began to take action.

In 1529, Guzmán expediently removed himself from investigations into his misconduct and swooped westwards from the capital, hoping to win new land, and thus regain favour with the Spanish crown. Unlike the more subtle Cortés, he didn't bother to negotiate with those in power, preferring to pillage and destroy his way to victory. The genocide was staggering and many tribes perished in their entirety. Of all Mexico, no area had such a brutal conquest.

THE MAKING OF A MODERN STATE

Colonized, and given the name Nuevo Galicia, Western Mexico continued to be isolated. The impassability of its approaches meant that the region remained something of a backwater until the 18th century. The journey to Guadalajara from Mexico City was too arduous to attract casual travellers until a road was cut through in 1794. Even then, the journey in a four-seater coach drawn by 12 mules took an uncomfortable 12 days. The railway between Mexico City and Guadalajara was opened in 1888 but was so slow that honeymooning couples were said to have their first child before getting there.

Ironically, the fight for independence, which shook the centre of the country in 1812 and cut off supplies from Mexico City, gave the west a new lease of life. The ports of

San Blas and Manzanillo flourished and, as a major trading centre for merchants, Guadalajara saw a great upsurge in its fortunes. Outside the powerful ports, industry was slow to take a hold. The area developed a tradition of conservatism and was only a pusher for liberalism when pressed.

Fervently Catholic, the west was finally rattled when a group of militant Catholics, the Cristeros, determined to have the rights of the Church restored by the new secular revolutionary government of the 1920s. Jalisco, in particular, became the centre of the movement. In 1927 the Guadalajara–Mexico City train was blown up, killing over a hundred people. Guadalajara itself cannily avoided open combat, though its conservative stalwarts covertly aided and abetted the Cristeros with arms and money, until the movement was suffocated by a combination of military force and a relaxation of government policy against the Church.

In the 1930s, suspicious of the popular left-wing president, Lázaro Cárdenas, who touted dangerous ideas of land for all and God for none, the establishment bestirred itself to found the ultra-Catholic Autonomous University of Guadalajara. It also played a key role in forming the opposition party PAN (National Action Party) which had strong links with the Church. Left-wing dissatisfaction in the 1960s spawned a student movement which organized urban guerrilla units to patrol the streets of the city. This insurrection was quickly wiped out by security forces and the right re-established control. In the 1980s, Nayarit stepped out of line and flirted with the radical politics of Cuauhtémoc Cárdenas and his PRD party (Revolutionary Democrats), but a series of bitterly disputed and corrupt elections ensured that the establishment regained control.

The State of Jalisco

With exuberant Guadalajara as its attention-grabbing capital city, the rest of the state is unfairly overshadowed. Spreading like an outstretched hand from the Pacific coast up to the Sierra Madre on its northeastern border, Jalisco holds fertile valleys, deep lakes and rugged hills within its grasp. In the remote past, almost the whole state was submerged under the vast expanse of a great lake, its surface pierced only by the peaks of volcanic mountains. Lava and alluvial deposits from these slowly filled up the depths until water finally burst forth, cutting deep gashes which became the valleys of today.

In case the state's blessings should be unappreciated, Jaliscans constantly reiterate the figures: theirs is the most temperate climate in the world; in a country of small lakes, Jalisco has the biggest, Chapala, which is fed by Mexico's longest river, the Santiago. It is also the home of the Mexican staffs of life—tequila and mariachi music.

To the south of Guadalajara, Mexico's second biggest city, the gentle banks of Lake Chapala have been colonized by North Americans escaping from long winters and a high cost of living. Jalisco has 300 km of Pacific shoreline but only two coastal towns of any size, glitzy Puerto Vallarta and ramshackle Barra de Navidad. Away from these towns, on vast ranches and in hidden hill villages, life goes on as before, more concerned with producing champion cowboys and bulls (in that order) than with issues affecting the rest of the country.

GUADALAJARA

Mexico City drew the politicians and Monterrey the money, but Guadalajara kept Mexico's soul. It is ebullient undistilled Mexico, renowned for its frankness, devout Catholicism and inbred machismo. The capital of the state, Guadalajara is a day's journey (1520 km) south of Ciudad Juárez on the US border and 5 hours (340 km) east of the Pacific, on a high, wide plain in the fertile valley of Atemajac. It presides over the whole of the north and west as a surrogate capital, independent of Mexico City 530 km away, and carrying enormous political clout.

Guadalajara, throughout its history, has been a bastion of conservativism and tradition, content to follow the lead rather than take it. Never a revolutionary city, it has been the scene of revolutionary action. When Miguel Hidalgo cried for freedom from Spain, Guadalajara was one of the first cities to fall, and it was from here that he proclaimed the abolition of slavery, 50 years before Abraham Lincoln abolished it in the US.

At a height of 1590 m, with a population of 4 million, two universities, a month-long festival and ceaseless mariachi music, Guadalajara is a city of great ease and tradition. The squares overspill with shoe shiners, frocked friars and serenading mariachi players. The state university, with its policy of free tuition, has filled the streets with a constant stream of articulate graduates. The mechanic, soldering an exhaust back on, will talk with immense authority on the latest developments in biochemical engineering and everyone extols the excellence of the city's most famous native son, the iconoclastic muralist José Clemente Orozco.

GETTING AROUND

Guadalajara dominates the highways in western Mexico. Like a vast roundabout, it scoops everything up and sends it on its way again, with clear directions north, south, east and west. In a vain attempt to make the city less congested, long-distance buses have been kept out. The train station is near the centre. Trains are slow and stately and tickets must be booked well ahead.

By Air: The airport is 16 km south of the city on the road to Chapala. Airport minibuses provide an hourly service to and from the central hotels. There are daily international flights to and from six US cities including Houston and San Francisco and daily national flights all over Mexico, with six to and from Mexico City.

By Bus: The bus station has been moved 15 km east of the centre, as far as the toll booth at the end of Av Revolución. Urban minicabs and buses connect the two and taxis charge a reasonable fixed rate. Express buses go to and from Mexico City (8 hrs, hourly), the United States border, Puerto Vallarta (6 hrs), Colima (4 hrs), Morelia (6 hrs) and Guanajuato (5 hrs).

By Train: The train station is at the Parque Azul end of the Calzada Independencia Sur. Trains take up to twice the time of the bus. Daily trains run to and from Mexico City (the 'Tapatio' takes 12 hours, departing 20.55), the US border towns of Nogales and

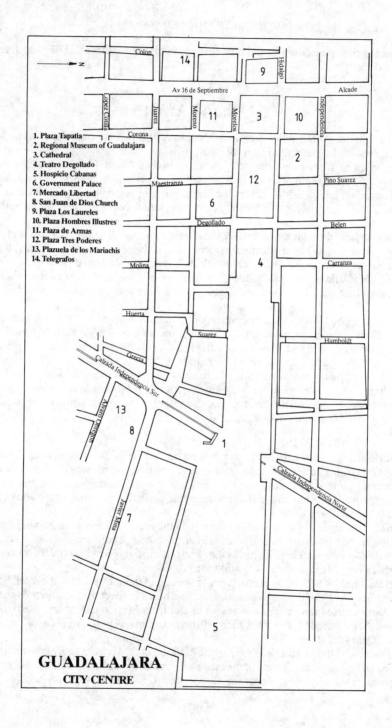

1. Plaza Tapatia
2. Regional Museum of Guadalajara
3. Cathedral
4. Teatro Degollado
5. Hospicio Cabanas
6. Government Palace
7. Mercado Libertad
8. San Juan de Dios Church
9. Plaza Los Laureles
10. Plaza Hombres Illustres
11. Plaza de Armas
12. Plaza Tres Poderes
13. Plazuela de los Mariachis
14. Telegrafos

GUADALAJARA
CITY CENTRE

Mexicali (the 'Tren Estrella', seated only, takes 30 hours, departing 19.00) and south to Manzanillo (the 'Colimense' takes 5 hours, departing 09.00). All tickets must be booked, at least 24 hours in advance, either at the train station itself or in the Hotel Universo travel agency on López Cotilla and Degollado.

In Town: Guadalajara is easier to enter than to avoid and the rigid system of one-way streets leads inexorably to the centre. All the main roads point like arrows towards the cathedral, but move at a considerably slower pace. These traffic artilleries trace a cross shape. Going from the east to the west, one-way Av Juárez turns into Av Vallarta. From the west to the east take one-way López Cotilla or Hidalgo. Calzada Independencia runs both ways north–south past the Parque Agua Azul down to the train station. Av Revolución goes east from Independencia towards the Mexico City road, past Tlaquepaque and the bus station.

Once in the centre, it is best to abandon a car in one of the underground car parks (the most central of all is on Morelos, to the right of the Teatro Degollado) and rely instead on taxis, buses and combis. Despite the great sprawl of Guadalajara, the interesting parts are fortunately close together, most within walking distance of each other, linked by cafés and markets. Ten blocks of the Spanish-planned core of the city have been turned into a pedestrian precinct and business keeps its distance from this 'old' part of town.

Taxis, Buses and Combis: Taxis within the centre cost little, and there is a fixed price to the bus station (about the same as to Zapopan and a little more than to Tlaquepaque). To anywhere else, the price is always negotiable and should be agreed before setting off. If it seems to be based on the size of your camera, wait for the next one to come along and judge the cost by the state of his fenders. Never leap into the smart, dark, pristinely clean taxis outside the large hotels. Their charges are definitely inspired by Texans.

Green and white buses rush efficiently from one side of the city to another in a belch of black smoke. It's better to be inside than to attempt to negotiate them as they briskly change lanes and defy the frantic whistles of the traffic police. 60A from Calzada Independencia goes to the train station, 15 to Zapopan and 616 to the bus station ('Nueva Central Camionera'). Combis are Volkswagen vans which act as minibuses, serving all districts of the city. The destination is written up on the windscreen and they leave when full. The central pick-up point is Calzada Independencia Sur by the market place.

TOURIST INFORMATION

There are two well-placed offices: Morelos 102, by the Plaza Tapatía (tel 14 43 56 or 14 86 86), or the more administrative SECTUR office at Degollado 50, almost opposite (tel 13 16 05). There are also booths at the airport, bus station and the Palacio Nacional. Guadalajara is used to visitors, encourages them and nurtures them with well-produced maps and down-to-earth advice about hotels, restaurants, buses and what's on.

WHAT TO SEE

In the colonial heart of Guadalajara, heavy, imposing buildings with lightly sculpted, roseate facades make way for a series of squares that surrounds the cathedral and leads eastwards to the Hospicio de Cabañas. This is the place to wander at any time of the day or evening. In October, with the month-long festival in full swing, the whole area between the cathedral and the Hospicio is filled with market stalls, street musicians, open-air sculpture competitions and street shows, with fireworks in the evenings.

José Clemente Orozco (1883–1949), one of the three great 20th-century Mexican muralists, was born in Guadalajara and painted his revolutionary murals in the very bastions of the city's institutions. His Museum Workshop has been closed for several years with no immediate signs of reopening, but many of the exhibits are still in the city. The Hospicio and the Government Palace have the most Orozco murals. Slightly further afield, the agonizing works in the university (12 blocks from the cathedral and 6 from the ex-convento del Carmen) more than compensate for the small effort needed to get to them.

The ceramic centres of Tlaquepaque and Tonalá, and Zapopan, the heart of Catholic Guadalajara, were once separate towns and are still far enough and distinctive enough to merit at least half a day's visit each.

Around the Plaza de Armas

The Cathedral

The grandiose bulk of the cathedral stands where Av 16 de Septiembre crosses Hidalgo, facing onto the Plaza de los Laureles with its fiercely manicured box laurels. Over the centuries since the first stone was laid in the 1560s, it has been adapted by many architects. The final mixture of baroque, mudéjar and neoclassical styles gives it an awkward, unwieldy feel. The 19th century was a bad time for the cathedral: just when the construction was almost complete, an earthquake in 1818 destroyed the original Tuscan bell towers (the present ones made of pumice stone were inspired by a design the bishop admired on his dinner plate). For the next 40 years, it was surreptitiously ransacked during various wars, culminating in the pawning of the silver high altar to help to pay for the cost of the Three Years War in the 1860s. One great work of art remains—Murillo's *Assumption of the Virgin* in the sacristy. A curious reverse Tardis effect takes place inside. The heavy mass houses a strangely shrunken interior, despite its elevating gothic vaulting and ornamentation. On Sundays, services inside compete with military bands in the Plaza de Armas outside, with the faithful swinging from one to the other.

The Government Palace

(Open daily 09.00–21.00.)

Facing on to the east of the Plaza de Armas, at right angles to the cathedral, is the 18th-century **Palacio de Gobierno** with its declamatory Orozco murals. The impressive, well-proportioned exterior, with water spouts carved like cannons and walls as thick as battlements, protected the incumbent royally appointed governors. It was here that Hidalgo proclaimed the abolition of slavery in 1810. José Clemente Orozco's monumental murals on the staircase commemorate the act. Hidalgo burnishes a firebrand above a sea of workers, who fight blindly amongst themselves—symbolizing the freeing of the oppressed and the confused conflict of ideals which impeded its progress. Cheap steel flick-knives spew forth from the monster that was the Spanish invasion. The artist believed that Hidalgo had put his money where his mouth was and had given his life for emancipation from Spain. He is framed on either side by the grotesque pantomime of 'the forces of darkness' (the army and the Church) and 'the political circus', which warn that the struggle is not over as crosses, scythes and swastikas juggle for space.

The ex-chapel attached was hastily reformed into the seat of Congress between February and March 1858 and from here Benito Juárez briefly ran the country. Here, too, the walls have been used to make a political statement. Juárez wields a quill above the bayonets raised against him. His championship of law is supported by the other popular heroes, Zapata and Carranza, solemnly to one side, with Morelos and a poor farmer to the other. A beatific Hidalgo presides over the proceedings surrounded by enchained torsos.

The Regional Museum
(On the north side of the Plaza de la Liberación; entrance on Calle Liceo, facing the Plaza de los Hombres Illustres; open 09.00–14.00; closed Mon; adm.)
This museum had the good fortune of an early inauguration, in 1918, and its collection is amongst the best in the country. Apart from the mammoth which children always want to see, there is an excellent lower-floor collection of pre-Hispanic figurines.

LOWER FLOOR
The first exhibit on the lower floor is an almost complete mammoth from the Pliocene age, which only came to light in 1962. Pushed against the far wall, to make room for the mammoth, are exquisite examples of pre-Hispanic sculpture from western Mexico (AD 200–800), found in local tombs and caves. Death and life were seen as a great circle, and dying only as a journey to another life. Each tomb was carefully filled with everyday and extraordinary objects to ease this voyage, such as food, guide dogs (the quirky pot-bellied type) and presents. The collection includes many funerary objects from Ixtlán del Río: one of the most precise is a necklace of 30 tiny naked figures hanging off a chain. Humans and animals were fashioned in every form, like the endearing Cojumatlán barrel vases, each with a tiny neck-spout marked with nose, eyes and mouth, surmounting a blown-up body. A meditative Nayarit figure (between AD 200 and 400) shows unusual sobriety, sitting with hands on knees, eyes closed, adorned with nothing but the simplest ornaments. Western sculpture never reached grand proportions and secondary details were often left out for simplicity, making them strikingly modern, even abstract, in their spareness.

UPPER FLOOR
The upper floor is given over to 'modern' Mexico, from the arrival of the Spanish in 1519 up to the present day. It begins with five rooms of colonial paintings influenced by Spain. European art was the touchstone and anything that hinted of a dark complexion or a tropical climate was immediately relegated to the second division. The style of the 18th century was one of excessiveness, forswearing rigidity and embracing the exuberance of the ultra baroque. **José de Ibarra** and **Miguel Cabrera** are the chief exponents, together with the transitional painter **Cristóbal de Villapando**. José de Ibarra (1688–1756), who was born in Guadalajara, has a whole room devoted to his large, allegorical oils. His paintings were very much the taste of the time—conventional and decorative, with light, delicate outlining that leaves all to the brushwork and highlighting of colours.

Ivory reliquaries from Manila are reminders of the wealth and importance of trading with the Orient across the Pacific Ocean. There are some glorious portraits of bishops whose noses make Pinocchio look ordinary. One of these, Felipe Galindo y Chavez, was the founder of the seminary in which the museum is housed.

191

East of the Plaza de Armas

The Degollado Theatre

Facing onto the Plaza de la Liberación, due east of the museum, is the 1866 **Teatro Degollado**. It opened triumphantly with a performance of *Lucia di Lammermoor* sung by Angela Peralta, the 'Mexican nightingale', and a cast brought over from Italy. It pales Covent Garden to a shadow, with neoclassical columns and a flowery interpretation of robust gods disporting themselves in a scene from Dante's *Divina Commedia* on the gold-edged ceiling. Downstairs a gilt telephone box demands to be used. Anyone can enter the foyer, although only ticket holders are officially allowed into the auditorium. (See Ballet Folklórico.)

Plaza Tapatía

Calle Morelos heads east from the right-hand side of the theatre down to the new Plaza Tapatía, which is in the shape of a Latin cross. Amidst shouts of hysteria and genuine delight, it was opened to the public in February 1982. Nine blocks of colonial buildings were knocked down to make way for car parks, chichi boutiques and restaurants. The arguments for and against this radical redesigning are still fiercely debated.

Hospicio Cabañas

(Open 10.00–18.00; closed Mon and Sun afternoon; guides free; adm.)
On the east side of the Plaza Tapatía, this neoclassical building was founded in 1801 by Bishop Ruiz Cabañas and designed by the Spanish architect, Manuel Tolsá. First a military garrison, then an orphanage, it is now a labyrinth of 23 courts set in gardens filled with orange blossom. The largest of these, a deconsecrated chapel boldly painted in searing colours by José Clemente Orozco, shows both the contradictions and the potential underlying the mixed Mexican inheritance. One can lie on the long hard benches and look up at the pantheon of gods, a catholic collection of the pagan and the Christian, with the pre-Hispanic alongside Christ, Jehovah and the Angel of the Apocalypse.

In the main dome Orozco symbolically depicted the four ages of man and the four elements of life, intertwined with a 12-m tall Man of Fire combining the Mexican Quetzalcóatl and the Spanish God. To the left of the dome is a futuristic Cortés, the bringer of metal to the New World, portrayed here as a robot warrior with nuts and bolts for knees and shoulders. Above the left-hand doorway are El Greco, on the right, and Cervantes, on the left, both much admired by Orozco as masters of their respective arts. Cervantes appears not to have a left hand, an oblique reference to a disability he shared with Orozco (together with deafness), having lost the use of his arm after a blast in the Battle of Lepanto. The many other rooms house Orozco's prints, drawings and studies for murals all over Mexico, including early sketches of the ones here.

Mercado Libertad

Victor Contreras' abstract metal sculpture of a soaring Quetzalcóatl stands outside the museum, and from here steps lead down to the maze-like Mercado Libertad, probably the largest market in Latin America. Its tiny stalls jostle together, hawking the very oldest natural herbal remedies and the very latest in contraband American sportswear. On the second floor, above the fruit and vegetable market, makeshift stands sell *pollo a la valentina* (chicken bathed in a hot sauce of tomatoes), fried potatoes with their skins on and drinks like the savoury *tesguino* (fermented maize with iced lemon).

Plazuela de los Mariachis

Across the busy Av Javier Mina (there is an overpass at the lights), south of the market and Plaza Tapatía, is the triangular Plazuela. A narrow funnel of inexpensive open-air cafés, like a wedge of cheese, fans out to a fountain at the far end. At night, numerous bands of competing mariachi players squeeze into the space. The Plazuela has become tawdrier than Tlaquepaque but the melancholic air of the songs is just as pervasive. Worn-out horses wait harnessed into their carriages, ready to pull the unsteady back home. The 18th-century church, which stands to one side of the Plazuela, has seen it all before and long ago put up a sign in the atrium, banning 'immoral thoughts, words or actions in this holy place'. (See Mariachi.)

South of the Plaza de Armas

Just off Av Juárez and facing Colón (one block south and one west of the plaza), the **Telegrafos building** (no fixed opening times) is temporarily out of a job. Originally a Jesuit church, it became part of the university in 1792. In the first quarter of this century, it was a symbol of progress and a focus for the conflict between liberals and conservatives, becoming, in turn, an institute of sciences and then a jurisprudence college. In 1924 David Alfaro Siqueiros painted the main hall with a declamatory mural on the Revolution and Zapata's cry for agrarian reform, bringing it firmly down on the side of liberalism.

Four blocks south of the Plaza de Armas, on either side of Av 16 de Septiembre, are the sumptuous churches of **San Francisco** and **Nuestra Señora de Aranzazu**. Aranzazu is the only chapel to remain of the four originally belonging to San Francisco. Built in the high Mexican baroque style of the mid-18th century, its three churrique-resque *retablos* are glitteringly overpowering, the finest and most ornate in the city. San Francisco itself was founded in the 1540s but the present baroque structure dates from 1684. The main door facing north was originally where the high altar stood, on the spot of an ancient, holy, mezquite tree venerated since pre-Hispanic times.

The Park

Av 16 de Septiembre merges with Calzada Independencia at the **Parque Agua Azul**, a large but not very soothing public park with distractions like a toy train, a children's zoo and occasional performances on an open-air stage. Sunday is family day and the whole park becomes a giant children's playground, littered with frazzled parents looking forward to Monday. The main entrance is on the Calzada, opposite which, on a small traffic island, is what appears to be an unassuming gentlemen's lavatory. On closer inspection, this turns out to be the miniscule **Museo de Arqueologia de Occidente de México** (open 10–13.00 and 15.00–19.00; closed Mon). Its meagre collection is charming and idiosyncratic, with a few pre-Hispanic pieces from each of the states of Jalisco, Colima and Nayarit: acrobats, warriors, dogs, diseased bodies and anthropomorphic figures in red, café and orange clay.

Beside it is the **Casa de la Cultura** (open 09.00–18.00) with its exhibition of modern Mexican art, and the extensive state library. At right angles, on Av Jesús Gonzalez Gallo, is the government-sponsored, up-market **Casa de las Artesanías** which backs on to the park (open 10.00–19.00, Mon–Fri; 10.00–16.00, Sat and Sun). Opened in 1964, the exhibition hall has some eclectic pieces from all over the world. Besides this are two generally unappealing floors of Jaliscan and Mexican crafts, with perilous shelves piled high with gaudy blown glass and unimaginative ceramics made to mass order.

West along Av Juárez
The **Ex-Convento del Carmen** is a lively arts centre with no reverence for its former calling, best visited during the busy weekends. Six blocks from the Plaza de Armas, on the right-hand side, it has a small art cinema, theatre, gallery and popular café. The billboard shows what's on, from baroque recitals to Buñuel retrospectives. On Saturdays there is a bazaar under the porticos where artisans from local villages sell bead jewellery and embroidered blankets.

Another six blocks on, the ancient and modern **universities** face each other. The soaring glass tower of the 20th century overlooks its older neoclassical partner with all the arrogance of the young. Inside the rectory of the older one, Orozco painted some of his most furious murals, known as *La Complejidad del ser Humano* (*The Complexity of Being*). On the cupola are painted four dizzy-making images: Orozco himself, with his hand raised, beside a man in a red bandana who sacrifices himself for his ideals, a technician and a man of action. On an adjoining wall, a group of naked, skeletal men are juxtaposed against porcine work managers, who hold rule books laying down rigid, unjust laws.

Northwest of the Plaza de Armas
Three blocks north on Av Alcalde and three west on San Felipe is a grim Victorian-looking military barracks, still very much in use, which has all but swallowed up the fine baroque church of **Santa Mónica** founded in 1733 for Augustinian nuns. The impressionable girls were kept in the back of the church behind a delicate wrought-iron grille. The highly ornate *salamónica* carving of the doorway is finely decorated with grapes dripping off the columns, angelic pilasters and a double-headed eagle, giving the impression of a permanent harvest supper. At the corner of the church is a curious niche sculpture of St Christopher, similar in many ways to the characteristic angels of the doorway, both coming from a strong pre-Hispanic tradition of folk art.

Two blocks further west along Calle San Felipe is the church of the same name, which, contrasting with Santa Mónica's exuberance, shows extraordinary sobriety in its execution, although of the same date. Tucked away almost out of sight, it has a delicate, evenly balanced plateresque facade edged by a row of acanthus leaves and gargoyles in the form of sea horses.

On the Fringes of the City

Tlaquepaque
Once a proudly independent municipality of wealthy merchants, Tlaquepaque is now an extension of the city. It can be reached by car or taxi southeast along Revolución (5 km,

20 mins from Independencia), or by bus 275 (which continues to Tonalá) from Av 16 de Septiembre.

San Pedro Tlaquepaque is renowned throughout Mexico for the quality of its crafts and its innovative Mexican designers. The shops buy in the best textiles, clothes, rugs, ceramics and crafts from all over the country and from Central America. The quality means the prices are higher than elsewhere, but they are competitive relative to the US or Europe, and the colourful, unique designs will turn heads in New York, London or Sydney. It's always advisable to shop around, as the standard isn't invariably high.

The two main streets of colonial houses are Independencia and Juárez. In **Independencia**, off the Zócalo, there is a ceramics museum (open 09.00–14.00; closed Mon; adm) at 237, where you can get your eye in before embarking on a shopping spree. Directly opposite is **Sergio Bustamante's** over-hyped gallery with sculptures in papier-mâché, bronze and ceramics. Half-way down at 232, **La Rosa de Crystal** is the oldest of the glass-blowing factories, straight out of Dante's *Inferno*. Hot pokers fashion molten glass into exquisitely delicate goblets and vases in blue, pink and green. The elegant **Hacinda Galindo** at 139 has a fine selection of distinctive Mexican ceramics and linens (they can also ship home). Two other shops with Circean charms are **Marquin's**, a rustic furniture shop at 186, and **Irene Pulos** at 224 with wearable dresses in bright primary colours based on traditional local patterns. **Juárez**, the street parallel to Independencia, continues the indulgence with cowboy boots at **Botas Michel** (160) and Mexican clothes at **El Aguila Descalza** (120).

Perhaps more enticing than all the shops is the fun and noise of the central plaza, **El Parian**. In effect it is no more than a series of interrelated bars and restaurants under one roof, with a kiosk in the middle, over, around and on which children play. Photographers wait to pounce on the tequila-sozzled, young women ply yesterday's roses, street-wise eight-year-olds sagely sell great bunches of balloons and caricaturists solicit models from the tables, all to the background of the soulful mariachi belting out their songs for a few thousand pesos. If this is too noisy, the **Restaurant Sin Nombre** (without a name) is a block north (Madero 80, tel 35 45 20) in a quiet corner, with classical music and a different menu every day. The food is imaginative, from *filet mignon* with a chocolate *mole* sauce to *queso fundido con rajas* (melted Oaxacan cheese with strips of mild green chilli peppers rolled in warm tortillas).

Tonalá

Easily combined in a day trip to Tlaquepaque, Tonalá can be reached by bus 275 from Tlaquepaque or 104 from the centre (on the corner of Moreno and Independencia). It is 30 minutes by car or taxi, along Av Revolución and north via La Piedad.

Tonalá has been known for its pottery for over 1000 years. The original earthy tones of browns and reds have now been crudely glazed over for commercial production. They may have lost much of their charm by foreign standards, but they are still bought for the local hotels by the truck-load. Only a few miles from the centre of Guadalajara, Tonalá has gradually been absorbed into the ever-growing suburbs but still keeps up its bargain-filled Sunday and Thursday pottery markets, in the main square and the streets leading off it. The many workshops continue to produce fragile figurines and delicate hand-painted flower and animal figures, whilst also displaying a pervasive fondness for glazed Batman logos.

The Virgin of Zapopan

Northwest of Guadalajara lies the suburb of Zapopan, famous for its Virgin who inspires pilgrimages from every part of Mexico. To get there take the trolley bus (marked 'Zapopan') from Juárez or bus 275D from Av 16 de Septiembre via Av Ávila Camacho. By car or taxi, take Av Vallarta and turn right/north on to Av de las Américas. The journey takes about 30 minutes.

Although closely associated with the Huichol, and often shown in beaded Huichol clothing, the Virgin of Zapopan is staunchly Catholic. She arrived in 1542 when Fray Antonio de Segovia took the little image he had been wearing around his neck and donated it to Zapopan, then a neighbouring Chimalhuacán village. Her miracles are legendary: giving blind men their sight, healing the incurable and, most incredible of all, bringing the prelate Manuel de Mimbela back to life for four days in 1721. This last miracle sealed her fate and she duly became the patron saint of the city in 1734.

The vast plateresque basilica which houses the miniscule virgin was built in the early 16th century by the Franciscans. In the atrium a monumental statue of a pursed-lipped pope holding his staff in his left hand and a *charro* boy in his right commemorates the 1979 visit of John Paul II. In the episcopal offices there is a small museum of the art of the Cora and Huichol people (open daily 09.30–13.00 and 15.30–19.00). The crafts on sale, masks, necklaces and rings, are brought in by the Huichol and the profits go to an artisans' cooperative.

Every year since 1734, from 13 June to 4 October, the Virgin has been paraded from church to church (13 in all) until she is finally escorted back to the basilica by trucks, all dangerously top-heavy with candles, altars and thousands of pilgrims. The serenading by mariachis, the dancing and the fireworks continue all night. The day to visit is Sunday, preferably at the beginning of October, when the church overshadows a plaza full of tamale stands, candy-floss boys and the inevitable lottery-ticket vendors.

Tequila

Fifty kilometres (40 mins) northwest of Guadalajara, on Highway 15, is the small town of Tequila, home of the Mexican national drink. Malcolm Lowry, who certainly had enough experience of it, wrote: 'It is a drink that if it does not make you drunk promotes meditation, not always of a cheerful nature.'

All buses going to Tepic and Puerto Vallarta, or points further north, pass through Tequila. **Panoramex** (Calzada del Federalismo Sur 948, tel 10 50 05) run tours to a distillery and a shop, leaving at 09.30 from Plaza San Francisco (Mon–Fri) and returning in the afternoon.

The fields around the town are spiked with the bluish-grey *agave tequilana Weber* plants, whose juices are fermented and distilled. Tequila has been drunk since pre-Hispanic times, initially for religious purposes. The Spanish found themselves acquiring a taste for it and in 1795 received a concession from the king of Spain to produce it. There are now 25 distilleries, many of them family-run, such as the Sauza and Cuervo firms which have been operating since the last century. Most of the tequila produced throughout Mexico is either from here or, at least, sold here. The tawny yellow *reposado*, a matured tequila, is far superior to the regular, clear, white brand. The difference is similar to that between malt and blended whiskies. Every shop in the village is stocked to the brim with bottles. Local brands, like Orendain and Siete Leguas, are proudly held up as the real McCoy, whilst imitations from Japan and Tamaulipas are greatly disdained.

BALLET FOLKLORICO
The Ballet Folklórico on a Sunday morning at the Teatro Degollado is a *sine qua non*. As always in Mexico, the theatre of reality threatens to outplay that of the stage. Crowds queue outside for the 10 am performance. No one has thought to buy a ticket in advance. Harrassed fathers clutch handfuls of delinquent children as tickets are sold fast and furiously. From the stalls to the gods, the regal gilt seats are within the reach of a modest budget, though hard enough to have been designed only for the ample bottoms of *condessas*. The dancers perform dances from the states of Michoacán, Yucatán, Veracruz, Chiapas and, finally, Jalisco, in a crescendo which has the audience in a frenzy of appreciation. A rival folk ballet is performed in the Instituto Cultural Cabañas at 20.30 on Wednesdays.

CINEMAS
It would be easy to live on an unadulterated diet of Beverly Hills cop movies in Guadalajara, but it is not too hard to find an alternative. Both the **Instituto Cultural Cabañas** and the **Ex-convento del Carmen** have cinema clubs. The **Cinematografo**, by the university on Av Vallarta, is the best of the rest, while the **Cine Charlie Chaplin** on López Mateos Norte 848 is usually up to date. All English films have Spanish sub-titles and there is no need to book ahead.

FESTIVALS
As well as celebrating all the many national high days and holidays, Guadalajara has taken the month of October for its own four-week festival. There are fireworks every night in the Plaza de la Liberación and cultural events day and night in every part of the city. The whole of the Plaza Tapatía becomes a great open-air market place, with craft stalls from every state in the republic, sculpture and photography exhibitions, busking, dancing and music. As in the Edinburgh Festival in Scotland, every grand theatre and spartan church hall becomes a stage for opera, mime, body building, folk dancing and disco competitions. The Championship Charro event is the most serious annual example of Mexican horsemanship—rodeo-style—and one which Jalisco proudly wins year after year.

It is an excellent time to visit the city. Hotels are harder to come by, but, because the festival lasts so long, not all the rooms are filled all the time. October, too, provides perfect weather, with balmy days and warm evenings. If another excuse was needed, it would be that it coincides with the festival of the Virgin of Zapopan at the beginning of the month, another great and colourful religious festival, close to the heart of all Guadalajarans. For all of these events and more, the tourist offices have programmes.

MARIACHI
The best evening's entertainment for Guadalajarans is listening to mariachi bands in the Plazuela de los Mariachis or Tlaquepaque's El Parian. The word comes from the French

mariage. Smart burghers in the 19th century, slavishly imitating the French, would call up musicians with guitars, violins, trumpets and occasionally a flute to serenade a newly wed bride and groom. Today, these strolling musicians, in tight, black bolero jackets and trousers piped with silver braid, high-heeled boots and wide wheelbarrow hats, are as much a part of Mexico as tortillas. The Plazuela de los Mariachis, together with the Plaza Garibaldi in Mexico City, are the best-known venues. The mariachi is an institution, almost a caricature, with thick black moustaches, an overflowing beer belly, peacock finery and a face so sad, solemn and serious that howls of sympathy are wrested from usually reticent listeners. Every song tells of love's labour lost, the perfidy of women and the agony of unrequited love. Double meanings thread their way through: each town has its own variations. If in doubt ask for the songs 'Los Arbolitos', 'La Guacamaya' or 'La Culebra'.

NIGHTCLUBS

It is usually only the rich young socialites (known as *fresas* or strawberries) who go all the way out to the Plaza del Sol in the southwest of the city, where internationally priced nightclubs cater to the conservative middle classes with mainstream rock, pop and hotter salsa. Several are clustered between the Holiday Inn and the Hyatt Regency, including **Gros, Jimmy's**, and **Daddy Oh!**. The Hyatt itself has a disco with an ice rink.

WHERE TO STAY   (area code 36)

Guadalajara has plenty of places to stay. Only during the month-long October festival is there a shortage, when all the best rooms disappear long in advance and reservations are essential.

Expensive

Business people patronize the luxurious modern hotels far from the centre, like the narcissistic **(GT) Fiesta Americana**, a monolithic glass-fronted structure overlooking the monument to Minerva (tel 24 25 68). The comforts are calmer at the **(GT) Holiday Inn** with its large gardens (close to the Plaza del Sol on Calzada Mariano Otero, tel 21 24 00). There is, however, a new contender for the throne which is making them all look to their laurels. The glorious **(GT) Quinta Real** (north of town at Av México 2727, off Av López Mateos, tel 30 17 97, tlx 684060) puts fresh flowers into every room and lights a log fire during the winter. The rooms have original prints and paintings on the walls, local ceramics in nooks and crannies and the odd discreet jacuzzi. A string quartet plays daily and can even be heard from the small tiled swimming pool which is surrounded by a cloud of jasmine.

Medium

In the heart of the city, the charming ****Francés (on Maestranza 35, one block south of the Plaza de la Liberación, tel 13 11 90) is Guadalajara's oldest hotel. Originally built in 1618 as a *posada* for merchants travelling back and forth between the coast and Mexico City, it became a landmark for liberal politicians and revolutionaries during Guadalajara's more turbulent years, before being refurbished in the 1980s when Charles Bronson descended to film *The Evil that Men Do* there. An ancient lift rises ponderously to the large rooms, which are filled with heavy wooden beds. Equally well positioned, the ****de Mendoza (at right angles to the Teatro Degollado, Venustiano Carranza 16, tel 13 46 46, tlx 682683), is a comfortable updated colonial hotel. Two Spaniards run the ****Don Quixote Plaza (Héroes 91, tel 58 12 99). Prints of Gustave Doré's windmill-jousting Don Quixote adorn the walls of the fussily restored but small and friendly Spanish mansion. Over the road is the colonial ****San Francisco Plaza (Degollado 267, tel 13 89 54) where tall rooms lead off a lobby filled with fountains and plants. A bustling restaurant sits in the middle of it all.

Near the university is the ***del Parque (Juárez 845, tel 25 28 00) which, despite an unprepossessing exterior, has good, big, modern rooms at a reasonable price. The tables of the modest restaurant attached spill out onto the street. The aged bell boy reappears in different guises as plumber, waiter or electrician as the need arises. This is a good choice for anyone arriving late and tired and in need of a reliable hotel which doesn't involve blowing a week's budget. The ***Universo (López Cotilla 161, tel 13 28 15) is a similar stalwart, with a big modern lobby and a cafeteria filled to the brim with families. The worn carpets are a testament to its popularity. Opposite the tour group Hotel Fénix is the little-adorned entrance to the first-floor *** Posada Regis (Corona 171, tel 13 30 26). The 150-year-old building has been a small hotel for 60 long years and has accrued bags of unorthodox character: the bathrooms have been hastily set up in the corner of the bedrooms.

Cheap

The lacklustre **Estación (Calzada Independencia Sur 1297, tel 19 00 51), beside the station, is clean, respectable, and conveniently placed. The rooms at the back are the quietest. The hotel most popular with young travellers is the well-run, brown-painted **Hamilton (Madero 381, tel 40 67 26). As it is often full, an acceptable alternative is the noisier but more central **Las Américas (Hidalgo 61, tel 14 16 04).

The cheapest accommodation still has the advantage of being in the centre, the grand hotels preferring the peripheries of the city. The only boast of the *Hotel Maya (López Cotillo 38, tel 14 54 54) is that it is '*absolutamente familiar*'. Although the paint peels off the walls, it does indeed have a family atmosphere and they make their own *pan dulce* in the small restaurant. The nearby *Occidental (Huerta y Villa Gómez, tel 13 84 06), in front of the Cine Avenída, is cheap and functional. The walls have been painted a bright lime green and the tiled bathrooms are clean.

EATING OUT

Some of the most characteristic of Mexican dishes come from Jalisco: chicken *pipián* made with pumpkin and sesame seeds, and *birria*, usually goat or lamb slowly baked in maguey leaves and then drowned in a sauce of chillies, cumin and tomatoes. *Pozole* and *menudo* are both very traditional broths. *Pozole* is made with chicken and pork and crushed maize, whilst *menudo* is a tripe and chilli-pepper dish, warming in the morning. Both are like fish and chips to the British and the best place to try them is the upstairs section of the Mercado Libertad. As for drinks, the town of Tequila is under an hour away and the national drink is available in as many varieties as Heinz. Apart from tequila, there is mescal (with or without the worm in the bottom of the bottle), beer served in great goblets called *chabelas*, and *tepache*, a cool drink of fermented pineapple.

In addition, Guadalajara's cosmopolitanism lends itself to French, Chinese, Japanese, Spanish and Argentinian restaurants as well as the ubiquitous American-style fast-food joints. Restaurants are spread all over the city, and many of them have to be reached by taxi.

Restaurants Around the City

North on Av de las Américas, the exquisite **Río Viejo** is at 302 on the left-hand side (tel 16 60 90). It is a beautiful, carefully decorated restaurant, filled with antiques from the owner's shop next door (religious art, candlesticks, dried hydrangeas in Pueblan vases, gilt mirrors), and a line of waiters in starched white. The daily suggestions are inspired: kebabs with wild mushrooms, grilled quail or red chilli shrimps. Well patronized at lunch, it is candlelit by night. Expensive. Closer to Av Vallarta but still on las Américas at 28 is the highly respected **Los Otates** (tel 52 04 81), renowned for regional food such as *machaca* (dried beef) tacos, *sopes*, *pozole* (hominy soup) and *chicharron* (deep-fried pork rinds). It is very informal with a no-nonsense seriousness. Moderate.

Luigi Capurro's **Recco** (Libertad 1981 as it joins Av Chapultepec, tel 25 07 24) is, as the owner proudly testifies, authentically Italian. The once-grand 1920s house has been painted a soft cornflower blue and the kitchens transformed to produce plates of *fettuccine* with *mariscos*, *zarzuela biscay* (an intriguing seafood casserole), *osso buco* in rich white wine and *zuppa inglese*, the glorious Italian interpretation of the English trifle which assumes an added piquancy so far from Europe. Expensive. A more modest Italian alternative is **La Trattoría** (Niños Héroes 3051, tel 22 18 17).

Restaurant du Pierre (Justo Sierra 2355, one block beyond Las Américas, tel 15 36 58) has charmed Guadalajara with its exquisite Parisian ways in preparing such dishes as a *sûpreme de Saint Pierre clouté aux truffes*. Expensive. **Chemary** (in Colonia Chapalito at Av Guadalupe 596, tel 21 29 51) is the Spanish restaurant where all the Spaniards eat and sounds more like Granada than Guadalajara. It serves hearty steaks as well as more traditional Spanish favourites like gazpacho and paella. Moderately expensive. **Rinconada** in Morelos, just down from the tourist office, is a quiet haven in which to have anything from courgette-flower soup to seafood pancakes. Moderate.

Seafood

Mexicans prefer to eat seafood in busy, bustling *marisquerias* rather than over-solemn, fussy restaurants. Of these, **El Pargo** (Av Francia 1302 at Federalismo Sur, tel 10 52 85) is forever bursting at its wide seams with a mass of large families around tiny tables, listening to music from Veracruz and sharing platefuls of *pescado sarandeado* (a split and grilled whole fish, occasionally served scales and all), oysters and shrimps. There is a second one at Av La Paz 2140. Both are extremely popular and consistently inexpensive. **El Délfin Sonriente** (Av Niños Héroes 2239 at Av Unión, tel 16 02 16) is another *marisqueria*, open all week to 23.00 and Sunday to 18.00. Their speciality is *parilladas*: a platter of octopus, squid, frogs' legs, grilled fish, and shrimps. Moderate.

Cafés

The **Copa de Leche** (Juárez 414 between Galeana and Ocampo, tel 14 18 45) is a Guadalajaran institution on three floors. Open all day from 07.00 to 23.00, it serves excellent breakfasts on the first-floor balcony. The thick white bowls of fruit and yoghurt, toasted croissants and cups of rich, dark coffee endlessly refilled make it hard to leave. Inexpensive. Another breakfast bistro is **Oui le Café** (just before the arches on the fringes of the Plaza Vallarta shopping mall, tel 30 01 88). The entrance is overhung with thick vegetation and hard to discern. It has a Tiffany glass interior with linen tablecloths and waiters wrapped in white aprons with black bow ties. At the small tables and booths all around, elegant women discuss hairdressers whilst the men are left to their lengthy business breakfasts. Mexican ingredients are combined to create an international menu, including omelettes such as the *Miki Takeshima*, with shrimps, oysters, carrots, bean sprouts and mushrooms. During the day one can go for a drink or for anything from sauerkraut sandwiches to the ubiquitous hamburger. Service is efficient and unobtrusive. Moderate.

The café in the Ex-Convento del Carmen on Av Juárez is frequented by students from the nearby university. Some of the most revered tacos come from the **Fonda Las Itacates** (on Av Chapultepec, just south of Av México), which offers a huge choice for a small price. **Café Madrid** (Av Juárez where it crosses with 16 de Septiembre) is always filled with *tapatíos* having breakfasts of *chilaquiles* and *malteados*, cheap, filling comidas or steaming coffees late at night from tall glasses.

There are two good vegetarian restaurants. The best is **Zanahoria** (Av Las Américas 538, a block up from the Río Viejo, tel 16 61 61, open 08.00–20.00). Closer to the centre is **Acuarius** (Priscilliano Sanchez 416, tel 13 62 77). Both do inexpensive comida corridas.

The **Gigante** supermarket (on Vallarta at Martínez) stocks exotic things like Evian water and tins of smoked oysters in amongst the biros, bras and bananas. Around the city are various **Polo Norte** ice-cream bars with irresistibly grainy guayaba ices. **Helados Bing** are altogether smoother and creamier for the cholesterol-deficient.

Charros competing in the Mexican equivalent of a rodeo

Lake Chapala

> Lake Chapala has tides and is subject to sudden and alarming squalls,
> but in the late afternoon it is smooth like gelatine and shot through with
> unexpected reverberated colours, ruby and amethyst, cornelian and
> reseda.

So wrote Sybille Bedford in the 1950s, when the lake was a bathing resort as famous for
the supposedly mild manners of foreigners who came to take the air, as for the mildness
of its climate. Lake Chapala, the biggest lake in Mexico, still offers a peaceful alternative
to the bright lights of the city and a place to rest, despite the fact that modern effluence
has now painted its waters a dull polluted green. Originally the domain of King
Chapalac, who gave the volcanic lake its name, today the villages of **Chapala**, **Ajijic** and
Jocotepec along the more clement northern shores have been colonized by retired but
not retiring North Americans. Notices everywhere announce weekly meetings of
Daughters of the American Revolution and Alchoholics Anonymous. Otherwise they
keep much to themselves and during the week there is little to do but take the air. The
villages only become truly Mexican at weekends, when droves of Guadalajarans come
down to puncture the silence with mariachi bands and broods of children.

GETTING AROUND
Lake Chapala is 48 km southeast of Guadalajara. Follow signs from the city centre on
Highway 23, past the airport. Buses leave regularly from the Central Camionera and the
journey takes half an hour. Ajijic is a 10-minute bus journey west of Chapala, and
Jocotepec a further 10.

Chapala
Chapala itself seems a strangely misplaced English suburb, with red brickwork and iron
railings. Activity is confined to spotting resident North Americans and eating. Try fish
from the lake, known simply as *pescado*, or *michi*, a broth made of catfish. Both are sold in
the restaurants by the pier. Boats go from here out to the two scraggy islands thrown up
by volcanic eruption, in the middle of the lake.

Ajijic
D H Lawrence wrote his heavy, somnolent novel, *The Plumed Serpent*, here in 1926.
Despite the satellite dishes and increasing selection of expensive craft shops, it's still,
just, a fishing village with narrow, cobbled streets and red tiled roofs. There's a small
archaeology museum displaying local pieces found in and around the lake, with a Casa de
Cultura attached, selling colourful Huichol bead work and national handicrafts. The
best buys, however, come and go. Mixtec women from Oaxaca hitch babies onto their
backs and come over 1000 km north in an attempt to sell their work. They set up looms
under the shade of trees, outside the Posada Ajijic, and weave intricately woven shawls
and brightly coloured wrist bands. At least one is likely to speak some Spanish, but no
English: bargain with ready notes or fingers when Spanish fails.

Jocotepec
Further round the lake shore is Jocotepec, a less colonized village for the fringe members
of the lake elite. The main square is at once both busier and more Mexican. Still famed

for its white *sarapes* (blanket-shawls), it now offers more of a hotchpotch choice. Calle Hidalgo has *sarapes*. Calle Miguel Arana (the road in from Ajijic) has quantities of leather sandals, shoes and belts for sale, particularly at No 21 and just along from there, a giant sandal outside the door announces a *maestro huarache* or sandal maker.

WHERE TO STAY AND EAT
(area code 376)

The red-brick facade of the **Gran Hotel Nido** (tel 52116), opposite the church in **Chapala**, resembles a Victorian station hotel. It has big sensible bedrooms and a no-nonsense dining room with white tablecloths, wooden wicker-bottomed chairs and walls lined with photographs of Chapala at the beginning of the century. The lunchtime comida corrida is always full.

The best place to stay in **Ajijic** is the ***Posada Ajijic** (16 de Septiembre 4, tel 53395) on the lakeside. Once a tequila factory, it is now run by Canadians who have put fireplaces and small kitchens into all the *cabañas* (garden cottages), which are set amongst tropical fruit trees. The restaurant is justifiably popular. The prices vary as much as the rooms but are always reasonable with a large breakfast included. The overpriced *****Real de Chapala** (PO Box 333, La Floresta, tel 52468) is set in lovely gardens outside the centre, towards Chapala. It's quiet enough to hear a pin drop until a convention of hoover salesmen from Mexico City turns up. The rooms are looking a bit jaded and the hotel is more favoured for long-drawn-out Sunday lunches in its lakeside garden restaurant. The ****Danza del Sol** (tel 52505), on the other side of the village, has been pleasantly remodelled with weathered wooden tables and waxy red tiled floors. All rooms have a well-equipped kitchen and a fireplace.

In **Jocotepec**, the lakeside **Posada del Pescador** is all that is on offer, but the rooms are reasonable and the owners friendly.

Tapalpa

For a slice of unselfconscious rural life, it would be hard to beat the hill village of Tapalpa, set high up in the Sierra de Tapalpa between Guadalajara and Colima. It would certainly be worth altering any well-thought-out itinerary, just to fit in a couple of nights in this peaceful place. On a gentle slope, its cobbled streets patiently bear donkeys laden with wood, cattle returning for milking, horses top-heavy with far-from-sober cowmen and enormous jeeps driven with consummate ease by 10-year-old boys in 10-gallon hats.

GETTING AROUND

From Guadalajara take the toll road (*cuota*) south towards Colima. After 34 km, at Acatlán de Juárez, the road divides. Make sure to take Highway 54, the old road south to Colima, and not the fast new toll. Some 44 km from here the road for Tapalpa bears right off Highway 54 and begins its climb up into rolling hills. Buses for Tapalpa leave from the Central Camionera in Guadalajara and take 1½ hours. Buses back leave every 1½ hours from the left-hand side of the parish church.

VILLAGE LIFE

In the morning cocks crow and the village awakens. Shops open which anywhere else would be deemed 'quaint' but are here a living, working part of daily life. The mass of dairies testify to the area's renown for milk and cream. During the week, visitors are so few and far between that everyone quickly becomes intimate. In this they are aided and abetted by the garrulous operator of the only phone in the village (on the corner of the plaza). Whilst dialling a number, she keeps her eyes firmly fixed on the television screen where the latest soap opera unfolds with high drama. Once the call is connected, however, her attention switches rapidly. The television is turned down as she cranes forward to participate in the long-distance whispered nothings.

Surrounded by flower-filled pastures and resinous pine forests, Tapalpa is a place for walking, relaxing and sipping hot chocolate or shots of tequila. Some 6 km out of town are mysterious giant boulders, calmly weighted down in fields of purple, pink and red wild flowers, where most walks begin and end. An accessible dirt road leads off to the left just after the bridge on the road out, passing an ex-paper hacienda, a few weekend homes and a former nuns' seminary.

WHERE TO STAY
There are three enchanting hotels. The most expensive is the ******Posada La Fuente** on the main square. This serene hotel has only six rooms which sleep either four or six. Sensitively renovated back to the basics, it is built with adobe walls, wooden beams and clay tiles. The rooms, smelling of pine, are filled with local furniture. The large sitting room has a crackling fire every night. As there are no telephones, the best way to book is to write well in advance to Posada La Fuente, Tapalpa. It is usually full at weekends but quiet during the week. *****Posada del Carratero** in Calle Carratero, 50 m from the main square, is the oldest hotel. All rooms lead off the main courtyard and have tiled bathrooms. The more modest ****Hotel Hacienda**, on the main square, has sparklingly clean rooms down steep steps overhung with bougainvillaea. The manager is full of information on the best walks, hidden waterfalls and the state of the dirt tracks.

EATING OUT
On the main square, **Paulinos** and **La Hacienda** are on second-floor balconies. Inexpensive. From here one can gaze unobtrusively at the sheriff, gun tucked into his belt, who in turn watches wistfully as cars refuse to acknowledge the new one-way system. Shy young couples perambulate in full view of benignly approving parents. The best food in town, however, is in the flower-filled courtyard of the **Posada La Fuente**. Open to non-residents, it serves breakfasts, lunches and dinners to linger over. Moderate.

The Jalisco Coast
Between Bahía de Navidad in the south and Puerto Vallarta in the north, Jalisco's ·212-km stretch of Pacific coast still remains undeveloped and often inaccessible. Don't be deluded by travel agents' claims that Puerto Vallarta is anything other than a tropical flesh-pot. It is the most attractive and appealing of all Mexico's resorts, generously blessed by nature, but a resort nonetheless. If it seems too hyper or too crowded, the road continues south.

Along the way, a few of the many bays have been opened up for expensive getaway hotels but there is no large-scale development after the razzmatazz of Puerto Vallarta.

The road follows the coast where it can but heads inland to avoid the mountains of the Sierra Lagunillas. For 100 km, only the occasional side road leads down to the sea. The Bahía de Navidad, on the border with the state of Colima, is the only other populated part of the entire Jalisco coast. The exact opposite of Puerto Vallarta, it hasn't yet heard the word 'condominium' and still bumbles along in a haphazard fashion, as content to let people stay as it is to let them move on.

Puerto Vallarta

Puerto Vallarta is one of those rare resorts that hasn't sold its soul to Mammon (although every other part of its body may be in hock). The old town still retains its charm, despite the hype, the condominiums, the tourists and the development on its northern and southern sides. Built beside the waters of the 40-km-long Banderas Bay, in the folds of the hills, it had no choice but to scramble upwards away from the sea lapping at its toes. Once it had been discovered by the Hollywood groupies, hoteliers grasped land to north and south but kept the original village in the middle 'picturesque'. What this means is that even the supermarkets and petrol stations have obligatory red-tiled roofs and white-washed walls, and the town has been protected from high-rises. Don't be fooled by brochure-writers' hastily got-together 'history'. The town begins and ends with tourism and its greatest hero should, by rights, be John Huston who brought the world here (much to his chagrin and dismay), with the filming of *Night of the Iguana* in the early 1960s.

GETTING AROUND
Puerto Vallarta is on Highway 200, 170 km($2\frac{1}{2}$ hrs) from Tepic, 400 km (6 hrs) from Guadalajara, 210 km (3 hrs) from Bahía de Navidad and an exhausting drive from the US border at Nogales (1200 km away).

By Air: The vast majority of foreign tourists fly in from the US or Guadalajara. There are daily flights to and from Mexico City and Guadalajara, and direct flights to and from Chicago, Los Angeles, San Francisco, Dallas, Denver and Houston. Two Mexican airlines have offices in town opposite each other on Juárez: **Mexicana** (tel 21707) and Aeroméxico (tel 20031). **Continental** (tel 23096) and **American Airlines** (tel 23787) have offices at the airport.

By Bus: There is no train (the nearest station is in Tepic, tel 321 34861). Nor is there a central bus station, but the various companies disgorge and pick up passengers from Av Insurgentes, the south side of Río Cuale. Buses leave hourly for Guadalajara and Tepic, and four times a day for Mexico City. Buses heading north to the US leave in the early evening.

Local buses run by Transportes Pacífico leave hourly for Punta Mita, and combis (No 2) depart every 15 minutes from Calle Piño Suárez to Mismaloya and Boca de Tomatlán in the south.

By Ferry: There is a daily ferry to and from Cabo San Lucas in Baja California (21 hrs). Recently privatized, the company has changed its time-table three times in the last three months, but departures usually leave in the early afternoon. For the most up-to-date information, ask at the tourist office.

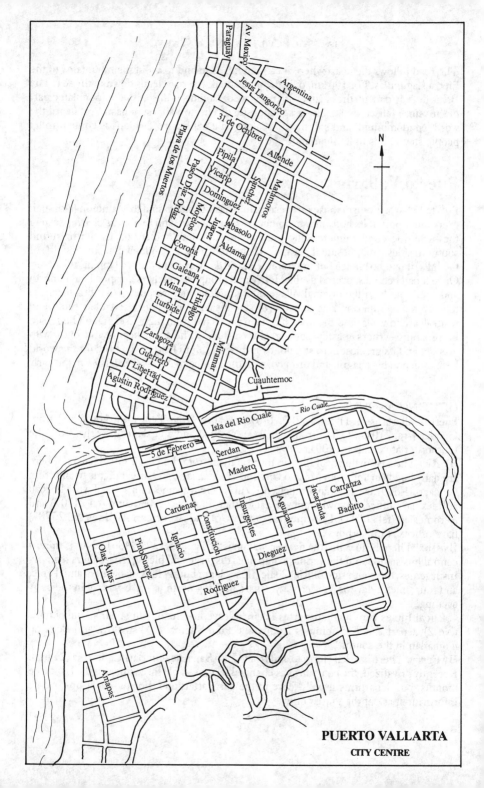

PUERTO VALLARTA

CITY CENTRE

In Town: The town is split into three parts, linked by an efficient bus service which runs from the airport and hotels in the north, to the old town in the middle, and the beaches and hotels in the south. Driving can be hell. Cobblestoned streets rise almost vertically, cratered with pot-holes, choked with traffic and squeezed narrowly into funnels, a permanent Saint Tropez on Bastille Day. To hire a jeep or car, ring Hertz (tel 20473), Ansa (tel 23395), Avis (tel 21107), Dollar Rent-a-Car (tel 30001) or National (tel 21107).

TOURIST INFORMATION
As well as the hawkers along the Paseo Díaz Ordáz, offering free information for the price of a time-share condominium, there is a good official tourist office around the back of the town hall (*palacio municipal*) on Juárez (tel 20242).

WHAT TO SEE
Apart from craning your neck to the improbable crown of the church, NS de Guadalupe (purportedly a replica of one worn by the ill-fated Empress Carlota, wife of Maximilian), there really is no more to contemplate than everyone else's navel on the various beaches. The old town is neat and orderly along its 1½-km sea-front, the Malecón. This leads down past the town hall to the river, Río Cuale. Above the two flat streets nearest to the sea (Juárez and Morelos), all is anarchy. The lanes and streets lead up and around, shooting off in any direction. The northern bank of the river is known as Gringo's Gulch, named after the hordes of North Americans who have moved down here since the 1950s. Elizabeth Taylor still has a house (which has reputedly been on the market for years), although she rarely comes down. Even here, the streets are narrow and cars can only squeeze through if everyone breathes in and out at exactly the same time. The narrow river splits the town in two. It is spanned by two bridges and steps lead down from both to a long, thin island, Isla Cuale, which has a poor archaeological museum on its southern tip and rather better shops and restaurants.

BEACHES
The beaches are the main attraction. One long stretch, the **Playa Norte**, runs from the marina in the north, past the hotel strip, to the centre of town. In town, **Playa de los Muertos** is the most popular beach, filled with bodies, bars and bargaining. To the south, the main road continues its twist, rattle and roll up and down past condominium after condominium, high above small coves hemmed in by hotels. One of the most pleasant of these bays is in front of the Camino Real Hotel, the **Playa las Estacas**, enclosed by two rocky points. Ten minutes along the road, the natural splendour of **Los Arcos** rises out of the water—arched rocks that have become a beguiling landmark of Puerto Vallarta and a favourite stop on snorkelling trips. Round another couple of bends the *Night of the Iguana* beach, **Playa Mismaloya**, counts as the end of Puerto Vallarta proper. The restaurant just over the bridge has wonderfully fresh lunchtime shrimp cocktails.

Further south, still on the route of the No 2 combi, is the small community of **Boca de Tomatlán**, 20 minutes from town. Occasionally there are rooms for rent but usually no-one stirs to reply to questions, content merely to have a little fishing, a pretty bay and no hotels. From here the road leaves the coast, passing the last of Puerto Vallarta's domains, **Chico's Paradise** (see Eating Out), before leaving all behind for the next 100 km.

Inaccessible by road but often visited by boats are two other beaches, **Playa las Animas** and **Yelapa**, two hours from Puerto Vallarta (see Boat Trips). Yelapa is a small fishing village, backed by jungle. Few fishing boats now leave from here. It is easier and more profitable to stay at home and sell a few warm Coca-Colas or a frightened iguana to tourists. Far prettier than the village is the waterfall and swimming hole, but it is a strenuous half-hour walk upstream and the boats back to Puerto Vallarta leave no later than 15.00.

North of Puerto Vallarta

Far beyond airport, marina and hotels, and into the state of Nayarit, is a much less developed stretch of coastline where possibilities are still more tantalizing than real. Although in the next-door state, it is best approached from Puerto Vallarta. One easy morning's journey, by car or bus, is **Punta Mita**, where the road falls into the sea. Turn left off north-bound Highway 200 at **Cruz de Huanacaxtle** (30 km). Punta Mita really is the end of the road: a no-frills-attached tiny fishing village of thatched-roof houses whose beach is the domain of butterflies, children, cockerels, dogs and Brahmin cattle, with not a bottle of Hawaiian Tropic in sight. A local man offers to take a boat and snorkelling equipment out to the **Tres Mariettas Islands**, which provide some very good diving, or along the coast to yet more isolated beaches further north. Be careful swimming off the point: it is full of coral which, by the same token, makes it excellent for snorkelling. Just before the road peters out, there is a dirt track on the left which bumps down for 100 m to a safer cove with a couple of restaurants. The **Coral** cooks what it catches, including the freshest of lobsters for a third of the price of anywhere else.

Seven km before the road meets the sea is the fantastical restaurant **Amapas**, set in a small jungle clearing. An extraordinary couple from the capital moved there 15 years ago, eating only what they hunted or planted. Out of this has grown an exotic kitchen restaurant run by the original colonists. There is no menu as such. Pots bubble on the stove: lifting a lid might reveal iguana, a wild boar's head, armadillo or snake. Simpler things can be reluctantly rustled up for more delicate stomachs, like *crepas de flor de calabaza* (courgette-flower pancakes). The requisite drink is 'bat's blood', a cool pomegranate punch.

THE NIGHT OF THE IGUANA

The film which hurled Puerto Vallarta into the spotlight is on every evening at 19.30 in the terrace bar of the **Jolla de Mismaloya Hotel**. As you watch, the film set is right behind you over the beach. The slow, heavy, torpid heat of the film still draws one in. Although everyone assumes she was, Elizabeth Taylor was never in it. Richard Burton, as the irreverently Reverend Lawrence Shannon, actually played opposite Deborah Kerr and the impossible Ava Gardner (brilliantly typecast). It is vintage Huston out of vintage Tennessee Williams: suppressed passions and viperish dialogue that sear through the social niceties of the Texas Baptists Ladies College.

SPORTS

Puerto Vallarta, by its very nature, has lots of water sports. Parasailing, scuba diving, fishing and snorkelling are usually on offer at the large hotels or available from their stands on the north beach and on the Playa de los Muertos. Playa Mismaloya must be the best for parasailing, offering not just a 10-minute viewpoint of high-rise hotels but a wide sweep, high in the air, over tropical jungle. Here, too, are the crumbling film sets on the far point. There is an 18-hole golf course, **Los Flamingos Country Club**, 12 km north of the airport, but reservations must be made at least 24 hours in advance (preferably through your hotel) (tel 20959). Many hotels have tennis courts: it is also possible to play at the **John Newcombe Tennis Club** (tel 227670) or the less grand **Vallarta Tennis Club** (tel 227676). There is some feeble horse riding on the beaches. **Rancho White Horse** (tel 25973) can arrange 3-hour rides through banana and mango plantations, with a swim in the middle.

BOAT TRIPS

Excursions leave from the Malecón or Mismaloya beach for snorkelling off Los Arcos or for beaches, like **Yelapa**, that can only be reached by a 2-hour boat ride. Most trips include some snorkelling, drinks, lunch and a few hours on the beach. They tend to be very crowded. A more peaceful alternative is to arrange a deal with the boatmen at Mismaloya or Tomatlán, for a trip out to the less-visited **Playa las Animas**, where the sand is fine and clean (Yelapa is coarser). Two other places to have lessons, rent equipment or go on trips from are **Chico's Dive Shop** on Díaz Ordáz 772 (tel 21895), or **Paradise Divers** at Olas Altas 443 (tel 24004). The fishermen have a cooperative which operates from the north end of the Malecón, with set prices for fishing trips.

SHOPPING

Forget cruise wear and designer clothing, forget lurex bikinis and spangled sombreros, and hunt out the shops which make Puerto Vallarta a cut-above. In Calle Corona, for example, a dangerous cluster of unusual shops includes the **Gallery of Huichol Art** at 164. Beaded masks, rings and necklaces come in strident red, yellow and orange and even the postcards are collectable. Just up the street is **Majolica** at 191 with distinctive handcrafted Pueblan pottery in the Italian and Spanish traditions. On the same side, **L'Aguila Descalza** at 179 has ceramics, belts and clothes by the Mexican Josefa. On the main street, Morelos, is **Galería Uno** at 561, with six rooms of paintings by Mexican artists and exhibitions of graphics and sculptures. Close by, **Nebaj** at 223 is something of an anomaly, concentrating on Peruvian and South American arts as much as Chiapan and Guatemalan crafts. **Veryka**, just over the river, is owned by the same couple. Also south of the river, **Olinala**, Calle Cárdenas 274, is a gallery of masks from heaven and hell and everywhere else in between. The collector is a Kent-educated Mexican with an English accent, rarely heard in America's back yard.

WHERE TO STAY   (area code 322)

The vast majority of holiday-makers opt for packages from the United States or Canada which can halve the cost of flight and board. However, the big tour-group hotels can easily be avoided, as there are several more comfortable, personal places to stay in the centre of town, never more than 5 minutes from the beach.

Undoubtedly, the loveliest place to stay in Puerto Vallarta is the ******Casa del Puente**, above Cuale Island (Rodríguez and Libertad, tel 20749). Molly Stokes has two apartments overhanging the river, each with an open drawing room, kitchen, bedroom and all the sybaritic extras—such as someone to look after you who'll also go and queue in the bank on your behalf, to say nothing of liquidizers, toasters and shelves full of English books.

Hidden in a tropical garden right beside the river are the attractive, rustic cottages of the ******Molino de Agua** (Vallarta and Serdán, tel 21957, tlx 065543, fax 26056). Each cottage has been decorated with inlaid wooden furniture, hand-painted bed boards and pewter- and yellow-tiled bathrooms. The ocean-view rooms are larger, with rocking chairs on the terrace. The complex has two restaurants, two pools and a jacuzzi.

The family-run *****Posada Río Cuale** (Serdán 242, tel 20450), on the south side of the island, is famed for its restaurant, **Le Gourmet**, which serves lobster *á l'orange* and *camarón al diablo* (shrimps in a hot chilli sauce). It also has a small pool and a few rooms with enthusiastic Mexican decor. *****Los Cuatro Vientos** (Matamoros 520, tel 20161) is a little hotel tucked away on a clattering cobbled street. With only 16 colonial-style rooms and an imaginative Indonesian-influenced restaurant, it is always full in season. The rooftop bar, **El Nido**, is a good spot for watching the sun set over the crown of the church. Two sister hotels which are similar, central, comfortable, family places are the *****Fontana del Mar** (Dieguez 171, tel 20583), with a pool, and the ******Playa los Arcos** (Olas Altas 380, tel 20583) on the beach. An old-timer, the *****Rosita** (Paseo Díaz Ordáz 901, tel 21033) caters for students and families. It's pleasant enough, on the town beach where the sea wall begins.

****Posada de Roger** (Basilio Badillo 237 at Insurgentes, tel 20639) is the best cheap buy in town. Rooms teeter above one another in disorganized fashion and there is a small pool at the top. All the rooms are extremely clean, with air conditioning. When the hotel is fully booked, as is often the case, the management will provide a list of other cheap hotels. The good, inexpensive restaurant attached has a dedicated following but closes off season. There are plenty of inexpensive posadas and hotels south of the river, including the ***Yasmin** (Basilio Badillo 168, tel 20087), which is plain but comfortable.

EATING OUT

The standard is high in Puerto Vallarta, with seafood at the top of most menus. On Cuale Island, **Le Bistro** (tel 20283) is Californian-owned and run. Slick black tiles are juxtaposed with irrelevant columns and overhanging greenery. Breakfasts are long and lazy. Dinner and lunch are more elegant: an excellent spinach and lemon soup could be followed by steak Lena, a butterfly cut of choice tenderloin nestled in spinach and mushrooms with a creamy wine sauce. Moderately expensive. Also on the island, **Franzi's** (tel 20689) can't be faulted for its breakfast, which has become an expatriate institution: crusty buttered rolls, orange juice, lots of coffee, eggs, bacon and a plate of papaya. The service too is excellent. On Wednesday evenings (between 18.00 and 21.00) the cruise ship musicians come over for jamming sessions. Inexpensive. **Chef Roger** (tel 20819) is on the road between the north and south bridges of the island. Only open in season, it is as popular with other chefs as it is with tourists. This is another place where breakfast can go on all day. Moderate.

On a back street in the south of town, deliberately out of the way, the **Balam** (Basilio Badillo 425, between Aguacate and Jacaranda, tel 23451) is a small restaurant run by a husband and wife with superlative home cooking. The *tostadas* heaped with fish marinaded in lime juice and spiked with chilli and coriander are particularly good, as is the dorado fish cooked in lots of garlic. Inexpensive. One of the oldest and most typical fish restaurants is the central **Moby Dick** (31 de Octubre 128, tel 21444) where practised waiters in white serve platters of fresh fish like *cazuela de mariscos a la veracruzana*, a mix of octopus, clams, shrimps and rice in a thick tomato and onion sauce. Moderate.

Californians like Puerto Vallarta and Californians like sushi, so there is more than one Japanese restaurant in the town. Set on an open-air patio, **Kanpai** (on the corner of Carranza and Pino Suárez, tel 21092) is the most respected. Although the six chefs are all Mexican and the waitresses Canadian (in requisite kimonos), the food is definitely Japanese: *misoshiro* soup with tofu, beef *yakatori* and even Japanese beer. Moderately expensive.

South of town are several more restaurants which may require a taxi. Furthest of all is **Chico's Paradise** (tel 20747), 20 km south and only open during the day. It is built beside the Tomatlán River where a series of boulders turn the mild stream into a roaring channel, pummelled and funnelled through the rocks. The food is unashamedly lavish, from spare ribs, jumbo prawns and stuffed crab to coconut pie and cinnamon coffee. Avoid it on the days the cruise-ship crowds take it over (from 14.00 on Tues, Wed and Sat). Moderately expensive. Tomatlán, at the end of combi route 2, also has a pleasant café, the **Primitivo**, run by a couple of Englishmen and offering steak sandwiches, crêpes, fresh fruit drinks and utter tranquillity.

Taking to the Hills

The villages up in the Sierra Madre of Jalisco, where there is nothing to do but walk, ride, talk and explore, are quite the reverse of the town's cosmopolitanism. Separated from themselves and the rest of the state by mountain chains, these villages are extremely difficult to get to. This, perversely, has made them a favourite retreat for a small handful of Hollywood stars, who have 360 days on a year and finally want five off, far from any possible autograph-hunters.

GETTING AROUND

All journeys to and from the Sierra Madre start and end at Puerto Vallarta. There are no bus services. Jeeps or logger's trucks go in and out and the locals hitch a ride with them. The simplest way is to fly. San Sebastian is 20 minutes away and Talpa 30. Five-seater **Cessna planes** fly in season (December–April), with secheduled flights on Saturday and Monday (they can also be chartered). Aero Vallarta (tel 22210) has an office on the second floor of the Banamex building on the main square. Otherwise it is a day and a half's horse ride (camping out overnight, arranged with the hotels) or longer by four-wheel-drive car (the roads are abysmal).

San Sebastian del Oeste

San Sebastian was once Jalisco's state capital, elevated because of its wealthy silver mines which ran out long ago, leaving the population to shrink down from 40,000 to the 750 or so still living there today. The little town is set in a small cleft in the hills, watered by a stream which runs through its length and guarded by a 300-year-old church, the tallest structure in the sierra. Nothing has been built since the mining days and the low white-washed houses all have the characteristic, long, floor-to-ceiling windows introduced by the Spanish. It is wonderfully fertile, the combination of a high altitude and a tropical latitude allowing pine trees, orchids and bananas to grow alongside coffee beans.

There are two moderately expensive converted haciendas to stay in, arrangements for which should be made through the tourist office in Puerto Vallarta (tel 20242). El Pabellón de San Sebastian (tel 338 60022) is in the town, across the plaza from the church, with 10 rooms in a fine, once-wealthy silver miner's mansion. The Hacienda Jalisco, owned by a long-resident Texan, is 20 minutes down a bumpy road beside the feeble runway (only 2 minutes faster in a jeep than it is by foot). There are rooms for six couples and a large kitchen garden in which lettuces, tomatoes and turnips grow beside orange and lime trees. There is no telephone and no electricity, only oil lamps, gas lights and fireplaces in every room.

The two haciendas can arrange horse-riding trips into the mountains (La Bufa, the highest peak, is 2450 m above sea level), or around the old mine shafts and haciendas which dot the countryside.

Talpa de Allende
High in the mountains where three spurs meet, above the Sierra del Desmoronado, the guayaba-producing town of Talpa is all but inaccessible in the rainy season. It's a larger place than San Sebastian, with a population of 7000, just as remote, but better known because of its big annual fair for its miraculous Virgin on 19 September. No-one can remember why she is miraculous but she is certainly very ancient and extremely delicate. In 1644, the village priest tried to swap the deteriorated image for another, but when he touched it, 'he was hit by a shaft of intense light and the Virgin repaired herself.'

An American couple have turned a hacienda into a very private hotel. Again, the tourist office in Puerto Vallarta can get in touch; otherwise write well ahead to Apt 25, Talpa de Allende, Jalisco 48200. There is another spit-and-sawdust hotel which the loggers and chewing-gum gatherers use after spending weeks deep in the hills.

South towards Colima
Highway 200 curves all around the Pacific coast to Acapulco. Manzanillo, the next large city along the coast, is 260 km south of Puerto Vallarta, a 5-hour car journey or 6 hours by bus (5 daily). The road heads inland to avoid the mountains, only returning to the coast at ****El Tecuan (Highway 200, tel 333 70132), 60 km (90 mins by car) south of Puerto Vallarta. This solitary, rustic hotel, with beautifully designed, wooden beamed rooms, is set on a hillside, overlooking the ocean. There are horses to ride, tennis courts and a pristine beach to surf off.

Costa Careyes
Some 30 mins further south (2 hrs from Puerto Vallarta) hidden away off Highway 200, this bay once sheltered the galleons of gold-hungry buccaneers. Today it is one of the

few remaining natural habitats where marine turtles come to lay their eggs. Along the shore, Italian architect Gian Franco Brignone has created a get-away-from-it-all retreat at the hotel *****Costa Careyes. It's a favourite haunt of Mexican politicians who can be heard getting back into it all around the swimming pool.

With no telephones or satellite dishes, and no identikit rooms, the small villas spread out upon the surrounding cliffs deliberately convey the atmosphere of an Italian hill village. There is plenty to do if the joy of doing nothing ever palls: an excellent stable for rides along the beach, tennis courts, scuba diving, windsurfing, deep-sea fishing and even two manicured polo greens complete with 30 polo ponies.

The Bahía de Navidad

The Bahía de Navidad takes a long, lazy sweep along the coastline, leaving a golden stroke of sand which joins the villages of Barra de Navidad and San Patricio Melaqué. **Barra** is blessed with two fronts, one looking onto the sea and the other onto the Navidad lagoon. **Melaqué**, a little larger, is more worn and lived in. Both have been popular for over 50 years with families from Guadalajara, who come down for their summer holidays, yet it never takes more than 5 minutes to walk to a quiet spot on one of the loveliest bays in Mexico. There may be a disco open if there are enough people to warrant it, but most of the time a few stories told over beers in the shore-front bars will be the evening entertainment. The pace is very low tempo, rising to a hum only at weekends, Easter or Christmas. Few foreigners bother to come here but those that do come back year after year.

History

The first Spanish ships to find a return passage from the Orient set sail from the Bay of Navidad in 1564. On the easier outward voyage, the fleet was under the command of Miguel López de Legazpi. He founded the city of Manila and named the islands he discovered, the Philippines, after his king. Having decided to remain, he handed over the captaincy of the arduous return voyage to his young nephew, Felipe de Salcedo. Within days of leaving Manila, disaster struck. Both the pilot and the sailing master died of disease, the crew were decimated by scurvy, and the helm was left to the care of an Augustinian friar, Fray Andrés de Urdaneta. He wore his habit throughout the voyage, and from within the fragile frame of a Don Quixote found the courage and strength to battle his way back through the trade winds and northwest gales down the coast to Acapulco. When they arrived, there was no one with the energy left even to drop the anchor. Only two men were standing, the captain and his friar, the gentle Basque man who had opened the way to the silk, spices and ivory of the Orient.

GETTING AROUND

Buses run hourly to and from Puerto Vallarta (212 km, 5 hrs) and Guadalajara (via Manzanillo, 5 hrs). In Barra they leave from Av Veracruz and in Melaqué from Gómez Farías. The two villages are 2½ km apart, a 40-minute walk along the beach or a quick hop on the bus. They are both small enough not to get lost in, fronting the bay and not more than five streets deep.

TOURIST INFORMATION

The Barra de Navidad office is on the road into the town, Av Veracruz, opposite the park. Although the office is tiny, its staff are generous with leaflets and well versed in local history. The less switched-on office in San Patricio Melaqué is on the corner of Morelos and Vallarta.

WHERE TO STAY
(area code 333)

Barra has a fair selection of modest little hotels, used to families and familiar faces. The ***Sand's** (Morelos 24, tel 70018), run by an American married to a Mexican, peacefully overlooks the lagoon. The garden is abundantly pretty with a good semicircular swimming pool and a lively evening bar, Coco Loco. This is the best place for renting snorkelling equipment and wind-surfing boards. The manager can also arrange fishing trips out in the bay if he has 24 hours' notice. Opposite is the **Delfin** (Morelos 23, tel 70068) with big rooms, a miniscule pool and a German owner. Foreigners are very popular and any German is always treated like a long-lost cousin. Another attractive little hotel, scrupulously clean and cheap, is the **Bogavante**, facing the beach on Legazpi (tel 70384). Some sea-facing rooms have a small kitchen area. The **(CE) Posada Pacífico** (tel 70359), behind the bus station, is the simplest of the lot: the rooms are spartan but so is the price.

Melaqué accommodation is less good. The loud, raucous, blancmange-pink ****Coco Club Melaqué** (tel 70001) is like a summer camp, with all-inclusive packages and a nauseating 'party team', intent on everyone Having A Good Time with nonstop aerobics, booze and a patter of well-rehearsed jokes. Two calmer hotels are the ***Legaspi** (Av de las Palmas, tel 70397) and the **Vista Hermosa** (Las Palmas and Gómez Farías 110, tel 70002), both with views onto the bay and swimming pools. The ***Orientales** (Abel Salgado and Obregón, tel 324028) is a new endeavour—a weird but wonderful Mexican rendition of Japan on the beach, with bamboo furniture, low-lying beds and a small pool surrounded by palm trees. Five minutes away, in its own bay, is the *****Coco Royale Costa Sur** (tel 70085), a sedate replica of the one in the village, but with more to offer and less to prove.

EATING OUT

The restaurants begin and end with seafood. **Barra**, again, has a distinct edge. On the sea facing Calle Legaspi are **Mariscos Nacho** and **Pancho's**, two doors down. Salads of octopus and shrimps, and red snapper tacos are followed by whole grilled fish washed down with bottle after bottle of the west coast's favourite beer, Pacífico. Cheap.

In **Melaqué**, palapa huts along the far end of the bay serve fish during the day. At night, **Kosonoy**, the best of these, spruces itself up for dinner, decorated with sea shells and fishing nets and lit by candles. Cheap.

The State of Colima

The tiny state of Colima perches on a bite-sized piece of the Pacific coast, caught in a bear hug between Jalisco to the north and Michoacán to the east. A country cousin to its grander neighbours, Colima is keener on the agricultural than the academic. It's a beautful state to explore and discover, well off the beaten tourist track. There are only two towns of any size, and when the bright lights of the city are left behind, rural Mexico reasserts itself with jumbled fields of maize. From the northernmost point, the volcano Nevado de Colima, to the Pacific Ocean, it is a land of green. Pines and meadows in the hills give way to a tropical coast with waving palm trees, waxy banana leaves and languorous mangrove swamps. A smart new toll road leading to the south of the state sears through low-lying hills and spans crevices with feats of Mexican engineering. The Colimense are impressed. Lemonade vendors make excuses to push carts along the inside lane and ice-cream salesmen squeeze extended families onto their newly motorized carts to depart for sales forays into the country.

History

This diminutive state nonetheless produced a David to defend itself against the Goliath of invading Purépecha from next-door Michoacán. In the 13th century, Colimotl, King of the Tecos, led his people to victory over the Purépecha, who, flushed with triumph after a recent victory over the Aztecs, hadn't thought twice about extending their territory into defenceless Colima. This victory gave the tribe enormous status within the surrounding area. On the strength of it, Colimotl became undisputed leader of a confederation of tribes extending as far as northern Jalisco. Patriots later gave his name to the state.

The glory was shortlived and Colima was colonized without difficulty by Hernán Cortés' nephew, Francisco, in 1524. In 1792, after two centuries of calm, its torpor was briefly disturbed when a young (though not yet heroic) Miguel Hidalgo arrived. He had been expelled from a seminary in Morelia for his radical utterances. Colima was considered a sufficiently rural backwater for him to kick his heels in for a few months. When he departed, he characteristically left his house to the town, to be turned into a free school for local children.

It was only in 1910, during the Revolution, that the whole nation looked to Colima, as first the strategic port of Manzanillo and then the state capital fell to the people. Centuries of inaction were as a spark to dry tinder for the citizens, who had had their fill of oppressive landowners controlling their lives. Manzanillo, as a main Pacific port, attracted such luminaries as Pancho Villa to its defence. Colima then bowed out of national politics, with a brief nod in the direction of the ultra-Catholic Cristero movement. In the lull which followed, a succession of unscrupulous governors managed rapidly to destroy most of its cultural heritage, pulling down the ancient Tecos site of Chanala, stone by stone, and selling off a large area to the English millionaire, James Goldsmith.

Colima

Colima itself is an unpretentious state capital with a university, a jumble of good if musty museums and modest hotels. It's untarnished by tourism, lazily curious of foreigners, but educated enough not to point and stare. The main square is dominated by a modern cathedral and turn- of-the-century neo-gothic portals. Here, in the cool of the evening, the townspeople sit outside at the wrought-iron tables of the Café Moneda, sipping *guayaba licuados* and playing backgammon. On Sundays the square fills with Colima dressed in its Sunday best. The strains of the municipal band have to compete with the hooting of horns jubilantly celebrating a wedding procession or the loud ranchero music emanating from the jeeps of local farmers.

GETTING AROUND

By Bus: The modern bus station is far out to the east of the city. Urban buses marked 'Centro/c.c.' travel to and from Calle Madero. There are four buses an hour to and from Manzanillo, two an hour to and from Guadalajara and eight a day to and from Mexico City.

By Car: Highway 54 runs from Guadalajara through the north of the state. It has two tolls and a good surface, apart from a treacherous 45-km section between Cuauhtémoc and Atenquique, where a large paper mill in a narrow gulley forces the road and the railway lines to converge suddenly. To the south, Highway 110 is a swift dual carriage-way leading to Manzanillo. The railway lines continue to run parallel to the road and impede its progress all the way to the coast. In places, the tracks suddenly rip across the fast road with no more than a cursory *alto*, and unwitting cars are forced to screech to a halt in front of the daily goods train.

By Train: Colima is midway on the Guadalajara–Manzanillo line. The railway station is in the south of the city opposite Parque Hidalgo, and has two trains daily. They arrive together at 14.00 from either direction and both take 3 hours. The most magnificent part of the journey north is the 1½-hour stretch between Colima and Ciudad Guzmán, which crosses gulleys and mountainous land that no road can reach. The train often sets forth with only the engine and one carriage. The air conditioning has a mind of its own and it's best to get a seat near the door.

TOURIST INFORMATION

The tourist office at Calle Hidalgo 75 (tel 24360) is more concerned with painting its nails than helping visitors, but it does have maps.

WHAT TO SEE

Colima has some wonderful crumbling museums which are covered in dust and seldom visited. The most up to date is the regional museum which has recently been opened on the main square. From here one can walk a circuit of the various other museums in about half an hour. From Constitución north of the square, the Mask Museum is six blocks to the north in Valle. Continue east down Valle to Av San Fernando, and turn right. By a large roundabout, often dotted with uniformed cadets from the local military college, the Museum of Western Culture and the Casa de Cultura sit side by side. To return to the main square, head south down Carranza and turn right along Madero.

Regional Museum
(Open 09.00–14.00; closed Mon.)
Set round the courtyard of a proud colonial building, this is a museum of vernacular and popular art, from pre-history to the present. The displays are clear, including re-creations of dwellings and period costumes. There is a Spanish bookshop attached.

Museum of Dance, Masks and Popular Art (INBA)

(Open 09.00–14.00; closed Mon.)

This musty one-roomed museum displays a unique collection of costumes and masks from throughout Mexico. Originally made for festivals, many of which are no longer celebrated, the masks offer a tantalizing glimpse of dying traditions. The ruddy-cheeked faces of Spaniards, always topped by a shock of straw-coloured hair and given piercing blue eyes, represent the early invaders. These sit side by side with skeletal figures of death and representations of animals like the jaguar and the coyote. The Coliman masks are almost all the work of one man, Herminio Candelario, who is still to be found carving in nearby Suchitlán. Many local exhibits are for sale and an excellent Fonart shop sells ceramics, weavings and other artisania from all over the country, at very reasonable prices.

Museum of Western Culture

(Open 09.00–14.00; closed Mon; adm.)

Despite an ugly concrete exterior, this influential museum gives an excellent insight into pre-Hispanic life in Colima.

LOWER FLOOR

Clearly labelled cases are filled with Coliman ceramics, showing how a rural people developed into an organized civilization. Starting with Capacha in the north of the state, ceramics dating from as far back as 1500 BC give a tantalizing glimpse of the domestic life of the sedentary farmers who lived in the area. Originally, ceramics had to be utilitarian and there was little room for artistic creativity. Early primitive vases for carrying water have a distinctive undulating hour-glass shape, supported at the waist by three tubular columns. In later, more sophisticated pieces from Comalá (AD 300–600), both life and death are given a central role. One memorable ceramic shows a fisherman casting his nets and then being consumed by a giant shark.

Excavations indicate that after AD 600 a new immigrant group overturned the life of these simple farmers, introducing formalized religion, building temples and defences against other marauders. The ceramics lost their vigour as war, not art, dominated life. At Chanala, a site near Colima dating from AD 1000, an elaborate ceremonial centre was found. Here pyramids, images of Tlaloc, the God of Rain, and traces of a calendrical system all indicated Toltec influences from the centre. Sadly, the site was destroyed brick by brick this century, for no apparent reason, and no longer exists.

UPPER FLOOR

The second floor is arranged in themes of life and death, detailing what early Colimans ate, wore, grew and worshipped, and how they died. The liveliness of the figures of dancers, acrobats and musicians playing tambours and flutes is balanced by daily scenes of women grinding corn or breast-feeding, whilst men are shown hunting, drinking and wrestling. Women tended to wear a long skirt with nothing on top, whereas men wore a long shirt and loin cloth. Both painted their faces, wore jewellery and made decorative incisions on their faces. One of the most beautiful of all the sculptures represents a young woman as Nature, lying on her side with her long, sweeping hair blown across her face by the wind.

Religion was dominated by the worship of cults and ancestors, until more advanced forms filtered in from central Mexico. One apposite god was the ascetic, cross-legged god of fire and volcanoes, Huehuetéotl. Many gods were believed to hide in animal shapes—spiders, dogs, iguanas, armadillos or fish—and these were often invoked. At times their very movement is captured: a dog gnawing on a corn husk, a snake uncoiling or a parrot screeching. Of all the many themes, none is as common as the *tepescuintle* dog, the simplest, most realistic and most exquisitely observed. It was a domestic animal, occasionally fattened up to be eaten, but above all it was a touchstone for the emotions, embodying happiness, illness, death or sadness as well as magic and mysticism. They were sculpted again and again, curled up, sleeping, growling, scratching, sitting on hind legs or feeding pups.

Casa de Cultura
Behind the museum, the Casa de Cultura encompasses a workshop, a small cinema and a café, **Dali**, which has music every evening between 20.00 and 23.00. One room is dedicated to the works of Alfonso Michel, Colima's greatest painter and one-time pupil of Tamayo, whose large canvases were influenced by the time he spent in Paris. Whilst they seem derivative to a European eye, here they are revered for their cosmopolitanism—a painter of his time if not his place.

WHERE TO STAY   (area code 331)
Except during the agricultural fair in early November, the hotels are more than usually quiet. The ******América** (Morelos 162, tel 20366) is a modern hotel behind an attractive colonial facade. On the main square, the neo-gothic ****Ceballos** (Portal Médellin 12, tel 24444) is justifiably popular. There are grand high-ceilinged boudoirs overlooking the square or single rooms the size of broom cupboards, and plenty of space to sit out and discuss the price of cattle with the local farmers. On Av Rey Colimán, to the south of the city, is the ****Gran Flamingos** (tel 22525). Whilst the '*gran*' has to be left at the door, this is a clean, characterless hotel, filled with travelling salesmen, no more than an acceptable alternative if the Ceballos is full.

On the Guadalajara road are three motels serving through traffic in need of a bed for the night. All on the Blvd Camino Real, in quick succession, are the ******María Isabel** (tel 26262), with restaurant, bar, pool and parking, and the *****Villa Rey** and *****Los Candiles**, which are just as comfortable but more moderately priced.

EATING OUT
For breakfast, lunch and dinner, Colima offers nowhere better than **Los Naranjos** (Gabino Barreda 34, parallel to Constitución), a cornflower-blue restaurant open all day, all week, and run entirely by an ever-changing selection of motherly waitresses. It is used by businessmen for informal morning think-tanks, and its plain homecooking is consistently reliable. Inexpensive. On Av 27 de Septiembre, three blocks south of the Mask Museum, **La Fonda** is pleasant for lunch, offering Colimense specialities such as *sopes* (savoury maize boats filled with spicy sauces). Moderate. Calle Constitución, leading northwards from the cathedral, has one block closed to traffic. Along here are **Livorno's**, serving crushed-ice lemonades, pizzas and quesadillas with mushrooms, and **Walter's Caffee** for coffees, fruit drinks and cakes. Cheap. Further up the same street is

Giovanni's Pizzas. Always full, especially on Sunday evenings, this offers a menu confined almost unremittingly to pizzas, but they are thin-crusted, thick on sauce and come quick and cheap, which explains their popularity with students. Cheap.

North Towards the Volcanoes

Only 10 minutes' drive north of Colima, the town is forgotten and the country reasserts itself with green pines, orange marigolds and fields of corn. A narrow road winds upwards through the villages of Comalá, Suchitlán and on to the park of Laguna María. This used to be the entry point for the conical volcanoes, Volcán de Fuego de Colima (3960m) and Volcán Nevado de Colima (4330m), whose smoking summits are visible for miles. However, the land around the park is now owned by James Goldsmith, and access is blocked beyond the lake. It's a beautiful road, though, and worth going as far as you can—about half an hour by bus or car.

Comalá is a pretty whitewashed town with a portalled main square and lopsided church. At the entrance to the town is the **Centro Artesanías** where local craftsmen sell masks and wooden furniture (open 09.00–18.00, Mon–Sat).

A few kilometres further north is the little-visited village of **Suchitlán**, the home of mask-maker Herminio Candelario. Ask directions in the main square to his corrugated iron hut, a *casa de cartón* where he and his seven children spend all day sitting on the ground, fashioning and painting crude wooden masks and hobby horses. He sticks rigidly to patterns learnt from his father and his grandfather before him. This village has nothing and everthing: desperate poverty has provoked a strong adherence to tradition. Candelario's masks are used throughout the area during the festivals of Easter week and Christmas. Children and adults perform the dances of their forefathers, dressed in coyote and jaguar costumes, with immense seriousness.

The main road winds on through banks of wild flowers up to the **Hacienda San Antonio**, a 19th-century coffee hacienda. Rumour has it that this is to become a smart hotel. It has a charming chapel and an aqueduct which brought water to wash the coffee beans. From here a four-wheel-drive vehicle may be able to carry on, fording a couple of streams to **Laguna La María**. Set in lush tropical vegetation, the lake is surrounded by tall trees which shade coffee plants. Weekenders often bring tents to camp, although there's never anyone there during the week. A small restaurant operates idiosyncratic hours—don't rely on it.

The snow-clad **volcanoes** are no longer accessible from Laguna La María. Anyone wishing to make the ascent should instead leave Colima on the Tonaya road and turn off at Fresnito. (The Colima–Tonaya bus will drop passengers off at the Fresnito junction.) A trail from the village of Fresnito leads up to the summit of the Nevado. It takes two days to climb, so come well prepared. There is a simple place to stay, **La Joya**, a few km from the summit.

Manzanillo

Manzanillo, with the title of 'resort' uncomfortably foisted upon it, is the costume jewel in the crown of the state of Colima. A strip of gaudily grand hotels looks askance at the busy workings of the port, whose pinch-nosed houses tower over the narrow streets.

Countless railway tracks cross and recross themselves, trying to find their way, as do the bewildered tourists stumbling across them. As there is little to do but relax, Manzanillo is recommended only for aficionados of aquatic sports and sun-soakers. Once the main port of call for ships on their way to the Philippines, the town now attracts deep-sea fishermen. Hotels will supply equipment for this, parasailing, windsurfing and numerous other sports.

GETTING AROUND
By Air: Aeroméxico and Mexicana run daily flights to Manzanillo from most major cities in Mexico. The airport is off Highway 200, to the west of the town and the suburb of Santiago.

By Bus: Buses arrive from Colima every half-hour and the trip takes an hour. There are six daily first-class buses to and from Guadalajara and two to and from Mexico City. The bus station is to the east of town, on the road in from Colima, and regular combis go from here to the centre. Second-class buses to Mexico City and Lázaro Cárdenas drop passengers in Armería for local connections to Paraiso and Cuyutlán.

By Car: Follow Highway 110 south from Colima. At the Playa Paraiso junction, the road for Manzanillo turns to the right along the shores of the Pacific, slipping gently past the mangrove-lined Laguna Cuyutlán and coconut palms before arriving at the town, which lies between two bays. The journey takes a little over an hour (101 km). Manzanillo is on the main coastal highway, 200, which leads northwest to Barra de Navidad and Puerto Vallarta and southeast (over a bad surface) to Ixtapa and Acapulco.

By Train: One train a day arrives from Guadalajara, via Colima, at 17.00. Another leaves for Guadalajara at 11.00. Both take 6 hours. All tracks lead to the railway station to the east of Juárez in the centre.

In Town: Most of the hotels are to the northwest along Highway 200, towards the suburb of Santiago and the airport. Buses and combis run from north to south and are marked 'Centro' or 'Santiago'. The Miramar bus goes along the coast, past the various beaches to Playa Miramar.

TOURIST INFORMATION
The tourist office is at Juárez 244 (tel 20181; open 10.00–15.00, Mon–Sat).

BEACHES
Playa Las Brisas is the closest beach to town. A long curve of sand, it has not yet been covered in hotels, possibly because of its proximity to the port. Beaches such as Playa Azul and Olas Altas further north are firmly under the aegis of the hotel strip, and as a result they are clean, well tended and full of tourists. Furthest north, Playa Miramar has the biggest waves and concentrates on surfing. Boards can be rented off the beach. South of town there are two small villages on the coast, Cuyutlán and Paraiso. Only Mexicans come here and the facilities are rougher and readier to please.

WHERE TO STAY
(area code 333)

Manzanillo became a landmark in the 1970s when the ivory towers of **(GT) Las Hadas Hotel** (Rincón de las Hadas, 28200, tel 30000, tlx 62506, fax 30430) rose above the cranes of the working port to create a pleasure dome more fit for Xanadu. Built as a folly by the Bolivian tin magnate, Don Anteñor Patiño, the Moorish domes and minarets erupt from palm, mimosa and hibiscus to overshadow the cobbled streets below. It is a superbly executed con: pay more and you too will turn into one of the rich and famous. On the beach, shady pavilions laid out like the Battle of Agincourt flutter temptingly in the wind, the ranks aligned in jumbled order to confront the foe of mediocrity. But in them lie not the Bo Dereks of the film that was shot here, but the ageing middle classes filled with borrowed airs and graces and a little too much lunch. The blindingly white rooms have marbled floors and expansive terraces. Bell boys dressed in red fez hats bear trays of food in the little cars which transport guests from one side of the hotel to another. There are endless tennis courts, an 18-hole golf course and three pools. One pool has an island where iguanas indulgently eat trance-inducing red hibiscus flowers. There are a variety of restaurants, from **Los Delfines** with its fresh catch of the day, sushi, scallops and tarragon, to **Legazpi** which serves classic international food with great ceremony. Very expensive.

Returning to earth, there are any number of bland resort hotels but only a couple of more modest establishments for those who fall for Manzanillo's dubious charms. The friendly *****Posada** (Playa Las Brisas, tel 22404), painted a shocking pink, has 23 rooms which have been well furnished with carefully chosen Mexican furniture. The main room is filled with English books, backgammon boards and chess sets. Run by North Americans, it has the feel of a private house. In town, where the port monopolizes the shore, the ****Colonial** (Fco Gonzalez Bocanegra 28, just behind the main plaza, tel 21080) has rooms leading off an open courtyard. They've seen better days and the bathrooms are basic, but the dining room downstairs (open to all-comers) serves delicious home cooking. The catch of the day is always included in the comida corrida. Inexpensive.

EATING OUT

Restaurant **Willy's** (up the road from the Posada, two blocks from the Las Brisas crossroads, tel 31794) is owned by a French couple and is in itself an excellent reason to make a detour to Manzanillo. Set on the sea front, it is an unpretentious bistro, serving dishes such as sea bass in mango and ginger sauce, or seafood salads of squid, crab and scallop to a constantly packed house. It's wise to reserve. Moderately expensive. **Roca del Mar II**, on the main plaza, is a good café for coffees and breakfast. Inexpensive. The **Ultimo Tren**, on the main road to Santiago, is a family cantina where plates of *botanas* (Spanish *tapas*) appear like magic with the drinks. Moderate. Further up the same road, **100% Natural** serves yoghurts, fruit juices and salads under a wide palapa roof. Moderate.

The State of Nayarit

The state of Nayarit lies awkwardly on the western coast, its elbow resting on the mountains of the Sierra Madre. Beginning just south of the Tropic of Cancer, its lush coastline is kept in check by the rugged Sierra Huichol to the east. This mountainous spur of the western Sierra Madre crooks Nayarit in its arm, creating a natural barrier between it and Jalisco to the southeast.

The little-visited state can be crossed in a few hours or explored for weeks. The island of Mexcaltitan, legendary home of the Aztecs, lies hidden in a mangrove swamp. The Cora and the Huichol peoples, driven into the remote Sierra Huichol to avoid the Spanish, still live in these inhospitable lands. To the south the Ceboruco Volcano towers over the ancient post-Classic site of Ixtlán del Río and the deeply sunk lake of Santa María. Apart from the village of San Blas, the coast remains largely undeveloped, despite having Novillero, the longest beach in the whole of Mexico, stretching 82 km along it.

Tepic

Tepic, the capital, is a dull provincial town to the south of the state. It wouldn't be worth a visit were it not for its fine regional museum and its access to the Cora and Huichol peoples, whose mountainous zones can only be reached by light plane or long trek. As a major crossroads, it is usually swept through by tourists intent on changing buses, trains and dollars. Even the Spanish gave it short shrift because of its proximity to the Huichol and Cora. It wasn't until the 20th century, when it was linked with the railway, that the town started to expand. Today its suburbs have stretched but the tourist office, museum and hotels are all in Av México which leads off the main square.

GETTING AROUND
By Air: Tepic has a tiny airport for the small planes which fly to the Cora and Huichol territories in the Sierra Huichol (see Visiting the Cora and the Huichol).
By Bus: The bus station is on Av Insurgentes, on the main road to Guadalajara, 10 minutes' walk from the centre. There are regular buses to and from Guadalajara (5 hrs), Puerto Vallarta (3 hrs), Mazatlán (5 hrs) and San Blas (1 hr).
By Car: Highway 15 between Guadalajara and Tepic (226 km) is usually a 3-hour journey. Much of this is invariably done through gritted teeth as cars and buses are pressed to the exhausts of trucks and lorries, crossing the hair-raising Barrancas pass. It's an unavoidable part of their journey between Guadalajara and the US border. Highway 15 continues north to Mazatlán, 295 km away. There's a swift splurge of toll road after Tepic which stops after 20 km.
There is a **clock change** at the state boundary between Nayarit and Jalisco: Jalisco is one hour ahead.
By Train: Trains for Mazatlán and Guadalajara stop here—the northbound at 11.00 and 13.00, and the southbound at 14.00 and 18.00.

TOURIST INFORMATION
The office at Av México 32 (tel 29545 or 29546) is not used to foreign tourists. The staff will try to arrange trips to the mountains to visit the Cora and Huichol, although hardly anyone goes.

WHAT TO SEE
The Regional Museum
(Av México; open 09.00–14.00 and 16.00–18.00; closed Mon.)
Between the tourist office and Sierra de Alica hotel, Tepic's small regional museum sits demurely in the courtyard of a 19th-century house. Here a confused jumble of cases is

filled with some of the most exhilarating pieces to emerge from western Mexico. The figures speak for themselves and the lack of clear labelling is almost a relief.

The rooms are devoted to ceramics. From the classic period, AD 400–600, come distinctive undulating vases incised with deep geometric patterns which are unique to Nayarit. These serene people often portrayed realistic figures of men and women in states of ecstasy. Other figures found at the site of Ixtlán del Río express every vicissitude of emotion from puzzlement to pain. The benign faces as often as not exude a shy smile. A woman sips a tisane while on her right a kneeling man stares intently at his sculptor. A section devoted to the representation of diseases shows men clutching aching bellies and bodies covered in venomous pustules.

Santa Cruz
(Calzada del Ejército, at the western end of Av México.)
The Cora and Huichol come to town today to venerate a cross of grass which grows in an otherwise barren patch of land outside the church of Santa Cruz, formerly part of an 18th-century Franciscan convent. Paper flowers, left as offerings, float on the iron railings which surround it.

WHERE TO STAY AND EAT   (area code 321)
Tepic has a few acceptable hotels. ****Fray Junipero Serra (Lerdo 23 Poniente, on the main square, tel 22525) is comfortable and provincial, the best the town has to offer. The more modest ***Sierra de Alica, round the corner in Av México, has a cavernous tiled entrance and the feel of a French *pension* in its simple bedrooms.

The Café Diligencia, opposite the tourist office, provides good coffee and breakfast. Cheap. For a change of menu, try the Cantonese Fu-Seng, round the corner from the Sierra de Alica at Sebastian Lerdo de Tejada Ote 78. Cheap.

The Cora and Huichol Communities

The Cora and Huichol, some of Mexico's most reclusive peoples, remain hidden high up in the Sierra Madre. Having escaped extermination during Nuño de Guzmán's bloody conquest of western Mexico, and survived the subsequent Spanish exploitation, they still prefer to keep themselves to themselves in these remote mountain territories. They can be visited with permission, and their festivals, which have changed little in centuries, are an exhilarating sight. Camera-touting tourists are actively discouraged. In practice, the difficulty of arranging a trip puts most people off, so that those who make it tend to have a genuine interest in and sympathy for these dwindling cultures.

Of the many rebellions which followed the Spanish conquest of their lands, the most famous was led by Manuel Lozada, the Tiger of Alica, in 1854. He continued fighting for freedom and took the unusual step of supporting the European Emperor Maximilian, years later, against the wishes of the Mexican government, in a desperate attempt to regain his people's rights. Lozada's capture and execution finally persuaded the Cora to give up the struggle and they accepted the dictates of the Mexican government. The Huichol, however, continued to fight against white and mestizo supremacy until the beginnings of the 20th century.

Both are survivors of the spiritual conquest and are intensely spiritual peoples. The Huichol in particular stick firmly to their ancient beliefs. The Cora and the Huichol languages derive from the Nahua Cuitlateco group and are linked to northern tribes such as the Tarahumara and Tepehuanes from Chihuahua.

The Cora

The Cora remain aloof from contemporary Mexico, hidden high up in deep canyons cut by rivers into the peaks of the Sierra Huichol. They subsist by simple farming and apart from some trading have little contact with the outside world. In contrast to the women, with their brightly coloured necklaces and full skirts, the men are more austere, in bleached cotton trousers and shirts.

The Christian elements that still survive in their religion were brought by the Jesuits in the 17th century. The priests converted the Cora to Christianity but had to leave them to their sins on the expulsion of all Jesuits from Mexico in the next century. Today the Cora interweave remnants of this Catholicism with the worship of their ancient gods of nature. Tayao, God of Fire and Sun, equates with the Christian God the Father; Tati, Mother Earth, with the Virgin Mary; and Tahás, a Venus figure, with the Archangel Michael.

The religious festivals of the Catholic calendar are celebrated with exhausting and deeply significant dances. Only the young men have the stamina to perform the *Danza de la Urraca* (Dance of the Magpie). For this they eat a quantity of the hallucinogenic peyote plant, rubbing their bodies with the remainder, and then dance nonstop for three days. Christian and non-Christian elements intertwine during Holy Week. The combat of the Jews and the Pharisees is re-enacted by naked men painted with savage bold black and white stripes. During Lent, a dance symbolizing the persecution of children by Herod reflects a similar persecution of the Cora by the Spanish.

The Huichol

The Huichol also live in remote mountain villages, south of Cora territory and stretching as far as Jalisco. The northern Huichol of Nayarit, being more isolated, are more traditional. They farm corn and cattle but devote a great deal of their time to observing religious rites. The women look similar to their Cora counterparts, whilst the men have elaborate costumes for high days and holidays: feathered hats, shirts embroidered with symbols, rings, earrings and at least four woven bags around the shoulders.

More than any other people in Mexico, the Huichol have remained faithful to the spiritual beliefs of their forefathers. Having seen off evangelizing Franciscans in the 17th century, they keep muddled traces of Christianity in the form of two Christs. Their most important gods remain their own: Nakawé, Goddess of Fertility; Father Tayaupa, the sun; Grandfather Tatewari, the creator; and Kuayamare, the sacred deer. The shamans or *maracámes* in charge of each village organize a pilgrimage each spring to Wirikuta, birthplace of their gods, 500 km to the northeast. Here they collect the trance-inducing peyote plant, which doesn't grow in their own infertile soil.

Whilst the Huichol nod in the direction of Catholicism during Easter week, their most important festivals revolve around Nakawé and the planting and harvesting seasons. Every element of Huichol life is filled with symbolism, from flora and fauna to rivers and mountains. In the bright geometric patterns of their weavings, the three most important symbols of the peyote, deer and corn constantly recur. They cover *kukure* (gourds) with beaded pictures to let the gods know exactly what it is that they most desire.

VISITING THE CORA AND THE HUICHOL
Neither the Huichol, nor in particular the Cora, welcome unsolicited visitors. It is necessary to ask permission of the governor of the particular area. The tourist office in Tepic will help with the formalities. Cameras are considered an intrusion, particularly during religious festivals at which visitors will be tolerated if not welcomed. There is one small hostel to stay in, in Jesús María, run by the Instituto Nacional de Indigenista (INI), anthropologists working in the area.

Small planes fly from Tepic's tiny airport to Jesús María (administrative centre of the Cora, in the northeast of the state) and Guadalupe Ocotlán (in Huichol territory, to the southeast), on Mon, Thurs and Sat, leaving at 07.00. Ring the tourist office beforehand as flights often change schedule.

Southern Nayarit

In the south of the state, luxuriously abundant folds of hill and valley cradle undisturbed colonial villages, a towering volcanic peak which plunges down to deep lakes, and the ancient site of Ixtlán del Río. Highway 15, the main road from the US border to Guadalajara, cuts through the region, but it is worth getting off this well-worn track to explore the unknown.

GETTING AROUND
Highway 15 runs from Tepic to Guadalajara (226 km), curving round gorges and bearing belching lorries. The journey takes 3 hours by car and 4 by bus. These leave hourly from both Tepic and Guadalajara. Whilst the region is easiest to explore by car, there are local buses from Tepic to Laguna de Santa María. First-class buses will drop passengers in Ixtlán and from there the Guerrero bus to Rancho de Arriba de San José will take passengers to the site, picking them up on its return an hour later.

Laguna de Santa María del Oro
Thirty-two km south of Tepic, the Santa María road leads off to the left, goes through the small village and then begins a rapid descent down to the lake (follow signs to Laguna). It's an enchanted place, an ancient volcanic lake of great stillness occasionally broken by jets of hot water bubbling to the surface. Gnarled trees and wild flowers flank the banks. The water is cool and refreshing to swim in.

The few restaurants around the lake are empty outside of weekends, but will always cook up fresh fish. The only place to stay is ***Koala (tel 321 23772), owned by an English couple. Small self-catering cottages are set in an orange grove, on the shore of the lake. A garden of Eden.

Jala and the Ceboruco Volcano
Some 84 km south of Tepic, still on Highway 15, Jala is a beautifully preserved colonial village with stalwart houses, cobbled streets and not much happening—except for children rampaging through the centre chasing balls and errant cattle. From the village a

terraced road spirals its way up into the hills, past bewildered oxen and hives of bees, to a microwave station (*micro onda*) 18 km away. From there it is a 30-minute walk to the crater of the Ceboruco Volcano through burnt sand and clinging vegetation. All around erupted rock casts a furious glare at having been wrested so summarily from its eternal peace. A guide can be found by asking at the town hall (*palacio municipal*) opposite the ice-cream shop. As it is way off the beaten track, however, the journey will be made by foot, horse or spivvy jeep as fortune dictates. Traces of Ceboruco, which last erupted in 1870, can be seen back on the main road where rolling pastureland is suddenly interrupted by an angry scar of blackened lava. There is nowhere official to stay, although simple rooms can be rented above the lollipop shop opposite the town hall.

Ixtlán del Río

Just north of the border with Jalisco, 85 km south of Tepic, the town of Ixtlán is no more than a bottleneck for traffic. There are a few hotels and restaurants but none that can be recommended except *in extremis*. The reason for stopping is 4 km south of town, on Highway 15, at Ixtlán's small straggle of an **archaeological site** (open 09.00–16.00; closed Mon). The Guerrero bus to Rancho de Arriba de San José will drop off passengers and returns an hour later. The site's few remains will only be of interest to archaeology buffs, and others should stay on the bus.

Although Ixtlán was occupied in the 7th century, the structures now visible belong to the post-Classic period (10th–12th centuries). Only a small nucleus remains of what was once a ceremonial centre stretching over 10 km. The ruins of a sturdy wall can just be distinguished on the hills behind. The marked influence from central Mexico and the Toltecs can be seen in the brickwork, the monumental columns and the L-shaped low-platformed temples. Unique to the site is the roundel, built in three phases, known as the **Temple of Quetzalcóatl** (or Ehecatl, the Wind God), towards the back of the complex. The outer wall, broken by stairs, encloses the interior. This interior wall has an unusual cruciform motif that runs around the entire wall in a series of 36, repeated again on the inside of the uncovered tomb. On the inner platform are two identical facing structures dedicated to the Sun and the Moon (each approached up eight steps flanked by a balustrade). A presumed ball-court site has been delineated but still not excavated. Hundreds of examples of idiosyncratic ceramics and sculptures were found here and are now displayed in the Tepic Regional Museum.

The Nayarit Coast

Nayarit's undeveloped coast has been overshadowed by the resort towns of Puerto Vallarta in neighbouring Jalisco, and Mazatlán, to the north in the state of Sinaloa. Apart from the port of San Blas, there is nowhere to stay on the coast north of Tepic, without camping equipment.

GETTING AROUND

All beaches are best explored by car, particularly north of Tepic. Highway 15 connects Tepic with the north of the state: San Blas is 32 km and Novilleros 35 km west off this road. Highway 200, a beautifully tropical road, lushly overhung with palms and banana trees, connects Tepic with the southern coast right down to Manzanillo. Second-class buses from Tepic and Puerto Vallarta make regular journeys to even the most inaccessible of the beaches mentioned, but the last bus back is rarely later than 16.00.

South of San Blas
South of San Blas, a rough road follows the coast. From Santa Cruz, only jeeps can get through the 50 km that eventually join up with the main coastal road, Highway 200. Although superb, the beaches are completely unadulterated, without even a glimmer of a restaurant. The developed beaches begin at this junction, with Chacala, La Penita and Rincón de Guayabitos following in quick succession. These are essentially Mexican summer holiday resorts, and most of the houses are private. On the border with Jalisco at **Nuevo Vallarta**, a huge amount of money has been poured into building up a resort to match Puerto Vallarta, a few km to the south, but it is unremittingly bland, a diet of condominiums aping the worst of its southern neighbour with none of its glamour. Highway 200 bypasses **Punta Mita**, the point which sticks out into the ocean above Nuevo Vallarta, and it has thus escaped the building rush. It is best approached from Puerto Vallarta (see North of Puerto Vallarta).

San Blas
The port of San Blas lies at the end of a glorious road that twists through lavish jungle where vines hang off the electricity cables. It suffers for its beauty: the heavy, still afternoons induce a languid torpor begging nothing more than an endless siesta. Then, as soon as the sun begins to set, the bugs come out and suddenly it's clear why that nice German couple packed up and left, welted and scratching, as you drew into town. Nature has otherwise outdone herself around the decaying town, with spectacular beaches and jungle. So, come well-stocked with insect repellent, and insist on a room without even a millimetre hole in the mosquito netting.

History
The present is nothing compared to the once proud and glorious past of the great port of San Blas. It was founded by the Spanish in the 16th century but was forgotten about until needed in the 1760s. Reports filtered back to Spain, via St Petersburg, that the Russians were beginning to nose down into sensitive Californian waters. San Blas was then expanded to protect Spanish interests in northwestern Mexico. Its sheltered bay was surrounded by cedar trees, perfect for building boats. It was also used as a base for exploration. One of the first ships to sail from the port, in 1768, carried 12 Franciscan monks. Led by Fray Junípero Serra, they had been given charge of the inhospitable Baja California missions (see Querétaro).

The port provided a constant source of booty for English and Dutch pirates, feeding off Spanish galleons returning from the Philippines, and in the 1780s it was fortified with a garrison. Ever patriotic, San Blas gave up its cannons to the fight for freedom from Spain in 1810. In 1825, the republican president, Guadalupe Victoria, founded the Battalion of San Blas which went on to defend the country from the 1847 North American invasion of Mexico City. The troops fought down to the last man and, despite their defeat, became a byword for nationalism and courage. A Naval College still maintains a low-key presence. At 5 uniformed sailor-cadets emerge to walk slowly home, picking their way through the pot-holes, like the white herons all around.

GETTING AROUND
San Blas is 69 km northwest of Tepic and 32 km west of Highway 15. Take the toll road north (Highway 15) and turn off to the left at the first petrol station (Pemex). There is no railway line to San Blas but buses connect the town with Tepic (6 daily, 1hr), Guadalajara (2 daily, 6 hrs) and Mazatlán (2 daily, 4 hrs). The bus station is on Calle Sinaloa.

To get to the **beaches**, take a bus from Calle Sinaloa for the village of Santa Cruz, less than 30 km to the south. They leave on the hour until 13.00. The road follows the beaches, curving round the great bay of Matanchen through pin-head-sized fishing villages. From the first village, Matanchen, a hard-packed road kicks back 2 km towards San Blas and the **Playa las Islitas**. The last bus returns at 14.00.

TOURIST INFORMATION
The small tourist office in the Palacio Municipal (tel 61998) is less helpful than the endlessly informed proprietors of the Hotel Las Brisas.

WHAT TO SEE
The town, lying on the Pacific between two salt-water estuaries, is distinctly the road-end. Tarmac stops dead at the plaza and pot-holed dirt-tracks continue to the sea. It has the potential of a tropical Eden, surrounded by lagoons and filled with coconut, mango and banana trees, but, because of the dreaded mosquitoes, it sees only the fleeing backs of potential tourists and has never grown more than 10 blocks in any direction. Calle Juárez crosses its breadth and Av Batallón de San Blas its length.

San Blas won the sympathy of Henry Longfellow, who wrote his last poem, 'The Bells of San Blas', about the long-silent chimes of the Roasario church, now in ruins. On the hill above the town, the Cerro de la Contaduría, are the remains of the fortress which, together with the customs house on Juárez, the red and white lighthouse (across the El Pozo estuary), and the grand church are all that now remain of better days.

BEACHES
Surfers love San Blas. They reckon it's worth a couple of welts to ride what they claim to be the longest wave in the world, in the Bay of Matanchen. At all times of year there are a few stalwarts somewhere in the town, and far more during the summer. San Blas is not actually on the sea. The **Borrego** beach divides the town from the Pacific. It is not the best but it is the closest, a 1-km walk along Av Heroico Batallón de San Blas, past the Naval College. Continue away from town and the beach quickly empties. **Playa las Islitas**, the first in the bay of Matanchen, 1 km south of San Blas, is completely undeveloped. Hemmed in by a wide bay, with the lights of Santa Cruz shining across the water, it has nowhere to stay or eat, and the only sound is of wave after wave pounding home on the sands. Pristine sand beaches stretch out to either side. The little village of **Aticama**, continuing south past the Oceanography School, was once the haunt of pirates but is now no more than a long row of palm-thatched huts, serving freshly caught fish with quantities of rice and avocado.

EXCURSIONS
Sport-fishing boats go out (on demand) to **Las Tres Marías** islands, 130 km away. One of these is an off-bounds open prison. The closest island to land is **Isabela**. Of volcanic

origin, it has a lagoon, an ecological station and a bird reserve. It can be visited in a day (the journey takes 3 hours), although there is a rudimentary hut to sleep in. The crew would expect their food and drink to be provided.

The boat trip up through jungle and mangrove swamps to the **Tovara fresh-water spring** is straight out of *The African Queen*. It leaves from the bridge crossing the estuary (on the way into town) and takes 30 minutes to meander up-river, past turtles basking on the banks, to the cool, clear spring where jaguars are said to drink at night. There is a small restaurant, open for lunch. The tourist office set the price for the boat, which carries a maximum of 6 people.

Trips to the islands and the spring can be arranged through Las Brisas Hotel (tel 50112).

WHERE TO STAY   (area code 321)
There is only a handful of hotels and restaurants in San Blas. The most elegant is *****Las Brisas** (Cuauhtémoc 160 Sur, tel 50112), with a few large, cool rooms (where the netting works), a lush garden, good restaurant and helpful staff. In its days of splendour, San Blas had a German consulate which now masquerades as the ***Flamingos**, a pleasant, quirky old building at the end of Calle Juárez. The ****Posada Casa Morales** (Cuauhtémoc 197, tel 50023) is the only hotel on the water, with a restaurant, palapa bar and pool.

EATING OUT
Macdonald's (Juárez 36), neither of hamburger fame nor Scottish, is a modest restaurant where plastic roses come in Grecian urns and the fish is grilled with garlic. Cheap. Around the corner, **Chef Tony's** is more imaginative with hot devilled shrimps and grilled fish *a la veracruzana*. Moderate.

North of San Blas
Plans are afoot to develop **Novillero** on the northern shores of the state. The longest beach in the country, its 82 undisturbed km of fine white sand are fringed by palm trees. The plans are likely to remain on the drawing board, fortunately, as there are no protected bays for hotels and the full force of the Pacific crashes on to the sand.

Mexcaltitan

The island-village of Mexcaltitan, 100 km northwest of Tepic, might have been created as the back-drop for Marquéz' *A Chronicle of a Death Foretold*—more at home in the Amazonian jungle than in a mangrove swamp on the shore of the Pacific. Although it is a full 25 km from the ocean, it seems more of the sea than the land. The car-less streets have high banks to keep the water out, and during the rainy season, the level invariably rises 4 m, flooding everywhere. From August to November, canoes navigate the streets and fishermen can wait at home for the catch.

History/Legend
Local belief places Mexcaltitan as Aztlan, the original model for the Aztecs' capital city, Tenochtitlán. The first inhabitants of this island were fishermen, known as Tenochas,

another name given to the Aztecs. According to legend, these Tenochas or Azteca were told by their god, Huitzilopochtli, to find a similar island in a distant lake. There an eagle would be sitting on a nopal cactus devouring a serpent and it was here that they were to establish themselves until the end of their days. Like Mexcaltitan, Tenochtitlán was an island, riddled with canals, divided into four parts with the fifth section, the main plaza, being the centre. However, no Aztec artefacts have been found in Mexcaltitan and there is little to support the legend (although it has been endorsed by the last two presidents of the republic helicoptering in for a few publicity shots).

GETTING AROUND
Mexcaltitan is well off the road from anywhere and to anywhere. It demands a special expedition but, for a taste of the extraordinary, it is definitely worth it. From Tepic, a bus to Santiago Ixcuintla leaves every 30 minutes. From there, second-class buses run three times a day to the pier, La Batanga, in the middle of nowhere (officially at 8.00, 13.00 and 16.00 but they tend to depart as soon as they are full; the last bus back is at 16.30). By car, turn off Highway 15 between Acaponeta and San Blas at the junction to Mexcaltitan and Santiago. It is a further 40 minutes via Santiago, past banana and tobacco plantations. There is no road to the island. Open boats ferry people from the pier, a journey of some 15 minutes.

VILLAGE LIFE
From the air, the tiny island is revealed as an oval, 350 m across and only a little longer, hidden away in the middle of a large lagoon fed by the San Pedro River. Four streets dissect it, all meeting head on in the plaza, where the gleaming white church thrusts up above the red-tiled roofs of the 400 houses, which cling to the island like shipwrecks to a lifeboat.

The island is in a time-warp. The basketball nets in front of the church are almost the only clue that it has ever entered the 20th century. Despite its glorious history, the future lies in the video machines being played furiously by pre-pubescent boys, whilst their fathers and grandfathers sit out in the shade, hand-sewing the fishing nets.

WHERE TO STAY AND EAT
There is nowhere to stay but floor or hammock space in the town hall. Santiago has two basic hotels, both on Calle Ocampo by the main square: the *Casino at 40 (tel 50850) and the *Santiago on the corner of Arteaga (tel 50625).

Las Garzas is the place to eat. On a miniscule island between Mexcaltitan and the pier, La Batanga, its only access is by canoe. The family serve up quantities of shrimps in half a dozen ways: dried in the sun, raw in lemon juice, with a hot *diablo* sauce or the wickedly mouth-burning *cascabel chile* of the *salsa huichol*. Then comes the fish. Smoked over mangrove wood, it is imbued with a delicate, distinctive flavour from the leaves, roots and bark of the mangrove, which is its unremitting diet.

Part VIII

MICHOACAN

Detail from the portal of the church at Angahuán, near the volcano of Paricutín

Michoacán is Mexico's most gentle state, a land of immense beauty and peace, content to meander along at a slower pace. There are no bright lights and no big cities, but a thousand villages and a hundred lakes. Morelia, with its elegant colonial buildings, cloistered convents and many parks, is the Spanish capital. Pátzcuaro, its close neighbour, on the shores of Lake Pátzcuaro, is the original capital, a smaller town with cobbled streets and clear air. All around the state, green hills slope down to lakes, rivers and valleys. Each village hidden amongst the hills produces its own highly individual crafts. Even at the petrol stations, where vendors with huge woven baskets covered in palm leaves sell their pumpkin-seed cakes, craft becomes art. It is a state for the old, the young and the curious: those who can't pace themselves move to other lands and then mourn their homeland in poignant songs.

Throughout this century, foreigners have been seduced by Michoacán. André Breton and León Trotsky came here during the Second World War, and since then artists, writers and families have slowly moved in, clustering around the lake shores or set apart in A-shaped *trojes*, the log cabins of the Purépecha. Yet, foreign visitors and tourists are still relatively few and far between, and those that come do little to disturb the calm, making it one of the most charming of all states for a short visit or a lifelong commitment.

History

PUREPECHA

The Purépecha of Michoacán were an idiosyncratic people who never bowed to the Aztecs, though they were brutally defeated by the Spanish. Led by Iré Thicatame, they came down from the northwest to settle in Michoacán in the 12th century. They spoke a

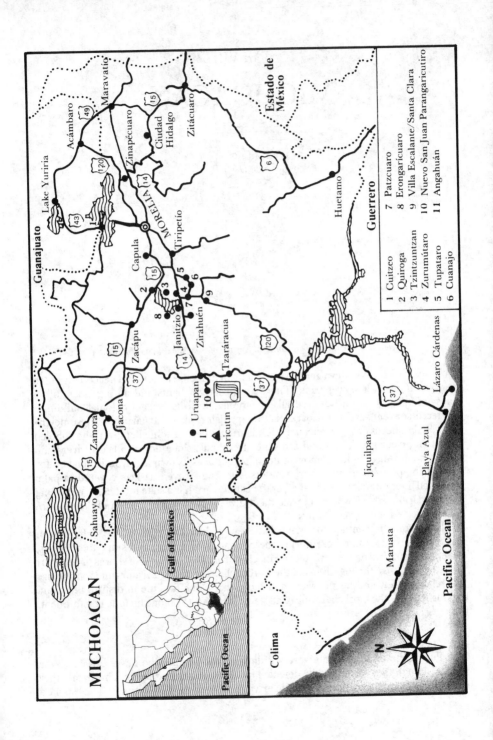

tongue which was quite distinct from the common Nahuatl and had striking similarities to the Peruvian Quechua language. They also had distinctive profiles, shaving their heads and removing all body hair, and wearing only loose shirts. In the 15th century their semi-legendary hero, Tariácari, crushingly defeated the Aztec leader, Axayacatl, and thwarted the Aztecs' attempt to colonize Purépechan lands. He built himself an imposing capital at Tzintzuntzán on the shores of Lake Pátzcuaro, confirming the authority of the Purépecha empire until the arrival of the Spanish.

The golden age of the Purépecha ended with the quivering Tangaxoan II. He was a weak man with a Nancy Reagan array of star gazers who induced him to put his own brothers to death on a trumped-up charge of adultery. When the Aztecs came to beg for help in defeating the Spanish, he, like Moctezuma, did nothing, convinced that the Spanish had been sent by a god. His terrified men believed that the clothes of the Spaniards were the skins of men and surrendered to the Machiavellian Nuño de Guzmán (see Part VII). Tangaxoan was dragged through the streets of Tzintzuntzán by the Spanish, before being garotted. The empire collapsed and Purépecha lords were forced to hand over their daughters to the sex-starved Spaniards. To salvage some shreds of honour from this pillage, the Purépecha called the Spanish 'sons-in-law' or *tarascue*. The Spanish, misunderstanding the word, named the conquered people Tarascans. Though synonymous with Purépecha, the name is still considered one of shame.

VASCO DE QUIROGA

Smarting from the iniquitous effronteries of the first president of the Audiencia, the grotesque Nuño de Guzmán, the Dominicans hand-picked their next representatives in the New World with kid gloves. Of these remarkable men, Quiroga was the most remarkable of all. He believed that the 'children of nature' were God's innocents, who needed not only to be saved from hellfire in the life to come, but to be raised above the misery of their present lives as slaves on Spanish haciendas in their own land.

Quiroga became bishop of Michoacán in 1537, shortly after his arrival in New Spain. He found a region still suffering from the devastation of Guzmán. In an attempt to restore the land and the people, Quiroga gave training in matters spiritual and practical. He founded communes where everyone, including Quiroga himself, worked six hours a day on communal land. Although the villages declined after his death, the legacy of his encouragement of arts and crafts continues to this day. The town of Santa Clara del Cobre still lives on the copper industry which he initiated.

His good work alone was not enough to counterbalance the devastation brought about by Spanish commercial and religious colonization. The native population was decimated by the influx of new industry, new ways and, above all, new diseases, such as typhoid, smallpox and measles. More than half of the non-Spanish were wiped out by a plague of typhus in the year 1643. Out of every six people, five died, and Tzintzuntzán shrivelled down from 20,000 to 200 inhabitants in four months.

THE TWENTIETH CENTURY

Despite the wars of independence and the Revolution which raged through Michoácan, it wasn't until the 1930s that the Purépecha heard his voice raised above a whimper. This was thanks to Lázaro Cárdenas, who is beloved and revered in Michoacán as much today as when he was governor of the state in 1928 and then president of Mexico. Cárdenas did more for the impoverished rural populations of Mexico in one presidency than the combined forces of all presidents since the 1910 'people's' Revolution. He instituted huge land reforms, giving 49 million acres back to the people, twice the amount restored by all his predecessors. Of Purépecha descent, he was a man of deep conviction and high principles. On becoming president he refused to live in the grandiose palace of Chapultepec and cut his salary by half. When governor of Michoacán, he opened over a hundred rural schools, and as president would receive delegations of field workers whilst foreign dignitaries fumed in the waiting room.

Michoacán is today the most controversial and politically angry of Mexico's states. Its popular PRD party (formed by Cárdenas' son, Cuauhtémoc) is consistently defeated by electoral fraud. In Michoacán they wryly tell the old joke that Mexico has a far more advanced democracy than the United States. In the latter, the result of an election is known some hours after polling. In Michoacán, the result is known months before the elections take place.

MORELIA

Morelia is the very Spanish capital of a very indigenous state. For once, the Spanish chose not to build their city over the ruined temples of their vanquished enemies. Instead they created their own town, built by Purépecha labour to Spanish design. Sitting in a café under the Zócalo's portals, it is easy to drift off into an Andalucian dream, far from Mexico, as the coffee gets cold. Yet, despite the imposing stamp of Spanish colonialism in the architecture, Morelia is very much of today. The buildings, of a warm pink stone, may have the look and feel of Salamanca, but none of the details do. The past isn't allowed to intimidate but is used to effect. Woolworths have a restaurant in a deconsecrated chapel (the high altar is now a kitchen) and the bus station is inscribed with red and black gothic lettering.

The city was founded in 1541 by the first viceroy, Antonio de Mendoza, and named Valladolid after the Spanish town where he was born. Pátzcuaro, the older Michoacán city, was ousted from power and had to be content with the pole position. In 1571 even the seat of the bishop was moved to Valladolid and Pátzcuaro quietly sulked. The name of the city was changed on 12 December 1828 in homage to its most famous son, José María Morelos y Pavón, the priest who assumed Hidalgo's mantle to become the military leader of the independence movement in 1810.

GETTING AROUND
By Bus: For once, the bus station is central and efficient, with decent hotels just outside the entrance. It is two streets north of Madero on Eduardo Ruíz where it crosses Calle Gómez Farías. There are three main inter-city companies: Flecha Amarilla, Norte de Sonora and Tres Estrellas. First-class buses leave every 2 hours to Uruapan and Pátzcuaro, hourly to Mexico City and five times a day to Tijuana. Second-class buses run to more places, more frequently, for less money and less comfort.
By Car: Morelia is well placed, with good connecting roads. It is a swift 303 km from the capital, 317 km from Guadalajara, 176 km from Guanajuato and 62 km fron Pátzcuaro.

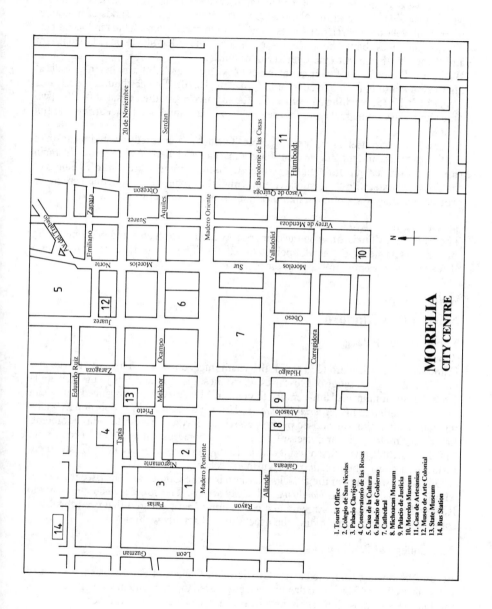

MORELIA
CITY CENTRE

1. Tourist Office
2. Colegio de San Nicolas
3. Palacio Clavijero
4. Conservatorio de las Rosas
5. Casa de la Cultura
6. Palacio de Gobierno
7. Cathedral
8. Michoacan Museum
9. Palacio de Justicia
10. Morelos Museum
11. Casa de Artesanias
12. Museo de Arte Colonial
13. State Museum
14. Bus Station

From Mexico City, the fast toll road to Toluca becomes Highway 15 and continues to Morelia via Zitácuaro and the National Butterfly Park, where thousands of migrating orange and yellow monarch butterflies come down to breed from Canada in December. The journey takes about 4 hours. This same highway meanders slowly on to Guadalajara and thence up the coast to the United States border.

By Train: The efficient '**Purépecha**' leaves Mexico City at 22.00, arriving in Morelia at 06.30, and continuing to Patzcuáro and Uruapan (10.10). The eastbound train leaves Uruapan at 19.15, reaching Morelia at 21.40, and arriving in the capital at 07.20. Two other first-class trains make the journey by day. The station is on Av Patriotismo (tel 21068).

In Town: The city itself is easily manageable. The bus station is only two blocks north of the tourist office, and the Zócalo three blocks east along Madero. Av Madero is the main east–west road that cuts through the centre. All points of interest are within 10 blocks of the Zócalo. **Taxis**, with the distinctive emblem of the arches of the aqueduct, are never expensive and always around. There is a rank in the Plaza San Francisco.

TOURIST INFORMATION

The **Galería de Turismo** is on the corner of Av Madero Poniente and Nigromante, in the Palacio Clavijero (tel 32654; open 09.00–20.00). The post office is at the other end of Av Madero Oriente, 369, at Serapio Rendón.

WHAT TO SEE

North of Av Madero

The Clavijero Palace
(Open all day.)
Francisco Javier Clavijero (1731–87), the Jesuit intellectual, was born in Veracruz and died in Bologna. A reader of Descartes, Cervantes, Newton and Sor Juana Inés de la Cruz, he revolutionized 18th-century thought in Mexico with his advanced European ideas, expounded in his *Historia Antigua de México*. The beautifully proportioned building named after him was praised by the wandering German, Alexander von Humboldt, for the symmetry of its architecture and its exceptional use of space and proportion. Finished in 1660, it was first a Jesuit college (until they were expelled in 1767) and then, variously, a house of correction and a primary school.

On the far west side of the Palacio Clavijero is Calle Goméz and the **Sweet Market** with its *chongos*, *cajeta* and *morelianas*, all sticky sweets. The street leads on to Eduardo Ruíz and the bus station. Enlightened city planners have ensured that even this has a sober neocolonial facade, hiding the usual flurry of activity within.

The College of San Nicolás
(Open all day.)
Across Nigromante from the Palacio Clavijero, the College of San Nicolás was founded in Pátzcuaro in 1540 by Vasco de Quiroga, but moved to Valladolid in 1580. It has one of the longest and most illustrious histories of any college in the Americas. The 18th century was its golden age in terms of intellectual endeavour, but its notoriety and present-day fame is rooted in the 19th century. Miguel Hidalgo studied Thomistic

theology, Latin and rhetoric here as a young man, returning as a 28-year-old priest in 1781 and going on to become the rector. His unorthodox views and way of life ensured, however, that he was kept under constant suspicion by the tireless Holy Office of the Inquisition. Not only did he doubt the veracity of the Virgin birth and question the omnipotence of the pope and the Spanish kings; he danced, gambled and spoke out against the celibacy of the priesthood. He was sacked and sent first to Colima and then to Dolores, Guanajuato, from where he was to launch the independence movement in 1810 with his cry for Mexican autonomy. As one of the seminal institutions in his life, the college has become a virtual shrine to patriotic Hidalgo worshippers (and that includes almost every Mexican in the world).

The Conservatory and Church of Santa Rosa
(Open all day.)
Both buildings are behind the Palacio Clavijero (along Nigromante), opening onto the Jardín de las Rosas where a statue of a ruff-collared Cervantes looks somewhat quizzically across at Don Vasco de Quiroga.

The convent of Santa Rosa was built originally in 1590, although the present church was not completed until 1756. As with all convent churches, the double doors open from the length of the church directly onto the street. The reliefs of saints (including Sta Rosa de Lima and St Martin) and the Sacred Family keep a sober face beneath the crocodile gargoyles. Inside are three sumptuous *retablos*, never able to shine out as they should through the all-pervading gloom. The 1743 conservatory attached was one of the first in the Americas, originally used for music lessons for the town's orphans. It is still the home of the children's choir, with voice classes, piano symphonies and guitar strummings going on all around in the main courtyard. In a smaller courtyard, a row of five antiquated washing basins and scrubbing boards are a reminder of a more austere past.

The Museo del Estado
(Jardín de las Rosas and Guillermo Prieto; open 09.00–13.00 and 13.00–20.00; closed Mon.)
Across the garden from the conservatory, the small state museum is in an 18th-century house, built with left-over brick from the aqueduct. This was once the home of Ana Huarte, who later married Agustín de Iturbide and briefly became the Empress of Mexico. The museum has an interesting approach—a counter-attack to cultural colonialism which revalues and celebrates the state's differences.

The very first exhibit is a replica of an 18th-century chemist, complete with scientific instruments, jars, labels and decoration. The rest of the ground floor illustrates the development of the state, from the early farmers who created gods as their needs arose, to a more organized social stratification between AD 200 and 900. Small, solid figurines, generally female and often pregnant, were decorated with clay, wood or bone—a form associated with fertility. One outstanding exhibit is the black obsidian mask from Tiristirán, with sublime Teotihuacán features, in a state of almost transcendental meditation. The period between 900 and 1521 saw the rise of militarism and the introduction of metal working. The Purépecha took control and used metals such as copper, gold and silver for weapons and jewellery. The second floor has exhibits celebrating the regionalism of Michoacán, with costumes, masks, photographs and maquettes from villages and towns all over the state.

Museo de Arte Colonial

(Leave the Museo del Estado along Santiago Tapia and take the second left into Juárez; open 09.00–13.00 and 16.00–20.00; closed Mon.)

Set in a small 18th-century house, this museum, despite its broader title, is wholly religious in context—as almost all colonial art was. Representations of Christ impaled on the Cross are displayed in almost every form: painted wood, sugar cane paste, maize or mezquite wood. Dominating the courtyard is a painting by **Miguel Cabrera**, which pays homage to Juan de Palafox y Mendoza, the quasi-saint of learning, who was considered to be the height of Catholic perfection in the 18th century.

The Casa de la Cultura in the Ex-convento del Carmen

(Av Morelos and Eduardo Ruíz; open Mon–Sat, 09.00–19.00.)

This graceful ex-convent is now Morelia's cultural centre. Its patios and cupolas, open and enclosed, are architectural delights, and it is also blessed with a huge bright sunny courtyard, which is used for open-air performances of plays and concerts (the Spanish play, *Don Juan Tenorio*, is an annual tradition on Hallowe'en). One of its cavernous vaults houses a small mask museum. Masks were associated with magic and the power to defeat death by taking on another's form, uniting nature with abstraction. Here, pinned harmlessly on the wall, they lose some of their dynamism: they really need fiestas, dances and drunken sprees to come alive. Upstairs, a doctor dispenses natural medicines, alongside temporary art exhibitions. A cheerful café in the main courtyard sells frothy capuchinos and sandwiches.

Palacio de Gobierno

(On the corner of Madero and Morelos, opposite the cathedral; open all day.)

Originally a seminary, this building was begun in 1770, following a plan that combined solidity with elegance: the impregnable walls are softened by the French Bourbon doorway. Around the second-floor walls and staircase of the main patio are a series of chalky murals by the Michoacán maestro, Alfredo Zalce. Those on the south wall begin with the arrival of the first Spaniards and the Franciscan missionaries, Juan de San Miguel and Antonio de Lisboa. The north wall forgets chronology and depicts the indigenous life of the state.

South of Madero

Cathedral

The cathedral is very much of the 17th century and one of the most uniform of its kind, with an underlying classicism firmly supporting its baroque exterior. Set between two plazas and facing north, it is built of a pale rose trachyte. The blue checks of the tiled dome add a welcome splash of colour to the sober decoration of the facade. The imposing 18th-century towers, added later, project a distinctly neoclassical air, with massive urns resting on squared pedestals.

The Doric interior houses a huge churrigueresque organ, two paintings attributed to Cabrera (in the sacristy), and the hat and staff of the beloved bishop, Vasco de Quiroga. Both Morelos and Iturbide were baptized in the silver font, one of the few valuables to remain. In 1814, impoverished troops fighting for independence took some of the silver, with the consent of the bishop. Liberal troops headed by the infamous General Huerta— never one to miss a trick— ransacked the rest in 1858.

From behind the cathedral, Calle Hidalgo, lined with market stalls, leads to the church of **San Agustín**, originally a 16th-century Augustinian monastery. Inside the church, the main *retablo* is boldly neoclassical, attributed to Francisco Eduardo Tresguerras. To the right of San Agustín is a porticoed passageway where public writers tap out letters on aged Remingtons.

West of the Cathedral

Museo Michoacáno (open 09.00–13.00 and 16.00–20.00; closed Mon) is behind the cathedral, one block to the west in Allende. Although this is the main state museum, the exhibits are rather sparse, giving a quick run-through of the state's history. The rooms downstairs are devoted to pieces from the archaeological sites of Opeño, Chupicuaro, Ihuatzio and Tzintzuntzán, whilst upstairs, past Alfredo Zalce's mural of the life of Cuauhtémoc, are colonial paintings, rusted arms, faded silks and delicate imported ceramics.

Abasolo, a street filled with stalwart colonial buildings, separates the museum from the **Palacio de Justicia**, a 17th-century law court. Above the stairs, a mural by Agustín Cárdenas, commemorating the first tribunal of justice, overlooks a sea of clattering typewriters and yawning plaintiffs despairing of equity amidst the anarchic bureaucracy of the place today.

One block behind, in Corregidora, is the **Casa Natal de Morelos**, the birthplace of Morelos. It is filled with Morelos' papers and letters and is of limited interest other than to Spanish-reading aficionados of the hero. The museum of his effects, **Casa Museo de Morelos**, round the corner in Av Morelos Sur, is only slightly more user-friendly, displaying old carriages, an exhibition of engravings from the Mexican wars of independence and portraits of Morelos.

East of the Cathedral: the Ex-convento de San Francisco

Three blocks east of the cathedral, an ex-Franciscan convent faces onto Vasco de Quiroga, built like a solid fort but with a 17th-century Mexican baroque facade. It has been converted into a **Casa de Artesanías**, acting both as museum and as shop, and as such is a showcase for a thrilling collection of local arts and crafts. Finely worked wooden columns from Ahuiran, huge Ali-Baba ceramic jars from Cocucho and ebullient glazed pineapples from San José de Gracia are but a few of the works littering the courtyard. Staff can arrange to pack and ship work worldwide (tel 21248), whether bought here or elsewhere. It's an ideal place to go for a taste of what is being made where, before setting out for some of the more remote villages.

The atrium in front of the church was once the burial ground for the worthiest citizens. When the church was secularized in the 19th century, the cemetery was closed, the 14 surrounding chapels were razed to the ground and a lively market place was built to shake the eternal peace. Today the square is renowned for *pollo plaza*, a chicken and tomato dish served from the hot braziers which dot the square.

WHERE TO STAY (area code 451)

Expensive
With views over the city and the cathedral from its eyrie above, the *****Villa Montaña in Colonia Vista Bella is the height of splendour (tel 40231, tlx 69624). Run by a French count, Philippe de Reyset, and patronized by presidents (both the home-grown Salinas de Gortari and the gringo George Bush), it has combined the best of Europe with the best of Mexico. The rooms are the size of Manhattan apartments, filled with fresh flowers and ablaze with the uncompromising colours of Mexico. Prices are usually all-inclusive in high season. The superb restaurant is also open to non-guests.

Moderate
Morelia's elegant colonial mansions, built for Spanish noblemen, now house international tourism. The stagecoach from Mexico drew up at the ****Soledad (off the main square at Ignacio Zaragoza 90, tel 21888, telex 69633), to allow exhausted passengers to rest for the night. It has retained its charm and is as likely to be full of Russian ballet dancers as Japanese anthropologists. ****Virrey de Mendoza (on the main square, Portal Matamoros 16, tel 20633) keeps its colonial splendour as floor after floor rises above an interior courtyard. The floorboards creak in the idiosyncratic tall rooms, haphazardly furnished in the 1940s. The ****Alameda (Av Madero Poniente and Guillermo Prieto, tel 22023), opposite, is extremely professional. Spread over two adjoining houses, a series of patios and terraces have become breakfast bars and dining rooms. The 36 new rooms, painted in strong colours, are altogether better than the older ones. The ****Catedral (Zaragoza 37, tel 30783) is a comfortable, converted colonial hotel, with rooms around a burnt-ochre patio filled with flowers, and a lobby with fat sofas and chairs in a covered courtyard.

Cheap
Around the bus station are three cheap and comfortable hotels: the **Plaza (Gómez Farías 278, tel 23095), the **Concordia (at 328) and, directly opposite the bus-station entrance, the **Del Matador (tel 24649). Despite the latter's macho name, the beds have frilly covers and all the staff, apart from a lift-operator, are female. South of Madero and facing each other across Vasco de Quiroga are the **Posada Don Vasco (at 232, tel 21484), a jumble of rooms above a flower-filled courtyard, and **Mintzicuri (at 227, tel 20664), whose swirling tiled facade announces it as the public baths as well as a hotel. Modern and efficient, it reeks of soap. Opposite the Casa de la Cultura is a small, tidy hotel looking onto the park, *El Carmen (tel 21725). The *Colonial (20 de Noviembre, tel 21897) has a few cheap rooms around a courtyard. The (CE) Central (behind the Museum of Michoacán at Abasolo 282, tel 20139) is a huge colonial building which survives on bags of character and little else. The upstairs rooms, overlooking the football-pitch-sized courtyard, are the best but have no bathrooms.

EATING OUT
Morelians mostly eat at home or in cafés, and the Villa Montaña has the only restaurant to cater for the gourmet. On Sunday mornings, the Posada la Soledad goes to town and lays out a huge buffet in its courtyard. During the week its menu is always reliable.

Moderate. Tucked in off Hidalgo, **Acuarius** is a vegetarian restaurant, set in a colonial courtyard topped by Delft-blue tiles, with daily inexpensive comida corridas.

Cafés line the porticoes facing the cathedral. Here Morelians set the world to rights over cups of coffee and an endless variety of things to eat. **Las Costillas de Don Luis** provides *sopas de fideo* and *juliana* (rich soups), served with warm tortillas prepared at the table. Next door, **El Rey Tacamba** specializes in Purépechan dishes such as *juruikata* (spiced rice) and *k'uiripita uirikikata* (marinaded and grilled steak). Both cheap. Close by, **Los Comensales** (at Zaragoza 148) is in a courtyard filled with rose trees and caged birds. The menu is traditional, including the salty *tamales* of Michoacán (ground corn pancakes stuffed with meat and wrapped in a banana leaf), and a heart-warming *caldo tlalpeño* (soup). Cheap.

North towards Guanajuato

The state of Guanajuato is only an hour's drive north of Morelia, along Highway 43. The road passes two lovely Augustinian monasteries, at Cuitzeo and Yuriria, both built early in the colonial period as physical reminders of the spiritual conquest. These can easily be visited in a day trip from Morelia.

GETTING AROUND
By Bus: First-class buses leave Morelia for Guanajuato throughout the day, stopping at Cuitzeo. Only second-class buses, Flecha Amarilla, go to Yuriria, but both monasteries are easy to hitch to, once outside the environs of Morelia.
By Car: Take Calle Morelos, which runs the length of Morelia, north onto Highway 43. After 30 km, it crosses over a 4-km-long dyke spanning Lake Cuitzeo to the town of Cuitzeo and its Augustinian monastery. After 29 km, a road leads off to the right for Yuriria, 3 km further on. For a round trip, return to Morelia via Acámbaro, 62 km southeast of Yuriria. The round trip is a little over 200 km.

WHAT TO SEE
Cuitzeo
The town straddles a finger of land pointing into the shallow, 48-km-long Lake Cuitzeo, parts of which dry out for much of the year. It is still fished for the delicate *charal* (which is promptly rushed off to the restaurants of Morelia and Mexico City) and for the fibres of the tule plant, a poor man's palm, which are woven into baskets and hats. The town is worth visiting only for its monastery.

Although the Franciscans were the first to introduce Catholicism to the area in the early 16th century, the land was assigned to the Augustinians in 1550. They laid the first stone of the monastery the same day. The magnificent facade is, unusually, signed with a Latin inscription by one of its Purépechan craftsman, Francisco Juan Metl. It is decorated with an interlacing network of stern cherubs and rosettes, interspersed with the Augustinian symbol of a pierced heart. The large atrium (originally over twice its present size) and the open chapel speak of congregations too large for the church (or too wary to enter). In the small entrance hall to the monastery are a couple of pre-Hispanic Purépechan sculptures which have been recovered from the lake bed. One is the water dog, Uitzimengari, who guided the drowned to the Water God deep below the surface. Around the two-storey cloister are drain gargoyles in the form of griffins, angels and rams. The staircase and some of the walls still have the remains of frescoes, including *The Last Judgement* to the left of the entrance.

Yuriria

Yuriria, across the state border in Guanajuato, is 32 km north on the Acámbaro road. The monastery was built under the direction of Fray Diego de Chávez in the 1550s (although the buttresses were not added until 1625), on the site of the already established Purépechan city of Yuririapúndaro. The northern Chichimec tribes were still making periodic sweeping attacks southwards and so the church was built defensively, with spikes of merlons topping thick, impenetrable walls. In contrast, the facade has a gentle network of strap patterns melding into foliage, disappearing up the wall and running away out of hand. As if disapproving of this ornamental plateresque facade, the square tower to the right and the roof-top battlements serve as a reminder that the Chichimec weren't finally 'subdued' until the end of the 16th century.

On the underside of the entrance arch are sculpted plates of fruit, a theme which Chávez is supposed to have copied from the sacristy of Seville Cathedral. Inside, the coffered vault in the nave is traced over with rib vaulting. This vaulting continues through the first level of the cloisters, echoed in the tall arches topped by stubby, foreshortened ones in the second level. In the convent's patio, the gargoyles have taken on fantastic animal forms.

Southwest to Pátzcuaro

There are two ways to get from Morelia to Pátzcuaro. The less direct route is to take Highway 15, the main road to Guadalajara, and turn down to Pátzcuaro at Quiroga. Eighteen km out from Morelia, the highway passes **Capula**, a village of potters. The houses on the main (and only) street open their doors to sell ceramics—dark brown plates and pots decorated with tiny brushstroke flowers and fishes. At the far end of the street is the village co-operative, the **Unión Estatal de Artesanos**, which is run by the potters themselves. The highway continues for 22 km to Quiroga: turn south here for Pátzcuaro via Tzintzuntzán.

Generally, cars and buses take the 1990 dual-carriageway Morelia–Uruapan road, which passes through Pátzcuaro (54 km, 40 mins). It is worth making a short detour to the village of **Tiripetío** (after 24 km), where the first university in the New World was founded in 1540 by the Augustinians. They also introduced hot water, a hospital and a cemetery, which all proved longer-lasting than the short-lived university.

Some 20 km (15 mins) further on, the village of **Tupataro** makes another delightful 3-km detour (on the left, signposted Cuanajo and Tupataro). The village church is very small but very charming. Its walls, and those of its churchyard, are constructed of adobe bricks. From outside, the few gravestones, the air of neglect and the bare white-washed facade are reminiscent of the simplicity of the dour Scottish kirk. Only the emblems of the sun and the moon on either side of the doors give a clue to the enchanting interior, where the ceiling is painted with Purépechan interpretations of the Passion of Christ, as told by the Augustinian missionaries. On its saint's day of Santiago (25 July), the church is bedecked with garlands and ribbons.

Tzintzuntzán

In Tzintzuntzán, onomatopoeically named after the humming birds which used to haunt its skies, the imposing remains of a once-glorious Purépechan city gaze wistfully across to the aged olives in the atrium of the Spanish monastery below, which was built in its stead. The modern town gets on with making the distinctive, crudely fashioned moss-green ceramics which attract buyers from all over the world.

Tzintzuntzán was once the ancient capital of the Purépechan kingdom. Now, all that remains of its pre-Hispanic glory are the ruins of five *yacatas* or **temples**, set high on a terrace overlooking the eastern shores of Lake Pátzcuaro. On the Day of the Dead, the whole platform is illuminated in a glow of candles. Built in 1200, the *yacatas* display a distinct Purépechan style found nowhere else in Mexico. They were circular, constructed on a rectangular stone base, with a passage projecting out, so that from the air they look like robust frying pans. The entrance was originally by a huge stairway which stretched 100 m wide.

In two tombs at the base of the temples, highly worked obsidian lip and ear ornaments, symbols of nobility, were found, together with depilatory tweezers made of silver, unknown elsewhere in Mexico but common in Peru. The highly stylized pottery buried beside the body was decorated with unique abstract motifs, which confirmed that these were a people apart. According to Aztec chronicles, the Purépecha were fine woodworkers, engravers, painters and lapidaries. The women were famed weavers. This benign people originally sacrificed only animals to appease their gods, although the tombs of kings reveal that sacrificed wives and servants were buried beside their lord, which doesn't say much for equal opportunities. Latterly they were to sacrifice humans to the God of Fire, Curicaveri—an Aztec influence.

The Purépecha claimed to have accompanied the Aztecs on their pilgrimage from lands in the north. When they went to have a swim in Lake Pátzcuaro, the Aztecs stole their clothes and ran off without them. And so the Purépecha went unclad, cutting themselves off linguistically from their treacherous companions by evolving a different language. This story may reflect more on the contemporary Spanish prurience for nakedness than the need for a creation myth.

Below the temples, the Franciscans built a 16th-century **monastery** in whose atrium Vasco de Quiroga planted olive trees—despite the Spanish law prohibiting olive growing, in order to maintain a home monopoly. Now gnarled and bent with the passage of time, they lend the monastery an air of mystery, furthered by the tantalizing fragments of burnt-ochre frescoes on the walls of the cloisters. Two larger chapels were added to either side of the original primitive chapel. In the one with a three-bay portico, San Francisco, the tourist office claim there is a Titian, though they omit to mention the great trade in skilled copies of the great masters. This painting disappeared in the 1970s but was mysteriously restored some years later, which has only enhanced its local fame.

In the town itself, there is a swarm of shops selling teapots, plates, rough round bowls and misshaped jugs, all made of porous clay on which earthy brown swans are painted in bold brush strokes over a green glaze. Make sure any purchase is wrapped well if you plan to travel far, as the solid-looking plates crack at the drop of a heavy suitcase.

Pátzcuaro

Pátzcuaro is the perfect complement to the carefully planned and ordered city of Morelia. It is a happy jumble and muddle, where streets wind up, down and around past once whitewashed houses. Capped by red-tiled roofs, on the uneven edges of cobbled streets, the houses, like the town, have weathered gracefully into a comfortable decrepitude, ready to tell their life histories but just as happy to let people pass right on through. Pátzcuaro is almost unbelievably picturesque: boats ply back and forth to the islands in the lake, while stalwart Spanish mansions around the plaza have been turned into comfortable, if musty, hotels. Amazingly, it isn't self-conscious (although the island of Janitzio is becoming so). That life goes on without the need for the tourist dollar can be seen all around. Whitewashed houses are often daubed with stark political slogans, tiles slip from roofs, and a hint of dilapidation lingers that would have been starched out in many other Mexican 'destinations'.

Well known, but relatively free of the stigma of tourism, Pátzcuaro's brief moment of glory comes but once a year when foreigners and locals alike swarm in to celebrate the Day of the Dead. The people engage with visitors, the buyer and the seller coming together in an appreciation of crafts which hold their value intrinsically and not just because of some much-thumbed price tag. Throughout the rest of the year, Pátzcuaro remains the nerve-centre of placid Purépecha life and may even be too quiet for some, offering nothing more than an amble around the plaza, freshwater fish from the lake and time to catch one's breath.

GETTING AROUND

Pátzcuaro is 56 km southwest of Morelia (see Southwest to Pátzcuaro) and 54 km east of Uruapan. From the terminal at Ahumada 63, one block north of the Plaza Gertrudis Bocanegra, first-class buses leave for Morelia and Uruapan every 30 minutes, and for Guadalajara and Mexico City four times a day. The smaller villages around the lake can all be reached by indestructible second-class Flecha Amarilla buses from the same terminal. Boats leave from the docks in the north of town for the lake islands. The railway station is at the entrance to the docks. The westbound train for Uruapan leaves at 20.45, and the eastbound train for Morelia and Mexico City at 09.10.

TOURIST INFORMATION

There are two helpful tourist offices, one in Portal Hidalgo 9 (tel 21818) and the other in Casa de los Once Patios (tel 21214).

WHAT TO SEE

Around the Plaza

All roads lead to the **Plaza Principal**, the largest square, edged with ancient trees and some of the oldest buildings in the state. The busy **Palacio Municipal**, next to Los Escudos Hotel, looks askance at the self-important bureaucrats with which it is filled, remembering the days when it housed the Marquises of Villahermosa. Past this, Calle Ponce de León leads to the **Mercado de Ollas** where reams of cooking pots wait to be sold. Opposite the Palacio Municipal sits the imposing 17th-century **Casa del Gigante**, now housing the crudely carved polychrome figures of a huge soldier ('*gigante*') and a water bearer. Although it is a private house, the residents are used to people coming to peer up through their courtyard.

Turn left and left again up Quiroga, where a cobbled incline leads to the enormous **Basilica of Nuestra Señora de la Salud**. The honest priest, Vasco de Quiroga, started building it in 1543. He had ambitions for a cathedral which was to be three times larger than Notre Dame in Paris, with five naves representing the fingers of the Lord. Neither were the authorities willing nor the people able to complete this ostentatious project and it was given up after 100 years. Opposite is **Galería Dos**, for expensive but high-quality crafts.

Museo de Arte Popular
(Open Tues–Sun, 09.00–19.00.)
In the same street, Arciga, this museum is housed in one of Quiroga's triumphs. Convinced that education would help to end the suffering of his flock, in 1540 Quiroga founded the successful Colegio de San Nicolás to teach them Spanish. Today, the fine building houses a large collection of crafts from the whole state. The entrance courtyard is paved with what look like white pebbles: closer inspection reveals them to be cows' vertebrae, laid down instead of paving stones. Within the museum there is a reconstructed *troje*, the typical wooden house of the Purépecha, as well as masks, ceramics and weavings.

Opposite the museum, **Chocolate Joaquinta** (Enseñanza 38, tel 21104) has won prizes for its thick dark chocolate, made from cocoa beans, cinnamon and vanilla, and sold in rounds. When heated in milk and swirled with a wooden whisk, it gives off a spicy odour, redolent of time long since past. Moctezuma and Cortés spent many an evening deliberating on the fate of Mexico over cups of such foaming chocolate. Turn right and go back downhill to the **Plaza de los Once Patios**. Here little boys rush to tell the history of the house which was famed for its eleven patios. After contorted additions and subtractions, they will finally beam with proof that what look distinctly like five patios are in fact eleven and will expect a small reward for this illumination. There are some glitzy up-market shops inside. The hill leads back down to the main square.

Plaza Gertrudis Bocanegra
Calle Zaragoza leads north from the Plaza Principal up to the town's second square, the Plaza Gertrudis Bocanegra. Sprawling onto its right-hand side is the market. It is officially open on Friday but its enthusiasm has spilled over to include the rest of the week. Dark tunnels lead into the nether regions, to the fishmonger whose most curious ware is a disconcerting fish with distinct feet. Back on the square, the former church of San Agustín is now a library. On the far wall, Juan O'Gorman's floor-to-ceiling mural (finished in 1942) depicts the state's history. Purépecha warriors look down to the degradations of Guzmán below. It is all painted in the earthy tones of the land around.

Excursions Around the Lake
Around the lake shore are several villages, serviced by hourly buses (from the bus terminal) and boats, or inexpensive taxi rides. A road circles the lake, crossing the northern edge of town, near the railway station. Heading west, it passes through

Huecorio, Arocutin, Uricho and round to **Erongaricuaro**, 17 km away. There, in the ancient, unadorned plaza (with a large Sunday market), the tarmacked road stops. It seems fantastic that André Breton, unaccustomedly bucolic, spent several months here during the Second World War, only to discover that he had nothing to teach the Mexicans about surrealism that they didn't already know. Buses strive on, northeastwards, along progressively worse roads, through San Andrés and San Jeronimo, before finally joining up with Highway 15, the main Morelia–Zamora road.

Heading east around the lake, the road divides after 4 km at **Tzurumútaro**, where there is a small agricultural museum in the patio of the church and a solemn but enchanting family cemetery which blazes with light on the Day of the Dead. Heading north, across the railway tracks, the road continues to Tzintzuntzán (21 km). After 10 km, a bumpy side road leads off to the left, rejoining the lake shore at **Ihuatzio**. Here, in a seldom-visited archaeological site, there are five brick *yacatas*, the unusual Purépechan temples (see Tzintzuntzán). They are smaller than those at Tzintzuntzán, and closer to the lake, providing an excellent view over it. When the site was first excavated, a Chac-Mool statue was discovered which, as the most characteristic symbol of the Toltecs, provided evidence of their influence in the area.

In the centre of lake are the **islands** of Janitzio, Tecuen, Yunuen and Pacanda. **Janitzio**, the largest, is also the most visited. It is overpowered by the souvenir shops along its cobbled streets and a vast, monolithic statue of Morelos, visible from every point along the lake shore.

THE DAY OF THE DEAD

Although the Day of the Dead, on All Souls' Day (2 November), is celebrated throughout Mexico, it is particularly poignant in the state of Michoacán. Here, tradition stretches back beyond history and into legend. Death has always been seen as nothing more than a continuation of life, for which the soul has to be properly prepared. When a Purépechan monarch died, his whole cortege had to go with him. One king, whose burial tomb was uncovered at Tzintzuntzán, was accompanied by seven wives, a cook, a retinue of servants and even a hairdresser. Exempt from the list were the doctors who had failed to cure him. Horrified by these pagan beliefs, the evangelizing friars effected a compromise, whereby celebrations were reduced to one night in the Christian calendar, All Souls' Eve, when spirits were acknowledged to come back to the world.

Legend has it that every year on 2 November, at the sound of the church bells, a funeral cortege passes through the island of Janitzio. At the head is the Purépecha warrior chief, Itzihuappa, mourning his wife, the Princess Mintziata, daughter of the last Purépecha king, who died of grief at the coming of the Spanish. This attracts thousands of visitors to Janitzio, crashing and barging for places on boats, craning necks, suffering cold feet and mosquitoes. Any aura is broken by the constant flash of bulbs. Avoid it and visit instead the smaller surrounding villages, which are quiet and welcoming. Relatives will happily offer visitors glasses of warming punch as they relate Uncle Juan's last moments on the busy Mexico City to Morelia road.

The night of 1 November is a night of vigil. Families sleep out beside the graves until dawn. The earth around the graves is freshly turned and strewn with elaborate offerings, such as bread in the shape of skulls, *pan de muerto*. It all comes together in a blur of marigolds, incense, bonfires, hilarity and happiness, offset by a sense of tranquil meditation. The heartwarming family group heating tortillas round a fire contrasts poignantly with the solitary man keeping silent vigil over a sorely missed wife. There are candles everywhere, so that Death can be looked squarely in the eye and not remain hidden under a veil of darkness or social nicety. It is important to talk through last moments, smile over imperfections and bring the dead back into today.

In every village a special place is dedicated to the memory of Lázaro Cárdenas. Four men slightly the worse for glasses of warming punch will heave a life-size portrait to an already decorated place of rest. Everyone, from stranger to Purépecha, will feel the magic of the man who kept his word and gave the land back to the Purépecha.

WHERE TO STAY AND EAT   (area code 454)

Pátzcuaro hotels leave a strong aftertaste of log fires, heavy furniture, musty secrets and a sense of the unpredictable. On the Plaza Principal, the ***Mansión Iturbe (tel 20368) offers large, genteelly laced but erratic rooms, leading off from a light, open patio. A few rooms overlook the lively square. Its restaurant serves up excellent breakfasts of yoghurt and granola or hot cakes and eggs, and continues throughout the day with trout and white fish, corundas and quesadillas. Under the opposite portals, the ***Misión San Manuel (tel 21313) has large, old rooms with chimneys, wooden-beamed ceilings and tiled bathrooms. Off the plaza at José Ma Coss 20 is the small, quiet ***Mesón del Gallo (tel 21474), with pleasant rooms leading off a long corridor.

Up by the Basilica, **Posada la Basilica (Arciga 6, tel 21108) has a lovely patio lined with mismatching wooden chairs, from which to contemplate the town. All the rooms have fireplaces. The restaurant has a good view and less good food, although the best view of all is from the lavatory. The spankingly modern 1990 ***Fiesta Plaza (Plaza Gertrudis Bocanegra, tel 29876) attractively replicates the colonial style. In the same square, the *Concordia (Portal Juárez 31, tel 20003) is the cheapest hotel in town—which is the best that can be said for it.

Pátzcuaro's long-term stalwart, the ****Posada de Don Vasco (Av Lázaro Cárdenas 450, tel 20694) has big practical rooms, table tennis, billiards and even an antique bowling alley to keep its guests on their toes. Its restaurant, the Tarasco, offers an extensive if standard menu. ***Hostería San Felipe (up the road at Lázaro Cárdenas 321, tel 21298) has plain rooms with fireplaces but the best restaurant in town. It is always packed on Sundays, when everyone eats *pescado blanco* (the white fish from the lake), cooked in garlic. The *sopa tarasca* (a spicy bean soup with strips of crisp tortilla on top) is unmissable.

There are restaurants all around the square, mostly adjuncts of hotels. Of these, El Patio does good coffee and breakfast as well as the ubiquitous *pescado blanco*, Spanish omelettes and thick steaks. Next door, the Posada San Rafael has an upstairs restaurant to watch the world go buying from. Both are moderately cheap.

South of Pátzcuaro

Santa Clara del Cobre

South of Pátzcuaro, on the Ario de Rosáles road, is the small village of Santa Clara del Cobre (the official name is Villa Escalante but people ignore it). It has lived, breathed and eaten off copper for centuries, ever since Vasco de Quiroga established it to encourage

Purépechans to profit from their skill in copper turning. Today it trades from back-street workshops and stalls on the main street. Copper, not the most cherished of metals, takes on a new perspective, basking in the admiration of the villagers who live or die by this single industry. They profess their thanks at every given opportunity: even the lampposts are made of copper, as are the doors, portal and lettering of the small museum (closed Mon). During the middle weeks of August, every coppersmith in Latin America (not so very many) descends on the village for the National Festival of Copper.

Zirahuén

There are two ways to reach beautiful Lake Zirahuén. The quickest is to turn south off the Morelia–Uruapan road (Highway 14), but a lovely alternative is from Santa Clara. At the far end of the village, a larger-than-life bust commemorates Cuauhtémoc Cárdenas (made, of course, of copper) and from here a country lane leads off to the right to Zirahuén, 11 km away.

This peaceful lake, set in a gentle depression, is indeed enchanted. Fields of corn slope down towards the water, and there are no more than a few houses dotted around its shores. It is said that the Purépecha king, Tzitzipandácuare, had many beautiful daughters of whom Zirahuén was the most beautiful. A young, noble Pátzcuaro chief came to ask for her hand in marriage. First, her father said, he must defeat the Mexica king to prove his love. So overwhelming was the brave warrior's hatred for the Mexica king and so intoxicating his love for Zirahuén that he conquered his enemy's entire army in one battle. Jubilantly returning for his bride, he was struck by an arrow at the palace gates. Zirahuén was inconsolable and retired to this hollow to mourn for ever. The gods created a water spring from her tears and her spirit was transformed into the waters of the lake. Some say the lake appears to breathe at night, and those same people say it is the murmur of the princess sighing still with love.

WHERE TO STAY AND EAT

There are wooden *cabañas* on the shores of the lake, both on the village side and on the far side. The ***Cabañas Zira (tel 451–43139) are the more isolated, and it's necessary to stock up with provisions from the village before climbing into the launch which ferries guests across. The same launch will also ferry passengers to **La Troje de Ala** restaurant, inaccessible other than by boat. You can see a menu before embarking, though even if you decide not to eat the 20-minute ride will cost next to nothing. A French chef was imported to teach the staff of this remoter than remote restaurant how to produce the *je ne sais quoi* of their excellent onion soup and *coquille St Jacques*. A Mexican flavour still persists in the fish cooked over smoking wood and then covered in a garlic, tomato, anchovy and parsley sauce, *a la Troje de Ala*. There is an excellent selection of wines, both national and international, and an afternoon can slip all too quickly away. The restaurant is open Friday to Sunday and on national holidays, and known only to a few Mexicans. Moderate.

Uruapan

Set on roller-coaster hills, the small but busy town of Uruapan is a pretty 62-km drive from Pátzcuaro through the pines of rural Michoacán. Bustling, provincial and profitable, it is an important commercial centre in a very uncommercial state. Its prosperity depends on the farmers and their crops of avocados and coffee. Although the shops are filled with chiffon evening gowns, there is little evidence that anyone is buying the latest creation. Outside of its chokingly compact main square, there is little to see but a pleasant national park and alpine scenery. It has been used as a base for visitors ever since the volcano of Paricutín, an hour to the northwest, exploded in the 1940s. Seeing an opportunity for tourism, the town authorities quickly painted the face of the centre whilst the muddy streets all around were left unabashedly with their curlers still in.

GETTING AROUND
There are regular buses from Morelia (2 hrs, 6 daily), Pátzcuaro (1 hr, 6 daily), Guadalajara (3 daily) and Mexico City (6 daily). The 21.30 train from Mexico City via Pátzcuaro and Morelia arrives at 10.00. The central bus station is on the main road to Pátzcuaro and the rail station is to the east of town. Town buses for the bus station leave from Alvaro Obregón on the Zócalo (marked 'Los Reyes'). Buses for the railway station leave from the same point (marked 'Panteón'). It's often quicker to walk.

TOURIST INFORMATION
The office is at Cinco de Febrero 17 (tel 20633).

WHAT TO SEE
Most of the sights of Uruapan are actually in the countryside around. The one exception is the **Casa de Artesanías** (on the Zócalo; closed Mon; adm), a 16th-century hospital known as **La Huatapera**. It was built by the Franciscans under Fray Juan de San Miguel, and claims to be the first in the Americas. The delightful building has notable mudéjar windows and a plateresque facade that was handed over to the lively Purépecha to decorate. A series of midget doorways lead into the small rooms, filled with examples of lacquer which, gnarled with age, are less garish than most, particulary the attractive old chests covered in intricate patterns. There is a small market behind, filled with shawls, sacks of coffee, citrus fruits and avocados.

WHERE TO STAY AND EAT
Uruapan is the only town of any size in western Michoacán and a large commercial centre. Accordingly, its hotels are generally dull, solid overnighters, ideal for travelling salesmen and itinerant farmers. The ****Hotel Plaza** (Ocampo 64, tel 30333, telex 69334), on the Zócalo, is the best in town, with comfortably spacious rooms—even its telephone kiosks are of elaborately carved wood. The ***Nuevo Alameda** (tel 34100), professing '*moralidad*' as its highest virtue, is just off the square, with private parking. The **Villa de Flores** (Emilio Carranza 15, tel 21650) is much the most characterful of all, with large rooms set around a pair of garden courtyards.

Outside town are two more hotels, orientated towards the weekenders who come to enjoy the parks. At the western end of the national park, Eduardo Ruíz, the ***Mansión del Cupatitzio** (tel 32100, telex 69331) is a lovely colonial-style hotel, with lots of plants and lots of stairs, and a large swimming pool and gardens. The ***Pie de Sierra** (on the Carapan road) also has large gardens, wide views and, at weekends, a big, noisy pool full of children (it's very quiet during the week).

Hotel restaurants in Uruapan, such as the **Plaza** or **Cuapatitzio**, offer above-average hotel food. Moderate. The **Nutrivida** in Independencia is a small café serving whole-meal sandwiches, yoghurts and *licuados* of fresh fruit. Under the portals of the Zócalo, the cafés **Pergola** and **Emperador** are always busy, with hearty breakfasts and comida corridas. Cheap. For a taste of the excellent coffee on which Uruapan's reputation stands, served in a traditional coffee house, try one of the 20-odd varieties in the **Café Tradicional de Uruapan** (Calle Emiliano Carranza, just north of the Zócalo). Sadly, it offers no more than coffees and cakes, but what coffee! and what cakes! Cheap.

West to the Paricutín Volcano

The Volcano of Paricutín exploded on 20 February 1943 and didn't calm down for eight years. It took a year for the lava to drown the village of San Juan de Parangaricutiro and everything else within 20 km. Some months after the initial explosion, another crater opened up, called Zapicho (the Child), which still lets off steam. Ever since the first murmurings, people from all over have been coming to marvel at the molten lava forms and the brave spire of the village church, now covered in graffiti, which was the only thing to rise above it all.

GETTING AROUND

By Bus: The village of Angahuán is the nearest access point to the volcano. It is an hour's journey from Uruapan via the local 'Los Reyes' bus, which departs from the Zócalo every 2 hours (07.30–19.00) on weekdays, and every hour at weekends.

By Car: Leaving Uruapan on Independencia, take the Carapan road north (Highway 37), turning left after 20 minutes towards Angahuán. Cattle trucks grind their way round tortuous bends as the road spirals through pine forests. *Trojes* sprinkle the surrounding hills—the real thing and not the fancy imitations which have restaurants inside. Look out for the turn: it's a dirt track and easily missed.

The church spire at Paricutín

250

WHAT TO SEE

Angahuán

The village of Angahuán is used by most people as an unpronounceable map reference and no more. In fact, it is an unalloyed Purépecha village, where only a fifth of the people speak Spanish and nearly everyone lives in square, pine, A-shaped *trojes*. Only the church and the hospital are made of brick, both 16th-century Spanish additions from the time of Vasco de Quiroga. The white-walled church still relies on adobe for much of its plasterwork, set within a brick framework, and the doorway combines Moorish influences with stylized Purépecha decorations. For their festivals (mainly 30 January and 25 July), the villagers wear their bright woollen shawls of black or red on white, which take a month to work.

Paricutín

From Angahuán, you can either hire a horse from the endless stream of people anxious that you should do so, or walk to the look-out, 15 minutes away. Here there are some *cabañas*, which can be hired, and a small, deliciously earthy restaurant. From this point you can see the church tower rising above the tormented lava. The tower is a 30-minute walk with a small boy to act as guide, or a 45-minute bump on a plodding horse. Rates are negotiable and it's worth asking around. To get to the crater takes longer—about 6 hours there and back by horse or a little longer on foot.

The Waterfalls of Tzaráracua

As an antidote to the heat and dust of Paricutín, nature has thoughtfully provided cascades, pools and waterfalls along a bottleneck of the Cupatitzio River, only 10 km southwest of Uruapan. Buses (signed 'Tzaráracua') leave from Uruapan's Zócalo. From the bus stop, it's either a steep climb down or a jolt on horseback: both take 5 minutes.

San Juan Nuevo

Strictly for volcano buffs, this new village is the replacement built for the one destroyed by the explosion, with an enthusiastic museum devoted to the volcano. Buses leave from Uruapan's central bus station. The drive there is delightful, past orchards and brickworks (producing hand-made bricks), conifers and freshly ploughed red earth.

The Michoacán Coast

Michoacan's long stretch of coast has largely been left as nature intended, with only one small resort, Playa Azul. Consequently, there are few hotels and few bright lights—and also few life guards for those caught in the powerful pull of Pacific tides.

GETTING AROUND

By Bus: Shaky and intrepid buses run four times a day between Manzanillo and Acapulco, stopping at Maruata and letting Playa Azul passengers off at the turning to the town, leaving them with a 1½-km walk in. The nearby industrial shanty town of Lázaro Cárdenas is the transport centre for the region, with connections to Morelia, Guadalajara and Mexico City. From its bus station, local buses leave every 20 minutes for Playa Azul.

By Car: One of the most hauntingly beautiful and isolated in Mexico, the shoreline of Michoacán is also cursed with one of its worst stretches of road. Between Acapulco in the east and Manzanillo in the west, the coastal Highway 200 is terrifyingly unreliable. During the rainy season, stretches of road may finally give up their fight against pot holes the size of craters and disappear entirely, dropping down cliffs to the sea below. The surface of the road from the state capital to Playa Azul (360 km) is considerably better, although recent political troubles in southern Michoacán have led to hold-ups and road blocks. Ask about the current situation before leaving Morelia, and don't travel after dark.

WHERE TO GO

Playa Azul
This is the one resort along the entire length of Michoacán's coast. The village only wakes when extended Mexican families come down for long weekends. Otherwise, it dozes in the midday sun. The tarmac gives out at the Pemex petrol station and the few buildings—a smattering of seaside hotels together with palapa huts serving fresh fish—are scattered around sandy tracks.

Maruata
Some 200 km further up the coast, the white sand on the long, wide strip of beach at Maruata is favoured by turtles coming to nest in privacy, and by the occasional ecologist or schoolchildren who come to watch them. It's strictly for those who want to camp and get right away from everything. All in all, this distant coastline has little to offer but itself and it is only the well-prepared traveller who can take advantage of it.

WHERE TO STAY AND EAT
In Playa Azul, the *****Delfin** (Av Carranza, tel 2 19 54) is modern and efficient, with a tiny pool fringed by coconut palms, close to the long sandy beach. The practical restaurant sticks to what it knows, which is fish, without going in for anything very fancy. One block back, the ****Costa de Oro** (Francisco Madero, no tel) is cheaper as it doesn't have a pool but is otherwise much the same. Of the palapa restaurants which front Playa Azul's beach, the **Marita** is considered the best, largely because of the size of the plates which come heaped with rice, beans and avocados as well as freshly caught and grilled fillets of red snapper and the pike-like *robalo*. Cheap.

Part IX

QUERETARO, GUANAJUATO, AGUASCALIENTES AND ZACATECAS

Miguel Hidalgo y Costilla, the parish priest who led the country to independence from Spain

Querétaro, Guanajuato and Zacatecas were once the jewels in the Spanish crown, the darling and much cherished children of the adoring mother country, the subject of proud letters home to the courts of Hapsburgs and Bourbons. Wealth poured out of the mines, fabulous churches were rapidly built and lowly prospectors became solid burghers within a matter of years. During the 19th-century independence movements, all this changed. The creoles, who had provided the wealth, now demanded some of the rewards. The first murmurs of dissent came from the heart of Guanajuato in 1810 and the last Hapsburg to set foot in Mexico was summarily executed in Querétaro in 1867.

Since their founding in the 16th century, the silver cities—and the productive agricultural land in between them—have often held the balance of power and public opinion. Today the cradle of modern industry, it is an area of dynamism and prosperity, offset by rural villages and unmapped sierras. With so much to see and do in the cities, the quiet provincial towns such as Jérez in Zacatecas or the missions of the Sierra Gorda in Querétaro should not be forgotten.

Often overlooked by first-time visitors searching for the elusive pre-Spanish Mexico, once discovered, the area seduces because it holds so many of the roots of the Mexican character and nation. Every month there is a major festival. In late April the whole country hears about the great agricultural fair of San Marcos in Aguascalientes, when prize bulls leave their lordly haciendas for the bloody ritual of the bullring and strutting

253

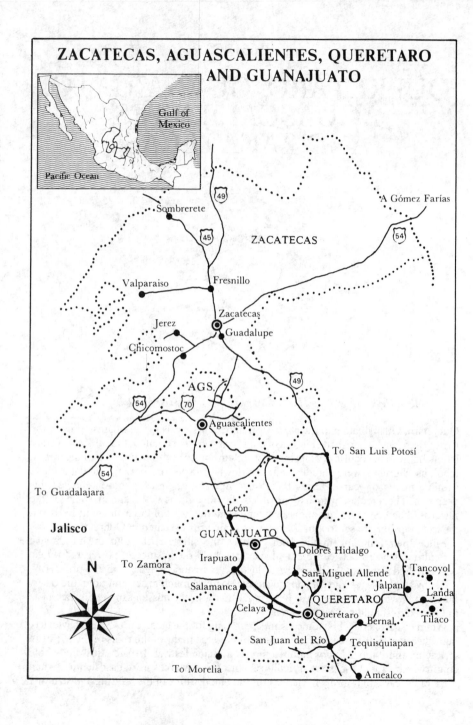

ZACATECAS, AGUASCALIENTES, QUERETARO AND GUANAJUATO

toreadors have their moments of infamy and glory. In September, bells ring out to celebrate Independence, and in October it is Guanajuato's turn for the limelight with the month-long Cervantino festival of plays and *entremeses* in the streets and plazas.

The landscape north of Mexico City is hidden under vast Kimberley Clark and Coca-Cola assembly plants until it opens out into the high, flat plains, clear of the volcanic peaks surrounding the capital. Zacatecas is the second-highest city in the country, and Guanajuato the most perpendicular, but the land between is fertile and well cultivated. Dry and gasping in the hot season, it comes to life with the summer rains.

The State of Querétaro

The state of Querétaro is the wise old man of Mexican history, witness to many key developments in the creation of the modern republic. Early Franciscan missionaries climbed high into its sierra to carve elaborate monasteries out of unyielding rocks, Emperor Maximilian met his death in its capital, and revolutionaries successfully plotted independence from Spain behind the closed doors of its large haciendas. Today it is a prosperous state, with thriving industries which have overflowed from Mexico City, and a colonial capital which makes a stimulating stop on the way north or south.

History

THE 1810 REVOLUTION AND THE CORREGIDORA

In the heady days after the French Revolution, when anything seemed possible, revolutionary groups began to gather in Mexico under the guise of literary coteries, to discuss the prospect of independence from Spain. A leading role in these secret negotiations was taken by the parish priest Miguel Hidalgo and the dashing officer Ignacio Allende. Their conspiracy was discovered by the *Corregidor* or Mayor of Querétaro. He made plans for their arrest, having first locked his wife, whom he suspected of liberal sympathies, into her room. She managed to whisper a message out through a keyhole, warning Hidalgo. This precipitated the struggle for independence which eventually brought freedom from Spain, and assured Josefa Ortiz, the *Corregidora*, an inviolable position in the popular history of Mexico.

THE END OF MAXIMILIAN

In 1867, the misguided and despised Hapsburg Emperor Maximilian fled to Querétaro. He had previously toyed with the idea of abdication, but his wife Carlota worked on his sense of Hapsburg dignity and persuaded him to struggle on. She travelled to Europe to appeal on his behalf. Napoleon III was obdurate: under threat from Otto van Bismarck, he was rapidly recalling troops from Mexico and had little time for her pleas. The Pope was equally unsympathetic, citing Maximilian's failure to help the beleaguered Church in secular Mexico. It is said that during this audience, the desperate Carlota finally lost her mind.

Meanwhile, in Querétaro—the conservative heart of Mexico, Maximilian and the 1600 men who remained loyal to him were besieged for a hundred days, by the republican troops of the anti-imperialist Benito Juárez. They cut off the water supply from the aqueduct and deliberately polluted the river with corpses. Although elaborate plans were made for his escape, Maximilian found them ignominious (he was asked to shave off his tell-tale blonde beard). He would have preferred to surrender, but was betrayed by one of his generals. Juárez decreed that he should be court-martialled and that the state would request the death penalty. Despite pleas for clemency from European monarchs, New World presidents and Garibaldi, he was found guilty of violating Mexico's sovereignty and causing the death of innumerable Mexican citizens (50,000 Mexican lives had been lost during the struggle against French domination). He was put before a firing squad in the Cerro de las Campañas outside Querétaro. His last words were to wish Mexico happiness.

TREATIES AND CONSTITUTIONS

A conservative stronghold, Querétaro suffered the ignominy of witnesssing the signing of the treaty of Guadalupe Hidalgo in 1848. A tremendous blow to national pride, this gave away almost half of Mexico's territory (including Texas, New Mexico, California and Arizona). However, to counterbalance this disgrace, Querétaro can boast that when the dictator Porfirio Díaz was finally overthrown in 1917, the new liberal Mexican constitution was drawn up in the city.

Querétaro

The capital of the state, Querétaro is a very Spanish city, filled with tree-lined plazas and splendid mansions, with a beautiful self-contained colonial centre. On the outskirts of the city, multinationals such as Kellogs and Singer have constructed huge plants, which have brought it an easy prosperity. It's a calm city to wander round for a day or to stop in for the night.

GETTING AROUND

By Bus: There are regular buses to and from Mexico City (2½ hrs), Guanajuato (2 hrs), San Luis Potosí (2½ hrs) and San Miguel de Allende (1 hr). The bus station is in Constituyentes Pte, opposite the Alameda, a 15-minute walk from the Plaza Principal down Corregidora. Town buses connect the station with the centre, marked 'Burocrata' or 'Central Camionera'.

By Car: Querétaro is on Highway 57, midway between Mexico City (215 km, 2 hrs) and San Luis Potosí (202 km, 2 hrs). Highway 45 leads west to Irapuato and then north to Zacatecas. San Miguel Allende is 58 km to the northwest (off the San Luis Potosí road) and Guanajuato 115 km northwest (off the Zacatecas road).

By Train: The railway station is in the north of town, with a daily train to Guanajuato (1½ hrs) and Mexico City (2 hrs).

In Town: Although the industrial suburbs seem endless when driving into Querétaro, fight to get to the centre and don't leave its environs. It is compact, laid out on a grid, and easy to negotiate on foot. Calle de la Corregidora cuts the town in half, running from the bus station in the south, past the Plaza Principal (also known as Jardín Obregón) to the Teatro de la República in the north. The oldest and most interesting part of town is north of Jardín Obregón, behind the regional museum. Andador Libertad, to the right of the museum, is filled with arts-and-crafts shops and leads to Plaza de la Independencia (also called Plaza de Armas). This square is the most redolent of old Querétaro, lined with heavy colonial buildings where the spirit of the Corregidora lingers still.

Car hire is available at Budget (southwest on the Carretera Panoramica, tel 21570).

TOURIST INFORMATION

The tourist office is in 5 de Mayo (tel 40179), next to the San Francisco church in Jardín Obregón. It organizes excellent city tours which leave the tourist office every day at 10.00 and last about 2 hours, visiting all the main places of interest at a spanking pace. They cost nothing and are given in both English and Spanish.

WHAT TO SEE

It is easy to while away the hours wandering through the small squares and alleys which lead one into another around the centre. When this palls, there are a number of museums and convents well worth visiting, all perfect examples of 18th-century baroque. Caryatids and atlantes are a Querétaro trademark, used as supports on almost every 18th-century building in town.

Museo Regional

(Corregidora 3 Sur, tel 22031; open 10.00–15.30 and 16.00–18.00, Tue–Sat; 10.00–15.30 Sun; closed Mon; adm.)

Housed in a 17th-century Franciscan monastery, Querétaro's regional museum is in some disarray, as many of its exhibits have been removed to the Museum of Art. What remains are illuminated manuscripts, huge hymnals big enough to be read by entire choirs, baroque furniture and carved ecclesiastical figures. The 16th-century church beside it is one of the oldest in the city. Inside, a statue of Christ flutters with photographs of women holding babies, pinned to it in thanks for the birth or to pray for health.

Museo de Arte

(Allende 14 Sur; open 11.00–18.00; closed Mon; adm.)

Originally built as an Augustinian monastery in 1731, this museum is housed in a superb example of baroque architecture. Its cloister is worth going to alone. The two storeys of arcades are linked by columns bearing caryatids, their long human shapes honed down to delicately pointed feet. The intended symbolism of the figures can seen in their hands. Some raise three fingers while joining the other two in a circle, expressing the mystery of the Trinity; others raise four fingers, evoking the four Evangelists. On the dome of the church are exquisitely garbed men with feathered headdresses: these are often thought to represent Indian caciques, but were in fact copies of ballet costumes from the French court of Louis XIV. Don't miss the grotesquely grinning faces of the gargoyles underneath the fountain.

The ground floor of the museum concentrates on 16th- and 17th-century religious works, which continue through the centuries upstairs. One room is devoted to the art of Abelardo Avila, including desolate prints of the monks forging their way through to build missions in the Sierra Gorda. The museum also has a growing collection of modern Mexican art. A guide gives free tours at 17.00 every day.

257

Arcivo
(Guerrero with Suárez, off Corregidora.)
In a stalwart colonial building where Juárez briefly held court and Maximilian was sentenced to death, the modern version of the mural is a 16-minute light and sound show. Fernando Castro Pacheco from the Yucatán has painted enormous murals of the history of the state, from the fall of the Chichimec chief Conin in the 16th century to the present day. These are lit up in turn, while a deep voice intones the sequence of events. It is a good 'idiot's guide' to the state's history.

Convento de la Cruz
(Northeast, in Plaza de los Fundadores: follow 5 de Mayo out of the centre and turn right into Najera; open 09.00–14.00 and 16.00–18.00.)
This, the first mission to be built in the area, is still a working monastery, with 30 friars. It sits on the site of the last battle of the doomed native Chichimecs against the Spanish and their fierce Otomí allies. Wishful legend has it that at a critical moment in the campaign, lightning in the shape of a cross shot through the air. This so impressed the Chichimecs that they laid down their weapons and embraced Catholicism there and then.

Today, the courtyards are filled with the music of canaries in cages and the chanting of monks. A statue of a Franciscan wearing a sombrero illustrates the mixture of the ecumenical and the quotidian which characterizes the monks' iife. The monastery has become a place of pilgrimage because of its miracle tree, which has thorns in the shape of crosses growing out of it. It is said to have grown from the staff of an elderly monk who spent a night here. Maximilian was imprisoned in this monastery before being shot. His cell is on display, as are Pueblan tiled baths, a big kitchen and even a replica cell with a bed, habit, and bible—and a skull to remind the monks of their earthly frailty. The 75th arch of the aqueduct runs through the grounds, and used to provide water for the monks.

Santa Rosa Church
(Av Arteaga, southwest of Jardín Obregón.)
This baroque fantasy is bolstered up by a pair of inverted arches. Tresguerras, their architect, was derided for his plans and told that he was unlikely to succeed. When he did, he put two sneering gargoyles on his arches, to laugh at his detractors as they passed. The Moorish tower lays claim to the first self-winding clock in the Americas.

Like all 18th-century conventual churches, Santa Rosa has double plateresque doors, in this case distinguished by pointed mudéjar arches. Inside, the lavish gilt church contains *retablos* designed by local craftsmen but influenced by Tresguerras, which for their imagination and verve form the high point of the 'Querétaro style'. Beside them is a collage of the Apostles by Miguel Cabrera. In the sacristy to the left hangs a full-length portrait of a beautiful nun, Ana María de San Francisco. The architect who built the aqueduct was madly in love with her and commissioned the painting. At the back of the church is the grille through which the nuns would watch Mass. The old convent next door was a hospital for many years and still smells institutional, although it is now an Institute for Graphic Arts.

258

Acueducto
Querétaro is bordered to the east by a long aqueduct, which with 76 arches claims to be the seventh longest in the world. Funded by a benefactor named Antonio de Urrutia, it was constructed in 1738 to bring much-needed water to the city.

Cerro de las Campañas
To the northwest of town, a small chapel (paid for by the Austrian government) commemorates the spot where Maximilian was shot. More noticeable is the vast statue of diminutive Juárez which towers over the small hill, making the trees look like saplings. Even his wrinkles are gigantically amplified. Buses to the Cerro de la Campañas from the centre are marked 'Carillo' or 'Satelitte'.

WHERE TO STAY   (area code 463)
Accommodation in Querétaro ranges from splendid colonial conversions to the cheap and not so cheerful. Anyone planning a long stay in the area would be better advised to make a base in San Miguel and come to Querétaro for day trips.

The ex-hacienda *****Jurica (on the road to San Luis Potosí, 9 km from the city, tel 80022, tlx 0121110, fax 89136) is emphatically exclusive but retains the atmosphere of a working hacienda, with horses wandering loose around the stables, manicured gardens and a deconsecrated chapel with an exquisite *cantera rosa* cross. The 179 modern rooms are built around various patios, one with orange trees, another with mosaic tiled floors. Guests can swim in the large pool, go horse riding, or play tennis or golf.

The ****Mesón de Santa Rosa (Plaza de Armas, tel 43078) is a treasure of a hotel, recently renovated and right in the heart of colonial Querétaro. The streets outside have been closed to traffic, so it is always peaceful. Rooms lead off courtyards filled with fountains and birds. It hasn't been overdone and still feels like a comfortable mansion. Less corporate than most others in the chain, the *****Holiday Inn (on the road to San Luis Potosí, Constitución 13 Sur, tel 60202) is extremely comfortable with light airy rooms, but best avoided at the weekends when it fills with obnoxious capital-city escapees.

Outside Querétaro is another weekend retreat in an ex-hacienda, the **Mansión Galindo** (52 km, 30 mins southeast, near San Juan del Río on the road to Mexico City, tel 467 20050). The russet-red 18th-century buildings have been restored, though the rooms are mostly modern. It's a peaceful spot, with large grounds and a small chapel.

Bland middle-range hotels cluster around the bus station. Try the ***Mirabel (Constituyentes 2 Ote, tel 43535) for comfort, or the cheaper **Impala (Corregidora Sur 188, tel 28604). In the Jardín Obregón, the *Plaza (Juárez 23, tel 21138) has seen better days but still provides 29 simple rooms, each with a bathroom. Another cheap alternative is the *Hidalgo (Hidalgo 14, a block north of Jardín Obregón, tel 20081), with modern rooms around a quiet courtyard.

EATING OUT
The Spanish introduced grapes to Mexico. The vines flourished, giving rise to fears that grapes (and wine) from the New World might ruin the home market, and in 1771 grape growing was banned throughout the country. It was reintroduced at the turn of the

century and a recent boom has established Querétaro as an important centre. For *pechugas de pollo a la uva* (chicken breast in a grape sauce), try **Josecho**, on the Celaya *cuota* road west (Highway 45). This restaurant has the best food in Querétaro, invariably patronized by expense-account executives. Expensive. **El Estancia** (on the road to San Luis Potosí) is another restaurant of the highest calibre, with one waiter per person, a little orchestra, a good wine cellar and a mass of different mushroom dishes, steaks and even caviar. Expensive.

Off the main square, **Fonda del Refugio** (Jardín Corregidora 26, tel 26190) specializes in typically Mexican dishes, such as *carnitas de cerdo*, (squares of pork to be doused in sauce). Moderate. It is also renowned as the spot where the Scots, visiting for the World Cup, danced in kilts round the fountain during a party that lasted a week. **Al Corregidora** (Av 16 Septiembre) specializes in fish, and lays on lavish comida corridas. Cheap.

Tequisquiapan

Tequisquiapan is the official geographical centre of Mexico. A small town of cobbled streets, radioactive hot springs and vineyards, it fills up at weekends with people escaping from the city. They come to lounge around the thermal pools, discussing diabetes and stomach complaints to the endless fascination of all concerned. The annual high point is the wine and cheese festival at the end of May.

GETTING AROUND

Tequisquiapan is 72 km east of Querétaro: turn left off Highway 57 at San Juan del Río. Flecha Azul run buses every half-hour from Querétaro's bus station on Constituyentes and Pasteur (45 mins). Hourly buses run from Mexico City's Terminal del Norte, via San Juan del Río (3 hrs).

WHERE TO STAY AND EAT   (area code 467)

Most of the 22 hotels clustered around the thermal waters have their own natural pools. The top hotel is ******Las Cavas** (Paseo de la Media Luna 25, tel 30804), on the far side of town, set in its own extensive gardens with tennis courts, a putting green and a large thermal pool. The conservatory-style restaurant specializes in *parilladas* of seafood, steak and home-made cakes. In town, the majority of hotels are musty boarding houses, with well-worn pool tables, domino sets and chess boards waiting for the weekend influx. The *****Posada del Virrey** (Guillermo Prieto Nte, tel 30239) is a notch above, with a good restaurant and lovely views from the top rooms. The ****Tequisquiapan** (Calle Moctezuma 6) is homely: its garden pool is blocked up during the week by the simple expedient of placing a huge block of wood over the hole. Cheaper hotels include the ****Mezquites** (Av Centenario 2 Nte) and the ***Mejía** (Guillermo Prieto 8, tel 30236).

The **Maridelfi** (tel 30052), on the plaza, serves regional *enchiladas querétanos* with *frijoles negritos* and local wines and brandies. Cheap. The market-place stalls, half a block down Independencia, sell *tostaditas de cueritos* and *tacos de cabeza de buey*, which taste infinitely better if left untranslated.

The Missions in the Sierra Gorda

Between Querétaro and Jalpan, there are five Francisan missions hidden in the middle of the wilderness of the Sierra Gorda. Anxious to prove their faith in adversity, the founding fathers looked for land that was as inhospitable as possible. The Sierra Gorda had even been left alone by the Aztecs, warned off by rumours of the barbaric ferocity of the Jonaces, the region's original inhabitants. The Spanish didn't attempt a conquest until 1750, when a fanatical Franciscan father from Mallorca, Junipero Serra, set off into the mountains with a small band of fellow monks. He founded the mission of Jalpan and was the driving force in evangelizing the area. (He later went on to evangelize California.) Four further missions were built by a handful of his followers, who had nothing to work with but their hands and what they could carry on their backs. The results are a unique expression of Latin-American baroque, interspersed with the native art of those who helped them. To see all five, it's best to spend the night in either Jalpan or Concá.

GETTING AROUND
By Bus: There are six buses a day between Querétaro and Jalpan. Local buses from Jalpan go to the other missions.
By Car: Jalpan is 190 winding km northeast of Querétaro. There are no petrol stations on the road until Jalpan, so fill up before leaving. The trip takes between 4 and 5 hours, depending on whether there is a bus on the road (which has no passing places). Take Highway 57 for Mexico City out of Querétaro, and turn left (north) down a straight road to Bernal. The road then starts climbing up into the foothills of the Sierra Gorda. The Peña, an impressive monolithic peak, looms mysteriously in the background. The sierra is arid and barren, a virtual moonscape alleviated only by cactuses, the occasional blue bus, or a scattered group of brightly clad goatherds. From the village of Toliman, the road climbs up through fertile plains covered in red earth and pine trees, into the Sierra Gorda proper. The views are breathtaking, the road spiralling so high that it reaches the clouds. The highest point (2375 m) seems to be at the top of the world. Early Franciscan missionaries who walked all the way from Querétaro with crosses on their backs must have finally felt that the trip was worth their while. The road from Jalpan, Highway 120, coninues to Ciudad Valles in San Luis Potosí.

VISITING THE MISSIONS
Jalpan
This is the oldest and finest of the missions, and the only one to be built under the direct auspices of Fray Serra, between 1751 and 1758. With scarcely an inch left uncovered, its stuccoed facade is eloquent with Franciscan symbolism and churrigueresque swirl. The theme of the facade is the defence of faith. Peter and Paul, founders of the Catholic Church, stand either side of the door. Above them are St Dominic and St Francis, the latter holding his identifying skull. Above the door are the crossed arms of Christ, dripping with blood from his stigmata, and St Francis, who is trying to absorb the pain (the Franciscan insignia). A Franciscan knotted cord runs above the diamond-shaped choir window. The double-headed eagle with a Hapsburg crown and snake in its mouth

261

is a clever illustration of the melding of European and indigenous traditions—an eagle eating a snake was an important Aztec symbol. To the right of the church are the portals where weary pilgrims would rest before beginning the long journey back to habitable territory. The interior of the church was destroyed during the 1910 Revolution. Its pride is a tubular organ which has been there since the founding of the mission. The fathers brought it on their backs, bit by bit, from Querétaro.

Landa

The mission of Landa is 20 km east of Jalpan on Highway 120. Its rose-stuccoed facade is the most elaborate of all, resembling a painstakingly iced cake, and the only one to be built by a Mexican friar. The church is dedicated to the Virgin Mary, who is surrounded by philosophers such as the 13th-century Duns Scotus, who devoted a lifetime to her study. Presiding over the entire facade is a figure of the Archangel Michael, holding a sword and scales, and standing triumphantly on top of a demonic-looking dragon. The mermaids below him symbolize evil defeated by good. Only emaciated dogs stir on the streets of the village of Landa, although there is a small general store selling drinks.

Tilaco

To go on to the mission of Tilaco, return to Highway 120 for 10 km, turn right down 4 km of paved road, and then follow 12 km of dusty track. At Tilaco, the most dignified of all the facades is topped by an exuberant crown. The figures of the saints seem distinctly American rather than European, and were carved by local craftsmen. Mermaids bear the weight of the portals on their shoulders.

Tancoyo

Continue along Highway 120 for 7 km, and then turn left, down 4 km of paved road and 12 km of dirt track, for the mission of Tancoyo. Unusually, an open chapel still remains within the imposing white-walled atrium, which is topped by Moorish coned merlons. The facade is dedicated to the Virgin Mary.

Concá

To reach the mission of Concá, return to Jalpan and take Highway 62 towards Río Verde (in San Luis Potosí). After 34 km, turn left down a 1-km track. Here, above the mudéjar arch of the door, the Archangel Michael triumphs over a ghoulish-looking gryphon, while indigenous angels cling to the foliage below.

WHERE TO STAY

In Jalpan, a small posada—the **Fray Junipero Serra**—has 37 simple rooms set around a garden. The dining room specializes in fish and shrimps from the local rivers. In Concá, the ***Ex-hacienda of San Nicolas** has been converted into a charming hotel, the more comfortable of the two, with 42 rooms and a swimming pool. Neither has telephones: reservations can be made through the tourist office in Querétaro or by ringing an agency (43078).

Callejón del Beso, Guanajuato

The State of Guanajuato

The state of Guanajuato is blessed with agricultural and mining riches. As soon as it was discovered that Guanajuato had silver in its hills, the Spanish zeroed in, building the beautiful, historic towns of San Miguel de Allende and Guanajuato. Renowned for the number of festivals they manage to squeeze into one calendar year (including the month-long Cervantino in Guanajuato in October), they have found favour today with many North American and European immigrants who have come for a week and stayed for a lifetime. Still retaining a decidedly Mexican flavour in their street life and architecture, these towns are excellent both for cultural visits and lazy meandering, and as a base for excursions into the wild country that surrounds them.

Guanajuato

Guanajuato isn't on the road to anywhere but has more going on within its narrow confines than any other city of its size. Long and thin, the city seems to have been poured into its niche between steep, harsh walls of dry rock, seeping into any pinch of flat ground it can find and clambering back up the sides. Bursts of multicoloured houses tumble down the surrounding hills—a Cézanne canvas with cubes of burnt ochre and sienna, side by side with pastel pinks and faded blue. There are no suburbs: the road leads straight into the labyrinth of multicoloured houses on multiple hills. It has a Mediterranean feel, and could by rights, be Andalucian or Tuscan, with narrow cobbled streets winding and bending to negotiate the hills. Little passageways lead off in all directions or turn into a square with only one exit. Roads are never straight. They bulge into a plaza only to be squeezed back into a corridor again.

A maze of underground tunnels lies beneath the city, and one shares Alice's doubt in Wonderland of never quite knowing where and when to emerge. When driving through

263

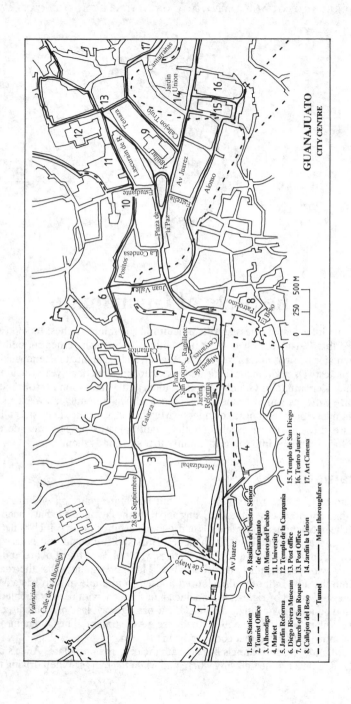

GUANAJUATO
CITY CENTRE

1. Bus Station
2. Tourist Office
3. Alhóndiga
4. Market
5. Jardín Reforma
6. Diego Rivera Museum
7. Church of San Roque
8. Callejón del Beso
9. Basílica de Nuestra Señora
   de Guanajuato
10. Museo del Pueblo
11. University
12. Templo de la Campania
13. Post office
14. Jardín la Unión
15. Templo de San Diego
16. Teatro Juarez
17. Art Cinema

- - - - Tunnel   ——— Main thoroughfare

0   250   500 M

them it is hard to imagine a busy city on top. It is rather like seeing a medieval town through the periscope of a time-submarine.

GETTING AROUND

By Bus: The pastel-pink bus station is a block west of the tourist office, on Juárez 131. Hotels can be booked from here and taxis wait outside. There are regular first-class buses to Mexico City (4 hrs), Guadalajara (4 hrs), Zacatecas (5 hrs) and Querétaro (2 hrs), and hourly second-class buses to San Miguel de Allende (1 hr).

By Car: Highway 45, a swift dual carriageway, swoops down from Mexico City (432 km) and Querétaro (115 km), continuing north to Zacatecas (311 km). Guanajuato is 22 km northeast of this highway, along Highway 110: the turn-off comes after Irapuato and just before Silao. Highway 110 is more curvaceous, taking its time to wend in from Guadalajara (302 km) in the west and continuing eastwards on a switchback of a road to Dolores Hidalgo.

By Train: The railway station is to the northwest of town in Tepetapa, a continuation of Juárez. There is a daily first-class service, with dining car, to Mexico City, a soothing 4-hour ride. When coming from Mexico City, the train divides at Querétaro, half going to San Luis Potosí and half continuing to Guanajuato.

In Town: Guanajuato is impossible to map. Bemused tourists pop like moles out of the myriad of tunnels undermining the city. In 1962 the bed of the Guanajuato River was turned into an underground street, Calle Miguel Hidalgo, with numerous tunnels leading off it in all directions. To add to the confusion, Guanajuato doesn't have one big main square, but a series of *plazuelas* (small squares) set around churches. Jardín Unión is the most popular of these.

The most important street is Juárez, which runs west to east from the bus station, past the tourist office and the market and through Plaza de la Paz to Jardín Unión. Parallel to and north of Juárez, above the Alhondiga, Positos runs past Diego Rivera's house to the university. From here Calle Estudiante leads down to Plaza de la Paz.

Don't even try to negotiate the centre by car. Leave it in one of the underground car parks in the tunnels and walk. The town is self-contained and much more easily seen on foot. Taxis are cheap and plentiful, though don't be surprised if they leave you short of your destination. Many squares are impassable by car.

For an overview, take the Carretera Panoramica which circles round in the hills above the town, past old mines and the monumental statue of El Pipila, the boy who stormed the Alhóndiga.

TOURIST INFORMATION

The office is on 5 de Mayo and Juárez (tel 20086). Ask for Desmond O'Shaugnessy, an Irishman, who came over to see the 1970 World Cup and never left. He now works for the tourist office, speaks fluent Spanish with a brogue and is full of inside information. Opposite, there is a booth which has maps and someone snoozing on duty during lunch hour when the tourist office closes.

Whatever way you arrive, within minutes small boys will accost you, anxious to act as guides, to anywhere in the city, but most particularly to the ghoulish exhibition of mummies. '*Ven a ver las momias*', they'll cry. Some years ago, a primary-school teacher decided to teach his pupils the history of the town, to create pocket-money jobs for them.

The young guides soon got cash registers in their eyes and the philanthropic scheme has turned into big business.

WHAT TO SEE AND DO

East of Juárez from the Tourist Office

The Market
Originally planned as a railway terminal, the market billows with wrought iron and vaulting glass. The ground floor is filled with baskets of eggs, fresh flowers, strawberries from Celaya, sugar-sweet effigies of the mummies, sweet-smelling herbs and endless chatter. Upstairs, more circumspect stalls sell local arts and crafts. Crackly old films are often shown at night, on the steps outside. A whitewashed wall serves as the screen and crowds gather to chat all the way through.

Callejón del Beso
From the market, Patrocinio, to the right, leads to the Callejón del Beso, where two balconies on opposite sides of the narrow passageway are close enough for lovers to exchange a kiss (*beso*). Small boys earn pocket money intoning the Romeo and Juliet scenario of thwarted love. Couples who kiss on the third step can expect 15 years of good luck (but seven of bad if they don't).

Plaza de la Paz
The chief attraction of this wide plaza is within the saffron-coloured church of the Virgin of Guadalupe, which shelters a 'miraculous' virgin. She was hidden in a cave in Granada for 800 years to prevent her being desecrated by Moors in the 8th century. Philip II of Spain subsequently sent her to Guanajuato to thank the city for making him rich beyond his wildest dreams. No-one seems to complain about the fairness of the deal and she is highly venerated. The body of Saint Faustina was also sent over from Spain and lies in musty state. The great wooden doors are more indigenous, with naive carvings of luridly grinning gargoyles.

Jardín Unión
In the heart of it all, Jardín Unión is a fairy-tale plaza which someone has wound up and let play a life of its own. A brass band belts its heart out on the stand, as Europeans try to saunter as nonchalantly as Mexicans around the tiny square. Girls go arm in arm one way, boys swagger the other, stopping only to flash eyes or exhange greetings. Sweethearts sit cheek to cheek on a park bench, kids tear past on skate boards, old ladies walk their dogs, a grandfather ambles by hand in hand with his grandson. You can watch it all from the terrace of the Posada Santa Fe, where a runny-nosed boy tries to sell his posy of weathered and yellowed rosebuds, while the waiter brings plates piled high with *nachos*. In the Bar Luna, men play dominoes and slam tequilas. The whole scene is framed by a backdrop of beautifully cropped Indian laurels and tall engulfing houses.

To one side is a grandiose neoclassical theatre, Juárez, complete with nine muses on its cornice. Its sickly green hue comes from the much-prized local stone. Beside it is the ornate Franciscan church of San Diego. Inside, a large glass box is filled with children's toys, poignant offerings to Santo Niño, who presides over the health of ill children.

East along Positos from the Tourist Office

Alhóndiga

(Positos, up the hill from the tourist office; open 09.00–14.00 and 16.00–18.00 Tues–Sat; 10.00–16.00 Sun; adm.)

This solid impressive granary, built to store grain and prevent famine, now houses a large museum. It is more famous for its bloody role during the War of Independence from Spain. Only 13 days after Father Hidalgo's *'grito'* roused the oppressed peasants, Spanish soldiers and their families were barricaded inside the Alhóndiga, whilst Hidalgo and his Mexican-born mob roared for blood outside. When it seemed as if the Spanish would be able to withhold attack for some time, a young miner, Pipila, rushed at the gates with dynamite strapped to his back. This kamikaze trip cost him his life but succeeded in opening the gates, and in return he became a national hero. The ensuing massacre was ruthless: no life was spared nor prisoner taken. Over 500 Spanish and 2000 Mexicans were killed and the town was pillaged by a rabble driven insensible with fury. Hidalgo was excommunicated by the Bishop of Michoacán for his role in the slaughter.

The Spanish later took their revenge and returned to Guanajuato, ordering the death of every man, woman and child captured. Furthermore, the severed heads of the four leading insurgents (Hidalgo, Allende, Jiménez and Aldama) were displayed in iron cages on the four corners of the Alhóndiga for eleven years, as a grim warning against further rebellion. The hooks remain in position today, one on each corner. When Mexico finally won independence from Spain, the heads were taken to Mexico City in a crystal urn and given a state burial.

The highlights of the museum include some exquisite portraits by Hermengildo Bustos, who portrayed his family and friends with a painful honesty, unsmiling, warts and all. He rarely painted life-size but concentrated on miniature postcard-sized portraits. Other exhibits include the turn-of-the-century photographs of another realist, Ramondo García, with one particularly beautiful shot of a mournful, haunting *charro*.

Plaza San Roque

From Positos, Galarza leads to Plaza San Roque. This square was originally a pantheon where the insurgents were buried. The restrained church with its mudéjar doors is the scene of *Estudiantinas*, plays of Spanish origin performed by students on Friday and Saturday nights, fuelled by wine in special flasks. Down from San Roque, **San Fernando** is an open square surrounded by brightly painted houses, at its busiest in March, when a small book fair takes place.

Diego Rivera Museum

(Positos 47; open 10.00–13.00 and 16.00–18.00 Tues–Sat; 10.00–14.30 Sun; adm.)

As a communist, Diego Rivera (1886–1957) was an embarrassment to deeply conservative Guanajuato, particularly at the height of the ultra-Catholic Cristero movement. More recently, they have been keen to own up to him and have opened his parents' house as a museum. The family lived here until he was seven, moving to Mexico City in 1903.

The first floor is filled with family furniture. It seems surprising that this narrow house could ever have contained the larger than life Rivera, with its pinched tight rooms cluttered with heavy wooden furniture, redolent of solid bourgeois preconceptions. The broad sweep of his paintings contains something of this doll's house world, in which every inch is utilized and a sense of order prevails.

The second floor is devoted to his work, exhibiting many paintings, sketches, self-portraits and photographs. A double portrait was inspired by Piero della Francesca's *Count of Montefeltro* in the Uffizi in Florence: one side represents Rivera's twin sister who died in infancy, entitled *Hermana de la Caridad* (sister of mercy); the other side is a self-portrait, called *Bohemio*.

Rivera went to Europe as a young man and studied one school after another, absorbing, reproducing, and then moving on to the next. His ability to assimilate other styles can be seen in the portrait of the revolutionary hero Zapata, who is conceived as a Renaissance Italian. On his return to Mexico in 1926, his European experience acted as a filter for his view of Mexico, during a time of talk, counter-talk, promise and revolution. He was to become one of the foremost artists of post-revolutionary Mexico.

Museo del Pueblo
(Next to the university on Positos 7; open 10.00–14.00 and 16.00–19.00 Tues–Sun; adm.)
This former home of the Marquis of San Juan de Raysas has been turned into a small, intimate museum by Chavez Morado, the muralist (who was born in the state). It houses examples of his own work, along with a collection of paintings (many of which are religious), and both pre-Hispanic and contemporary ceramics.

University
Rebuilt by Urquiaguy Rivas in the 1950s, the university towers above the narrow streets. A seemingly endless flight of stairs soars up to its entrance. One of the oldest universities in the country, it owes its origins to a Jesuit seminary, and sits incongruously next door to the churrigueresque facade of the original church. Two paintings by Miguel Cabrera are inside the church. Otherwise the plain interior has little to recommend it, other than a towering 19th-century cupola.

On the Fringes of the City

Guanajuato is squeezed into a gulley, and consequently some of its greatest attractions are outside the centre—including its two most interesting churches, a working mine, a gruesomely Mexican museum, an ex-hacienda and a refurbished village.

La Valenciana
The road northeast to Dolores Hidalgo (Highway 110) passes the mine and church of La Valenciana. Local buses leave from the Alhóndiga. The church was built by the owner of the richest mine in the area, the self-styled Count of Valenciana, in the latter half of the 18th century. Renowned for squandering his money on wine and women, he financed it in a supposed act of pious contrition, intending it to be the most splendid church in Mexico. He seconded a mass of hapless miners to build it, who were also required to contribute a large lump of silver every week to defray costs. It is, indeed, one of the most dramatic (and expensive) churches in Mexico, set conspicuously on a hill high above the town. The classic Mexican black and white film *Bugambilias*, with Pedro Armendáriz,

Dolores del Río and the beautiful photography of Gabriel Figueroa, was shot in and around Guanajuato. The climax takes place on the steps of this church, as the desperate father shoots his daughter's husband moments after they have exchanged vows; thereafter the film spirals downwards into tragic proportions.

The facade of the church is delicate and restrained, but inside three *retablos* explode with gilded cherubs, curves and flourishes. An elaborate side portal, built in the same pale rose stone as the church, blossoms with wild cascades of ornamentation, blending in with the billowing landscape around. The count's house is next door and has been recently restored. Unfortunately, it isn't open to the public: try to glimpse inside through the thick wooden doors. Opposite the church, a dusty track leads to the mine of La Valenciana, which is still working. There is a small museum and shop at the top and the battlements around it are shaped into the prongs of the Spanish crown.

Iglesia de los Mineros/Mineral de Cata

Take the Carretera Panoramica to Cata on the north side of town. Here, there is a modest church for the miners, at the bottom end of the social scale and quite the opposite to grand Valenciana. Utterly unpretentious, it sits in a small square, next to a vintner, well away from the hurly-burly of the centre. Inside the church, hand-painted *retablos*, painted on tin plates with naive detail and bright colours, speak eloquently of the perils of mining, showing roofs caving in and miners suffering from respiratory diseases. Every square inch of the walls is lined with mementos, given in thanks for recovery and as an insurance against future illnesses. They include braids of hair, children's shoes and even a pickled appendix.

Museo de las Momias

(On the Carretera Panoramica, northwest of town beyond the railway station: take a bus from the centre marked 'Panteón/La Rocha'; open 09.00–18.00; adm.)

Guanajuato is renowned throughout Mexico for its mummies. In this museum high above town by the cemetery, the curiously Mexican preoccupation with death is displayed in all its gloom. Every day, tourists flock to shuffle past its collection of mummmified corpses in glass cases.

In the 1890s, when more space was needed and impoverished relations could no longer afford to pay the upkeep on a grave in the public cemetery, the authorities disinterred the corpses. To their surprise they found that chemicals in the soil had mummified the bodies, clothes and all. Cashing in on the Mexican love of the macabre, they decided to display the unfortunate deceased to the public. This ghoulish collection of over 100 preserved corpses has a disturbing fascination. As at Pompeii, life seems to have been switched off unexpectedly. The bodies are fully clothed, even down to their socks. Men show signs of an unshaved beard, while women have their pigtails tied. Foreigners didn't escape: there are two French doctors in suits and even a tiny Chinese woman. The most missable parts of the collection are the women who died in childbirth and the tiny children with the haunting look of Victorian china dolls.

Ex-Hacienda de San Gabriel de Barrera

(Take Calle Hidalgo out to the Silao road, Highway 110, which leads southwest to the hacienda and then on to the village of Marfil.)

Once a prosperous hacienda, San Gabriel is now a museum. The rooms look as if they've been taken by surprise and little has been touched since their heyday in the 19th century. The extensive gardens, employing four full-time gardeners, were laid out to European design for nostalgic Spaniards.

Marfil

Early in the 20th century, the River Guanajuato burst its banks. The ensuing flood devastated the marshy area southeast of town, known as Marfil, leaving behind only half-drowned churches and crumbling walls. Subsequently, an Italian architect, Giorgio Belloli, embarked on an ambitious project to restore the houses, using as many original details as he could. Such was his charm and skill that he persuaded the wives of many wealthy North Americans to buy his houses. Today, the village oozes Italian allure, with its ochre-domed churches and cypress-covered slopes.

SHOPPING

Finely worked, autumnal-coloured **ceramics** from Guanajuato are highly prized. Two distinguished ceramics maestros sell from home. Gonzalo Gorki, who trained in Japan, lives near the Embajadores to the east of town, by the baseball field (tel 24306). Sr Capeto has a workshop in Carcamanes, a side street off Positos, up from the post office.

Behind the church of San Diego in the Jardín Unión, a small *Casa de Artesanías* (Mineral de Cata, tel 21524) has a good selection of thick rough-cut glasses, another speciality of the region.

CINEMA

International films (subtitled in Spanish) are shown in a small art cinema in Calle Cantarranas, west of Jardín Unión.

DON QUIJOTE

Anxious to maintain links with home, Spanish settlers established a tradition of performing *entremeses cervantinos*, early plays by Cervantes. These are still performed weekly by students, in the streets. In turn, Cervantes' hero, Don Quijote, has become inextricably linked with Guanajuato. There are several statues of him in the city, and even a **Museo Iconográfico**, which is filled with over 600 artistic interpretations of this one character. It's a jumble, with works by Dali, Picasso, Daumier, Doré and Posada, as well as less prestigious local artists.

FIESTAS

The main festivals are Easter and the big international Cervantes festival in October, the Cervantino. The latter comprises an eclectic mix of cultural events, from cinema in the streets, students singing in alleyways—dressed as swaggering Spanish gallants, international theatre, special exhibitions in museums, café talking and sidewalk walking, to processions, re-enactments of Christ's journey from Gethsemane, book fairs, courtships and one hundred other incidentals. Plaza San Roque is always at the heart of things.

ORCHESTRA

Guanajuato has two of the best orchestras in Mexico. Unfortunately, they don't perform in their home town as frequently as they perform in other parts of the country: check with the tourist office.

WHERE TO STAY (area code 473)

At Easter and during October the town is filled from top to toe, and advance booking is essential. At other times there is always a bed to be found. Hotel prices have not been hiked up for tourists, and compare favourably with the rest of Mexico.

Guanajuato's smartest hotel is the colonial ****San Javier (Plaza San Javier, tel 20626, tlx 12327), which has 129 rooms, swimming pools, green gardens and a huge dining hall with log fires and starched waiters. Ask for one of the older bedrooms which have fireplaces and tiled bathrooms.

The ***Posada Santa Fe (in the Jardín Unión, tel 20084) has the best location. The colonial hallway is let down by disappointingly small rooms, but it's comfortable and family run. The restaurant outside is more expensive than some, but there is nowhere better for watching the world go by. Still in the Jardín Unión, the ***San Diego (tel 21300) was a convent 200 years ago and then a private home, before becoming a hotel. Sadly, the rooms are lacklustre, though they have the distinct advantage of a central position. It has a first-floor restaurant with views over the square. Just off the Jardín Unión, the ***Hostería del Fraile (Sopeña 3, tel 21179) is the most attractive three-star hotel, with big airy colonial rooms in what was a 17th-century coin factory.

If you go underground (anywhere) and follow signs for the Embajadores tunnel southeast, you will find the road surfacing at the ***Motel Embajadores (tel 20081), set in a peaceful courtyard, next to the Parque Embajadores where a lively market takes place on a Sunday morning. A 10-minute walk from the centre, it's clean, simple and quiet, with an excellent restaurant. For a view and a margarita, try the ***Motel Guanajuato (tel 20689), high above the town on the road to Dolores Hidalgo. The plain tiled rooms have panoramic views.

**Hotel Mineral de Rayas (Alhóndiga 7, tel 21987) has 90 rooms on five floors with no lifts. It is a little dark but central, overlooking the Alhóndiga. Also near the bus station, the **Hacienda de Cobos (Hidalgo and Juárez, tel 20143) has 40 small but charming rooms. It was once a 17th-century silver magnate's mansion. Next to the monument to Don Quijote is a pretty hotel on three floors, set around a courtyard, the **Molino del Rey (Calle Padre Belaunzarón and Campanero, tel 22223; take underground Hidalgo and come up at the monument). Family run, with high brick ceilings and heavy wooden furniture, it has a good restaurant at a moderate price.

*Casa Kloster (Alonso 32, tel 20088) is popular with young Europeans. The 16 rooms open onto a patio filled with plants and canaries singing in cages. There is only one communal bathroom.

Out of town, next to the Hacienda San Gabriel, the ****Hotel San Gabriel (tel 23980) has colonial-style rooms, tennis courts and a swimming pool.

EATING OUT

Guanajuato doesn't go in for fancy restaurants. Around Juárez and the Jardín Unión, there is a mass of small restaurants, all serving generous comida corridas and Mexican

271

stalwarts. The town is best known for its *cebadina* (root beer) and *enchiladas mineras* (made with chicken, potatoes, carrots and lettuce). The **Santa Fe** does these par excellence. Also in Jardín Unión, on the corner opposite the Sante Fe, a small restaurant with no name prepares hot spicy *chilaquiles* (a tortilla casserole). **El Retiro** in nearby Sopeña (up from Teatro Juárez) is the place for cheap comidas.

The San Javier hotel owns the restaurant **Venta Vieja** opposite it. It's an old favourite, specializing in meat with dishes like *corazón de filete Rossini* (steak smothered in a creamy mushroom sauce). Expensive. **Tasca de los Santos** (Plaza de la Paz 28, tel 22320) is Spanish rather than Mexican and serves a variety of *taberna* food. Moderate. The **Motel Guanajuato** is highly rated for its Mexican cooking as well as a more international range of steak and fish dishes. Moderate.

In Sopeña, the **Dolce Vita** offers Italian pastas with a distinctly Mexican hallmark. Cheap. **Nutricional Vegetariano** is a vegetarian restaurant in Plaza de la Paz, to the north of the church, offering a choice of comida corridas and fresh fruit juices. Cheap. East of the market in Juárez, a *rosticería* provides plates of roast chicken with salad and tortillas. Cheap. Nearby, **El Callejón** serves seafood (moderate) and next door, the sweet shop **La Cajeta de Celaya** sells the sticky fruit sweets of the area, *cubiletes*.

On the road to Dolores Hidalgo, past Valenciana, **Restaurant de la Sierra** (Mineral de Sta Rosa) is high up in the hills. It is a popular spot to walk from: in the morning, hikers sit in front of raging fires sipping nips of tequila. Family run, with plain tables, it serves up endless plates of *enchiladas suizas, carne a la tampiqueña* or *guacamole*. Cheap.

Dolores Hidalgo

A dusty, colonial town on the route between Guanajuato and San Miguel de Allende, Dolores Hidalgo is known for its glazed tiles and, more importantly, for being the birthplace of Father Miguel Hidalgo. An ardent defender of the underdog, he proclaimed his famous '*grito*' for independence here, in 1810, which ultimately freed Mexico from Spanish rule.

GETTING AROUND
By Bus: The bus station is two and a half blocks south of the main square, down Hidalgo. Second-class buses connect the town with Guanajuato (60 mins) and San Miguel de Allende (40 mins).
By Car: Dolores Hidalgo is 54 km northeast of Guanajuato on Highway 110, and 40 km northwest of San Miguel de Allende on Highway 51.

WHAT TO SEE
An imposing church stands guard over the main square. The '*grito*' is still proclaimed from its doors every 16 September with a great flourish. It was built in the early 18th century, with an elaborately columned, churrigueresque facade, to which two towers were added as an afterthought. Joseph and Mary are on the front. Mary (the Virgin of Dolores) grieves over Christ on the Cross. The Evangelists stand by, books in hand. An empty shield once housed the arms of Spain, which were subsequently ripped down once independence had been won. Inside, there are two elaborate wooden *retablos*, one lavished with gold, the other plain.

The airy square is lined with a haze of pale purple from its jacaranda trees and ice-cream vendors. Its bandstand is edged in the thick glazed tiles for which the town is famous. To find out more about them, visit the **Asociación de Ceramistas** (Ceramics Association), in Puebla 52, two blocks southeast of the cathedral (tel 20222).

Hidalgo's house, around the corner in Calle Hidalgo, has been turned into a museum (open 09.00–13.00 and 16.00–18.00, closed Mon). The house is very much as it was, with a traditional kitchen and some beautifully carved wooden furniture. Memorabilia include his distinctive round steel glasses.

Always a radical, Hidalgo questioned priestly celibacy, doubted the veracity of the Virgin Birth, believed that fornication out of wedlock was not necessarily a sin, and thought the King of Spain was a tyrant. His lover, Josefa Quintana, bore him two daughters: one died in infancy, the other went on to marry a Mendoza whose descendants still live in the town today. He did a great deal for his home town, introducing new industries such as the tile making for which it later became famous. It was here that he formed a 'literary club', which preferred plotting the independence movement to discussing the latest works of Wordsworth and Schiller.

WHERE TO STAY AND EAT
(area code 468)

Whilst it is not somewhere to linger long, the town does have a couple of hotels. The best of these is ****Posada Cocomacán** (on the main square, tel 20018), which is old, colonial and cheap, with big light rooms. An unnamed fish café, up the hill in the same street, serves hearty platefuls of fried fish and avocado. Dolores Hidalgo is famous for its *nieves* (ice creams), avocado and mango ices in particular. There is always a stand with wooden tubs in the main square.

San Miguel de Allende

San Miguel de Allende has to a certain extent been obscured by its own myth. Extremely well known, it is usually associated with the gringos and second-rate artists whose invasion of the town has spawned numerous language schools and art galleries, and a succession of crowded bars and cafés. However, its many foreign residents (students, retired artists and loafers, both European and American) are not overnight tourists but are there to stay: they have adapted to San Miguel and have watched it adapt to them. Both because of and despite this foreign influx, San Miguel remains a comfortable and fascinating place to visit.

As a town it spends a lot of time contemplating its own navel. With a preservation order stamped on it, it has developed into a self-conscious architectural image of colonial Mexico, complete with cobbled streets and an urban plan which radiates from the central Jardín. Close to Guanajuato and its wealthy silver mines, but considerably less perpendicular, San Miguel attracted many colonial families and became a wealthy supply centre for the mines. A handful of important families sponsored lavish churches, fountains and monasteries, and built themselves thick-walled mansions with heavy wooden doors, studded with brass knockers and heraldic shields, set around the Jardín.

Filled with Indian laurel trees and crisscrossed by paths leading in every direction, the Jardín is the focal point of the town today, the place where everyone comes to see and be seen. During the day, retired Mexicans and North Americans doze in the sun under wide-brimmed hats, but in the evenings it is taken over by the courtship rituals of the young. The girls, arms linked, go endlessly round and round, studiously avoiding but slyly noting the boys rotating in the opposite direction.

History

San Miguel was founded by the barefoot Franciscan friar, Juan de San Miguel, in 1540. It was quickly built up into a garrison to defend Spanish interests along the silver route to Zacatecas and rapidly expanded. The population was made up of indigenous Mexicans and Mexican-born Spaniards, hampered by the restrictions imposed on them simply because they were creoles born in Mexico and not Spain. First the American Revolution, then the French and finally Napoleon's invasion of Spain made them restless.

Ignacio Allende was a creole, born in San Miguel on 20 January 1779 and baptized in the Parroquia. He joined the army at 18 and was later put in charge of the local militia in Querétaro. Here he set up a literary club which was really an underground movement for independence. At the age of 35 he met the 57-year-old parish priest of Dolores, Miguel Hidalgo, and together they plotted the overthrow of the colonial government. On the night of 13 September their plan was discovered by the Mayor of Querétaro (see History, Querétaro). A rider was sent to warn Allende. He wasn't at home, but the rider continued to Dolores, found both Allende and Hidalgo together, and advised them that their plan had been uncovered.

The only option was to bring the insurrection forward by three months. With Hidalgo's famous shout for freedom, the raggle-taggle army set off the same day, via Atotonilco, to San Miguel. The town fell without a struggle and the local militia joined the rebels. That night, however, the rebels became a mob. Inflamed by Hidalgo's words, and holding the Spanish responsible for all the sufferings of the last three centuries, they raced through the streets, armed with scythes, machetes and clubs to pillage the town. Hidalgo was powerless—only Allende could calm them down. This scene was to be repeated wherever the revolutionary army attacked. Subsequently, Allende, as the military man, may have expected to lead the troops, but in fact it was Hidalgo, the religious leader who had spoken out the first words of insurrection, who was chosen as the popular leader. Allende continued to fight throughout every one of the early independence battles. He was captured by government troops in March 1811 in the northern state of Coahuila, walked in chains to Chihuahua and summarily executed. Independence was still a bloody decade away. In 1826, the town added his name to its own.

GETTING AROUND

By Bus: Buses are not a strong point in San Miguel. Only a couple of daily first-class buses run to Mexico City and Querétaro. Second-class buses link the town with Dolores Hidalgo, Guanajuato, San Luis Potosí and Aguascalientes, but services tend to be unreliable.

By Car: San Miguel is 52 km north of Celaya on Highway 45, which leads west to Aguascalientes (276 km) and the northwest, and east to Querétaro (63 km). From Mexico City, take the periférico and Highway 57, turning off 28 km north of Querétaro onto Highway 11 (278 km, 3 hrs).

By Train: San Miguel is on the Mexico City–Querétaro–San Luis Potosí line. A

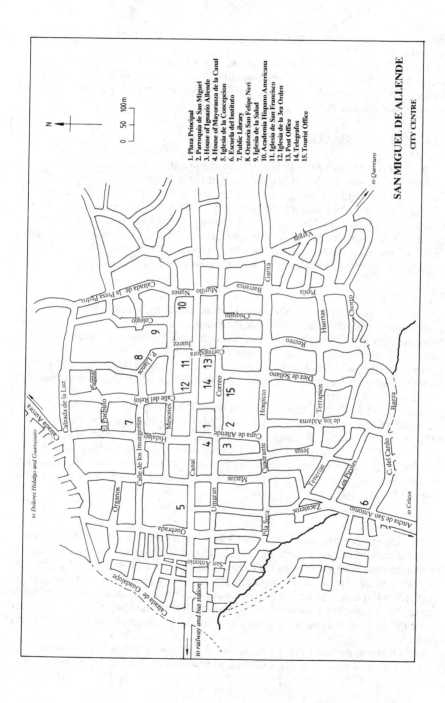

SAN MIGUEL DE ALLENDE

CITY CENTRE

1. Plaza Principal
2. Parroquia de San Miguel
3. House of Ignazio Allende
4. House of Mayoranza de la Canal
5. Iglesia de la Concepcion
6. Escuela del Instituto
7. Public Library
8. Oratoria San Felipe Neri
9. Iglesia de la Salud
10. Academia Hispano Americana
11. Iglesia de San Francisco
12. Iglesia de la 3ra Orden
13. Post Office
14. Telegrafos
15. Tourist Office

to Queretaro

to Dolores Hidalgo and Guanajuato

to railway and bus station

to Celaya

comfortable train leaves Mexico City early in the morning (breakfast included) and returns in the evening.

In Town: The much-improved bus and train stations are both to the west of town, on either side of the Libramiento ring road. Although San Miguel is most definitely a walking city, the cobbled streets can be murderous and it isn't just Dr Scholl who recommends sensible shoes.

TOURIST INFORMATION

The tourist office is on the southeast corner of the Jardín Principal and Canal (tel 21747; open 10.00–14.30 and 17.00–19.00). It is small but enthusiastic, providing good maps and organizing 2-hour tours of the city. In a town where dollars and pesos want to change hands fast, the **banks** make the process as ponderous as possible. The quickest is Multibanco Comermex, half a block east of the Jardín on San Francisco, which will change money between 09.00 and 12.00. Otherwise try the hotel receptions. Shops and hotels sell English newspapers and the weekly English paper, *Atención*, which gives details of what's on where, including classes and rooms for rent. The Biblioteca Publica (library) (Insurgentes 25) has more than 30,000 titles in English.

WHAT TO SEE

The small, busy Jardín Principal is the magnet in the centre of town, dominated by the **Parroquia** (parish church), which was modelled on a postcard of Notre Dame—an amazing flight of fancy to the more extreme regions of the Mexican imagination. The national bank, **Banamex** (Canal 4; open 09.00–13.00), has taken over the Casa de Canal, a mansion of soft pink quarried stone, with a neoclassical facade, studded with the family coat of arms. The bank's entrance is on Canal, beneath an arcade of overhanging wrought-iron balconies.

Southwest of the Jardín, at the junction between Umarán and Cuna de Allende, stands the **Museo Casa de Allende** where the great Mexican patriot was born. An inscription above the door reads '*Hic natus ubique notus*' ('Here was born he who is known everywhere'). The museum is filled with memorabilia. Four doors along, the **Casa de los Perros** (Umarán 4) now houses one of the better galleries, Casa Maxwell. The mansion's name refers to its balcony, which is supported by corbels carved into the shapes of dogs.

The Churches

Either side of Mesones, northeast of the Jardín, four churches are within a couple of blocks of each other. **San Francisco**, two blocks east of the Jardín, was originally known as San Antonio. The excesses of the estípite facade, topped by an image of St Francis, contrast with the clipped laurels around its atrium. The church of **Tercer Orden**, to the west of San Francisco, in the same garden, was once part of the Franciscan monastery. It was used as a convent for lay people who wanted a life more in line with that of the friars and nuns, and was left deliberately bare and simple, in contrast to San Francisco next door.

The **Oratorio de San Felipe Neri** is a block north of Mesones. It was known as the mulattos' church until it was embellished with a distinguished baroque doorway and salamonic columns, to became one of the smartest churches in town, changing its allegiance to San Felipe Neri. Its facade of pink stone, *cantera rosa*, was of uneven quality, at times rose and at times dull brown, and was painted over with a pink wash to hide the imperfections. Five apostles flank the door. There is a fine *Virgin of Guadalupe* by Miguel Cabrera in the east transept. The 33 oils along the nave trace the life of the Florentine, San Felipe Neri, who founded the order. In the west transept is the sumptuously garish chapel, **Sta Casa de Loreto**, built by Manuel Tomás de la Canal for the then astronomical sum of 36,000 pesos. It is a copy of the Holy House in Loreto, Italy, the legendary home of the Virgin Mary, which was believed to have flown miraculously from Nazareth to Loreto, in a fit of pique over Moslem reoccupation of the Holy Land. The chapel is a chocolate-box extravaganza, with gilded rosettes, ornate twisted columns and heavy gold cloth on the walls. Needless to say, the Canals had penitent statues of themselves sculpted in niches on either side of the altar, below which are their tombs.

Around the corner is the modest little **Iglesia del Salud**, whose churrigueresque facade faces a market overspilling with gladioli, oozing wild honeycombs and piles of avocados. The doorway of the church is recessed and crowned with a shell. In a separate chapel inside, Mass is celebrated in English on Sundays at 11.30.

FESTIVALS

San Miguel seems to have more festivals than days of the year, celebrating its own variations as well as the main religious and national festivals. The animals are blessed on 17 January, Allende's birthday is celebrated on 21 January, and the whole of Easter Week builds up to the Good Friday processions through the streets. The anniversary of the independence movement, 16 September, is especially loud here, so close to Dolores Hidalgo where it all began. Each of the many churches has its own festival, while the whole town celebrates its namesake, San Miguel Arcángel, on 29 September.

EVENINGS OUT

Many of San Miguel's restaurants double up as bars or film houses (see under Eating Out). The language schools and *Atención* list live music, exhibitions, concerts and films.

LANGUAGE COURSES

There are three well-known language and art schools as well as countless language-exchange classes. The **Centro Cultural El Nigromante**, better known as Bellas Artes, is the most Mexican of the schools, and the closest to the Jardín, attached to the church of La Concepción. David Alfaro Siqueiros taught there in the 1940s and began a never-completed mural. The **Instituto Allende** (tel 20190), built by the Medici-like Canal family, is closely affiliated to US universities and the University of Guanajuato, and holds important exhibitions in its galleries. The **Academía Hispano Americana** (Mesones 4, tel 20349) is one step behind in such august company, relying on the short-sharp-shock approach to learning Spanish.

TOURS

At 11.30 on Sundays, an interesting 3-hour walking tour of some of the private houses and gardens of San Miguel leaves from the Biblioteca Publica (Calle Insurgentes). Tickets can be bought there, from the tourist office or from the Instituto Allende.

WHERE TO STAY

San Miguel has every sort of hotel. Bookings should made in advance for the period between Christmas and Easter, but at other times finding a room should present few problems. For longer stays, the tourist office, the various language schools, and Mama Mia's restaurant can provide lists of families who rent out rooms.

Expensive and Moderate

The ****Casa de Sierra Nevada (Hospicio 35, tel 20415, fax 22337) is an exclusive cosmopolitan hotel comprising four elegant colonial houses, which prides itself on Mexican style and European service (the staff are largely Swiss, apart from a Philippine acupuncturist). Its restaurant is superb. Above town, the ***Rancho El Atascadero (tel 20206) has pretty rooms with fireplaces and simple Mexican furniture, set around garden terraces and a swimming pool. The hotel runs a minibus in and out of town and can arrange horse riding.

Draped in bougainvillea, colonial ***Posada San Francisco (Jardín Principal, tel 20072) rests on the laurels of its excellent position in the heart of town, with a patio restaurant and comfortable rooms. The apartment-sized suites, ***El Patio, each have a jacuzzi, cable TV, domed windows and brick-faced *boveda catalina* (domed) ceilings. The bland ***Aristos, right behind the Instituto Allende (tel 20149), has large peaceful gardens and a swimming pool. Still in the southern end of town, the ***Villa Santa Monica (Baeza 22, tel 20427) dates back to the end of the 18th century. The Mexican film star, José Mojica, converted it in the 1930s, shortly before he became a monk and retired from public life.

Cheap

The **Central (Canal 19, tel 20851) is a lovely, small hotel, half a block from the Jardín, tucked away behind arches. Its excellent restaurant serves particularly good fresh fruit and papaya-juice breakfasts. The **Posada Carmina (half a block from the Jardín, in Cuna de Allende, tel 20458) is a simple, 10-room hotel and restaurant, with orange trees in the courtyard. **Posada de la Fuente (Calle Ancha, tel 21453) is quiet and inexpensive, in the San Antonio district of town. *Quinta Loreto (Calle Loreto 5, tel 20042) has long been established as the budget choice, for its rooms, its swimming pool and its restaurant, which is usually full of longer-term language students. Next door to Bellas Artes, the *Sautto (Dr Macías 55, tel 20251) is a pleasant little hotel set around a garden courtyard, offering weekly or monthly rates.

Outside Town

At the smart ****Hacienda Taboada (km 8 to Dolores Hidalgo, tel 20850), the swimming pools and jacuzzis are filled with crystalline water from a thermal spring. At weekends, the garden restaurant serves up lengthy brunches and swimming is included in the price (there is a hefty charge during the week). A couple of miles up the road, the modern colonial ***Posada del Cortijo Spa (tel 21700) also has its own thermal springs.

EATING OUT

A mass of restaurants caters for the many foreigners going out to eat in San Miguel.

Moderate

The perennially popular **Mama Mia** (Umarán 8, tel 22063) is decidedly international, offering thick, crusty pizzas, grilled fish and steaks. At weekends, it puts on live salsa, jazz or flamenco music, and films in French and English. During the 1986 World Cup, a Scotsman stood the whole packed bar to a drink and spent the rest of his holiday washing up in the kitchens to pay for it. **Pancho and Lefty's** (tel 21958) is another evening place which has better music than food. It keeps late hours: anyone still awake at 1.00 am ends up here. **El Jardín** (San Francisco 4, tel 21706) is a patio restaurant with an imaginative cook, whose spinach soup with a hint of garlic is worth going back for again and again. The dark cavernous Spanish **Rincón Español** (Correo 29, tel 22327) serves sangria, *paella de fideos* (a heaped plate of paella) and an enormous *plata mariachi* of steak. **El Patio** (Correo 10, tel 20017) has several bars, including the Toreador, full of bullfighting memorabilia, and a piano bar with orgiastic, diabolic panel doors.

Cheap

The **Chapala** is always full of locals working their way through its large four-course set-lunches. The **Dolce Vita**, in a patio off Canal, is a steamy café providing coffees, fruit juices and stuffed croissants as well as masses of magazines. For inexpensive shrimps and fish, the **Caribe** (Juárez 33) is a well-worn favourite. The **Colón** café (opposite San Francisco Church, tel 20989) is cheap and cheerful, serving omelettes, salads and sandwiches. Both the hotel restaurants in the **Central** and the **Quinta Loreto** offer good food at low prices. For freshly squeezed carrot juice in ½-litre glasses, walk a block down Umarán from the Jardín to an inauspicious, unnamed shop on the first corner.

North to Guanajuato

The hill road to Guanajuato takes a little over an hour: leave San Miguel on Calzada Aurora in the north of the town.

Eight km along the road, the warm springs at Taboada are wonderfully therapeutic. Large, cheap municipal baths are surrounded by gardens. More hot springs are further along the road at La Gruta. Both of these are only minutes from town: hourly buses leave from the Oratorio de San Felipe Neri.

Atotonilco

Eleven km further on, the dust-bowl village of Atotonilco emerges out of dry fields. It was built as a retreat in 1740 but has since become part of Mexican folklore. Ignacio Allende was married in the village church in 1802. In 1810 he returned with Miguel Hidalgo, who snatched the banner of the Virgin of Guadalupe from above the altar. She, the first Mexican Virgin, became the figurehead of the national movement. The interior is covered in folk paintings and the frescoed walls are hung with small naive oil paintings depicting the lives of various saints. Some of the altars in the six adjoining chapels are decorated with painted Venetian mirrors.

The State of Aguascalientes

This tiny state, formerly part of Zacatecas, was granted its independence in 1823 when, so the story goes, the charismatic president Santa Ana granted it freedom in exchange for a kiss from the mayor's wife. Her lips are now incorporated into the state shield. One of the smallest states in Mexico, less than 0.3 per cent of the total, it is named after the hot springs, *aguas calientes*, which are dotted around the capital. It was once on the Spanish silver route, but now that the silver is no longer mined, it concentrates on producing fighting bulls, wine, and the little green fruit known as *guayaba*. Famed above all for its great spring fair of San Marcos, it tends to be overlooked throughout the rest of the year.

Aguascalientes

For some obscure reason, people can't help liking Aguascalientes. It really is no more than a large, prosperous farming city, but its warm people, lack of formality and colonial heart make it a pleasant stop on the way to Zacatecas or Guanajuato. In particular, it is well worth seeing the collection of Posada's prints in the museum in the Jardín Encino.

GETTING AROUND
In the middle of the country, Aguascalientes is easily accessible. It is on the main US to Mexico City road, Highway 45—520 km from the capital and 1350 km from the border. Guadalajara is 232 km southwest on Highway 54, and San Luis Potosí 168 km east on Highway 70. There are daily Aeroméxico and Aerocalifornia **flights** to the capital and Tijuana from the small airport on the east side of the city. **Buses** stop in the Central Camionera, near the ring road to the southeast of the city, with regular services to Zacatecas, Durango, Guanajuato, Guadalajara and Mexico City.
In Town: The bus station is just off the ring road, where it crosses Quinta Avenida. Local taxis and buses run to the Plaza de la Patria. The railway station is also on the ring road, on the eastern side of the city (take the Madero bus). The cathedral, looking out over the double Plaza de la Patria, is the centre of the city. Hotels and restaurants in every price range are all around, and the best of Aguascalientes is within walking distance. Hertz has a **car hire** office in the Hotel Francia, at the far side of the square.

TOURIST INFORMATION
The office is next to the cathedral (Plaza de la Patria 145 Pte, tel 51155). It is well armed, but besieged during the San Marcos festival.

WHAT TO SEE
Plaza de la Patria
The broad double square is dominated by a great piercing Ionic column, which was built for Charles IV of Spain in 1807. Within three years, Mexico was fighting for its independence and the citizens hastily swopped the king's head for that of an eagle, the national symbol.

The **Palacio de Gobierno**, begun in 1665 under the aegis of Manuel Tolsá, has a graceful facade of deep red sandstone, set off by the soft pink of the balconies and arcaded courtyards within. The Chilean Oswaldo Barra Cuningham, a pupil of Diego Rivera, painted the murals in the early 1960s. Those on the ground floor show scenes from the state's history, from the pre-Hispanic conquest of the wandering Chichimecs to present-day industries, such as the production of guayabas, brandies and fighting bulls. On the right are the luminaries of Aguascalientes, from Guadalupe Posada to the one-armed sculptor, Jesús Contreras. The upper floor bursts out with all the fun and debauchery of the San Marcos Festival.

At right angles to the palace, the **cathedral**, begun in 1704, is being noisily destroyed by pigeons. The salamonic-baroque facade, squeezed between two three-tiered towers, has become a nesting ground for thousands of birds. The cathedral, however, houses a fine collection of religious art, including Cabrera's *Virgen de Guadalupe* and Juan Correa'a *Inmaculada Concepción*.

The Teatro Morelos

On the left-hand side of the cathedral, this theatre was built in 1884. In November 1914, leaders of the various revolutionary factions chose it as a venue for hammering out proposals for an armistice. Doubts about the opposition's intentions led the great revolutionary hero, Pancho Villa, to take up arms and the theatre got badly bruised in the process. It was renovated in 1964 for the calmer pursuits of concerts and plays.

The Casa de la Cultura and Museo Regional

This terra-cotta building (in Calle Carranza, behind the cathedral on the right-hand side) was, in turn, a convent, a seminary and a school, and now houses the city's cultural centre. Jesús Contreras' mighty bronzes of pre-Hispanic gods act as a backdrop to films, exhibits, and classes in every conceivable subject. The centre produces a monthly news sheet.

On the same street, the **Museo Regional de Cultura** (open 09.00–14.00 and 16.00–20.00, closed Mon) includes a reproduction of the infamous *Tienda de Raya* or farm shop. *Campesinos*, working on someone else's land for the privilege of living there, were forced to barter beans for soap, food and candles, in the one shop within walking distance. Inevitably, they notched up unpayable debts, thereby becoming economically dependent upon the landowner.

José Guadalupe Posada Museum

(Jardín Encino, six blocks south of the Plaza de la Patria on Colón; open 10.00–14.00 and 16.30–20.00.)

This typical white-washed colonial house, with fluted drains and long, grilled windows, houses a large collection of Posada's prints. Born in Aguascalientes in 1852, Posada had already made his mark as a political satirist and caricaturist by the age of 19, when he had his first lithographs published in the newspaper, *El Jicote*. His macabre engravings, infused with black humour, captured the misery of contemporary society, at a time when the middle classes had never had it so good while the working classes saw little improvement. His works are spare and incisive, stark and humorous. Rivera believed that he 'was so outstanding that one day even his name may be forgotten. He was so closely associated with the spirit of the Mexican people that he may end up just as an abstraction.' Indeed, Rivera put him in the forefront of his most famous mural, *Dream of a Sunday Afternoon in the Alameda* (in Mexico City), arm in arm with his own well-known creation, the skeletal figure (*calavera*) of a fashionable lady.

Next door to the museum is the **Templo del Encino**, a church favoured by bullfighters. The windows are framed with buttercup-yellow tiles, and the dome is tiled in blue and white. Inside, a black Christ, found within an oak (*encino*) tree, is venerated before every fight.

Museo de Aguascalientes
(Calle Zaragoza 505, four blocks east of the plaza on Madero and four north on Zaragoza; open 10.00–14.00 and 16.30–20.00; closed Mon.)
Francisco Zuñiga's pre-emptive Henry Moore-like sculpture, *Sitting Woman* (1913), marks the front entrance. The graceful neoclassical building was designed in 1904 by the self-taught architect, José Refugio Reyes, whose other works include the far less restrained, neo-Byzantine Templo de San Antonio opposite, and the Hotel Francia.

The museum concentrates on contemporary art, devoting four rooms to native-born **Saturnino Herran**. Born in 1887, he moved to Mexico City at the age of 16, on the death of his inventor father, and went to study in Bellas Artes, alongside Diego Rivera. Unlike so many of his peer group, he never left the country, and was one of the first to be inspired by Mexico rather than Europe. Although his work never reached the polemical proportions of the great muralists, he is still one of the most revered painters of his generation. He died tragically young at the age of 31.

FESTIVAL OF SAN MARCOS
Cock fights, bullfights, gambling and dancing all feature prominently during this great festival, one of the best known and oldest in Mexico. It officially begins on 25 April, continuing into early May, but the excitement builds up throughout the whole of April. Gambling is illegal in Mexico. Each year, the Casino de la Feria asks for a gambling permit for cock fighting in its massive *palenque*—too late for the inevitable refusal to arrive in time.

HOT SPRINGS
The springs after which Aguascalientes was named are all around the state. Most have been turned into municipal baths with naturally heated pools. Some of the largest are at Jesús María, 14 km north of the city. Second-class buses leave every hour for Jesús María (30 mins) via Valladolid or Emiliano Zapata. Check with the tourist office, as the baths close for cleaning and holidays.

WHERE TO STAY AND EAT   (area code 491)
The hacienda-style *****La Troje (tel 61620), north of town on Highway 45, is the smartest hotel in the state, with a large garden, swimming pool and steak restaurant. In town, hotels of every description cluster around the Plaza de la Patria. The modern, well-run ***Río Grande (José Ma Chavez 101, tel 61666, tlx 125638) and the older Porfirian ****Francia (corner of Madero, tel 56080) both look onto the plaza. The Río Grande has a very good restaurant. On the other two corners, facing each other

diagonally across the square, are the ***Imperial** (5 de Mayo 106, tel 51650) and the ****Señorial** (Juan de Montoro and Colón, tel 51630)—both several notches down the ladder but central and cheap.

Outside the hotel dining-rooms, there are few smart restaurants in the centre, but plenty of bars and cafés, such as the **Mitla** (Av Madero 220) with its popular five-course lunches. Cheap. The Jardín San Marcos (where the fair is held each year) has several restaurants around it, including the *torero* **La Tasca** (Calle J Pani), whose walls are hung with the tools of the bullfighting trade. Moderate. Next door, **Kiko's** is keener on drinking than eating, but each drink comes with a tableful of *botanas* such as guacamole, nopal salad and *cueritos* (pickled pig skin, deceptively like onion rings). Cheap.

North of Aguascalientes

Highway 45 leads north to Zacatecas (135 km)—an easy drive, taking only a couple of hours. San Francisco de las Romos, 22 km north of Aguascalientes, is known by every truck driver as San Pancho de las Carnitas, because of the amount of pork sold in the town. Ten km beyond, a turning to the right leads off to the village of **Pabellón de Hidalgo**, built around the ex-hacienda of San Blas, 8 km from the highway. Here the rebel troops, led by Miguel Hidalgo, stayed overnight in 1811. Its Museo de la Insurgencia is filled with blunderbusses and important-looking documents. There is also an important craft school and shop, specializing in regional weaves and yarns.

Highway 45 continues north for 9 km to Rincón de Romos (41 km from Aguascalientes), where a desolate side-road leads east to the abandoned mines and villages of Tepezalá and **Asientos**. Just short of Asientos, a monastery has been renovated and turned into a holiday home for children. In the village, the Santuario de Guadalupe is still inhabited by four silent nuns. In the cemetery behind the convent, there is a large pit filled with skeletons, backed by morbid murals relating tales of a doomed eternity. This ghoulish collection is the pride and joy of the local boys, who love to slip in unseen by the nuns and shock visitors with their fearlessness.

The State of Zacatecas

Unlike the city of Zacatecas, which seems softened by the wind, the state is buffeted by it, making its vast, lonely stretches feel desolate and unwelcoming. Apart from the charming capital, the site of Chicomóstoc and the enchanting town of Jeréz, the state has little worth lingering over. A major crossroads, the capital is closely linked to San Luis Potosí and Aguascalientes. The route west, to Durango and the Sinaloa coast, passes the ex-mining town of **Sombrerete** with its lavish Franciscan church and monastery.

Zacatecas

The university city of Zacatecas has a distinctly medieval air. Cobbled alleyways wind around narrow streets, crawling past baroque churches and opulent mansions, up hills rich with silver, iron, copper and zinc. It makes an excellent stop for a couple of days, with a peaceful atmosphere and one of the greatest collections of colonial art in the country. Strangely, it receives few visitors, which means that it is all the more pleasant for those who do make it. Until a few years ago, no one knew what they were missing, and few bothered to find out. Recently, a preservation order was stamped on the city, and Gregory Peck and Jane Fonda came to film *The Old Gringo* in the boutique-free centre. Slowly more people are following to see it for themselves and the city has dusted down the red carpet, converted the old bullring into one of the most exquisite hotels in Mexico and opened galleries showing the extraordinary artistic wealth of Zacatecas in the 20th as much as the 17th century.

Silver, the foundation of Zacatecas, is no longer mined. The last mine is now a disco, deep in the bowels of the earth. At a healthy 2500 m, the city is the second highest in Mexico, which has encouraged an alarming propensity for medical establishments: doctors, surgeries, dentists and chemists abound, making it seem as if the whole town is loudly dying or filled with hypochondriacs.

Silver History
Zacatecas marks an ancient, invisible boundary, between the forbidding, unpopulated lands of northern Mexico and the southern civilizations of Mesoamerica. The precious metals worn as jewellery by nomadic tribesmen spurred prospectors on in the fulfilled hopes of finding silver. In 1546, Juan de Tolosa struck a vein in a gorge of the Cerro de la Bufa and founded the city on the spot. By the early 17th century, Zacatecas was the third-wealthiest city in the country and by the end of the 18th century over 2000 mine-shafts had been sunk. The mines were almost entirely worked by enforced labourers, who had to crawl along dank, dark shafts, hauling the ore up notched ladders wrapped in the very blankets that they slept in at night.

Zacatecas was not an easy option. Several days' journey from the capital, it was on the very edge of the pre-Hispanic civilizations and northern wastelands. Even in the 19th century, running shoot-outs were part of the job:

> The wagon in which [silver bars] were carried was drawn by six mules galloping at their utmost speed. Eight or ten men with muskets between their knees sat in the wagon facing outwards, and as many more galloped alongside armed to the teeth. Bands of robbers 300 or 400 strong have been known to attack.

GETTING AROUND
Zacatecas is 600 km from Mexico City–7 hours by car, 8 hours by bus and 12 by train.
By Car: Zacatecas is crossed by three major roads: Highway 54 from Saltillo (370 km) in the northeast to Guadalajara (320 km) in the southwest; Highway 49 from San Luis Potosí (186 km) in the east to Torreón (386 km) in the northwest; and Highway 45, the main road from the capital (600 km), which continues to Durango (290 km).
By Public Transport: The **airport** (tel 20643) is 25 km southwest of the city, with daily flights to and from the capital and Tijuana. The modern **bus station** (tel 20684 or 20225) is above town on the ring road, with hourly services to and from the capital, stopping in Aguascalientes (2 hrs), Léon (change for Guanajuato) and Querétaro. Buses

also connect the city with San Luis Potosí (2 hrs), Guadalajara (4 hrs), Chihuahua and the north. The **railway station** is just south of the main ring road, Blvd Mateos. The northbound train leaves Mexico City at 10.00, arriving at Zacatecas at 21.30. Southbound, it leaves Zacatecas at 18.00, arriving at the capital at 07.00 (tel 20294).

In Town: Zacatecas fits like a wedge between two hills, the Cerro del Bosque and the Cerro de la Bufa. The thin end of the wedge narrows in on the Plaza de Armas and the cathedral, fanning out to the Alameda and Jardín Independencia. The principal street, Av González Ortega, leads off the Blvd Mateos ring road, changing its name to Av Hidalgo as it hits the centre. Zacatecas is an eminently walkable town. The *'centro histórico'* around Av Hidalgo and the cathedral is small and compact, and nowhere is more than 10 minutes' walk, apart from the bus station (take a taxi or 'Ruta 7' minibus from Blvd Mateos).

TOURIST INFORMATION
The office is opposite the cathedral, at Av Hidalgo 606 (tel 28467 or 26683).

WHAT TO SEE
Within the heart of the city, almost every building is noteworthy. The tourist office is helpfully situated, right in front of the cathedral and the café Acropolis, where reviving coffees are served up in 12 different guises at a low-slung soda fountain.

Cathedral
Begun as a parish church in 1567, it was reconstructed in the 1750s and upgraded to a cathedral. The pinkish-brown stone changes colour according to the light, lending contours and depth to the myriad shapes and forms. In an echo of the Holy Trinity, there are not one but three facades, each split into three sections, divided by sets of three columns, reiterated inside by the three naves. The front facade, opening directly onto the street, is shaped like a shield with twisted columns and a great rose window. It is the most wildly exuberant of all. None of it is left unsculpted, as if a frenzied hand was working on a commission per centimetre. Christ crowns the facade, flanked by the 12 Apostles and surrounded by a profusion of cherubs, angels, grapes, shells and every conceivable symbol of the abundance of faith. In contrast, the interior is vast and unadorned, stripped of its finery in successive anticlerical purges which left only a bleached skeleton, with massive, thick, fluted Doric columns and a paltry makeshift altar lost in the immensity of it all. The right-side portal, depicting the Virgin with the Child in her arms, faces the market. The left-side portal, of the crucified Christ, is much the most sober. Flanked by caryatid columns in the shape of women holding up Corinthian capitals, it opens out onto the Plaza de Armas. The twin towers were built 100 years apart but are exactly identical, apart from a lightness of colour on the left.

Plaza de Armas
At right angles to the cathedral is the 18th-century **Palacio de la Mala Noche**. Its name comes from the night when mine-owner Manuel Rétegui, having made more than one fortune and lost it, was once again down to his last penny. This he gave away to a widow and her starving family. Unable to pay his workforce the next day, he sat in the dark, contemplating suicide, when his gaffer knocked triumphantly on his door: his men had

struck a vein, and his fortune was secured. This apocryphal story secured large amounts for the heaving coffers of the Church. Rétegui, nevertheless, built a false door in the Callejón de Veyna, so that he could get in and out unseen by the importuning riffraff. On the far side of the square is the sober 18th- century facade of the **Palacio de Gobierno**, once the home of Don Vicente de Saldívar Mendoza, now bureaucratic offices. Around the stairwell, the tradition of painting the state's history in murals has been kept up by Antonio Pintor Rodríguez.

The Other Churches

Much of the wealth of Zacatecas' mines found its way to the churches. Many, like the cathedral, have since been stripped of their altars, *retablos* and baptistries.

At the far north end of town, where Av Hidalgo becomes Calle Juan de Tolsá, just after the Fountain of the Conquistadors, the beautiful ex-convent of **San Francisco** has been turned into a mask museum. It was the first church to be built in Zacatecas in the 16th century and one of the richest. Today, behind its churrigueresque facade, lies only a roofless reminder of what it once was. The church and monastery surrounding it have been completely renovated to house the 6000 Mexican masks which Rafael Coronel, the painter and collector-brother of Pedro, collected and donated to his native city. It is one of the biggest collections open to the public in the country.

Follow Calle Codina back to **Santo Domingo** (one block west of the cathedral). This church, begun by Dominicans, was in fact finished by the Jesuits in 1749, when they were given an injection of cash by the wealthy Counts of San Mateo. Although poorly lit, the eight churrigueresque *retablos* along the side naves still shine out ostentatiously. **San Agustín** (Calle Hierro, the continuation of Codina; open 10–14.00 and 16.00–18.00) makes up the triumvirate of orders which evangelized the city. The narrow side portal, recently restored, has a charming child-like relief, framed by estípite columns in which St Augustine is accompanied by musicians and an inquisitive sun. Its treatment has been rough: it was first pulled down stone by stone in the 1860s, on Juárez' orders, and then turned into a casino. Today, structurally if not ecumenically repaired, it is a conference centre and exhibition hall.

The Pedro Coronel Museum

(The old Jesuit College, at right angles to Santo Domingo; open 10.00–14.00 and 16.00–19.00; closed Thurs; adm.)

The brothers Pedro and Rafael Coronel have been great patrons of their native city, donating their lifelong collections and works. Pedro Coronel, the artist and sculptor, died in 1985. His marvellous and eclectic collection ranges from pre-Hispanic pieces (particularly from Guerrero) to Goya's *tauromaquia* etchings and Piranesi's architectural drawings. In the 20th-century room, the modern masters, Giacometti, Chagall, Picasso and Miró, are contrasted with artefacts from the Far East.

Pedro Coronel's last commissioned work is in the Congress building, above the church of San Agustín. Constructed in the late 1980s, the Congress is an exact replica of the 18th-century treasury which was destroyed by a bomb during the 1914 battle of Zacatecas. His vast, glass Miróesque mosaic is suspended from the ceiling in the Chamber of Deputies.

Avenida Hidalgo

Av Hidalgo, the main street, was closed to traffic for days to film Jane Fonda, Gregory Peck and Jimmy Smits in *The Old Gringo*, Carlos Fuentes' powerful story of two North Americans caught up in the cataclysmic events of the 1910 Revolution. Although the film is purportedly set in Chihuahua, Zacatecas was chosen because of its excellently preserved centre, arrested at the turn of the century.

The contemporary passion for Art Nouveau and French architecture was combined in the Teatro Calderón. This sumptuous Porfirian legacy was built in 1891 with stained-glass windows and frescoed walls. The stylistically similar market opposite straddles an upper and lower street level. Remodelled (the present market is in the Jardín Independencia), it has opened its doors to restaurants, cafés and ritzy shops as well as a row of video games.

Museo Francisco Goytia

(Open 10.00–14.00 and 17.00–20.00; closed Mon; adm.)

The southern end of Av Hidalgo leads to the aqueduct and park where the ex-Governor's Palace has been turned into an art gallery. Six 20th-century Zacatecas artists have been given the limelight. For a city so small and so far from the main stream of artistic life, it is an impressive collection. Common ground is represented both by their native city and by the lengthy trips each took to Europe.

On the ground floor are works by **Julio Ruelas** (1870–1907), who belonged to the Mexican *fin de siècle* school and spent many years in France. **Pedro Coronel**'s bold colours and abstract work sear off the canvas in his vermilion and indigo *Birth of Fire*. **Manuel Felguerez**, born in the late 1920s, twists colour into shape, segmenting triangles, cubes and squares.

On the upper floor, there is a copy of **Francisco Goytia's** (1882–1960) most famous work, *Tata Jesucristo*. Goytia spent four years in Barcelona studying with Francisco Gali, but returned to fight with Pancho Villa in the Mexican Revolution. He spent the rest of his life in great poverty in the capital. **José Kuri Breña's** onyx, marble and bronze sculptures lead through to the paintings of **Rafael Coronel**, the brother of Pedro. His monumental *Bishops*, in purple and burnt sienna, is the only oil. His medium is acrylic, exuberantly applied from thick palettes of paint: distorted animal and human faces are caught out of focus, incorporating a record for a mouth, toothpaste tops for eyes and twigs as the lashes.

The Mine and the Cable Car

(Open 12.00–19.30 daily; disco Thurs–Sun from 22.00, with an entry price equal to the minimum daily wage for today's miner.)

The **Mina El Eden** is northeast of the city, near the modern hospital, a cheap taxi or bus ride from Jardín Independencia (marked 'Seguro Social' or 'IMSS'). Small mine trains take visitors down the shafts for tours of the mines by day and by night, finishing up at the incongruously situated El Eden Mine disco. The guide quotes hair-raising statistics of daily deaths on rickety ladders and dangling ropes. Opened in the 16th century, it was last worked 20 years ago but has been kept as it was, with flimsy wooden bridges over chasms of gloom and slimy, narrow tunnels that riddle the foundations of the city. There is a lift up and out to daylight.

Some 100 m to the right, by the Motel Bosque, is the *teleférico* or **cable car** (open 12.00–19.00, Tues–Sun, adm), which swings high across the city to the Cerro de la Bufa. It is closed in strong winds (which are frequent), but even on a calm day it is an exhilaratingly scary ride, over the cathedral and roof tops 800 m below. The Cerro de la Bufa has a **museum** (open 10.00–14.00 and 17.00–19.00) commemorating Pancho Villa's victory over Victoriano Huerta's federalist troops in 1913. This great and decisive battle, in which conservative Zacatecas backed the wrong horse, is so much a part of modern Mexican history that the labelling is non-existent: the contemporary newspapers, photographs, testimonials and clothes speak for themselves.

FESTIVAL
The last week of August and the first week of September are given over to the city's festival, with bullfights, dancing and, on 27 August, a loud, colourful pageant re-enacting the final fight between the Moors and the Christians.

WHERE TO STAY   (area code 492)
The *******Quinta Real** (Av González Ortega, tel 29189, tlx 684060, fax (36) 416263) is Zacatecas' most prestigious hotel and makes staying anywhere else a poor second. Hidden under the arches of the aqueduct, it incorporates the second-oldest bullring in the Americas into its design. Each room is exquisitely decorated with colonial opulence in the Mexican colours of terra cotta and peach. In the Plaza de Armas, the ******Paraiso Rattison** (Av Hidalgo 703, tel from Mexico City 533 1195) is an elegant alternative— entirely modern behind an 18th-century facade.

For more down-to-earth prices, the well-run *****Posada de la Moneda** (Av Hidalgo 413, tel 20881) has 36 comfortable old rooms in a colonial building, 2 minutes from the cathedral, next door to the Teatro Calderón. *****Posada de los Condes** (Av Juárez 18, tel 21093), topped with defensive white merlons, is just behind the lively Plaza de la Independencia: its restaurant is better than its rooms. The ****Condesa** (Av Juárez 5, tel 21160), opposite, looks sober and steady from the outside, but hides a depressingly dilapidated interior. The ***Río Grande** (Av González Ortega 302, tel 20479) is basic but decent.

EATING OUT
Again, the **Quinta Real** wins hands down. The restaurant is built into the tiers of the bullring and large bevelled glass windows look out onto it. Musicians play in a cove on the first level, their melodies rising upwards. It specializes in oysters Rockefeller and cuts of beef from the rich Zacatecas pasture lands. Expensive. On Blvd Mateos, the **Zacatecas Grill** has a short but carefully prepared menu with shrimps from Mazatlán and local beef. Start with *queso fundido con rajas* (melted cheese and strips of chillies rolled in hot tortillas). Moderately expensive.

In the centre, the Covent Garden-style renovation of the old covered market has spawned a handful of places to eat. On the ground floor, a cellar restaurant, **La Cuija** (tel 28275), takes great care in preparing traditional dishes such as *puerco en mole verde* (pork in green *mole* sauce). Many of the wines are from Fresnillo (none are unmissable but the Carrera label is the better one). Moderate. Up above, the cosmopolitan bar of the **Paraiso** is invariably packed. Its psychedelic cocktails are lethal, although the *chimichangas* (shredded beef and guacamole in flour tacos) limit the damage. Moderate. This market also has the definitive coffee bar, **El Acropolis**, with 12 different coffees and autumnal platefuls of filling food like *enchiladas huicholes* (stuffed with cheese). Cheap. For the most delicious breakfasts, climb up Calle de Chepiñque, above the Alameda, and join the queues for Doña Lupe's famous *gorditas* (fat tortillas split and stuffed with anything from beans and cheese to nopal cactus and chilli). Very cheap.

Guadalupe and the Museum of Viceregal Art

To the east of the city, Guadalupe was once separate but is now merely a continuation of Zacatecas, hemmed in as it is on every other side by hills. It is a pleasant place to spend a morning or afternoon, and its museum, with its concentration on the masters of colonial art, is rated by many as the outstanding example of its kind in the country.

GETTING AROUND

Take the 'Guadalupe' bus from Blvd Mateos, or drive down Blvd Mateos/Highway 45 for 6 km, turning left down Calle Begoña to the Plaza Principal.

WHAT TO SEE

The town square is dominated by the ex-Franciscan convent of N S de Guadalupe, founded in 1707 for the propagation of the faith by the intrepid friar Antonio Margil de Jesús. Now the **Museum of Viceregal Art** (open 10.00–14.00 and 17.00–20.00, closed Mon, adm), it houses an important collection of colonial paintings, sculptures and antiquarian books. Most of the paintings were designed expressly to decorate wealthy churches and convents, competing with the baroque splendours of the facades. The silver barons endowed the Franciscans with enough money to commission the best artists of the 17th and 18th centuries—Juan Correa, Cristóbal de Villalpando, José de Ibarra and Miguel Cabrera.

Two monumental oils of Cabrera's (1695–1768) line the stairway, which leads up to his series, *The Life of the Virgin*, on the second floor. These 14 works in oval frames rank amongst his greatest, most mature works, playing with light and shadow, daringly separating the woman from her iconic role. The second-floor **Capilla de la Enfermería**, close to the sanitorium for those too ill to make it to church, is dominated by Juan Correa's *N S de Zacatecas*. Patronized by the counts of San Mateo, the artist thoughtfully slipped their daughter into the bottom left-hand corner of the painting.

A handful of Franciscan monks still live on the ground floor, surrounded by the **Cloister of the Passion** where several anonymous paintings, stamped with *decimas* (10-line poems), unravel the Bible for new converts to Christianity. Patrons often acted as models, particularly the Conde de Laguna, José Calvo's benefactor, whose miserably twisted nose crops up two or three times. The adjoining **Capilla de Napoles**, covered in gold stucco with signs of the zodiac hidden in the mesquite-wood parquet floor, houses the diminutive *Virgin del Refugio*, donated by Isabella Farnese.

In a part of the old convent, to the right of the main entrance, an ex-orphanage is now a **Regional History Museum** (open 10.00–16.30, closed Mon), with a display of Huichol art and a collection of antique coupés, cars and railway carriages. Porfirio Díaz's fender rubs Francisco Madero's bumper, proof that these two political opponents shared one passion in common—they both drove Mercedes.

Southwest of Zacatecas

The Guadalajara road, Highway 54, speeds southwest away from Zacatecas. At Malpaso, Highway 70 leads off to Jeréz (57 km), whilst Highway 54 continues past the archaeological zone of Chicomóstoc (42 km), also known as La Quemada.

Chicomóstoc

(Open 09.00–17.00; closed Mon.)

The hill site of Chicomóstoc is unusual, little visited, little explored and little known. Most tourists are local or intrepid and few foreign names are etched into the dusty visitors' book. It is, however, well worth a trip from Zacatecas, and its lofty eyrie will probably be all your own.

It is difficult to get to the site. The tourist office in Zacatecas (tel 28467) runs occasional and irregular tours. Guadalajara-bound buses prefer to forget its existence and even second-class buses speed up past the entrance, taking visitors on to the next scheduled stop and making them walk the 3 km back in the heat of the midday sun. Taxis are cheap in Zacatecas and always open to negotiation, but hitching isn't recommended because of the lack of cover from the sun. The somnolent guards sell dusty and obscure archaeological books alongside crisps and soft drinks.

The ruins are etched into the side of a windswept hill, easy to miss until you are right on top of them, as the raw colour of the stones and bricks blends into the thin topsoil. Chicomóstoc is considered the northernmost point of pre-Hispanic Mesoamerica. It was never large, merely a well-fortified staging post. Primarily a defensive site, it controlled the Malpaso valley, hemmed in by the double wall of the Sierras Zacatecas and Fria. The steep-sided slopes of the hills were used as natural barriers but, in addition, a thick wall was built to brace the citadel, whose remains are still clearly outlined on the skyline. Pre-Hispanic history is riddled with myths, and one such claims that the Aztecs originated from here before moving south to Lake Texcoco. Architectural evidence suggests that it was a frontier post of the pre-Aztec Toltecs. They built their great capital, Tula, along the same lines, including layers of sun-dried bricks instead of monumental slabs of stone to make up the columns.

Jeréz

Jeréz, 26 km from the Malpaso junction and 57 km from Zacatecas, is a delightful, quiet, provincial town, where cowboys under great, wide sombreros still ride three abreast down the street. The main square, lined with wrought-iron benches, is filled with old-timers chewing the cud and young girls intriguing. Sunday comes seven days a week, the shops stock nothing but bridles, hats, whips and lassoes, and the clock stopped ticking 100 years ago. Second-class buses from the main Zacatecas terminal stop in the town on their way to Tepetongo in the Sierra Los Alamos.

In the 16th century, Jeréz was a front-line settlement between the conquered lands in the south and the unknown north. Soon Spanish silver interests clamoured for a permanent garrison to be set up to protect the *camino real* to the capital. Architecturally, it belongs to Andalusia, as did many of the original settlers. Elegant, low houses with wrought-iron balconies are still smartly white-washed and the cobbled streets are kept pristinely clean. The small museum is frozen in the time of the 19th-century poet,

Ramón López Velarde, who was born here and baptized in the baroque parish church. The gothic folly of a library in Calle Serdán was a flight of fancy for the otherwise sober architect, Damaso Muñeton, better known as the man who built the second tower of Zacatecas' cathedral. Two blocks from the library is the romantic little 1878 Hinojosa Theatre, an exact replica of Washington's Ford Theatre where Abraham Lincon was shot. In the main square, underneath the porticoes to the right of the Palacio Municipal, is an unmarked café serving famous huge, knickerbocker glories of fresh strawberries, crushed ice and ice cream.

Part X

THE NORTHWEST

Tarahumara children

To squeeze the six states of the northwest into a single chapter is an indignity, particularly when two of them, Chihuahua and Sonora, are the biggest in the country. Most of this land mass, however, is parched desert or high impassable mountain. The Sierra Madre forms a formidable barrier between Sonora in the west and Chihuahua in the east, falling straight between the states like a bolster in a four-poster bed. There are few roads, and they run mainly north–south, not east–west.

The big attraction is the Chihuahua–Pacífico railway which claws its way from Chihuahua, through mountain ranges, past Tarahumara villages, resinous pines and searing canyons to Sinaloa and the coast. The shores of the Gulf of California are almost entirely undeveloped: even the road runs well inland. The long rangy Baja California peninsula, to the west, is all desert and beach. Californians use it as their backyard with weekend barbecues on the beach, off-the-road motor-cycling championships and ceremonies initiating the young into the joys of being an adult (principally legal alcohol in vast quantities).

The State of Chihuahua

Chihuahua is vast. At 244,938 sq km, it is the largest state in Mexico and not much smaller than Spain. The rugged mountains of the Sierra Madre in the west cut off Chihuahua from the Pacific. No road has yet been able to forge a pass and the only way through is by rail, on a track that took 100 years to complete. The thrill of this journey

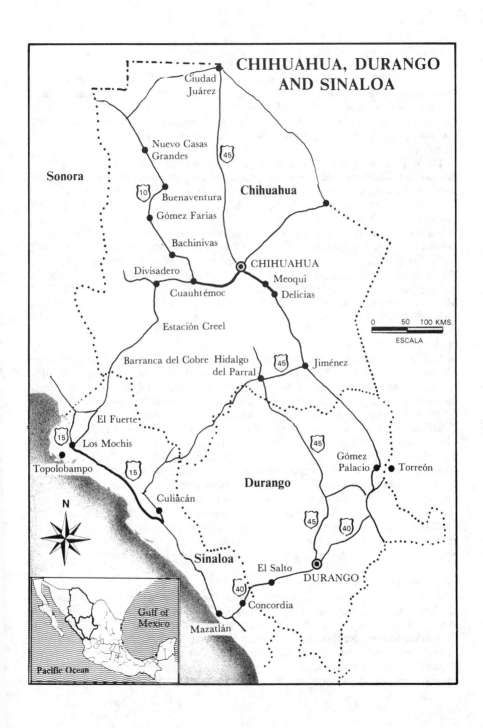

CHIHUAHUA, DURANGO
AND SINALOA

alone makes it worth visiting the state. It runs through canyons that dwarf Arizona's Grand Canyon, stopping off along the way in isolated mountain villages. North and east of the city of Chihuahua, excellent farming land is edged by a desert of parchment-white sand dunes. This stretches across to neighbouring Coahuila, through the Zone of Silence where a build-up of electricity in the rainy season cuts off all radio sound. Chihuahua's cloudlessly clear skies are magnificent, etched with shades of dying crimson and orange in the late afternoon, followed by ink-black nights lit by thousands of stars.

The resilient people of Chihuahua always have an eye to their northern neighbour. Able women wheel around in huge jeeps, displaying an independence unheard of further south. At the same time, anxious to keep up standards, they wear clammy nylon stockings in the stifling heat. The tall northern men, filled up on beef, milk and cheese, are avid supporters and players of basketball, a sport rarely seen in the south.

Within this enormous area there are huge haciendas. Before the Revolution, landholdings encompassed millions of acres and even today some ranches run to 60,000 acres. Yet Chihuahua still has the feel of virgin land, waiting for the hoe and plough. When the Spaniards arrived in the 16th century, they found various independent and isolated peoples: Tarahumara, Tepehuano, Comanche and Pima. Today, immigrant Mormons and Mennonites have risen to the challenge of turning desert into fertile land with incomparable success.

History

In 1527 a Spanish ship grounded off the coast of Florida, leaving only four survivors— Alvaro Núñez Cabeza de Vaca, Dorantes, Castillo and Estebanico, a black Arab. After seven years of wandering across the great plains and deserts they reached Chihuahua, the first Europeans to be seen there. Reports filtered through to the Spanish further south of the seven gold cities they had found. In 1539, Friar Marcos de Niza took Estebanico back to search for these fictitious cities. He described the glories of one, which he called Cíbola, so lyrically that hundreds went in search of it. The Tarahumara, the original inhabitants of Chihuahua, were chased into the sierra, hotly pursued by missionaries on the one hand and prospectors on the other. No cities were ever found. Núñez Cabeza de Vaca died in Seville in a monk's habit and Friar Marcos became renowned as the greatest liar in New Spain, but the missionaries and prospectors never stopped. The Franciscans evangelized the deserts and the Jesuits the mountains. Settlements grew up around the prospectors' camps and wise men gave up panning for gold in order to raise beef cattle. As the Spaniards moved in, so too did the Apaches, driven down from the north by European settlers in Texas and Arizona.

THE REVOLUTIONARY YEARS

The Apache wars raged for 250 years, but all the time mines were being exploited, ranches built and fortunes made. The great wealth of the state didn't extend much beyond the hands of a few—one landowner had an estate the size of Belgium. Chihuahua was ripe for revolution and when Francisco Madero announced in 1910 that he had 'designated Sunday, the 20th day of next November, for all the towns in the Republic to rise in arms', Chihuahua was ready. Town after town fell to straggling groups, composed of peasants, mechanics, beggars, miners, servants, students, idealists

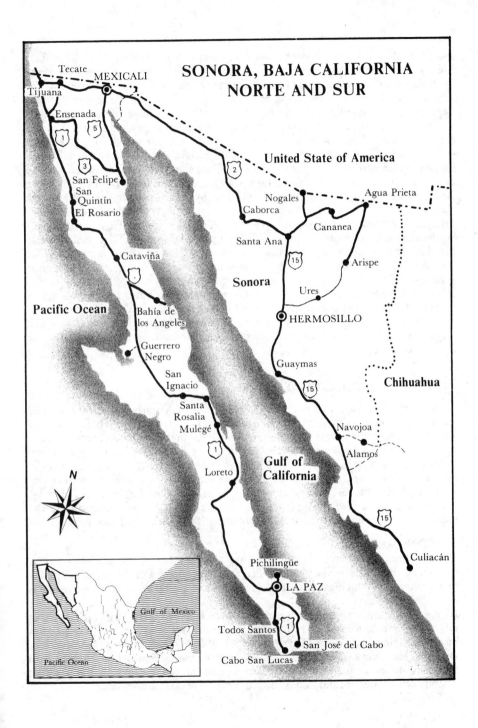

SONORA, BAJA CALIFORNIA
NORTE AND SUR

and all the dissatisfied in the state. For a few, it was a chance to wrest Chihuahua from Mexico City's control. For most, it was a fight against the landowners, but for everyone, the president, Porfirio Díaz, was the embodiment of all the ills of despotism.

These rebel armies, without uniforms or proper weapons, were marshalled into fighting forces first under the leadership of Pascual Orozco, a mule skinner, and then by the outlawed Robin Hood, Pancho Villa. Within five months, they had taken the border city of Ciudad Juárez in a decisive battle. Both Díaz and his vice president resigned within a month. But Madero couldn't control the revolution he had unleashed. Orozco became titular head of a further rebellion in Chihuahua, asking not just for political democracy but for agrarian reform, higher wages, restrictions on child labour and a 10-hour working day. Madero was assassinated by political opponents and his loyal supporter, Villa, clamoured for more say in the increasingly middle-class revolution. When little seemed to change, Villa's tactics became more brutal. He crossed the US border and burnt and looted the town of Columbus, New Mexico. US General Pershing marched 6000 troops through the deserts of northern Chihuahua in search of Villa but spent $130 million in vain. The Mexican government was now embarrassed by the great general-bandit and as soon as it was decent they gave him a large hacienda, on the condition that he laid down his arms. For several years he did, but in 1923 he was shot in Hidalgo del Parral, two months after he had hinted at coming out of retirement.

The modern state has lost its revolutionary fervour and its great landowners are much diminished, but it continues to jibe at Mexico City politicians, preferring to vote for the right-of-centre opposition party, PAN.

Northern Chihuahua

Coming over the border from El Paso to Ciudad Juárez isn't nearly as much of a shock as leaving the confines of the big cities altogether and heading into the Mexican country-side. The north of the state is defiantly cowboy country: in the few towns, boots, belts and saddles are on sale everywhere, even at the vets. In the midst of all this agricultural industry, the ruins of Paquimé, some 360 km ($4\frac{1}{2}$ hrs) into Mexico, are a testament to an earlier age. Blending the Pueblo cultures of the southern US and the glorious civilizations of Mexico, they are the first example of the haunting sites further south. Close by, the Mormons have set up a replica Little America, but the language, landscape and music are definite reminders that this is no longer Tex–Mex but Mexico for real.

GETTING AROUND

Get away from the border towns of El Paso and Ciudad Juárez as fast as possible, unless you want a cheap dentist. To enter Mexico, you need a tourist card (available from the immigration office, on most buses and all planes) and a valid passport. The crossing is open 24 hours a day.

By Air: There are large airports in both El Paso and Ciudad Juárez, with flights to most US cities from the former, and daily flights from the latter to all major Mexican cities including Chihuahua, Mexico City, Monterrey, Mérida, Guadalajara and Acapulco.

By Bus: Trailways and Greyhound buses cross the border hourly from their El Paso terminals to Ciudad Juárez's long-distance bus station (the Central de Autobuses) at Triunfo de la República and López Mateos. From here there are departures to all major towns in Mexico, including Chihuahua (hourly, 5 hrs), Nuevo Casas Grandes (the stop for Paquimé) (4 hrs) and Mexico City (26 hrs).

By Car: As a direct, nonstop route to central and southern Mexico, the Ciudad Juárez–Mexico City route (1866 km) has little to recommend it, as it takes far longer than the northeast roads and doesn't have the beaches of the western route. However, if your destination is the city of Chihuahua and the railway, take flat, straight Highway 45 from Ciudad Juárez, through 160 km of desert and then another 180-odd km of fertile farming lands. The drive takes 4½ hours.

By Train: The train between Ciudad Juárez and Mexico City takes 36 hours (the bus takes 26 hours), leaving Ciudad Juárez at 17.00 and Mexico City at 19.50, and passing through Chihuahua, Zacatecas, Aguascalientes and Querétaro. The station is a 15-minutes walk from the border, where Corona crosses Insurgentes.

Nuevo Casas Grandes

This town is the major agricultural centre for the northwest of the state, but for tourists it is no more than the transport and hotel base for the trickle of visitors to Paquimé.

GETTING AROUND
Nuevo Casas Grandes is 352 km (4 hrs) southwest of Ciudad Juárez along Highway 2, and the same distance from Chihuahua along Highways 45 and 10. Two bus companies, Omnibus de México and Chihuahuenses, have terminals close together on Obregón in the compact centre. Eight buses a day go to and from Ciudad Juárez's Central de Autobuses, and eight to and from Chihuahua's Camionera Central.

A local train runs between Ciudad Juárez and Nuevo Casas Grandes, but it takes twice as long as the bus and is more laden with animals and logs than with people.

The ruins of **Paquimé** are 6 km west of Nuevo Casas Grandes, near the old village of Casas Grandes. The road crosses rich farming land, grazed by herds of Aberdeen Angus and Hereford cattle, interspersed with crops of alfalfa (strictly for animals), peaches, apples, nuts and chillies. Buses leave east of the main street, 5 de Mayo, on Constitución and go to the main square of the old village. From here it is a 15-minute walk to the ruins (signed). The buses continue to Colonia Juárez, passing the entrance to the ruins, and may unofficially let passengers down at the gate.

WHAT TO SEE

The Ruins of Paquimé
(Open 09.00–17.00; closed Mon.)
By far the most important and exotic site in northern Mexico, Paquimé belongs to the American Pueblo–Oasis culture, which spread all over Arizona, New Mexico, Utah and Colorado. It reached its peak in AD 1000 with the advent of trade with the Mesoamerican Toltecs from the south. The Toltecs brought ornate plumes and headdresses, reflected in the plumed-serpent motifs that adorned the buildings, but more importantly they brought new ideas. Paquimé's highly mystical pantheon was expanded to incorporate new gods, and the Toltec rituals of the ball game and human sacrifice were adopted.

Paquimé's glory was short-lived. In 1340, the Apaches swooped down from the north, sending the placid farming people fleeing to the hills, and leaving the site to be covered over with the rich, red dust of centuries.

On the edge of the sierra, in a semi-desert valley of cactus and mezquite, Paquimé is open to the most extreme of weathers, with long, hot summers and frigid winters. Like pliant putty, the shapes and form of the baked-earth buildings have been softened and pummelled by the elements. The labyrinth of interlocking, rectangular and L-shaped rooms is set around patios housing ancestors buried in the corners and beds raised up by steps. Excavations have unearthed clusters of ant-hill houses, some several storeys high with curious T-shaped windows and doors. The river, less than a km away, was harnessed for a network of canals and drainage and an elaborate winter-heating system.

Less than 1 km further west, on the left-hand side of the road, is a hastily erected 'STOP AND SEE GOOD POTTERY' sign. Manuel Olivas (tel (169 43975) and his family work, design and sell enchanting ceramics, copied from the mystical emblems and symbols of Paquimé. The work is crude and irregular yet far more pleasing than the polished, highly finished pottery sold elsewhere.

Colonia Juárez

This Mormon community is a 10-minute bus journey west of Paquimé. Although tiny in numbers, the Mormons have made themselves an enclosed microcosm of the United States, complete with high school, cheer leaders, American football, lollipop-sucking blonde girls in pigtails and roses creeping up the white clapper-board houses. Twenty Mormon families, inspired by Joseph Smith (1805–44), came to Mexico in 1884, to this barren god-forsaken piece of semi-desert which they have transformed, like the Menonnites, into prime agricultural land. As their numbers regularly increase, they are looking for more and more land, but the government is now disinclined to sell to this closed community.

Hacienda de San Diego

A rough but much travelled road leads southwest to this dilapidated but still fine hacienda which Chihuahua businessmen may turn into an hotel. It originally belonged to the biggest landowner in the north, Luis Terrazas who, when asked 'Do you belong to Chihuahua?', replied 'No, Chihuahua belongs to me.' He owned over 17 million acres, 500,000 head of cattle, 225,000 sheep, 25,000 horses, textile mills, mines, railways and meat-packing plants. His 12 carefully married children made dynastic alliances worthy of empire builders. This meagre hacienda alone would have employed 1000 *peones*, members of the landless peasant class who formed the backbone of Pancho Villa's División del Norte army. It still draws the community together for its northern rodeos, known as *jaripes*, which take place most Saturdays. Couples ride with the woman in front and the man behind, guiding the horse and protecting the woman with his arms.

Mata Ortiz

Four km (10 mins) further on down an increasingly bumpy track, Mata Ortíz was once a wealthy mining town and still boasts a railway from Nuevo Casas Grandes. It is now known for its Paquimé-inspired pottery, vaunted by a few North American dealers. It has become a sad, decrepit village where artisans, like the young Jaime Dominguez, still work from home.

WHERE TO STAY AND EAT (area code 168)
Neither cheap nor exciting, the most recommendable hotels in Nuevo Casas Grandes are on Av Juárez. The ****Motel Hacienda (at 2603, tel 41046) is fully Americanized with comfortably large rooms, cable TV, drive-up parking, steak house and swimming pool. Others include the *Paquimé (at 401, tel 41320), the **Piñon (at 605, tel 40655), and the **California (Constitución 209, tel 41110).

Restaurant Malmery, where Av Juárez crosses Calle 8, has a Belgian owner and echoes of European food. Moderate. El Canton, where Juárez crosses Juan Mata Ortiz, offers Chinese and Las Vigas (16 de Septiembre and Hidalgo) more typical food. Both cheap.

Chihuahua

With its wide boulevards, stately colonial centre and fantastical gothic suburbs (built by wealthy ranchers), the city of Chihuahua comes as a great relief after the tedious, monotonous miles of arid scrub and cactus desert to the north and south. It is not very exciting but definitely pleasant and a convenient stop at the beginning or end of the Chihuahua–Pacífico railway. There are none of the famous dogs in sight. Apparently the governor has the only six in the state and they never leave his house.

The city was founded in 1709 on the strength of its rivers and mines but today makes its money from lumber and beef. Yet for such a calm city, it has had a bloody past. In 1811, the father of the Mexican independence movement, Miguel Hidalgo, was shot here and his head severed, to be displayed in the city of Guanajuato. One hundred years later, Chihuahua was the centre of Pancho Villa's revolutionary army, the División del Norte, which became the most effective in the country, decisive in overthrowing the corrupt president, Porfirio Díaz.

GETTING AROUND
By Air: Flights link Chihuahua to the major northern cities, Mexico City (3 hrs) and the US. The two airline companies, Aeroméxico and Noroeste, have offices at the airport, although tickets can be bought and booked in any hotel travel agency. The airport is a 20-minute taxi ride (tel 154559) east of town.
By Bus: The bus station, Camionera Central, is west of centre, within walking distance along Av Niños Héroes. Long-distance buses connect Chihuahua with all parts of Mexico: Ciudad Cuauhtémoc (hourly, 1½ hrs), the US border (hourly, 5 hrs), Zacatecas (6 a day, 10 hrs), Mexico City (8 a day, 21 hrs). Local buses connect Chihuahua with the villages of Santa Isabel and Aquíles Serdán every hour between 07.00 and 19.00 and then every 2 hours until 23.00.
By Car: Chihuahua is on the El Paso–Mexico City road, Highway 45, 710 km (5 hrs) from the border and 1479 km from Mexico City—a solid two days' drive (similar to

London–Istanbul). For **car rental**, try Hertz (Av Revolución 514, tel 166473), Budget (Av Independencia 1205, tel 160909) or Avis (Av Universidad 1703, tel 141999). Tourists can **park** for free wherever there is a large E on a blue sign (usually outside museums and hotels).

By Train: Chihuahua is the start of the fabulous Chihuahua–Pacífico railway which runs down to the coast at Los Mochis in the neighbouring state of Sinaloa. The station is near the city prison, 2 km south of the Zócalo (for details see Western Chihuahua).

The station for 'El Fronterizo', the train that runs between the border at Ciudad Juárez and Mexico City, is in the south of the city, reached by buses to Colón or Ferrocarriles. There is one daily train in each direction. The journey from Ciudad Juárez to Mexico City takes 37 hours. The southbound train leaves Ciudad Juárez at 18.00 and Chihuahua at 23.53, arriving in Mexico City a day and a half later at 06.55. The northbound train leaves Mexico City at 19.50.

TOURIST INFORMATION

The SECTUR office is at the northern entrance to the city, at Tecnológico 7901 (tel 178972), and has endless supplies of leaflets. The central office is in the Edificio Agustín Melgar (Calle 13, 1300, tel 159879). From the cathedral, walk along Libertad to the post office, *correo*, and turn into Calle 13. The staff are justifiably enamoured of their state and do everything they can to convince doubting Thomases.

WHAT TO SEE

All work and no play hasn't encouraged creativity and Chihuahua doesn't go in for art galleries. Instead, it celebrates its role in the Revolution, making a museum out of Pancho Villa's house. The centre is formal and businesslike, with little room for frivolity in the buildings or squares. For a night off, the Chihuahuenses go to one of the neighbouring villages where they eat fruit ices and dance to the frenetic music of accordions.

Plaza de Armas

In the centre of the city, the Plaza de Armas is flanked by a stalwart baroque **cathedral**. Built of weather-worn volcanic stone, the facade is bolstered by two substantial bell towers. The name of the stonemason responsible, Naba, is clearly etched on the top right-hand corner of the facade. Inside, the Doric interior drips with signs of Chihuahua's wealth and respectability. The eclectic collection includes chandeliers from Capri, marble scenes of Christ's journey to the Cross from Carrara and a German organ capable of filling the cathedral with the sounds of a full symphony orchestra. The greatest splendour is indigenous, an 18th-century cupola lined in 23-carat gold from local mines. The rose in the middle is a lump of pure gold. A small chapel to the left of the main doors displays a Christ dripping with black blood—the first crucifix to be brought into the state by Spanish troops, anxious to impress the serious nature of Catholicism on the susceptible natives.

In the crypt is the **Museo de Arte Sagrado** (Museum of Religous Art) (open 09.00–15.00, Mon–Fri). An underground gallery is filled with the works of 18th-century religious painters, such as Miguel Cabrera, José de la Paez and Antonio de Torres. It's a

300

surfeit of baroque: even Cabrera, who usually shocks and surprises with his realism, seems muted and conservative.

In the middle of the square, beside a French-inspired bandstand, stands a statue of Antonio Deza Ulloa, founder of Chihuahua. His finger points dramatically to the ground, signalling that 'here' is the place to build the city. Opposite the cathedral are the Presidencia Municipal and government offices whose heavy Porfirian exteriors proclaim a firm stamp of power.

Palacio de Gobierno

From the cathedral, walk a block east to Independencia; turn right and then left into Victoria. The government palace was built in 1890, though its neoclassical facade looks older. The murals of Aaron Mora cover the whole of the ground-floor courtyard, giving a pictorial history of the state. The Arab, Estebanico, searches for the seven cities of gold, and the Spanish conquer the state after harsh fighting with the Tarahumara, Apache and Comanche. A beatific Hidalgo suffers in his cell, before having his head cut off (by a Tarahumara slave, as no-one else would do it). This head was preserved in a saline solution and taken on the three-day journey south to Guanajuato, where it was hung from the Alhóndiga. The murals curve round the actual cell where he was executed, bedecked with flags. Then the chains of servitude break to reveal the great revolutionary hero Pancho Villa, who saves the state before finally being assassinated in Hidalgo del Parral. By Villa's side stands a naked Pascual Orozco, who gave his all to the Revolution.

Paseo Bolivar

Seven blocks south of the cathedral, this is one of the oldest streets in town, lined with absurd gothic mansions. At 401, the **Museo Quinta Gameros** (open 10.00–15.00, Mon–Fri) is a complete replica of a Parisian house, built by the Francophile owner of a goldmine, just before the Revolution. He didn't have long to live in it, as it was quickly appropriated and used as a military barracks. Recently restored, it is filled with Louis Quinze and fin-de-siècle furniture, more French than France. Whole rooms are carved in undulating arches of Art Nouveau. Nowhere has been spared decorative touches of 24-carat gold. A child's room is a shrine to Little Red Riding Hood: she appears on the ceiling, cupboards and bed. The bathroom next door is an extravaganza of Pueblan tiles and the latest in bathroom accessories, such as a wonderful circular shower of the sort usually found only in municipal baths.

Museo Historico de la Revolución

(Three blocks south of Paseo Bolivar and one block west, in Calle Décima (or 10) 3814, tel 162958; open 09.00–14.00 and 16.00–19.00; closed Mon.)

The museum cataloguing Chihuahua's part in the Revolution is appropriately in Pancho Villa's house, which later became his military headquarters. Pancho Villa lived here with Luz Corral, his second wife (of three, or 22, depending on which reports you read) and their one son. The two sons by his first wife still live in Mexico City. Though consistently unfaithful to Luz Corral, he kept returning to the woman who taught him how to write. (One of his demands during the Revolution was that education should be freely available to all.) The front of the museum is in his house proper, including a well-equipped and much-loved music room. In the bedroom, a holster is slung over the big brass bed. The

301

car in which he was shot is parked in the courtyard, bullet holes still scarring the side but in perfect working order. Behind here were the quarters of his 50 bodyguards (known as Dorados, a name the local baseball team have taken on). This was blown up during the Revolution and the museum itself is housed in a recently restored wing. It is filled with memorabilia: Colt and Winchester rifles, well-worn saddles, even pictures of the dead Pancho Villa. John Reed, a North American who travelled with Villa whilst writing *Insurgent Mexico*, took a lot of photographs of Villa and his men, cataloguing the pride and despair of those who fought. These line the walls: Pancho Villa bears a marked resemblance to Orson Welles.

Aquíles Serdán (formerly Sta Eulalia)

Spanish miners from Mérida founded the original Chiuhuahua in this hill village, 18 km (20 mins) southeast of the present capital, off Highway 45. The silver and zinc mine is still worked but people come simply because it is a very pretty village, straggling uphill along narrow, cobbled streets with overhanging balconies and drainpipes popping like cannons out of the walls. On Fridays and Sundays a band plays *ranchera* music in the square from 19.00 to 21.00. The bands, made up of trumpets, saxophones, guitars and drums, have a clear beat and a decided rhythm. The dancers follow with a double-quick polka that is all hips and shoulders, cheeks pressed to cheeks, whirling and spinning around the bandstand like Beryl Cook figures come to life. There is a an all-out fiesta on 16 September but every weekend is fun.

An excellent regional restaurant, **El Mesón de Chihuahua el Viejo**, 50 m up the hill from the square, serves roast kid in chilli sauce and the small, northern *tamales* filled with pork and *chiles anchos*, flavoured with cumin seeds. Moderate.

On a damp day, the sweet smell of the herb *gobernadora* scents the hills around the village. The Japanese use it in their cooking and produce it in vast quantities, but the Chihuahuenses prefer it as tea.

Santa Isabel

Santa Isabel (often referred to as General Trías) is 49 km southeast of Chihuahua. The heart of the colonial, cobblestoned village is hidden in orange groves. Here cars are double-parked outside **Germania's** (on the corner of Centenario and Libertad), renowned purveyors of frozen fruit and milk ices. One is never enough and family feuds have developed over the respective merits of avocado, guayaba and nectarine. The walnuts are hand-picked by the family themselves. On Sunday evening the band plays in the square as people suck their melting ices, which drip in time to the frantic northern tempo.

MUSIC AND FESTIVALS

Calle Aldama, one block south of the Plaza de Armas, is the mariachi-band centre of the city. On Thursdays, the state band plays in the main square from 19.00. Close by, in Calle 13, is **Aristos**, a hill-billy country disco where anyone is lost without cowboy boots, a cowboy partner and a wide stetson.

The main festival celebrates Santa Rita at the end of May. There is also a big agricultural fair in the second week of October, when all hotels book up fast.

WHERE TO STAY

The *****San Francisco (Calle Victoria 409, tel 167770, tlx 349631) is an excellent modern hotel which treats its guests with care and calm and has the advantage of being right in the centre. The *****Castel Sicomoro, a long taxi-ride away (Blvd Periférico Ortiz Mena 411, tel 135445, tlx 349605, fax 131411) is proud of its conference facilities, banqueting hall and swimming pool in the shape of the state, and is hard to fault as a luxurious business choice. The ****Victoria is a better choice for travellers. Closer to the centre and in amongst the restaurants, it is popular with groups travelling on the railway. The gardens are large and spacious (tended by the same gardener for 20 years) and the pool long and tempting with a high diving board. The lobby is very grand but the rooms have different, rather dubious styles, so check several for taste and noise (the best are facing onto the garden, on the side furthest from the road). The hotel travel agency specializes in visits to the Mennonites and the sierra and can make reservations at all the hotels along the railway.

The modern ***del Cobre (Calle 10a and Progreso, tel 151660) and *** Dorado (Calle 14a and Julian Carrillo, tel 125770) are good for late arrivals as they are close to the bus station, but have little else to recommend them. The run-down **San Juan (Calle Victoria 823, tel 128491) was built in 1940 by a wealthy miner for his beautiful wife, who died before it was finished. Lots of 1940s details remain—in the chimney place of the café, the manager's office and the Andalusian tiled patio and fountain studded with Art Deco frogs. Mennonites use it when they come into town on Saturdays, approving of the spartan, clean rooms. The *Reforma (also in Calle Victoria 809, tel 125808) is less characterful. A large covered turn-of-the-century patio serves as reception, ruined by an eyesore of a staircase plonked in the middle. The bedrooms are enormous, quiet and sparsely furnished, with creaking wooden floors. Still in the same street, the (CE) Casa de Huéspedes Aida is cheaper still and deserves its good reputation.

EATING OUT

Chihuahua prides itself on the best beef, milk and cheese in the country. A local speciality is *chile con queso* (strips of green chilli covered in dripping cheese). The so-called Zona Dorada (in Av Juárez between Colón and Pacheco) has the better restaurants including the Cantonese Los Vitrales, set in a miner's mansion (opposite the Hotel Victoria), and La Calesa (Av Juárez and Colón, tel 128555) which serves superb cuts of meat. Both expensive.

Enter El Galeón (Av Juárez 3312–B, tel 152050) and walk onto a ship in full sail. The waiters are in sailor's uniform (complete with leery eye) and the downstairs bar has the port-holes and curved beamed walls of the bows. Try the grilled red mullet or the sea bass which comes on a bed of smoked salmon. Moderately expensive. Also in the Zona Dorada but considerably lower-key, the Café Ajos y Ceballos has an electric-blue front and serves Mexican staples such as *enchiladas suizas* and chicken in the spicy chocolate sauce, *mole poblano*. Deals are made over northern breakfasts in the tartan Rincón Escoces restaurant of the San Francisco Hotel, which stays open for rib-eye steak lunches and quieter dinners. A meatless choice is the Restaurant Vegetariano where Libertad crosses Calle 13.

The Chihuahua–Pacífico train

Western Chihuahua and the Chihuahua–Pacífico Railway

Western Chihuahua is frontier country. Beyond the Mennonite communities at Ciudad Cuauhtémoc, the land abruptly forgets the vast, flat expanses of the plain and begins to climb up into the Sierra Madre Occidental. Slicing through the mountains are gorges four times the depth of the Grand Canyon. Rivers meander along a full day's journey below the canyons' rim. One of the most awe-inspiring railways in the world—the Chihuahua–Pacífico line, also known as the Copper Canyon Railway—provides the only link for hundreds of kilometres beween central Mexico and the Pacific, cutting through mountains that make Scotland's seem like pimples on an adolescent's chin. No roads other than rough tracks have yet been able to cross this part of the sierra. The train can cross in 13 hours but by car, via Durango or the US border, it would take two days. Much of this territory remains unexplored, inaccessible even to the Tarahumara who still live in caves high up in the sierra. From Creel, several tracks radiate out across the sierra, where houses, trains and people are no more noticeable than grains of sand in the vastness of it all.

GETTING AROUND

By Bus: Hourly first-class buses from the Camionera Central in Chihuahua take 2½ hours to Ciudad Cuauhtémoc, but only the second-class buses stop in Santa Isabel/General Trías (see Chihuahua) or continue to Creel (4½ hours, every 2 hours). Nearly everyone prefers the train. Buses from Creel go to Batopilas and Guacochi. The journeys are unremittingly bumpy and subject to every conceivable vagary. The Batopilas bus leaves from the far side of the tracks, 50 m from the Chihuahua stop, at 07.00 every Tuesday, Thursday and Saturday, taking most of the day. It returns at 04.00 every Monday, Wednesday and Friday. Loggers go more frequently in their trucks and are generous with lifts.

By Car: Highway 16 loops in and out of the railway tracks to Ciudad Cuauhtémoc. The railway and road march together into the sierra as far as Creel, but only the train bravely continues through the mountains to the Pacific. A road of sorts tackles the sierra, through Cusararé to Batopilas or down to Hidalgo del Parral. The majesty of the mountains indubitably diminishes the might of man and the hire car won't make it. In the rainy season (late July to early October) these roads are impassable to all but loggers' trucks and four-wheel-drive jeeps, and even in the dry season it is advisable to go well prepared.

By Train: The first-class Chihuahua–Pacífico train chugs off from the Ocampo station in Chihuahua at 07.00 every morning, its passengers blearily clutching at cups of coffee. It takes 2½ hours to Ciudad Cuauhtémoc, 5 to Creel and 13 to Los Mochis. First-class trains cost a little more than the second-class but are quicker and far more comfortable, providing properly padded seats, a restaurant car, air-conditioning, and a complimentary breakfast.

To get to the Ocampo station, take a bus marked Colonia Rosalía or Sta Rosa to the prison and walk around to the back. Tickets should always be booked long in advance, either from the station office (tel 122284 or 157756 and open until 18.00) or from the travel agency in the Hotel Victoria. Cars can be taken on the train but the process is expensive and bureaucratic: they have to be booked in and brought to the station several hours before departure.

There is a **time difference** between the mountains of Central Mexico and the plains of the Pacific. Los Mochis is on Pacific time but all train schedules (including the one below) work on Central time, which is one hour ahead.

From Chihuahua	07.00	*From* Los Mochis	07.00
Cuauhtémoc	09.30	El Fuerte	08.18
Creel	11.45	Bahuichivo	11.49
Divisadero	12.57	Divisadero	12.53
Bahuichivo	14.17	Creel	14.200
El Fuerte	17.43	Cuauhtémoc	16.35
Los Mochis	19.00	Chihuahua	19.05

For those who eschew time and comfort, the second-class trains leave at 07.20 and 12.00. Both arrive in Los Mochis after dark.

The Chihuahua–Pacífico Railway

Better known as the Copper Canyon Railway, this 650-km (13-hr) journey is without peer in Mexico. The track corkscrews through the Sierra Madre Occidental, cleaving a narrow path between mountains and canyons, twisting through narrow passes, and slipping over delicate bridges. It was the dream-child of some Kansas City businessmen who, as early as 1872, planned to link the mid-west to the Orient via Topolobampo Bay on Mexico's Pacific coast. Ninety years later it was finally opened, an awesome engineering feat complete with 36 major bridges and 87 tunnels.

The most dramatic view-point is at Divisadero, where the train stops for 20 minutes to let passengers look out over the Copper Canyon far, far below the track. Once in the mountains, every moment is spectacular, particularly if you have enough Spanish to persuade the driver to let you ride in the engine cab for a while. It makes little difference whether you leave from Los Mochis or Chihuahua, but do try to spend a couple of nights in Creel to explore the sierra. If there is time, it is also definitely worthwhile stopping in Divisadero, overhanging the magnificent Copper Canyon, Bahuichivo or El Fuerte, where the few hotels (all ***) arrange trips and horse rides down into the canyons, out to waterfalls and over to deserted mining villages.

Ciudad Cuauhtémoc and the Mennonite Communities

Before hitting the mountains, the train calls in at this prosperous Mennonite town. In the heat of the desert, this Nordic race, with pallid complexions, blond hair and wiry figures, speaking a guttural Low German, seems like a mirage. In appearance and lifestyle, the Mennonites are far removed from Latin-American Catholics, a state of affairs both are keen to preserve. They place themselves outside civil law, refusing to do military service or attend state education, guided only by their own conscience and the words of the Bible.

The sect was founded in the 16th century by the Dutchman Menno Simons. In 1776 they were granted lands in the Ukraine by Catherine the Great, but a hundred years later were commanded to join the army. In protest, 100,000 accepted land in Canada from the British government. After the First World War the Canadians demanded state education for Mennonite children, provoking a further emigration. Alvaro Obregón, president of Mexico, sold 2500 Mennonites 100,000 hectares of marginal, arid land around Cuauhtémoc for $43 per hectare. Since then the community has grown to 30,000 (forcing many to move on to South America) and has transformed the land into highly productive fields and pastures. The town now has more banks per head than any other city in Mexico.

The Mennonites live in communities along Highway 23 to Nuevo Casas Grandes. During the week, the entire family is out working in the dairies, creameries and fields. (At km 6, Campo 2B, a shop called the Sello d'Oro sells their salty feta-like cheese.) Their eminently practical clothes haven't changed in generations. The men wear overalls and long-sleeved shirts, without a hint of nonconformity. The women dress in long, dark skirts, long-sleeved shirts and a plain headscarf or hat (white for single women, black for married). Sunday, the great day of rest, sees the young men lounging around town with a beer and cigarette (both distinctly frowned upon by the conservative Elders). Modern life is now eroding their sectarian heritage: microwaves are found in kitchens and American pick-ups are preferred to horses and carts. Most shocking of all, a beautiful 6 ft 2 in Mennonite recently walked off with the title of Miss Chihuahua.

The Hotel Victoria travel agency in Chihuahua organizes small group visits for a large price (tel 128893).

WHERE TO STAY   (area code 158)
The hunting and riding lodge of ****Rancho La Estancia (tel 141 22282, tlx 034875) is 10 km west of Highway 23, in the hills. The price includes meals and riding but you can go just to ride.

The comfortable ***Cumbres Inn (Av Aldama and Calle 11, tel 24480), a taxi ride from the centre, is built loftily above the town with spreading views over the countryside to the mountains beyond. At the southern end of town is the ***Posada del Sol (Calzada Chavez, tel 23333), an extraordinary Disney-fantasy extravaganza. On the main street, Allende, is the large and friendly Tarahumara Inn (at the corner of 5a, tel 22801) and the small, pokey *Unión opposite (tel 21114).

EATING OUT
Equs (13 and Allende 1310, tel 25200) is a surprisingly grand restaurant with Mennonite butter, Sicilian coffee with *amaretto*, trout from Canada and the very best of local beef, like the Rib-Eye Special. Expensive. Otherwise the main square is the answer with a good farmers' café, El Den, popular for breakfasts.

The Sierra Tarahumara

There are some 40,000 Tarahumara, who call themselves *raramurí*, spread over the sierra crossed by the railway. The land they live on has made them magnificent runners,

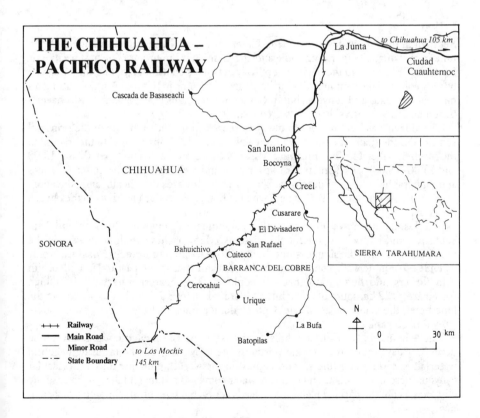

THE CHIHUAHUA –
PACIFICO RAILWAY

La Junta
to Chihuahua 105 km
Ciudad
Cuauhtemoc

Cascada de Basaseachi

San Juanito
Bocoyna
CHIHUAHUA
Creel

Cusarare
El Divisadero

SONORA
Bahuichivo
San Rafael
Cuiteco
BARRANCA DEL COBRE
SIERRA TARAHUMARA

Cerocahui

Urique

N

+++ Railway
— Main Road
— Minor Road
– - – State Boundary

La Bufa

Batopilas

to Los Mochis
145 km

0   30 km

easily out-running horses in the rugged canyons. Races have long been part of their traditions, weaving the magical with the physical and lasting from hours to days. There is a report from 1892 of one runner who carried a letter from the village of Guazapares (1000 m above sea level) to the city of Chihuahua (1500 m) and returned with a reply within five days, having covered 850 km. Their diet hardly credits their stamina, relying largely on corn, mice and over 200 species of plants growing in the hills. *Tesgüino*, a crude, low-alcohol corn brew which they drink in liberal quantities, provides as many nutrients as the rest of their diet put together.

Many still live in caves, particularly around Divisadero. Although those near villages now wear western-style clothes, out in the hills and valleys the men wear *huarache* sandals and a nappy-like cloth around their waists, crossed between the legs and left hanging in a triangle down the back. The women seem synonymous with babies, carrying them strapped on their backs in a tight shawl, looking like a pile of firewood. Their skirts are thickly bunched and flower-patterned, worn with long-sleeved shirts and headscarves. The Tarahumara are a reticent people but are delighted by attempts to talk their language, *raramurí*. Some of the most common phrases are: *quira!* (hello), *naté taraba* (thank you), and *chimiviguacavatu* (what is your name?).

Creel

Set high in the mountains (at 2338 m), Creel is an ideal Tarahumaran village to spend time in, walking, hiking, riding and exploring. Timing is important. The best weather is from early February to the beginning of May, when it's cool and dry. The winter can be bitterly cold and the summer stinking hot. The rains come in July and August, cutting off many of the roads and canyons, but by September the rains have gone, the visits haven't begun and the countryside is at its greenest.

The village was built to house railway workers and named after one of the principal sponsors of the track. It is small, with the few hotels and shops parallel to the tracks, on the southern side. The **Tarahumara Mission Store** on the Zócalo (open 09.30–13.00 and 15.00–18.00) sells Tarahumara woven pine and reed baskets, dolls, rough ceramics and topographical maps of the sierra. The profits go towards their health and education. Jesuit Father Verplancken runs it and, when at home, blasts out Vivaldi from the church speakers.

The Jesuits attempted to convert the Tarahumara throughout the 17th and 18th centuries, and left behind several old missions. Many of these are hidden away in the mountains, but one, the simple, stone-built, 400-year-old **San Ignacio Mission**, is only a gentle 45-minute walk, south along Av Mateos and on through pastureland filled with wild flowers and huge, smoothed-off boulders. The nearest waterfall, 30-m high **Cusararé**, is 22 km south of town: hitch a lift or take a tour. It is an hour's walk from the lone hotel, the Cabañas Cañon del Cobre, along a track that meanders past boulder-strewn river-banks.

The 4-hour trip (140 km) and hike northwest to the **Basaseachic waterfall** can be done in a day from Creel. In the northern Sierra Madre, this fantastically beautiful waterfall is 250 m high (the second highest in the world), plunging into a spectacular canyon. Incredibly, it makes no roar: the water comes so fast that it falls 3 m clear of the cliff face. From the parking place, a trail leads across the river on an elevated bridge and winds through alpine forest to the top of the falls. From here a breathtaking hike plunges down to the bottom of the falls (1 hour's walk down and 1½ back up).

The hotels run numerous **tours**, to waterfalls, lakes, hot springs and caves, ranging in price depending on numbers and comforts. The cheapest tours are with the Casa Margarita but for comfort go to the Parador de la Moñtana (see below).

WHERE TO STAY

The ***Parador de la Montaña** (at the south end of Av López Mateos 44, tel 60075) is a well-managed tour-group hotel with an indifferent restaurant and comfortable, dark rooms. The manager is rumoured to be opening his own place, **Just a Little Resort**, with log cabins and fully equipped kitchens. *Casa Margarita, opposite the station, is a family house that has grown and grown as travellers pass on the word. It is nearly always full. Guests eat together in the kitchen and dinner can run to three sittings. The rooms, built on over the years whenever there was money around, range from the cheapest of bunk-bed dormitories to high luxury. The tours are also the least expensive in town. If these are full, the **Korachi and **Nuevo Barrancas del Cobre, with log fires in most of the rooms, are on the other side of the tracks.

Some 22 km down the road at Cusararé, the ***Cabañas Cañon del Cobre** (tel 158214) is a Tex–Mex hotel with no electricity but lovely cabins and a big dining room where guests meet for candlelit dinners.

Batopilas

Although out on a limb (118 km south of the railway station at Creel; 7 hrs by bus or truck), Batopilas makes a good base for experienced hikers who want to explore deep into the canyons. Between Creel and Batopilas, pine trees and bracken grow high up in the mountains while roses, peaches and guayabas line the valley floor. The road, twisting and bending through crevices and cracks, attains heights that look insurmountable and depths that never seem to end. Wave after wave of hallucinogenic rock forms echo the work of local potters. La Bufa, the magnificent overlook for Batopilas Canyon, is 4½ hours from Creel. Batopilas is only 24 km further but it is the longest stretch of the journey as the road winds and curves round ever-decreasing bends to the river at the bottom.

Silver was discovered here in 1632, some veins yielding pieces of ore which were 80 per cent silver. In the late 19th century, a mining magnate had a piano brought from Chihuahua (a 20-day journey) on the backs of Tarahumaras, for his children to learn Chopin on. There are still extravagant, crumbling houses and haciendas around the village, including the magnificent ruins of an unaccountably large 400 year-old church, 6 km down the river. The mines continued to be worked until the 1940s but production dropped off rapidly after the 1910 Revolution. Today there are two or three hotels for loggers or tourists but little else in the quiet, riverside village.

WHERE TO STAY

Hotels in Batopilas are cheap and basic—the **Batopilas** and the **Parador** (booked through the Parador de la Montaña at Creel), both on Juárez, and a little, nameless place on Calle Zarco.

Southeast of Batopilas, in the village of Guachochic—the gateway to the Barranca de Sinforosa on the Río Verde—there is a simple hotel called the *Chaparro (Calle Villa, tel 30004). Further south again, in Guadalupe y Calvo, is a rough loggers' inn, the **(CE) Díaz** (Juárez 47). Both these villages are accessible (just) from Hidalgo del Parral (see South on the Durango Road).

Barrancas de Divisadero

Some 44 km southwest of Creel, and the next stop on the train, Divisadero is the highest point on the track (over 2460 m), providing an overview of the six interlocking canyons of the Barranca del Cobre. Far below, the Urique River snakes through its subtropical base, in a canyon five times as deep as the Grand Canyon. Up above, it is fringed by blood-red *manzanita, madroño*, pine and oak trees. The train stops for 20 precious minutes when hopelessly inadequate photographs are taken over the sheer drop. Then the lenses swing round to catch fleeting shots of the Tarahumara women selling their woven baskets, wooden dolls and piping hot *tamales* (long, thin corn dough stuffed with tomato). The train beeps twice and promptly leaves as stragglers race to jump on. Some people stay for two hours and then take the slower, second-class train to their next stop, using the time to explore further along the canyon's rim and the woods around. There is a small café at the stop which hasn't hiked its prices up too exorbitantly.

WHERE TO STAY
There are three hotels around Divisadero but only one right on the canyon's edge. This, the **Cabañas Divisadero Barrancas** (tel 141 123362), has a glass-fronted restaurant that hangs over the cliff face, leaving nothing but wings to the imagination. The cabins are charming, with log fires and piles of blankets, and the setting is incomparable, but the food is uninspired. Many Tarahumara rely on the hotel and the 20-minute tourists, for employment and to sell their crafts. The hotel pays its staff appallingly; the tourists treat them a little better.

Two other hotels have their own short stop (called Posada), 10 minutes down the track. The ***Posada Barrancas** can be booked through the Santa Anita in Los Mochis (tel 681 20046) or directly (tel 141 166589). The ***Mansión Tarahumara** (no tel: book through the Chihuahua tourist office, tel 159879) is a medieval castle in the unlikeliest of settings. Circa 1987, it comes complete with red turrets and a huge banqueting hall. Log fires are prepared in each cabin and the home-cooking is excellent. These hotels are all expensive because of their inaccessibility, but meals are included and walks and horse riding are on offer.

Along the Railway from Divisadero to Los Mochis

Forty km from Divisadero, the train stops at **Cuiteco** (1800 m), where there is one rustic hotel, the **Cabaña Pinar del Cuiteco** (tel 125080) with just 15 rooms.

A few km along, the train stops at **Bahuichivo** (1750 m) to let out passengers for Cerocahui, 12 interminable km from the station. The ***Mission Hotel** (booked through the Santa Anita, tel 681 20046) sends an old school bus for its guests. The hotel is in a fine, 18th-century building opposite a church founded by the Italian Jesuit,

Salvatierra, in 1680. It organizes trips to the edge of the vast Urique Canyon, at 1880 m the deepest of them all. Truculent horses led by prodding and cajoling boys take guests through valleys and across rivers to waterfalls and mines. Although a favourite haunt of bible-belt groupies from the mid-west, the small hotel is still pretty and peaceful.

El Fuerte is the last major stop before Los Mochis but makes a far more peaceful stop for the night, still basking in the peace of the mountains while benefiting from the warmth of the coast (the rise in temperature is noticeable even when arriving by night). The ***Posada (booked through the Santa Anita, tel 681 20046) is a lovely colonial mansion, with patios and gardens, which has been turned into a successful hotel.

A paved road follows the railway tracks between El Fuerte and **Los Mochis**—the unappealing but unavoidable terminus for the railway line and a major crossroads on the west coast (see The West Coast to Mazatlán).

South on the Durango Road

Highway 45, the main road south from Chihuahua, is long and unremitting to Zacatecas (see Part IX). Hidalgo del Parral in southern Chihuahua and Durango in the state of the same name both make good stops. Parral—the town where Pancho Villa was shot— offers little more than somewhere to rest. Durango is far larger, the capital of a rural state made up of ranches and wild-west film sets, with comfortable hotels and a fine, colonial heart.

GETTING AROUND
By Bus: Five buses a day go in each direction on the Chihuahua–Durango road, stopping off in Hidalgo del Parral. From there, second-class buses leave once a day, early in the morning, for Vergel (3 hrs) and Guadalupe y Calvo (7 hrs).
By Car: At Jiménez, 220 km south of Chihuahua on Highway 45, Highway 49 branches off to the southeast for Torreón and Saltillo (see Part XI). Highway 45 veers west to Hidalgo del Parral (330 km from Chihuahua) and then continues south to Durango (711 km). Fill up with petrol at every chance. A new highway now provides a more direct link between Chihuahua and Parral (220 km) via Satévo.

Hidalgo del Parral

To travellers from Durango, the old mining town of Hidalgo del Parral provides a 'welcome to Chihuahua' that might make them want to scupper any plans for going further north. It is an introverted, messy town, always blown by a dusty, desert wind which funnels up the streets and chases visitors on their way. The town spruces itself up to its Sunday best for the Zócalo, but lets its hem show everywhere else. Its only claim to fame is that the outstanding bandit revolutionary, Pancho Villa, was shot here in 1923. On Calle Gabino Barreda, the retired general had a long-time girlfriend whom he often visited. His assassins waited 103 days for his last visit, on the way back from his godson's christening. As his 1919 Dodge car pulled away, eight assassins with repeating rifles peppered the car and murdered the hero of the landless peasants of Chihuahua. No-one knows to this day whether it was a political or personal vendetta.

Northwest into the Mountains

The loggers' roads from Parral into the heart of the Sierra Madre are redolent of children's stories, as *The Little House on the Prairie* meets *Butch Cassidy and the Sundance Kid*. There is no specific aim to such a journey, other than a beautiful drive through the foothills of the Sierra Madre. The area is frequented by loggers and raw army recruits as well as narco dealers, who take these back roads to the coast during the September marijuana harvest.

The road divides at Puerto Justo. A bumpy unpaved track heads northwest to Balleza and Guachochic, and then on to Creel (see The Chihuahua–Pacífico Railway). This is not an easy drive, requiring a four-wheel-drive vehicle and considerable planning. The road southwest to Vergel and Guadalupe y Calvo is reasonable as far as km 114. By then the green grasses have given over to pine forests, and a Pemex petrol station marks the end of navigable road in anything but a jeep or truck. Guadalupe y Calvo (241 km), a once-wealthy 16th-century mine, is another 4 hours on (see Batopilas, The Chihuahua–Pacífico Railway). A mint was established there in 1842 but lasted less than a decade, subjected to endless attacks by Apaches and Comanches. Today's wealth comes from logging in the largest sawmill in Latin America. The Pacific coast, deceptively close on the map, is a two-day journey from Parral, along unmapped tracks.

WHERE TO STAY AND EAT
(area code 152)

Hidalgo del Parral offers two motels: the *****Camino Real** (on the Durango road at the Pemex station, tel 22050) and, on the southern edge of town, the ****Villa Cariño**. The ****Turista** (Av Independencia 14, tel 24447) is a small, family-run hotel. The 19th-century masonic lodge, to its right, was once a theatre but is now split between the traffic cops and the local masons. The **Restaurant Moreira** (Herrera and García, in the centre, tel 21070), the best on offer, is open for coffees and enchiladas from 06.00 to 23.00.

In Jiménez

A nondescript town at the junction between Highways 45 and 49, 80 km east of Parral, Jiménez has a smart motel, ******Las Pampas**, actually on the crossroads, and another motel in town, the ****Río Florido** (Av Juárez and 20 de Noviembre, tel 20400). Two cheap hotels in the same street are ***La Gran Via** (600, tel 20567) and ***Avenida** (309, tel 20562).

Durango

Durango, capital of the state of the same name, is set in a high fertile plain below the Sierra Madre Occidental, at a height of 2000 m. Whilst the suburbs are choked with cheap shops, the Zócalo and the streets fanning off it have kept their colonial grandeur. Once a key staging post for Jesuit missions and Spanish mines, it is just as important today for ranchers and their families, coming in from outlying reaches of the state to get a month's supply of goods. A busy, large town, it is also the last place of note for anyone embarking on the highly recommended roller-coaster drive over the Sierra Madre and down to the coast at Mazatlán (see Mazatlán to Durango).

Durango has long been a haunt of Hollywood film producers because of the quality of its light. Its fantastic locations are ideal for Westerns, while production costs are still only a fraction of those in California. Durango's greatest export to Hollywood was Dolores del Río, a leading Mexican film star, 'discovered' here and taken off to fame and fortune in the States.

GETTING AROUND

By Bus: The bus station is in the northeast of town. First-class buses connect Durango with most major cities in Mexico, including Chihuahua, Zacatecas, Mazatlán, Guadalajara and Mexico City. From the station, 5 de Febrero (parallel with 20 Noviembre) seems to take for ever to wind in to the centre. Buses to the station are marked 'central camionera' and go from 5 de Febrero, one block south of 20 Noviembre.

By Car: Durango is on the crossroads of Highways 45 and 40. Highway 45 whizzes straight as an arrow from Hidalgo del Parral (411 km), through apple orchards, cattle ranches and pin-prick villages, continuing southeast of Durango to Zacatecas and Mexico City (903 km). Highway 40 leads southwest to Mazatlán (294 km) and northeast to Torreón (253 km).

In Town: The road running from east to west past the main square is 20 Noviembre. Constitución and Juárez run north–south on either side of the cathedral. It is quickest and easiest to walk around the centre.

TOURIST INFORMATION

The tourist office in Hidalgo Sur 408, two blocks west of Constitución (tel 12139), is more interested in prospective film producers than tourists, but does have maps. Dolores del Río's house is in the same street.

WHAT TO SEE

The Centre

In the airy colonial centre, an 18th-century baroque **cathedral** teeters on the edge of absurd ostentation in the manner of Churriguera, with elaborate baroque lateral doors and a plethora of finely carved estípites. The tower above the side door opening onto Constitución is haunted by a white nun, who tended a young, wounded Spanish captain. He recovered and returned to the fray, leaving her to retire heartbroken to a convent, where she waited forlornly for him to return. The bandstand in the main square is topped by the national symbol, gleaned from Aztec legends, of an eagle on a nopal cactus devouring a serpent. All around it people devour steaming corn on the cob, covered in mayonnaise, cheese and chilli, and sold on every corner.

To the south of the square, in 5 de Febrero, is the massive 17th-century colonial palace, **Casa del Conde de Suchil**. Behind its heavy wooden doors the local tribunals of the Inquisition were carried out to devastating effect. The courtyard inside is exquisitely decorated with finely carved columns and terracing, and filled with orange and lime trees. For several years it stood empty, maintained in pristine condition, whilst the city fathers debated the perfect use for it. It now houses a bank.

313

Regional Museum
(Victoria 100 with Serdán, 15 minutes' walk or a cheap taxi ride from the Zócalo; open 10.00–17.00, Tue–Sun; adm.)
This big museum proudly details the history of the state from its pre-Hispanic past to its cinematic present. The Spanish arrived in the area to find descendants of the Chalchi-huita, the Tepehuano and others: they put up a notable resistance but were finally conquered and put to work down the gold and silver mines. The museum recreates the caves where early Chalchihuita settlers sought refuge from the elements in prehistoric times. The display includes a mummified corpse, which was found buried in one of the caves, and was used as protection against marauding animals. (This was common practice.) One room is devoted to the modern-day life and work of the Tepehuano. Downstairs, there is a catalogue of the films which have been shot in the state: the walls are lined with endless photographs of Dolores del Río.

Villa Oeste Film Sets
Some 14 km north of town, Highway 45 passes the film sets at Villa Oeste. Suddenly, under an outcrop of cactus-covered hills, emerges a Bank of South Texas, a clapper-board church, Ryan's Hotel, and El Descanso Café. The thin walls wobble in the wind as one piece of plyboard evokes every western ever seen on rainy Sunday afternoons.

WHERE TO STAY AND EAT   (area code 181)
Posada Duran (to the right of the cathedral in 20 Febrero, tel 12412) is a wonderful, shabby colonial hotel. The big, high-ceilinged rooms look over a courtyard. Each room has lashings of hot water and creaking wooden floorboards. On the other side of the cathedral, **Posada San Jorge** (Constitución 102 Sur, tel 33257) is an alternative, modest, colonial hotel. The comfortable ****Presidente (20 Noviembre 257 Ote, tel 10480, tlx 066303), where the film crews and directors stay, is considerably more up-market but still retains a modern-colonial style. Alternatively, try the well-estab-lished ***Casa Blanca (20 Noviembre 811 Pte, tel 13539) and the newer ***Plaza Catedral (Constitución Sur, tel 32480).

All the hotels are good for breakfast, but for something more try the colonial Casa de la Monja (Negrete 308 Pte, one block behind 20 Noviembre, tel 17162) which serves regional food like *caldillo durangueño* (beef in its own juice with green chilli). Los Condes (on Negrete) is an attractive café in a pretty interior courtyard.

The West Coast to Mazatlán

The roads running parallel to the west coast from the US border to the Tropic of Cancer are the stuff of Westerns, dominated by heat and dust. Cutting through parched desert and scattered cacti, they are relentlessly flat and straight for hours on end. The lone cowboy on his horse has been replaced by the four-wheel-drive jeep: stetson-bearing farmers race along, listening to loud *norteño* music and stopping for occasional breakfasts of scrambled eggs and steaming tortillas.

Running along the coastal plain, these roads are hemmed in by the Gulf of California on the west and squeezed by the vast bulk of the towering Sierra Madre on the east. The copper-coloured desert of Sonora in the north, dotted with squat, spiky barrel cacti, finally gives way to the humid tropical plains of Sinaloa and the resort of Mazatlán, which is just below the Tropic of Cancer. No road attempts to cross the high range of the Sierra Madre mountains to the east until as far south as Mazatlán.

Possible breaks on the trip south are Hermosillo, the capital of the state of Sonora, and the colonial town of Alamos in the hills. The tranquil bays of Bahía Kino and San Carlos offer a stop by the sea in the company of the motor-home crowd. Los Mochis is a necessary evil for those crossing to Baja California by ferry, or going up the Cañon del Cobre by cliff-hanging train (see The Chihuahua–Pacífico Railway). Mazatlán itself is a well-worn coastal resort with a tacky charm, which provides a welcome burst of sea and sun after the arid north.

GETTING AROUND

Crossing the Border: There are three main border crossings. Californians cross over at Mexicali (in Baja California) while those coming from Arizona use either Nogales or Agua Prieta. Don't linger in these unexciting border towns but head on down to either Hermosillo or the preferable Alamos (well worth pushing on an extra couple of hours for). To cross the border you'll need a tourist card (available from the immigration offices at the border and in buses and planes) and a valid passport. The crossings are open 24 hours a day.

By Air: From Mexicali there are daily flights to Guadalajara and Mexico City. Hermosillo is more international with daily flights to Tucson in Arizona as well as to Chihuahua, Mazatlán and Mexico City.

By Bus: First-class buses thunder down Highways 2 and 15, bearing passengers from Mexicali, Nogales and Agua Prieta to Hermosillo and then on down to Mazatlán via Guaymas. They leave hourly and are swift and efficient.

By Car: Nearly all the traffic from the northwestern border ends up in Hermosillo and is then funneled southwards down Highway 15.

Highway 15 begins at Nogales and leads due south to Hermosillo (275 km, 3 hrs). From Mexicali, long, hot Highway 2 runs parallel to the US border for 165 km, through the desolate Altar desert, part of the 2½ million square km of desert in the area. The roadside is dotted with *saguaro* and organ cacti and the road itself is punctuated by endless routine narco-traffic checkpoints. They will ask for passports and visas and may want to check the car. (These may get worse in the state of Sinaloa where the capital, Culiacán, is known as Little Chicago because of its busy drug trade.) Highway 2 then veers southeast to cross Highway 15 and go on to Agua Prieta. Highway 15 continues south to Hermosillo (623 km, 7 hrs from Mexicali). A minor road from Agua Prieta winds its way down past villages and through hills and gorges to Hermosillo (see The Agua Prieta Road).

After Hermosillo, Highway 15 follows the coast, going through Guaymas, Los Mochis and Mazatlán before heading inland to Guadalajara and Mexico City.

By Train: The Ferrocarril del Pacífico railway line shadows Highway 15 from Nogales to Guadalajara, stopping off at all the major towns on the way. It's ponderous, hot and better avoided. The buses are much quicker. There is also a rail link from Mexicali.

315

The Agua Prieta Road

The scenic route from Agua Prieta on the Arizona border down to Hermosillo is a long wind through desert grasslands, canyon country and once-rich colonial villages. The road is pretty, if not well kept, and the drive takes about 6 hours.

Arizpe

Cradled between two canyons, the little-visited backwater of Arizpe was founded in 1646 by Jesuits. Reinforced to resist attack from the Apaches, it was never conquered and became the most important town of the northwest (which included Arizona) for decades. Today, hidden in the hills, it is a charming spot in which to spend the night. The streets are dusty and unpaved, although a keen sense of civic pride emanates from the small hospital and large baseball pitch.

WHAT TO SEE
The Franciscan church, in the centre, has a roller-coaster beamed roof which tips and tilts drunkenly but somehow keeps standing, and an ornate *retablo* behind the altar. The *pièce de résistance* lies in a glass vault in the central aisle. The body of Juan Bautista de Anza, who went on from Arizpe to found San Francisco in California in the 17th century, was brought back, fully dressed, to be displayed in the church for all to see. There's a festival on 4 September, when all the girls in the village dance around a beribboned pole outside the church and the women dance more circumspectly within. The men watch indulgently, tippling glasses of tequila.

In Av García Morales, the remains of an old *tienda* (general store) are filled with ancient spurs, cigarette advertisements, saddle soap, stetsons, nails and revolving stools on which ranchers would wait as orders were made up. In the days when the town was rich, Chinese immigrants set up shop here, only to be booted out in 1910 by a suspicious government which resented the commercial success of all Asians in the state. The store is not open to the public but Señor Pesqueira from the hotel can get the key and point out the Chinese characters etched into the drawers and tables.

WHERE TO STAY AND EAT
De Anza, run by the Pesqueira family (Lerdo de Tejada 30, tel 12), next to the church, provides a warm welcome and six clean simple rooms. In the main plaza, the café **Kankun** has good homecooking.

Ures

South of Arizpe, the road passes through several other colonial villages. Between Aconchi and Baviacora it enters the fertile valley of the River Sonora. In the summer, row after row of red chillies are strung up to dry along whitewashed walls. At Mazocahui, turn right and continue through the hills to Ures.

Anxious not to disappear off the map, Ures calls itself the 'forgotten Athens', because of the number of intellectuals it purports to have produced. Its pleasant square may well have stimulated study, with a 17th-century church and solid colonial houses whose heavy wooden doors open to reveal light, airy courtyards. It's a place of old town values, where solitary horsemen doff their caps as they pass the church.

The road from Ures continues to Hermosillo (74 km, about an hour).

316

Hermosillo

Capital of Sonora, Mexico's second-largest state, Hermosillo is a boom town with wide streets, low-slung colonial houses and box-like 1930s buildings with Rennie Mackintosh windows. It is also a city of forthright people, huge flour tortillas the length of an arm and breathlessly hot sun. July and August are the hottest of all. In the still dead heat of the afternoon, no-one, anywhere in Sonora, does anything. The first big town on the road south, it is particularly equipped to deal with well-heeled visitors. The Ford Motor Company has a plant in Hermosillo and the town is only too delighted to accommodate their executives with big hotels and expense-account restaurants. Budget travellers are compensated by some of the best tacos in Mexico, which can be bought off the street.

GETTING AROUND
By Bus: The bus station (tel 70580) is southeast of town on Blvd Transversal 400. First- and second-class buses go to Guaymas and Bahía Kino, north to the border (Mexicali, Nogales and Agua Prieta) and south along Highway 15. A white bus marked 'estación' shuttles between Blvd Rodríguez and the bus station on an endless round.
By Car: Hermosillo is 275 km south of Nogales and 460 km north of Los Mochis on Highway 15. The highway goes straight through the town centre, becoming a wide boulevard lined with palm and orange trees, changing its name from Kino to Rodríguez to Rosales, before continuing south. For **car hire**, try Hertz (tel 48500) on Blvd Rodríguez and Tamaulipas, or Budget (tel 43033) round the corner in Tamaulipas 26.
By Train: The railway station (tel 43830) is off Highway 15, to the northeast of the city. The northbound train leaves at 08.00 for Mexicali (10 hrs), and the southbound train at 20.00 for Guadalajara (24 hrs).
In Town: The smart **hotel strip** is out on Blvd Kino, a 15-minute walk from the centre. Otherwise nowhere is more than a couple of minutes' walk.

TOURIST INFORMATION
There is a small office in Blvd Rodríguez 138 Nte (tel 47399) whose staff speak excellent English and have a wide range of maps and literature.

WHAT TO SEE
Whatever the loyal tourist office may tell you, there is not much to see and it is better to press on. In the main square, Zaragoza, lined with orange trees, the **cathedral** has recently been lavishly renovated at the cost of millions of pesos. Hermosillo is as Catholic as they come and donated the money without batting an eyelid. Sadly, the bland neoclassical interior now looks plastered with too much make-up. Across the square, the **Palacio Municipal** has a bit more spark, with Moorish arches and a courtyard painted with bright modern murals.

The state history museum, **Museo de Sonora** (Calle Jesús García; open 10.00–17.00; closed Mon; adm), is on the eastern side of a tall hill known as La Campana (the bell), topped by a radio antenna and visible from all over town. The building is a converted penitentiary, which was still in use in the early 1980s. One cell remains to show the spartan conditions endured by the inmates: a three-tiered bunk, a bucket and a basin in a room the size of a cupboard. One of Sonora's proudest and most emotive moments is given a room to itself. In the 1930s, a tearful President Cárdenas formally restored land to the Yaqui people, whose numbers had been almost decimated by previous regimes. The rest of the museum is devoted to the history of the state which is dry for non-Sonorans, despite the odd costume and colourful display. There are short four-line summaries in English in every room.

The redeeming feature of the **Iglesia del Carmen,** nearby in Calle Jesús García, is the stall outside selling *tostadas* (fried tortillas) filled with the freshest of shrimps. The church itself has a curiously eclectic facade, with a bit of everything thrown in, from neoclassical to Moorish and postmodernist.

WHERE TO STAY   (area code 621)
Hotels are expensive in the north and those in Blvd Kino (a continuation of Highway 15 from the north) are smart business hotels. The best and most comfortable is the *****Pitic Valle Grande** (Blvd Kino 369, tel 51112), with a large garden and pleasant service. Politicians come for coffee and breakfast in the café. Over the road, its cheaper sister hotel, ****Bugambilia Valle Grande** (tel 45050), caters for middle management, not top executive.

In the centre, the ***Kino** (Pino Suárez 151, tel 24599) is a family hotel with modern rooms in a colonial building. Try for one nearest the top, both cooler and less noisy. ***San Alberto** (Serdán and Rosales, tel 21800) was once the grand old man of Hermosillo hotels but is now a poor relation. The cheaper **Monte Carlo** (Juárez and Sonora, tel 20853) and **Washington** (Dr Noriega, tel 31183) are reputedly 'where the soldiers go'.

WHERE TO EAT
Motel La Siesta (in Blvd Kino, tel 43989) has an excellent steak restaurant serving the local beef, which is rated the best in the country. Expensive. Alternatively, **Mariscos Los Arcos** (Michel 43) is famed for its seafood, particularly the *mariscada*, a banquet of grilled fish with 12 attendant side dishes. Moderate. Tourists are sent to eat in **Zamboz** (Calle Serdán), for endless hearty mariachi music and pool tables, but a good fish and steak grill. Moderate.

Even those who purse their lips and say they never eat ice cream may find themselves addicted to **Helados Bing.** Made of thick cream with huge chunks of real fruit, such as peach, mango or guayaba, they can be chain-eaten all the way down the coast. The shops are easily recognized by their pink and white candy-striped roofs: cars have been known to screech to a halt just outside. There is one close to the tourist office in Blvd Rodríguez. Cheap restaurants in the same area are the Mexican **La Fiesta** which comes complete with loud mariachi music, **Lai Wah** modelled on a pagoda, with big platefuls of Chinese food, and **Callejoncito** for tacos. These come any way but are delicious filled with mushrooms, herbs, garlic, black pepper and Chihuahua cheese. In Niños Héroes, off Rodríguez, there's a **Tienda Naturista** health-food shop and vegetarian restaurant. The three-course comida corrida comes on one plate like a TV dinner.

Bahía Kino

The bay of Bahía Kino faces the Isla Tiburón, with a broad, thick sweep of white sand, fringed with the low-rise sproutings of a small holiday village. It is divided into two segregated parts: the clam and shrimp fishermen still live in the older part whilst the new section is a strip of bijou bungalows and trailer parks, reflecting the imported tastes of Arizona and California (definitely the Chevy set and not the jet set).

Sandpipers and frigate birds wheel and dive all day long whilst grey pelicans glide by with an air of matronly boredom. In the winter months the town is filled with North Americans, but the summer months are too hot for all but the accustomed Sonorans.

GETTING AROUND
Bahía Kino is 120 km southwest of Hermosillo on Highway 16. The only buses come from Hermosillo (every 2 hrs, 1½ hr).

WHAT TO DO
For such a small village, Bahía Kino offers a lot of water sports. Diving, snorkelling and fishing can all be arranged through the Kino Bay Trailer Park (tel 621 53197), either in groups or individually. Given time, they can also organize boat trips out in the Gulf of California to Tiburón Island, now a national park. Many people just go clamming as the tide goes out and spend the rest of the day sleeping in hammocks. Others take long walks along the beach or through groves of tamarisk trees and swarms of black and orange butterflies. The only distraction away from the sea is the small Seri Museum.

The Seri and the Museum
Father Eusebio Kino, a Jesuit missionary, established a small colony here for the Seri in the second half of the 17th century. They never accepted Catholicism or Spanish land rights, fighting fiercely against both throughout the 18th and 19th centuries. At the beginning of this century, the government was ruthless in its attempts to make them settle. When they refused, their women were shipped off to the Yucatán and Guatemala, and their children were boarded out with Sonoran ranching families. Their numbers had shrunk to less than 200 by the 1930s: one Seri was executed for every head of cattle that was rustled.

Having traditionally lived a nomadic life, hunting deer and rabbits in the desert or fishing from Tiburón Island in the Gulf of California, the Seri were increasingly hemmed in this century by encroaching landowners, who pushed them out to Bahía Kino. Here many of them settled and hunted for shark livers. Slowly North Americans discovered the bay and its excellent sports fishing. Anthropologists studied the Seri's way of life, evangelists claimed their souls, and the Seri sold them woven baskets, shell necklaces and sculpted animals and birds made from *palo fierro* (iron wood). Today there are over 500 Seri but few still live in Bahía Kino. Most live further up the coast at Desemboque, or Kin.

The single-room **museum** (on the main street; open 09.00–13.00 and 16.00–19.00; closed Mon) is largely photographic. The Seri no longer keep up their customs: in the 1960s, Protestant missionaries persuaded them that painting faces wasn't Christian, while their reed boats have been replaced by dinghies with outboard motors. Their baskets, now sold commercially to tourists, have a long history. They were originally associated with virginity, every girl being expected to complete one before she met her man. They are made from the fibres of the desert plant *torote*, which are woven into spiral, snake-like patterns. All those who watch a ceremonial basket being made must ask the artisan's permission and drop something of value into it (sunglasses, money and cassettes all find their way in). When there is only one more spiral to be completed (some grow 1.20 m tall and 1.30 wide), everyone comes to celebrate.

WHERE TO STAY

(area code 624)

There are very few hotels and no cheap accommodation, other than camping. At the junction of the old village and the new, the ****Posada del Mar (tel 20155) is an attractive, comfortable hotel and the only one not centred around a trailer park. The main street of the new village runs along the edge of the bay, where a big billboard announces the expensive ***Posada Sta Gemma (tel 20026). It has 14 beach-front cottages, each with two bedrooms, bathroom, balcony, huge fridge, fireplace and kitchen, disturbed only by the roar of the sea. At the end of the 11-km bay road is the ***Motel Kino Bay and Trailer Park (tel (621) 53197). It is well organized, with a late-night shop, fish-cleaning room, laundry and international telephone, designed for long-term trailer campers but with half a dozen rooms as well.

San Carlos and Guaymas

If San Carlos is the beauty, then Guaymas is the brawn. These two towns are only 12 km apart but whilst San Carlos, on the edge of a broad, sweeping bay, is for holidays, the busy port of Guaymas is for work. They appear from nothing in a searing clash of parched land hitting the warm wetness of the Gulf of California.

GETTING AROUND

By Air: Guaymas airport has three weekly Noroeste flights to Phoenix and Tucson, Arizona, and daily Aeroméxico flights (in the afternoon) to and from La Paz, Mexico City and Tucson.

By Bus: The bus station in Guaymas is on Calle 14 and Rodríguez. Inter-city buses provide hourly connections with Hermosillo (1 hr 45 min; change there for Bahía Kino) and with Mazatlán (12 hrs) and all points south. Buses run every 30 minutes between San Carlos's plaza and Guaymas (45 mins) from 07.00 until 21.00. After that taxis, from the rank on Guaymas' Tres Presidentes Plaza, are the only link.

By Car: Guaymas is on Highway 15, 136 km south of Hermosillo (1½ hrs on a fast 4-lane road) and 414 km (5½ hrs) from Nogales. Highway 15 continues down the coast to Mazatlán (780 km, 10 hrs) and on to Guadalajara. The turning west to San Carlos is 12 km north of Guaymas. Although the two towns are the next stop on the coast from Bahía Kino, there is no direct road. Either return to Hermosillo and take Highway 15, or retrace 50 km and take an unmarked right-hand turn through well-irrigated farming land to pick up Highway 15 further south.

By Ferry: The daily 8-hour ferry between Guaymas and Sta Rosalia (Baja California) (tel 22324 or 23393) leaves the docks at 11.00. Tickets are on sale from 07.00 to 10.00.

By Train: The southbound train for Mazatlán and Mexico City stops at 21.30 and the northbound train for Hermosillo and Mexicali at 05.30. Although tickets can be bought in Guaymas from the office on Av Serdán at Calle 29 (tel 24980), the station itself is 10 km east in god-forsaken Empalme. During the day regular buses run along Serdán, marked 'Empalme', but at night take a taxi from the rank on Tres Presidentes Plaza.

In Town: Highway 15 cuts through the centre of Guaymas, becoming Blvd López. To get to the centre, turn right down any of the numbered streets to Av Serdán, parallel to the boulevard.

Car hire isn't necessary but is convenient, particularly to explore the further beaches: try Budget (Blvd López, tel 21450 or the airport, tel 25500) or Hertz (tel 21000).

TOURIST INFORMATION
Guaymas has an office behind the Palacio Municipal (tel 22932).

WHAT TO DO
Guaymas was founded in 1701 by the missionaries Eusebio Kino and Juan Salvatierra. An important working port, it has little intrinsic charm today, although it is a cheaper place to stay in than San Carlos. The tree-lined square is cool and pleasant, with statues of Sonora's three presidents of the republic—Abelardo Rodríguez, Elías Calles and Adolfo de la Huerta—looking like dripping chocolate in the sun. A couple of banks have bought up grandiose 19th-century mansions: Banca Serfin at Calle 22 Sur, next to the Palacio Municipal, and the Banca Comermex, further north on Av Serdán.

San Carlos is the glamorous face of Guaymas. Suddenly the monochrome palette of Sonora's desert gives way to colour. The bay backs on to tenacious scrubland seared by raw, red mountains and faces the sharp, sapphire Gulf of California with its sprinkle of green islands. Like Bahía Kino, it has been discovered by Arizonans and Canadians. Although it remains small, they have built condos, moored yachts and made the desert look as if it has been sprayed with garden sprinklers.

The main road in from Highway 15 to the marina sweeps around the bay. The more secluded beaches are further on, behind the Tatakawi hill. The road passes the beach known as Algodones which was used as the set for the film of Heller's *Catch-22*. Although it has now been taken over by a Howard Johnson hotel, the beach is still big enough to get lost on. Club Med have built their complex next door but there are plenty of deserted beaches still further west that no-one visits.

SPORTS
Cortez Sea Sports (the San Carlos Marina, tel 60230) runs professional scuba-diving, fishing and whale-watching trips. The **Sociedad Cooperativa Tetabampo** (San Carlos Marina, tel 60011) organizes daily boat trips at 08.00 and 14.00 for up to 6 people, including the ice and drinks, bait and tackle.

WHERE TO STAY   (area code 622)

In Guaymas
The large, colonial ****Playa de Cortés (tel 20548 or in the US (213) 391 6354) is actually on the shores of Bacochibampo Bay, in Colonia Miramar, the northern end of town, signposted off Highway 15. The cool, elegant rooms, each with its own fireplace,

look out onto the mountains or the bay. The grounds include a swimming pool, golf course and tennis courts, and the recent addition of a trailer park. The hotel staff will book cabins or vehicle space for ferry passengers, and make sure they get there on time.

Guaymas concentrates on cheaper hotels. The ***Flamingos (just off Highway 15 north, tel 20690) has clean, bright rooms and the advantage of a pool. Closer to the ferry (4 blocks) is the air-conditioned and practical **Rubi (Av Serdán, between Calles 29 and 30, tel 21069) or the **Impala (Calle 21, No 40, just off Av Serdán).

In San Carlos

The best beach, Algodones, has now been taken over by an unimaginative Howard Johnson complex and an exclusive, luxurious *****Club-Med village (tel 60166) with its hush of self-importance. Bookings must be made 24 hours in advance. The ****Fiesta San Carlos (km 8, tel 60229) has big, wholemeal rooms with views over the bay and sun-soaked balconies but is a long walk from the shops and restaurants. The motel **Creston (tel 60020), on the main road in, is the only cheaper place and is often full in the winter season.

EATING OUT

In Guaymas

Although the Motel Armida is bland, its restaurant L'Oeste (Blvd López Norte, tel 23050) serves succulent steaks and whole grilled red snapper. Moderate. Close by, the Xochimilco (Av Serdán, tel 27800) offers Mexican dishes in its garden restaurant and mariachi music every night. Moderate. The Del Mar (Av Serdán and Calle 17, tel 20226) is popular both for its fresh oysters and for the baseball games displayed on a giant satellite screen. Moderate.

There are seafood cafés around the plaza and Av Serdán, good for long, cheap, multi-course lunches. Try Tony's (near the post office; where Av Rodríguez crosses Calle Miguel Alemán). The ferry terminal has a last-minute café serving *quesadillas* and *burritos* and there are day-and-night fish-taco stalls beside the Fisherman's Monument on the main plaza.

In San Carlos

Restaurants in San Carlos promise a lot but often fail to come up with the goods. Exceptions are the raucous San Carlos Grill (Plaza San Carlos) which insists on keeping the margaritas flowing but does serve excellent Sonoran beef steaks and spare ribs. The Chinese Beijing (tel 60550) prepares stir-fried squid with ginger and local shrimps. Many of the motor-homers just use the supermarkets which now stock nostalgic cookies and peanut butter.

The Yaqui Reservation

Some 26 km southeast of Guaymas, the village of Cruz de Piedra marks the beginning of the Yaqui reservation. Yaqui history since 1519 is horrific. During colonial times, there were 150,000 Yaqui living in Sonora, predominantly along the banks of the Yaqui River. When Spanish mining and ranching infringed on their territory, they fought back fiercely. They were protected and pacified to a large extent by Jesuit missionaries who acted as intermediaries between Yaqui chiefs and the Spanish crown, restricting Spanish settlements and ensuring that basic land rights were recognized. With Mexican independence in 1820, the Yaqui lost their only support. Nevertheless they continued to farm their land and pay their taxes, even sending soldiers to fight for the Republic against the puppet-emperor Maximilian in the 1860s.

In the second half of the 19th century, renewed harassment turned into a holocaust. Yaqui land was sold by the dictatorial government of Porfirio Díaz, in his march for modernity, to friends and political allies, both Mexican and foreign. The incoming ranchers cared little for pre-independence Yaqui land rights. The Yaqui fought back. An army of 6000 Mexican soldiers was sent to 'subdue' them. Those that weren't killed outright were deported to the Yucatán as slaves on the henequen-rope-producing ranches, 3500 km away. Turner, a Californian writing in 1910, records that in 1892 the entire Yaqui population of Navojoa was imprisoned: so many of the men, women and children were hanged that the town's supply of rope was exhausted, even though each rope was used five or six times.

During the 1910 Revolution against Díaz, the few remaining Yaquis fought with General Obregón's revolutionary army to get their lands back. Promises were made but not until 1930 did President Lázaro Cárdenas make a reservation on the northern bank of the Yaqui River. In recent years, President Alemán dammed the river, to irrigate the southern bank and turn it into one of the most profitable regions in Mexico. It is said that when Cárdenas returned 30 years later, and saw that the water from the Yaqui River had been diverted away from the reservation, he could not hold back his tears.

Alamos

In a lone valley surrounded by the Sierra Madre Occidental, the peaceful colonial town of Alamos is so beautiful that it has been declared a national monument. It is reached by a gently winding road bordered by cacti and small trees. There are splashes of colour, the Schiaparelli pinks of the *amapa* trees or the white blooms of the *palos santos*, even during the hottest, driest months. One of the richest towns in Mexico in the 18th century, with abundant gold and silver mines, Alamos fell into a sad state of disrepair at the turn of this century when the mines closed. It was rediscovered in ruins by silver prospectors from Arizona in the 1940s. The Andalucian architecture, with crumbling Moorish arches and windows covered in magenta and vermilion bougainvillea, caught their imagination and others followed. Today, many of the stately white stuccoed colonial houses, once the palaces of gold miners, have been proudly restored by North American immigrants and they look much as they must have done in their prime. This restoration has not been overdone and there are still many derelict houses. Nor has the town become a big tourist 'destination', because the road stops at Alamos and few drivers bother to deviate from Highway 15. Donkeys and horses are more common than Nikon-filled tourist Pullmans. The best time to see the town is off season (April to October) when there are next to no visitors.

Almost all from Arizona, the North Americans range from consul to hippy, Wall Street success to nonentity. These self-styled aristocrats meld in with the local community as little as possible and most of them are only here during the winter. On the whole the Mexicans are delighted. They've done a lot for the town, providing a library, educational scholarships, theatre and English lessons. Nonetheless, the incomers are conscious of criticism, which a local magazine does its best to dispel. 'Unlike many expatriate colonies, drinking is not done to excess. Although intimate friendships develop, flirtations between one another's husband or wife is not condoned.' Anyone staying more than a day may well get caught up in the social intrigue of it all and wonder for months whether Bill, the ex-senator, is speaking again to John, the young but retired stockbroker.

GETTING AROUND
Modern Navojoa on Highway 15, 195 km south of Guaymas, has petrol stations, ice cream parlours, wide boulevards and hamburgers. The road to Alamos leads due east through 50 km of rolling hills.

There are hourly **buses** to Alamos from Navojoa and from Navojoa to all the towns on Highway 15. The Navojoa bus station is at Guerrero in the centre. Buses in Alamos come and go from the Alameda (northeast of the main square).

TOURIST INFORMATION
The tourist office (tel 80211) is on the main square under the Hotel los Portales (open 09.30–13.00 and 15.00–17.00). They can arrange horse riding and trips into the hills, with a day's notice.

WHAT TO SEE AND DO
A man in the main square draws his cart, selling *raspados*, scratchings of ice drowned in a sticky fruit syrup. Children pour out of every doorway clutching fistfuls of coins while benign grandmothers watch from the wrought-iron seats which line the park. The cathedral which overlooks it has the wide beaming face of a simple country cousin, with an afterthought of a tower stuck to the left-hand side. The plain neoclassical interior is disappointingly austere. Below the main square, the locals gather in the **Alameda** where the market has a flurry of chickens and a mass of small food stalls selling tacos and avocados. The shops around are filled with lassoes, boots and bridles for farmers who come in from the hills. It's a far cry from the tranquil splendour of the splendid American palaces above.

Museo Costumbrista de Sonora
(Open 10.00–13.00 and 16.00–18.00.)
The museum on the main square has a homely feel. Old clothes, typewriters and sewing machines have been proudly donated by the older families. It all gives a wonderful sense of place and a feeling of how things were in more prosperous days. Dr Alfonso Ortiz Tirado is given a whole room to himself. This son of Alamos reached international fame as a tenor. A 19th-century kitchen has been recreated complete with a 20th-century maquette of a blonde Stepford housewife, whose stiffened joints make her lurch with unintended lasciviousness in one corner.

324

The Prison

Up above the Palacio Municipal, prisoners, padding lion-like behind bars, are kept incarcerated on the top of Guadalupe Hill, passing the interminable boredom of their days making horse-hair keyrings. No one is in for more than drunk-and-disorderliness and visitors are always a welcome relief—to the guards as much as the prisoners.

Camino Real

There are still traces of the cobbles of the old coach road linking Alamos to El Fuerte, another rich mine. Today the dusty track is only passable by horse, jeep or the sporadic bus which goes to Tojibampo. It is worth going along for the ride as much as anything. The Mayo hamlet of Tiachibe takes about 2 hours. Cirilo Solis Escalante, half-Yaqui and half-Mayo, can organize trips (contact him through the Casa de los Tesoros hotel). The villagers sell masks and woollen blankets. They speak some Spanish but mostly Mayo. A smattering of phrases which may help are: *ketcham alea* (hello, how are you?), *kyeta* (very well, thanks), *chokori* (thank you), *aye ki si wata* (how much?) and *ah kum bi cha se* (where?).

Inside Information

For the curious, many homes and gardens are open on Saturday mornings. Most of them look as if they've stepped out of the pages of glossy magazines. Contact Elizabeth Nuzum (Comercio 2). Her own delightful house is filled with pieces from all over the country showing a loving eye for Mexican detail. Money from these tours is being used to build up the public library.

SHOPPING

Elizabeth Nuzum also has a craft shop below the church at the end of Calle Comercio, acting as agent for whatever the locals want to sell. Fifty per cent of the price goes to the artisan and everything is made in the area.

FIESTAS

The town celebrates the festival of Purissima Concepción from 8 to 12 December with candles and processions. Nearby Aduana has its festival on 20 November.

WHERE TO STAY   (area code 642)

Once the treasury, then a convent, the ****Casa de los Tesoros (Av Obregón 10, tel 80010) has 16 high-beamed bedrooms with rounded chimney places and tiled bathrooms. They lead off ample patios filled with mango trees, where old-timers assemble every evening to chew the cud over margaritas. Opposite what was once a Japanese silk factory, the ****Mansión de la Condesa Magdalena (Av Obregón 2, tel 80221) is the beautifully restored hotel where presidents stay. The 13 rooms open onto an airy courtyard. ***Los Portales (Av Juárez 6, tel 80211) was once the place to be, with log fires blazing welcomingly in every bedroom and drinks on the balcony, but recent family disputes have allowed it to become run down. It's still worth having a look, as the colonial courtyard and rooms used to be lovely and may have recovered themselves. Under the Portales there is a wide courtyard where the family rent a couple of basic rooms, which smell of the chickens which have been hastily shooed out. It's a bed and no more, but the

325

family is friendly. ***Acosta (on the road to Navojoa, tel 80246) is a trailer park which also has motel rooms and a swimming pool.

EATING OUT
Elsa Duarte de Grajeda of **Las Palmeras** (on the main square, Cárdenas 9, tel 80065) is an ample señora with a generous smile, who serves her guests plate after plate of home-cooking. These include chillies stuffed with cheese, enchiladas in a red colorado chilli sauce and bone-shattering black coffee. Her cheery blue and white café is to one side of the museum. Cheap. The dining room in the **Casa de los Tesoros** is warmed by log fires in the winter. They serve set meals for guests but are open to all-comers for Mexican home-cooking. Moderately expensive. The hotel **Mansión** has a good dining room, serving tumblers of freshly pressed grapefruit juice with plates of eggs, bacon and fried banana for breakfast. Moderate. The **Caracol** on the road in from Navojoa is a good restaurant worth stopping at. It serves an international mix such as cream of onion soup (often with oysters slipped in) and fresh fish chowder. The owner was married to a North American and speaks excellent English. Moderate. **Polos** (Zaragoza 4, tel 80001) is a café with a telephone, patronized more for the spice of its long-distance conversations than for its food. Cheap.

Los Mochis

Knowing that Los Mochis is going to be Bedlam makes it bearable. For anyone caught unawares, it can turn into a nightmare of missed connections and closed hotels. Just inside the state of Sinaloa, it's a modern sprawl which squats ignominiously on a promontory, leaning towards the Baja California peninsula. Spider-like, it controls a web of communications, and the tourist is bound to get enmeshed in its clutches. It's the terminus for the Chihuahua–Pacífico railway and the La Paz ferry and a major town on coastal Highway 15. Don't even attempt to connect train with ferry or bus with plane. A night stop is almost inevitable. It's not impossible that the whole thing is a conspiracy to get tourists into a town that they would otherwise avoid like the plague. To add to the confusion, Los Mochis is on Pacific time (like Baja California and Sonora), one hour behind the rest of Mexico. It is easiest to surrender at the beginning and blow out on taxis and a good hotel for the night.

GETTING AROUND
By Air: The airport is southwest of the city, with daily flights for Mexico City, La Paz and Tijuana. The carriers are Aeroméxico (Leyva 168 Nte, tel 52582) and Aerocalifornia (Hidalgo 440, tel 28466).
By Bus: The first-class Tres Estrellas bus station (tel 21757) is in Alvaro Obregón, two blocks southeast of Leyva. It is open 24 hours a day, and buses come and go every half-hour for Mexico City, Mazatlán, Guadalajara, Hermosillo and Tijuana.
By Car: On Highway 15, Los Mochis is 460 km south of Hermosillo and 432 km north of Mazatlán. A 78-km paved road leads northeast into the foothills of the Sierra Madre, passing through El Sufragio and El Fuerte.
By Train: There are two railway stations. The Chihuahua–Pacífico (tel 29385), for the Copper Canyon, is 2 km southeast of town (see The Chihuahua–Pacífico Railway). The

Ferrocarril Pacífico, for trains going up and down the coast, is some 50 km inland at El Sufragio. There are two northbound and two southbound trains a day. To give the tourist a nervous tic, they've added the extra challenge of putting El Sufragio onto Central time, one hour ahead, so make sure to check the timetable. In any event, few want to take the coastal railway from here as the bus is much quicker.

By Ferry: The daily ferry (tel 20141) to La Paz in Baja California goes from **Toplobampo**, 24 km south of Los Mochis. It takes 8 hours and leaves at 08.00 hours, though it's usually a couple of hours late. There is a ticket office in town (Juárez 125, tel 20035) which is only open from 08.00 to 12.30. Tickets for cars must be booked well in advance. **In Town**: Av Leyva is the main street, running southwest from Highway 15. No hotel is more than 3 minutes' walk from here.

Local buses for the railway station at **El Sufragio** (marked 'San Blas') and the ferry terminal at **Topolobampo** leave from the second-class bus station, Alianza de Autotransportes del Norte, in Alvaro Obregón, between Leyva and Angel Flores. However, the safest bet is to take a taxi, as almost all connections (the train and ferry) leave so early in the morning that the buses won't be running. There are always taxis outside the Hotel Santa Anita on the corner of Leyva and Hidalgo.

WHERE TO STAY   (area code 681)
Los Mochis has few hotels and those are all either expensive or dingy. The ****Santa Anita (tel 57046, tlx 53254, fax 681 20046) is a large, modern hotel in the centre, where the train staff and tour groups stay. Cheaper hotels are around the Tres Estrellas bus terminal, such as the **Los Arcos or the *Hidalgo. All these are a taxi ride from the railway station, although the Santa Anita sends a minibus to meet booked guests.

Mazatlán

Just below the Tropic of Cancer, Mazatlán unwinds lazily along 23 km of coast. Its long beaches stretch the length of a peninsula between Bahía Urias to the east and the Pacific ocean to the west. The modern northern end of town, the Zona Dorada, is an unashamed resort, well worn in by package tourists. It is not a very ritzy resort but an affordable second-best, and a welcome break after the long drive from the north. The older southern part of town is anxious to cast off the lager-lout image of the resort and is starting to refurbish its colonial buildings. It also hosts an international cultural festival every November.

The original town is much the more interesting. As an important fishing port and trading station, Mazatlán grew up in carefree splendour and filled its centre with large elegant houses, once painted with a bright disregard for colour. Now worn and faded, they still disdain the modern purpose-built towers of the present. Balconies teeter dangerously and railings twist off at angles. Old doors lean awkwardly and houses sag under the weight of their years. Most have been abandoned by the prosperous, for modern American-style villas. The town faces north, turning its back on the busy port in the south where the shrimp industry flourishes.

The much-feared Spaniard Nuño de Guzmán colonized the port in the 16th century but it was such barren terrain that it lay dormant until the 19th century. Just as it was becoming established as an important Pacific port, it suffered a series of blockades. In

1847, US forces marched down from the northeast border and closed the port. Then in 1864 the French, busily fighting to install the puppet-emperor Maximilian, bombarded the city and controlled it for a couple of years. Later, during the American Civil War, there were plans afoot to turn the whole of Sinaloa into a slave state. The plans didn't materialize and the port was subsequently taken over by Germans. The land was cheap and they brought new-fangled agricultural techniques which made the barren soil fertile. Their influence is everywhere today. The big brewery which produces Pacífico beer is of German origin. The Sinaloan *corrido* is danced back and forth to the music of the *banda* (band music), whose solid underlying rhythms come from German-introduced brasses and drums. These can be heard in the main square every Sunday night from 19.00. So keen are the descendants of these early settlers to advertise their origins that many cars sport German stickers.

GETTING AROUND
By Air: The airport is 16 km south of town, a 40-minute trip by bus or taxi from the Zona Dorada. There are daily flights to the US (San Francisco, Los Angeles, Houston and Denver) as well as to all major cities in Mexico. Three airlines use the airport: Mexicana (at the airport, tel 25767, or in Av Camarón Sábalo, tel 35554), Aeroméxico (Av Camarón Sábalo 310, tel 41111) and Delta (at the airport, tel 23354).

By Bus: The first-class bus station is in Calle Río Tamazula where it crosses Carretera Internacional Norte (tel 17625). It's a 5-minute walk from Av del Mar. Buses leave hourly for destinations all over the republic, principally between Mexico City and Nogales.

By Car: Mazatlán is on Highway 15, 1202 km south of Nogales on the US border and 522 km north of Guadalajara. It is a 5-hour drive from Los Mochis (432 km) and 3 hours from Tepic (278 km). Mazatlán is also the junction for a winding 6-hour journey eastwards through the Sierra Madre to Durango, along Highway 40, which many claim to be the most beautiful road in Mexico (see Mazatlán to Durango, below).

By Ferry: The ferry sails daily to and from La Paz in Baja California, taking 16 hours. It costs next to nothing to cross as a foot passenger, but it's more comfortable to rent a cabin. With two bunks and a bathroom, these cost less than a night in a two-star hotel. The terminal is on Playa Sur Prolongación Carnaval, by the port (tel 17020).

By Train: The 'Ferrocarril del Pacífico' runs daily between Nogales on the US border and Mexico City. The southbound train leaves Mazatlán early in the morning and the northbound in the early evening. The station is to the south of town, next to the port, and tickets can be bought here (tel 15892) or from Viajes Harsuna (in Av Camarón Sábalo 3315, tel 41239).

In Town: Mazatlán is divided into two distinct areas, an apt reflection of its split personality. The new Zona Dorada in the north was built as a resort. Running the length of Av Camarón Sábalo, it consists entirely of beaches and hotels, the haunt of red-legged tourists, most of whom don't move out of its neon lights. The old town, in the south, around the port and Cerro de la Nevería, is a maze of small streets, winding and twisting over two hills. It is cooler and more dignified, with a slumbering charm. A coastal road connects the two, called Av del Mar in the north but becoming Olas Altas shortly before it arrives at the port in the old town.

Town buses marked 'Sábalo' go up and down between the centre (from Juárez next to the market) and the Zona Dorada: they run every 10 minutes between 06.00 and 23.00. In Mazatlán the taxis are called *pulmonías*—open jeeps shaded by striped canvas, which are constantly going up and down the coastal road.

Car and Bike Hire: Cars can be rented by the day or week from: Hertz (Av del Mar 1111, tel 36060), Avis (Av Camarón Sábalo 314, tel 36200) or Budget (Av Camarón Sábalo 402, tel 32000). Mopeds and bicycles can be rented from a number of places up and down Av Camarón Sábalo.

TOURIST INFORMATION

The office in the Zona Dorada (Loaiza 100, tel 32545) is hidden away in a courtyard, opposite the Los Sábalos Hotel. The staff are helpful and efficient, speaking better English than the English. Another less informative office is in Olas Altas 1300 (tel 51222). There are US (tel 12685) and Canadian (tel 37320) consulates for emergencies. (The British use the Canadian consulate.)

WHAT TO SEE AND DO

New Mazatlán is above all a beach resort, concentrating on package tourists who want to surf, parasail and fish. The old town is largely ignored by tourists. It's pleasant to wander around its streets without constantly being offered a breakfast for two in exchange for buying a time-share condominium.

Acuario

(Two blocks behind Av del Mar in Av de los Deportes, tel 17815; open 10.00–17.00; closed Mon; adm.)

The aquarium is filled with moray eels, sea horses, turtles and every colour and shape of fish from the tropical seas. The lack of space makes one want to put them all back where they came from, but there is nevertheless an eerie thrill in being nose to nose with a bull shark. The auditorium shows films every hour and there is also an eminently missable performing seal show in the afternoon.

The Old Town

The colonial heart of the town stretches behind the Hotel Siesta, down Calle Venus where the military hospital is, around the museum and toward Plaza Malacada where the old theatre is being given a face lift. Until the Revolution, a large European community— French, Italian and German—lived in the area and their architectural influence has rubbed off, particularly in the theatre and the Italian portals.

The tiny **Archaeological Museum** (Sixto Osuna 76, tel 53502; open 10.00–13.00 and 16.00–19.00; closed Mon; adm) has four airless rooms with a scattering of pre-Hispanic pieces found in the area. The earliest nomadic inhabitants were tall and corpulent, renowned for their longevity. They wore little clothing other than loincloths and, for decoration, arm and leg bands, earrings, nose pieces and a feather headband, the *tocado*. They lived near rivers or the sea, eating seafood and cactus fruits, or deer and berries in the mountains (Mazatlán means 'place of the deer'). A room is devoted to the *ulama*, the pre-Hispanic ball game in which the ball was propelled by the hips. It is still played in exactly the same way today, in the hills around Mazatlán.

The main square is tiny but lush, filled with mango trees, royal palms and Indian laurels. Classical music belts out from loudspeakers on the bandstand, and old men snooze on benches all around. In a small café under the bandstand, sweethearts hold hands, children fight and eat ices, and off-duty shoeshine men read their newspapers. The square is dominated by an enormous neo-gothic cathedral which is only worth a visit for the cool inside. There is a busy market round the corner with a mass of small cafés on the top floor.

BEACHES
The quietest beach is **Playa Los Cerritos**, at the northernmost point of town. The waves are often rough and it tends to be a surfer's haunt. Three small islands face the Zona Dorada. The **Isla de los Venados** is surprisingly empty, particularly on the southern side which is indented with small sheltered coves. There are no hawkers and no facilities. It is only a 10-minute ride over from the Zona Dorada hotels: a boat leaves from the El Cid every 1½ hrs. Few people tear themselves away from the most popular strip of beach, **Playa Sábalo**, which runs in front of the hotels and is always filled with sunbathers, hawkers and novitiate scuba divers.

Chico's Beach Club on Camarón Sábalo (tel 40777) hires out all manner of **beach equipment**, from rubber rings to parasails.

HORSE RIDING
Horses can be hired from Guadalupe Ranch in Calle Gaviota, behind the Zona Dorada. They mostly go up and down the beach but can be persuaded to go further afield, riding ability permitting.

CARNIVAL
Mazatlán claims to have the third biggest Mardi Gras carnival in the world (after Rio and New Orleans). During the day it is fairly circumspect, as formal processions of floats bear costumed dancers through the streets. During a popular dance, the Queen of the Carnival is elected, along with her opposite number, the *Rey Feo*. At night the people take over. Olas Altas is packed with dancers, singers, drinkers and visitors, all wearing masks and intent on keeping the party going for as long as possible. The carnival lasts a week (the week before Lent), after which, bleary-eyed, Mazatlán sleeps it off and returns to normality. Book a hotel well in advance.

WHERE TO STAY   (area code 678)
The best time to go to Mazatlán is off-season (April to November), when the rates are low. In September and October there are so few people that prices are reduced by over 50 per cent. For an overnight stop on the way south, it is worth pressing on an extra half-hour, past Mazatlán, to Copala (see under Mazatlán to Durango, below).

Zona Dorada
The smartest hotels are all in the Zona Dorada. A common alternative to a hotel room is a suite with basic kitchen facilities. Hotels are used to extended families squeezing into tiny rooms. Painted in unmistakable pastel shades, *******Pueblo Bonito** (Camarón Sábalo, tel 43700, tlx 66741) is new but filled with colonial detail, with tiles in the bathrooms and terraces dripping with terra-cotta pots full of plants. All rooms come with

a kitchen (well equipped with coffee makers, toasters, orange squeezers and Mexican ceramic bowls) and cushy sofas. *****El Quijote (Camarón Sábalo, tel 43609, tlx 66792) is smaller and more intimate, with well-decorated rooms facing the sea. All rooms have kitchens. A white and pink building covered in brilliant flowers, ***Suites La Misión (Camarón Sábalo, tel 32533) is just across the road from the beach and well run with little fuss. An alternative on the sea front opposite is ****Suites Las Flores (Av Loaza 212, tel 35011): the kitchens are spartan, and some smell rancid, but there is a good view and the windows can be kept open.

Avenida del Mar
Between the hotel strip and town, still on the sea front, ***Las Arenas (Av del Mar 1910, tel 20000, tlx 66768) is a well-respected older hotel with a small pool, only 2 minutes from the bus station. The smallish rooms with fridges are a reasonable buy. Similarly, ***Las Jacarandas (Av del Mar 2500, tel 41177) is a family-run beach hotel with a small heart-shaped pool and big bedrooms. Characterless, but serviceable and respectable, ***de Cima (tel 27311) looks over the sea midway between the old and the new town. It has a large secluded pool and a good restaurant, El Galeón.

The Old Town
On the sea front, the **Siesta (Olas Altas 11, tel 12640) is undeterred by the bright lights down the road. The courtyard inside looks like a Louisiana showboat with wooden lattice work and rows of deep bottle-green doors set into white walls, leading into large rooms. Clean and simple, it is the best buy in Mazatlán. Nearby, ***Belmar (Olas Altas 166, tel 20799) is a rambling rabbit warren—old and worn but still going strong, always popular with Mexicans and Europeans. The older section is more interesting, and more dishevelled, than a more recent addition with dark panelled rooms. The higher up the room, the less the buses drown out the lapping waves. Worn rocking chairs line the reception which is filled with cavernous nooks and crannies. The generous swimming pool compensates for the tiny strip of much-used beach.

EATING OUT
Restaurants in the Zona Dorada cater for the passing tourist trade and most are either lacklustre or gimmicky. Food is much better in the old town.

Moderate
El Marinero (Av del Mar) is Mazatlán's most famous fish restaurant. Nets hang down from the ceiling and it is always packed to the brim with locals. Try the seafood platter which comes on a hot charcoal burner with shrimp, frogs' legs, oyster and fillet, or a *habachi* with four kinds of jumbo shrimps. It also serves excellent fish chowder, smoked marlin and whatever is in season. El Mirador, on top of the Cerro del Vingia, offers more seafood, unpretentious and home-cooked. Try the *ceviche* of shrimps marinaded in lime, coriander, onions and tomato.

The Shrimp Bucket (Olas Altas 11, tel 16350) is a Mazatlán institution that has been going since the 1950s. True to its name, it serves clay buckets filled to the brim with fried shrimps. The barbecued ribs are also good. Set in the cool garden courtyard of the Hotel La Siesta, it is less riotous than many of its counterparts in the Zona Dorada. Fully

Mexican **Doney** (Escobedo at 5 de Mayo) has nothing Italian about it except the owner's memory of a Roman restaurant, which inspired the name. Opened in the 1950s, it has a solemn dignity with a high brick ceiling and starched tablecloths. Sepia tints of old Mazatlán line the walls. It specializes in *chilaquiles* (a casserole of tortilla with a chilli sauce) and *cortadillos* (chopped steak with potatoes in a green tomato sauce). **Tres Islas**, on the beach under a wide palapa, between the Holiday Inn and El Cid hotels, serves enormous seafood platters, smoked oysters or octopus. It's a popular haunt with families and is always busy.

Cheap

Just down from the Siesta Hotel, the **Copa de Leche** is a good café to sit and sip coffee in while the waves roll to the shore. It also serves shrimps, fish tacos and *quesadillas*, and an infinite variety of tequila combinations. **Janito** (Serdán 1809, tel 12983, on the corner with Ocampo, just around the corner from the market) looks like a dive from the outside, but serves authentic Cantonese food within. A lot of Asiatics came to work on the railways in the 19th century and a large and prosperous Asiatic community still lives in Mazatlán (their business interests include the supermarket chain, Casa Ley). Many of them come to eat here. **Casa Naturista** (Zaragoza) is a small vegetarian restaurant, serving lunches only. Alternatively, **Vegetariano Plus** (Leonero Valle 208, one block behind the cathedral) provides a three-course comida corrida which runs out by 15.00.

If cooking for yourself, buy fresh fish off the boats in the port first thing in the morning. The central market is filled with fresh fruit and vegetables and the Zona Dorada has many small supermarkets. The lager to drink is Pacífico, which is made in the large white brewery beyond the port.

Mazatlán to Durango

East of Mazatlán, Highway 40 cuts inland, over the Sierra Madre to Durango (313 km) and the colonial heart of central Mexico. It's the first road south of the border to attempt the crossing. The journey still takes over 6 hours, winding and twisting up through the mountains from the humid tropical coast, past colonial mining villages, through gnarled oak to pine forests at the top.

GETTING AROUND

By Bus: There are eight buses a day between Mazatlán and Durango (7 hrs).
By Car: Take Highway 15 south out of Mazatlán to Villa Unión; then head east on Highway 40, via Concordia and Copala, up into the sierra. There are petrol stations at Concordia and Revolcadero.

WHAT TO SEE

Concordia

Some 30 km from Mazatlán, this colonial mining village is famed for its ceramics. The 18th-century church in the centre has an elaborate baroque facade propped up by a stalwart tower. A secret passage allegedly runs from here to the nearby Capilla del Carmen, used by the Xixime tribe when fleeing from the Spanish in the sierra. Banamex, the bank, has cornered the best building in the square, its windows capped by Moorish arches.

The best place to buy ceramics is **Chendopiña**, which supplies whole sets to the better hotels and restaurants in Mazatlán. It has been going since the turn of the century and everything is still made by hand. The yard is strewn with half-finished pots and shards of pottery. The workshop is a couple of blocks behind the church, in an unnamed street: ask directions from the main square.

Copala

Copala is a tiny village of cobbled streets and red-tiled roofs. Nothing much happens, and the arrival of a few tourists is invariably greeted with a genuine concern for their welfare. There is no telephone, no rush and a pervasive, sleepy smell of horses. The 18th-century church is cracked and stripped of adornments, barring a faded wooden *retablo*. The creaking old seats are made of wooden slats with iron grilles at the end. A small museum in the square displays a few archaeological bits and pieces, some relating to Copala's foundation as a mining village in 1565.

The road continues into the state of Durango, climbing higher and higher into the lovely National Park of Puerto de los Angeles, past the rustic village of El Salto. (For Durango, see South on the Durango Road.)

WHERE TO STAY AND EAT

In **Copala**, the small colonial *Posada San José (no tel) is a delight. There are only four rooms, each with a four-poster bed, leading off a terrace which looks out over the village square. The old house is built on the side of a hill so that everything is at a confusing level. The restaurant downstairs serves big helpings of home-cooking. Another restaurant, **Daniel's**, is Tex–Mex-run by a North American who took it over from his mother. He continues to serve good home-cooking, including his famous banana and coconut pie.

Cactus overlooking a grave, typical of the northwest

High in mountain pines, 10 km up the road, the **Hotel Villa Real** (no tel) was originally run by a Bavarian couple, though now it is mainly in the hands of their Mexican staff. Guests are treated like members of the family and everyone eats sauerkraut, *bratwurst* and *nudels* together in the small dining room.

Baja California

If it were lush and rich, one could understand the pull, but it is fierce and hostile and sullen. But we know we must go back if we live and we don't know why.

John Steinbeck found himself reluctantly hooked to this knobbly finger dipping into the warm waters of the Gulf of California. Some 1300 km long—longer than Italy—Baja California is commonly referred to as Mexico's land apart. For many years the Spanish thought it was an island. Even today, politically, geographically and mentally, it has little affinity with the mainland and is far closer to California.

Until the paved road was completed in 1973, it was an inaccessible, unexplored mystery. Nowadays, when heading south in a hot, crowded bus, it is hard to imagine any reason to stop. The peninsula is one of the most inhospitable in the Americas: large parts of it are arid, waterless desert, filled with sharp rocks, rattlesnakes and cactuses. So dry is it that the hurricanes which come between late August and mid-October are seen as benevolent sources of rain. Throughout the rest of the year, it may rain only three or four times. But for thousands of rugged, outdoor Californians, complete with motor-homes, surfboards and mountain bikes, it has everything: sea, fish, peace and space. Without these trappings, Baja California hasn't much to offer. The secret bays will remain secret unless you have a four-wheel-drive truck to get to them. The average tourist, with his red neck and white shorts, won't have a chance to get off the road and will simply be bored by most of it and fleeced by the rest of it.

Chaparral-covered hills rise from the sea up to the mountains in northern Baja California, but the road continues remorselessly south to the true desert between San Quintín and La Paz. Without the time or the resources for more than a taste of Baja California, bypass the north and stick to the southern half: the oases of San Ignacio and Mulegé, the mission town of Loreto and prosperous bay-side La Paz. These can all be seen in a week, perhaps as a beach extension to the Chihuahua–Pacífico railway trip, taking the ferry from Los Mochis to La Paz and then travelling north to Sta Rosalía from where another ferry returns to Guaymas on the Sonoran mainland.

History

Baja California's history has been shaky ever since it was torn away from the mainland by the San Andres Fault, 20 million years ago. Again and again, brave attempts were made to conquer the desert but they consistently came to nothing.

The first people to wend their way down Baja's length were nomadic groups, pushed south in search of game and land, leaving behind cave paintings in brilliant hues of red, yellow, black and white. They lived off cactus fruits, fish, rabbits and deer. When meat was scarce, it is said that they tied string around each morsel, chewed it, swallowed it and then pulled it back up to hand on to the next person.

In the 1520s the audacious conqueror of the Aztecs, Hernán Cortés, sent explorers over who came back with mythic tales of 'an island rich in gold and pearls, inhabited solely by women, who permitted only occasional visits from men and ruthlessly cast forth all male children born among them.' The land was named in reference to an 11th-century romance, which told of a mythical island paradise—California. Cortés himself came in 1535. He found nothing, and left a short-lived colony in La Paz to the Jesuit missionaries.

PIRATES

Spanish galleons, returning with exotic booty from the Philippines, sailed down the coast, chased by English and Dutch pirates and privateers—among them, Francis Drake in the *Golden Hind*. In 1587, the Spanish saw two sails waiting for them under the arched rocks of Los Cabos and were horrified to find that they belonged to 'an English corsair and thief Don Tomás Candiens of Tembley, a young man of little age'. The intrepid Thomas Cavendish, following in the footsteps of Drake, had lain in wait for a month, hidden by rocks that reminded him of the Needles off the Isle of Wight. He savagely attacked the overloaded Spanish galleon, sailing off with a fortune in silks, pearls and spices. Not to be outdone, the Spaniards felt they had to try again with the forgotten peninsula. They sent heavily armed expeditions to found settlements, but these were thwarted again and again.

THE CHURCH

The Church took a surprisingly long time to establish itself in Baja California. Early missionaries didn't have the strength to do more than make a sign of the cross, beg for some water and expire on the spot. One of these, just before he died, wrote that the peninsula was 'a pathless, waterless, thornful rock, sticking up between two oceans'. It was left to the Jesuit, Juan de Salvatierra, a man of unshakable faith, to make the first inroads. The son of an aristocratic Lombard and a Spanish noblewoman, he was born in Milan in 1648 and was ordained a Jesuit priest at the age of 20. In the New World, he first spent a decade in the Sierra Tarahumara of Chihuahua, before joning the Jesuit colleges of Guadalajara and then Tepotzotlán. In 1697 he left for the dry, cactus-studded land of Lower California. Accompanied by ten men, including six soldiers, he founded the first mission in Loreto. For the rest of his life he continued voyaging up and down the Californias, only returning to the mainland to die in Guadalajara in 1717.

When the Jesuits were expelled by the Spanish crown in 1768, the Franciscans, under Fray Junipero Serra, took up their mantle for five years before giving up and handing over control to the Dominicans, who built nine more missions between 1774 and 1834. These missionaries kept rough population estimates which recorded that the indigenous people shrank in numbers from 42,000 in 1697 to 5500 in 1777. The Europeans had brought over cattle which ate the meagre food that the people lived on. They also introduced diseases, ranging from the common cold to syphilis and smallpox. In 1864, in a desperate bid to combat depopulation, a North American, Jacobo P Leese, was granted leave to colonize the land between latitude 24° 20' and 31° (roughly between Ensenada and La Paz), in return for 100,000 pesos of gold and the promise that the 200 families accompanying him would consider themselves Mexican citizens. This colony also failed, limping on for a mere seven years. Only in this century has the trend been reversed, particularly around the burgeoning tourist resorts of Los Cabos and La Paz.

WILLIAM WALKER
Despite its manifold disadvantages, many people have attempted to make something of the peninsula. In October 1853 the bigoted, egocentric and charismatic William Walker, a journalist for the *San Francisco Herald*, recruited an army of southern sympathizers and sailed for Baja California. His aim was to seize Sonora and Baja and make them into slave states. Unopposed, he 'took' La Paz, proclaimed himself president and moved his paltry 46 troops all over the sparsely populated peninsula. Within weeks, 230 more men joined him, mostly from Kentucky and Tennessee, but also from Germany and Ireland (the only two countries outside the United States of which Walker approved). His men starved, his cattle died and he eventually had to surrender to US troops. Although he was acquitted of inciting racial tension, the event only aroused growing Mexican suspicions that North Americans wanted more than just investment in Baja California's land and mines.

The Border Towns

Tijuana made its money during the US prohibition years when gambling and prostitution were legalized and visitors came in droves. It has been pulled up by its boot straps by a PR-conscious local council, but nothing can turn it into a 'destination' for anyone but weekending college students and day-tripping shoppers. Its one saving grace, for a late breakfast or lunch, is the Yoghurt Place (Calle Cantera 4, tel 82006; take a bus or car to 'Playas' and the bull ring). This excellent and cheap vegetarian restaurant offers freshly squeezed fruit drinks and mountainous salads, as well as sorbet ice creams and large set lunches.

Mexicali, the other border town, has no saving graces. It is a dustier version of Tijuana, less grasping but just as dire. San Felipe, 190 km (2½ hrs) south of Mexicali on the Gulf of California, is another weekend haunt. It has a reputation (which it is trying to lose) for rowdy, all-night tequila parties on the beach.

All land traffic from California must pass through one of the two border towns, but avoid lingering in either. Tijuana, 109 km (1 hr) north of Ensenada, is the more convenient crossing.

GETTING AROUND TIJUANA
Over 30 million people a year cross the San Ysidro/Tijuana border, making it the busiest crossing in the world. Most of these simply walk across to Tijuana but those travelling further south or staying more than 72 hours must have a tourist card. These are free, validated by a birth certificate or passport, and normally available at any of the border crossings, travel agents, Mexican consulates or tourist offices (eg Los Angeles, tel 213 659 8730).
By Air: Tijuana airport is to the east of the city, by the Otay Mesa border crossing. Daily flights leave for all cities in the west of Mexico, the capital (10 daily), Villahermosa in

Tabasco and Mérida in the Yucatán. Tickets can be bought in travel agents or at the airport: Mexicana (tel 832850), Aeroméxico (tel 832700), Aerocalifornia (tel 842006). **By Bus:** The modern depot in Tijuana is 5 km southeast of the centre, on the airport road. To get there, cross over the dried river bed on the first pedestrian bridge after the border post and take an urban bus marked 'Buena Vista' or 'Central Camionera' from Calle 2a as it crosses Revolución. Tres Estrellas de Oro and Transportes Norte de Sonora run first-class services all over Mexico, and Autotransportes de Baja California (ABC) to Ensenada and throughout the peninsula. La Paz is 22 hours away, Guadalajara 36 hours, and Mexico City 48 hours.

By Car: Car permits are unnecessary in Baja California but they are required on the mainland and hence for ferry travel. The permits are free and available at all crossings but must be accompanied by proof of ownership of the car. Mexican insurance is not compulsory but is a good idea: anyone involved in an accident who does not have an acceptable policy or immediate proof of payment is liable to be held by the authorities. Non-Mexican insurance is not valid in Mexico. *In extremis*, last-minute insurance is sold at the border.

Interstate 5 from San Diego leads to the San Ysidro/Tijuana border. At weekends this crossing can be very congested. If so, try Otay Mesa, east of the airport and Interstate 5. There are two roads south to Ensenada, the fast 109-km toll road (*cuota*) Highway 1-D, or the old, slower 106-km Highway 1. Calle Internacional runs west along the fenced-off border to Highway 1-D, past a no-man's land constantly marshalled by US helicopters and police, where illegal immigrants (known as '*pollos*') are willing to risk everything to cross into the US.

Car rental in Mexico is universally expensive, equal to the US, although the price of petrol is very low. Many San Diegan companies offer rental and insurance for Mexico: try Fullers Ford in San Diego (tel 426 4440).

By Train: The San Diego trolley, a swift overland train (tel toll-free in the US (800) 872 7245), is the cheapest way to travel to the San Ysidro border. There is no rail network in Baja California.

GETTING AROUND MEXICALI

The border formalities are the same as in Tijuana. Mexicali and Calexico, its sister city in the US, share absurd hybrid names (from California and Mexico) and the status of duty-free ports. This encourages day-trippers who walk over the border, take the waiting taxis or minibuses to the centre, and leave again within a few hours.

By Bus: The bus station (Central Camionera) is southeast of the border, on the edge of the Zona Rosa shopping area, at the junction of Av Independencia and Calzada López Mateos. Greyhound buses from the Calexico terminal go to the Central Camionera every hour. Tres Estrellas and Norte de Sonora service the mainland and ABC services the peninsula.

By Car: Interstate 111 from Calexico crosses the border to the east of the Río Nuevo. It then bears right, changing its name to Calzada López Mateos. Stick with it through the business area of the city for 6 km until the junction of Highway 5 (to the rough-and-ready beach resort of San Felipe) and Highway 2. Highway 2 heads west to Tijuana or east to the mainland of Mexico, joining up eventually with Highway 15 to Guaymas (836 km), Mazatlán (1616 km) and Mexico City (2750 km).

337

By Train: Mexicali is the only railway station in Baja California (tel (656) 572386). The station is on Calzada López Mateos, opposite the bus station, at the junction with Calle Ulises Irigoyen. Urban buses ply to and from the border every 20 minutes. The Mexico City Express (which is anything but express) leaves at 08.00 (tickets are on sale at the station from 05.00), arriving in the Pacific-coast resort of Mazatlán at 06.55 the following day, Guadalajara at 19.05 and Mexico City at 07.55, 48 hours later.

TOURIST INFORMATION
The tourist office in **Tijuana** is in the Plaza Patria on Blvd Agua Caliente (open 10.00–19.00, Mon–Fri; tel 681 9492). There are more central offices at the airport, the international border and the Chamber of Commerce (Calle 1 at Av Revolución). The Procuraduría de Protección al Turista in the Centro de Gobierno (tel 684 2138) can help sort out any legal wrangles.

The tourist office in **Mexicali** (open 10.00–19.00, Mon–Fri; tel 72561) is on Calzada López Mateos, where it crosses Calle Camelias, an inconvenient 2 km south of the border.

Ensenada

Ensenada, 109 km (1 hr) south of the US border, is a relaxed version of frenetic Tijuana, with wide open boulevards and beaches, fringing the shore of the Bay of Todos Santos. Every weekend under-age Californians come down to drink and surf, but during the week it reverts to calm. It is a much better overnight stop than Tijuana and the last town of any size on the way south, before La Paz.

History
Ensenada was discovered in 1602 by Sebastián Vizcaíno, who was determined to found a permanent settlement there. Lack of fresh water put paid to his hopes and it wasn't settled for two centuries. Spanish galleons, laden with silks and spices from the Orient, stopped off on their way down to Acapulco but were plagued by pirates. Later on, whalers and fur traders called in, and in the early 19th century ranchers settled the bay area. For a brief moment, in 1870, Baja California held its breath as gold was discovered in the hills nearby. Ensenada promptly became the capital of the region but the mines gave out within 30 years and the capital was moved to Mexicali. When prohibition was rife in the US during the 1920s, Ensenada made its fortune providing legal drink, gambling and prostitution. The harbour carried on with freighters and fish canning, but the town concentrated on entertainment. Today Ensenada still has these two industries, the gringo and the sea, and does very well out of both of them.

GETTING AROUND
Highway 1-D ends in Ensenada, 109 km from Tijuana. Highway 1 continues to Cabo San Lucas, the southernmost tip of the peninsula.

The **bus station** is on Riveroll between 10th and 11th, 10 blocks from the boulevard. There are departures every 30 minutes to Tijuana ($1\frac{1}{2}$ hrs) and Mexicali (3 hrs) and four times a day to La Paz (18 hrs), stopping at all points south. **Local buses** leave 5 blocks to the right of the bus station, at Calle 7.

Fixed-route **taxis** (bumble-bee yellow) display a sign on the windscreen. The main rank is on Riveroll, at the corner of 4th, in front of the gas company. Blue and white taxis leave from Gastelum between 4th and 5th: they are expensive and a price should always be negotiated first.

Ensenada faces its port and harbour. Highway 1-D curves around the bay and becomes Blvd Lázaro Cárdenas around the port. One block behind is Av López Mateos with all the shops, cantinas and restaurants, and many of the hotels.

TOURIST INFORMATION

The tourist office (open 08.00–19.00, Mon–Sat; tel 63718 or 62222) and Procuraduría de Protección al Turista (tel 63686) are side by side, at Av López Mateos and Espinoza, next to the excellent FONART craft shop.

WHAT TO SEE

Bodegas de Santo Tomás
(Av Miramar 666 at Calle 7, tel 82509.)
The wines of Baja California have none of the fame of Californian wines, nor do they yet deserve it, but the quality is improving all the time as Californian techniques filter south. The three biggest wineries in the country are all around Ensenada. Of these, Santo Tomás is the most acclaimed. Thirty-minute tours of the winery start at 11.00, 13.00 and 15.00, and end with samples of the wine (the red is far better: the white is a little sweet), brandy, bread and cheese. Wines are on sale at trade price. The small village of Santo Tomás, where the grapes come from, is half an hour south of Ensenada in a lush, wide valley. The vineyard was started up by the Dominicans in the 17th century.

Riviera del Pacífico
(Blvd Lázaro Cárdenas and Av Riviera.)
This one-time casino is now the town's cultural centre, used largely for wedding receptions and ballet classes. It had an inauspicious start. It was planned in the 1920s when prohibition in the US meant big business for legalized gambling, betting and booze in Mexico. By 1930, when it was completed, the morality code in Mexico had tightened. Although the boxer, Jack Dempsey, was brought in as manager, it closed when the Mexican government outlawed gambling in 1938. The building is still fabulous. It echoes southern Spain with painted wooden ceilings and Venetian tiles on the wall. The casino itself is octagonal: murals of bacchanalian disportings act as a backdrop to the ghostly click of counters and sighs of despondency.

BEACHES

Following Highway 1 south, the best beaches are at **Estero**, 10 km from Ensenada (local buses leave on the hour from Riveroll and Calle 7). Continuing on to Maneadero, turn right for Punta Banda and **La Bufadora**, 20 km along a winding road. This natural geyser spouts up great jets of water, compressed by jagged rocks which act as a funnel, shooting the surf up through a small vent in the ceiling of the underwater cave.

WHERE TO STAY   (area code 667)

Hotels aim for the market they know they can get, and as a consequence prices are high, usually given in dollars and only reluctantly translated back into pesos. Just outside town, sandwiched between the sea and Highway 1-D, *****Roses by the Sea (km 105.5 to Tijuana, tel 44310) is a pastel extragavanza with a double swimming pool that seems to cascade over into the sea, jacuzzis, a gym, tennis courts and cool, soothing rooms. Close by, ***Quintas Papagayo (km 103, tel 44155) has grown to be a village. Run by the Hussong family, it has ocean-front cottages, a small apartment block and a large log cabin. All the rooms have their own kitchen and there are swimming pools, jacuzzis and tennis courts. Its restaurant, El Pelicano, serves fresh lobster *thermidor*, scallop steaks with crab-meat sauce and *linguini Todos Santos* (lobster, shrimps, scallops and baby clams in butter and white wine sauce). Moderately expensive.

In town, the ****Travelodge (Av Mateos and Blancarte 130, tel 81602) is a comfortable, not too corporate hotel, right in the centre, with powerful showers and coffee-machines in the rooms. The ***Misión Santa Isabel (Av Castillo 1100, tel 83616) is colonial in style, its corridors lined with attractive ceramics.

Both the pistachio-green motel **America (Av Mateos 1309, tel 61333) and the dark brown **Sahara are bang opposite the tourist office, nothing special but central and reasonable. Cheapest of all, *Pancho's is on Calle 2 and Av Alvarado 211, one block behind Av Mateos.

EATING OUT

Virginia Geffroy was born in Santa Rosalía, studied in France, and ran El Rey Sol (Av Mateos 1000 and Blancarte, tel 82351) until she died in 1989. The menu includes *lechoncito adobado* (roast suckling pig) and seafood such as *matarraya au beurre noir* (sting-ray). Expensive. China Land (Av Riveroll 1149, between 11 and 12, tel 86844) is owned by a couple from Hong Kong but specializes in Peking dishes, using traditional duck and unusual partridge. Moderate. For Mexican food, there is the informal El Macho (Av Macheros) for steak and lobsters, *nachos* with melting cheese and strips of chilli or enchiladas in *salsa roja*. Moderate. Las Cazuelas (Blvd Lázaro Cárdenas) is more formal and the food is less bastardized: the steaks are from Sonora, the wines from Santo Tomás and the Mexican dishes, such as *pollo pipián* (chicken in a pumpkin seed sauce) and *pavo en mole* (turkey in a dark chilli and chocolate sauce) are treated with a seriousness hard to find in the amorphous border region. Expensive.

For fish, there are any number of places, but the Casamar (Blvd Lázaro Cárdenas 987, tel 40417), on the waterfront, outranks the rest. Expensive. The locals, however, prefer the Bahía de Ensenada (Av Riveroll and Mateos 109, tel 81015) which isn't at all smart but is always busy. Waiters race between tables with tortilla chips and red-hot salsa, ice-cold Tecate beers and whole fried sea bass, grilled lobsters, squid in its own ink or abalone steaks. Cheap.

Señor Salud (Calle 9 and Espinoza) is a wonderful, wholesome vegetarian café offering pitta pockets stuffed with Chihuahua cheese and alfalfa sprouts as well as big salads and home-baked cakes. Cheap. On Calle 6, a line of taco stalls '*de la sexta*', open all day and almost all night, provides the simplest of Mexican staples, a tortilla rolled around chicken, pork, beef, tripe or even fish.

Three kilometres south of town, in Playa Hermosa, is the award-winning Cueva de los Tigres (Acapulco and Las Palmas, Col Playa Hermosa, tel 62450), which combines abalone steak with crab meat and a touch of cinnamon. The quail is from San Quintín and the dates are fresh from Mulegé. Moderately expensive. The small coastal village of

Puerto Nuevo, on the old road between Tijuana and Ensenada, survives on its well-established reputation for lobsters. Now the lobsters come from Australia and the prices are imported from California, but people still flock into **Ortega's** for Sunday lunch. Moderate.

Bars

With a drinking age of 18 in Mexico and 21 in California, it is inevitable that Ensenada's bars are filled with young Americans most weekends. **Hussong's** cantina (Ruíz and Av Mateos) has been around for over 100 years and is probably the best-known place in Ensenada. The walls may not have changed a great deal since it opened but the people have, and every evening there is a mariachi band playing soulful songs for the maudlin to sing along to. Opposite, **Papas and Beer** is a restaurant and cantina that has no chandeliers to swing from although the intention lingers on.

South from Ensenada to Loreto

The road south, Highway 1, is narrow with no shoulders to speak of. Anything and everything uses it, from the odd rattlesnake or cow to the more frequent bus or trailer. If driving, fill up with petrol at every opportunity: stations are few and far between and the next one may not have any petrol in stock. There is no other reason to stop on the 600 km between Ensenada and Guerrero Negro.

San Quintín

San Quintín, 191 km south of Ensenada, clings tenaciously to the roadside for about 10 km but is only a few streets wide on either side. In 1883 a North American company was granted land concessions here: finding no water, it was delighted to sell to a gullible British company, which bought the land after a rainstorm had made it green. The British found not a drop to drink and left behind only a sorry cemetery. There is water now. It was discovered 25 m below the surface in the 1930s and has transformed the valley into fields of tomatoes, chillies, wheat and corn. Impoverished Oaxacans have travelled from the south of Mexico up to Baja California to look for work in the tomato harvests. Cheap labour is scarce so close to the US: for an 8-hour day, the Oaxacans are paid the equivalent of the minimum hourly wage over the border. To the south of town are some superb sand-dune beaches beside a rough sea, where Californians have bought second homes.

Cataviña to Guerrero Negro

Some 180 km further on, around Cataviña, the boulder-strewn landscape is peppered with *cirios*, long, thin cacti, native only to Baja California, whose branches curl like elephant trunks towards the sky. At a junction 100 km further south, a narrow road leads to the small fishing and camping village of **Bahía de los Angeles**, surrounded by *cholla* cactus, elephant trees and *yucca valida*.

Guerrero Negro, 232 km further south, sits on the 28th parallel, the border between southern and northern Baja California. Scammon's lagoon, south of town, is a breeding ground for the grey whale (see Los Cabos). Between the lagoon and the town are some of the biggest salt works in the world. The town itself is only worth stopping in for petrol or a night's rest (see Where to Stay).

San Ignacio

After Guerrero Negro, Highway 1 veers southeast across the stark, dusty Vizcaíno Desert, through a landscape of volcanic peaks and cacti. After 142 km, an oasis suddenly appears, set in a grove of date palms, as if blown in by the wind. San Ignacio is by far the prettiest village in Baja California. The main square is the beginning and the end of it with a charming mission, pastel-coloured houses and large shady trees to rest under. The first Europeans to arrive were Jesuit priests—the Italian Francisco Marío Piccolo and the Spaniard Sebastian Sistiago—who had riden by mule for four days from Mulegé without finding water.

San Ignacio was a logical centre for evangelizing the surrounding area, and each of the three orders had a hand in constructing the mission. It is unostentatiously baroque, built of lava with 1-m thick walls that were easy to carve. The paintings and the impressive gold leaf *retablos* came from the mainland. Impish cherubs who have long since shed their wings smirk down at the congregation. The elongated horse-shoe buildings to either side served as schools, monasteries and, during the harvest, as warehouses.

Santa Rosalía

Santa Rosalía is incongruous in the extreme. Overlooking the Gulf of California, 73 km east of San Ignacio, it is surrounded by a mountain mass of volcanic cones. It was built in the 1880s by the French, who discovered rich copper deposits in the surrounding hills. El Boleo became one of the richest copper-mining companies in North America, with joint German and French owners, who drafted in the Seris from Sonora as enforced labour.

Today, Santa Rosalía is a curious amalgam of French elegance and German discipline in a Mexican town that is so stiflingly hot, still and dusty that no-one puts a toe out of doors between dawn and dusk in the long summer months. The most striking of many oddities is the church of prefabricated iron, designed by A E Eiffel for the 1898 Paris World Fair, then dismantled, shipped out to Baja and reassembled here. The clapper-board houses, draped in bougainvillea, and the elegant French Palacio Municipal echo the past, but today rich yachts dock in yesterday's harbour.

A daily 7-hour **ferry** leaves at 23.00 for Guaymas in Sonora.

Mulegé

Between Mulegé and Loreto are some fabulous beaches with crystalline aquamarine waters. In the summer, the dolphins come out and play with the boats. In the winter, Canadians and North Americans bring their camper vans down to the beach, earning themselves the title of 'snowbirds'. They have made the gentle town of Mulegé a motor-home service station, selling BBQs, muffins, cookies, gas cookers and unleaded petrol.

Along the banks of the wide river, towering date palms provide the town's principal crop, a profitable relic of seeds first planted by the Jesuits in the 18th century. The Jesuits also introduced grapes and olives, and the oasis now counts citrus fruits and avocados amongst its crops. A simple mission overlooks the town, begun by the Jesuits in 1705 and completed in 1766. To see it, go past the square on Calle Zaragoza, over the bridge, and turn sharply to the right.

WHERE TO STAY
Between Ensenada and Loreto, a distance of some 635 km, there are four government-sponsored ****Pinta hotels, at San Quintín (116 km), Cataviña (229 km), Guerrero Negro (375 km) and San Ignacio (465 km) (tel in US 800 262 2656). These are well-designed pit-stops with rare petrol stations, swimming pools and restaurants. All, except San Quintín, can be seen from the road.

San Quintín's Pinta is on the old highway, overlooking the sand dunes. The town has some dishevelled duck-shooting hotels around the bay and motels along the road. **Cirios is a basic candy-stripe pink motel (to get there, turn right off the highway at 'Muebleria Metralla').

Guerrero Negro also has a couple of motels on the road into town, as well as its Pinta. **El Morro (tel (667) 857 0414) is plain but comfortable with a decent restaurant, La Casita. Others are the *San Ignacio (first on the right) and *Las Dunas. Malarrimo is an unpretentious restaurant at the entrance to town, which serves excellent breakfasts and large dinners of steamed octopus and blue crab *au gratin*.

San Ignacio's Pinta is on the road into the village. Another motel, the **Posada San Ignacio, is on the far edge of the village (signposted from the square)—a scruffy family-run place that organizes trips to see cave paintings.

In Santa Rosalía there are two hotels in the town—the pink clapperboard ***Del Real (tel 20829) and, at right angles, the (CE) Olivera (tel 20057). Out of town, on the road south, ***El Morro (tel 20414) is an up-market anglers' hotel.

Mulegé has some very cheap, insalubrious guest houses and the respectable, tidy **Terrazas (Calle Zaragoza, tel 30009).

Loreto

Loreto was the first successful European settlement of the Californias and its capital, until a hurricane ripped it to pieces in 1829. It wasn't only the Spanish who colonized it. In the 19th century three Welsh brothers, called Davis, jumped ship here. Two stayed, married and began a clan of Davises: a street is named after them. Stephen Green jumped ship in Los Cabos and made his way up to Loreto. His son did his bit to counter depopulation and had 52 children before he died at the age of 105 in 1931. There are Drews, Taylors and Cunninghams as well. The breeze that comes up from the south in the summer is known as the Cromwell, because of the buccaneer who arrived with it. The beach he landed on has kept his name.

Today the small town depends on tourism, with deep-sea fishing and scuba diving the main attractions for visitors. Recent developments to the south of town in Nopoló have brought more money into the area, but the luxury hotels and the fishing village are worlds apart.

GETTING AROUND
Loreto is 136 km south of Mulegé, 1111 km south of Tijuana and 337 km north of La Paz. The bus station is on the corner of Calle Salvatierra (the main road in from Highway

1 south) and Calle Independencia. Four daily buses go to and from Tijuana (13 hrs) and La Paz (4 hrs). Nopoló has a tiny airport with one daily flight to La Paz and one to Los Angeles.

TOURIST INFORMATION
Loreto's coolly air-conditioned tourist office (open 09.00–15.00 weekdays; 09.00–13.00 Sat) is in the main square, near the Bancomer Bank.

WHAT TO SEE
Museo de las Misiónes
(Open 09.00–17.00; closed Mon and Tue; adm.)
This modest museum, hidden within sturdy stone walls, is just off the main square, in what was the first mission to be built in Baja California. Four stiflingly hot rooms, ineffectively cooled by overhead fans, detail the history of the peninsula from top to toe, from the early settlers, through the arrival of the Europeans to the establishment of missions. The endurance of the Jesuits, who transformed desert into fertile plain, is well illustrated with artefacts, pictures and diagrams. It was they who introduced the technology of the wheel and the use of animals for labour.

The Mission of San Javier
The 37-km side road to the Jesuit Mission of San Javier takes about 2 hours, but it is one of the most lovely trips on the peninsula, passing through the magnificent Sierra de la Giganta. At one point there are palms on one side of the track and cacti on the other, as the landscape shifts from the coast to the mountains and drops down into the valley of San Javier. High-clearance cars or jeeps are advisable as the road is rough. The turn-off is 2 km south of Loreto on Highway 1.

The mission was the second to be built in Baja by the Jesuits. Begun in 1699, it wan't completed until 1758 but continues to be used as the parish church today. Incongruously beautiful in its rugged, dry valley setting, its stalwart facade is etched with simple Moorish embellishments. If it is locked, ask for Rosa Guadalupe (better known as La Chiqua), who has the key. She, or her brother, can also guide walkers to some nearby cave paintings in the mountains.

FISHING
Loreto Divers (Calle Salvatierra, by the mission, tel 30029) or the hotels can organize trips. Overfishing by local shrimp fishers and international trawlers has depleted the once endless stocks of roosterfish, marlin and sailfish and there is constant pressure to impose controls so that tourists don't disdain the waters. In the hot summer months, the town is very soporific and the fishermen raise more than an eyebrow at the bold Californian Hemingways keen to be out wrestling with fish from dawn to dusk, day after day.

WHERE TO STAY   (area code 683)
Prices in Loreto are inflated by the many sport-fishing Californians who come down. The ****Pinta (Francisco Madero, tel 30025) has lovely villa rooms with sea views, log fires (scarcely ever needed) and brick floors. Hacienda rooms are cheaper. The

344

***Oasis** (tel 30211, tlx 52581) is the oldest hotel. The rooms front a strip of beach that looks over to the towering bulk of the Isla del Carmen. The day starts at 4 am when the boats leave, by torch light, and lunch begins at midday when they come back with their catch of electric-blue finned sailfish and the mottled yellow and purple dorado. The ***Misión de Loreto** (Lopéz Mateos 1, tel 30048, fax 30648) has been popular with families for years because of its informal atmosphere, restaurant and swimming pool.

The only cheap places in town are the basic *Motel Salvatierra** (Av Salvatierra 223) and the *Junipero** (Calle Hidalgo).

In Nopoló
A few km south of Loreto is the airport and tourist development of Nopoló. Heavily funded, it has been long in the planning stages. The only completed hotel is the extremely sybaritic *****Stouffer Presidente** (tel 30700, tlx 52584, fax 30377), an all-inclusive resort. Drink, food and sports (including excellent riding and water-skiing but not scuba diving or deep-sea fishing) are all included in the exorbitant pay-once price.

EATING OUT
Loreto is not a large place and many visitors eat in their hotels, so there is little to choose from. **Cesár's** (Calles Zapata and Juárez, opposite the supermarket, tel 30203) is a very recommendable seafood restaurant, where even George Bush has eaten. Come here for clams the size of a fist, or reasonably priced special lunches of bass smothered in butter with garlic bread and bean soup. Moderate. The **Café Olé**, half a block from the main square, serves large breakfasts and simple light lunches. Cheap.

La Paz

The only large town in the south, La Paz is set on a beautiful bay on the Gulf of California, backed by mountains and fronted by hilly islands, which merge until one seems to fade into another. It is a vivacious town, bouyed up by tourism, yachts and the influx of mainlanders from Durango, Zacatecas and Sonora, who have jumped onto a profitable band-wagon.

GETTING AROUND
By Air: The airport is on the north side of town, 20 minutes from the centre. Aeroméxico and Mexicana have daily flights to Guadalajara, Puerto Vallarta, Tijuana, Chihuahua, Mexico City and Los Angeles.

By Bus: The central bus station is in the southwest of town (tel 24270 or 23060). Two companies, Tres Estrellas and Autotransportes Aguila, run first- and second-class services. Four buses a day go to and from Tijuana and Mexicali, stopping at Loreto, Sta Rosalía and Mulegé, and several a day go south to Los Cabos.

Frequent **town buses** run between the station and the town centre: take a 'Centro' bus into town, and a 'Central Camionera' bus out.

By Car: La Paz is 337 km south of Loreto on Highway 1. The road climbs up over the Sierra Giganta to the western side of the pensinsula and then turns sharply at Villa Insurgentes to head straight for La Paz, back on the east coast. Cars can be taken on the ferries to and from the mainland.

By Ferry: The daily ferry to and from Topolobampo, near Los Mochis in Sonora, takes 8 hours, leaving La Paz at 20.00 and Topolobampo at 08.00.

The daily ferry to Mazatlán in Sinaloa takes 16 hours, leaving La Paz at 17.00 and Mázatlán at 15.00. (See Santa Rosalía and Los Cabos for other ferries.)

Buy tickets at the office (tel 20109) in Ramírez, between Ejido and Héroes de 47, as long in advance as possible. If told that the ferry is booked up, wait till 15.00 and try to pick up one of the many last-minute cancellations or returns. The tickets are cheap—for passengers and for cars. A cabin costs twice as much for two people as the deck, but is infinitely preferable, and includes a bathroom.

The **ferry terminal** is 17 km from town along a good paved road (Highway 11) on the Pichilingue peninsula. The blue and white 'Pichilingue' bus to the ferry leaves from the old station on the waterfront at Independencia.

In Town: La Paz is a geographically confusing city because one assumes that the water to the east is the sea, but it isn't: it's a bay within a gulf, and the sea is in fact to the north. The waterfront, Paseo Alvaro Obregón, is the main street. To the right, just after the tourist office, is Av Independencia which leads up to the main square, Plaza Constitución, four blocks from the waterfront.

There are several **car hire** firms: Hertz (half a block from Hotel Los Arcos, tel 22345), Avis (Riviera Hotel, tel 22345), Budget (tel 21097) and Auto Renta Sol (16 de Septiembre, tel 24545).

TOURIST INFORMATION
The tourist office is on the waterfront at Av Independencia (tel 21199). The post office is on Revolución and Constitución.

WHAT TO SEE
La Paz is concentrated on the bay but the town itself is pleasant to walk around, with a network of cobbled streets leading up from the bay-front Paseo Alvaro Obregón to the main square, Plaza Constitución. Banks, shops and restaurants have carefully taken over most of the older buildings. This means that those still in their original shape are also in the least good condition (such as the one-time Jesuit mission, now the Hostería del Convento, see below). The modern cathedral in the plaza was built over the remains of another Jesuit mission which was razed this century. Further from the bay, the town's **Museum of Anthropology** (Altamirano and Cinco de Mayo; open 09.00–18.00) is more than usually dull for a foreigner. The displays are badly laid out, weighty with Spanish explanation and long on local history.

BEACHES
The fishermen leave daily from the town beach in front of the Hotel Los Arcos, so it is busy and not very clean. They will take trips to less well-known beaches, such as **Isla Espíritu Santo**, to the north of town, where there are natural swimming pools and empty beaches. Trips should be organized the day before as they leave at dawn. Book

through **Viajes Palmira** (a kiosk on the beach in front of Los Arcos, which can also arrange fishing, diving, boating and water-skiing). Better still, ask the boatmen personally and avoid the middle men. They congregate on the corner of Rosales and the front, Alvaro Obregón. The head of the cooperative, José Luis, can be rung at home (tel 28097), as can his colleague Hugo Fisher (tel 28097), whose grandfather was English. Other uncrowded beaches are a bus ride away, beyond the ferry terminal at Pichilingue. The good, paved road ends at the terminal and only rough tracks continue round the peninsula. On the way, the smart La Concha Hotel (5 km from La Paz) has the best small beach and a restaurant good enough to use as an excuse for going there.

EVENINGS

A walk along the front isn't all La Paz has to offer. There is often live music a taxi ride away in the **Old West** (La Católica and Juárez), or at **Las Barritas** or **La Paz Laza**. Live jazz and film shows take place at **Kabuki's Art Café** (on Independencia, near Plaza Constitución).

WHERE TO STAY   (area code 682)

The *****La Concha Beach Resort** (5 km from town on the road to Pichilingue, tel 26544, tlx 52233; in the US ring toll-free 800 999 BAJA) is a calm, relaxing hotel that is switched on to switching off, with every sport under the sun from deep-sea fishing or kayaking to dominoes and Monopoly. The rooms are wholesome and the beach towels enormous. The restaurant is orientated towards seafood: the fresh daily catch comes with baked potatoes and *chayote* (a soft vegetable pear). Breakfasts are anything from papaya and coffee to buttermilk hot cakes and locally grown *damiana* tea. *****Los Arcos** (on the front, Alvaro Obregón 498, tel 22744) is the nearest La Paz gets to colonial, with a large courtyard around a fountain. Aspirant beauty queens are housed here during the city's pageant. ***La Perla** (Alvaro Obregón 1570, tel 20777, tlx 52533) is also on the front, with minimally decorated rooms, a small pool and sunset views over the bay. The date-palm-fronted, cheap and cheerful ***Gardenias** (Serdán and Guerrero, tel 23088) has rooms that are wearing thin and institutional bath rooms.

The cheapest places in town are also the most central. The **(CE) Posada San Miguel** (half a block from the main square, Belisario Domínguez) has a hopeful tiled entrance but disappointingly barren rooms. Around the corner, the **(CE) Pensión California** (Santos Degollado 209, tel 22869) is a bee-hive of constant activity from children, cats, washerwomen and vendors. The patio is flooded with plants and large, plain rooms open onto it, each with its own primitive bathroom. Close by, the **(CE) Hostería del Convento** (Fco Madero Sur 85, tel 23508) is on the site of a Jesuit mission founded in 1720; it now offers no more than white-washed walls and naked light bulbs for a rock-bottom price.

EATING OUT

The seafood café, **El Taste** (Alvaro Obregón and Juárez), includes beef and lobster on its long menu and many of the famous white wines of northern Baja California such as El Aceto and Calafia. Moderate. There are two Chinese restaurants, **El Jade** and the **Nuevo Pekin**, behind the La Perla hotel. Moderate. The **Bismark 11** ((Degollado and Altamirano) is eight blocks inland, five west of the museum, but worth finding for its oysters or whole grilled fish *a la veracruzana*. Moderate. **El Quinto Sol** (Domínguez and the main square) is an informal vegetarian restaurant offering thick yoghurt and granola drinks and chunky wholemeal sandwiches with slabs of cheese and avocado. The La Perla Hotel's open café does the best breakfasts in town.

Todos Santos

On the opposite coast of the peninsula, south of La Paz on Highway 19 (85 km, 1 hr 20 mins), Todos Santos is a pretty, vaguely colonial town set in a rich mango orchard. Famous for its mango sweets and open-air fish restaurants (particularly the **Sta Monica**), it also has a fine Jesuit mission and a hotel which the owners claim was the inspiration for the Eagles' song, 'Hotel California'. It isn't very inspirational now but the bar, restaurant and pool tables are still the most exciting things in town.

The nearest beaches are only 1½ km out of town. Further south, wide, open beaches such as Pescadero and Los Cerritos lie exposed to the crashing waves of the Pacific Ocean, and are much loved by surfers. There are a couple of taxis in Todos Santos (ask at the hotel) which will take people out to these further beaches in the morning and pick them up in the evening.

Los Cabos

The towns of San José del Cabo and Cabo San Lucas are 32 km apart, on the southern tip of the peninsula. San José was founded in 1730, as its old church and plaza attest, but is now a modern resort complete with large hotels, condominiums, a golf course and beautiful beaches. Cabo San Lucas was created around a tiny harbour, a favourite haunt of English pirates. Now it is the favourite haunt of holiday-makers as hotel after hotel rises up to dwarf the tiny, original nucleus. The population has grown ten times in ten years and one in three people works for a construction company.

GETTING AROUND

By Air: Los Cabos airport is 11 km north of San José del Cabo, with flights to Mexico City (stopping in Guadalajara), Tijuana, Chihuahua, Monterrey and several southern US cities, including Los Angeles and Houston. Taxis and hotel minibuses link the airport to both towns.

By Bus: Buses to and from La Paz (3 hrs, 4 daily along both routes) use the San José terminal on Calle Doblado and the Cabo San Lucas terminal on Calle 16 de Septiembre. Local buses between the two towns run from the same terminals every 30 minutes but tail off from 18.00. In the evening, taxis are the only connection.

By Car: San José del Cabo is 181 km (3 hrs) south of La Paz, on Highway 1. Cabo San Lucas is 32 km southwest of San José, at the end of the highway. From Cabo San Lucas, Highway 19 follows the west coast of the peninsula as far as Todos Santos before heading inland to rejoin Highway 1 some 30 km south of La Paz. Any hotel in either resort can arrange **car rental**.

By Ferry: A daily 18-hour ferry (tel 684 20109) leaves at 11.00 for Puerto Vallarta in Jalisco.

WHAT TO DO

The main attraction is **sport-fishing**. However, although the general policy is 'catch and release', Japanese trawlers, commercial fishers and the shrimping fleet have all taken their toll and the numbers of fish in the water are falling each year. Tourists are looking for yellowfin tuna, snapper, marlin and rooster fish, but the shrimping fleets take anything they can in their fine-meshed nets, including dolphins, and discard the dead left-overs.

Glass-bottomed boats leave from the dock, taking trips out to the colonies of sea lions basking on the rocks and around these to the beaches on the far side. **Diving** in Los Cabos took off when Jacques Cousteau filmed the undersea walls just offshore in the late 1970s. There are agencies in every hotel and along the promenade by the pier which can arrange all manner of sea trips, including whale watching.

WHALE WATCHING

Each winter grey whales come down to breed off Baja, after spending the summer months feeding in the Bering and Chukchi Seas near Alaska—the longest migration undertaken by any mammal. Hunted voraciously between 1850 and 1938, grey whales came perilously close to extinction. They are now protected by international agreement and their numbers have grown back up to almost 20,000. Grey whales are toothless, occasionally prodding a boat out of curiosity but never attempting to overturn it. They are enormous animals, eight times the size of an African elephant. Even the calves are up to 4 m long, while fully grown adults may be four times longer. These vast animals rise and fall in the water, showing the utmost grace as they heave up out of the ocean and shoot jets of warm air and water out of their spouts. Immediately they take a great gulp of air, and another, and then dive back in with a graceful flick of the tail. Both the exhaling and the inhaling, sounding like soulful fog horns, can be heard from 100 m away.

There are some necessary controls on whale watching but several operators are licensed to take people out. In Cabo San Lucas, try **Amigos del Mar** (Blvd Marina, tel 30869) or **Cabo Divers** (Plaza Cabo San Lucas on Madero, tel 30747). January is the best month to see them.

WHERE TO STAY   (area code 684)

Los Cabos is an American winter-vacation resort which means, in one word, expensive. The season runs from November to May when room prices are 40 per cent higher than during the rest of the year. Travel agents in the US or Europe may be able to arrange cheap packages with flight and car hire included.

In San José del Cabo

San José is a little cheaper than San Lucas. Beach hotels are designed for packages and overworked holiday-makers. The ******Calinda** (Blvd Mijares, tel 20077) is the best value. A cluster of cheap hotels, including the ***Colli** (Hidalgo, tel 20052) and the ****Ceci** (Zaragoza 22, tel 20051) is near the post office, just off Blvd Mijares which runs down to the sea.

In Cabo San Lucas

The hotels here are spankingly modern, engaged all the time in fierce competition which doesn't lower prices but does add frills. The *******Finisterra** (tel 30100) is

349

long-established, high above the harbour with a popular bar and the Blue Marlin Restaurant where trios and mariachis play every night. The *****Solmar (tel 30383) is on the Pacific side of the point, by a secluded bay. Every room faces the ocean, and in the winter months the whales snort, blow and play right outside. On the road to San José is the *****Clarion, on a bluff above the sea, with jacuzzis bubbling and tennis courts in the garden. Many of the rooms have balconies overhanging the ocean where guests can see the whales cavorting and disporting themselves.

The colonial-style ***Mar de Cortez (Calle Cárdenas, tel 30232), in the centre of town, is not mind-blowingly over-priced, while the **Casablanca (Calle Revolución, off Calle Morelos, 3 blocks north of the bus station) is the cheapest place in town.

Part XI

SAN LUIS POTOSI AND THE NORTHEAST

Huastec girl

This chapter encompasses the four states of Nuevo León, Coahuila, Tamaulipas and San Luis Potosí, an enormous stretch of land from Texas to below the Tropic of Cancer. Much of the northern half is ranch land, interspersed by industrial cities. The real excitement begins in the state of San Luis Potosí and little of what comes before is worth lingering over.

The Tex–Mex border

The Texas–Mexico border is frontier country indeed, definitely more Tex than Mex—an amorphous region dedicated to assembly plants, with cheap over-the-counter drugs, dentists, opticians, and an anaesthetized version of Mexican culture, safely marketed for Mexico's northern neighbour and employer. The towns are curious cultural crossovers in which Texan diners are decorated with Mexican sombreros, where the beef must be American but the beer Mexican. Texans and Mexicans alike wear stetsons and high-heeled cowboy boots, sport large bellies with the requisite stomach ulcers and drive around in massive Japanese pick-up trucks. Their 'lady friends' are encouraged to exult in mythic tropicality by ordering piña coladas and tequila sunrises. There are any number of hotels in the border cities but all of them are twice as expensive as far better hotels further south. Costs are dollar-defined and ludicrously inflated, particularly in taxis, hotels and restaurants.

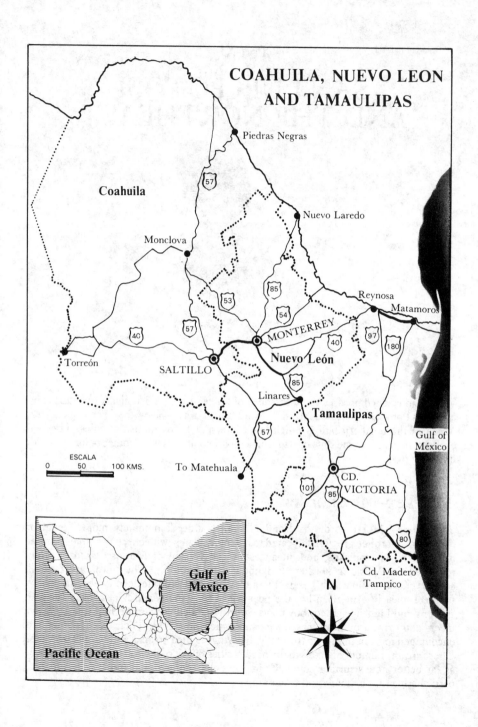

COAHUILA, NUEVO LEON AND TAMAULIPAS

Piedras Negras

Coahuila

57

Nuevo Laredo

Monclova

85

53

54

57

40

57

Reynosa

Matamoros

MONTERREY

40

97

180

Torreón

SALTILLO

Nuevo León

85

Linares

Tamaulipas

57

Gulf of México

ESCALA

0   50   100 KMS.

To Matehuala

CD. VICTORIA

101

85

80

Cd. Madero
Tampico

N

Gulf of México

Pacific Ocean

Gulf of México

No more than a few hundred km south of the border, towns such as Saltillo, Ciudad Victoria, Monterrey or San Luis Potosí show the resilience of the Mexican temperament in the face of a barrage of consumerism from the north. Older, proud cities in their own right, they are never Anglo-Saxon, always Hispanic. If entering Mexico from the northeast, try to arrange your travel plans so that the first day in Mexico can be started early, with time for a good run south, away from the clutches of the border mentality.

BORDER CROSSINGS
The main border towns in the northeast are Piedras Negras in Coahuila, and Nuevo Laredo, Reynosa and Matamoros in Tamaulipas. Nuevo Laredo is linked to Monterrey by Highway 85 and to the other border towns by Highway 2. Matamoros is linked to Ciudad Victoria and the south by Highway 180, and Reynosa by Highway 87 to Ciudad Victoria and by Highway 40 to Monterrey.

To enter Mexico, you need a tourist card (available from the immigration offices, on most buses and on all planes) and a valid passport.

GETTING AROUND
By Air: Every major city in the north has an airport (Monterrey, Piedras Negras, Nuevo Laredo, Reynosa, Matamoros, Saltillo, Ciudad Victoria and San Luis Potosí). Domestic flights within Mexico are considerably cheaper than flights from the US, with daily departures for the capital and other major Mexican cities. These connect with flights to and from Houston, Dallas, Chicago, San Antonio, McAllen and Brownsville.

The two major carriers, Aeroméxico and Mexicana, have offices at all the airports (from Mexico City, tel 207 8233 for Aeroméxico, or 660 4444 for Mexicana).

By Bus: US buses cross the frontier and continue to all major Mexican cities. However, Mexican buses are invariably cheaper and often quicker—immigration delays on long-distance buses can be interminable. The best first-class bus companies are ADO, Omnibus de México and Transportes del Norte, whose services link the northern towns to each other and to Mexico City (16 hrs), Guadalajara (14 hrs) and all other cities in the country. ADO buses travel up and down the Gulf coast from the border to Ciudad Victoria, Tampico and Veracruz (18 hrs from Matamoros). All bus stations in the border towns have 24-hour left-luggage lockers.

By Car: Northern Mexico is a vast territory with very litle population outside the four state capitals (San Luis Potosí, Saltillo, Monterrey and Ciudad Victoria) and the border towns. This means that the vital north–south artery, Highway 57, is fast-moving. Nearly all traffic between the northeast and central Mexico uses this main road. The alternatives are to drive down the Gulf coast, avoiding central Mexico altogether, or to veer west from Saltillo into the south and west of the country.

Mexico City is approximately 16 hours' drive from the Texas border, 1302 km via Highway 57 from Piedras Negras/Eagle Pass through Saltillo. Alternatives are Highway 85 from Nuevo Laredo via Monterrey (1187 km to Mexico City), or Highway 101 from Matamoros via Ciudad Victoria, followed by Highways 80 and 57 via San Luis Potosí (1030 km to Mexico City). The latter route is often tortuous and winding.

The **Gulf** route, from Matamoros/Brownsville to the Yucatán, bypasses central Mexico completely. Take Highway 101 to Ciudad Victoria (315 km), Highways 85/80 to the port of Tampico (550 km) and continue south on Highway 180 to Veracruz

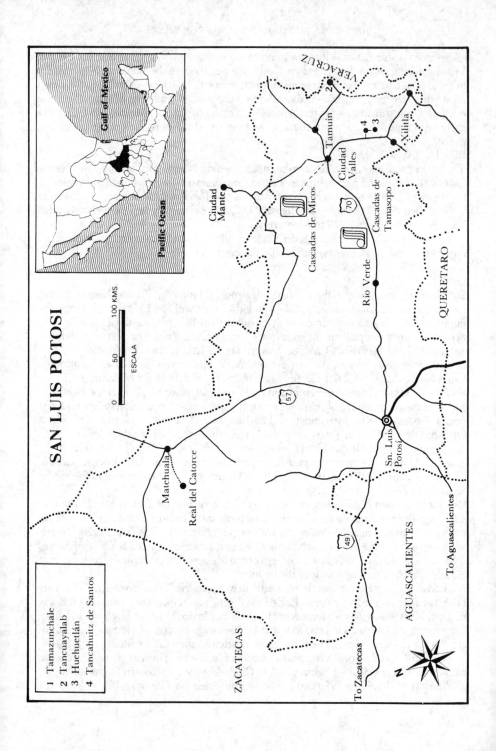

SAN LUIS POTOSI

1 Tamazunchale
2 Tancuayalab
3 Huehuetlán
4 Tancahuitz de Santos

ESCALA

0   50   100 KMS.

Gulf of Mexico

Pacific Ocean

VERACRUZ

Tamuín

Ciudad
Mante

Cascadas de Micos

Ciudad
Valles

Cascadas de
Tamasopo

Xilitla

Río Verde

QUERETARO

Matehuala

Real del Catorce

Sn. Luis
Potosí

To Aguascalientes

AGUASCALIENTES

To Zacatecas

ZACATECAS

57

70

49

N

(1024 km). For the **southwest**, take Highway 57 from Piedras Negro to Saltillo (445 km) and Highway 54 through Zacatecas to Guadalajara (1120 km).

By Train: Trains are slower and a little more expensive than the long-distance buses but a great deal more comfortable. The overnight sleeper from the border town of Nuevo Laredo to Mexico City, the 'Regiomontano', is an excellent way of cutting through the north. It has recently been dragged up by its heels and offers a much-improved service (first-class accommodation only, with bunk-bed cabins and a dining car). It has to be booked in advance. Southbound, the sleeper leaves Nuevo Laredo (tel 28097) at 14.00, arriving at Monterrey (tel 754653) at 18.00, Saltillo (tel 35584) at 20.10, San Luis Potosí at 01.50 and Mexico City at 08.45. Northbound, it leaves Mexico City (tel 547 89 72) at 18.00, arriving in San Luis at 01.00, Saltillo at 06.30, Monterrey at 09.00 and Nuevo Laredo at 13.00.

A less comfortable ride, with first- and second-class seats but no sleeper, is the 'Aguila Azteca' which takes 24 hours for the journey between Nuevo Laredo and Mexico City. Southbound, it leaves Nuevo Laredo at 18.55, arriving at Monterrey at 23.30, Saltillo at 02.30, San Luis Potosí at 10.00, San Miguel de Allende at 13.10, Querétaro at 14.40 and Mexico City at 19.15. Northbound, it leaves Mexico City at 08.00, arriving at Querétaro at 13.45, San Miguel de Allende at 15.15, San Luis at 17.45, Saltillo at 24.00, Monterrey at 02.20 and Nuevo Laredo at 07.15. A similar train connects Matamoros with Reynosa at regular intervals (3 hrs).

The State of Nuevo León

Sandwiched between the vast expanse of Coahuila to the west and the long, thin state of Tamaulipas to the east, Nuevo León missed out on the coast and only got a nibble of the US–Mexico border, which nevertheless throws a long shadow right across the state. Nuevo León is far closer to Texas than to Mexico City, and economic lessons have been quickly learnt. The state capital of Monterrey has become the nation's third largest and most productive city. The draw of prosperity has seen a migration from the sparsely populated countryside into the great urban mass, leaving the land to goats, which are reared on wild grasses and fed to Monterrey businessmen.

Monterrey

Monterrey is the ugly duckling of Mexico, showing every inclination to turn into a swan. It is young, self-opinionated, wealthy, huge and aggressive. First established in 1596, it took three centuries to get off the ground. Today, with a population of three million, it is Mexico's third largest city and its industrial nerve centre. Tension between the capital and this northern bastion of business is legendary. Regarded further south as penny-pinching capitalists, the 'Regiomontanos', as its citizens are called, are sick to death of hearing their Mexican Pittsburgh maligned and point to their industries which keep the economy on its feet: steel and iron, car assembly, textiles, cigarettes and brewing. Monterrey can also lay claims to being the most expensive and least relaxing of all

355

Mexican cities, leaving tourists yet to be convinced that there is any point in battling with its traffic and high prices.

GETTING AROUND
By Air: With daily flights to and from every major US and Mexican state, Monterrey is a popular entry point for those wanting to see the length of the country. The airport is on the Ciudad Alemán road, to the northeast of the city. Minibuses wait outside the main entrance and ferry passengers to the central hotels. Reservations and bookings can be made with hotel travel agencies, who will also arrange transport to and from the airport.
By Bus: The bus station is confusing, with a plethora of ticket offices for umpteen routes. All tickets must be bought from there and, for weekend travel, booked as many days in advance as possible. It's best to stick to the well-known companies: Tres Estrellas de Oro, Transportes del Norte and Omnibus de México. Frequent first-class services run to the border at Nuevo Laredo (3 hrs) and Reynosa (4 hrs), Saltillo (1 hr), San Luis Potosí (6 hrs) and Mexico City (12 hrs). Urban buses (17 and 18) leave every 10 minutes from Colón, the street fronting the terminal, for the Macro Plaza.
By Car: Monterrey is well positioned on Highway 85, the main road between Nuevo Laredo (230 km, 3 hrs) and Mexico City (990 km, 12 hrs). Saltillo is a fast hour away (85 km) on Highway 40.
By Train: The station is close to the bus station, five short blocks west along Colón and three north on Nieto. The overnight train between Nuevo Laredo and Mexico City, the 'Regiomontano', has to be booked well in advance (tel 754653). Southbound it leaves Monterrey at 18.00 and northbound at 09.00.
In Town: Monterrey is in a basin, surrounded by the mountains of the Sierra Madre and dominated by the Cerro de la Silla or Saddle Mountain. Although impressive to look at, they entrap the industrial smog which seals the city in its own pollution. Its complicated traffic system has been tidied up by giving each route a number (displayed on green signs): route 3 comes in from Nuevo Laredo, route 5 goes out to it and route 6 leads to Saltillo. The centre of the city is a recent innovation, a vast 100-acre Macro Plaza, lit up at night by a green laser shining out of the pinnacle point of a red obelisk. Around here are the cathedral, government offices and top hotels. The Zona Rosa, or smart shopping zone, is in the streets to the southwest (Hidalgo, Morelos and Padre Mier). The bus station and the train station are close together, 3 km northwest, connected to the centre by buses 17 and 18.

TOURIST INFORMATION
The INFOTUR office is on the edge of the Macro Plaza (Matamoros and Zaragoza, tel 450902; open all week 09.00–19.00). It organizes tours and provides lists of what's on.

WHAT TO SEE
The Bishop's Palace or Obispado
(Open 10.00–18.00, Tues–Sun.)
Tantalizingly in sight from all parts of the city, this magnificent palace is difficult to reach. Take bus 4, west along Padre Mier, and get off when it turns left to Degollado; walk up the hill and take the first left and then the first right. Keep asking as there is only one entrance.

The palace was built in 1789 by the second bishop of Nuevo León, Fray Rafael José Verger, who also designed the high baroque estípite facade. He died within two years and his palace didn't last long in its original calling. In turn church, prison, fort, hospital and HQ for Pancho Villa, it is a testament to the changing fortunes of 19th-century Mexico. In 1956, it became the Regional Museum.

Unfortunately, it is only the palace's exterior that rates a mention, with a wonderful facade and great views over the city. The historical museum inside (covering the period from the Spanish conquest to the present day) is loaded down with regional memorabilia. Although fascinating for Regiomontanos, proud, for example, that their city was given its coat of arms by Maria of Austria, it is of scant interest to anyone else.

Cervecería Cuauhtémoc
(Av Universidad 2202; take bus 1 from Juárez or buses 1 or 17 from the bus station along Cuauhtémoc; open 09.30–17.30, Tues–Sun.)
Monterrey's brewery was founded in the 1890s by the Mexican-born German, José Schneider, and rapidly became the largest in the country. When beer production outstripped the available bottles, the company began producing its own glass, metal caps and labels. Today it has expanded further, nursing a sports museum and art gallery under its wing. Tours of the brewery begin at 11.00, 12.00 and 15.00, finishing with free beer in the gardens (strong, dark Bohemia, Tecate and Carta Blanca lagers). The English are well known here. They played football in Monterrey in the 1986 World Cup and drank the brewery dry. Maradona's hand ball, in the same event, outraged Monterrey, confirming the Argentinians as the butt of many a Mexican joke.

Centro Cultural ALFA
(Av Roberto Garza Sada 1000; ALFA buses leave from the Alameda on the hour and return at half-past; open 15.00–21.30, Tues–Sun; adm.)
In the past, culture was given a rough ride in this hard-working city, but now that it has money in its pocket, Monterrey is keen to fill the gap. The largest business consortium of all, ALFA, has built a superb cultural centre, combining a hands-on museum with a planetarium and 180° screen. The cylindrical building, which looks as if it is sinking into the ground on one side, is an unmistakable landmark from any part of the city.

It is a challenging museum, questioning presumptions and teasing the jaded museum buff. One lower-floor exhibit illustrates the development of the Mexican home, from a pre-Hispanic cave to a modern 1990s house complete with microwave and computer— both taking up the same amount of space. The fourth floor plays with physics and actively encourages touching, smelling, pressing and pulling, with running ropes, optical illusions and magnetic forces. The fifth level displays sculptured figures from the southwestern state of Colima (200 BC–AD 200). They are a delight, with wide eyes, proud noses, high cheekbones and chunky, round, muscular bodies painted a deep, earthy red. Outside the museum itself is Rufino Tamayo's *Universe*, a vast stained-glass window, housed in a huge aluminium barn.

WHERE TO STAY   (area code 83)
Monterrey is full of extremely comfortable hotels at extremely uncomfortable prices, designed for those who don't pay their own bills. Top of this list are the *****Crowne

357

Plaza (Constitución Ote 300, tel 446000, tlx 382009), the *******Gran Hotel Ancira** (Hidalgo and Escobedo, tel 424806, tlx 382872) and the *******Ambassador Camino Real** (Av Hidalgo Ote 310, tel 422040, tlx 382875). The ******Monterrey** (Zaragoza and Morelos, tel 435120, tlx 382562), on the Macro Plaza, is one of the older hotels in town with magnificent views from the ninth floor. Considerably cheaper, the ******Royal Courts** (Av Universidad 314, Highway 85 north, tel 762710) is a popular motel with rooms set around a swimming pool.

Inexpensive hotels are clustered around the bus station. The ***Del Norte** (Democracía and Juan Mendez), the ****Soles** (Jiménez 1120 Nte) and the ****Patricia** (Av Madero 123 Ote) share the same management and telephone number (tel 727248), and are the best on offer, with parking, air conditioning and quite pleasant rooms. The cheapest hotels are in the street leading south away from the main entrance of the bus station, Amado Nervo, beginning with ***Posada** (tel 723908) on the right at 1138 and ***Nuevo León** (tel 741900), on the left at 1007.

EATING OUT

The better restaurants are southwest of the city centre, in the exclusive San Pedro/Colonia del Valle area which spreads up the slopes of green, wooded hills (take the San Pedro bus from the corner of Ocampo and Pino Suárez, or a car along Constitución and route 77). Three huddle on the corner where Av Roble meets Gómez Morin: the Italian **Rugantino** (tel 785978), the seafood **Guacamaya** (tel 787300) and the exotic **Hawaii 5 0** (tel 786405). The Guacamaya, looking like the hull of a beached ship, serves lobster *thermidor* and paella with crayfish. Moderately expensive. Hawaii 5 0 is utterly over the top and very jolly. Its Polynesian flavour extends to seafood with tropical fruits, such as Paradise shrimps which arrive on half a pineapple, and lobster with cashew nuts. The Bao-bao tray is loaded with tempura shrimps, strips of beef, lobster pancakes, fish bread and lots of satay sauce. Moderately expensive.

In the centre, the attractive Spanish **Mesón del Olivo** (Dr Coss, on the east side of the Macro Plaza) takes three days to prepare its duck *a la sevillana* with a sauce of delicately blended spices and herbs. Moderate. On the west side of the centre is **Das Bier Haus** (Hidalgo and Rayón) which has every conceivable brand of Mexican beer and a restaurant attached to the more popular bar. Inexpensive. Kid is roasted on a spit at the macho **El Tío** (a short taxi ride west, Hidalgo and México, tel 460291), which brings its tables and chairs onto the patio whenever the weather is warm enough. Inside, the walls are covered with sepia photos of matadors and polo players. Moderate.

The **Gran Hotel Ancira** lobby bar plays up to its old-world elegance with tightly buttoned bell boys and dismissive waiters. **Sanborn's** (Morelos and Escobedo 920 Sur) is the answer for homesick westerners. An American-style soda fountain with rotund waitresses, it is soothingly maternal. Close by, the vegetarian **Sr Natural** (Escobedo 713 Sur) is tiny but central, serving food that is cheap and extremely filling.

The State of Coahuila

This enormous but deserted state is the third largest in the republic and the least visited by pleasure-seeking tourists. It watches traffic pass through but can't hold on to it for more than a night. It is not unattractive, but its very size and barren loneliness make it seem unwelcoming to the average traveller. Coahuila once produced Francisco Madero, the instigator of the 1910 Revolution. Today, it sticks to nuts and bolts, soldered in the *maquiladores* (machine-assembly plants), where labour costs are but a fraction of those of their Texan equivalents across the border.

Saltillo

It is the capital of one of those lonely vast territories stretching from the US frontier roughly to the Tropic of Cancer ... the limbo and ante-room to Mexico.

—Sybille Bedford, 1953

Saltillo is spread over a large valley ringed by arid mountains. Once capital 'of all the northern land up to the Pole', its sovereignty shrunk to the state of Coahuila in 1948, when Texas was lost to the USA. Although of sorely diminished influence, it still has a beautiful colonial heart, hidden by the prosperous jumble that has grown up around it. A world apart from neighbouring Texas with its six-lane highways and drive-in Mc-donalds, Saltillo offers the Mexican alternative: cheap labour in Chrysler and General Motors assembly plants. It is not yet full-blown Mexico, but in its beautifully restrained Plaza de Armas it offers a taste of what is to come, and is a far better place to stay the night than any border town.

History

It was only as a result of the war with the United States in 1846–8 that Mexico lost control of Texas and the territory between the Río Bravo and Río Medina. Saltillo suddenly became a fortified frontier town rather than the influential capital of the outposts of the empire. With the link-up of the national railway between Mexico City and Monterrey, in the closing years of the last century, Saltillo became more involved with national politics. Within 10 years, Coahuila-born Francisco Madero had come forward as the mouthpiece of the reform movement, dedicated to ending the protracted presidency of Porfirio Díaz, then in its 35th year.

In the spring of 1908, Madero published his inflammatory treatise, *The Presidential Succession of 1910*, which questioned the mortality of the almost deified dictator-president. Madero wanted to re-establish democracy in Mexico: from Saltillo, he declared himself the democratic opponent to Díaz in the forthcoming elections. Locked up for his presumption, he triumphed the following year, when the dictator was overthrown. Madero's victory, however, was short-lived. Betrayed by one of his army leaders, he was murdered in an organized scuffle, and control of his revolution passed into the more ruthless hands of Huerta.

GETTING AROUND
By Bus: The station for first- and second-class buses is on the southwestern outskirts of town. There are regular services to and from Nuevo Laredo (4½ hrs), Matamoros (7 hrs), Monterrey (1½ hrs), Matehuala (4 hrs), San Luis Potosí (5 hrs), Guadalajara (9 hrs) and

Mexico City (11 hrs). Second-class buses are often full: first-class buses are safer bets as seats can be booked in advance. Minibuses and combis marked 'centro' wait outside the bus station to ferry passengers into town. No 9 goes back out again, leaving from the corner of Aldama and Hidalgo.

By Car: Saltillo is well positioned and seems to be on the way to everywhere. Highway 40 runs northeast to Monterrey and west to Torreón (277 km). Highway 57 runs north to Monclova and Piedras Negras and south to Mexico City (852 km), via San Luis Potosí (451 km). Highway 54 leads southwest to Zacatecas (363 km) and Guadalajara (680 km).

By Train: The railway station is also southwest of town, just off Carranza. First-class trains pass through Saltillo on their way to and from San Luis Potosí (5 hrs), Mexico City (12 hrs), Monterrey (2 hrs) and Nuevo Laredo (7 hrs). The 'Regiomontano' leaves Saltillo southbound at 20.10 and northbound at 24.00. To make reservations well in advance, tel Monterrey 754604; alternatively, book tickets at the station. The centre is a 15-minute walk or short taxi ride from the station: walk up Carranza to Madero; turn right across the Alameda park and continue straight up Victoria to Allende; Plaza Acuña is then three blocks to the left.

In Town: The city centre is small and walkable, and revolves around two squares, the Plaza de Armas and the Plaza Acuña.

TOURIST INFORMATION

The tourist office is efficient but inconveniently far from the centre (on the second floor of the Convention Centre on Highway 57, tel 54504).

WHAT TO SEE

The area around the **Plaza de Armas** has a calm order and elegance, which is sustained for about two blocks in any direction. The **cathedral** faces onto the plaza from Calle Hidalgo. It is one of the biggest in the country, built between 1746 and 1801, and more solid in form than many similar churches further to the south. It tries to show good northern resistance to loose frilliness, but the great conch shell capping the main entrance is unabashedly baroque, and is echoed inside by a sumptuous gold altarpiece and a pulpit draped in gold leaf. It was built to honour the patron saint of Spain, Santiago (Saint James), although the modern city's main **festival** (from the end of June to the beginning of August) prefers agriculture to religion.

Opposite the cathedral stands the fine **Government Palace**, a three-storey roseate building which is an exact reproduction of colonial might and majesty, built in 1928. The **Visual Arts Centre**, on the Juárez side of the plaza, shows occasional films. Its fine print collection includes works by Leopoldo Mendez of Aguascalientes, which pack a powerful political punch. He was influenced by the legendary 19th-century printmaker, Guadalupe Posada, whose skeletal figures can be seen all over Mexico.

The city's commercial life is centred around **Plaza Acuña**, named after a local poet, Manuel Acuña. A melancholic medical student, he committed suicide at the age of 23 by imbibing vast quantities of arsenic, which he had hoarded from the university laboratories.

WHERE TO STAY (area code 841)

Drive-through traffic tends to stop off at the motels on the highway, not deeming Saltillo worth a detour. The best of these are the *****Camino Real (Carreterra 57, tel 52525) and the mushroom-inspired ****La Torre opposite (tel 53333), both with large gardens, trailer parks and swimming pools.

In the city itself, the central ***San Jorge (Aldama and Manuel Acuña Norte 240, tel 30600) has a decent restaurant with magnificent panoramic views, which serves a northern breakfast of *machacada con huevo* (dried beef with scrambled eggs). Close by, and within spitting distance of the Plaza de Armas (one block west), the **Urdiñola (Victoria Pte 207, tel 40940) boasts an imposing stairway worthy of Scarlett O'Hara.

EATING OUT

Saltillo's excellent restaurants redeem some of its drabness: the girth of its citizens is a testament to its kitchens. Baby goats (eaten when one month old) figure prominently on the menu. Saltillans won't eat kid anywhere else, claiming that only the grasses of Coahuila can provide meat of sufficient succulence and tenderness.

The most attractive restaurant is El Tapanco (Allende Sur 225, a block southwest of the cathedral, tel 40043; closed Sun). Expensively rustic, set in a colonial house with log fires, it provides excellent food and calm service. The speciality is *filete tapanco* (a thin fillet of beef in a rich, dark chilli sauce). Moderately expensive. Boca del Río (on the north side of Allende where it crosses Lerdo, tel 24105) is often full. The menu is 100 per cent seafood, including squid in its own ink and oyster soup. Moderate. La Canasta (V Carranza 2485—the road out of town, tel 58050) is the preferred haunt of businessmen. It is a ranch-style affair with turn-of-the-century furniture, serving *arroz huérfano* (rice with bacon, pecans and pine nuts) and *pechuga rellena* (chicken breasts stuffed with cheese and parsley). Moderate. A vegetarian café (Gral Melchor Muzqui Pte 376; open 13.00–16.00, closed Sundays) provides granola, yoghurt and wholemeal sandwiches.

The State of Tamaulipas

The most easterly of the US border states, Tamaulipas snakes down the Gulf coast to its southern boundary with Veracruz. Topped and tailed by the rivers Bravo and Tamesi, it is sealed off to the west by the mountains of the Sierra Madre Oriental. Often ignored by the far-distant centre of the country, Tamaulipas nevertheless managed world headlines for a brief moment in 1989. The border town of Matamoros, a popular weekend spot for US students, was identified as the scene of a Satanic death cult when the gruesome remains of one US holiday-maker were found on the municipal rubbish tip, nibbled at by human molars. Cross-border traffic came to a grinding halt and Tamaulipas is still trying to forget the perhaps-mythical story that created such a media bonanza.

Ciudad Victoria

Only a palpable 45 km north of the Tropic of Cancer, Ciudad Victoria comes as an oasis after the hot, flat journey down from the border. Dust, heat and wind constantly gust straight from the Gulf over the plains to the city and on to the mountains of the Sierra Madre that finally loom into sight. It is a quiet, provincial state capital, peopled by solid citizens and prosperous farmers delighted to see any stray foreigner who blows in with the wind.

GETTING AROUND
By Air: The airport is east of town on the Tampico road. Aeromar fly to Mexico City on weekdays, and Aeroméxico fly to Nuevo Laredo and Monterrey. The Aeroméxico office is on the corner of Hidalgo and Calle 13.
By Bus: The bus station is on the ring road, northeast of the centre, where it crosses Av Carrera Torres. First-class buses connect Ciudad Victoria with all major towns in the northeast and on the Gulf coast, including Mexico City (12 hrs), the US border (5 hrs), Tampico (3 hrs) and Monterrey (4 hrs). Minibuses and taxis connect the station with the Zócalo.
By Car: Ciudad Victoria is 312 km south of Matamoros on Highway 101 and 242 km northwest of Tampico on Highways 85/80.
By Train: The railway station is to the west of the city, where Hidalgo becomes the Plaza Héroes de la Independencia. There are only two daily trains: one from Monterrey to Tampico and the other to Mexico City. Both are more used to goods than people and painfully slow.

TOURIST INFORMATION
The eager and helpful tourist office is on the ring road, on the 11th floor of the Dallas-inspired government tower (tel 21057, fax 25135).

WHAT TO SEE
There are few reasons to linger in Ciudad Victoria, except to draw breath after a long journey. A visit to the **Anthropology, Archaeology and History Museum** (Av Matamoros, just after the Teatro Juárez; open 10.00–16.00) is like a wander through an overfull antiques shop. The collection includes haphazardly arranged pre-Hispanic artefacts (mainly from the Huastec Sierra de Tamaulipas), grand carriages, and remnants of the Spanish days when Tamaulipas was known as Nuevo Santander. The exhibits may be rehoused in a smarter home, but the move isn't imminent. The **Centro Cultural**, in the Plaza Juárez, is a feather in the cap of the proud city. It houses the state library, an art gallery, cinema and theatre, as well as a **casa de artesanías** with some fine pieces of Huastec art and some pretty, elaborately worked lace collars. An excellent leather shop, **Artesanía Tamaulipeca**, to the left-hand side of the entrance (Pino Suárez 402 Sur, tel 21954), sells soft leather jackets, skirts, boots and trousers in any colour or design.

El Chorrito
Take Highway 85 north of Ciudad Victoria and turn left at Hidalgo for El Chorrito (23 km). The road leads ever upwards into the hills, through fragrant orange groves and

past a fabulous waterfall, to this small village, swelled by souvenir shops and pilgrims coming to pray to the miraculous Virgin of Guadalupe. This most Mexican of all Virgins was first seen in Mexico City in the 15th century. She appeared on a rock at El Chorrito at the beginning of this century, and a church was built around her image etched onto the rocks, which now forms the back of the altar. Every religious festival is celebrated with great ceremony but the Virgin's feast day (12 December) is the climax of a jamboree that lasts for a week.

Padilla

Some 54 km northeast of Ciudad Victoria, on Highway 101, is the vast Vicente Guerrero dam, peppered with hunting lodges once patronized by George Bush. Second-class buses make the 40-minute journey from the bus station in Ciudad Victoria.

The dam flooded the village of Padilla where the self-proclaimed emperor Iturbide was shot by a firing squad in 1824. His ostentatious imperial court (at which his birthday and those of his extended family were declared national holidays) was recognized as a travesty in newly independent Mexico, and lasted only months. He was unceremoniously bundled out of the country in 1823. After a brief exile in Italy and England, he attempted a comeback, but was captured on arrival and summarily executed. Today, only the remains of the hacienda and the church rise hauntingly above the water, like unwanted guests who refuse to leave.

WHERE TO STAY   (area code 131)

Ciudad Victoria has several good pit stops. The snazziest, *****Motel Las Fuentes (on the road to the airport and Tampico, tel 25655), has a trailer park, steak house and swimming pool. The ****Panorama (Av Lomas del Santuario, km 698, tel 25888) is a popular hotel, overlooking the town, with spacious rooms all leading off the swimming pool. The restaurant serves hefty breakfast such as *huevos tarascos* (layers of eggs, tortillas, ham and cheese with a hot green pepper sauce).

More modest hotels are in the main square, Plaza Hidalgo. The ***Sierra Gorda (Hidalgo Oriente 990, tel 22280) has pretensions to grandeur, with deep-pile carpeting on floor and ceilings, cable TV and air conditioning. Unassuming **Los Monteros (Hidalgo 962 Ote, tel 20300) has a lovely tiled lobby and clean, simple rooms with fans, leading off two sunny courtyards.

The most attractive hotel in the state is the ****Hacienda Sta Engracia (off Highway 85, 30 mins north of Ciudad Victoria; reservations should be made through the office in Ciudad Victoria, Aldama 1062 Ote, tel 24356, tlx 031214; advance booking advisable Aug–Nov). The Martínez family still own this small country hotel, set in the heart of orange-growing country, where the camellias hang off the trees. The rooms are redolent of the days of wealthy landowners, with heavy wooden furniture and fires crackling for each guest. Ask for a room in the older section, which is hung with portraits of young women, all former secretaries. There is blissfully little to do—a pool to swim in, some horses to ride and some tennis to play. The dining room, where all the guests congregate for massive dinners, is presided over by family portraits.

363

EATING OUT
The dining room at **Posta Plaza** (11 Zaragoza 701, tel 21444; two blocks south and three west of the main square) is filled with sunlight and plants. The food is consistently good, particularly the quail grilled with bacon. Moderate. An octagonal building resembling a beach café, on the road to Monterrey, makes an unprepossessing setting for the fine food of **Los Cotorros**, which includes dishes such as river trout stuffed with shrimp and squid. Moderate. University students meet after classes in the café of the Centro Cultural. Cheap.

Tampico

The port of Tampico is a breezy old tar which has seen better days. World-weary and jaded, it nevertheless retains a strangely alluring sea-shanty air. On the north bank of the Río Pánuco, it emerges from the lushness of the tropics with belching factories, oil refineries and power lines. It announces its antecedents loud and clear. Oil is all. Nevertheless, it is a lively place to stop for a day or two, with a fine Huastec museum and long beaches within easy reach of the centre.

History
The Spaniards sailed up the Gulf coast from Cuba to the mouth of the Río Pánuco in 1518 but waited 10 years to establish a colony. French filibusters, who didn't accept Spanish hegemony in the New World, came in from the Gulf and destroyed the small settlement. It wasn't rebuilt until ranching families moved to the lush river banks in the 1820s. Surface seepages of petroleum were spotted by the Californian oil magnate, Edward Doheny, in the 1880s. He immediately bought 600,000 acres, turning it overnight into a boom city with a port to rival Veracruz. Other multinationals followed— Standard Oil, Royal Dutch, and the Pearson company (owned by Lord Cowdray), dominating the industry until it was spectacularly nationalized by President Cárdenas in 1938.

GETTING AROUND
By Air: Tampico airport is 15 km north on Highway 80, the Ciudad Victoria road. Mexicana and Aeromar run daily flights to Mexico City, Veracruz, Nuevo Laredo and Monterrey. Both have offices at the airport. Airport minibuses leave from the Hotel Inglaterra on the Plaza de Armas (tel 133614).
By Bus: Tampico's main bus station is in the north of the city, linked to the centre by Chevrolet communal taxis. First-class buses provide frequent daily services to towns in the north and on the Gulf coast, including Mexico City (9 hrs), Veracruz (10 hrs), the border at Matamoros (8 hrs) and Ciudad Victoria (3 hrs).
By Car: A Gulf coast crossroads, Tampico is halfway between the US frontier and the port of Veracruz and only 9 hours from Mexico City. Highway 81 from Ciudad Victoria (242 km) crosses the Pánuco River at Tampico, over a gracefully arching bridge, and continues as Highway 180 to Veracruz (502 km). Inland routes to Mexico City (Highway

105, 468 km) or San Luis Potosí (Highway 70, 392 km) have to cross the mountainous barrier of the Sierra Madre, through the heart of the Huasteca region.

TOURIST INFORMATION
The tourist office, no more than a sub-office, is on the east side of the Zócalo, on the second floor of Olmos Sur 102 (tel 122668).

WHAT TO SEE
The elegant **Plaza de Armas** is the centre of town. In the evenings, cruise-ship crowds admire the Andalusian kiosk with its tiled dome and wildly flying buttresses, echoing to the sound of the mariachi bands. Here too is the 19th-century cathedral, whose twin towers encase a Byzantine-inspired mosaic of the Last Supper. The evening service is packed every Sunday, with the fans whirring loudly throughout. A mad scram of children is always first out, rushing across to the soda fountain opposite the Hotel Inglaterra.

The **Plaza de la Libertad** is one block south on Olmos and one east on Madero. This is Tampico's oldest square, where trams ran until the 1970s. The buildings date from the turn of the century, when Porfirio Díaz was president and France was the arbiter of taste. This influence can be seen in the post office (on Madero) and the telegraph office next door, as well as in the iron-railed, creole-style balconies of the Hotel Del Rey, where members of the oil aristocracy once disported themselves. On the southwest Aduana corner is the Edificio Luz, a prefabricated building brought over from England and built on a base of palm trunks.

Museo de la Cultura Huasteca
(In the Tecnológico Madero; open 10.00–17.00, Mon–Fri.)
This unpublicized Huastec museum is the most important of its kind in all Mexico: only the Huastec room in the Museum of Anthropology in Mexico City comes close to the range and exquisite delicacy displayed in its collection of sculptured forms. It is in Tampico's twin town of Ciudad Madero, 7 km from the Plaza de Armas. Follow the Monterrey road to the Camino Real hotel and turn right after 700 m into Av Ejército Nacional. Alternatively, take a northbound beach bus (eg 'López Mateos' from López de Lara, three blocks east of the Plaza de Armas).

There are still 50,000 Huastecs in southeast San Luis Potosí, northern Veracruz and southern Tamaulipas, but in their heyday (over 1000 years ago) their influence extended to the Maya in Guatemala (where there is still a strong linguistic link), central Mexico, the Toltecs and later, the Aztecs. Their pantheon of gods was copied by others, particularly the Goddess of Love, Tlazoltéotl, and her partner, the God of Flowers, Xochiquetzal. The Huastecs were a prickly people, quick to anger, almost continually at war with the Aztecs. This led them to make a foolhardy alliance with the Spanish, which in turn resulted in their near-obliteration by the tyrant-conqueror, Nuño de Guzmán, who went on to destroy the Purépecha of Michoacán.

The museum's earliest Huastec ceramics are pots dating from 1100 BC. Their form was gradually developed, first with incisions in the smooth clay, representing eyes and mouths, and then with tripod feet. They were later dyed orange, red and brown, with coffee-bean brown eyes, before finally taking on animal shapes around 50 BC. The museum displays extensive collections of ceramics, costumes and shellwork. It also

365

includes some sublime sculptures, which concentrate on the gods but are earthy enough to show a few deformities (and a few beauty marks, with big-thighed women coming top of the list).

BEACHES
Miramar beach stretches languorously along the coast for 10 km, 15 km from the centre. Buses marked 'Recreativo' go from López de Lara (three blocks east of the Plaza de Armas) to the quiet **Playa Mar**, where ex-oil-union boss, La Quina, built a 16-room hotel and restaurant for the families of his members. It is very cheap, and foreigners would be welcomed, though they never come.

The beaches show the Mexican passion for family and companionship: privacy is not a Mexican concept. Those by the river mouth are filled with families who can't imagine a day at the beach without grandma, grandpa, aunts, uncles, vast amounts of food and cases of beer, all driven straight on to the sand (where every learner driver has his first lesson). There are a few, old, clapboard beach houses with rocking chairs swung by the wind. Deserted bandstands may conjure up the sound of Glenn Miller, but stereos on the Playa Rol compete with Madonna.

WHERE TO STAY
(area code 121)

Tampico offers two sorts of hotels. Around the staid Plaza de Armas are the formal, smart hotels such as the efficient ******Inglaterra** (Díaz Mirón 116 Ote, tel 125678, tlx 14735, fax 140556). Between this and the more ebullient Plaza de la Libertad is the ******Colonial** (Madero 210 Ote, tel 127676), a pleasant, modern hotel with large rooms and good bathrooms. A few doors along, the once attractive *****Posada del Rey** (Madero 118, tel 24464) has been carved up into boxes, tastelessly upgraded room by room.

The other sort of hotel leers and winks like an ageing tart at all and sundry. The **Tampico** (four blocks west of the cathedral, Carranza 513 Ote, tel 24970), built to the latest 1944 fashions, has a fine sweeping tiled lobby and a ball room reminiscent of *thé dansant*, silk stockings and red lipstick. The **(CE) Gran Hotel Rivera** (Héroes del Cañonero 102 Pte), built in 1925, used to be one of the greats, the haunt of politicians, film stars and the gilded cruise-ship set. Now it lets its rooms by the hour, sunk into resigned degradation. Only echoes remain of former elegance. The *****Capri** (two blocks north of the Plaza de Armas, Juárez 202 Nte, tel 22680) is a more comfortable, less atmospheric alternative.

On the road to the airport are several more oil-directed motels and hotels. On the beach is the *****Posada de Tampico**, a vast resort with cool, fresh rooms, baths, swimming pools and a bookshop offering discounts on books like *El Arte de Amar en la Pareja* (*The Art of Making Love in a Couple*).

EATING OUT
Seafood is the order of the day. The elegant **El Jardín Corona** (one block from the Camino Real on Av Hidalgo) eschews frozen fish: the red snapper, shark and dog fish come straight from the boats to the table. Expensive. For Chinese seafood, **La Gran Muralla** (by the Posada Tampico, Av Hidalgo 5201) is the best in Tampico, combining Mexican and Chinese traditions to great effect. Moderate. There are two

well-established seafood **Diligencias**: the oldest is to the north on Calle Ayuntamiento 2702; the other, draped in nets and lobster pots, is in the centre at Calonero Ote 415. Moderate. The fish restaurant **Pikio**, at the mouth of the river and south end of the beach, is packed at weekends, serving up endless *brochetas de pescado adobado* (baked fish kebabs). The Sunday brunch in the Posada de Tampico is equally popular. The Posada del Rey has two busy but modest restaurants—the Spanish **La Troja**, and **La Tasca**, which serves crab, shrimps and *gringas* (flour tortillas stuffed with bacon, spicy sausage and cheese). Inexpensive. Underneath it is the 1930s **Café Selecto**, one of the oldest in town, buzzing from 7 o'clock in the morning. Politicians go first to the appropriately named café **Elita** (just off the main plaza at Díaz Mirón 211), shifting in the afternoon to **Mundo**, two blocks down the same street. Inexpensive.

The State of San Luis Potosí

After the barren north, the state of San Luis Potosí, below the Tropic of Cancer, is the first to look south rather than north, proud of its Mexican ancestry and far removed from the modern would-be Texan towns near the US border. It stretches from the centre of the country towards the Gulf, and rewards exploration with tantalizing tastes of 17th-century splendour, markets in hidden villages and waterfalls in tropical jungle. Unused to foreign tourists, it's a state where one is unlikely to meet Bob from back home. In prosperous, colonial San Luis Potosí, the state capital, an abundance of gold and silver mines provided the wherewithal for the extravagant baroque churches and dignified buildings which line its streets. The town makes a good overnight stop on the way south, with enough to see to entice visitors to spend an extra night.

In the north of the state, on the way down from Monterrey and Saltillo, the eerily empty ghost town of Real de Catorce was once an affluent mining centre. The doors of the abandoned bank flap aimlessly in the breeze and those who knew better days now lie in its rambling cemetery. It has a charming hotel which is well worth making a break for, from the border. To the east lies the luscious green land of the Huasteca, where small Huastec villages nestle amongst waterfalls, jungles of bamboo and rolling hills, with colourful markets every Sunday. Families often walk 20 miles to attend, the women with their hair elaborately bound in bright woollen turbans. The eccentric English artist, Edward James, lived amongst all of this, creating his surreal sculptures in the jungle near Xilitla.

SAN LUIS POTOSI

Sprawling unceremoniously across the flat San Luis valley, the city of San Luis Potosí tries hard to hide its glorious lights under the bushels of dust which blow in from the deserts all around. Industry is kept hidden on the outskirts, fringing a colonial centre of narrow balconied streets and elaborately carved rose-pink churches. Exuberant facades and carvings impart a medieval atmosphere, making up in enthusiasm for what they lack in architectural discipline.

Today, San Luis Potosí is a quietly prosperous political nerve-centre and an active backbencher. It is fiercely pro-PAN, the conservative party which opposes the government. This is sheer cussedness, as San Luis Potosí has always been nonconformist and is really a liberal at heart. Proudly self-supporting, it doesn't like being told what to do by the centre of the country. It is also something of a cultural whizz kid, encouraging composers, dancers and actors to its festivals with well-attended performances. By day, the centre bustles with self-important government officials; at night, fringe theatres burst at the seams with enthusiastic audiences.

History

Until the Spanish discovered gold in 1592, no-one had given a second glance to the arid plain of San Luis Potosí, apart from the semi-nomadic Guachichil tribes, who had liked it enough to break with custom and settle for 300 years. The land-hungry mestizo captain Miguel Caldera decided to try his hand at appropriating the area in 1550. In the 40 years it took him to establish a hold, the Franciscans, on the lookout for wild, untamed areas to evangelize, moved in and founded a monastery. In 1592, their sleepy outpost received a sudden jolt when whispered rumours of gold drew hordes of fortune hunters to the valley. Caldera had opened a mine which proved lucrative beyond his wildest dreams. He founded the city of San Luis around the Franciscan monastery, giving it the name of France's saintly king. He added Potosí a little later, after the fabulously wealthy Bolivian silver city, hoping that his own mines would be as lucrative.

By 1633, San Luis Potosí had become the third most important city in Mexico. Despite the odd flutter in its fortunes, it remained prosperous, becoming capital of Northern Mexico in the 17th century. Wealthy citizens subscribed to elaborate churches to assuage their guilt, and built elegant houses to announce their new-found status.

In the 19th century, San Luis Potosí was the capital of the republic twice. In 1867 President Juárez signed Emperor Maximilian's death warrant here, despite the pleas of the deranged Empress Carlota and European intellectuals such as Victor Hugo. Later in the 19th century, San Luis Potosí became a centre for liberal factions plotting the end of the dictator Porfirio Díaz's long regime. Francisco Madero, unwitting author of the Revolution, was imprisoned in San Luis Potosí on election day to prevent him standing against Diáz. Enraged, he hatched his 'San Luis Potosí plan' which culminated in the 1910 Revolution.

GETTING AROUND

By Air: There are daily flights to Mexico City and three a week to Monterrey. The Mexicana office (Madero and Uresti, tel 41119) will book flights and also runs a combi to and from the airport, which is north of the city on the Saltillo road. There is also an airport taxi service (on 5 de Mayo, tel 40054).

By Bus: The bus station is to the east of town, where Highway 57 bypasses the city on its way from the north to Mexico City. Combis and town buses connect the station with the Alameda in the centre. Excellent first-class buses leave for destinations all over Mexico almost every hour, including Zacatecas (3 hrs), Monterrey (6 hrs), Reynosa on the US border (8 hrs), Mexico City (5 hrs) and Guanajuato (4 hrs).

By Car: Highway 57 connects San Luis Potosí with Piedras Negras and the US border (889 km) via Saltillo in the north, and with Mexico City (413 km) via Querétaro in the

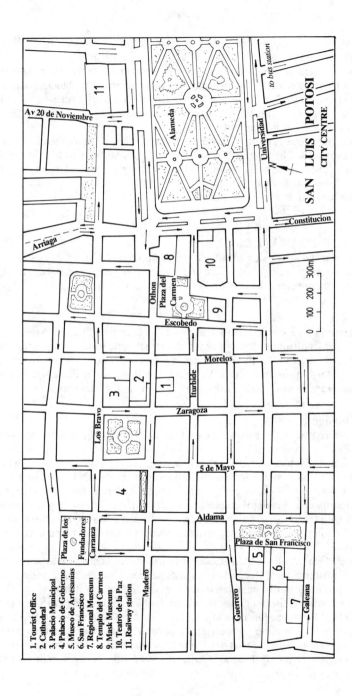

SAN LUIS POTOSI
CITY CENTRE

to bus station

Av 20 de Noviembre

Arriaga

Constitucion

Universidad

Alameda

Othon

Plaza del Carmen

Escobedo

Morelos

Iturbide

Zaragoza

Los Bravo

5 de Mayo

Aldama

Plaza de los Fundadores

Carranza

Plaza de San Francisco

Madero

Guerrero

Galeana

0   100   200   300m

1. Tourist Office
2. Cathedral
3. Palacio Municipal
4. Palacio de Gobierno
5. Museo de Artesanias
6. San Francisco
7. Regional Museum
8. Templo del Carmen
9. Mask Museum
10. Teatro de la Paz
11. Railway station

south. Highway 70 passes through San Luis Potosí on its way from Tampico to Aguascalientes and Highway 49 leads northeast to Zacatecas.

By Train: The railway station is to the east of town, opposite the Alameda park. It is a short walk from the centre: from the cathedral, take Othón for five blocks, past the tourist office, and turn left into Av 20 de Noviembre. San Luis Potosí is well connected. First-class trains leave daily for Aguascalientes in the west and Tampico in the east, and for Laredo on the US border and Mexico City.

In Town: The centre is most easily seen on foot: nowhere is more than 5 minutes' walk from the cathedral. The main streets are one-way: Othón runs east to west and Iturbide west to east. San Luis Potosí is surrounded by a bypass and any road out of the centre will eventually join up with this.

For **car hire**, try Rente del Centro (Carranza 757, tel 21248) or Rente un AutoKar (Carranza 757, tel 22606).

TOURIST INFORMATION
The office on the south side of the cathedral (in Othón 130, tel 23143) is a fund of information, and provides good advice on planning trips outside the city. A notice board displays programmes for theatres and entertainment in general.

WHAT TO SEE
The epicentre of the city is **Jardín Hidalgo** (also known as Plaza de Armas), bursting with intricate negotiations in every corner. Priests struggle to save souls in the cathedral, and politicians machinate in the Palacio de Gobierno opposite, both breaking for leisurely coffees in the café **de la Virreina**. To the east, in Plaza del Carmen, the Carmelite church and eclectic mask museum both vie for attention.

Jardín Hidalgo
On the eastern side of the square, the **cathedral** in Jardín Hidalgo has been squeezed by the Palacio Municipal next door, and blows its cheeks out in disapproval with an unusually protuberant baroque facade. The Italophile Bishop Montes de Oca supervised its remodelling on his return from Rome. No expense was spared: the four Apostles on the front, copies of those in the Lateran chapel in Rome, are made of Carraran marble. Inside, the marble San Sebastian is a copy of a Roman original, while the wooden choir was carved by Italians brought over to do all the woodwork. Today the choir is the favourite haunt of those who want to sleep off an over-indulgence of pulque.

Bishop de Oca was also responsible for the turn-of-the-century embellishments to the **Palacio Municipal**, next door. Italian artists painted chocolate-box ceilings and even created reproductions of Pompeian mosaics at the foot of the stairway.

Across the square, the neoclassical **Palacio Gobierno**, finished in 1816, now houses wax models of President Juárez being implored by the Teutonic beauty, Princess Salm Salm, to spare the life of her compatriot, Emperor Maximilian. (An unimpressed Juárez signed his death warrant the next day.) The adjoining room houses banks of portraits of past luminaries, including Idalfonso Díaz de León, the first governor in Mexico to abolish slavery (in 1837).

East of Jardín Hidalgo
Follow Othón down from the cathedral to Plaza del Carmen, which opens out in front of the **Templo del Carmen**. Originally the whole square formed part of the atrium of the Carmelite monastery, which was the pride of the city. The church, finished in 1764, is an outstanding example of late Mexican baroque.

Its facade is elaborately decorated from the tip of its illicit tower to the toe of its unusually florid base. Nicolas Fernando de Torres earned his surname by building this vast tower. They were normally forbidden on Carmelite churches, but in this case palms were greased and the authorities managed to overlook its construction. It is divided into three levels: at the top of the facade, the Virgin (del Carmen) and her son represent the future. Halfway down, the reformers Saint Teresa and Saint John of the Cross represented the 18th-century present and below, in niches either side of the door, Elias, founder of the order, and Elijah symbolize the past.

Inside, past a pink volcanic-stone *retablo* edged with gold, are two baroque *retablos* covered in shining 24-carat gold, either side of architect Tresguerras' neoclassical altarpiece. The main treasure, however, is the breathtaking, gloriously self-indulgent Chapel of the Virgin or House of the Five Lords, covered in carved figures. In a swirl of garish colour, four of the five 'lords', Mary, Joseph, Jesus and Saint Anne, gaze down from the ceiling. St John is represented symbolically by a large conch shell. Five and seven are particular numerical favourites of the Carmelites. The entrance to the chapel is known as the Door of the Seven Princes, an unmissable baroque extravaganza. God presides from the top and was originally lit by the soft glow of many candles, whose holders still remain. Unfortunately they cast their light rather too enthusiastically upon his glory in 1957 and the whole facade was badly damaged by fire.

In the same square is the **Museum of Masks** (open 10.00–14.00 and 16.00–18.00, closed Mon), with the best collection in the country. Room after room is hung with ritual masks from every region. Pink-cheeked, fair-haired effigies of conquistadors look angelic beside the snarling bloodstained fangs of jaguars. Opposite, the neoclassical **Teatro de la Paz** has concerts and plays most evenings. Huge mosaics by Fernando Leal line the walls, dominating the lobby, treating of pre-Hispanic dervishes, 17th-century pastorals and a favourite Mexican farce—the dialogue between *La Gorda* (the fat woman) and *El Flaco* (the thin man).

Behind the square are the benched gardens of the **Alameda**, once the orchards of the Carmelite monastery and now a place to sit and watch children chase balls.

West of Jardín Hidalgo
Southwest of the cathedral, one block down Othón and then left into Aldama, **Plaza San Francisco** opens onto the street. A cool sheltered square with fountains and leafy trees, it is a perfect foil for the gentle baroque facade of its Franciscan church. The interior was once rich in paintings, now lost or stolen. All that remains of the original Franciscans is a carved and knotted girdle around the stone font. The most interesting piece is a statue of St Francis which bends at the joints like a mannequin. It was used to encourage novices in their prayers, genuflecting with the boys. A huge crystal chandelier in the shape of a galleon hangs from the dome, a gift from a wealthy patron who survived a shipwreck. At the back of the church, the sacristy is filled with 18th-century furniture, paintings, baroque carvings and estípites. Above the door there is an unusual relief of St Francis

having his stigmatas tended to. It is packed full of symbols, such as lambs, water and skulls. The tropical birds in the trees (unknown to Europe) are an exotic local addition. On the other side of this door, another baroque flurry is dedicated to the Virgin, who is flanked by her symbols of the sun and the moon. The relief also depicts the theologian Duns Scotus, who defended her honour by proving the Immaculate Conception. It's best to ask permission to enter the sacristy from the padre, who sits in his office inside.

In the same square is an incongruous Presbyterian chapel, built for Anglo-Saxon miners (the John Wesley chapel down the road now sports an ignominious 'garage and spare parts' neon light), and a **Casa de Artesanías**. Here you can buy the fine silk *rebosos* (shawls) for which San Luis Potosí is famous. Tradition has it that a woman should be able to pass a shawl through her wedding ring. Looms have been set up to show how it's done and the prices are cheaper than in any of the tourist-oriented shops.

Round the corner in Galeana is the excellent **Regional Museum** (open 10.00–13.00 and 15.00–18.00, 10.00–12.00 weekends, closed Mon), which has a fine collection of Huastec art. Upstairs, the elaborate churrigueresque decoration of the Aranzazu chapel contrasts to the plainness of its white walls. It was designed to impress novices who were contemplating entering the order.

Back towards the centre, up Aldama, is the saffron-walled **Caja Real** where the king's fifth (*quinto*) was measured out. The Spanish monarch was entitled to a fifth of everything coming out of the mines. The staircase is an oddity, its steps low and widely spaced to accommodate the paces of the unfortunates who lugged the gold and silver up to be weighed.

Northwest of Jardín Hidalgo

The **Plaza de los Fundadores** was once dominated by the black gowns of young Jesuits going in and out of their seminary. Now it is an empty open square, edged on the west by the neoclassical Edificio Piña. Escaping plans to turn the whole square into a grave neoclassical quadrangle, the Jesuit **Capilla de Loreto**, on the northern side, has kept its fine naive baroque facade. A particularly Mexican touch is the carving of a domestic cat, used instead of St Mark's more common symbol, the ferocious lion. Local craftsmen couldn't get the hang of the foreign animal the Jesuits kept asking for and the cat was a compromise. Inside is one of the few remaining Jesuit altarpieces in Mexico, a feast of green and gold. Most of them were destroyed when the Jesuits were recalled to Spain in 1767. A small wooden doorway leads through to the **Iglesia de la Compañia**, another earlier Jesuit church built in 1675. Between the two, a cross carved from rock survives from the foundation of the city. The courtyard of the Jesuit college next door is now the rectorate of the university and clacks with typewriters.

FIESTAS

On Good Friday, the streets fill in an eerie procession of silence. Figures dressed in hoods reminiscent of the Klu Klux Klan and cloaks of different hues, each representing a different neighbourhood, march in silence and the air is suffused by a heady incense. In the San Juan de Guadalupe district, a livelier representation of the Passion of Christ is re-enacted on the same day. Jews and Pharisees accompany the condemned Christ on his journey to the Cross. Concerts and exhibitions are held all over town during Easter week. In May there is an international arts festival with concerts, theatre and cinema.

The day of Saint Louis of France, patron of the city, is celebrated on 25 August, and always coincides with a big agricultural fair, complete with bull fights and *charreadas* (Mexican rodeos).

WHERE TO STAY   (area code 481)

Hotels aren't a strong point in San Luis. The hoteliers have eschewed antiquity for modern, stolid hotels of little character, to cater for the overnight needs of businessmen and families. What the hotels lose in crumbling, colonial charm, they gain in comfort and service. The ****Panorama (Av Venustiano Carranza 315, tel 21777, tlx 13655) is the most central and up-market, with large rooms looking out over the city. It has a small pool, a smart restaurant and a swift efficient café which fills with paper-reading Potosinos every morning. Further down the scale, ***Concordia (Othón and Morelos, tel 20666, next to the tourist office and the cathedral) and ***María Cristina (Sarabia 110, tel 29408, by the Templo del Carmen) are both mediocre, with clean rooms that don't make one want to linger.

The **Progreso (Aldama 415, tel 20366) and the **Filher (Universidad and Zaragoza, tel 21562) are the nearest the town gets to quirky hotels. The Progreso has creaking wooden floorboards and turn-of-the-century furniture, and seems surprised to have got as far as the 1990s. The Filher looks promising, with a colonial facade and an interior courtyard, but unfortunately it has been badly modernized, with rooms squeezed into every nook and cranny. The **de Gante (Madero and 5 de Mayo, tel 21492, off the main square) has corridors of swirling carpet where many have trodden before and standard, spartan rooms.

The cheapest hotels of all are by the train station: try the Anáhuac first (Xochitl 140, tel 26504), then the Jardín Potosí (Los Bravo 530, tel 23152) or the Guadalajara next door.

EATING OUT

San Luis Potosí is famed for its *enchiladas potosinas* (small fried tortillas dyed red with *chile ancho* and filled with cheese, served with strips of avocado and fried beans). At Easter they're known as *enchiladas del santuario* and are sold outside the steps of the cathedral, filled with piping-hot creamy cheese and sprinkled on top with a drier salty cheese. Another favourite is *fiambre potosino* (a combination of chicken, tongue and boned pig's trotter marinated in thyme and marjoram). Dishes from the state include delicious *cabuches*, the buds of the *biznaga* cactus which taste like artichoke hearts and look like tiny soft green pine cones. *Tuna* or prickly pear is eaten a great deal, either fresh, turned into cheese (*queso de tuna*) or as *calonche*, a fiery, throat-burning drink.

Expensive

La Lonja (Madero and Aldama, tel 28119) is the best restaurant in town. Politicians sit in neoclassical splendour over long lunches of the most delicately prepared regional food. Starched waiters flurry to the snapping of fingers. The food is worth all the fuss. To start, try a salad of *cabuches* with palm hearts and yucca flower buds (*chochas*), or a *sopa de elote con huitlacoche*, a blackened corn soup tasting of creamy mushroom, which becomes addictive after a mouthful. The huge range of steaks is often ignored in favour of the most popular of all dishes, *gusanos de maguey*. These are the worms found in the heart of the maguey cactus, which are fried a deep golden brown in butter and then rolled in tortillas, served with lashings of *guacamole*. They taste of barbecued sausages and even the squeamish can be won round to them.

Los Vitrales is similarly elegant, with an extensive international menu and a consistent local following. The marinaded *fiambre potosino* is refreshing and light in the heat of the day.

Moderate
For regional food in more practical surroundings, try **El Cielo Potosino** (Julian de los Reyes, tel 42428, to the north of centre). *Enchiladas potosinas* are always on the menu. On the main square, the **Posada de la Virreina** is a popular café in which to sit and sip coffees or beers. It's one of the oldest buildings in the city, named after a tenuous connection to Francisca de la Gandara (whose uncle lived here), the only Mexican national ever to marry a Spanish viceroy and become first lady. Ask to see the elaborately carved baroque stove which still survives in a back room on the first floor.

Cheap
There is an abundance of small cafés in the centre, all serving large comida corridas and coffees. One of the best is the friendly **El Bocolito** on Plaza San Francisco, which is run by a cooperative to raise funds to help young students. They take it in turns to serve the food, which is regional, cheap and always filling. **Café Tokio**, on the Alameda by the train station, is wholeheartedly Mexican despite its Japanese name and decor. It is always packed to the brim with families and young couples consuming quantities of enchiladas, tortas and even elaborate fish dishes. For a cultural change, **Fuk Chong** (Carranza 875, tel 41919) is an authentic Cantonese restaurant, while the **Yu Ne Ni Sa** (Arista and Independencia, tel 43631) is vegetarian, with a good comida corrida at lunch time.

Maguey cactus used to make pulque

North to Real de Catorce

The only way to enter Real de Catorce is via a long black shaft of tunnel. In the bright sunlight at the other end, one blinks and steps back a hundred years. Like a movie set, it has banks, dusty cobbled streets, ancient cars and frothing horses. By rights, a 10-gun John Wayne should walk bow-legged down the street. Unlike a movie set, it's the real thing. Once a rich gold town, the richest in the state, its prosperity dwindled and the 1910 Revolution finally finished it off. Most of the inhabitants left, leaving behind a sad bullring, a cemetery of faded grandeur and poignant balconied buildings as testaments to better times. Only the shops are still in use, their wooden counters and shelves stocked sparsely with tins.

Real de Catorce is a holy place, high up in the mountains, with a curious tranquillity in the air. Pilgrims and penitents come on their knees to worship the St Francis in the church. On 4 October the town fills for his week-long festival. In April, the Huichol make a 43-day pilgrimage all the way from Nayarit, in search of their sacred *peyote* (*lophophora williamsii*), a hallucinogenic plant found high up in the hills, which doesn't grow in Nayarit. They used to come the 500 km on foot, but nowadays often complete the journey by bus or truck.

GETTING AROUND

A 3-km narrow tunnel, once a mine shaft, provides the only entrance to Real de Catorce. It is low enough to prevent big tourist buses passing through, with room for single-file traffic only. The odd bus or car is controlled at each end by men with radio telephones.

By Bus: Real de Catorce is 30 km west of Matehuala on Highway 57. Regular buses ply up and down the highway between San Luis Potosí and Saltillo, stopping at Matehuala (3 hrs from each). From Matehuala, there are three buses a day to Real de Catorce (1½ hrs), leaving morning, noon and mid-afternoon, from Hidalgo, near the Hotel Matehuala. The last bus back from Real de Catorce leaves at 16.00.

By Car: Real de Catorce is 280 km from Saltillo and 230 km from San Luis Potosí. Turn west at the Matehuala junction on Highway 57 (1 hr's drive via La Paz).

In Town: The village is small, with no formal street plan. Lanza Gorta is the main street, leading from the tunnel to the church. Beyond this Gorta curls on round to the cemetery, 1 km on from the church. There aren't any signs but it's an easy place to nose around.

TOURIST INFORMATION

All phone calls go through the operator (known, like an 007 agent, as Caseta 4) who will relay messages, like a Chinese whisper, through the village. It's better not to rely on them reaching their destination intact. Jorge Quijano Leyva is the town's information officer and delightful guide. He is usually in the mint, but can be reached through Caseta 4. Now in his 60s, he has lived in Real de Catorce all his life and witnessed the dwindling of its fortunes. He isn't paid and never asks for money, but desperately needs help to keep up the museum.

WHAT TO SEE

The Parish Church

Dedicated to the Virgin, the 18th-century church is better known for its shrine to a miraculous St Francis. The walls are lined with *retablos*, small votive paintings offered to the saint in thanks for near misses in the car, effective cures and other favours. They are a marvellous example of naive Mexican art, particularly the older ones painted on tin which line the bell tower. Beside these hang locks of hair, cut off in penance. Thanks to the generosity of these pilgrims, the neoclassical interior of the church has been restored, its gleaming paint highlighting the disrepair all around. Its original *mesquite* (wood) floor is the only one of its kind in the state.

Casa de Moneda

Opposite the church, the imposing old mint was the most important building in town for one year, in the mid-19th century, when it produced its own coins. It had taken so long to build that the mine's fortunes were already on the wane by the time it opened. Today it is a temporary art gallery, with a small studio next door where Italians make and sell jewellery.

Museum

In the street below the mint, and completely disorganized, is the town's museum. It resembles a Victorian attic, filled with dusty bits and pieces from the last century—tarnished medals, sepia photographs curling up at the edges and even an old car. Everything is piled in heaps with a singular lack of ceremony. It's a fascinating jumble of the last hundred years.

Church and Cemetery

There is another smaller church out by the cemetery, past the restored bullring and cockfighting *palenque*. It stands in the midst of a ramshackle cemetery and is buttressed at the back to prevent it sliding into history. Inside, the cupola is painted with faded church dignitaries. Donkeys loaded with wood and flowers wander past on the track outside, which leads up to the most recently closed mine and to villages in the hills. On the way, scattered stones are threaded with silver, making hope spring eternal.

WHERE TO STAY AND EAT

There are two hotels. The ***Real (Caseta 4 or Matehuala 22593) is an old house in the centre, which has been converted without fuss into an utterly delightful hotel. The owners put wild flowers in the bedrooms and make all their guests feel more than welcome. There are quilts on the beds and tiles on the floor. Downstairs, the Italian-run restaurant serves wholemeal bread, salads and yoghurt as well as a variety of pastas. It's the best place to eat in town. Moderate. **Quinta La Puesta del Sol is out towards the far end of town, by the cemetery. It is littered with signs telling people to enjoy themselves, whilst at the same time warning them in four languages not to steal the towels. The rooms are reasonably priced but spartan, with flood-the-bathroom showers, redeemed to some extent by excellent views of the valley below. In town, there are a couple of **cafés** with no name, the front rooms of houses, where the food is fresh and home cooked.

East to the Huasteca

Highway 70, from San Luis Potosí to Tampico, twists over the heights of the Sierra Madre before descending to the fertile plains and rolling hills of the Huasteca. It is a breathtaking rollercoaster, which finally comes to a gentle halt in a swelter of tropical heat. The rural Huastec have lived in this area for centuries, driven to villages and hamlets in the foothills after the Spanish invaded and appropriated the best of their rich lands. Ciudad Valles, a characterless but substantial town, is a good base from which to explore the area.

On the way from San Luis Potosí, there are unbelievably azure-blue waterfalls and lakes to swim in. To the south are the Huastec villages with their big bright Sunday markets and the surreal sculptures of Edward James, whilst to the east are the sulphur baths and spartan remains of the Huastec site of Tamuín. Although the local bus network extends to most of these places, they are sufficiently remote to make it worth hiring a car for a couple of days.

GETTING AROUND

By Bus: Regular first-class buses run between Ciudad Valles and San Luis Potosí (5 hrs), Tampico (3 hrs), Ciudad Victoria (4 hrs), Monterrey (7 hrs) and Mexico City (10 hrs). Ciudad Valle's bus station is out of town, to the southeast, on the road to Mexico City (Highway 85). Local second-class buses go to the markets: check at the bus station for times. Town buses connect the main square with the station, marked 'Central de Autobuses'.

By Car: Ciudad Valles is 265 km east of San Luis Potosí and 142 km west of Tampico, on Highway 70. Ciudad Victoria is 232 km north on long winding Highway 85, which continues southwards to Mexico City (477 km).

By Train: One daily train leaves San Luis Potosí early in the morning, stopping at Ciudad Valles en route for Tampico. It returns in the afternoon. The journey is spectacular, but takes forever. The train stops at the waterfalls of Tamasopo.

WHAT TO SEE

The Climb into the Sierra

Just outside San Luis Potosí, the road starts its climb out of the dusty, flat valley into the Sierra Madre Oriental. The earth takes on rich terra-cotta tones and a rumpled blanket of rolling pine-clad foothills stretches all around. In the distance, the narrow thread of road can be seen forging its way through what seems to be an inpenetrable pass. Extravagantly shaped stone boulders loom large on either side. For 100 km the road spirals past high hamlets with smoking chimneys, before beginning its descent into the fertile plain around Río Verde. The air fills with the scent of oranges and tangerines, grown in grove after grove in the fields around.

Laguna de la Media Luna

A couple of km before Río Verde, a small sign points right to Laguna de la Media Luna. It's easy to miss: if you overshoot, it is only a short drive back from Río Verde. After 11 km, a bumpy track reaches the banks of the lake, which is shaped like a half-moon and surrounded by pines. Its water is so translucent that the bottom is always visible. In the afternoon the light casts a sheen on it, making it a deep rich blue. The silence is only disturbed at weekends when families arrive with tents and snorkels. There's a small shack selling the saccharine drinks that Mexicans are fond of, but little else.

Río Verde
Río Verde is a quiet, small, provincial town, bemused by the juggernauts which pass on the highway. In the centre, horses and *solkis* (brougham carts) are used as much as jeeps and the pace of life is slow. The cafés serve tankards of freshly squeezed local orange juice for next to nothing. There is a small hotel in the main square, the **Plaza** (Plaza Constitución Pte, tel 487 20100), which is cheap and respectable. The attached restaurant serves gallons of orange juice and hearty helpings of eggs and beans.

Cascadas de Tamasopo
East of Río Verde, the road starts to pick its way back into the hills, past small farming communities dotted over a flat basin at the top of the sierra. The colours are perennially autumnal and the fields full of cane and maize. Small boys stumble precariously down the road, carrying bundles of chopped cane. This is Huastec country proper. In the heat of the day, you can turn off the main road to find little-known waterfalls and pools to swim in. Some 77 km from Río Verde, a small road leads off to the left, signposted Agua Buena and Tamasopo.

The **Tamasopo waterfalls** are 2 km north of the tiny flower-filled village. Triple falls pour into a large pool of water, edged with sandy banks. At weekends, follow the river a couple of km south to even quieter spots. From the village, a dirt track cuts its way up the hill for 4 km to **El Cafetal**, a tiny hamlet set around a gnarled tree, where an abandoned train is now home to four families. A track leads from behind the train to a curved arch of rock, hidden in the hills, which spans two deep, refreshing pools of water on either side. It's a steep, 1-km climb down. The track is unsigned and difficult to find: few people know about it and even fewer make it. Ask any of the children for *el arco* and they'll be only too pleased to guide you down.

Tamasopo has one simple hotel, **Cosmos** (Calle Allende, tel 40), and a *casa de huéspedes*. Families will also put people up: ask when you arrive. The train stops here en route between San Luis Potosí and Tampico.

Cascadas de Micos
For yet more waterfalls, continue on Highway 70 for 64 km. The road descends into the tropical Pánuco valley and the heat becomes sweltering. Nine km before Ciudad Valles, turn left for Cascadas de Micos, continuing up a dirt track for 11 km. The road deteriorates towards the end and only jeeps can make the last km or so. There are five falls, running into each other. The crystal-clear water gathers in a huge pool and is shaded by overhanging trees. It would be a paradise, were it not for the litter which has been left all around.

Ciudad Valles
Ciudad Valles is no more than a pit stop. A centre for sugar cane and citrus fruits, it is resigned to people passing through as fast as possible and does little to detain them. Its only redeeming feature is the **Museo Regional Huasteca** (in Blvd Sur, on Highway 85,

the main Mexico City–Nuevo Laredo road; it has no fixed timetable but is usually open in the morning). Set up by an amateur enthusiast, Oralia Gutiérrez de Sanchez, who has walked the length and breadth of the Huasteca, this small Huastec museum displays ancient and contemporary pieces and costumes. It includes a mass of tiny clay heads, many looking strangely Negroid or Caucasian. Each was created as an individual portrait, with distinctive facial characteristics, like a collection of photographs. The dates are uncertain, though they are undoubtedly pre-Hispanic. The museum also includes de Sanchez's findings from the nearby site of Tamuín.

Tamuín

Highway 70 continues east from Ciudad Valles to Tamuín, 28 km away. Set amongst large fenced fields of plump cattle, the Huastec site known as 'El Consuelo' is 6 km out of the village of Tamuín. The entrance is blocked by a fierce barbed-wire fence, but this is intended to deter cattle, not visitors, and can be lifted up. The site is always open, though its straggling remains are of little interest other than to archaeologists. It was a Huastec ceremonial centre, stretching for 17 mostly unexplored hectares. Low platforms are surrounded by crenellated 'talud' walls. Until as late as 1946, these bore traces of stucco and painted frescoes, with key patterns and figures, but they were subsequently either stolen or largely destroyed by the weather. The long low structure to the left of the entrance gate was painted with a procession of 11 male priests or god figures, in red on a white background, dating from AD 900. Tombs were discovered below them, with figures in foetal positions facing east. A channel led from the river to a round space in the middle of the site, which is believed to have been used for purification rituals.

The post-Classic Huastecs of the northern Gulf area were a mysterious people, who have evaded research. Linguistically related to the Maya, they evolved apart, building round structures which they dedicated to the plumed serpent god, Quetzalcóatl. Their people dressed in bright colours, wore spectacular jewellery and painted their hair red and yellow. The Aztecs, who conquered them in the 15th century, found them too sensual and decried their sexual immorality. (They can't have been too horrified, however, as they quickly began worshipping the Huastec goddess of love, Tlazoltéotl.)

WHERE TO STAY AND EAT
(area code 138)

Hotels in **Ciudad Valles** are centred on the main Mexico City–Nuevo Laredo road (Highway 85), and on Hidalgo which leads off the main square. The best hotel in town is the hacienda-style ****Posada Don Antonio (Blvd México Laredo 15, tel 20066), with a welcoming swimming pool and all-important air conditioning. It has a good café in which to try *bocoles* (maize cakes filled with cheese, ham and nopale cactus) for breakfast. Cheap. The more formal restaurant specializes in seafood from the Gulf and local beef. Moderate. Next door are the cheaper and less exciting ***Boulevard, ****San Fernando (tel 20184) and *Casa Vitela (tel 20128). *Rex (Hidalgo 418, three blocks off the main plaza, tel 20345) is unspectacular but good value for money. For an alternative restaurant to the Posada Don Antonio, try **Malibu** on Hidalgo, just off the main square. Cheap. The **Pizzeria Bella Napoli** (Juárez 210, just off the main plaza) serves up Mexican-tasting pizzas. Cheap.

On the road to Tamuín, 15 km outside Ciudad Valles, the comfortable ***Taninul (tel 20000) is in the middle of the country, close to the archaeological site. Its main claim to fame are its foul-smelling sulphur thermal baths, which purport to work wonders for stiff bones. With the soothing feel of an F Scott Fitzgerald sanitorium, it is a peaceful place to rest up in. There are rocking chairs on the veranda, horses to ride and opportunities for walking trips into the nearby Huastec mountains. The restaurant caters for fresh-air appetites, with hearty helpings at moderate prices.

Tamuín offers the basic (CE) Casa de Huéspedes La Villa and the more upmarket if unremarkable ***Villa Guerrero (Juárez 14, tel 80451). El Ganadero, on the road to the site and announced by an unsubtly large sign of a bull, does good steaks. Moderate.

South of Cuidad Valles

The hill villages south of Ciudad Valles can be explored in a day, though there are simple hotels for those who linger or continue on to Hidalgo or Mexico City.

GETTING AROUND
By Bus: It is easiest to explore the area by car. Local buses run from Ciudad Valles to each village, but getting from one village to another is more difficult. Check timetables at the bus station before setting off, or do what the locals do and hitch a lift, paying a small pre-agreed sum.

By Car: From Cuidad Valles, take Highway 85, the Mexico City road south, turning left after 50 km to Tancanhuitz. Alternatively, for a winding rural route which doesn't take much longer, continue from Tamuín on the San Vincente Tancuayalab road. Drive through the village, with its whitewashed houses and brightly painted doors, and turn right to Tanquián de Escobedo (18 km), through rich agricultural land where horses graze on gentle hills dotted with palms. From Tanquián, it's 24 km to Tancanhuitz, through a patchwork of green forested hills, blue rivers and orange groves.

After Tancanhuitz, continue down Highway 85, turning right for Xilitla. To go on to Mexico City, return to Highway 85 and continue south through Tamazunchale. It's a long winding road through some of the most beautiful sierra in Mexico and will take the best part of a day.

WHAT TO SEE
Tancanhuitz de Santos
On Sundays, the roads into Tancanhuitz are lined with Huastecs, coming in for the big weekly market from far-flung villages. Many of the women wear their traditional Sunday best. Their long, dark hair is swept up in bright skeins of wool. Uniform black skirts act as a counterpoint to the *quechquémels*, white diamond-shaped shawls embroidered with crimson animals and flowers. The Aztecs highly prized the art of embroidering these shawls, which were originally far more elaborate. Wicker baskets are filled with fruit and vegetables, chickens squawk and boys have their hair cut by the barber. Although stalls selling nylon dresses and jeans are becoming ever more popular, Tancanhuitz is still a place for locals to gather and barter, swapping gossip, buying fanciful ribbons or powders to make the unfaithful return. Men, in modern clothes, gather in groups to drink fiery *aguadiente* or *nectar*, a fruit-based intoxicant, before the long stagger home. Foreigners are still a rich and rare breed, to be stared at open-mouthed.

Xilitla

Some 15 km west of Highway 85, the Huastec village of Xilitla clings to its lofty perch above the road, set imposingly high on a cliff above the valley of Río Moctezuma. The main square is haunted by the ruins of a 16th-century Augustinian monastery, whose thick walls were built as defence against persistent attack from the Huastecs. Today the market is filled with Nahuatl and Huastec voices bargaining over copal incense or tobacco, weighed on a scale made of stones. There is a smell of rich local coffee everywhere.

Xilitla's greatest recent excitement began in 1949 with the arrival of the English sculptor, Edward James, whose unusual British habits never ceased to fascinate the villagers. He, in turn, was entranced, remaining until his death in the 1980s. Surreal spires still spike above his house in the village. Down the hill, he built huge concrete follies in the jungle. Doorways open onto empty space, spiral staircases lead nowhere. Grotesque and glorious, it's an unmissable fantasy, inspired by the frenetic growth of the jungle that surrounds it, and made more fanciful still by his friend, a Yacqui, Plutarco Gastelum, who is often found on site. His wonderful tales reach realms untouched even by James. To get to the follies, take the main road out of the village which leads back down the hill. At the bottom, a dirt track leads off to the left: after 100 m, skeletal buildings appear on the right.

Tamazunchale

Tamazunchale means 'place of the governor', who in this case was, unusually, a woman named Tomiya. Once a remote Huastec village, Tamazunchale expanded rapidly when the main highway was built in the 1930s, and is now a prosperous town. It has its own sprawling Sunday market, which has become something of a tourist attraction. It is also popular with ornithologists and butterfly collectors, as the forests around teem with different species.

WHERE TO STAY AND EAT

There is one small hotel in Xilitla, *La Favorita, on the main square. To eat, return to the main Ciudad Valles road (15 km) and turn left towards Ciudad Valles. After a couple of km (before Huichihuayan), at a place known as Acamaya, five or six small restaurants sell mouthwatering freshwater prawns from the local river. They are sold by the kilo, cooked up with tomato and chilli and served with hand-patted tortillas. To finish off, buy oranges from the piles which line the road. From here it is about 70 km back to Ciudad Valles.

Part XII

OAXACA

Hand-weaving Trique woman with a waist loom

Outside the boundaries of the city, the state of Oaxaca provides endless surprises. The city of Oaxaca is stately and colonial, with the autocratic stamp of the Spanish on every paving stone, but the countryside around is rural and indigenous. The most monumental buildings are those of Spanish precursors, the Mixtecs and Zapotecs, whose power and influence may have long disappeared but whose descendants have remained.

Oaxaca's geography doesn't make life easy. Villages and pre-Hispanic sites sprawl in ungainly fashion over the rocky central plateau. This plateau is set between two mountain chains which create the valleys of Tlacolula, Etla, Zaachila and Zimatlán. The best way to explore the valleys is to take a series of individual forays out from the city, which lies at the heart of the plateau (at 1550 m). Village markets on different days of the week provide an optional way of focusing trips. To the east, the state narrows into the flat, fertile Isthmus of Tehuantepec. In the south, the Oaxacan coastline provides a perfect antidote to the frenzy of cultural and commercial exhaustion that monuments and markets bring on. The long journey from Oaxaca takes up most of a day (unless you take a short flight), along narrow roads that curl through mountain passes, to a world far removed from the rest of the state.

Seventeen distinct peoples live within Oaxaca's state boundaries, each with their own language, religion, dress and culture. Side-stepped for centuries, despite being the home state of Mexico's most famous presidents, Benito Juárez and Porfirio Díaz, Oaxaca has always found it difficult to adjust to the fast-developing world. Paradoxically, this lack of progress is its greatest attraction today. Differences in language, dress and custom are now being encouraged by visitors turned amateur-anthropologists, whilst the government wrings its hands in despair.

Many households in Mexico are filled with reminders of Oaxaca's native art: hand-dyed woollen rugs from Teotitlán, Ocotlán sashes, raw silk scarves from Yalalag, black Coyotepec pottery, green glazed ware from Atzompa and fantastic wood carvings. It is also well known for its artists, the foremost in Mexico: Francisco Toledo of Juchitán, Rufino Tamayo of Oaxaca City and Rodolfo Morales of Ocotlán.

A first visit to Oaxaca is never long enough. It is only on the second or the third, when sights have been seen and presents bought, that there is time to wallow in it. Ten days are enough for a first visit to the state, spending half the time in the city and valleys and the rest on the coast for a few days' relaxation. There is no bad time to go but July is the busiest month in the city (see Festivals) and autumn is the most beautiful (after the rains). The markets happen on different days and it is best to plan visits around them (see below).

MARKET DAYS
Monday: Miahuatlán
Tuesday: Atzompa
Wednesday: San Pedro y San Pablo Etla
Thursday: Zaachila
Friday: Ocotlán, Sto Tomás Jalieza
Saturday: Mercado de Abastos, Oaxaca (and all week)
Sunday: Tlacolula

Atzompa starts at 14.00, but for all the others, try to get there as soon after 09.00 as possible.

TRAVEL AGENCIES
Whatever your personal feelings about group tourism, think again in Oaxaca. To arrive exhausted in mid-afternoon at the village market you'd set your heart on, only to find it has packed up already and the last bus left 5 minutes before, is no fun. Oaxaca is well endowed with travel agencies who have learnt from experience that air-conditioned 60-seater tour buses aren't everyone's cup of tea. They have adapted to small 10-seater minicabs, either with a professional guide to show what's what or merely a driver to take you there and back. A guide will cost the same for one or ten, so try to join a group. The main hotels all have travel agencies in their lobbies and there are several others around the city. **Centroamericana de Viajes** (Portal de Flóres 8, tel 632725, tlx 018826, fax (951) 64269) is the most competent with the best guide, Luís Angel Sorrora.

History

PRE-HISPANIC
Oaxaca's earliest history seethes with internecine rivalry. Dynasties were created and became, like all good dynasties should, despotic and interbred. From the many disparate groups in the valleys, the Zapotecs emerged as the strongest around 200 BC, building their monumental ceremonial centres on the high ground of Monte Albán, San José Mogote and Yagul. They extended their influence over the whole of Oaxaca, and established trading links as far south as the distant Maya and as far north as the great city of Teotihuacán. When Monte Albán exhausted its supplies of water and space, the

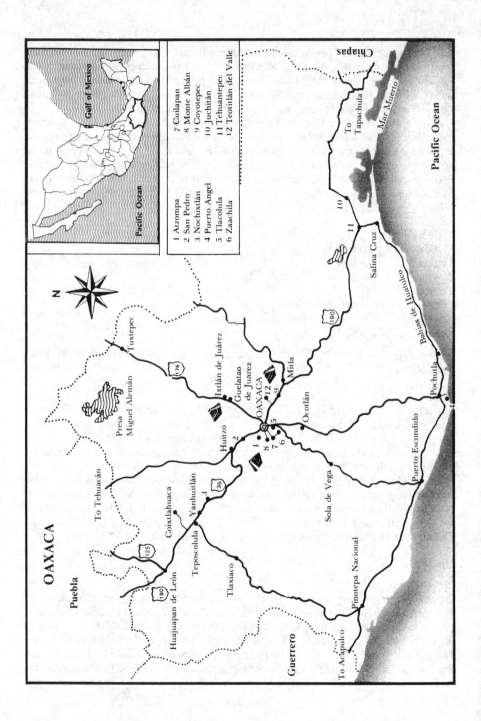

Zapotecs began to decline and the nobility moved down to the valleys to rule over smaller, satellite states.

The Mixtecs, long suffered as the woolly neighbours from the hills, came down to taunt the straitened Zapotecs around AD 800. They began to invade the happy valley people, and consolidated their position by marrying royal Zapotec princesses. Impressed by the monumental architecture, they emptied Monte Albán's ancestral tombs and replaced Zapotec bodies with their own. Thought to be aggressive and unruly, in fact they proved the contrary, fashioning the most delicate metalwork ever seen in Meso-america. They disdained monumentality for intricacy, temples for palaces. They introduced mosaic tiles into architecture, colour into pottery and precious stones into jewellery: gold, turquoise, jet, amber and coral. In the second half of the 15th century, the Aztecs swept down from the northwest, lured by merchants' stories of ornate jewellery and rich farming land. Not content with an empire the size of Italy, they absorbed Oaxaca and Chiapas into their territories. The Zapotecs and the Mixtecs, ancient antipathy still smouldering, were loath to become allies, and inadvertently smoothed the way for others by maintaining local animosities. The Spanish, who sent expeditions down to the south as soon as Tenochtitlán fell, exploited this division. The conquests of Francisco de Orozco in 1521 and Pedro de Alvarado in 1522 sealed the fate of the still warring Mixtecs and Zapotecs.

LIFE UNDER SPAIN

Divided by language and geography, Oaxaca is not easy to govern. The Spanish found over 570 distinct communities, which they lumped together under the umbrella term of Oaxaca for ease of administration. The Spanish church and noblemen imprinted 'colonial' rule on the state, imposing divisive boundaries in the 1520s which have lasted till today.

In 1529, Charles I of Spain demoted Hernán Cortés, the original conqueror of Mexico. He was no longer to be governor of the whole of New Spain but, as a palliative, was offered the lands of his choice. Cortés chose Oaxaca, becoming the Marquis of the Valley of Oaxaca. Charles I gave him a grant of 11,550 square km and the souls of 23,000 indigenous people to save (which he interpreted as unpaid labour in the mines and fields of his vast estates).

Monasteries were encouraged in the hope that people could be forced into manage-able order around the churches. The Dominicans came in 1527 and built at an incredible rate, getting a good start over the Franciscans and Augustinians. Many areas, like the marginal land of the Mixes, had nothing for the friars, but they developed the Mixteca Alta with mining, silk worm farming and cochineal production. The silk industry was so successful that the protectionist Spanish government was finally driven to ban it in the 18th century, after producers in Spain complained of undercutting by cheap imports from the colonies.

OAXACA

Oaxacans say that there are 20 earthquakes a day but only occasionally is one strong enough to be felt. Occasionally, unfortunately for Oaxaca, comes around once a week.

The architecture of its churches has lent new meaning to the word seismic: heavy stones, thick walls and low towers. Every generation since Oaxaca was founded in 1529 has had to rebuild the city after earthquakes, creating streets full of single-storied houses, solidly rooted churches and cool cucumber-green masonry.

The city has borne up well: the cracks are more noticeable in the minds than in the streets. For Oaxaca is a very Spanish city in the middle of a very indigenous state. It has had to struggle to keep its identity as a Spanish island in a state where 17 ethnic groups coexist. Every building in the city proudly announces a colonial past. Oaxaca was built (and rebuilt and rebuilt) by the Spanish, and continues to be seen as the centre of colonial government in a state that has had its autonomy wrested from it, first by the Aztecs and then the Spanish, and now by the bureaucrats of far-distant Mexico City. The streets are filled with brightly costumed people from the country who have to use the big city to pay taxes, barter and buy. From 7 o'clock in the morning, the Zócalo becomes the happy hunting ground of Triques, Zapotecs and Mixtecs who have come to sell their shawls, shirts, blankets and jewellery to international coffee-drinkers delighted to buy for the chance to stare.

Oaxaca has a long artistic tradition, stretching back 2000 years to the Mixtecs and Zapotecs. Rufino Tamayo, Rodolfo Morales from Ocotlán, Francisco Toledo from Juchitán and the younger generation of Ariel Mendoza, Justina Fuentes and Eddie Martínez have continued to uphold Oaxaca as the centre of modern Mexican painting. The artistic tradition triumphantly announces itself. Artisania is sold on street corners, in fine galleries, open cafés or the single room of the artisan's house. The markets are a riot of colour, light and animation in every corner. Stalls aren't just vehicles to sell vegetables: they're works of art put together with geometric precision. Mountains and pyramids of papaya and mangoes are piled high, the fruit sliced in half to show off the oozing flesh.

GETTING AROUND

By Air: Four flights daily connect Oaxaca to Mexico City, two to Huatulco and one each to Acapulco, Villahermosa, Puerto Escondido and Tuxtla Gutiérrez. The small airport is south of the city and mini-buses leave every hour for the central hotels. Travel agents will make bookings and sell tickets. **Aeroméxico** (tel 64055) is at Hidalgo 917. **Mexicana** (tel 68414) is one block north and another east on the corner of Independencia and Fiallo. **Aerovías Oaxaqueñas** (tel 63824), for flights to the coast, is at Armenta y López 209, one block east of the Zócalo. **Aeromar** (tel 51500 ext 296) has an office at the airport.

By Bus: There are two stations. The first-class station, for long journeys, is on the Panamericana where it crosses Pino Suárez. In general, the ADO company covers routes to the west of Oaxaca with daily services to Huajuápan, Puebla (7 hrs) and Mexico City (9 hrs) (tel 50903), and the Cristóbal Colón company covers routes to the south and east with daily services to Tehuantepec (4½ hrs), San Cristóbal (12 hrs) and the Guatemalan border (12 hrs) (tel 51214).

The second-class station, by the Mercado de Abastos (take combis from Hidalgo marked 'Abastos'), has almost a hundred different companies under one roof. Several daily buses go slowly south to Pochutla, Puerto Escondido and Puerto Angel (try Estrella del Valle at Gate 22) or to the Isthmus of Tehuantepec (try Fletes y Pasajes or

to Mexico City

Panamerican Highway

N

13

OAXACA

CITY CENTRE

to railway
station

Gomez Farias

Humboldt

Berriozabal

Carranza

Garcia Vigil

Allende

12

Constitucion

Gurrion

Porfirio Diaz

Bravo

Alcala

Abasolo

Matamoros

Cinco de Mayo

Murguia

11

Juarez

Pino Suarez

14

Morelos

Reforma

8

Madero

7

6

Galeana

Mier y Teran

Garcia

5

3

4

Independencia

10

Armenta

Hidalgo

Diaz Ordaz

20 de Noviembre

Trujano

Magon

1

2

Guerrero

Ocampo

Las Casas

Colon

Bustamante

9

River Atoyac

to Monte Alban

1. Zocalo
2. Palacio de Gobierno
3. Alameda
4. Cathedral
5. Post Office
6. Palacio Municipal
7. Church of San Felipe Neri
8. Chuch of Soledad
9. Market
10. Theatre
11. Museo de Oaxaca
12. Church of Santo Domingo
   and Regional Museum
13. Bus station
14. Rufino Tamayo
   Museum

0   150   300m

Oaxaca-Istmo). Combis leave every 20 minutes from the outside of the station for any village within an hour of the city and set off just as soon as the chassis is dragging on the ground.

By Car: The roads in from Mexico City, over 500 km and 8 hours away, have to cross the spiny back of the Sierra Madre del Sur. The equidistant routes are either via Izúcar de Matamoros (Highway 190) or Tehuacán (Highway 150). The Panamericana, Highway 190, continues to the Guatemalan border via Comitán in Chiapas. The poorly surfaced Highway 200 runs along the coast, west to Acapulco (and eventually on to Tepic), and east to Guatemala. The roads connecting coast to city are not good. Take Highway 175 via Ocotlán; the alternative, via Sola de Vega, is slow, unpaved and teeth-clenching.

Renting a car invariably costs more than expected, particularly as there is a scarcity of cars. Avis (tel 65030) is on the Alameda and Budget (tel 60611) at the Stouffer Presidente. Hotel porters often prove to be a mine of alternative information with much better deals.

By Train: The station is out to the west, along Independencia to Calzada Madero (combis 'Estación/Centro'). Trains have improved in the last few years and the comfortable night sleeper from Mexico City (leaving at 19.15) gets in in time for breakfast in the market at 09.30. Always book far ahead (tel 62676 in Oaxaca or 597 6177 in the capital).

TOURIST INFORMATION
The main office, one of the most helpful in Mexico, is on the corner of 5 de Mayo and Morelos, two streets north and then two streets east of the Zócalo (open 09.00–15.00 and 17.00–20.00; closed Sun).

Oaxaca is organized for tourists. At right angles to the post office, on Independencia, the International Friendship Centre (tel 60123) can sort out legal problems and robberies; alternatively try the combined consular offices on Hidalgo 817/5 (tel 65600). **American Express** have an agent in Viajes Micsa on Hidalgo (tel 62700), by the Zócalo, and all the banks will change traveller's cheques. An English-speaking **doctor** is on duty 11.00–13.00 and 18.00–20.00 (tel 56354) and a **dentist** at Alcalá 102–15 (tel 69365). There is a 24-hour **chemist**, Farmacia Soriano del Sur, on Colón where it crosses Bustamente (tel 64041). **Laundry** is wickedly expensive in hotels: for those who don't mind carrying a dirty bag of travel-worn clothes through the streets, there is an efficient laundrette at 20 de Noviembre 605 (one street west of the Zócalo, open 09.00–20.00, Mon–Sat).

WHAT TO SEE

The Zócalo

Oaxaca was set out like a chequerboard by the mathematician, Alonso García Bravo, who also redesigned Mexico City after the fall of Tenochtitlán. He made the square, known as the Zócalo, the pulse of city life. (He was so pleased with his design that he lived here for the rest of his life.)

The pistachio-coloured **cathedral**, on its north side, was the oldest church in Oaxaca. Work began in 1553 but it was rebuilt in 1730 after a crippling series of earthquakes. It has been modified since, leaving the towers asymmetrical. Despite its antiquity and its position, it is not one of Oaxaca's most-loved churches: foreigners prefer the ostentation of Santo Domingo and natives the romance of La Soledad. The interior is sombre and exalted and the five naves, like a basilica, give it immense stature and space. It is still used for tranquil moments, sleep or prayers, in the heat of the day.

The 19th-century **Palacio de Gobierno**, on the south face of the Zócalo, has a mural around the stairwell depicting the state's history and its romantic and not-so-romantic citizens. The right wall is dominated by women, including the native-born poet, intellectual and nun, Sor Juana Inés de la Cruz. A great wit and beauty, she was a favourite at the viceregal court. Suddenly, at the age of 20, she took orders and retired to a convent to produce her poems and plays until even her learning seemed to prevent communion with her God and she burnt every book but the Bible. In the lower left corner of the same panel is the decapitated head of the last Zapotec princess, murdered on Monte Albán. When her lover, a Mixtec prince, found her, he committed suicide on the spot and, it is said, their blood mingled and dripped into the Atoyac River far below.

North of the Zócalo

Museo de Oaxaca
(Two blocks north of the Zócalo on Macedonio Alcalá; open 10.00–14.00 and 17.00–20.00; closed Mon.)
The museum is housed in what is grandly called the 'Casa de Cortés' although Cortés certainly never lived there. The Andalusian facade is of beautifully sculpted stone encrusted with 18th-century family shields. Most of the exhibits are temporary, concentrating on the many young Oaxacan painters. There is one permanent room devoted to the quirky artist Miguel Cabrera (1695–1768), born in nearby Tlalixtac but whose best works are out of the state. Most famous of all are his oval-shaped canvases in the Metropolitan Cathedral in Mexico City.

Santo Domingo
(Five streets north of the Zócalo on Alcalá.)
Santo Domingo was described by Aldous Huxley as 'one of the most extravagantly gorgeous churches in the world'. It was begun in 1572 but the plan was so grand that the first communion wasn't held until 1608 and work continued for another 200 years. The high, almost medieval facade is squeezed into a tall, narrow space between mighty, thick towers, classically topped with domes and cupolas. There is little suggestion of the richness of the interior. Inside, a stuccoed tree of Jesse takes up the whole of the choir vault. Distinctly naive in its naturalism, it sports a hundred gold-leaf branches reaching out to the four corners, set against a background of the purest white. Some 64 polychromed, gilded and stuccoed Dominican missionaries take up the vault adjacent to the tree, much spruced up since their initial painting. The army converted the church to stables in 1869, destroying the 14 side altars which have been replaced by replicas. It didn't reopen until 1902 and the main altarpiece, inspired by that of Yanhuitlán, is a 1959 copy. The church moves from the sublime to the sublimer. The **Capilla del Rosario**, off to the right, finished in 1729, is a hectic frenzy of foaming white, edged with gold piping.

389

Museo Regional
(Open 10.00–18.00, Mon–Fri; 10.00–17.00, weekends; closed Mon; adm.)
Housed in the adjoining monastery, this is a big museum and one worth leaving time for. Faint traces of a frescoed Peter and Paul remain in the entrance to the lovely Dominican building. Founded in 1548, it was expropriated by the army in the 19th century and used as a barracks. They defaced and whitewashed many frescoes, lending the quadrangle an air of faded silk embroidery.

Huge stelae from Mitla and Monte Albán dominate the ground floor. Figures were carved with inverted commas coming out of their mouths, indicating speech, though sadly it's mostly indecipherable. There is a room for temporary exhibits where regional arts and crafts are for sale. Upstairs, a large room exhibits the many costumes of the area. Next door is the most important room of all, dedicated to the treasure found in tomb 7 at Monte Albán. The red portals of the original entrance are flanked by two guarding jaguars. Inside, copies of the intricate jewels are displayed: masks set with turquoise, a glass made of a single piece of crystal, jade necklaces, pearl earrings, gold filigree pendants (even false nails made of gold) and exquisite ivory codices with dates and minute carvings etched on to them.

Institute of Graphic Art
(Opposite Sto Domingo; open 10.00–14.00 and 16.00–19.00; 11.00–17.00, Sun; closed Tue; adm.)
Artist Francisco Toledo is an avid collector of prints and has now opened his house to the public. Over 300 exhibits include paintings by Dürer, Delacroix, Kokoschka, Miró, Posada, Rivera and the English artist Leonora Carrington. Toledo was born in Juchitán in 1940. Rich in magic and myth, his engravings and lithographs have hung all over the world. He now dedicates himself to woodcuts and designs for tapestries woven by the artisans of Teotitlán del Valle.

With your back to the museum, turn left and left again, to see Trique women sitting weaving woollen shawls on waist looms. The original intricate patterns, as worn by the women themselves, take an age to weave and are consequently expensive. They have started to produce mass-market shawls for tourists.

Casa Juárez
(García Vigil and Carranza; open 10.00–14.00 and 16.00–19.00; closed Mon; adm.)
In 1818, a small Zapotec boy, later to become president, arrived in Oaxaca. Benito Juárez had walked the 74 km from Guelatao, his village in the hills, to visit his sister and look for work. Antonio Salanueva, who lived in this house, gave Juárez a job and, recognizing his potential, paid for his education. The house is now a museum with rooms kept much as they were in the early 19th century, the walls graced with a few portraits of Juárez.

East to West along Av Independencia

The **Teatro Macedonio Alcalá** (named after a romantic troubadour) is a late Porfirian construction, finished in 1909, curving round the corner of Independencia and 5 de Mayo. European was the order of the day—the Italian Opera Company of Miguel Sigaldi was brought over to inaugurate the theatre with *Aida*. The lobby is Mexican

Louis Quinze with a 1957 dome mural of seven muses in diaphanous scarves, encircled by an aghast Bach, Wagner et al.

Also on Independencia, next to the biggest funeral parlour in the city, the church of **San Felipe Neri** is famed for its anachronistic facade. Inside, Saint Gaudencio, an early Christian martyr, lies dressed in full Roman regalia. Benito Juárez married the 17-year-old Margarita Maza here in 1843. He had lived with her parents before she was even born. Ten years after their marriage, when she already had five children, Juárez had to flee the country as a political exile. For the next two years she moved constantly, finally setting up shop in Etla to support her family and send money to Juárez in New Orleans. Reunited with her husband, she had two more sons but was to endure several more separations before Juárez finally gained the presidency. She died, exhausted, in 1870, at the age of 45.

Museo Rufino Tamayo
(Morelos and Díaz; open 10.00–14.00 and 16.00–19.00; closed Tue; half-day Sun; adm.)
This wonderful display of Rufino Tamayo's unique pre-Hispanic collection is one street behind the church. Tamayo's portraits of Oaxaca life and paintings of fleshy, scarlet water-melons have been hung in galleries around the world, but his monument in Oaxaca is this collection of pre-Hispanic sculpture. It took 20 years to bring together. The mounting of the pieces, the colours of the rooms (rose, lilac, burnt sienna, etc) and the design were all the work of the painter. He loved the art of the southwest with its concentration on the human figure in daily poses. A maquette from AD 650 (in the second room) shows a ball-game in mid-play as the players, like Sumo wrestlers, fight it out. They are surrounded by chunky spectators including a loving couple with his arms entwined around her waist. The third room has a hunch-backed dwarf from Colima and a recycled stela—one side is pre-Classic Teotihuacán, the other, sculpted by the Aztecs, 1000 years later. The fourth room embraces pieces from the Maya, the Huasteca and southern Veracruz cultures.

The Church of La Soledad
This church, at the west end of Independencia, is dedicated to the Virgin of La Soledad, the popular patron saint of the city. Construction began in 1682. The facade was sculpted from the local, green cantera stone to look like a baroque altarpiece. Screen-like, it folds around the contours of the church, pushing the towers back into second place. The interior is drenched in gold leaf and the altarpiece has an image of the Virgin with a crown of gold weighing a hefty 3 kilos. Almost opposite is the **Escuela Primaria** where Porfirio Díaz, of infamous memory, was born. Don't leave without trying the ice creams of rose, lime and papaya sold outside the church.

FESTIVALS
During the last two Mondays of July, the town gives itself over to its most important festival, the **Guelaguetza**, with dances from the seven regions of the state in a vast open-air auditorium on the Cerro del Fortín hill. It culminates with the Feather Dance, a high stepping re-enactment of the disputes between the Zapotecs and the Mixtecs, arbitrated by Moctezuma, in which all the dancers wear bright feather headdresses. The

festival itself goes back to a pre-Hispanic ceremony for the Corn God, Centéotl, when a virgin was sacrificed to ensure a good harvest. True to form, Spanish missionaries melded the festival with that of the Virgin of Carmen (traditionally 16 July). It begins at 10.00 and ends at 14.00, thereby spanning the hottest hours of the day. Hotels fill long in advance and tickets must be booked seven days ahead, either from the tourist office or from a travel agent. Dates for the Guelaguetza in 1991 are 22 and 29 July and in 1992, 20 and 27 July.

For anyone who can't make it in July, various hotels put on shows that lack the thrill but still have the spectacle of the real thing. The **Monte Albán** hotel on the Zócalo has a show every night at 20.00. Alternatively, the deconsecrated chapel of the **Stouffer Presidente** creates an exalted setting for the dances and holds a massive buffet on Friday evenings.

LEARNING SPANISH
Oaxaca has some good language schools and an understanding population who may themselves speak Spanish only as a second language. The **Instituto Cultural Oaxaca** has month-long courses including workshops, lectures, and the rudiments of Mixteco and Zapoteco (Av Juárez 909, tel 53404, fax 951 61382). The tourist office also has the latest information on university courses for foreigners (three a year) and Spanish-speaking families to stay with.

NIGHTLIFE
At night a band discourses from the kiosk ... the Indians squat on the pavements to listen, their dark faces melting into the night—invisible. High-heeled, in every tender shade of artificial silk, the flappers stroll giggling under the electric light. There is a rolling of eyes, a rolling of posteriors. The young men stroll in the opposite direction.
—Aldous Huxley, *Beyond the Mexique Bay*, 1932

Still, for many, the best entertainment of all, the state band plays in the Zócalo on Sundays at 12.00 and almost every night at 19.00. The whole square fills up with families and the cafés around bulge with students, politicians, foreigners, latter-day hippies and villagers.

Later on, try **Los Guajiros**, a restaurant with live music that starts at 22.30, and salsa (Wed–Sat). Similarly, **El Sol y La Luna** (Murguía 105, tel 62933) has hot, live jazz and salsa music every night in its open courtyard. Both the **Centro Cultural Juan Rulfo** (Independencia 300, tel 63456) and the **Centro Cultural Oaxaqueña** (González Ortega 403, tel 62483) put on dancing, plays and films (the tourist office has monthly programmes). The **Teatro Macedonio Alcalá**'s plush, marble theatre (on the corner of Independencia and 5 de Mayo) is used by both local and national companies. Performances are always in Spanish: the tourist office can recommend or dissuade.

HORSE RIDING
Travel agents or the tourist office can make arrangements for riding at the **Rancho El Estafuste**, up in the northeast of the city, on the edge of open country and the sierra. The riding is excellent, through villages, gulleys, forests and farm land, usually taking half a day, sometimes stopping for a picnic along the way. The tack is western, with

saddles big enough to have a tea party in, but check that the stirrups are long enough before you start. Take a hat or scarf as the sun scorches.

SHOPPING

Oaxaca offers more temptation to buy and be damned than any other state in Mexico (except neighbouring Chiapas). The range goes on and on, from pre-Hispanic black pottery and Spanish-introduced green glazed pottery to weavings, textiles, filigree jewellery, *huipiles*, ceramics, sculptures and baskets. Visitors' interest in crafts has had a two-fold effect. It has provided a strong market for arts that may otherwise have died but also introduced mass-marketing so that Mona Lisas are woven into ancient weaves and fluorescent pinks and yellows have crept into natural clay and earth colours.

The **Mercado de Abastos** is a cacophony of sound, taste, colour and smell: pyramids of pineapples, coffers of cacao beans, shining red tomatoes, green glazed urns, intricately interwoven shirts, sweet-smelling herbs, stinking cuts of meat, nylon petticoats, salsa music competing with Bruce Springsteen, sharp green limes, red hot chilli peppers, a dozen cures for insomnia, hassle, hawking, heat and total intoxication. Permanently set up by the second-class bus station, it's alive and firmly kicking every day but especially so on Thursdays and Saturdays.

The old market in the centre, on 20 de Noviembre, is much the same if on a smaller scale. The **Mercado de Artesanías** is not so tempting. On the corner of Calle García and Zaragoza, it is a shed-like building with exhibits on sale that are no different from anywhere else. Trique women from the southwest of Oaxaca sit and weave their vivid red shirts on back-strap looms, looking decidedly disgruntled at their lot.

The streets north of the Zócalo have some high-quality shops, more expensive than the villages but often offering better workmanship. A few shops concentrate on individual artists whose pieces consequently become 'collectable', such as the carved wooden animals of the Mormon, Manuel Jiménez from Arrazola. The government-sponsored **Aripo** is at García Vigil 809 with a weavers' workshop at the back. **Fonart** is on the same street where it crosses with Bravo. **Yalalag** at Alcalá 104 has a small patio creeping with vines and walls covered head to toe in masks, with little rooms leading off, filled with artisania from ten different states. On the Parque Juárez, at Pino Suárez 58, **Casa Brena** produces its own glazed pottery painted over with gold. For reproductions of the Mixtec gold jewellery, try **Oro de Monte Albán** (tel 64528) by Santo Domingo. **Shipping** can be arranged from any of the shops mentioned or through **SIACI** (Periférico 1017, tel 62556) who will also do the paperwork.

WHERE TO STAY   (area code 951)

Oaxaca has no end of places to stay, with a hotel, posada or boarding house on every street. The **Stouffer Presidente** is outstanding. The **Marqués del Valle** an old favourite, and the **Principal** a more modest alternative.

Expensive

The ex-convento de Santa Catalina, now the excellent *****Stouffer Presidente** (5 de Mayo 300, tel 60611, tlx 18845), has been turned from cloistered nunnery to first-rate hotel. Other costume changes in its tortured history include a jail and a cinema. From when nuns were banned in the anti-clerical 1860s, it had to wait till the 1970s to be put back to its former, sombre elegance with cloisters, arches and gardens. It can get cold in the winter but there are fireplaces and warm colours in the far-from-monastic rooms, some with the remnants of original frescoes. The larger hotels like the ****Misión de los Angeles (Calz Porfirio Díaz 102, tel 51500, tlx 018850), and the ****Fortín Plaza (Av Venus 118, Col Estrella, tel 57777, tlx 18623) have extensive gardens and are thus some distance from the centre. The ****Victoria (Carr Panamericana km 545, tel 52333, tlx 18824) has wonderful views over the city and the valley beyond. There are bungalows in the garden as well as pretty rooms in the hotel.

Moderate
The ***Marqués del Valle (tel 63474, tlx 18608), over the Portal de Claveria, is ideally situated with one side looking over the Zócalo and the other over the Alameda and the cathedral. Once the city's grand hotel, it is now a well-run, family place with little pretension. In its time it has played host to such disparate guests as Haile Selassie, the Prince of Wales, Pedro Infante and John Wayne. It is not a place for late sleepers, as the Mexican flag is raised outside at 08.00 with all due pomp and circumstance. Also on the main square, with a colonial feel and regional dances every night, is the ***Monte Albán (Alameda de León 1, tel 62777). ***Señorial (Portal de Flóres Magón 7, tel 63933) is over-used by tour groups but does have a swimming pool and parking (rare in the centre). The ***Calesa Real (García Vigil 306, tel 65544, tlx 18623) is a pretty hotel with a charming restaurant, a sun-soaked terrace and swimming pool, but indifferent rooms.

Cheap
The **Principal (5 de Mayo 208, tel 62535) has 16 simple, cool rooms around a light courtyard filled with pots of flowers. Highly thought of, it books up early in the morning. If full, the **Plaza (Trujano 112, tel 62200; second floor), off the Zócalo, is similar with bold, bright Mexican colours. Further up the same street, at Trujano 212, the ***Mesón del Rey (tel 60033) has been snazzily done up with a travel agency and parking for its 22 rooms but keeps its price low. One block from the Zócalo, the **Francia (20 de Noviembre 212, tel 64811) is a rambling colonial building, with large, basic rooms (the exterior ones are noisy) and a TV in the big, open lobby showing non-stop Mexican soap operas. Cheaper hotels in the centre include the *Colón (Colón, tel 64726), the *Aurora (Bustamente 212, tel 64726), and the *Reforma (Reforma 102, tel 67144).

EATING OUT
There is an endless choice of restaurants and an infinite variety of local dishes from grasshoppers to iguana. Oaxacan regional variations provide embellishments on the most established of national dishes. The chocolate-based sauce, *mole oaxaqueño*, is lighter in colour and sweeter than the more famous *mole poblano* because of the bananas added to the usual chocolate and chilli negro. Mescal is the local, rawer equivalent of tequila, a sharp *aperitivo*. Coffee is drunk *a la olla* with vanilla, and chocolate is made with water (it was the Spanish who introduced milk).

For breakfasts, the markets are an adventure. Many people start the day at dawn with a coffee and then breakfast in the middle of the morning on eggs, beans and tortillas in the markets. The enormous Mercado de Abastos on Saturday mornings has a whole area of cafés touting for business. In the central market, ask for **Abuelita's** stall.

In the Centre

Overlooking the Palacio de Gobierno, second-floor **El Asador Vasco** (tel 69719) is an elegant restaurant with tables on the terrace and wandering minstrels every night. It may be touristy but it is also deservedly well known. The house wines are Rioja, the menu daring with stewed calf's tongue or *corazón de filete* (steak) followed by solid chocolate profiteroles. Moderately expensive. Underneath, the **Menu del Jardín** has seats in the sun or the shade, vast *tortas cubanas* (open sandwiches) and slapdash service, bored by tourists but delighted with old friends. Inexpensive. **Mi Casita** (tel 69256) is at the other end of the arcade, but the entrance is on Hidalgo. The food is distinctly regional with a nopal (cactus leaf) soup and rich grasshoppers in the rainy season. Moderate.

Los Danzantes (on the corner of Trujano and 20 de Noviembre, tel 66880) is a dishevelled restaurant with hearty platefuls of Mexican food. The *caldo de gato* is more of a stew than a soup with whole green beans, chayote, tomatoes and thick chunks of pork. Cheap. Another regional kitchen for enormous brunches is **El Mesón** (Av Hidalgo 805), with vats of *chilaquiles, mole* and red beans. Cheap. For inexpensive lunches with lots of courses (comida corridas), the **Alameda** (two blocks from the Zócalo on J P García 202, tel 63446) is a good choice. Cheap. **La Galera** (Colón 613, two blocks south of the Zócalo, tel 66834) does lunches only in a large, wholly Mexican restaurant, with good prices and a huge range. The *tacos de pescado* (tortillas filled with fish and coriander) are especially good. Inexpensive. To the north of town, at B Dominguez 508, is the Argentinian steak house **El Che** (tel 51999). The wines are Spanish: Sangre de Torro and Riojas. Steaks are preferred but the spinach cannelloni is superb. Moderate. **Ajos y Cebollas** (Av Juárez 605, tel 63793) is run by the director of the Instituto language school, whose wife is an eminent historian. It's a very well thought-out restaurant specializing in whole pineapples topped with jumbo prawns, with live music after 22.00 in the evenings.

Worth a Detour

Getting to these restaurants will require a taxi. Although difficult to find, they are all worth it. Well known to Oaxacans, they rarely see other tourists.

Cabo Kennedy ($3\frac{1}{2}$ km from the centre on the road to Mitla, tel 50111, open 365 days a year) may look like a camp site but don't be deceived. It is owned by the Ramírez family, who found themselves entertaining so frequently that they decided to open a restaurant. The owner's mother does all the cooking and produces the best *mole verde* in the whole state. Made of herbs which give it a rich green colour and white haricot beans, it is less piquant than most sauces and is used on pork and chicken. Her *sopa de guias* is a delicious courgette-flower and sweetcorn soup. To finish off, she makes home-made vanilla ices spiced with cinnamon. In season they serve the caviar of Mexican food, *chapulines*, tiny red grasshoppers which feed off alfalfa plants, fried in garlic and lemon and eaten rolled in piping hot tortillas. They are surprisingly good. Check with Sr Ramírez as he plans to run a taxi to and from the centre. Moderate.

Clemente (Av Cuauhtémoc 205, a narrow potholed street off the road to Mexico City in Colonia Mateo, tel 65296) is a small informal restaurant set in a garden overhung with bougainvillea, always filled at lunch. Ask for a *botana* and a feast of food will appear: tortillas filled with chicken and laced with avocado, *memelitas* (small doughy tortillas to be filled with various sauces and meats) and even the great Mexican speciality, *patas de puerco* (pigs' trotters). A big plate of fruit arrives on the table to finish up with. Moderate.

   Los Pacos (B Dominguez 108, tel 53573, a taxi-drive north of the Panamericana) provides traditional Oaxacan cuisine. The rustic palapa belies a sophisticated kitchen which offers three different *moles*, *memelitas* or *cecina* (sliced beef with a spicy sausage sauce). Start with a *botana* (a selection of appetizers) to try a little of a lot. Moderate.
   Nuu-Luu (Iturbide 100, San Felipe del Agua, tel 53187; tell the taxi driver it's beyond the Fountain of Seven Regions—*Fuente de la Siete Regiónes*) is another family-run restaurant, set in a flowering garden, high up in San Felipe, to the north of the city. Guests are greeted by a large grey dog. Home-cooking includes carrot soups, spicy pork kebabs and endless salads using local vegetables. Daughter Fatima is a vegetarian and always has an imaginative non-meat dish on the menu. Moderate.

Seafood and Vegetarian
For seafood, the **Ostióneria Mar de Plata** (towards the train station, Av Ferrocarril 619, tel 68198) is a no-nonsense place with formica tables, tankards of beer and barrels of mescal to accompany the freshest of fish. The whole family (chefs, owners and waiters) is vast, fuelled on octopus tails *al mojo de ajo* (garlic), cod's roe baked in the oven and the ultimate hang-over cure, a cocktail of oysters, shrimps, octopus and chilli. Moderate. Somewhat fancier, **Mariscos la Morsa** (Calz Porfirio Díaz 240, Colonia Reforma, tel 52213; closed Mon) specializes in innovative seafood dishes. They have at least ten ways of preparing oysters as well as seafood pasta and oriental seasonal fish, cooked with peppers, onions and rice. On Sundays they prepare a huge paella. Moderately expensive.

   There are two vegetarian retaurants, one by the Tamayo museum (Av Morelos 509), and **El Arca de Emmanuel** which is unusually elegant (opposite the ADO bus station on the Periférico, tel 56412). Moderate.

Monte Albán

Monte Alban is the work of men who knew their architectural business
consummately well.
   —Aldous Huxley, *Beyond the Mexique Bay*, 1932)

Monte Albán, the mountain with the top sliced off, towers above the city of Oaxaca. Majestic and imposing, it dominates the flat valleys all around from its eyrie up in the clouds. There is nothing demure or subtle about its grandeur: it shrieks of monumentality, power and the wealth of ages. The Zapotecs who built this great religious centre chose not to build on the mountain's summit but dug down into the bedrock, creating a vast, level plateau, so that the buildings appear to have been spawned by the mountain itself. Although Zapotecs still live in Oaxaca, with their own language and communities, their ancestors left no written evidence, no codices and no history to tell us of their great heritage. The temples, pottery and tombs of Monte Albán must speak for themselves.

GETTING AROUND

Monte Albán is 9 km west of Oaxaca. Scheduled buses take 20 minutes and run every 2 hours from 09.30 from the Hotel Mina del Angel (tel 66666, Mina 518 where it crosses Mier y Terán). Taxis cost double. It may be cheaper to join a group through the travel agencies or, cheapest of all, take the early morning buses from the second-class bus station at 07.30 with the guides and groundsmen and hitch back down.

If you have a torch, take it for some of the dark tombs. The late afternoon light is the most attractive, but there is not much time to linger as the site closes at 17.00.

History

THE BEGINNING

Without any natural water supply, this mountain-top site seems an absurd choice but, amazingly, it was continuously occupied for a full 15 centuries. It was first inhabited after 600 BC by a branch of the Olmecs from Veracruz and Tabasco, who had been driven south by flooding on the flat, gulf plains. The *danzante* figures, the grey clay pottery, jade, the jaguar god effigies, the numbering by a dot (representing one) and a dash (five) and the calendrical systems all come from the Olmecs, the Mother Culture of Mesoamerica.

Building began gradually from 300 BC. The rocky surface was flattened and paved by hand, graced on its edges by temples and palaces, platforms and pyramids, plazas and sunken patios. Only Building J, known as the observatory, shifted the general north–south axis of the site to point due southwest, for obscure astrological reasons.

THE CLASSIC

Most of today's remains were in place between AD 350 and 600. By AD 350 it was already a large city of great refinement, influenced by the Maya from the south, who brought the colour blue, and the Teotihuacános from the north with their cinnabar red. The buildings in general followed the *talud-tablero* style of Teotihuacán, with vertical panels topped by a flat surface giving solidity and strength to already imposing structures. Impersonal geometric forms, stepped fret designs, and animal and bird motifs decorated the brightly painted buildings, covered over with stucco and painted with reds, blues and greens. The population rose to 25,000 with trading links extending to the ends of the known world. The Zapotecs explored and expanded beyond their hill-top boundaries and absorbed satellite states of over 50,000 people. Carved jades, polychromed frescoes and elaborate tombs all come from this period. The ceramics show more female deities than in any other part of Mexico, a phenomenon that persists today with the almost deified matriarchs of Juchitán, in the Isthmus of Tehuantepec.

DECLINE

Between AD 600 and 800, the way of life began to change. Any creative pride was concentrated more on the gilding than the lily. Monte Albán was gradually abandoned. The nobility set themselves up in vassal states such as Zaachila and Mitla. Militarism was on the rise, directed resentfully against the Mixtecs from the Cholula–Puebla area who were moving into the valleys and intermarrying with Zapotec nobility. Mixtec brides brought a whole retinue of servants to the Zapotec court and Mixtec princes married several times, always with an eye to the dowry.

397

By 1100, the Mixtecs had dominated the site. Under their leadership, Monte Albán took on a cultural renaissance. The Mixtecs reused the old Zapotec tombs and replaced the incumbents with their own ancestors' figures and jewels, intricate goldwork and delicately engraved bones. Their written history was inscribed on deer-skin codices, read top to bottom, like a rebus. They constructed little, content to use the already existing temples and palaces. The arts of lapidary, metal smithing and codex writing reached unparalleled heights. They too, however, found an easier life on the valley floors and Monte Albán was deserted once again. Invasions from the north, by the Aztecs in the 15th century and then by the Spanish in 1521, completed the collapse.

VISITING THE SITE
Sybille Bedford, never one to shirk the unpalatable, thought that 'If the Nazis had not been so cheap, had their taste been better and their instinct for self-dramatization less Wagnerian, this is the way they would have built.' Certainly the massive bulk of the structures clearly announces man's attempt to conquer nature. It must have been at tremendous cost. The entire mountain top was levelled to form one vast terrace on which the city was built—using neither beast of burden nor the wheel.

The site begins with the climb up from the city of Oaxaca, 400 m below. Terraces flattened out of the mountainside provided the housing and drainage for most of the population: only the high priests and noblemen actually lived in the ceremonial centre itself. Beside the car park, there is a small **restaurant** and **museum**, with replicas of the *danzante* figures and maquettes of the site and tombs. Guides and books also promise to unfold the mysteries of the site for a small price.

Every building is clearly marked with an unromantic number or letter, and this has been kept to in the text below. The buildings were set out on the long, thin terrace, with a grand plaza in the middle and a platform on the southern edge. The northern end of the plaza also ends with a raised platform, and behind this are further structures and the majority of the tombs. Begin with the north end, walk through to the plaza, going round anti-clockwise, and take the road out past the ball court.

THE TOMBS
The earliest tombs on the site were no more than pits, with a simple stone slab covering the body and a few offerings of beads and food to send it on a journey to a better life. The northern tombs show a progression of the art, with antechambers leading into the actual chamber in the shape of a cruciform. The stairways down to the tombs were often sealed with a monumental stone slab and then filled in with rubble. Originally undecorated, these tombs soon became monuments in their own right, painted with exotic friezes. Excavations have uncovered hundreds of urns, finely sculpted with elaborate head-dresses, incised glyphs and specific gods, such as the Corn God with a cob on each side of his breast. The Zapotecs did not practise cremation. Bodies were buried whole and over time each tomb may have had several tenants. The Mixtecs who replaced the Zapotecs and, later still, the valley people brought bodies up to the mountain top to be buried, making the northern end more of a necropolis than an acropolis.

Tomb 105 is the only one not within the confines of the site. It is across the road from the car park, on the hill known as the Cerro del Plumaje. Its walls are decorated with one of the best preserved friezes, with a concentration of red tones, depicting nine couples, each with their name glyphs beside them—the Nine Lords of the Underworld and their companions. The whole tomb has been reproduced in the Museum of Anthropology in Mexico City.

A path leads north and right of the Visitors Centre to a small temple with column supports. **Tomb 7** is under the main steps. In this tomb, the Mexican archaeologist, Dr Alfonso Caso, discovered an amazing cache of over 500 pieces of Mixtec jewellery in 1932, currently on display in the Museo Regional in Oaxaca. (The state sued the Mexican Federal Government for possession of the jewels and won the suit.) Finely wrought gold jewellery, pearls the size of pigeon eggs, alabaster, silver, jade and turquoise made up the greatest treasure to be found in Mexico. Like so many of the tombs here, it was built by the Zapotecs but used by the Mixtecs.

The path continues northwest along the edge of the terrace, past the Sunken Court of the North Platform, to the second great tomb to be prised open, **Tomb 104**. Above the entrance way is a funerary urn to Cocijo, the Rain God. The door is one massive stone slab, etched in glyphs. The tomb itself is covered in blue and yellow murals of stylized creatures including Xipe Totec, the God of Reincarnation and spring, and the Corn God, Pitao Cozobi, which must have been painted while the body was in place, with drips of paint sprinkled in the hurry to finish. Directly under this tomb is another, **Tomb 172**, an earlier construction in which the offerings and the skeleton have been left exactly as they were found. A path leads south towards the Grand Plaza, along the west wall of the North Platform.

THE GRAND PLAZA

Most of what is shown today comes from Classic Monte Albán, built between AD 350 and 600 over previous constructions. The Danzante Building and Building J are earlier. The whole area is 320 m long and another 140 across. Every inch of space on the mountain top was used, so that buildings perch on the edge of the terrace, looking onto the plaza like guards of honour.

The strange arrow-shaped mound in the middle of the plaza, known as **System J** and pointing sharply southwest, is an early building, associated with astronomy and possibly an observatory. Several times remodelled, it is riddled with tunnels roofed by stone slabs joined at the top. Like the Danzante Building, it incorporates carved slabs both within and without, decorated with writing recording dates and details of battles won. The carving also depicts bodies both naked and dressed, often genitally mutilated. One figure, dressed in a jaguar skin, holds his own name glyph, a jaguar's head, in his left hand. The other large mound neatly covers a rocky rise which couldn't be levelled and was thus given prominence, topped with temples and graced with wide staircases on each of its fronts.

THE NORTH PLATFORM

The North Platform's broad staircase is over 12 m wide, with a generous balustrade. Heavy columns once stood in front of the structure and, at the top of the steps, are another two sets of six columns, some 2 m in diameter. The Sunken Court behind is a vast square built around an altar in the centre. To the left are the remains of Building B, probably a later Mixtec addition, which once rose through seven levels to a temple at the top.

THE WEST SIDE
Like System M, at the other end of the west side, **System IV**, the first complex on the west side, was set out around an enclosed courtyard, with a pyramid turning its back to the mountain's edge. Small, perishable, covered buildings once surmounted the top of the low pyramids, where ceremonies would have been performed. Wide stairways face onto the plaza. Stela 18, north of the pyramid, is the earliest carved stone monument at the site, still undeciphered and badly worn.

The broad stone-faced **Danzante Building** is one of the most important structures because of its stone bas-relief slabs, which show the earliest examples of writing in Mexico as well as writhing figures. These were once thought to represent loose, freely moving, dancing figures and the misnomer, *danzante*, has stuck. Later they were classified as swimmers, or dead prisoners of war, or a generation of children born deformed because of incest and inbreeding. Theories circulate but no archaeologist has found a hard and fast answer. The tortured sculptures of the figures portray the Olmec physiognomy, with slanted eyes and mouths drooping at the corners. There were some 140 in the building, facing onto the plaza, lining the narrow corridor and even making a stairway. The figures are haunting, painful, boneless and limp. All are male, all are naked (a great stigma: nudity was considered scandalous) and many are mutilated.

THE SOUTH PLATFORM
Past **System M**, the south platform blocks the end of the plaza. Although the largest structure, it is not greatly excavated. The broad stairway leads up steeply to the uneven platform with views over the plaza and valleys around. There were once stelae with glyphs on them in each of the four corners. All four are now in Mexico City. One remaining stela is on the right-hand side of the platform, on the plaza floor. Carvings and hieroglyphs are arranged in two columns with numbers based on the early Olmec line and dot system.

THE EAST SIDE
The **Palace** is one of the few temples which may have housed a great dignatory or priest: the divisions of various rooms have been marked out on the top of the platform. It was built over an earlier structure which had caved in underneath it. In the patio facing it, a cruciform tomb was uncovered, the interior walls lined with niches for effigies of the gods.

The **Pyramid** is next in line to the Palace. A tunnel runs from its south side to the complex in the centre of the plaza, with several tombs leading off it. On the altar in front of the main steps, there was once a jade Bat God, able to see in the dark and so associated with the Underworld. This has now been removed to the Museum of Anthropology in Mexico City.

The **Ball Court** is to the right of the road leading back from the Grand Plaza to the museum. In the shape of an I, it was constructed around AD 200 but subsequently improved. The game itself, known in Zapotec as *lachi*, was played with a hard rubber ball, hit off the hip and the elbow into the goal. This court is unusual in having two niches for gods at diagonal opposites and a circular stone in the centre of the court, but no round goal rings. The sloping, stepped sides of the court were probably covered in stucco and the matches were watched from the neighbouring temples.

East to Tlacolula and the Mixe Region

Highway 190, the road southeast to Tehuantepec, crosses the flat plain of the valley of Tlacolula. In the 40 km between Oaxaca City and the ruins of Mitla, there is more to see and do than on any other road in Oaxaca, with villages, sites and markets every few kilometres. However, once past Mitla, the road has no choice but to climb up and over the Sierra Madre, with no reason to stop until it reaches Tehuantepec (250 km) far below on the Pacific. It is a nightmare of a journey and not one to attempt by night if driving.

GETTING AROUND
Oaxaca and Mitla are 40 km apart. Second-class buses, Transportes Valle del Norte or Oaxaca-Istmo, leave for Mitla from the Oaxaca station every 25 minutes, taking 40 minutes. All the places mentioned are on Highway 190, or a short detour off it. It is easy to hitch but often hot and shadeless. Traffic stops early (including the buses).

On the other hand, east of Mitla in the Mixe region, there are next to no amenities— only a very sporadic bus service from Mitla and the scarcest of accommodation. The sulphur springs of Hierve el Agua are 2 rough hours from Oaxaca. Hector Pérez, of the Agencia Camacho in Oaxaca (tel 58594), makes an excellent guide for this unexplored territory.

The Valley of Tlacolula

Santa María El Tule
The tree with the widest perimeter in the world is in the churchyard of this small village, 14 km from Oaxaca. A conifer, *taxodium mucronatum*, it has a wider girth (42 m) than height (40 m) and continues to grow. Two thousand years old, it has a tortured shape, its branches shorn on one side and sprouting growths on the other. It has immense water problems. The roots are approximately three times the height and there is no longer water to replenish it. Since the 1950s, an English company, Worthington's, has pumped water down but it is a sad reminder of how the valley once was. Nomadic tribes settled here in 2000 BC to hunt and fish. The forest was gradually chopped away until, by the time the Spanish arrived, it was denuded. This is one of the few trees to remain. If travelling by bus, with no time to stop, sit on the left-hand side.

Tlacochahuaya
Eight km further east along Highway 190, a right turning leads to the village of Tla-cochahuaya (2 km). Its 16th-century church was originally part of a monastery, built by the Dominicans as a halfway house between Oaxaca and Tlacolula. The founder, Fray Jordán de Sta Catalina, designed it as a place of devotion and penitence, with none of the opulence of the other monasteries. The church is the size of a pocket handkerchief and the cloister is simple and crude. The walls and ceiling were painted by local Zapotecs with a profusion of Dominican roses. The *retablos*, restored by a German corporation, are accredited to the Zapotec, Juan de Arrue, whose most delicate work was in minia-tures and oils. The small organ, frivolously painted and carved, looks like a children's toy. In the 1530s, the Zapotec King Cocijoeza's son was married here to the daughter of the local bigwig. He never left the church. During the ceremony, a fight broke out: he was garrotted and died on the spot.

The village has a week-long religious festival that starts on 30 September.

Dainzú
The Zapotec site of Dainzú is some 2 km further down the main road, along a 1-km track to the right. It was founded in 350 BC, but reached its splendour between AD 500 and 600. It was a strategic site, controlling a narrow pass in the valley with look-outs for miles around. Largely unexcavated, the site has adapted to its topography: the shape of the hill emphasizes the pyramid, and its red soil is reflected in the stucco on the buildings. The things to see are the tombs (one of which has a jaguar's-head lintel, with its legs and paws as jambs) and the stone-sculpted ball players. These sculptures, leaning against the base of the pyramid under a corrugated-iron roof, are of irregular shapes and sizes and may well have come from somewhere else. As if caught in mid-play, they are dressed for the ball game, with helmets, and elbow, knee and hip protection.

Teotitlán del Valle
After 3 km, turn to the left and continue for 4 km to this traditional weaving village. Some 5000 weavers, at home or in the weaving market, produce 75 per cent of Oaxaca's wall hangings and rugs. Most of the weavers are men, but as demand is increasing for their ancient art, whole families are joining their fathers at the loom. Amongst the many, two traditional workshops are **Casa Santiago**, one of the first houses on the right, and, further into the village, **Benito García Hernandez**. Casa Santiago has a large collection for sale, ranging from place mats to rugs, all produced from the three looms constantly worked by father, mother, sister, nephew and son-in-law. The colours are pastel pinks, blues and caramel, with only a few of the bright modernist Picasso-like reproductions (painstakingly woven for Texan tour groups). Generally, the women make the yarn, the best still using natural vegetable dyes: indigo, pomegranate rind, pecan nutshells, moss and the episcopal purple of cochineal.

Lambityeco
The seldom-visited ruins of Lambityeco are only 7 km on from Dainzú, to the right of Highway 190. Populated since 700 BC, Lambityeco came into its own in the 7th and 8th centuries, when the Zapotecs moved down to the valleys from Monte Albán. Behind the pyramid is a group of small patios with the remains of four chambers. The tomb in the first patio has two exquisite stucco busts, presumed to represent the last rulers—the woman on the left with the name glyph (10) Cane and the man on the right with the glyph (1) Earthquake. Behind the tomb are two sculptured panels: the right-hand panel depicts a man lying on his chest holding a femur bone (a symbol of power) with his name glyph (8) Owl, and a woman with a bead necklace and the title (3) Turquoise. The left-hand panel shows another couple: his name would have been (4) Human Face and the woman's (10) Monkey. In the second patio are two large, well-preserved Cocijo (Rain God) masks, made of terra cotta and stucco. The mask on the right—a jaguar mask with a quetzal feather headdress—is in better condition, but the one on the left shows more clearly the god's symbols, with the wind in his right hand and lightning in his left.

Tlacolula
Four km beyond Lambityeco, Tlacolula is the long-established trading centre for the valley and its Sunday market still calls the shots locally. The market has everything but

concentrates on weaving and textiles (mainly from the neighbouring villages of Teotitlán and Santa Ana del Valle). The 16th-century Dominican church has a charming naive Mexican baroque chapel. The stonewood technique was used to decorate the ceiling, as in Santo Domingo in Oaxaca. Wood was moulded and covered with a layer of clay, and then painted and edged with a thin layer of gold leaf to resemble stone.

Tlacolula has become a self-styled mescal centre. On the main street, Calle Zaragoza, Señor Pensamiento's shop is popular with tour groups, who try shots of fruit-flavoured mescal in the back bar (guayaba, orange, apple, grape or *sapote*). Serious mescal drinkers may prefer the better quality, less gimmicky firewater drunk in the cantinas, such as **Joyas Oaxaqueñas**, two doors down.

Yagul

The high, commanding pre-Hispanic site of Yagul is the last stop before Mitla—35 km from Oaxaca and 3 km on from Tlacolula, down a 1½-km road on the left. At the turning, on the escarpment to the right-hand side, ancient petroglyphs testify to the very early date the site was first occupied. It is dramatically situated, dug deep into the hillside, and naturally defensive, having control over all it could see without being seen. It became one of the main Zapotec strongholds after the decline of Monte Albán at the end of the 6th century.

From the parking place, a path climbs steeply up to the look-out point on the hill, providing an invigorating aerial view over the site below and the valley beyond. The path passes a tomb with jaguar-head sculptures and the remains of brick wall-bracing in the hill. The site itself begins with the **Patio of the Triple Tomb**, on the left when entering from the car park. Here, a single-entrance burial chamber opens into three tombs with stone heads on the doorways and sculptures on the lintels. The Mixtecs took over the earlier Zapotec burial grounds to inter their own nobility and reworked the stone decorations with mosaics similar to those at Mitla. Beyond this is the ball court, the largest yet uncovered in the state. Facing into the hill, north of the ball court, is the **Palace**, with six patios but only one doorway. The walls were built of an adobe core but faced with stone, to give the impression that they were solid stone throughout. Grouped around patios and quadrangles, rather than temples and pyramids, the palace is an example of the shift from outward- to inward-looking architecture in the post-Classic era.

Mitla

This scruffy village, 40 km from Oaxaca and 4 km to the left of Highway 190, was built over the ruins of the most magnificent of all Mixtec sites. For those who prefer intricacy to monumentality it is, without doubt, the most spectacular site in Oaxaca and one of the most delicately beautiful in the whole country. The villagers, when not concerned with tourism, weave *serapes* (blankets) and *huipiles* (rugs) in bulk, selling them to Oaxaca and Mexico City. The quality isn't up to much but the factories are all open for visits, and a cluster of stalls clings to the entrance gates of the site.

History

Although a late runner, Mitla was occupied by Zapotecs from the 1st century AD. As the power of Monte Albán declined in the 7th century, society became less centralized. A

403

more feudalistic system developed whereby a handful of smaller satellite city-states such as Yagul, Zaachila and Mitla were ruled by Zapotec nobles. Mitla was to become one of the most important of these vassal states. In many ways it continued the tradition begun at Yagul, putting palaces in place of pyramids to reflect the increasing importance of civil rather than religious rule. The Mixtecs took control in AD 850, absorbing the local Zapotec population. When the Spaniards arrived in 1528, it was still an active centre, in which both Mixtec and Zapotec were spoken. The Spaniards built their church on top of a razed palace, using what stones came to hand, particularly the lintels.

The 17th-century Dominican friar, Burgoa, believed that Mitla was the burial place of high priests and kings. Certainly, its name in Zapotec is Yoopaa, meaning 'the home of the dead', while the name Mitla comes from the Aztec Mictlán, which means the same. The friar's opinion has raised many questions but major burials have not been dis-covered and later friars have proved less interested in Mitla's antecedents: at the beginning of this century, some priests knocked down one room covered in pre-Hispanic frescoes in order to build a pigsty, and converted another into a stable.

VISITING THE SITE
(Open 09.00–18.00.)
Mitla was the converse of Monte Albán, neither grandiose nor monumental, bringing palaces to the plain, from mountain top to valley floor. The city, of creamy green limestone, centres on five groups above the Mitla River. Two groups remain in good condition, set around quadrangles with highly ornamented facades interwoven with the intricacy of filigree jewellery (a Mixtec talent). They lead back to courtyards and patios, turning in on themselves like a retreating snail. It is far removed from the sheer mass of Monte Albán but strongly reminiscent of the post-Classic Maya sites in the Puuc hills of the Yucatán, particularly Uxmal.

The **Column Group**, the first in the site, is the best preserved of the complexes. The patterns on the walls wind in whorls and spirals following some divine pattern, described by Aldous Huxley as 'petrified weaving'. Each tiny stone, put in place like a delicate mosaic, was fixed without the use of mortar. Some have kept their original colour, the faded crimson of cochineal. No other place seems to have been so conscious of its own design: over 100,000 tiny pieces of stone were used in this group alone. No animal appears in the decoration but the geometric motif, like the Greek key patterns, traces the abstract uncoiling of a serpent, snaking its way around the walls. Three doors lead into the **Hall of the Six Columns** where six monoliths would once have supported a perishable roof. From here, a dark, narrow passage leads back into a further courtyard, the **Patio de las Grecas**, with four small chambers leading off it, each with an echoing design both inside and out. The low doorways are made lower still by metal supports (to protect the lintels from earthquakes) which, unseen, have knocked several visitors unconscious.

The quadrangle to the south is built to the same plan, with galleries around a central patio. There are two **tombs**. One under the east gallery leads down to a cruciform-shaped chamber made up of monolithic slabs of stone. The other tomb, under the north gallery, is supported by a fat column to keep the roof from falling in. Both tombs are solidly constructed to cope with earthquakes, backed and topped with adobe so that the stone stayed solid while the adobe took the shock.

The **North Group**, behind the church over the road from the entrance gate, is a quadrangle. (The south wall was removed to build the church.) The northernmost gallery leads, via a small tunnel, into a further patio. The doorways have a few, small stucco remains, as delicate as codex writing, on the lintels.

The Frissell Museum

This small museum (open 09.00–18.00, like the site) has set out its pieces in dusty glass cases. In the first room, a corner display cabinet traces the evolution of the Zapotec Rain God, Cocijo, from a crude pre-Classic figurine to a very advanced late Classic head with jaguar and snake motifs worked into the symbolism. After AD 500, his cult suddenly took off, coincident with the drying out of the valley. Later pieces, including many clay statuettes, show how receptive the Zapotecs were to contemporary influences from the rest of Mexico, such as Xochicalco, Teotihuacán and the rest of the central Mexican plateau.

WHERE TO STAY

The ****Posada La Sorpresa**, adjoining the museum, is a little hotel often used by archaeologists. The home-cooking doesn't vary much, but it's fine for lunch or an overnight stay.

Xaaga

Right off every beaten track (8 km from Mitla on the Tepuxtepec road; turn right down a 2-km bumpy track), Xaaga is a Zapotec hamlet, built up around a now-defunct hacienda. From there it is a 20-minute walk across the fields to the craggy hills where 2000-year-old petroglyphs have been found etched into the limestone. Made of oxidized animal fat, the figures are no more than stick-pin animals and people. The dry valley floor, stretching back to the city of Oaxaca, would once have been covered in forest, of which little remains except the much-vaunted Tule tree.

The Mixe Region

Only for those with both time and a sense of adventure, a byroad from Mitla (signposted Tamazulapan) leads northeast into the harsh, barren Mixe region, the poorest and least advanced in Mexico. Unpaved until 1990, the road now has a rudimentary covering to ensure the delivery of corn, chillies, cacao and coffee, which were previously brought down by mules. Neither the Aztecs nor the Spanish ever conquered the region, and until 200 years ago it had never been entered by an outsider. The 75,000 Mixe live in settlements scattered over the mountains that extend northeast of Mitla towards the Isthmus of Tehuantepec. There is no firm sense of identity uniting the disparate villages: mountain barriers can make a distance of only 10 km impassable. Today the people suffer a new handicap, an unexplained genetic epidemic which causes blindness and the collapse of the nervous system.

On the way to the petrified waterfall of Hierve el Agua, the road passes mescal makers using original techniques. Mescal is a raw, traditional, throat-burning version of tequila, made from the maguey cactus. Each cactus takes 16 years to grow its spiky leaves. These spines are then cut off and the hearts barbecued underground. When caramelized, they

405

are put on a treadmill and pulped by a vast stone wheel, tirelessly pulled round and round by a scrawny horse. The pulp is distilled in a serpentine coil of pipes and tubes. This is the home-produced version. Further south in Mitatatlán, a modern factory using copper machinery has turned the horse and the stills into commercial anachronisms.

Hierve el Agua, the goal at the end of the journey (2 hours from Oaxaca), is a series of sulphur springs that have cascaded down into a frozen jet of calcium, a suspended stalactite. It is a magical place, an extraordinary natural phenomenon set in a wild, lonely landscape. It has long been a modest place of pilgrimage: on the rocky outcrop up above are pre-Hispanic ruins with traces of walls and ceramic shreds.

South to Zaachila and Zimatlán

Two very different day trips can be made south of Oaxaca to the valleys of Zaachila and Zimatlán, combining country villages with weekly markets and local customs with beautiful crafts. Zaachila is most fun on a Thursday when the agricultural market is on—the largest, oldest and most revered in the valleys, whilst Friday is better for Zimatlán, Ocotlán and the famous home of black pottery, San Bartolo Coyotepec.

GETTING AROUND
Local buses leave at least every half-hour from the second-class bus station, with extra buses on market days. (The railway is only suitable for goods.) Driving is the easiest way to explore the valleys at leisure—and the only way to take up on local suggestions to hunt out a particular artisan down a maze of country lanes. For the Zaachila valley, take Calle 20 de Noviembre out of Oaxaca and follow the signs to Zaachila and Cuilapan (Highway 147) over the Atoyac River. For the Zimatlán valley, take Calle Armenta y Lopez out to Highway 175, past the airport, and follow signs to San Bartolo Coyotepec and Ocotlán.

The Valley of Zaachila

Arrazola
Eight km from Oaxaca, a road leads off to the right (Highway 145) to Arrazola (another 5 km). Under the shadow of Monte Albán, the village is well known for its carved and painted wooden figures. Introduced by the Dominicans, for church decorations, the brightly polychromed sirens, armadillos, iguanas, dogs, snakes and monkeys now owe little to the Catholic canon of saints and angels. The Jiménez family, the best known, reserves its work for North American museums. The Morales family, particularly the young son, Arsenio, still works and sells from home (the second track on the right and first house on the left).

Cuilapan
Twelve kilometres from Oaxaca, Cuilapan was once considered to be the heart of the Mixtec civilization. Accordingly, in the 1530s, the Dominicans chose to build a great monastery there, on already holy (if pagan) ground. Construction of the monastery and its church was well advanced, the basilica begun, and straggling communities had been herded into one place, when the Dominicans realized that they had made a tactical error.

The Aztec garrison at Oaxaca proved to be far more influential than Cuilapan. They decided to ignore the Mixtecs and moved their attentions to Oaxaca, leaving the basilica in Cuilapan without a roof.

There are three facades. The first, to the basilica, is full of good Dominican symbolism, with fire-breathing dogs separated by fleurs-de-lys. Flanked by Faith and Hope, poor old Charity got lopped off in the 19th century. The Rapunzel towers were added during army occupation in the 1800s. The facade of the monastery entrance is more of a hybrid, in the Renaissance style but topped with *estípite* columns. The facade by the ticket office is different again, with a triangular fronton and Doric columns whose sobriety shows the influence of the Spanish architect, Herrera. Structurally, the monastery remains in good shape. However, most of the paintings have deteriorated and the kitchen smells as if cows have been wintering in it.

In their heyday, the Dominicans, under Domingo de Aguiñaga (a friend of Ignatius Loyola), baptized left, right and centre. The church at Cuilapan includes the Christian tombs of the Zapotec princess Donaji and her husband (and one-time enemy), a Mixtec prince of Tilantongo. She took the name Doña Juana Cortés, and both are buried under the church floor. The 16th-century tombstone reads 'MAIAONA [Maria Ioana] CORTES DIEGO AGUILAR'.

Vicente Guerrero, the former president and one of the heroes of the fight for independence, who deserved much more, was shot here on St Valentine's Day 1831, for being too liberal. He is commemorated by a large, neglected monument behind the monastery.

Zaachila

Zaachila, 6 km from Cuilapan and 18 from Oaxaca, grew important in the late Classic period, when Monte Albán declined and noble Zapotec families moved to lower ground. It was the capital of the last Zapotec kingdom. The Aztecs tried to conquer it in the 1480s but failed to intimidate the king, Cocijoeza. Despairing, the Aztec leader, Ahuitzotl, then tried to marry the Zapotec to his beautiful daughter. Cocijoeza wisely refused, only to change his mind as soon as he met her. The Aztec king planned to use his daughter as a spy, but she, too, fell deeply in love and would have none of it. Ahuitzotl died in 1503, but the Aztecs didn't stop the pressure. When the Spanish came, Cocijoeza saw a way of vanquishing his enemies in one fell swoop, and sent envoys to welcome them. The Spanish did indeed conquer the Mixtecs but turned on the Zapotecs as well. The broken old man died in Zaachila in 1529, at the age of 72. His eldest son, a pious Catholic, was all but ignored until he began a counter-revolt in 1555. Sentenced to death, he died of a cerebral haemorrhage on his return from the trial.

All that remains of the site can be seen on a hillock behind the church. When it was excavated in the 1960s, the villagers took up their machetes to prevent any finds being taken to far-distant Mexico City. Ignacio Bernal, the Mexican archaeologist, had to ask for army protection when he found two burial chambers in 1962. The larger chamber, in three parts, has an entrance decorated with geometric designs uncoiling like a snake, and a pre-chamber with reliefs of owls—the night birds who protected the soul in darkness. In the inner chamber are four wall sculptures, two of priests and two of rulers. The furthest wall is faced with a horizontal figure, like a swimmer, thought to be the emblem of an ancestor.

Zaachila has a Thursday **market**. In the Zócalo, the household market spreads its wares, from bread on the extreme left, through meats and flowers to wooden furniture. The old hands don't waste time here but instead make for the livestock market, at the entrance to the village, where the animals are still sold by barter and not auction. Fat sows scratch around for a few grubs and young bullocks arrive in medieval carts, as buyers and sellers practise their poker faces.

Opposite this market is a splendid country restaurant, **La Capilla**, with thick wooden tables and chairs set out under walnut trees. *Tasajo de herbas* (flat, grilled beef) comes with *asiento* tortillas, made with a salty lard. Moderate.

The Valley of Zimatlán

San Bartolo Coyotepec

This small village, 15 km from Oaxaca, is the home of distinctive black pottery. Shaped without a wheel from the iron-rich clay soil around, it has been worked for 2000 years. For centuries it was a dull, buff colour until Doña Rosa Valente Nieto Real polished the pots with agate and rediscovered the metallic sheen appreciated by her Zapotec ancestors. Some copies are sold in Oaxaca markets, painted with black boot polish for a 3-day glow. Doña Rosa died in 1980, a tiny, frail old lady, but her OAP son, Don Valente, gives practised demonstrations at 10.15 every morning, well patronized by visitors. Their shop in Calle Juárez (the first right turn after the sleeping policeman) has jars, pots, bowls and necklaces for sale.

San Martin Ticajete and Sto Tomás Jalieza

The road drops down to **San Martin Ticajete**, where tree roots are shaped and painted into undulating snakes. Just before the km 130 sign is a left turning to **Sto Tomás Jalieza**, 1 km away. Its small market is entirely made up of women weavers, some with looms around the waist. Held on Fridays, to coincide with that of Ocotlán, it concentrates on cotton weaving into belts, shirts, table cloths and bracelets, decorated with animals.

Ocotlán

Just short of Ocotlán (turn right 1½ km after the Pemex station), the village of **San Antonino** is well known for the embroidered shirts and dresses produced by women working from home. It is easy to get lost or misdirected but the Pérez family at 50 Cinco de Mayo (turn left in the square and take the third street on the right) are worth battling to find for their beautifully worked clothes.

Ocotlán, although not large, is the biggest town in the area and its Friday market, which starts setting up the night before, attracts people from all over the state. It has none of the rhyme or reason of Zaachila or Etla. It sprawls and spills over the square and beyond in a jungle of alleyways, tunnels and low-slung awnings. Everything is on sale, from horse tack (saddles, boots, spurs and chaps) to painted furniture and brightly coloured sashes. The fruits and vegetables are very seasonal: cactus flowers, fuchsia-pink pitaya (drunk with lemon and fizzy water), chamotes, and cherries the size of plums. Even the inmates of the local prison weave split bamboo baskets to be sold at the market. The four Aguilar sisters (Irene, Josefina, Guillermina and Concepción) fashion coloured

408

clay figures, from nuns to brides, birth to death. The artist Rodolfo Morales is from Ocotlán. Many of his works draw inspiration from the square, the market place and the church, as fantasy blends with reality and colours hit head on.

North to Etla and the Sierra Juárez

The Valley of Etla

To the northwest of Oaxaca, Etla was the granary store of the central Oaxacan valleys in pre-Hispanic times. It was also the most productive and populous. In the last 200 years, it has suffered considerably because of deforestation. Few people bother with this, the least visited of the valleys, and see it only as the beginning of the road to the centre of Mexico, but it does have a pre-Classic Zapotec site (at San José Mogote) and a lively market at Atzompa.

GETTING AROUND
Once again, buses to all the villages mentioned leave from the second-class bus station in Oaxaca, with extra departures on market days. By car, take Highway 190 (the Panamericana) from Oaxaca and follow the signposts off this road. The valley ends at Huitzo, before the Panamericana begins its wind and curve over the mountains on its way to Mexico City, 500 km away.

Atzompa
After 6 km on the Panamericana, turn off to the left for 3 km, following signs for Atzompa. The village is best known for its distinctive dark green glazed pottery. It lives and breathes by these pots, which are baked in wood-fired ovens. Teodora Blanca and her family, who live on the road into Atzompa, shot to fame when Nelson Rockefeller bought 67 of her light brown 'earth mother' clay figures on one visit. They also make

Earth-mother figure from Atzompa

409

strings of black beads and drainpipes, stoppered with carved animal heads. There is a market on Tuesday and Friday which starts at the unusually late hour of 14.00, beside the church.

San José Mogote

Ten kilometres from Oaxaca on Highway 190, the small village of San José Mogote encompasses an equally small pre-Classic Zapotec site, with long, clear views over the fertile valley to Monte Albán and the Sierra Juárez. It was one of the very first in the south: signs of inhabitation have been dated from 1350 BC. It reached a modest peak in 600 BC but had almost died out by AD 400. Artefacts found at the site indicate that it grew to about 250 hectares in size and traded long distances for marine pearl oysters from the Pacific and polished magnetite mirrors from the Olmecs. It was divided into ceremonial and secular areas with a separate cemetery and, like Monte Albán, was built on a hill to protect it from earthquakes and flooding. The workmanship is crude, with roughly carved stones and narrow stairways. The villagers were determined to keep any artefacts found during the digging and so manage the small community museum themselves. It is excellent. There are three delicately beautiful Olmec jade figurines and a funeral urn with the mask of the Zapotec Rain God, Cocijo. One huge red brazier still has its own incense burner.

A few km further along, the village of **San Pedro y San Pablo Etla** has a large Wednesday produce market where limestone is sold in blocks (it is used for making tortillas). Pyramids of avocados are arranged next to rows of carrots, and purple flowers are sold in arm-straining bunches. The market stretches below a 16th-century Dominican monastery designed by Fray Marin, with a very sober plateresque facade.

The long, thin village of **Suchilquitongo** and neighbouring **Huitzo** mark the end of the valley, and the beginning of the Sierra. This was also the end of Zapotec land. The remains of a barely excavated defensive site behind Huitzo show that it was strongly fortified. The remnants of a Zapotec tomb, excavated here in 1985, are kept under lock and key in the Palacio Municipal in Huitzo (ask for the Presidente: although everyone will be only too glad to help, it may well be a wild goose chase). The size of the Dominican church in the village implies that the Spanish, too, kept the town well defended.

The Sierra Juárez

For a long winding drive through pine-smelling sierra, take Highway 175 northeast of Oaxaca. The mountain range is named after Oaxaca's most famous son, Benito Juárez, who was born in the village of **Guelatao**, 74 km uphill. Buses from Oaxaca's second-class station leave every hour.

In Juárez's time, only 10 of the 150 villagers spoke any Spanish. Born on 21 March 1806, he was orphaned at 3 and raised by an uncle. When he was 12, he left the impoverished village to walk barefoot to Oaxaca, where he was befriended by a Franciscan lay brother. He trained as a lawyer, often defending his fellow Zapotecs without a fee, before entering politics, becoming the first indigenous and only Zapotec president of Mexico. The village has become a shrine to Juárez but non-Juárez buffs will also find it a peaceful place to stop and have a picnic.

One kilometre north, the quietly fraying village of **Ixtlán** clings to its former glory with a dominating parish church, whose 18th-century churrigueresque facade is decorated like an altarpiece. The village has a small shop to buy drinks in, and a surprisingly raucous primary school.

The Road from Oaxaca to Mexico City

Oaxaca and Mexico City are 507 km apart, a 6-hour journey by road which is usually done nonstop by people anxious to reach the city and with no time to explore the country. But for anyone with a day to spare, the northwestern corner of Oaxaca offers a surprising insight into this rural and complex state, with vast monasteries towering unexpectedly over valleys and villages. It is a poor region, but nevertheless got the full Catholic treatment in the 16th century when the Dominicans conquered the Mixtecs with their customary zeal. The soil is thin, the mountains high and the main road, Highway 190 (the Panamericana), snakes its way across the region as fast as the mountains will let it.

GETTING AROUND
Huajuápan is roughly halfway between Mexico City (285 km) and Oaxaca (222 km) and a good base for visiting the Dominican monasteries. First-class ADO buses from Huajuápan go to both cities every hour on the hour. Only second-class buses from Calle Nuyoor in Huajuápan go to the monasteries, all 1½ hours away. There are 8 daily buses to Yanhuitlán, 77 km southeast of Huajuápan on Highway 190. Coixtlahuaca is 22 km northeast of Highway 190, 77 km from Huajuápan, with only two buses in the early morning and two in the late afternoon. Teposcolula is 75 km southeast of Huajuápan, 13 km southwest of Highway 190 down Highway 125 (the road to the coast), and buses are frequent.

Huajuápan de León

Huajuápan, in the Río Mixteco valley, is the largest town in the Mixtec region though of little interest in itself. It is surrounded by the dry, parched Sierra Madre Sur and spiked with organ cactus sticking up like telegraph poles from the brick-red soil. It was flattened by an earthquake in 1980 and didn't have the strength to recover. Its fame, such as it is, rests on mescal, a fermented alcoholic drink, distilled from the silver-green maguey cactus grown in the fields around. Malcolm Lowry, passing through in 1946, didn't find any, which is perhaps why he pronounced it, 'absolutely and so utterly dark and sinister it was almost beyond belief'. Perhaps so, but not if your visit coincides with the Sunday market or one of the festivals, such as the celebration of Señor de los Corazones in the third week of July.

One km behind the ADO bus station, on a windswept pimple of a hill in the middle of the valley, is the **Cerro de las Minas**, a small, recently excavated Mixtec site. Local optimism that it will prove as large and important as Monte Albán is a sad reminder of the desperate need for tourism to boost the economy. The one factory for 100 km,

411

FIDEPAL, manufactures palm-fibre sombreros and is open for visits between 08.30 and 16.30.

The Monasteries of the Mixteca Alta

The Dominicans came to the area in the 1540s and immediately began to get their houses in order. The warm golden stone of **Yanhuitlán**, appropriately named 'in a wide valley', dominates a broad plain and was the first of the three to be completed. Made to last, the church was built on a raised platform constructed from masonry from the earlier Mixtec temples. Its huge flying buttresses had to withstand frequent earth tremors and, in 1812, when it was temporarily a fortress, an attack by anticlerical troops. Within the church, the rib vaulting along the nave leads up to the fabulous main altarpiece, decorated with archangels and prophets, the only verifiable work of the Spaniard, Andrés de la Concha. A small museum in the monastery attached protects the rest of the affluent monasteries' treasures, in the only part of the once-extensive building that is still standing (open 10.00–18.00). A big festival is held in the last week of May, with a fair, cock fights and masked, mescal-induced dances.

Coixtlahuaca is a complement to Yanhuitlán, with a better-preserved monastery but a sadly neglected gothic open chapel. Its two idiosyncratic, plateresque facades each have large rose windows. The one to the side is flanked by unusual reliefs of the Passion sculpted by the Mixtec, with Nahuatl speech glyphs coming out of their heads. The Aztecs introduced the Nahuatl language when they subjugated the Mixteca Alta at the beginning of the 15th century. Tribute sent to the Aztec Emperor, Moctezuma, included 80 bags of cochineal, the strong, crimson dye produced by a tiny insect that feeds off the cactus growing in the region.

Teposcolula, like Coixtlahuaca, was once a centre of the silk-worm industry introduced by the Dominicans in the 1540s, which later declined with the opening of the Chinese silk trade. The Dominicans left behind a monastery dating from 1570 and a Renaissance open chapel. A double row of arches is all that now remains of the grand design of the latter. In the centre is a hexagon, once covered over with a cupola, now open to the elements. The original church was destroyed by earth tremors but large sculptures of saints still survive, now set in niches on the new facade.

WHERE TO STAY AND EAT   (area code 953)

Although every village has somewhere to hole up for the night, Huajuápan is the best bet. The ***García Peral** (tel 20742) on the Zócalo has surprising luxuries, such as a disco and a swimming pool. The restaurant is the best around, serving *cabrito al pastor* (goat), *cecina oaxaqueña* (dried beef) and a regional, darker variation of the *mole poblano*. For a night, the **Linda Vista**, just before the ADO station, or the *Arellano**, by the second-class station, are spartan alternatives. **El Dorado**, by the Arellano, is a cheerful seafood café, where the crab and shrimp cocktails are spiced by the high tension of the local basketball final on the TV. Cheap.

The Oaxaca Coast

While Oaxaca's coastline may not be the most stunning, it is uncommercial and uncrowded, with good middle-range accommodation. Beaches in Mexico tend to be either deserted or the domain of some glitzy resort, but Oaxaca has managed to strike the middle ground.

The coastline bulges into the Pacific, forced out by the hunched backbone of the Sierra Madre mountains. Craggy foothills of barren scrub stretch its length, from the large town of Pinotepa Nacional in the west to Juchitán in the east. Pinotepa Nacional is not worth staying in but is a major stop on the coast road (Highway 200) between Acapulco and the more preferable beach town of Puerto Escondido. Along the coast long stretches of bleached sand are pounded by waves blown in from the Pacific. Before the road was built in the 1970s, the area was almost inaccessible and largely ignored. Political unrest fermented and the towns of Juchitán and Tehuantepec in the east are famed for their opposition to the government.

Until recently, little had been done to attract the tourist and the locals lived off the sea. In the 1980s, the Ministry of Tourism decided to cash in on the natural beauty of the area and began building the international resort of Huatulco in the most outstanding of many bays. Puerto Escondido is a smaller, more Mexican resort with an annual surfing competition in August. Puerto Angel is little more than a fishing village which received a huge word-of-mouth following in the 1960s.

The major drawback of the Pacific is the strong undertow. All the bigger hotels have pools and a flag (always red for danger) advising people when to swim in the sea. From Puerto Angel to Salina Cruz there are wonderfully tempting stretches of deserted beach, but only very strong swimmers should think about throwing off their clothes and jumping in.

GETTING AROUND

By Air: There are airports in Puerto Escondido and Huatulco. Mexicana operate four direct flights a week between Mexico City and Puerto Escondido. Aerovías Oaxaqueñas run a daily, 20-minute flight to Puerto Escondido from Oaxaca, leaving at 12.00. The 28-seater planes fill up quickly and should be booked in season (tel 958 20132). For Huatulco, Mexicana run a daily, direct flight to and from Mexico City, while Aeroméxico fly to and from Mexico City via Oaxaca on Mondays, Wednesdays, Fridays and Sundays, leaving Huatulco in the afternoon.

By Bus: Aged buses clatter up and down Highway 200 which runs the length of the coast, from Pinotepa Nacional in the west to Juchitán in the east. From Pinotepa Nacional, buses take an appalling, badly surfaced road north up Highway 125 to Tlaxiaco (212 km), where the road divides for Mexico City or Oaxaca. A faster route from Oaxaca is via Highway 175 to Pochutla. Ten buses a day run from 05.00 to 22.00 (7 hrs). From Pochutla, buses run every half-hour to Puerto Angel (30 mins) and hourly to Huatulco (1 hr), Puerto Escondido (2 hrs) and Juchitán.

By Car: All roads coming south to the coast have to twist through the jagged peaks of the Sierra Madre and none are as direct as they look on the map. Pochutla, 13 km north of Puerto Angel, is on the crossroads between Highway 200, the coast road, and Highway 175 which winds its way north to Oaxaca through mountains, pines and innumerable hairpin bends. Juchitán in the east connects Highway 200 to Highway 185 which heads north into the fertile plains of Veracruz.

By Train: There is no railway between Oaxaca and the coast, or along the coast west of Juchitán. A daily train connects Juchitán with Veracruz (see Isthmus of Tehuantepec).

413

Puerto Escondido

Puerto Escondido sprawls from hill to shore. Set around a wide, sheltered bay, the dusty fishing village has turned itself haphazardly into a low-key resort, in response to the surfers who came to crest its waves. The village didn't intend this to happen and still extends a welcome that isn't entirely determined by wallet size alone, whilst the lack of specific planning means that there are no big chains of hotels.

GETTING AROUND

By Bus: The first- and second-class bus stations are next to one another on the main Highway 200 (known as Carretera Costera), where it crosses with 16 de Septiembre, opposite Hotel Ribera del Mar. The Flecha Roja first-class station, for long-distance buses, is actually on the crossroads, while the Estrella del Valle second-class station, for local buses, is a block uphill.

By Taxi: Taxis meet aeroplanes at the airport (10 km west of town) but have to be booked to take passengers back (tel 20114 or get the driver's home number). They are collectives and will fill up with other passengers. Everyone pays a small set rate.

In Town: The main street, Pérez Gasga, runs parallel to the sea and is closed to traffic. All the central hotels and restaurants are here, on the main beach. Further stretches of beach are a short walk east. From Pérez Gasga, it's a 5-minute walk uphill to the main Carretera Costera, also parallel to the sea, which cuts the town in half. Above this are the cheaper hotels and the market.

TOURIST INFORMATION

At the west end of the main street, Pérez Gasga, the tourist office (tel 20175) keeps casual hours, closing from midday to 18.00 and all day Sunday. On the main street, travel agents Agencia García Rendón are open all day (tel 20114) and can organize snorkelling, boat trips, horse riding and surfing, as well as plane and bus tickets.

BEACHES

The best beach of all is Bacocho, out west below the Posada Real. Boats from the town beach will make the trip out here. It's a long stretch of sweeping sand, virtually deserted because of the undertow. Less strong swimmers can walk and sunbathe on it and then use the pool of the Posada Real at the eastern end. The main beach in town is lively: fish is bought and sold, small cafés vie for custom, and there is always room to squeeze in a sunbathe. For a quieter, less public spot, take a 5-minute walk further east to Zicatela near the Santa Fe hotel. Again, beware of the strong current. This is where the annual surfing competition takes place every August.

WHERE TO STAY   (area code 958)

The ****Santa Fe (1 km out on the east side of town, off the Carretera Costera, Apartado Postal 96, tel 20170) stands head and shoulders above the other hotels. American-run with an eye to Mexican detail, it has a mass of small tiled stairways leading off a central courtyard, which brims with flowers. It sits on a clean stretch of beach and has its own small swimming pool. The restaurant uses local ingredients but gives them a

414

wholesome international feel, offering plates of tropical fruit, yoghurt and crusty bread for breakfast or freshly caught lobster for lunch. It's rustic at a price, but well run and friendly. The town centre is a 5-minute walk along the beach.

****Posada Real** (Blvd Juaréz, Frac Bacocho, tel 20133, fax 20192), a couple of km to the west of town, sits in a large green garden with its own strip of deserted beach and two swimming pools. The rooms are small and functional but the location makes them worthwhile. The hotel hires out beach bikes for crossing the dunes of the Bacocho beach, stretching endlessly out to the west. Non-guests can use the pool and beach if they have a drink in one of the restaurants.

There are two good moderate hotels right in the centre on the beach front, off Pérez Gasga. The better buy is the ***Rincón del Pacífico** (tel 20056) which is plain and simple, with big fans rotating overhead. The ***Las Palmas** (tel 20230) next door is similar but slightly smaller, with darker rooms. Both have palm-lined gardens at the back, leading onto the beach.

To the north of town, beyond the Carretera Costera, are a number of cheaper hotels which can't command the prestige of their beach-front competitors. Of these, the **Luz del Angel** (1a Norte with Av Oaxaca, tel 20122) can be highly recommended for its big clean rooms with huge fans. Rooms on the top floor are cooler, with a view of the bay. The *Palacio Azteca** next door is neither a palace nor advisable, with dirty rooms and surly staff. As a last resort, **(CE) Trailer Park Neptuno**, right in the centre off the main beach, has nothing to recommend it but its location. It's a cheap place to hang a hammock or rent a *cabaña*.

EATING OUT

The main street is lined with restaurants and cafés serving fish and fish. Of these, the best is **Los Crotos** which buys fish off boats on the beach lapping at its feet. It is then cooked up in front of the tables, and often filled with rich seafood sauces. Moderate. Equally good is **Perla Flammante**, nearby, which buys in three or four different types of seasonal fish every day, cooking them to specific orders, from easy on the chilli to laced with garlic. The restaurant upstairs is breezy and open, with wooden chairs and tables. Moderate. Locals will always be found in unpretentious **Lolis**, a round palapa-roofed hut on the other side of the street, which specializes in *pulpo* (squid) and *ostión* (oyster), washed down with bottles of beer. It is alway crowded with families on Sundays. Moderate. Pizza and lasagne are always on the menu at the **Osteria Pizza del Viandante**, which is run by an Italian. It's also open for long lazy breakfasts of home-made yoghurt and fruit, or plates of egg, beans and avocado. Moderately inexpensive. Next door, **Il Cappuccino** is famed for its coffee. Moderately inexpensive.

Puerto Angel

Ever since the 1960s, Puerto Angel has been famed as a 'hang out'. Its long Zipolite beach in particular is the subject of many tall tales and fond reminiscences. Today's reality is a far cry from the hazy crazy days of its early visitors. Once the most beautiful bay in Mexico, it is now littered with coke cans and filth, and the cafés all along it are filled with hangers-on who feel the world owes them a living. Theft and disease are rife. Mexicans avoid it like the plague.

The villagers themselves are fed up with these international lotus eaters and would prefer to see the back of them. Consequently, they give all foreigners short shrift. Because of a desperate shortage of water, they are unable to build bigger hotels to attract the tourist boom to the east and west. For most visitors, it falls between two stools, being neither sufficiently rustic nor sufficiently comfortable to attract either way. Gloom and despondency pervade and after a quick drink, brushing flies off with one hand and feeding starving dogs with the other, many would-be lingerers decide to move on.

To the west of Zipolite, at **San Agustinillo**, there's a turtle-slaughtering compound. Giant turtles of the Olive Ridley breed (now almost extinct, having survived since the age of dinosaurs) are macheted to death or left to die on their backs in the sun. Female turtles are sliced open for their eggs whilst still alive. Strangers aren't welcomed and ecologists despair. The Japanese continue to import 98 per cent of this meat and pay high prices for the eggs, a supposed aphrodisiac.

Huatulco

The newest and most beautiful of all Mexico's mega-resorts, Huatulco is still on the drawing board. It won't become an ugly sprawl of high-rise blocks until the beginning of the next century. At present, some 50 km of beach are being developed, enveloping the village of Santa Cruz which is already swollen with builders, waiters and tour operators as the boom begins. Until 1982, the natural beauty of the seven bays of Huatulco was unknown to the outside world. The Zapotecs who lived there subsisted on fishing. Then, President López Portillo, passing on a cruise, got dollar signs in his eyes and decided to pump government money into the area, to reap the rich rewards of tourism. The Zapotecs were swept out of the way and building began. Although the scheme was ostensibly conceived to bring employment to an impoverished people, 90 per cent of the money leaves the area straight away.

There is no disputing the beauty and tranquillity of the seven bays. Cliffs drop sheer into azure water, interrupted only by silent, sand-swept shores. Francis Drake and Thomas Cavendish (whom the Mexicans refer to as pirates) moored here for shelter in the 16th century. Today, outside the resort, there is only a barren expanse and little to do but relax and swim. The best time to come is between May and October, off-season, when it is at its quietest.

GETTING AROUND
The resort of Huatulco is 35 km east of Pochutla along Highway 200. Santa Cruz Huatulco, the village which came before the resort, is 6 km south of Highway 200 and the bus stop for the resort: there is no public transport between the two, only taxis. Otherwise, it is an hour's hot walk. The hotels expect their guests to arrive by plane, and taxis and minibuses meet all arrivals. There are daily flights to and from Oaxaca and Mexico City.

TOURIST INFORMATION
The tourist office is in front of the Sheraton (open 09.00–14.00 and 16.00–19.00, tel 10326).

THE BAYS

Before development began, there was one small Zapotec fishing village in the bay of **Santa Cruz**. This has been largely ignored by the builders and is the place to go to hire boats for trips to the more deserted bays. To the east of Santa Cruz, **Chahue** has a trailer park to one side, with a café selling basic food. The beach itself, plummeting into the sea on a steep slope, is the one the Mexicans use. Next door, **Tangolunda** has been earmarked for development, though to date there are only three hotels on its long sweep.

The other bays of **Cacaluta** and **El Maguey**, to the west of Santa Cruz, and **El Organo** and **Conejos**, to the east, are best reached by boat from the pier in Santa Cruz. They are often deserted. Boats will drop passengers off and arrange a time to pick them up. Take water and sun cream, as there is nothing there and shade can disappear.

WHERE TO STAY AND EAT   (area code 958)
Huatulco is aiming high and there aren't any bargains to be had in the few hotels that have opened. In Santa Cruz itself, they are slowly building cheaper hotels. Ring the tourist office to check what is open. The *****Sheraton (Paseo de Tangolunda, tel 10055, fax 10113) oozes a soothing tranquillity. Bright breezy bedrooms are decorated in the best of modern Mexican taste, with terraces for watching the waves lap in from the sea. Large black polished pots and clay fertility goddesses from Oaxaca fill every nook and cranny. The bathrooms come with bathrobes and every conceivable extra. There are three large pools in front of the hotel and guards on duty to watch when people swim in the sea. The complex includes games rooms, saunas and health resorts, as well as four restaurants (ranging from candelit splendour to seafood grilled by the pool). Across the bay is an exclusive **Club Med** that can only be booked through a travel agent.

In Santa Cruz, ****Posada Binniguaenda (Blvd Juárez 5, tel 40077) is the oldest hotel and has weathered in well. The small swimming pool sits amongst an unruly garden filled with ceramic pots and bougainvillea. There's a restaurant and bar above, where the sunburnt sip cocktails by candlelight.

Santa Cruz has an increasing number of good, family-run restaurants and road side cafés. These cater more for hotel staff who live in the village than for tourists who are expected to stay in their hotels.

The Isthmus of Tehuantepec

This narrow isthmus is renowned for its dominant women and its rich, fertile lands, made richer still by the discovery of oil. Low-lying, hot and humid, it is usually passed through by travellers on their way to or from the coastal resorts to the west.

GETTING AROUND
By Bus: Juchitán's long-distance bus station is on the main highway, with daily buses to and from Oaxaca (6 hrs), Veracruz (8 hrs), Villahermosa (7 hrs), Tapachula (7 hrs) and San Cristóbal de las Casas (7 hrs). Local buses connect the town with Tehuantepec and continue west down the coast.
By Car: Tehuantepec and Juchitán are 30 km apart, on Highway 200. Fifteen km east of Juchitán, Highway 185 heads north across the isthmus for Acayucan (177 km) and the plains of Veracruz. From Tehuantepec, Highway 190 leads northwest to Oaxaca (242 km).

Tortilla-making in the Isthmus of Tehuantepec

By Train: A daily train connects Juchitán with Veracruz (13 hrs), cutting right across the Isthmus of Tehuantepec. This narrowest point in the country—the 'waist of Mexico'—has spawned many plans to link Gulf to Pacific. The rickety railway of today does little justice to the magnificent plans of the British who were responsible for building it. After a few brief years of glory, it ran into enormous debt and any hopes for a monopoly of trade between the seas were finally scotched by the opening of the Panama Canal.

Another daily train runs down the coast from Juchitán to Tapachula on the Guatemalan border (10 hrs).

Tehuantepec

Tehuantepec is especially famous for its outstanding women. Statuesque, confident and splendidly dressed, they are so unlike the norm of women in Mexico that they have become as legendary as Amazons. For fiestas, they wear long flowing skirts topped by short red and black shirts, embroidered with silk flowers. Round their necks they wear chain after chain of gold necklaces, and round their heads they wrap distinctive, brightly patterned turbans. The diminutive artist, Frida Kahlo, was often dressed as a Tehuana and many of her self-portraits show her wearing the traditional dress. The main **festival** is on 15 August. Others include the last week of June and the first 10 days of September.

The town itself isn't worthy of its women. The huge neglected square is surrounded by the decaying houses of once-prosperous merchants, supported by thick columns to resist earthquakes. Porfirio Díaz spent much time here with his lover, Doña Juana Romero, for whom he built the only two-storey house in the town. Railway tracks used to pass in front of her door, on Díaz's orders. For hoi polloi, the station is some distance away in a coconut grove. The market is a dark den of a place to one side of the square, where the women gather to chat or to sell chocolate. Many come in from the villages with great baskets of fruit on their heads, just as Rivera painted them over 50 years ago.

The ***Donaji** (two blocks from the main square at Juárez 10, tel 971 50064) is central and adequate for a night's stay, although the *****Calli** (2 km east of town on the highway, tel 971 50085) has the advantage of air conditioning and a swimming pool.

Juchitán

The people of neighbouring Juchitán are known throughout Mexico for their long history of opposition to central government. They are mainly of Zapotec descent, amongst the few never conquered by the Aztecs. At the turn of this century, Díaz could only overcome opposition by imprisoning all the women and starving the town into submission. In 1980, a communist-backed mayor was elected to great local acclaim—and to the horror of the government. Predictably, he was removed by the army for 'subversive behaviour'. (He refused to leave his office before his three-year term was up and lived in the town hall for four months.) The town remains strongly anti-government today.

Juchitán is a great sprawling town, with a large square flanked by local *lambimbo* trees, overlooked by a statue of the liberal and anti-clerical Juárez. The market is on the lower floor of the municipal palace: outspoken women crush pineapples, guayabas and papaya to make long refreshing drinks. Local specialities range from dried shrimps to iguanas.

Festivals overlap with those of Tehuantepec, with an extra one in the third week of May.

Part XIII

TABASCO AND CHIAPAS

Mother and child in San Cristóbal de las Casas

The two southeastern states of Tabasco and Chiapas are the entry points to the land of the Maya, a people whose culture is an integral part both of Mexico's past and of its contemporary life. The oil-rich Gulf plains of Tabasco give way to the pine-clad highlands of Chiapas, bordered to the south by the jungle plains along the Pacific coast, and to the east by some of the last remaining tropical rain forest in Mexico, where the long-haired Lacandóns (descendants of the Maya) fight it out for survival with the tree-logging companies.

The State of Tabasco

This tiny state, measuring only 330 km by 195 km, enjoys a wealth out of all proportion to its size, thanks to its fertile farming lands and, more particularly, to the discovery of rich oil deposits. Cacao beans to make chocolate, pineapples, livestock, chillies and maize are all produced on the land the oil derricks haven't plumbed or the sea hasn't reclaimed. Although there have been no earthquakes in the region, there have been terrible floods. The state is, in effect, more water than land, with a maze of lakes, waterfalls, rivers and lagoons, which all drain into the Gulf of Mexico. There are no stunning beaches but several quiet seaside fishing villages in tropical settings, which make a good day's break from museums and ruins.

Tabasco includes some of the greatest Olmec sites and the most westerly ruins of the Maya empire, many of which were uncovered during the search for oil. Museums were

420

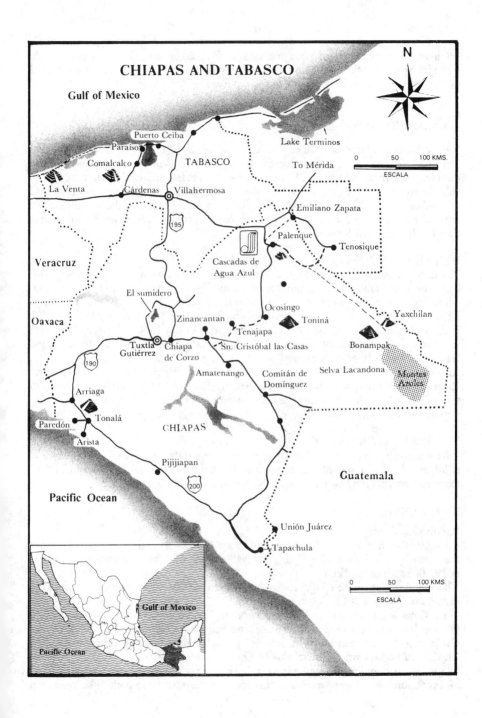

CHIAPAS AND TABASCO

Gulf of Mexico

N

Puerto Ceiba
Paraíso
Comalcalco   TABASCO
La Venta   Cárdenas   Villahermosa

Lake Terminos
To Mérida

0   50   100 KMS.
ESCALA

Emiliano Zapata

195

Palenque
Tenosique

Veracruz   Cascadas de
Agua Azul

El sumidero

Oaxaca   Zinancantan   Ocosingo   Yaxchilan
Toniná
Tenajapa
Tuxtla   Chiapa   Sn. Cristóbal las Casas   Bonampak
Gutiérrez   de Corzo
190
Amatenango   Comitán de   Selva Lacandona   Montes
Domínguez   Azules
Arriaga

Paredón   Tonalá
CHIAPAS
Arista

Pijijiapan
200
Guatemala

Pacific Ocean

Unión Juárez
Tapachula

0   50   100 KMS.
ESCALA

Gulf of Mexico

Pacific Ocean

set up to house the remains, so that profitable wells could be sunk without causing public outrage. As a result, the fascinating and unique open-air **Parque La Venta** in the capital of Villahermosa now counts as one of the top five museums in the country.

Villahermosa

Villahermosa is a large oil-rich city which spills out in all directions from its colonial centre. What was countryside a decade ago is now a permanent showground and the domain of international hotels. The heart of the city is in fact an island, surrounded on all sides by rivers and lakes, with wide tree-lined boulevards cutting swathes from one end to another. In this thriving town, tourists are left to get on with it by the welcoming but otherwise engaged citizens: once visitors have passed through the exceptional museums, they rarely linger any longer.

GETTING AROUND
Villahermosa is well connected by air, bus and road. The airport is north of town, with daily nonstop flights to and from Mexico City, Tuxtla Gutiérrez and Mérida, and connections to all the other main airports in the republic. Highway 186 leads east to Mérida (642 km) and the Yucatán, and Highway 180 west to Veracruz (480 km). The city is also within easy striking distance of Palenque (off Highway 180), and Tuxtla Gutiérrez and San Cristóbal (south, off Highway 195). ADO and Cristóbal Colón are the principal bus companies. There is no railway.
In Town: The two main arteries are **Paseo Tabasco**, which leads from the Carrizal River, through the centre and on to the Grijalva River, and **Blvd Grijalva**, the main through-road, which cuts across the centre from west to east, heading out towards the airport and Palenque, passing the Parque La Venta on the way.

TOURIST INFORMATION
Villahermosa has two tourist information offices—one at Paseo Tabasco 1504 (tel 50693 to 98, ext 116, 117 and 118) and the other at Av Méndez 718–2 (tel 27336). In addition, there are information booths at the ADO bus station and the airport.

THE MUSEUMS
Parque La Venta
(Blvd Grijalva, just north of the junction of Paseo Tabasco and Highway 180; 3 km from the centre by bus 'Tabasco 2000'; open daily 08.00–16.30; Light and Sound shows daily at 19.00, ex Mon and Wed.)
This open-air park is the reconstructed jungle home of 30 Olmec pieces saved from the damp, marshy land of La Venta.
La Venta is actually on the Tabasco–Veracruz border. It was first inhabited in 1500 BC, which makes it the earliest known site, and built by the Olmecs, Mesoamerica's first civilization. It was abandoned in 500 BC, probably after flooding from the Gulf of Mexico, and is now virtually inaccessible. Oil explorations were begun in the area in the 1950s, and after much public hue and cry, led by the poet-archaeologist Carlos Pellicer, 30 invaluable pieces were moved to this specially reconstructed park. The collection

includes a mosaic mask which was deliberately buried by the Olmecs themselves, under layers of clay and adobe bricks.

The park is superbly designed, complete with orchids, deer, cacao and a crocodile (called Papillon because he keeps escaping). From the entrance on the Bvld Grijalva, a jungle path leads past the 30 large pieces. The collection include three monumental basalt-stone heads, placidly rooted in the ground. No written records of La Venta remain and no skeletons have been unearthed, and these heads are perhaps the Olmecs' most impressive legacy. With no stone within 100 km, the monolithic pieces had to be rolled down from the Tuxtla mountains. They were sculpted—without any metal tools— in La Venta. Many of the other exhibits manifest another Olmec fascination—the jaguar. This animal was almost certainly the focus of a cult in Olmec society, granted divine status at a time when man had not yet decided that he was one step above the animals. As well as a jaguar cage, jaguar mosaic and jaguar child, there are smaller jaguar heads and humanized jaguars.

Natural History Museum
(Open 09.00–20.00, Tues–Sun.)
A short walk from the Parque La Venta, this innovative museum sees more groups of school children than tourists. It offers a quick whistle-stop run around Tabasco's natural history, from a slice of jungle life to the latest advances in the petrochemical industry. A huge revolving atlas of the world puts the whole thing into perspective.

CICOM (Centro de Investigaciónes de las Culturas Olmeca y Maya
(Av Carlos Pellicer Cámara, on the banks of the Grijalva River; from the Zócalo, the CICOM bus runs south beside the river; open 09.00–20.00, Tues–Sun.)
This museum is often known as 'the Carlos Pellicer'. Many exhibits came from his private collection and have since been expanded to create an important complement to the open-air park. On the second floor, explanatory photographs and maps place the various Mesoamerican cultures in the context of their 25,000 years of history. The collection includes a mass of little figurines from Tlatilco in the central highlands, alabaster masks from Teotihuacán, Olmec remains (basalt figures and jaguar symbols) and Maya sculptures.

Museo de Arte Popular
(27 de Febrero and Juárez; open 09.00–20.00, Tues–Sun.)
This small town house has been transformed into an exhibition space and shop, with examples of regional costumes and everyday objects from around the state. In the garden there is a reconstructed house with wooden walls and a thatched roof, of a type still inhabited by the Chontal, local descendants of the Maya.

Casa de los Azulejos/Museo de la Ciudad
(Juárez and 27 de Febrero; open 09.00–20.00, Tues–Sun.)
When Graham Greene came to Villahermosa in the 1930s, the avunculuar chief of police told him, 'You've come home. Why, everybody in Villahermosa is called Greene—or Graham.' One of these, José María Graham Macgregor, emigrated from Scotland with his parents in the 1860s, because of religious persecution. His father set

up a profitable exporting business to Miami, which enabled him to buy a modest town house with a thatched roof and adobe walls. His only son was sent on a Grand Tour. On his return in 1885, the young man took over the house and transformed it into an eclectic mishmash of all that he had seen. Tiles and patterns come from Valencia, Barcelona and the Orient, the balustrade is Parisian, the architect was Italian. There are mosaics copied from the Alhambra and Persia, Byzantine and gothic arches, doors from the Farnese Palace in Rome and a statue to Mercury. On the outside, a thread of Cleopatra profiles runs around the building (his only daughter was said to look like her). Along the balustrade, there are five small statues portraying each of his sons, and, at the corner, a statue of Mercury whose mercantile riches made it all possible.

The museum concentrates on the history of Tabasco, its invasion by Dutch and English pirates, its progressive role in the Revolution and its recent burgeoning wealth, but the most outstanding exhibit of all is the house itself.

FESTIVALS
The Usamacinta River marathon (strictly for well-heeled professionals) is run in the second week of May. For seven days at the end of April, the great state fair takes over the city, when the 17 municipalities of the four regions of Tabasco parade their beauty queens, livestock and artisania. There is dancing and music in the evenings.

WHERE TO STAY (area code 931)
The erstwhile oil barons stick to the Hyatt and the Holiday Inn. The towering *****Exelaris Hyatt (Av Juárez 106, tel 34444) knocks the spots off the competition, creating an international enclave in the middle of Villahermosa. The *****Holiday Inn (Paseo Tabasco 1407, tel 34400) is large, modern and blandly comfortable, but generally considered to have less finesse than the Hyatt. Presidents, however, stay at the ****Cencali (Paseo Tabasco and Juárez, tel 26000), superbly positioned on the edge of a lake in the centre of town. It feels small, loved and unhurried, with large gardens and patios surrounding the pool. The ****Maya Tabasco (Blvd Ruíz Cortines 907, tel 21111) is another elegant hotel, with a restaurant (specializing in southern cooking) set in a half-moon on the edge of the swimming pool. It also boasts a laser disco (far enough from the restaurant and hotel to be unobtrusive).

Somehow the cheaper hotels are uniformly unsettling. The ***Plaza Independencia (Independencia 123, half a block from the Plaza de Armas, tel 21299) is a notable exception, with a bright, breezy restaurant, lock-up parking and a swimming pool. If all its 90 rooms are full, try the 1950s ***Miraflores (Reforma 304, tel 20022).

Villahermosa is not a town for bargains, but it's worth looking around Madero and the pedestrian precinct area at the junction of Avs Juárez and Lerdo: the **San Miguel (Lerdo 315 and Madero, tel 21500), the **San Francisco (Madero 604, tel 23198) and the *Oriente (Madero 441, tel 21101) are the best options.

EATING OUT
These restaurants are spread all over the city but should be known to taxi drivers. For the best of regional Tabascan sea food, try Guaraguao (27 de Noviembre 947), where a packed house is informally served with sopa de mariscos (soup thick with crab, snail and octopus), acamaya (a type of river lobster), and tortillas al mojo de ajo. Moderate. The

steak house **El Ganadero** (27 de Febrero 1706, tel 32303) has adopted a simple formula, serving American cuts of grilled steak with baked potatoes and salads. Moderate. Spanish restaurants are currently in favour: the bistro-like **Mesón del Duende** (Av Gregorio Méndez 1703, tel 51324) is run by a Galician (cheap) and the more elegant **Mesón de Castilla** (Pagás Llergo 125, tel 25621) by an Andalucian (moderate). For late-nighters, the busy pizza place **Eduardo's** (Av Cedros 121, tel 23121) stays open till 01.00. A novel alternative to these is the river boat **Capitán Buelo**, which leaves from a dock on Lerdo de Tejada at 13.30, 15.00 and 21.00 (tel 35762 to reserve). It's a fun way to see the city from the Grijalva river, whiling away an afternoon or evening with good food and wine. Moderate.

In the centre, the day starts at either the **Café Casino** or **La Caldereta**. However, both the governor of the state and the shoe-shine boys prefer to grab drinks of *horchata* and sweet breads off the long-established stand at the corner of Av 27 de Febrero and Paseo Tabasco.

Comalcalco and the Coast

North of Villahermosa are the ruins of Comalcalco, the most westerly of all Maya sites, and the beaches and lagoons of coastal Tabasco.

GETTING AROUND

By Bus: ADO buses leave the first-class station in Villahermosa for Comalcalco (49 km) and the beaches at Paraíso (25 km further) every hour on the hour. The ruins are 3 km from the modern town—best reached by taxi in the heat of the day.

By Car: Leave Villahermosa on eastbound Highway 180, turning left at the first main junction (signposted Comalcalco and Nacajuca). The road winds through several small Chontal villages and along the edge of the Laguna Cantemual to Cupilco, with its charming church looking like a freshly iced wedding cake. Comalcalco is 12 km further on. The journey takes under an hour. Alternatively, leave Villahermosa on the fast two-lane westbound Highway 180 and turn right to Comalcalco at the junction with Highway 187. This route takes much the same time, although it covers a greater distance, but it is not such a pretty drive.

To continue to the coast, simply head north on Highway 187 for another 25 km.

Comalcalco

The ruins of Comalcalco, on the fortified banks of the Río Seco, were first rediscovered in 1880 by the French explorer-archaeologist Désiré Charnay, who compared them to Palenque. They were inhabited between AD 550 and 1250 by the Chontal Maya, who had contact with the Maya empire in the south and also with Xochicalco in the central highlands (present-day Morelos). Later, in the 9th century, the site provided a stepping stone for the Toltecs as they came down from Tula (in Hidalgo) to confront the Maya Itzá of Chichén.

VISITING THE SITE
(Open daily 08.00–17.00; adm.)
Comalcalco is an open site, with little shade, comprising several pyramids, unexcavated mounds and a broad, open plaza. Although the land was rich with the cacao bean, its situation, on sea-flooded plains, meant that there was no stone. The buildings were constructed with flat, kiln-fired bricks, made out of a mixture of clay, sand and shells, pasted together with burned oyster shell and lime mortar. These bricks, before being baked, were often incised with animals (monkeys, scorpions, crabs and crocodiles), or with architectural representations of the pyramids, gods and potentates, and even hieroglyphic sculptures. Many of these relief carvings are kept in the small **museum** at the entrance to the site.

This same paste was used to create stucco masks on the facades of the main buildings. Several of these still exist, protected by palm-thatched roofs, such as the Sun God mask on Temple VI. The best remaining examples, however, can be found by walking the length of the plaza and climbing up to the **Grand Acropolis** on the far right. This giant platform, 35 m high, has the remains of a palace on the top. Under one of its temples, a tomb, discovered by Franz Blom in 1925, is decorated with nine stucco sculptures representing the Lords of the Night.

The Tabasco Coast

Some 25 km north of Comalcalco, Highway 187 crosses a bridge over the Laguna Mecoacán at Paraíso (7 km from the sea) and branches off towards the seaside villages of Limón, Puerto Ceiba and Barra de Tupilco. Lagoons open out into the Gulf of Mexico and communities are split by mangrove-lined estuaries. There are no resorts, simply small fishing villages making a lazy living out of the sea. Life is easy. Along the road to the coast are plantations of bananas, copra and cacao, as well as mangoes and oranges, to supplement the daily diet of fish. In each village, you will find at least one person willing to take visitors out in his boat, to explore the watery land.

Paraíso has a small hotel and several seafood restaurants. The best of these is the government-run **Parador Puerto Ceiba**, on the banks of the Laguna Mecoacán, offering oysters in their shells which the locals then cover with tequila and tortillas *al mojo de ajo* (soaked in garlic), as well as stuffed crab and marinaded snails.

Tenosique to Guatemala

For the adventurous and the pragmatic, Tenosique, in the far eastern corner of Tabasco, offers the opportunity to head into northern Guatemala by river, and thence to the jungle Maya ruins of Tikal. This is the only reason to visit Tenosique. Although it is on the railway between Coatzacoalcos and Mérida, and at the site of an important bridge crossing the Río Usumacinta, it nevertheless has few attractions.

GETTING AROUND
To Tenosique: Tenosique de Pino Suárez is 210 km from Villahermosa. Take Highway 186 east to Emiliano Zapata (a godforsaken hole 145 km from Villahermosa), and then bear south.

To Guatemala: Buses leave Tenosique for La Palma (40 rough km, 9½ hrs), on the banks of the Río San Pedro. From there boats leave for Naranjo in Guatemala (6 hrs). Second-class buses from Naranjo to Flores/Santa Elena (7 uncomfortable hrs) leave once or twice a day: it is often necesary to spend the night in Naranjo's small, new hotel. Buses leave hourly for the hour-long journey from Santa Elena to Tikal.

Visas for Guatemala can be obtained from the office at the Santa Elena airport: you will need passport-size photographs, proof of financial solvency (a credit card will do) and a valid passport. Mexican pesos are not accepted in Guatemala and the exchange rates are worse over the border.

To Yaxchilán and Bonampak: Tenosique is the point at which boats from Yaxchilán on the Río Usumacinta emerge back into civilization. It also has a small **airport** which sends Cessnas to Yaxchilán and Bonampak if and when pilots and planes are available. Although it is a far less reliable departure point than Comitán, Palenque or San Cristóbal, it is closer and therefore cheaper.

The State of Chiapas

Chiapa ... exceedeth most provinces in the greatness and beauty of fair towns.
—Thomas Gage, 1648

Chiapas is a beautiful state, rich in lakes and rivers, highlands of pine and oak, jungle lowlands of orchids, rare butterflies and brightly coloured birds. Occupying the southernmost reaches of the republic, bordering Guatemala, it is more Central American than Mexican in outlook and remains one of the most indigenous states in the country. The Tzotzil, Tzeltal and Lacandón Maya maintain strong cultural traditions, which they are trying hard to preserve in the face of encroaching commercialism and tourism. The remains of the ancient cities of the Maya, such as Palenque, Yaxchilán and Bonampak, are hidden in its jungles and the whole state is littered with unexplored remains.

Visits to the state can begin at the graceless, modern capital, Tuxtla Gutiérrez, continuing swiftly to the attractive hill town of San Cristóbal and down to the marvellous ruins of Palenque on the plain. Alternatively, make the short trip to Palenque from Tabasco's capital, Villahermosa, and from there either head up to the highlands and San Cristóbal, or continue east to the Yucatán peninsula.

History

During the 7th and 8th centuries AD, there were several important Maya city-states around the Usamacinta River on Chiapas' eastern border, most notably Palenque, Bonampak and Yaxchilán. These glorious civilizations had been abandoned long before the arrival of the Spanish, and Chiapas formed part of the Aztec empire, which stretched across the present-day state and on south into Guatemala. Its fame as a coffee- and chocolate-producing area was well known to the Aztecs, for whom to have a chocolate was to have a Soconusco (the name of a village in Chiapas which is still renowned for its chocolate and coffee).

Luis Marín was the first Spaniard to attempt the conquest of this mountainous and tropical state, in 1523. He gave up after a few months, but was followed, four years later, by Diego de Mazariegos, who came armed with Aztec vassals and Spanish settlers. He founded his first capital on the marshy land of Chiapa de Corzo, before moving up to the cool, dry pastures of San Cristóbal (which he named Ciudad Real after his birthplace), creating there the influential town which became the bastion of colonial power between Guatemala and Oaxaca.

For most of the colonial era, Chiapas was administered by the Captaincy General of Guatemala, whose capital was in the much closer colonial city of Antigua. The resilience of its pre-Hispanic cultures is largely due to the state's general inaccessibility—originally it was a three-month horse ride from Mexico City, while its lack of gold and silver mines acted as a further protection against the greed of the conquistadors. Chiapas only separated from Guatemala in the 19th century, after Mexico had wrested independence from Spain and declared itself a nation apart.

Palenque

The small town of Palenque is little more than an adjunct to its marvellous ruins. Famed for their exquisite carvings and extraordinary beauty, they engender a sense of mystery which lasts long after any visit is ended. Many people believe that the Maya reached their apogee in Palenque. Neither the most important city, nor the latest, it is the most enduring and magical, a haunting testament to a lost civilization and to the rapidly disappearing rain forest which surrounds it.

Palenque is blessed by an incomparable setting. Hidden by luscious evergreen jungle, the site rises up on artificial terraces from a fertile plateau, backed by the Chiapas foothills. One of the most westerly of Maya sites, it flourished after AD 600 under the influence of Pacal and his sons, becoming the jewel in the crown of Mayan cities. Learning their lesson from the heavier architecture of sites such as Tikal in the nearby Petén region, its architects created their own distinctive style, renowned for its lightness, using roof combs and corbelled vaults to great effect.

GETTING AROUND

By Air: Palenque's small airport proudly displays the wrecks of planes along the length of its runway. Four-seater biplanes (fiendishly expensive and not very safe Cessnas) can be chartered for flights to Yaxchilán, Bonampak and Villahermosa.

By Bus: First-class buses run four times a day to and from Mexico City (14 hrs), and five times a day to and from Villahermosa (2½ hrs). The service to and from San Cristóbal is second-class only, and consequently extremely slow (7 a day, 5 hrs).

Combis to the ruins (8 km) leave from the corner of Calle Hidalgo and Allende every 15 minutes. At 10.00 they leave for the 15-minute trip to Misol Ha and on to the cascades of Agua Azul, returning at 15.00.

By Car: From Villahermosa, take the Río Grijalva toll bridge and Highway 186 towards Escárcega. At Catazajá (km 115), turn right for Palenque (28 km).

Palenque is 177 km north of San Cristóbal. Fill up with petrol before leaving, as there are no pumps between Ocosingo and Palenque (120 km).

By Train: Palenque is on the Coatzacoalcos–Campeche–Mérida line. The journey is a nightmare, in either direction. Don't be taken in by the romance of the idea—it is either freezing cold or boiling hot, interminable and very uncomfortable.

TOURIST INFORMATION

The tourist office is in the Palacio Municipal, just to the east of the Zócalo. The post office is to the left of the same building. Two money-changing banks (open 10.00–12.00) are four blocks west on Juárez. The best travel agent is Marco Antonio Morales, who can be contacted either through the hotel Cañada (tel 50102) or directly (tel 50411). He also organizes excellent trips to Bonampak and Yaxchilán, providing transport, food and camping equipment.

VISITING THE SITE

(Site open 08.00–17.00; Pacal's tomb open 10.00–17.00; adm.)
The entrance to the site is surrounded by makeshift stalls, where Lacandóns with their

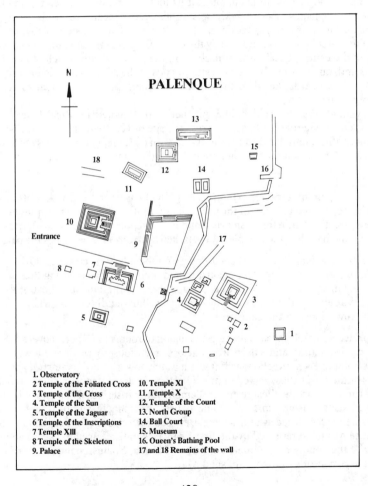

1. Observatory
2 Temple of the Foliated Cross   10. Temple XI
3 Temple of the Cross   11. Temple X
4. Temple of the Sun   12. Temple of the Count
5. Temple of the Jaguar   13. North Group
6 Temple of the Inscriptions   14. Ball Court
7 Temple XIII   15. Museum
8 Temple of the Skeleton   16. Oueen's Bathing Pool
9. Palace   17 and 18 Remains of the wall

long black hair and loose white shifts come to sell bows and arrows, wooden armadillos and beads to ever-inquisitive tourists.

TEMPLE OF THE INSCRIPTIONS

The first pyramid on the right is named after the panels of hieroglyphic texts on the temple walls. Some 21 m high, it was built on nine layers, the number associated with death and the gods of the Underworld, covering over the tomb of Lord Pacal (AD 603–683).

A painstaking exploration disclosed the great ruler's tomb in 1949. The archaeologist, Alberto Ruz Lhuillier, was intrigued by a stone at the top of the temple, which was pierced with round holes. He hoisted it up from the flagstone floor, to discover a flight of rubble-filled steps leading down through the pyramid. It took four years to excavate the stairway and discover the burial chamber at its foot. There, in a sealed crypt under an enormous sarcophagus, Pacal's body was submerged beneath 1000 pieces of jade, including a death mask, rings, necklaces and a pectoral. The vast stone slab making up the lid of the sarcophagus was framed by the celestial signs of the sun, the moon and the planets. In the centre, Pacal gives himself up to the jaws of death, watched over by his ancestors and, on the walls, by the nine stucco gods of the Night. Outside the crypt, the skeletons of six guards, killed so that their souls could protect the great ruler, were discovered intact.

The pyramid was almost definitely planned and designed by Pacal himself, long before his death. He ruled at Palenque from the age of 12, when his mother, Zac-Kuk, handed over office, until his death at the age of 80 in 683. He, in turn, was succeeded by his two sons, Chan Bahlum who died in 702, and the younger Kan Xul.

THE PALACE

The quixotic pair of explorers, John Lloyd Stephens and Frederick Catherwood, camped in the covered galleries of the palace in the 1840s, plagued by mosquitoes, gnats and a never-ending battle for fresh bread and lard. Stephens was astounded that such a great city could have been so completely overtaken by nature. He describes the palace as:

> richly ornamented with stuccoed figures on the pilasters, curious and elegant; trees growing close against it, and their branches entering the doors; in style and effect unique, extraordinary, and mournfully beautiful ... We selected the front corridor as our dwelling [and] turned turkey and fowls loose in the courtyard.

The palace was built in various stages. Cellar-like rooms have been covered over by later workings. Patios and courtyards enclose a curious three-tiered tower whose windows point in each direction, as if it was a watch-tower or observatory. Tablets line the walls of the four patios, carved in fine limestone or decorated with stucco reliefs. In the easternmost court (furthest from the Temple of the Inscriptions), a line of individually carved slabs bolsters up a wall. The figures, wretchedly humbled, appear to be captives, their faces turned away in shame. Between each slab are four explaining glyphs. This image was to be repeated by the first Spaniards in the Yucatán: carved above the doorway of the conqueror Montejo's house in Mérida, Spanish conquerors rest their feet on the gory heads of the vanquished Maya.

430

THE CROSS GROUP

From the palace a path leads across the Otulul stream. This tributary of the Usumacinta River was channelled by the Maya and crossed by a broad stone bridge. Recently, almond, guayaba, orange and avocado trees have grown along its banks, from seeds planted by the guards. The Cross Group is over the stream, on higher ground. The three lovely temples that make up the group each have towering roof combs, curved roof tops and an outer and inner vaulted room. They were built after the death of Pacal, and may have been constructed in AD 692, in honour of his son, Chan Bahlum.

In the **Temple of the Foliated Cross** (the furthest of the three), a superb sculpted tablet in the inner sanctuary shows a young man bearing a manikin sceptre (an insignia of office), in front of a stylized maize plant growing out of the head of an earth monster. Five rows of glyphs flank the figures on either side of the plant.

The **Temple of the Sun**, to the right of the path, was once entirely painted in stucco. Now only fragments remain on the upper facade.

The **Temple of the Cross**, on the left, housed the magnificent Tablet of the Cross which is now in the Museum of Anthropology in Mexico City. Lateral reliefs of Chan Bahlum still remain.

MUSEUM

Crossing the stream again, the path leads along the east side of the palace through the much dilapidated ball court (one of the oldest constructions) to the museum. Its most notable carving is the Tablet of the Slaves (AD 731), in which the *halach uinic* or ruler, seated on a human cushion, accepts offerings from the attendants to either side of him. The museum also houses various pieces of jewellery, stucco heads and clay figurines.

NORTH GROUP

The five temples of the north group, built on a raised platform, lack uniformity of style and structure, and may well have been used by merchants plying between Guatemala and Veracruz in the post-Classic years.

The **Count's Temple**, at right angles to the raised north platform, was named after Count Frederic von Waldeck. He lived there for two years in the 1830s, drawing and theorizing, embellishing and distracting, until he had convinced himself that the Maya warriors and their temples resembled the Phoenicians in dress and the Egyptians in architecture—with the odd elephant sculpture thrown in to complete the picture. His title was as misplaced as his theories but his heart was in the right place. Having started work at Palenque at the age of 66, he lived for another 43 years, dying only because he turned his head to look at a pretty Parisian and failed to see the carriage which ran him over.

WHERE TO STAY AND EAT   (area code 934)

In recent years, the small village of Palenque has mushroomed into a town, to cope with the steady stream of visitors. Rooms are hard to come by at Christmas, Easter and in the first week of August, when the village celebrates its main festival.

The excruciatingly bad drive up to the******Misión Palenque** (Rancho San Martin de Porres, tel 50241, fax 50499) is redeemed by large, minimalist rooms, painted in bright, bold indigo blues and oranges. The grounds include a swimming pool, natural spring

431

and floodlit tennis courts, and the hotel organizes horse-riding trips through the jungle. The restaurant's *pechuga de pollo* (chicken with chayote and avocado) is excellent. ***Chan-Kah** (km 3.5, tel 50318), on the road to the ruins, comprises 18 palapa-roofed cottages with stone-slabbed floors. Its garden has a series of pools, drained off from the stream—wonderfully refreshing after a day in the ruins.

The cottages of the long-established and very pleasant ***La Cañada** (Merle Green 13, tel 50102) are still thickly surrounded by trees, occasionally home to monkeys and marmosets. Its thatched restaurant, **María del Sol**, serves the best Mexican food in Palenque, with fillets of bass in almond sauce and chicken cooked with the bitter oranges of the region. Moderate. Its only rival is **La Selva** (to the right of the Mayan statue). Moderate. Next to the Cañada, the capable, modern hotel, ***Maya Tulipan** (Merle Green 15, tel 50201), has Maya reliefs around its entrance.

The cheap hotels are in Calle Juárez, the road running to the main square. Try the ***Casa de Pakal (10, tel 50102), **Misol-Ha** (14, tel 50016), or the *Regional** (113, tel 50183) with plain rooms set around a patio. On the far side of the square, the **Vaca Vieja** (42 Av 5 de Mayo, tel 50377) has pleasant rooms and a small regional restaurant. Cheapest of all is the dubious (CE) **Posada de Alica** (Av Velazco Suárez, tel 50322), next to the market (which starts up at 4 o'clock in the morning, because of the heat).

Many people (including, rumour has it, Margaret Trudeau back in the 1960s) wouldn't stay anywhere else but the cheap **Mayabel** trailer park (2 km from the ruins), famed by travellers for its hallucinogenic mushrooms, picked at dawn from steaming cowpats.

Bonampak and Yaxchilán

For lovers of the Maya culture, these two outlying sites are worth the stamina and preparation required to reach them. Bonampak is famed for its coloured frescoes and Yaxchilán for its dramatic position in the midst of jungle, high above the Usumacinta River.

GETTING AROUND
By Air: Small light aircraft leave from Palenque, Tuxtla Gutiérrez, San Cristóbal or Comitán, taking hours instead of days. They usually combine Bonamapak and Yaxchilán in one trip, for a very hefty price. The relevant tourist offices can arrange the flights. The small Cessnas have to leave and return early enough to avoid afternoon turbulence. Their safety record is fairly turbulent as well. Comitán has the better planes and pilots, but is off the tourist route.

By Boat: The most majestic way to arrive at Yaxchilán is by boat, down the Río Usumacinta, the natural river border between Mexico and Guatemala. This journey requires considerable forward planning and is best organized through a specialized travel agent, such as Viajes Pakal in San Cristóbal (tel 82818) or Viajes Shvialva, near and linked to the Hotel Cañada in Palenque (tel (934) 50411 or fax (934) 50392).

By Land: It is possible but difficult to get to Bonampak by land, although not during the rainy season, when roads turn into treacherous swamps. The Bonampak turning is 10 km south of Palenque on the road to Ocosingo, signposted 'Chancalá'. Second-class buses from Palenque take 7 hours to reach the turn off to Bonampak: even then, the walk from the turn off to the ruins takes several hours, and should only be undertaken with a guide.

No road leads directly to the ruins of Yaxchilán. Take the Bonampak road as far as Caribal (20 km short of Bonampak) and then turn left down a rough road to the small army base on the banks of the Usumacinta (18 km). From there, boats can be hired for the hour-long river journey to the ruins of Yaxchilán. The price is per boat rather than per person—high for one, but correspondingly lower for several people.

TOURIST INFORMATION

The guards follow visitors like shadows, explaining what they know and making up what they don't. There are no amenities, apart from stalls selling hot, sticky drinks. It is possible to string up a hammock in a thatched hut at Yaxchilán: come provided with everything you need.

VISITING THE SITES

Bonampak

When approached in a light Cessna plane, flying in over the jungle and the Lacan-Ha river, Bonampak remains hidden from sight until touchdown. The wings scrape the undergrowth on either side of the bumpy grass runway, and the doors are, as often as not, tied up with string. Palenque's most experienced pilot is too short to see the ground ahead over the height of the dashboard, and comes in to land standing on his tiptoes. The roar of the engine, the stifling heat and the suspension of credibility in the laws of nature make this a journey not to be undertaken lightly.

Bonampak was rediscovered in the 1940s. In 1946, Giles Healey photographed the miraculously conserved late Classic wall paintings. Their preservation was a lucky disaster. Within years of their completion (around AD 750), water seeped through the walls of the limestone chamber and calcified the paintings. The murals are in the three chambers of the **Templo de las Pinturas**, to the right of the first platform of the three-tiered palace.

The murals are unparalleled for their unfolding dynastic narrative and for the vividness of their colours: ochre, turquoise, red, black and vermilion. Over 210 people are depicted—warriors, rulers, prisoners, musicians, children and bearers.

The **first chamber** shows the mighty preparations for a great battle, presided over by a small child and his attendants. The **second chamber** portrays the battle: naked captives (on the wall door), bleeding and mutilated, sit at the feet of their vanquishers. One dying prisoner, his head thrown back on his shoulders, sprawls limply over the steps. The **third chamber** represents the thanksgiving: the captives are finished off on a pyramid, as the child and his court celebrate victory by running spiked ropes through their tongues. Nobles, draped in long, white robes, patterned loin cloths and exotic turbans, attend the child.

The murals of Bonampak are complemented by outstanding low-relief sculptures on the lintels and stelae. Each of the doors is surmounted by a niche for stucco figures, and their carved lintels repeat the bellicose scenes. On the lintels of the third chamber of

433

Temple I, a captive is impaled through the heart, his head pulled back by his superbly masked assailant. Both look distinctly Maya, with sharply sloping foreheads. On the top level of the structure are four more temples, once topped by roof combs. The middle temple includes a superb lintel of a lord holding a ceremonial bar of office, with twin manikin sceptres. In front of the monument stands a vast limestone stela dedicated to Chaan Muan, dating from AD 650. This same ruler reappears in stelae on either side of the first platform: on the left-hand side, he is accompanied by his mother on his right, and his wife from Yaxchilán on his left. On the right-hand side, he displays the regalia of office—a feathered headdress and a manikin sceptre.

Yaxchilán

On the Mexican bank of a great loop in the Usumacinta River, Yaxchilán is one of the most dramatic, isolated and inaccessible of Maya ruins. Its builders had to adapt to its position, carving space out of the jungle, grabbing flat land where they could and levelling terraces where there was none. The ruins trail up steep hills into high jungle canopy. Tropical birds, including the all-too-rare scarlet macaws, scream at being disturbed, and the occasional bellow from a reclusive howler monkey resounds like the roar of a jaguar.

Yaxchilán may have been occupied from the 3rd century AD. It achieved prominence during the Classic period, between AD 550 and 800, expanding rapidly under the ruler known as 'Shield Jaguar' and his son 'Bird Jaguar', both of whom are portrayed on several monuments. The excellent state of preservation of the carved lintels and stelae show that women played a prominent role here and performed important ceremonies, including shedding blood in sacrifice to the gods.

All visits are led by the guards. From the narrow runway, a path leads through ceiba and amate trees to the labyrinthine tunnelled palace and into the main plaza, where most of the standing structures, including the ball court, are arranged. Up above the main plaza, in the central doorway of Structure 33, a huge stone body stands sentinel, separated from its head. The Lacandóns, who live in the jungle around, believe that when the head is replaced on the body, the world will end. The last step leading up to this structure is carved with 13 hieroglyphic limestone panels. The faint outlines show a vast ball rolling down a stairway (perhaps the very one leading up to the structure), propelled by an ornately dressed ball-player. In the plaza facing the structure a long, thin stalactite has been incised with glyphs.

Behind and to the right of Structure 33, a rough winding trail climbs steeply up past several other ruins to the highest group. Here, three dramatically positioned temples (Structures 39, 40 and 41) would once have looked out over the river across to present-day Guatemala. The jungle has since obscured the sight-line and the river remains invisible 200 m below.

The Ocosingo Road

This beautiful but badly surfaced road winds its way from Palenque to San Cristóbal (177 km), passing two spectacular waterfalls—Misol-Ha and Agua Azul, and the ruins of Toniná.

GETTING AROUND

If driving, fill up with petrol before leaving, as there are no pumps between Palenque and Ocosingo (120 km). There are two daily second-class buses between Palenque and San Cristóbal (6 hrs). They pass both waterfalls, dropping passengers off 2 km from Misol-Ha and 4 km from Agua Azul. The walk back from Agua Azul, to catch the next bus, is uphill and tiring in the heat of the day. Combis from Palenque go to both the waterfalls. Alternatively, they can be visited on tours, run as day trips from Palenque and San Cristóbal (ask at the tourist offices).

Toniná is 14 km east of Ocosingo and difficult to get to other than by car or cheap, local taxi. From the church in Ocosingo, take Calle 1 Ote south and follow signs down a rough track to the site.

WHAT TO SEE

Some 22 km from Palenque, the **Misol-Ha** falls create a large pool, ideal for a refreshing swim after the sticky heat of Palenque. Some 33 km further south, the unbelievably blue waterfalls of **Agua Azul** cascade gently down over various levels of limestone, again forming pools to swim in. (In the rainy season, the waters turn a muddy brown.) There is a small café nearby.

The town of **Ocosingo** (116 km from Palenque and 61 km from San Cristóbal) has little to offer, other than cafés for lunch, and mechanics if the curves and potholes of the road have taken their toll.

The city of **Toniná** flourished between AD 500 and 800, and was quite independent of nearby Palenque and Yaxchilán. The site is little visited and largely unexplored: much of the city still lies hidden under grassy mounds. It is, however, well worth making a special visit to see the recent discoveries (of which there are more every season), most particularly the great stucco mask on the fifth level of the many-tiered palace. The site also includes a small ball court. The small museum at the entrance to the site houses the remains of the tomb of the last ruler of Toniná, Tzots Choj and his wife—imposing figures etched out of stone, along with various other sculptures and a maquette of the site, all explained to Spanish-speakers by the competent guards.

WHERE TO STAY AND EAT

Ocosingo has a few cheap hotels, although it is generally better to press on to San Cristóbal or Palenque. The best is the *Central on the Zócalo. Failing that, try the **Posada Agua Azul (I Ote Sur 127), which has modern rooms and a small swimming pool. The café **La Montura** on the Zócalo serves good breakfasts. Just short of the site itself, a ranch house has opened up as a restaurant, offering cold drinks, ice sticks and simple meals.

San Cristóbal del las Casas

The autumnal hill town of San Cristóbal is a world away from the tropical, jungle ruins of Palenque. It exudes a sense of well-being, enhanced by the suddenly cold, mountain weather. At night, the blankets are piled high, and in the early morning the Zócalo fills with townspeople breakfasting on hot chocolate and sweet breads. In the markets, the

Tzeltal official in Chiapas

most gorgeously woven cloths, shawls, dresses and textiles from Chiapas and Guatemala are sold by the women who made them, putting into every stitch a thousand years of history.

Any visit to San Cristóbal should be left open-ended. Because of its fortunate inaccessibility, with no airport and generally bad communications, the town has never been fully developed for tourism, and those many foreigners (particularly the French) who come to seek it out, don't try to change its calm, daily rhythm.

Surrounded by villages where over 10 different languages are spoken (principally Tzotzil and Tzeltal), San Cristóbal is a Spanish-created centre in the middle of a cultural melange, filled with opulent churches and sturdy, colonial mansions. It was named after the Dominican Fray Bartolomé de las Casas, the first bishop of Chiapas, revered for his opposition to Spanish exploitation of the Maya. Ironically, the plight of the marginalized indigenous Mexicans is today nowhere more apparent than in San Cristóbal, imparting an air of mournfulness to the town. Although traditional customs and languages are still clung to, they are under constant siege, as traditionally co-operative communities fight to maintain their own identity in the face of an alien bureaucracy.

GETTING AROUND

By Air: The nearest airport is 20 km west of Tuxtla Gutiérrez (103 km, 1½ hrs by car, 2 hrs by bus with a change in Tuxtla), with daily flights to and from Villahermosa, Oaxaca, Cancún, Mérida and Mexico City.

By Bus: The **first-class** bus station (tel 80291) is seven blocks south of the Zócalo, on Insurgentes where it crosses with the Pan American Highway (190). There is an hourly service to Tuxtla (1½ hrs), but only one bus a day to Tapachula (9 hrs), Oaxaca (12 hrs) and Mexico City (21 hrs): these should always be booked in advance. A new swift nonstop service to Mexico City cuts down on the hours of crushed travelling: it's more expensive, but worth it.

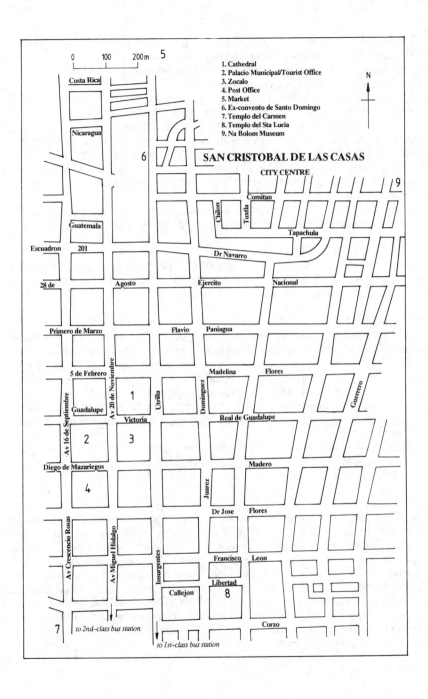

0   100   200m   5

Costa Rica

Nicaragua

1. Cathedral
2. Palacio Municipal/Tourist Office
3. Zocalo
4. Post Office
5. Market
6. Ex-convento de Santo Domingo
7. Templo del Carmen
8. Templo del Sta Lucia
9. Na Bolom Museum

N

6

SAN CRISTOBAL DE LAS CASAS

CITY CENTRE

9

Comitan

Chilon

Tuxtla

Tapachula

Guatemala

Escuadron   201

Dr Navarro

28 de   Agosto   Ejercito   Nacional

Primero de Marzo   Flavio   Paniagua

5 de Febrero   Madelina   Flores

Av 20 de Noviembre

1

Utrilla

Dominguez

Guerrero

Av 16 de Septiembre

Guadalupe   Victoria

2   3   Real de Guadalupe

Diego de Mazariegos   Madero

4   Juarez

Dr Jose   Flores

Av Crescencio Rosas

Av Miguel Hidalgo

Insurgentes

Francisco   Leon

Libertad

Callejon   8

7   to 2nd-class bus station   Corzo

to 1st-class bus station

The **second-class** bus station is on Allende with Moreno (five blocks south of the Zócalo down Hidalgo and two blocks west down Moreno). This is the station for buses to Palenque (6 hrs) and Agua Azul (4 hrs). These buses are slow, and rarely run on time: it's often quicker to hitch up the Ocosingo road.

To get to the outlying hill villages of San Juan Chamula, Tenejapa or Zinacantán, take a **combi** from the market (see Villages Around San Cristóbal).

By Car: San Cristóbal is on Highway 190, between Tuxtla to the west (83 km) and Comitán to the southeast (88 km). Rough roads lead from the town to many of the surrounding hill villages. These are passable even in a Volkswagen Beetle, except during the rainy season. Palenque (186 km) is a 6-hour journey to the northeast, on the winding Ocosingo road—one of the loveliest in Mexico. Potholes are deep and frequent, and it's better avoided at night.

In Town: The town is best seen on foot, as the centre is small and easily walkable. Taxis are cheap and plentiful. **Car hire** is avilable at Budget in the Hotel Diego de Mazariegos.

TOURIST INFORMATION
The tourist office (tel 80414) is on the main Zócalo. It is always full of enquiring tourists, and its staff are endlessly helpful. Good notice boards display up-to-date information on what is going on and where to go. Messages can be left here.

WHAT TO SEE
San Cristóbal is firmly stamped with its Spanish legacy. The Andalucians founded the town in the 1530s with the help of Aztec vassals and built their mansions of red-tiled roofs and whitewashed walls, opening into sun-filled patios and high-ceilinged rooms with brick and beam ceilings. Many of these have been converted into hotels and restaurants, but some are still lived in by the descendants of these Spanish grandees. San Cristóbal was also an important Dominican centre. Under their influence, an extraordinary number of churches were built, including the great Dominican church of San Domingo.

When you are ready to leave the gentle calm of the city, wander along to the market and take a minibus out to the villages surrounding the town. Or go further afield, to explore caves and waterfalls on horseback, truck or foot (see Horse Riding).

Zócalo
The Zócalo illustrates the architectural styles which have influenced the town. The oldest building is the 16th-century Hotel Sta Clara, originally the house of Diego de Mazariegos who first conquered Chiapas. Its sober plateresque facade, on Av Insurgentes, is carved with stylized eagles looking more like turkeys, sirens like vipers and lions like fireside pets—the closest the indigenous craftsmen could get to these mythological symbols. The Ciudad Real next door was given a firmly neoclassical facade, to symbolize independence from Spain and the throwing off of the yoke of Spanish baroque. Next to this, the Bancomer building has a definite turn-of-the century stamp, showing the influence of the dictator, Porfirio Díaz. In the middle of the square is the bandstand and garden so typical of Mexico, always full of children selling *pulseros* (woven wristbands), shoe shiners and women with vats of steaming corn cobs, served on a stick with mayonnaise and chilli.

The Cathedral

On the north side of the Zócalo, the 17th-century facade of the cathedral corroborates this mixed cultural background. Stamped in the centre is the double-headed eagle, the symbol of the Austrian royal house, surrounded by geometric Moorish patterns in the form of stars as well as indigenous flowers carved by local craftsmen.

The wonderful Moorish ceiling inside the cathedral is a 20th-century copy of the original. Under it the baroque wooden pulpit has a distinctively indigenous flavour. The figure holding it up has strong, thick Maya thighs, dark skin and a squint—considered a sign of great beauty. The *retablos* behind the altar, left behind when the Jesuits were expelled from Mexico, contain a mass of detail (including a portrait of Edward the Confessor of England, looking white and unsure of himself). While the interior paintings were the work of creoles, their outer frames were carved by locals, adorned by Maya-looking angels with long eyelashes.

Santo Domingo

(Utrilla, five blocks north of the Zócalo.)
The most important church in the town, this was the centre of the wealthy Dominicans, who were particularly powerful in Chiapas. The present building dates from the 17th century (the first was flooded and then finished off by a fire), although the rich decoration is 18th-century baroque. As there was very little stone around, it was built of adobe and covered in a mixture of sand and limestone.

Steps lead up to the atrium, whose walls are spiked with sharp merlons, deliberately conveying the impression that one is entering a fortified sanctuary. The facade is an outpouring of abundance. Salamonic columns restlessly spiral up towards the roof along its entire length. The saints' heads on the first level were decapitated in an anti-Catholic backlash during the 19th-century reform wars. Around them are local interpretations of the Catholic church, imparting a regional flavour to lions, sirens, suns, eagles and flowers.

The interior is splendid. Santo Domingo is the only church in town not to have a wooden roof, and is also the most lavishly filled with gilt *retablos*. Curiously, these are built into and not onto the walls. The pulpit too is totally exuberant; only the modern replacement altar departs from the theme of opulence.

This, and the smaller church down the steps to its right (originally built as a 12-bed hospital in 1636), have become the most important centres for locals, particularly for those from San Juan Chamula, who still talk (rather than pray) to the images and drink Coke to bring out the evil spirits hidden in their stomachs. (Originally they drank pulque, but this tradition has been eroded by the anti-alcohol movement led by local evangelists, and by the saturation achieved by Coca-Cola.) Bits of hair—a symbol of fertility—are hung on the figure of Christ to make him live again. Many of these Chamulans are in fact evangelized Christians, introduced to Protestantism by US teachers, and now expelled from their village.

There is also a good regional **museum** in the cloisters and convent of San Domingo, with a historical synopsis of the town on its ground floor and a much more interesting, explicative pair of collections on the upper floor—one on costumes and their history, the other on the art of lacquer work.

San Francisco
(Av Insurgentes, 3 blocks south of the Zócalo.)
Set back from its plaza, the unadorned, pure white facade of San Francisco, topped by a traditional red-tiled roof, belies the wealth of its dimly lit interior. Between its creaking, planed floorboards, threatened by rising damp, and its wooden ceiling are outstanding works of religious art. Lit by candle, the gold leaf gleams back and saints emerge from years of dust and grime. Incense hangs heavily on the air. The roundels on the ceiling are by Fray Moctezuma and around the walls are paintings of the 12 Apostles (four of the better oil paintings were stolen a few years ago). San Francisco is one of the most popular of San Cristóbal's 22 churches, patronized by those of Spanish blood.

Na-Bolom Museum
(Av Vicente Guerrero 33.)
The home of Swiss photographer Trudi Blom, and her archaeologist husband Franz (who died in 1963), Na-Bolom has become something of an institution in San Cristóbal. Born in Berne in 1901, Trudi Blom became a Socialist and was forced to flee to Mexico during the Second World War. She began to experiment in photography and subsequently, after a visit to the Lacandón jungle in eastern Chiapas, developed a life-long interest in the Lacandón people. Her photographs line the walls of the house, which is also filled with the archaeological finds of her husband.

Tours begin at 16.30, when guests assemble in the library. A young student gives a short history of the Bloms before detailing the work that is being done to preserve the rain forest and help the Lacandón. Although it is all a bit precious, these informal lectures are fascinating and deeply depressing at the same time ((70 per cent of the rain forest has now gone forever). The students often organize highly informative visits to the villages, which include meetings with the village elders and doctors, to discuss herbal remedies and the structure of the communities.

Museo Zul-Pepen
(Guadalupe Victoria 47; open 16.00–20.00; closed Mon; adm.)
The owner of the biggest butterfly collection in Chiapas opens his house in the afternoon. His collection includes local species and samples from all over the world.

SHOPPING
Although the villages are the most rewarding places to go shopping in, there is never a shortage of things to buy in San Cristóbal itself. Women from outlying villages offer their weavings at every street corner. Shops are filled with textiles, bags and masks from Chiapas and Guatemala. The plaza in front of Sto Domingo overflows with women and young girls selling woven purses, shawls and belts (little of which is local—nearly all is brought in from Guatemala).

Next to the church is the **Sna Jolobil** shop and museum, a co-operative run by Tzotzil and Tzeltal women, whose weavings are still based on the old patterns, incorporating pre-Hispanic symbols for gods, animals and fertility. Although the prices are higher than in the open market, the quality is infinitely better. The encouragement of this co-operative has resulted in the recovery of many lost traditions, and the creation of some ingenious new designs. Opposite it, the tiny Sna Jolobil Exhibition Centre has some outstanding weavings on display.

Just beyond this is the daily **market** (eight blocks north of the Zócalo on Utrilla), selling fruit, vegetables, ceramics, sandals and just about anything one could want, to a continuous background of loud *ranchera* music. **Real de Guadalupe**, the street leading off from the north side of the Zócalo, also has quantities of craft shops selling every imaginable design and weave of textile. It's worth exploring its full length, as some of the better shops (eg no 44) are several blocks from the Zócalo. The government-run **Casa de las Artesanías** (Av Hidalgo and Niños Héroes, tel 81180; open 09.00–19.00) is extremely competitive, with an imaginative and diverse stock ranging from prayer stools to book covers, cushions and jewellery.

HORSE RIDING
Horses can be rented from the Café Olulu or the Casa de Huéspedes Margarita (Real de Guadalupe 34, tel 80957), or from Amfitrones Turisticos (one block from the tourist office, on 16 de Septiembre, within the Restaurant Fogón del Jovel, tel 81153). The most popular rides are to the village of San Juan Chamula (10 km northwest; see Villages Around San Cristóbal) or to a huge cave 9 km south of town.

TURKISH STEAM BATHS
These can be found at Baños Mercedarios (Primero de Marzo 55), providing quite an extraordinary experience in this Catholic hill town.

WHERE TO STAY   (area code 967)
The hotels in San Cristóbal are amongst the best in Mexico. They are not luxurious, nor are they part of chains; instead, they possess those far more elusive qualities—charm and character. At Christmas and Easter, prices rise and rooms are hard to come by. The rest of the year, accommodation is easier to find and far cheaper.

Two of the best hotels are on the Zócalo itself. The ***Santa Clara** (Av Insurgentes 1, tel 81140 and 80871, tlx 78151) is the oldest building in town and one of the most attractive hotels, with 40 large rooms (the 19 newer ones are less interesting). It includes a travel agency, swimming pool, jacuzzi and parking, but there is also plenty of room just for sitting around and writing postcards, overlooking the Zócalo. Just along from it is the ***Ciudad Real** (tel 80187 and 80464), another pleasant colonial building converted into a well-run hotel.

Possibly the very best Spanish mansion hotel is the ****Posada Diego de Mazarie-gos** (5 de Febrero 1, tel 81825 and 80513), which is two hotels in one, run by an Asturian and patronized by the discerning French. The oldest hotel in San Cristóbal, and another colonial stalwart, is the ***Español** (1 de Marzo 15, tel 80412 and 80726, fax 80514, tlx 78156). All of these offer high standards of service, including restaurants, at rates much lower than they deserve.

Other medium-range hotels are further from the centre, not ideal for a first visit (particularly when without a car) but good second choices when the town is full. Of these, the most comfortable and welcoming is the ***Parador Ciudad Real** (Diagonal Centenario 32, tel 81886 or 83044, tlx 78148) which offers excellent home cooking in its restaurant, helpful staff and attractive brick and beam bedrooms.

Alternatively, some blocks from the centre, the ***Rincón del Arco** (Ejército Nacional 66, tel 81313 and 81568), round the corner from the Na Bolom museum, has a mixture of old and modern rooms, each with a chimney in the shape of an animal and all opening onto a flower-filled courtyard. The modern, colonial-style ***Mansión del Valle** (Diego de Mazariegos 39, tel 82581, tlx 78330, fax 82581) is a less charming but practical tour-group hotel. Similar to this but only a block from the Zócalo, the ***Posada de los Angeles** (Madero 17, tel 81173, fax 84371) is the newest hotel in town despite its colonial patio.

The cheaper hotels are congregated in the Calle Real de Guadalupe which leads off the Zócalo. Side by side are the *San Martín** (Real de Guadalupe 16, tel 80533), which halves its prices out of season, and the *Real del Valle** (Real de Guadalupe 14, tel 80680), with parking and good service. The most popular is undoubtedly the successful **Casa de Huéspedes Margarita** (Real de Guadalupe 34, tel 80957) which has long since established itself as the cheap option for hard-up travellers, offering basic rooms, communal bathrooms, and very low prices. Its café is surprisingly imaginative, serving carrot juice, quiches, granola and yoghurt. It runs horse-riding trips to Chamula, Agua Azul, Toniná or the caves, and has lots of good postcards on sale.

Other cheap hotels are on Insurgentes. The inconspicuous, 10-roomed **Posada San Cristóbal** (Insurgentes 3) is only half a block from the Zócalo, with the added advantage of a small restaurant. A little further down the same street is the **Fray Bartolomé de las Casas** (Niños Héroes 2 with Insurgentes, tel 80932), a private house until recently, run by the owners. Sixteen spacious rooms are set around the central patio and its cypress tree, with some less attractive modern rooms beyond.

EATING OUT

Elegance isn't San Cristóbal's forte. The better restaurants are few and far between, usually linked to one of the hotels (of which the **Conquistador** in the Posada Mazariegos is the best). On the other hand, there are plenty of wonderful small, steamy cafés serving large breakfasts and food throughout the day.

To begin the day, start at either **La Famiglia** (Utrilla) or **Madre Tierra** (Insurgentes) which both serve excellent breakfasts of yoghurt and granola, with wholemeal bread and fresh orange juice. The **Madre Tierra**, opposite the San Francisco church, is run by an Englishwoman and is consistently good for breakfast, lunch or dinner. Live music is often played in the small upstairs bar in the evening, but during the day it much more pleasant to be in the patio. There is a wholewheat bakery attached. Later on in the morning, the **Café Colonial** (Dr Navarro 1, on the corner of Utrilla) plays classical music on its large patio and serves *licuados* and sandwiches. **La Galería** (Hidalgo 3, half a block from the Zócalo) has home-made cakes, coffees and chocolates, as well as more substantial dishes such as chicken breast with peanuts. The French and Italians prefer **El Teatro** (1 de Marzo 8, opposite the Hotel Español). All of these are cheap.

For something more elaborate, **El Fogón de Jovel** (Av 16 de Septiembre 11, tel 81153) is a gallery-restaurant, where marimba players perform in the evening. Chairs and tables are set around a brightly painted patio. The menu is very regional, but each dish is given a lengthy description. Moderate. On Insurgentes, the **Tuluc** is a linguistic Tower of Babel, filled with travellers and dominated by the ubiquitous presence of its owner, who speaks four languages. Hearty platefuls of pasta, chicken, fish and salads are all surprisingly cheap. Also on Insurgentes, the **Misión del Fraile** is another busy restaurant, specializing in grilled meats brought to the table still cooking over a hot flame. Moderate. **El Bazar** (half a block south of the Zócalo on Hidalgo) is one of the most popular lunchtime restaurants which continues to serve a cheap daily menu into the evening. Right on the Zócalo itself, the **Plaza** is set on a second-floor balcony for inveterate people-watchers.

Villages Around San Cristóbal

Away from the growing city of San Cristóbal, the outlying villages uphold traditions which stretch back far beyond the Spanish conquest, although they have been encroached on ever since. The beauty and dignity of the Tzotzil and Tzeltal people who live here, and the outstanding quality of their textiles, have drawn many people to visit them, from casual tourists to heavy-handed missionaries and cautious anthropologists. These visitors are treated warily, recognized as an important source of income but also as a threat. To keep up good relations, whilst avoiding a constant deluge of patronizing tour buses, visits are restricted to market days (see below), which suits both parties. Obviously, snap-happy photographers and buttock-hugging shorts offend everyone's dignity. In particular, the Tzotzil-speaking San Juan Chamulans will only let outsiders into their church if they are decently dressed and carrying written permission to enter (obtainable from the tourist office on the main plaza).

GETTING AROUND

Good roads lead northwest to the Tzotzil villages of San Juan de Chamula (10 km) and Zinacantán (11 km), and northeast to the Tzeltal village of Tenejapa (27 km). These are the three closest and most visited villages, and combis, marked with the name of the village, leave from the market in San Cristóbal. Many other villages, such as Cancuc, San Andrés and Chenalhó, are further away from San Cristóbal and down considerably worse roads. To visit these, it is nearly always necessary to take a second-class bus or to

San Juan Chamula

443

hitch a semi-formal ride with one of the truck drivers who congregate around the market place. The buses often leave only once a day, making a day trip almost impossible, and no accommodation is available. It is best to plan any trip well ahead: the tourist office has timetables and will give advice.

VILLAGE LIFE

Festivals and religious services represent a mix between the pre-Hispanic and the Catholic. After the conquest, the Christian cross provided the link between the two cultures, having been used in both for centuries. Associated with the cardinal points, and with the ancient cult of the *ceiba* tree, where ancestors are believed to live, crosses were and still are a central focus in indigenous art and devotion. (Halfway along the road to Tenejapa, there is an extraordinary hill-top cemetery, visible from some distance because of the height of the carved crosses rising high above the graves.)

The Tzotzil-speaking Zinacantecans traditionally wear pink tunics and flat, berib-boned, handwoven straw hats, whilst the San Juan Chamulans wear black tunics. In the two Tzeltal villages of Tenejapa and Cancuc (26 km from Tenejapa, down a rough track), costumes are even more elaborate, including intricate shirts and shawls: those of Tenejapa are woven in muted, autumnal colours, while in Cancuc both men and women sport candy-striped pink and white. The women of Tenejapa have opened up a weaving co-operative, **La Lucha** (on the right, at the entrance to the village) to sell these works of art, although their independence is under threat from the village authorities. These elders come out in force on Sundays, wearing chains of silver buttons etched with the Virgin of Guadalupe (religious and civil authority are very closely linked): together with most of the other adult men, they then proceed to drink until they keel over.

MARKET DAYS

Tenejapa has a main market on Thursday and a lesser one on Sunday when the village elders parade through the streets in their finery. The markets at San Juan Chamula and Zinacantán are both on Sunday.

FESTIVALS

The most colourful festivals in Chamula are Carnival—just before Lent, Easter week, and the three days from 22 to 25 June when the town's Catholic patron saint is celebrated. Zinacantán's major festival also celebrates its patron saint, Lorenzo, on 11 August, while Tenejapa celebrates San Idelfonso on 23 January.

Tuxtla Gutiérrez

Tuxtla Gutiérrez, the capital of Chiapas, is an awful town, one to get in and out of fast. Its few attractions are peripheral and only the restaurants could make anyone want to linger. A visit, however, is almost unavoidable. It has the only national airport in Chiapas, almost all buses pass through it, and even those travelling by car will find it difficult to bypass. By way of consolation, anyone stuck there can visit the best zoo in Mexico, on the outskirts of the town, or take a boat trip up the Sumidero Canyon.

GETTING AROUND

By Air: There are daily flights to and from Mexico City, Oaxaca, Tapachula and Villahermosa, Cancún and Mérida. The airport is 21 km southwest of town, on Highway 190. Combis run between the airport and Av Central (stopping outside Hotel Humberto, to the west of the Zócalo).

By Bus: The **first-class** bus station is at the corner of 2 Norte and 2 Pte (only two blocks from Av Central), with services to and from San Cristóbal (2 hrs), Comitán (3½ hrs), Tapachula (7 hrs), Oaxaca (10 hrs) and Mexico City (a gruelling 19 hrs). In addition, a new, slightly more expensive, nonstop first-class bus service now runs between Mexico City and Tuxtla.

Second-class buses run from 3 Sur Ote, three blocks south of Av Central, to Palenque (9 hrs) and Mérida (18 hrs). As they go via San Cristóbal, it is generally better to change there, from second- to first-class.

Combis and buses to Chiapa de Corzo (20 mins) leave Tuxtla from the corner of 4 Ote and 4 Sur.

By Car: Highway 190 runs through Tuxtla on its way from Oaxaca (542 km) to Comitán (171 km). Chiapa de Corzo (14 km) and San Cristóbal (82 km) are east of Tuxtla on the same highway.

In Town: Tuxtla is divided by long, straight Av Central, which runs east–west past the cathedral and the Zócalo. Calle Central crosses this from north to south, just to the west of the cathedral. The streets are named numerically north, south, east or west of these main arteries. Most tourists will only need to use Av Central. Combis constantly go up and down its length, past the tourist offices and the Hotel Bonampak.

TOURIST INFORMATION

There are two tourist offices, both to the west of town near the Hotel Bonampak, on Av Belisario Domínguez (an extension of Av Central). The office nearest the centre, just east of the Hotel Bonampak, is bigger and better, and can supply maps for the whole country (tel 24535; open 08.00–20.00, Mon–Fri; 10.00–12.00, Sat). The state office, directly opposite the Hotel Bonampak (Belisario Domínguez 950, on the second floor of a tall, yellow building, tel 34837; open 10.00–20.00, Mon–Fri) is less helpful, providing local information only. Underneath it, the excellent, state-run **Instituto de la Artesanía Chiapaneca** is filled with crafts from all over the state, at very reasonable prices.

WHAT TO SEE

In Town

The main attraction of the modern whitewashed **cathedral** is its bell tower. Every hour, wooden figures of the 12 Apostles emerge to strike their chimes. Around it the recently refurbished **Zócalo** is filled with cafés and fountains. To the west, on Av Central, the **Hotel Bonampak** has reproductions of the murals of Bonampak in its lobby. Though not a patch on the real thing, they aren't a bad second for those who don't have the time or the energy to make the difficult trip to the site itself. In **Parque Madero**, northeast of the centre on 5 Norte, there is a good anthropology museum, an *orquíderío* filled with the orchids for which Chiapas is famed, and botanical gardens.

Zoomat

(20 mins from the town centre; take a cheap taxi or a combi which leaves every 20 mins from 1 Sur Ote, a block south of the Restaurant Pinchanchas; open 08.30–17.30; closed Mon.)
An unmissable experience in Tuxtla is a visit to its ecologically conscious Zoomat, founded and run by Miguel Alvárez del Toro. Considering a zoo to be a necessary evil, he opened the Zoomat in 1980, in an attempt to prevent the extinction of a number of regional species. Each species is given as much freedom as possible, in large open spaces recreating its natural habitat. Clear notices provide detailed information, in an attempt to create public awareness. Sadly, in many cases these include notices of imminent extinction. Amongst others there are regional varieties of jaguars, tapirs, ocelots, snakes and monkeys, as well as animals which are indigenous only to Chiapas. A large mirror invites one to look at the most dangerous species of all, which is destroying not only itself but all nature.

Chiapa de Corzo

Chiapa, the Spanish capital of Chiapas, is today no more than a pleasant adjunct to the monstrous modernity of Tuxtla Gutiérrez, 14 km to the west. It is set on the banks of the languorous Grijalva River, from where 2-hour boat trips wend their way up the Sumidero Canyon to the Chicoasen dam. A morning's stroll would exhaust its delights: a **lacquer museum** in the plaza, one grand church—the 16th-century gothic **Santo Domingo**, one ruined church and one little chapel.

When Diego de Mazariegos came to conquer the Chiapa people in 1528, he encountered tenacious resistance. Finally, seeing that all was lost but refusing to submit to the Spanish, they threw themselves—men, women and children—off the Peñón de Tepetchia into the canyon. The Spanish promptly built a couple of churches and decorated the plaza with a fanciful octagonal mudéjar brick fountain, in honour of and in the shape of the Spanish crown. The town was never a success, however. No wind came off the river, and the Spanish sweated feverishly in the heat and resulting animosity, before finally giving in and moving their capital to the cooler hill ground of San Cristóbal.

Maya Ruins

(From the Nestlé building on Highway 190, go three blocks down Calle Libertad and two blocks left at the old cemetery.)
Just outside Chiapa de Corzo are some excavations which have been carried out by the Church of Latter-Day Saints, better known as the Mormons. In their ceaseless quest to prove that the western hemisphere was first populated by the Jaredites, who came here from Mesopotamia, and then by the Lost Tribes of Israel, they have been generous sponsors of archaeological work. At Chiapa de Corzo they found one of the oldest of all Maya sites and, on one of the stelae, the earliest known recorded date—36 BC. It is now thought that proto-Maya groups separated from the older established Olmecs as early as 1500 BC, crossing over the Isthmus of Tehuantepec into Chiapas. By 800 BC, they had already built the first structures at Chiapa de Corzo.

Most of these Zoque-Maya temples were razed to build the colonial town and little is left at the nominal site, except for a couple of platforms showing different stages of superimposition. On Highway 190, directly opposite the Nestlé factory, is a burial mound, known as **Monticulo 32**, which was excavated in 1973. An intact skeleton was found inside the chamber, surrounded by ceramics and funerary urns. Everything is still just as they found it (the site guard has the key).

Cañón de Sumidero
North of Chiapa de Corzo, the Grijalva River enters a spectacular canyon, cut through 1500-m cliffs. The best way to see it is to float up-river in one of the boats which leave from the pier in Chiapa de Corzo. The trip lasts a couple of hours, passing waterfalls and entering caves. Payment is per boat and not per passenger.

WHERE TO STAY   (area code 961)
Hotels in **Tuxtla** take advantage of the town's spider-like ability to trap tourists. They are either cheap and dingy or expensive, with little in between. The top snazzy hotel is the Arabic-style *****Flamboyant (Blvd Belisario Domínguez 1081, tel 29311 or 29259), with a swimming pool and tennis courts. The ****Bonampak nearby is modern and comfortable, and also has a pool. At the other end of Av Central, ****Real de Tuxtla (Carr Panamericana km 1088, tel 25197) is the most pleasant Mediterranean-style hotel in Tuxtla, set in spacious gardens with a large pool.

***Posada del Rey (1 Ote Norte, tel 22871) boasts a quasi-colonial entrance hall and florid modern rooms. Two more modest hotels are **La Mansión (1 Pte Norte 221, tel 22151) and the **Internacional (Belisario Domínguez 16, tel 20110).

Anyone on a budget, or planning a trip up the Sumidero Canyon, will find it worth spending the night in the one cheap hotel on the main square of **Chiapa de Corzo**: the **(CE) Los Angeles** has big, bare rooms set around a courtyard, with no frills attached.

EATING OUT
Despite its distance from the sea, Tuxtla Gutiérrez has an excellent seafood restaurant, **La Palapa de Amado** (Libramiento Sur Ote 3125, tel 37670; a taxi ride from the centre, close to the zoo at the north end of town). Platefuls of shrimps, paella and the chef's special—*robalo alcaparrado* (sea bass in a creamy caper sauce) pour out of the kitchen as the waiters madly try to keep up with the demand. Moderate.

Las Pichanchas (Av Central 837, tel 25351) offers superb regional food, such as *tasajo con chimol* (strips of beef charcoaled with ground tomatoes and onions), or the tiny leaves of the *chipilin* steamed in a broth with maize balls and Oaxacan cheese. Mariachis play at night. Moderate. **Parachico's** (Blvd Corzo y Venezuela, tel 22478; a taxi ride from the centre) is studiously Chiapan, with pottery from Amatenango and exotic dishes such as *nucu* (black ants) or the *cuchuinuc* flower fried with beef and egg whites. The owner's aunt sits in a dark corner and reads people's fortunes. Moderate. At the other end of town, **La Selva** (Blvd Belisario Domínguez 1360, tel 26251) serves excellent regional dishes against a background of constant marimba music, and is always full. Moderate.

The curiously named **London** (2 Pte and 2 Norte) has tried to recreate a London club in Chiapas, with a predictable lack of success (except for the whisky). Wary of British beef, it specializes in *robalo relleno de mariscos* (sea bass stuffed with octupus, squid, shrimps and artichokes). Moderate.

447

Behind the cathedral, the **Cafeteria San Marcos** serves *licuados*, bulging buns and chocolate cakes. Cheap. Next door, the **Trattoria San Marcos** (tel 26974) is an example of Venice meeting Mexico and Mexico winning: gondolas are the only Italian thing on the menu. Cheap.

Comitán de Domínguez

Basking in its warm climate, under the clearest of skies, Comitán is a pretty little town, the last pleasant break on the road between Mexico and Guatemala. The narrow streets roller-coaster up and down past brightly painted ochre, pink and green houses, all dominated by the main square, where music pours out from speakers hidden in the bushes. Although established by the Spanish as early as 1527, Comitán was part of Guatemala until it became the seat of the Chiapan independence movement in 1821 and subsequently joined Mexico.

Today it is little more than a stopover on the way to Guatemala or the lakes of Montebello, surrounded by countryside rich in coffee, cotton and beans. Yet, for such an inconsequential town, it has produced some very forward-looking thinkers, including Belisario Domínguez (1863—1913) who spoke out against Huerta, malevolent hijacker of the Revolution, and had his tongue ripped out as a result. The poet and writer, Rosario Castellanos, also lived here for many years, writing lyrically about Comitán and its customs.

GETTING AROUND
By Air: There is a small airport on Highway 190 at km 1259 (tel 20390), which is used by four-seater Cessna biplanes flying to and from Palenque, Bonampak, Yaxchilán, Villahermosa and Tuxtla Gutiérrez. Flights from Comitán are slightly cheaper than elsewhere; views of the Lagos de Montebello, directly beneath the planes' flight path, are another advantage. For more information, contact the tourist office (tel 20532), Aero-Comitán (tel 22872), or the travel agent Viajes Tziscao (2a Norte Pte 62, tel 20824 or 20878, tlx 78155). All flights must be booked 24 hours in advance.
By Bus: The first-class Cristóbal Colón bus station is on bougainvillea-lined Highway 190, which skirts the west side of town (a 20-minute walk to the centre). Regular services connect the town with Tuxtla Gutiérrez and San Cristóbal (8 daily), Tapachula (3½ hrs, 3 daily) and Ciudad Cuauhtémoc (1 hr, 13 daily).

Second-class buses leave every 15 minutes from 2 Av Pte Sur 23 for the Chinkultic ruins, dropping passengers off at the entrance (from where it is a 3-km walk in). The same buses then continue to the national park of Montebello.
By Car: Comitán is on the Pan-American Highway 190, 88 km east of San Cristóbal, 171 km east of Tuxtla Gutiérrez and 243 km north of Tapachula.

The ruins of Chinkultic and the lakes of Montebello are both southeast of Comitán, off the same road. Leave town on southbound Highway 190 and turn left after 16 km, at the Trinitaria junction (signposted 'Lagos de Montebello'). The ruins of Chinkultic are 44 km from Comitán, down a 3-km signed track to the left. It is a 10-minute walk in from the car park and then a steep climb up to the pyramids. The lakes are 11 km further down the road.

To Guatemala: The Mexico–Guatemala frontier at Ciudad Cuauhtémoc is only an hour away from Comitán. The **Guatemalan consulate** in Comitán (2 Av Pon Nte 28, tel 21540 or 22669; open 08.00–18.00) can arrange visas, on production of passport-size photographs, proof of financial solvency (a credit card will do) and a valid passport. Mexican pesos are not accepted in Guatemala and the exchange rates are worse over the border.

The first-class bus from Ciudad Cuauhtémoc to Guatemala City (1325 km) leaves at 07.30. There are no hotels in the town: either take a 06.00 second-class 'Transportes Tuxtla' bus from Comitán, or cross over during the day and spend the night on the Guatemalan side of the border.

TOURIST INFORMATION
There is a small information booth (tel 20532) on the main square, between the church and the Casa de la Cultura.

WHAT TO SEE
Comitán itself has little to offer but churches (the main festival is on 4 August) and a couple of small museums. More compelling attractions are within an hour's journey from the town—to the east, the ruins of Chinkultic and the lakes of Montebello, and to the northwest, the pottery-making village of Amatenango del Valle.

In Town
On the main square, the **Casa de la Cultura** haphazardly exhibits remains from the ruins of Chinkultic, and hosts occasional performances by visiting bands or orchestras. There is a café nearby, opening onto the square. More rewarding is the **Museo de Arte** (Av Belisario Domínguez Sur 53; open 10.00–19.00; closed Mon). This small gallery houses an impressive collection of works by modern artists, of whom the vast majority are Oaxacans. It includes engravings and lithographs by Francisco Toledo, paintings by Rufino Tamayo and Rodolfo Morales, and several works by Justina Fuentes and Irma Guerrero. Morales' paintings are full of the strong colours of Mexico—indigos, peaty browns and bold reds.

The **Casa de Belisario Domínguez** (Av Belisario Domínguez 35; closed Mon; adm) was the home of a local doctor and subsequent martyr to the Revolution. It has since been converted into an attractive museum, set around a courtyard filled with flowers. Belisario Domínguez was born in Comitán in 1863. He left to study medicine in Paris, and returned with many new liberal ideas. Vehemently opposed to Huerta's corrupt regime during the Revolution, he published a speech denouncing the president, and for this he lost his life. The museum preserves his pharmacy (he was famed for treating patients for free) and his furniture intact, conveying a strong sense of the presence of this noble man.

Amatenango
Set in a fertile valley, 56 km west of Comitán on Highway 190, this 2000-year-old village is famous for its traditional ceramics, which are still shaped by hand, without the use of a wheel. Pots, stoves and animals are sold by the roadside. The village itself, set 50 m back, remains undisturbed, the domain of chickens and old Tzeltal women, in beautifully woven clothes, wilting in the doorways of their red adobe houses.

Chinkultic

Although Chinkultic reveals many similarities with other Maya ruins, such as Palenque and Yaxchilán, it was in fact inhabited earlier and for longer. It dates back to well before the time of Christ (some archaeologists date it to 300 BC) and survived into the late Classic period. Holding the balance of power over the nearby Lagos de Montebello, it was also a natural staging post on the trade route between the highlands of Chiapas and the jungle plains leading into Guatemala.

The site, however, has been little excavated—the supposed ball court is still uncovered—and is only rarely visited by tourists, despite its imposing setting and enormous 26 m-high temple. Although the climb to the top of the temple is steep, the splendid views it commands make it well worth the effort. The temple is surrounded by water: a lake semi-circles around the rear, while in front a huge, steep-sided pool (a *cenote*) drops sheer away as one peers, vertiginously, over the edge. This is one of the steepest *cenotes* to have been discovered, and many artefacts have been dredged from it (some of them are in the Casa de la Cultura in Comitán).

Lagos de Montebello

The National Park of Montebello begins a few km east of the track to Chinkultic. This whole uninhabited area, with its 59 lakes, marks the end of Mexico. To the south, the frontier is rigidly delineated by an arbitrary straight-line border; to the north, it follows the winding course of the Usumacinta River.

The lakes are the starting point for tracks leading into this inaccessible jungle region. Although it is possible to walk from here to Bonampak (and Palenque), across the Río Lacantún, the journey takes several days and most definitely requires a guide.

Several of the lakes, on the other hand, are within easy walking distance of the bus stop at the entrance to the park. Known as the Lagunas de Colores, they range in colour from royal blue to turquoise to moss green. The natural beauty of this region, and its scattering of makeshift restaurants, makes it a popular weekend excursion.

WHERE TO STAY

Comitán has a surprising number of hotels for such a small town, largely because of the through-traffic to Guatemala. On Highway 190, the ***Lagos de Montebello** (tel 21092) is a convenient, modern hotel for overnight travellers. However, a far better bet is the ****Real Balún Calán**, close to the Zócalo (1a Av Pte Sur 5, tel 21094), which provides comfortable rooms, a good restaurant—called Escocés (the Scottish), without any apparent reason—and a swimming pool. Cheaper hotels include the **Internacional** (Belisario Domínguez 22, tel 20112) with big, airy rooms and a café in the lobby, or the very cheap **(CE) Delfín Pensión** (tel 20013) which looks onto the park.

EATING OUT

There are no out-of-the-ordinary restaurants in Comitán. The Balún Calán hotel's is probably the best. **Helen and Enrique** has tables on a terrace fronting the main square, serving chicken breasts *a la parmesana* and exquisite mango tarts. **Nevelandia**, also on the main square, offers a *parillada* (a big grill with beef, pork, peppers, radishes and onions served on wooden boards). For the best Mexican food, take a taxi out to the well-known but difficult-to-find **Los Gallos** (at km 1285 on Highway 190, on the left across a ditch), which specializes in pork dishes and often has musicians playing.

The Chiapas Coast

The coast of Chiapas has changed little over the centuries. Bordered by low-lying fertile plains, it formed an important trading route between the centre and the south for early Maya and later Aztec merchants. The coastal plain is still verdant and bountiful, with abundant fields of mango and papaya, but the stretches of beach remain empty and undeveloped—largely because of the strong currents which can sweep swimmers out unawares. Cars travel through on the fast straight road southeast to Guatemala and only those who want to get right away from it all will linger.

GETTING AROUND
By Air: There is an airport in Tapachula, with daily flights to Mexico City, Oaxaca and Tuxtla.
By Bus: Frequent daily services connect Tuxtla with the two main towns on the coast, Tonalá (3½ hrs) and Tapachula (7 hrs).
By Car: Flat, straight Highway 200 runs down the coast for the 300 km or so from Arriaga in the west, through Tonalá to Tapachula. Highway 190 loops inland, winding in corkscrew curls through thickly wooded hills, from Tapanatepec (west of Arriaga) to Tuxtla and San Cristóbal, and then down through Comitán to Tapachula. The quickest route between San Cristóbal and the coast is via Arriaga.

Tonalá

Near Chiapas' western border, the small town of Tonalá is a convenient stop on coastal Highway 200 between Huatulco and Tapachula, offering little more than a couple of restaurants and one good hotel. Nearby is the deserted beach of Puerto Arista, with an excellent, small palapa restaurant which is worth a detour.

GETTING AROUND
Highway 200 runs through Tonalá. The bus station is at the junction between the highway and Av Hidalgo, with regular connections up and down the coast and northeast to Tuxtla. Puerto Arista is 21 km south of Tonalá: turn south off Highway 200, 4 km east of town, or take a combi or taxi from the centre of Tonalá.

TOURIST INFORMATION
The tourist office is in the Palacio Municipal off the Zócalo (Av Hidalgo, tel 30101: open 09.00–14.00 and 18.00–20.00).

BEACH
Puerto Arista is a huge stretch of mainly deserted beach which echoes to the sound of Pacific waves crashing onto its shore. It is always hot and humid, and the residents of the small village do little but fish in the early morning, lying in hammocks during the heat of the day. It is a good place for doing nothing. Swimmers should beware of the undertow which can be extremely dangerous, particularly during April and March.

WHERE TO STAY

The best hotel in **Tonalá** is the *****Grajandra** (Av Hidalgo 204, tel 30144), next to the bus station. The modest ****Galilea** in the Zócalo (tel 30239) is also clean and comfortable. In **Puerto Arista**, it is easy to find somewhere to sling a hammock, and every restaurant has a room to let. The more up-market *****Arista Bugambillas** (tel 30675) has a swimming pool and small restaurant.

EATING OUT

Both the hotels in **Tonalá** have restaurants, serving mostly fish and seafood. On the main street, the **Parillada Sal y Pimienta** (Hidalgo 85) provides huge plates of grilled meats, washed down with Cuban wines. Cheap.

In **Puerto Arista**, the beach front is lined with tiny palapa cafés serving seafood. Deserted during the week, save for the odd seagull, they come alive at weekends with families from Tonalá. Without doubt the best of these is **Sobre Las Olas**, run by Elsa Gutiérrez. Like a 1950s filmset, Jorge Negrete plays on a crackling radio, the canvas flaps in the wind and the sun sets in a haze over the waves, as she cooks up succulent, freshly caught shrimps with a touch of cream. Next come platters of *salsicha de macabil* (fish sausage packed with coriander) or *liza*, the local fish, baked in the oven. Her curried fish soup, *caldo de pescado*, is without equal. Cheap and unmissable.

Tapachula

As Highway 200 approaches Tapachula and the Guatemalan border, the vegetation becomes tantalizingly tropical: palms, bananas and coffee plantations stretch away from one side of the road, while craggy heights rear up on the other. Tapachula doesn't live up to this build-up. A border town with a strong Central American influence, it is as disappointingly transitional as its counterparts on the northern border, although much smaller and more provincial. In the rainy season its streets become rivers: torrents of water wash over the feet of pedestrians and cars skid to a halt. In Tapachula, people come and go with rapidity. Tourists cross to Guatemala and Guatemalans come over in the hope of finding work or getting themselves into the United States. Few who have the option linger longer than a night.

GETTING AROUND

The first-class bus station is to the northeast of town (17a Ote and 3a Nte, tel 62880), a 20-minute walk from the centre. Regular buses connect the town with San Cristóbal and Tuxtla, stopping off at towns on the way.

The route to Izapa and Unión Juárez is covered by second-class buses, marked 'Unión' and 'Progresso', which leave from Calle 9 Pte.

To Guatemala: From the first-class station, six daily first-class buses go to Talismán, the main border crossing for Guatemala, 20 km east of Tapachula. The journey takes 20 minutes and is not expensive by taxi.

The **Guatemalan consulate** (tel 61252) is near the tourist office, on Calle 1 Ote 33. To obtain a visa for Guatemala, you will need passport-size photographs, proof of financial solvency (a credit card will do) and a valid passport. Thus equipped, it shouldn't take longer than half an hour to get a visa—but allow at least a morning. Mexican pesos are not accepted in Guatemala and the exchange rates are worse over the border: change them in Tapachula, either into quetzals or into US dollars.

TOURIST INFORMATION
The tiny tourist office is tucked inside the Palacio Municipal on the west side of the Zócalo (tel 63543). The staff have maps of the town and will give advice on getting to Guatemala.

WHAT TO SEE AND DO
Tapachula has little to offer, other than a small museum. However, with a little more time, it is possible to take a day trip to the site of Izapa and the hill-top village of Unión Juárez.

In Town
Tapachula's small **regional museum** is next door to the tourist office in the Palacio Municipal. Although generally down at heel, it boasts the odd intriguing piece from the nearby site of Izapa. The ceramics are decorated with exuberant local flora and fauna. Of particular note is a skull decorated with a beautiful turquoise mosaic.

Izapa
Izapa is 11 km northeast of Tapachula on the road to Talismán. An early site (800 BC), founded by an Olmec splinter group, it was later taken over by the Maya, flourishing around the time of Christ. It was the main city in the area, graced with ball courts and important carved stelae. Its altars, which would have been used as thrones by rulers, take the anthropomorphic forms of toads and frogs. Carved deities on the stelae are represented as serpents and fish. One stelae depicts the origins of man in the form of a tree, with couples descending from its every branch. Many others have been badly eroded by the elements.

Ignored and unvisited, the site is divided by the main road, guarded only by a sleepy custodian. Stop first on the left-hand side of the road (by the 'Izapa' sign), where there is a large courtyard surrounded by stelae. On the other side of the road (a 20-minute walk through groves of cocoa and mango), there are two further areas worth visiting. (In the rainy season the rough track may be impassable: ask the custodian to point the way.) The **Lion Court** is a tantalizingly unexplored mound, with stelae scattered at its feet. Further on, the **Ball Court** is grazed by Friesian cattle and surrounded by fields of pineapple. One of the pieces which surround it is the huge head of a frog. The tree of life is at the far end.

Unión Juárez
Unión Juárez is 43 km north of Izapa on the Cacahotan road. The road passes through Santo Domingo, where a two-tiered Teutonic house is a reminder that Germans once owned huge coffee plantations in the area. It then climbs up into the clouds, leaving tropical jungle far behind and entering an alpine landscape, before reaching the rural village of Unión Juárez. Here a small hotel, **Cabaña Suiza**, serves home-cooked dishes in its restaurant. It is a good base for walks to waterfalls or a trip to the still active volcano of Tacaná.

WHERE TO STAY

There are a number of hotels in Tapachula, catering for every need. The best is ****Loma Real (tel 61440), on a hill to the west of the city, off Highway 200. Its big, white rooms are filled with wickerwork furniture, and it has a good, if simple, restaurant and a large swimming pool. To the east of town, the ****Kamico (Prol Central Ote S/N, tel 62640) is comfortable though with a little less character; it also has a swimming pool. ***San Francisco (Central Sur 94, tel 61494) only accepts travellers with suitcases. The manager protests a little too much about the respectable nature of his hotel, refusing to rent rooms by the hour. Nevertheless, the rooms are clean and comfortable, if somewhat shabby and overdecorated.

The nicest hotel in Tapachula, and the best value, is the **Fenix (Av 4 Norte 19, tel 50755). Its big hallway is filled with plants, and the rooms have been recently modernized. Cheapest of the cheap, and well run though run down, is the (CE) Las Américas (Av 10 Norte), with rooms opening off a courtyard.

EATING OUT

Tapachula is not renowned for its *haute cuisine*. If staying no more than a night, it is best to stick to the restaurants on the Zócalo. Many Chinese and Japanese immigrants live in Tapachula, and this has led to a correspondingly high number of oriental restaurants. The best is the Cantonese **Mandarin** (tel 62012), which is culturally mixed up with tartan wallpaper and both Mexican and Chinese food on the menu. It specializes in seafood. Moderate. The local community prefers to eat Chinese dishes at the **Casa Blanca** (Central Norte 118). Cheap.

Back on the Zócalo, the **Doña Leo** is popular for breakfasts and plates of roast chicken with the rich black beans of the south. Cheap. For pseudo-Italian, try the **Hostería el Capistrano** (1a Ote and 3a Nte), just off the Zócalo, which serves pizzas, pastas and salads. Moderate. There are plenty of other cafés for quick breakfasts and light meals in the main square.

Part XIV

THE YUCATAN PENINSULA

Barred antshrike

Land of the Maya, pristine coral beaches and the exhilarating ruins of once-glorious cities, the Yucatán peninsula is a place apart, and one which should not be missed on any first visit to Mexico. Thought to be an island by the Spanish, it remains isolated from the rest of Mexico today, more Central American than Mexican.

It is a flat, flat land, quite different to the valleys and peaks of the Sierra Madre which dominate much of the republic. The undramatic limestone landscape acts as a foil to the bright white embroidered dresses of the Maya women, whitewashed palapa-roofed houses, thick, dark green jungle and blue, blue sea. There are no rivers in the Yucatán, only underground pools—*cenotes*, formed by water dripping through the porous limestone. The plains are dotted with the startling facades of fortress-like Franciscan monasteries and abandoned haciendas. Mérida is the only city of any size in this predominantly rural peninsula. The gentle, dignified Maya, once a civilization as advanced as any in the world, remain true to their traditions, keeping alive their language and customs and the memory of their ancestors. The faces of villagers seen queuing in the shops seem to come straight off the portraits of Maya priests displayed in the museums.

The peninsula is split into three states—Yucatán, filled with the ruins of ancient Maya cities such as Uxmal and Chichén-Itzá as well as a myriad of lesser-known sites, Quintana Roo with its long stretches of white beach sheltered by the reef which runs its length, and Campeche, the least known of the three, with its walled colonial capital and ruined cities which still bear the scars of many invasions.

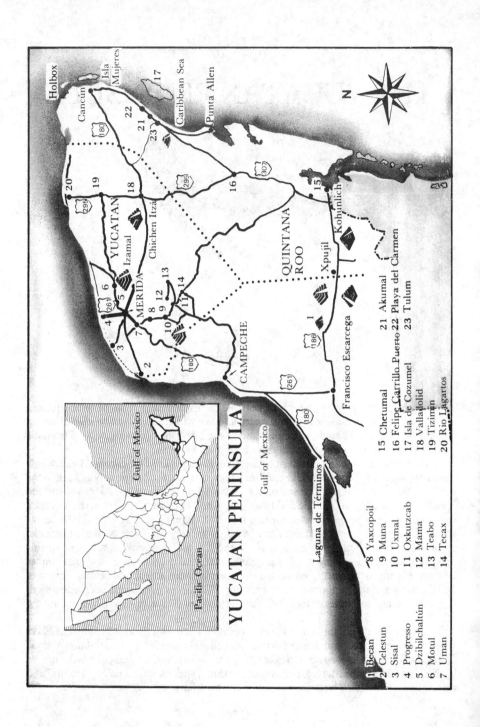

YUCATAN PENINSULA

1 Becan
2 Celestun
3 Sisal
4 Progresso
5 Dzibilchaltún
6 Motul
7 Uman
8 Yaxcopoil
9 Muna
10 Uxmal
11 Oxkutzcab
12 Mama
13 Teabo
14 Tecax
15 Chetumal
16 Felipe Carrillo Puerto
17 Isla de Cozumel
18 Valladolid
19 Tizimín
20 Rio Lagartos
21 Akumal
22 Playa del Carmen
23 Tulum

History

The early history of the Yucatán is inseparable from that of the Maya. Although Maya influences stretched as far south as El Salvador and the Ulúa valley in Honduras and as far west as the central highlands of Mexico, it was in the Yucatán peninsula that this civilization reached its greatest glory. The earliest-known Maya skeleton has recently been dated to 1200 BC—younger than the Olmecs but far more ancient than the Aztecs. Whilst Europe was still in the Dark Ages, the Maya were predicting eclipses of the sun and the moon.

THE WORLD ACCORDING TO THE MAYA

The Maya world was conceived as a flat square, sandwiched between thirteen heavens and nine underworlds. Each of the four points of the compass represented a specific colour: white for the north, red for the east, yellow for the south and black for the west. The Maya pantheon of gods was large and complex. The supreme god, the invisible Hunab Ku, created the Maya world through the heavenly pair, Itzamná, the Sun God and Ixchel, the Moon Goddess. Chac, the Rain God, with his long nose associated with lightning, is the most visual of the canon and his masks are often seen adorning the facades of Maya ruins, particularly in the desperately dry Yucatán. His role was similar to that of the other rain gods, the Central American Tlaloc or the Oaxacan Cocijo. The other common god is the plumed serpent Kukulkán, a fusion of the earth and the sky, bird and reptile. The God of Culture and Learning (similar to Quetzalcóatl in central Mexico), he was also the Wind God, breathing life into the world.

The scientific and artistic achievements of the Maya are spectacular. Their solar calendar, with 18 months of 20 days each, plus 5 'dead' days, was more accurate than the contemporary European Julian calendar. A 260-day religious calendar meshed with the solar one, like two cog wheels with well-oiled gears, creating a calendar round of 52 years, equivalent to our century. Zero (which was only invented twice in the history of the world) was in common usage with the Maya at the time of Alexander the Great.

Many sculpted stone monuments record dates and battles using the Maya vigesimal system, in which a dot represents one and a dash five. Numbers and glyphs were read from the bottom to the top, left to right. The recurrent human figures on these monuments, often carrying a manikin sceptre and a ceremonial bar across the chest, were the great rulers and leaders of the various city-states. At the top of the social system came the *halach uinic* or supreme leader, aided by a council and chiefs who collected taxes, raised armies and negotiated alliances. Women, needless to say, came low on the human and social scale. Yet, when compared with the more rigid hierarchies of Oaxaca and central Mexico, the Maya allowed women some say. Murals and sculptures, ceramics and codices portray women sitting close to the rulers, in their role as mothers, sisters, wives or, occasionally, governing caretakers for child-rulers. Although they are more often shown copulating with monkeys than holding any serious power, women nevertheless held the balance of power at various times in Yaxchilán and Bonampak, while shrines on the islands of Jaina, Cozumel and Mujeres were specifically devoted to women and goddesses.

The previously much-touted idea of the Maya as a pacific people has now had its day. The warrior class was held in high esteem, and murals at Bonampak and Chichén-Itzá bear witness to the ceremony and prestige afforded to battles. These wars, however, were short-lived and sporadic. They were most commonly provoked by disputes over boundaries, raids or internecine strife, and prisoners were only rarely sacrificed.

IN THE END

The fall of the magnificent Maya civilization has teased and plagued the modern world. Most of the cities were in ruins before the first Spaniards were shipwrecked on the Caribbean coast.

Dynasties became interbred and despotic, provoking palace revolutions. These became increasingly common around AD 600, when intensified agricultural techniques proved unable to support a rising population. Mesoamerican farming techniques relied on the slash-and-burn method of clearing jungle land and then moving on when the soil was exhausted. The increase in population meant that there was correspondingly less spare land available, and fiercer territorial battles over who owned what.

There was, however, nothing so sudden as an overnight collapse of the Maya. Maya cities in the Yucatán outlasted those in the central highlands, while the latest of all Maya cities, Flores in the heart of the Petén jungle, was still inhabited by descendants of the Itzá Maya in 1694. Today, the Maya still farm the land of their ancestors. The same broad, sloped foreheads and slanting doe-eyes portrayed on stone monuments of 1000 years ago mark out the native inhabitants of the Yucatán from all the many newcomers who have moved down to take advantage of the surge in tourism.

THE SPANISH CONQUEST OF THE YUCATAN

The Maya prophet Chilam Balam had predicted that men with beards would come from the lands of the east to conquer the Maya, so it was no surprise when the hirsute Spanish arrived on the Yucatán coast. The first Spaniards arrived in 1511, shipwrecked off a reef in the Caribbean. Cortés himself first landed in Cozumel but overlooked the peninsula, which he thought to be an island, in his rush to reach Mexico City and the Aztecs. In 1526 Francisco de Montejo, one of Cortés' soldiers, began to explore the peninsula and only then did the Spanish discover that it was not an island. Eight years later, a widespread Maya revolt put all the Spanish settlements in jeopardy and Montejo reluctantly withdrew, writing this dispirited letter to the Crown:

> In these provinces there is not a single river, although there are lakes and the hills are of dry rock, dry and waterless. The entire land is covered by thick bush and is so strong that there is not a single square foot of soil. No gold has been discovered, nor is there anything from which advantage can be gained. The inhabitants are the most abandoned and treacherous in all the lands discovered to this time, being a people who never yet killed a Christian except by foul means and who never made war except by artifice.

FRAY DIEGO DE LANDA

The Spaniards only delayed another decade before conquering the penisula and soon the flat limestone was dotted with the fortress-like monasteries of evangelizing Franciscan priests. The Franciscan and future bishop Diego de Landa (1524–79) repaid the Maya with immense cruelty, sentencing many to death and burning the codices which recorded their history. Finally repenting of this savagery, he attempted to salvage some of the culture he had single-handedly destroyed by rewriting their history in Spanish—the *Relación de las Cosas de Yucatán*. In this report, he wrote of his own Francisans that:

> They took the leading men, put them in stocks in a building and then set fire to the house, burning them alive with the greatest inhumanity in the world ... I saw a great tree near the village upon the branches of which a captain had hung many women, with their children hung from their feet.

WAR OF THE CASTES

Despite such reports the Spanish continued to dominate the peninsula, growing rich from the profits of their huge haciendas. Tension was mounting, however, and between 1847 and 1849, the Yucatán was ravaged by the infamous War of the Castes, caused in part by the exportation of the Maya as slaves to Cuba and in part by the expropriation of Maya land for the manufacture of sugar cane.

Threatened by a possible US invasion, the rich landowners armed their staff. For the first time the Maya had weapons in their hands, which they used to turn against their masters. The creoles and mestizos fled to the big cities, principally Mérida and Campeche, where they would have been slaughtered en masse—had it not been the beginning of the rainy season. Rather than pursuing them, the Maya returned to reclaim their stolen land and to plant the all-important corn on which they survived. The terrified landowners begged for help from central Mexico but had to wait two years before an army arrived to put an end to the uprising. France, Britain and the US were asked to help but showed little interest. Indeed, Britain was making a tidy profit selling arms to the rebels from nearby Belize. Finally, after two years of vicious fighting against government forces, the Maya were defeated, returning to a worse serfdom than before.

THE TALKING CROSS

In 1850, after the War of the Castes, Maya rebels (known as the 'Cruzob'), who wanted to remain independent from the rest of Mexico, rallied together under the symbol of the talking cross—'Chan Santa Cruz'. This was the invention of their leader, José María Barrera, who manipulated it like a ventriloquist, using it to incite his followers to fight against the Mexican army. Although Barrera himself was killed, the rebels continued the fight, even providing government troops with drinking water which had been infected with cholera. The resistance continued until 1901, when the eastern half of the Yucatán peninsula became Quintana Roo. Troops armed with machine guns broke in and destroyed the Chan Santa Cruz. Although the Cruzob later won it back, the area had by then become infested with smallpox, which killed many of the insurgents. The movement gradually lost momentum and had virtually died out by 1930. Quintana Roo remained a 'difficult' state until 1974, when it was finally incorporated into the Mexican republic.

The State of Yucatán

The most northerly of the three states which make up the peninsula, Yucatán is also the most cultural. It has taken care of its ruined cities, restoring to them something of their former splendour, and encourages visitors to explore its lesser-known sites with well-organized tours and carefully drawn maps. It expects enthusiasm and rewards this with the thrill of discovery. Its northern shore is filled with flamingos, ecological reserves and isolated beaches. Inland, amongst the sites, are villages with weekly markets, dominated by tall monasteries and brightened by Maya women being taxied around on tricycles.

Mérida

To most passengers arriving off an international flight, the humidity and acrid tropical smell of Mérida, together with the bustle and noise, are overwhelming and utterly intoxicating. This most un-Mexican of cities has a distinctly European feel, with streets of low-slung houses radiating out from its colonial heart. Although it is known in tourist brochures as the 'white city', its buildings are now a duller shade of grey, counterpointed by the white flashes of the *guayabera* shirts worn by the men and the embroidered *huipil* dresses of the women. It is voluble like all towns on the Gulf coast but tempers this with the gentleness of the Maya people. An unhurried air prevails, and men and women show open affection: an aged man in a battered panama will stroll hand in hand through the square with his capacious wife in her billowing dress.

There was no through road connecting the Yucatán with the rest of Mexico until a single road was built in the late 1950s. As a result of this isolation, Mérida has always looked to its close neighbours in Central America, Cuba and the United States, and further afield to Europe, and has little in common with the Mexican republic. Many still remember the excitement of ships coming into the port at Progreso, when strangers from as far afield as Mexico City would be seen sitting in cafés. Landowners grew rich from the production of henequen, sending their children to Europe for schooling. (This accounts for the distinct French influence apparent on many of the houses.) Its people, the Maya, have one of the oldest and strongest cultures in the country and remain indomitable, despite endless tribulations. Maya flourishes as a language and a way of life.

All roads lead to Mérida: as the capital of Yucatán, it is the focus for the whole peninsula. Calm and soothing, it is well prepared to meet its guests' every need, from good hotels and rich food to well-prepared tourist offices and efficient transport. It makes an excellent base.

GETTING AROUND

By Air: Mérida is well linked, both nationally and internationally. Flights come in from Mexico City, Cancún, Cozumel, Villahermosa, Acapulco, Guadalajara, Oaxaca, Havana, Miami, Los Angeles and Houston. The main carriers are Aerocaribe (Paseo Montejo 476, tel 280033), Aeroméxico (Paseo Montejo 460, tel 279455) and Mexicana (Calle 58 No 500, tel 246633).

The airport is to the southeast of town on the Campeche road. Minibuses meet most flights, but failing that, wide-beamed taxis wait greedily. Taxis in Mérida are more expensive than anywhere else in Mexico: it's worth finding someone else to share the ride with, which is what the Mexicans do. The journey into town takes about 15 minutes. A 'Ruta 67' bus also plies between the airport and Calle 60 with 67, but the service is often unreliable.

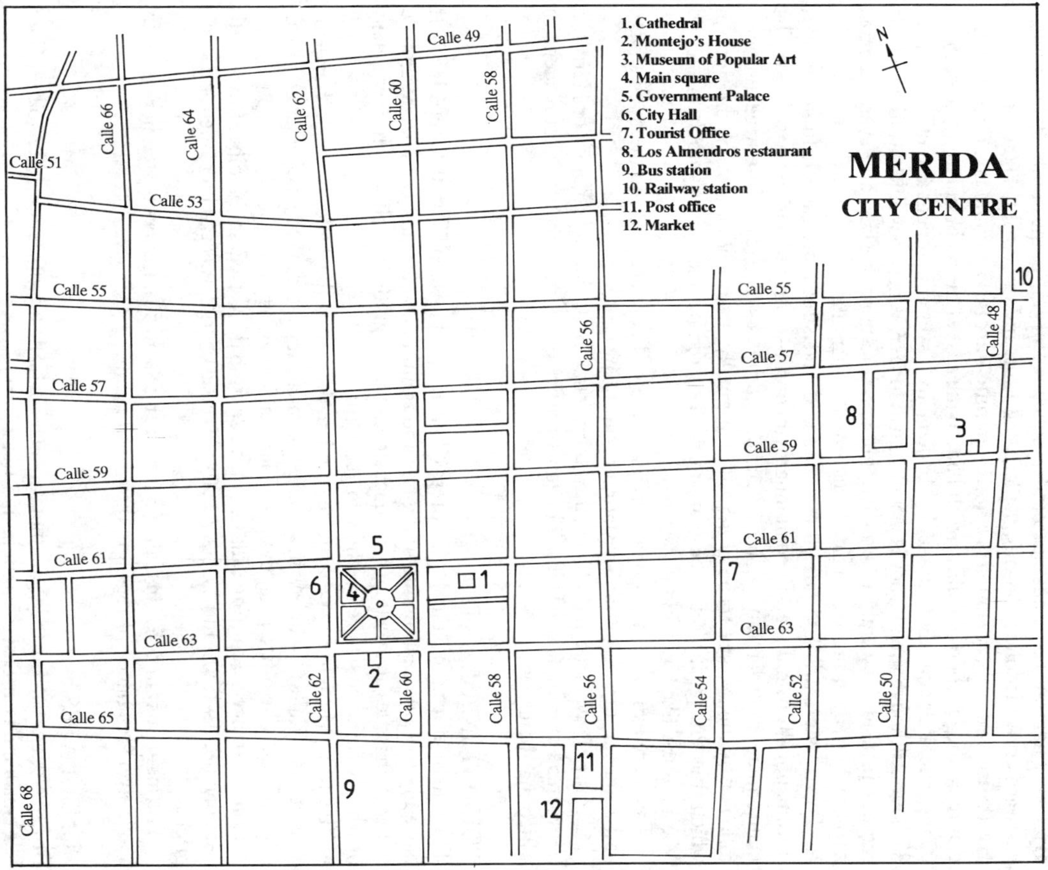

MERIDA
CITY CENTRE

N

1. Cathedral
2. Montejo's House
3. Museum of Popular Art
4. Main square
5. Government Palace
6. City Hall
7. Tourist Office
8. Los Almendros restaurant
9. Railway station
10. Bus station
11. Post office
12. Market

Calle 48

Calle 50

Calle 52

Calle 54

Calle 56

Calle 58

Calle 60

Calle 62

Calle 49

Calle 51

Calle 53

Calle 55

Calle 57

Calle 59

Calle 61

Calle 63

Calle 64

Calle 66

Calle 68

Calle 65

By Bus: The bus station is in Calle 62 between 65 and 67, two blocks south of the main square. Efficient first-class buses connect Mérida with almost every major city in the republic, including Campeche (2½ hrs), Cancún (5 hrs) and Valladolid (3 hrs). An over-night bus to Palenque leaves at 23.30, taking about 10 hrs.

By Car: Highway 180 leads in from Campeche (160 km) in the south and continues eastwards to Valladolid (160 km), Cancún (320 km) and the Caribbean coast.

By Train: The railway station is a hot 15-minute walk (or 5-minute taxi ride) from the centre, at the junction of Calles 48 and 55, to the east of the main square. The train for Campeche, Palenque and ultimately Mexico City leaves at midnight and officially takes 37 hours, although the journey is usually much longer. Where possible, avoid it and use the bus instead. The train is crowded, hot and interminably slow, and even the most hardened of adventure seekers have regretted embarking on it.

In Town: Mérida is laid out on a simple grid and streets are named functionally if unromantically by number. Even numbers run north–south and odd run east–west. The main square is bordered by 60, 61, 62 and 63. Addresses tend to give the street number, followed by the two streets on either side. Originally, areas were known by the trade in which they engaged. Today these are marked by red plaques with symbols of the old Maya names, like birds and butterflies.

Taxis are expensive and do not circulate freely. There are ranks in the main square and at the airport. Hotels and restaurants can easily call them up.

Car hire is available at Budget at the Holiday Inn (Av Colón, tel 255453) or Hertz (55 between 54 and 56, tel 249333). The tourist office has a list of reputable local agencies which may be cheaper.

TOURIST INFORMATION

The tourist office is next to the Contreras Theatre (60 between 57 and 59, tel 49389). It has a mass of information, including bus and train timetables, and can change money, too. It even issues an excellent free magazine, a tourist guide in itself, which gives details of what is going on where and how to get there.

Visas for Mexico can be acquired or lengthened in the Delegación de Servicios Migratorios (Calle 60 with 49, in a small shopping alleyway marked Pasaje Camino Real, tel 216714). The office is on the first floor, halfway down.

Long-distance **telephone** calls can be made from the Caseta sin Nombre (on 59 with 64; open 08.00–13.00 and 17.00–20.00). Reverse-charge calls can be made for a small price.

The main **post office** is in Calle 65 (between 58 and 56). Letters posted here have an above-average chance of reaching their destination.

CONSULATES

British citizens can use the Canadian consulate in Calle 62 with Colón (tel 256299). The US consulate is at Paseo Montejo 453 (tel 255011).

WHAT TO SEE

The Spanish founded the city of Mérida in 1542 on the ruined remains of the original Maya city of Ichkansiho or Ti'ho, which had flourished along with Uxmal and Izamal from AD 300 to 900. The conquistadors used the stone from a quadrangle lined with pyramids to furnish the centre of their city with a Franciscan monastery and the fortress home of Francisco de Montejo, the conqueror of the Yucatán. Both were built on the bases of pyramids. Mérida was so named by the Spanish in the hope that it would rival the statuesque beauty of its namesake in Extremadura, Spain.

Plaza Mayor

The Plaza Mayor or main square buzzes to the gossip of shoe shiners, newspaper vendors and hammock touters, framed by rich green laurels (a present from Cuba) and hemmed in by some of the oldest buildings in the republic. Old men shaded by panama hats or young lovers sit face to face on the S-shaped seats on every corner, known as *confidenciales*. Here nothings can be whispered in public, respectably.

On the east side of the square, the **Cathedral of San Idelfonso** dominates with its huge ungainly front. The oldest cathedral in Mexico, it was built from a desecrated Maya temple and finished in 1598. The enormous cost of building it was divided between the Crown, the Spanish landowners and the unfortunate Maya who were forced to contribute a large percentage of their already stretched budget. More fortress than house of God, it is imbued with a firm stamp of power, allowing little time for fripperies or decoration. The campaniles on top of its towers were added later, with a complete disregard for proportion between them and the heavy base.

The tall front implies a far greater height than actually exists inside, where heavy arches support hemispherical vaults and curious crisscross coffering. The plain interior conforms to a severe Counter-Reformation style, struggling in a heavy-handed way to be neoclassical. Most of the valuables were either looted or burnt during the Revolution. The sparse decoration focuses the eye on the vast 20-metre-high wooden Christ which hangs above the altar and was a present from Spain.

On the southern side of the square, the **Casa de Montejo** overshadows the cathedral with its extraordinarily decorative plateresque portal. This important example of 16th-century civil architecture now belongs to Banamex and its interior can be seen during banking hours. Dated 1549, it was built by a native master-mason and is renowned for the number of naively carved portraits included on its facade. The ground level is the earliest part of the building. The top corners of the door hold the portraits of a bearded old man and a young woman: it is debatable whether these are of Montejo and his wife, as the figure of the bearded man is repeated elsewhere. The keystone is a grotesque man, also bearded, who seems to support the weight of the whole structure on his back.

Above the doorway is the equivalent of a heraldic tapestry, carved in stone. This is a no-holds-barred reminder of who conquered whom. The pilasters framing the window are embellished with the caryatid figures of warriors in armour, standing on the heads of vanquished demons—the Maya. Each conquistador wears a helmet, morion and cuirass and holds a halberd and sword. They are flanked by two 'hairy men' carrying clubs and wearing the artist's representation of a close-fitting sheepskin suit, a common theme in medieval sculpture.

Another 16th-century mansion, the **Palacio Municipal**, is on the west side of the square. More interesting is the 19th-century **Palacio de Gobierno** on the north, with its startlingly graphic murals by Fernando Castro Pacheco. With a horrifying simplicity,

463

using shadowy colours, he portrayed the history of the state as a ghostly nightmare of subjection and domination.

From the Plaza Mayor to Paseo Montejo

Calle 60 leads north from the main square, past some of Mérida's older buildings. **Plaza Sta Lucia** is pleasant leafy square with a small unadorned church, where Mass is held in English on Saturdays at 18.00. Its cemetery was originally for negro and mulatto slaves.

Paseo Montejo, the self-styled Champs Elysées of Mérida, leads north from Calle 47. This wide boulevard is lined with *fin de siècle* mansions, set in well-appointed gardens where French topiary vies with Moorish arches built by nostalgic Levantines. It was built with much razzmatazz at the turn of the century, and generally believed to epitomize European elegance. Porfirio Díaz was brought down from Mexico City to open it in 1906: unfortunately, the Yucatán was then so isolated from the rest of the country that no-one recognized the diminutive president and the whole affair was a damp squib. A mishmash of fast-food restaurants, group hotels and tawdry discos now jostles for space amongst the mansions.

Museo de Arte Popular

(West of the main square, on 59 with 50 and 48; open 08.00–20.00, Tues–Sat; 09.00–13.00, Sun; closed Mon.)

The Museum of Popular Art is one of the greatest unsung treasures of Mérida. Nothing, not even a sign, announces from the outside that there is anything to see within. It stands opposite an abandoned military barracks, where crumbling arches and colonnades cringe around a green expanse, as gates flap listlessly in the wind.

The museum is a ramshackle jumble of local arts and crafts. Every room leads to a discovery—of hammock looms, local embroidery or basketwork, all with a distinctly abandoned feel. Naive paintings on the walls portray the village where each individual craft was made. A precarious recreation of a spartan *campesino* hut is filled with papier-mâché models of the family—the baby in a hammock and the children staring aimlessly into space. Best of all is the shop behind, which is crammed with bits and pieces from the Yucatán and from all over the republic. As always with these government-run shops, the prices are fair and the selection enormous.

Anthropology Museum

(North of the main square, off 59; open 08.00–20.00, Tues–Sun.)

Housed in the ex-penitentiary between the zoo and the Centenario park, this museum covers the whole Yucatán peninsula. Its exhibits range from a description of the evolution of the prehistoric limestone peninsula, which was probably attached to Cuba and Florida, to samples from some of the 2500 sites found in the area. Many of the pieces are replicas of originals which can still be found *in situ* on the sites. Recreations of the brightly coloured stuccoed sculptures, which would have ornamented the outsides of buildings, breathe life into the weather-washed ruins that now remain.

HAMMOCKS

Mérida is the hammock centre of the world. As they are light and easy to carry, it is worth buying some here—for a jungle trip, a budget trip or just a siesta back home. Avoid street vendors unless you know exactly what you're looking for. It is best to go to **Poblana** (65 with 60), where hammocks line the shop from floor to ceiling in every colour and size. Artificial fabrics wear out quickly and are uncomfortable to sleep in: look for henequen, sisal or cotton. A well-made hammock should survive six to seven years of constant use. Make sure that it is tightly woven, with five-thread strands, so that fingers can't slip through easily. A double for a Maya is a single for most others and it best to try to get the biggest size possible (you should be able to lie across the hammock, not just lengthways). Poblana charge a reasonable price and are generous with advice.

MARKET

The market (Calle 56, between 65 and 67) is four whole blocks of all that moves, including live beetles encrusted with semiprecious jewels, to be worn as brooches. It is big, brash and mostly tacky, but filled with the chatter of Maya from the women who bring their fruit and vegetables in from the villages. Its scope ranges from leather goods and ceramics to fruit and vegetables, animals and birds, the good, the bad, the legal and the illegal. The portals behind the post office are a good place to start looking for hammocks, sandals, shirts, hats and other traveller's requisites.

OTHER SHOPPING

Mérida is also the home of the *guayabera* shirt, the panama hat, and the traditional Maya *ipil* or *huipil* (a white dress bordered with floral embroidery). **Camisería Narvay** (62, just off the main plaza) has a good selection of *guayaberas*. The best are made of pure linen, though a cotton mix is cheaper and many Mexicans wear pure polyester. Genuine Panama hats are made of jipijapa palm: when rolled into a cigar shape, they will spring back into position undamaged. (Beware of doing this to imitations, which will unfurl full of jagged holes.) There is a selection of shops under the portals in the main square.

Huipiles are worn by women everywhere, particularly in the market which is a good place to start looking for them. The best are hand-embroidered and made of cotton, though most women use the cheaper more durable polyester, garishly embroidered by machine.

Coral, conch and tortoiseshell are widely on sale, but all are endangered species.

NIGHTLIFE

Mérida has several clubs for dancing or listening to the heady mix of Yucatecan and Cuban rhythms. Try **Ixta'Pi** (in Calle 60 with 55) for salsa and regional music. **Picadilly**, in front of the post office, is where young people go to dance salsa (Mon–Thur), on a dance floor behind the restaurant. The **Trobador Bohemio** (in Calle 55, Sta Lucia) is better still—a bit of a dive where Mexican musicians sing of love, the city and women. Trios play romantic music at the more formal **El Lugar** in Paseo Montejo, opposite the Palacio Cantón.

THE WEEK AT A GLANCE

Mérida looks after its visitors well and has laid on something for them to do or see every day of the week. It isn't just for the tourists: the Mexican love of a fiesta means that locals easily outnumber foreigners.

On **Monday** the main plaza is the setting for *vaquerías*, feet-stamping dances to the beat of a *jaranera* band, which come from the ranches. All along the Gulf coast from Veracruz to the Yucatán, the emphasis is on movement from the waist down. To prove their proficiency, men and women will shake their hips and click their heels in a frenzy of rhythm, while balancing glasses of water on their heads. The dances start at 21.00 and are free.

On **Tuesday** at 21.00, at the Teatro Peón Contreras (next to the tourist office), the Ballet Folklórico of the university dance a lively mixture of Spanish, Aragonese, Yucatecan and Cuban steps, which are all part of the mixed cultural heritage. The seats are unnumbered so it's a good idea to get there early. The performance lasts 1½ hrs and costs a small sum. Alternatively, trios, solos and orchestras play Latin-American music in the Parque Santiago (59 with 72) at 21.00. Free.

On **Wednesday**, the Casa de la Cultura (Calle 63 with 64 and 66) hosts a variety of events. Free.

On **Thursday** at 21.00, the Teatro Sta Clara puts on an extravaganza of music, dance and poetry, including the *Harana Yucateca* (a mix of Maya and Aragonese steps danced by couples). Free. Alternatively, Parque Sta Lucia (60 with 59) resounds to folk music with the *Serenata Yucateca*, when trios and solos sing of broken hearts and lost hopes. It is very roots Mexican and free.

On **Friday** at 21.00, the university puts on a free show of regional ballet in its central patio (60 with 57).

On **Sunday** from 10.00 to 22.00 the full length of Calle 59 from Parque Sta Lucia to the main square explodes with lively events, including the police orchestra blowing their brasses in Sta Lucia at 11.00, marimba in Parque Hidalgo at 11.30 and a representation of a traditional Yucatecan wedding in the Palacio Municipal at 13.00. There are also two morning markets, one in Plaza Sta Lucia and the other in 62 with 63.

WHERE TO STAY   (area code 999)
Mérida offers a rich choice for those who want something out of the ordinary without being out of pocket. Many mansions which were once the family homes of fabulously rich henequen barons have now become hotels, in varying states of repair.

Of these, the first to head for is the quirky ****Trinidad** (62 with 55 and 57, tel 213029 and 232033) where 20 colonial rooms harbour a haphazard collection of antique furniture, including wrought-iron bedsteads and Art Deco lamps. All the rooms are different and lead off a maze of courtyards, surrounded by a jungle of a garden. The indomitable doyenne of the establishment is Srita Lulu, who presides over the small café with great panache, wearing slightly too much make-up and a wide smile. As she serves up piping hot coffee and granola with yoghurt for breakfast, she entertains her guests with tales of a racy past or advice on out-of-the-way haunts.

The ******Casa de Balam** (Calle 60 No 488, tel 248844, fax 245011) has been refurbished in the best of taste, with handwoven curtains, Moorish arches, fountains, rich red floor tiles, local ceramics and carved door lintels. Its discreet swimming pool is hidden away in a small walled garden overhung with tropical drapery. With only 48 rooms it manages the difficult blend of efficiency and charm. Opposite, the ******Misión** (Calle 60, no 491, tel 239500, tlx 753835) is larger and less intimate, and often invaded by tour groups. The rooms are cool, with a comforting Scandinavian simplicity.

The ****Calinda Panamericana (59 with 52, tel 239111) has an impressively sweeping entrance, though the rooms behind belie the promise of faded colonial charm, being large, modern and comfortable. Proper bath tubs are supplied with lashings of hot water. The large swimming pool is next to a café, where the waiters in mufti will cheerfully overcharge.

The extraordinary ***Posada Toledo (58 with 57, tel 231690) has scarcely changed since it was refurbished by wealthy *haciendados* at the turn of the century. The family moved out a couple of decades ago, leaving behind a master bedroom filled with French furniture, a dining room lined with family portraits, and a patio overhung with clinging plants. The ***Gran Hotel (Calle 60 in Parque Hidalgo, behind the cathedral, tel 242622) claims to be the first purpose-built hotel in the Americas. The lovely old rooms are set around a flower-filled courtyard, linked by open passageways filled with an eclectic mixture of heavy 1930s furniture, old radios, Art Deco spitoons and birds in cages. Its neighbour, the ***Caribe (tel 249022), occupies an ex-college for priests of San Idelfonso—pleasant enough, though popular with loud groups. The main advantage of the ***Dolores Alba (Calle 63, no 464, tel 213745) is that rooms can be booked here for its sister hotel outside Chichén-Itzá. The 1920s-style ***Colón (62 with 57, tel 234355) was once reputedly a place of assignation. Its eggshell-blue facade is reminiscent of an Odeon cinema, and it still boasts 11 oriental tiled steam baths. Sadly, the rooms don't live up to its racy past, having been badly modernized.

Archaeologists and anthropologists desert pre-Hispanic ruins and villages for the colonial comforts of the **Reforma (Calle 59, tel 247922), at rock-bottom prices. Large high-ceilinged rooms with wooden doors and slatted blinds are set around an open patio, and it has a refreshing pool. The rooms on the street side can be noisy but are often the only ones available.

The *Mucuy (57, no 481, tel 211037) is family-run, basic and extremely clean. Shelves are well stocked with English books and there is a big garden to sit and read them in. The hotel organizes cheap tours to the sites.

The best budget buy in Mérida is a small, unnamed (CE) Casa de Huespédes (in 62 near the main square). This once elegant mansion was stripped of most of its fine furniture during the Revolution. What remains are high whitewashed rooms with large beds and fans whirring overhead, set on the first floor above a wide courtyard, with rocking chairs, tables and spitoons on the balconies outside. The only drawback is the queue for the one communal bathroom.

EATING OUT

Many consider the regional cuisine of the Yucatán to be the best in Mexico. Certainly, for any foreigner who hasn't acquired a taste for tongue-scorching chilli, its lack of hot spices and generous use of fruit comes as a gentle relief. The distinctive ebony-black beans of the south come, fried, with nearly every dish. Other regional specialities are *sopa de lima* (a chicken soup filled with slices of chicken and avocado and spiced with lime), *papadzules* (chopped egg and pumpkin seed rolled in a tortilla and covered in a tomato sauce), *pollo pibil* (chicken marinaded in annatto, Seville orange, pepper, garlic and cumin and baked in banana leaves), *relleno negro* (chicken or turkey stuffed with pork and covered in a dark sauce of oregano and other spices) or *poc chuc* (charcoal-grilled pork marinaded in bitter orange and served with a tomato and onion sauce).

There are four major immigrant groups in Mérida. The Lebanese came after the First World War and set themselves up as grocers, businessmen and moneylenders. The Koreans and Chinese worked on the henequen plantations, while the Arabs quietly made money, surprising the Méridans with their business acumen. Consequently, restaurants in Mérida cater for every kind of taste. Although there are no top-class restaurants, good home cooking is readily available, usually served in modest surroundings, with a wide range of Yucatecan, Mexican, Lebanese, French and international dishes.

Moderately Expensive

The Breton owner is also the chef in **Yannig** (62 between 57 and 59; open 17.00–23.30 and also for Sunday lunch; check with the tourist office, as his lease runs out soon and he may move to new premises). He keeps news from France pasted in the window, from the winner of the Tour de France to the progress of the Channel Tunnel, and cooks with aplomb, mixing Mexican ingredients with French *je ne sais quoi*. Try *crevettes Yanig* (shrimps cooked in cream, wine and ginger) or crêpes filled with fried plantains, breast of chicken, cream and marinaded onion. Meals are served in a small garden at the back or on tables at the front, beneath Toulouse-Lautrec posters.

Muelle 8 at the northern end of Paseo Montejo (Calle 21, no 142, tel 274976) offers a range of seafood, from jumbo shrimps, huge avocados stuffed with lobster, and smoked red-snapper pâté to fillets of fish smothered in garlic or fried in butter. The restaurant in the hotel **Casa del Balam** (Calle 60) is well regarded, serving good steaks as well as local specialities such as *cochinita pibil* (pork roasted in banana leaves, covered in an orange and chilli sauce).

Moderate

For real Yucatecan cooking, try **Los Almendros** (Plaza de Mejorada, tel 12851) for original *campesino* recipes such as the traditional *pollo ticuleño* (chicken with fried beans, tomato sauce, sweet peas, red peppers, slices of fried banana, ham and cheese) or *pavo en escabeche de pueblo* (baked turkey with black pepper marinaded in a garlic sauce). It is unpretentious and always full, particularly popular for big family Sunday lunches. If you can't get a table here, two other Yucatecan restuarants to try are **El Tucho** (60 with 55, tel 242323) or **Jaraneros** (56A with Paseo Montejo, tel 279856).

Patio Español in Parque Hidalgo is part of the Gran Hotel and hasn't changed much since the 1940s, with tiled floors and tables sheathed in white. Waiters bring plates of paella, squid and *poc chuc*. The front of **El Faisán y el Venado** (59 with 82) is studded with Maya figures but its food is contemporary, relying on a few, well prepared dishes such as *cochinita pibil* and *escabeche*. A comida corrida is available at lunchtime. The **Tulipanes** (Calle 42) has been around a long time and is set in a big tropical garden with a *cenote*. The food is Yucatecan (lots of chicken, banana and rice) but the main interest is provided by the evening show, when actors reenact a human sacrifice, with music and dancing. It now gets the tour groups. Just before Plaza Sta Lucia, **Portals** is a small Lebanese-run restaurant, serving chick peas and *köfte*, and a delicious *berenjena al orno* (rich aubergines baked in the oven). **La Casona** (Calle 60) has a pretty pink facade, with a large open doorway and the long tall windows typical of 19th-century Mérida, when stuccoed reliefs and fussy decoration became more fashionable than plain colonial. It serves home-made pasta washed down with wines from Tuscany.

Cheap
The best place for breakfasts, morning coffee and people-watching throughout the day is the **Express**, opposite the Parque Hidalgo. When it first opened in 1937, the presence of any foreigner meant that a ship had just come in and was a source of considerable excitement. Today, foreigners are easily assimilated into the confusion which reigns daily, as plates piled high with tropical fruit or frothy coffees find their way from table to table. Service is languorous but worth the wait. For breakfast, try *huevos motuleños* (a crisp tortilla layered with rich black beans, tomato sauce, peas, ham and avocado, and topped with a fried egg and cheese).

The smaller **La Carreta** (62 next to Yannig, tel 214633) appears to have remained in the 1930s, with heavy furniture and an original Art Deco interior. The menu ranges from shrimps with champagne to beer and eggs. **Cafeteria Pop** (57 between 60 and 62, tel 216844) is a modern black and white café, its chrome counter dominated by a mural of three Yucatecan faces. Customers read their papers as they eat pastries, sandwiches and salads. There are plenty of cafés around the main square: those upstairs have good views of evening performances. **El Cangrejito** (57 between 64 and 66) serves nothing more than tacos as they should be and is always popular.

Vegetarian
Ananda Maya Gynza (Calle 59 between 60 and 62, tel 282451; open 12.00–10.00, closed Sun) is blandly vegetarian but soothingly situated, with tables under a shady tree in a pleasant courtyard. An alternative is **Naturalmente** (Calle 64 between 57 and 59), whose small menu puts its vegetables to good use.

South along the Puuc Route

Over a thousand years ago, the Puuc hills, a low rise on the flat landscape of the Yucatán, were a major Maya population centre. The region prospered despite the lack of any surface water, for miles around. The Maya overcame this problem by catching the rainfall in *chultunes* or underground cisterns, which were carved into the limestone floor and plastered within.

Uxmal is the most important site in the region, and still the most spectacular. Kabah, Sayil, Xlapak and Labná are all close by, and the caves of Loltún are only a few km further east. It would be impractical to attempt to cover all these sites in one day, especially if relying on public transport. If time is short, concentrate on Uxmal, as the other sites have only one notable building apiece.

GETTING AROUND
Uxmal is 78 km south of Mérida, on Highway 261, the slow road to Campeche. Second-class buses leave Mérida's main terminal every 2 hours from 07.00, passing the ruins 1½ hours later. Return buses are, at best, erratic. They should leave from the driveway of the Hacienda Uxmal at 12.00, 15.00, 18.00 and 19.30 but are often delayed on the long Campeche road. Many people resort to hitching back with other tourists. Alternatively, take a standard tour, which includes the return journey, the services of a

guide, and tickets to the Sound and Light show (ask at the tourist office in Mérida, tel 249290). A local bus links Uxmal with Ticul every 2 hours, via Santa Elena.

Kabah is 21 km southeast of Uxmal, on Highway 261 and on the route of the same second-class bus (although it is not an official stop). There are no local buses to the other Puuc sites (Sayil, Xlapak and Labná) or to the caves of Loltún, and hitching can be difficult. For those without a car, hired cars, tours or taxis are the only answer.

Uxmal

There is little that can compete with an early morning glimpse of Uxmal. It is possibly the most gracious and exquisite of all Maya sites. The hard light of the Yucatán reflects and

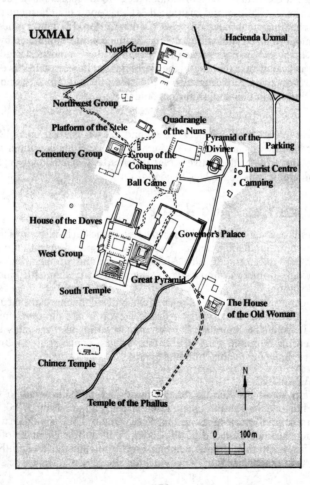

plays with the geometric designs incised on the warm golden stone of the pyramids and quadrangles. Elaborate filigree patterns and friezes, similar to those at Mitla in Oaxaca, lock together to form a mosaic facade. Double-headed serpents coil and writhe over the masonry. In this tinder-dry land the Rain God, Chac, is omnipresent. On every corner and every facade, the jutting angular features of his masks leap out, intoning the longing for rain.

History
Uxmal was founded in the 6th century AD. Although the late-coming Xiú dynasty, who ruled the site from the 11th century, belatedly took the credit for Uxmal's rise to prominence, the majority of the structures were completed by 10th-century Maya, long before the upstart Xiús were on the scene. The Xiú engineered the short-lived League of Mayapán between the great cities of Chichén-Itzá, Mayapán and Uxmal. When it collapsed in 1194, after a battle between the Itzá of Chichén and the Lords of Mayapán, the Xiú dynasty were held as gentlemen hostages in Mayapán, leaving Uxmal to decline. Later, when the Spanish arrived, the Xiú sided with the newcomers and betrayed their fellow Maya. Over 400 years later, the archaeologist, Sylvanus Morley, took the trouble to trace their descent from AD 1000 to the 1940s and discovered the last of the line, Dionisio Xiú, living in marital strife in nearby Ticul.

TOURIST INFORMATION
(Open 08.00–17.00 daily; adm; free Sun.)
The entrance hall houses a small museum and cinema, a restaurant and bookshop, and ice-cream vendors. The **Sound and Light** show begins at 19.00 every evening in the Nunnery Quadrangle (there is no public transport back). A colourful narrative, with musical accompaniment, provides a lively history of love and treachery, while the ruins are lit up as back-drops.

After Chichén, Uxmal is the most visited site in the state. However, the tour buses don't arrive until 10.30, leaving the early morning hours undisturbed.

VISITING THE SITE

PIRAMIDE DEL ADIVINO
'Rising like some New World Tower of Babel', the 30-m-high Pyramid of the Magician looms over the entrance. The base is oval, the edges rounded in a generous curve. It is built on three tiers, with monumental stairways on the east and west faces. The doorway to the temple on the west side is a great yawning Chac mouth, reminiscent of the Chenes style from southern Yucatán which also incorporates genitalia from later non-Maya Toltecs into the design. A long, well-worn chain runs up both stairways, giving courage to the faint-hearted. The steps are less than a shoe's depth and the height is distinctly vertiginous. The uppermost temple has a splendid view over the rest of the site, the swarming tourists and the Puuc hills beyond.

CUADRANGULO DE LAS MONJAS
From the west of the pyramid, a rubble path leads into the Nunnery Quadrangle between the corners of the east- and south-facing buildings (the main entrance is through the large corbelled arch in the south side). Nunnery Quadrangle is a misnomer, derived

from the Spanish notion that it housed the Maya equivalent of the Vestal Virgins. Of the four, long, low, 10th-century structures, the raised **north range** is probably the oldest, judging by the earlier structure beneath it. It is the only one to have roof combs and serpent masks in tiers above the doorway. Monkeys, birds, human figures and Rain God masks are framed by the lattice work. Carvings of traditional thatched huts mount the doorways.

Next in date come the south, the east and finally the west range. The lattice-work on the **east range**, reminiscent of the screen between confessor and sinner, is more sober than that of the north face. Chac masks in tiers mount the central doorway and the corners of the building, hanging over like elephantine water spouts. The frieze of the upper facade comprises six V-shaped designs, made up of eight vertical bands of double-headed serpents. Each of these is studded on the penultimate band with the head of an owl, the bird associated with death.

The **west range** is the most elaborate. A pair of stylized rattlesnakes, added later, wind across the front and a human figure appears from the feathered head of one. This was possibly the divine Quetzalcóatl-Kukulkán, the Wind God, who came to prominence with the arrival of the Toltec-Itzá in the Yucatán.

TOWARDS THE GOVERNOR'S PALACE

From the arch in the south range, a path leads past the sloped **Ball Court**, where the ceremonial ball game was played, up a steep path to an artificially raised platform. Here, the simple **Casa de las Tortugas** is dwarfed by its proximity to the Governor's Palace. This small temple is named after the frieze of turtles on its upper level. Turtles represented yet another cry for water, and were said to grieve with the Maya in droughts, their tears falling as rain. In Maya art the turtle also represents the flat earth surrounded by seas.

PALACIO DEL GOBERNADOR

John Lloyd Stephens came across the unexcavated Governor's Palace in 1840, and wrote:

> There is no rudeness or barbarity in its design or its proportions; on the contrary, the whole wears an air of symmetry and grandeur. If it stood this day on its grand artificial terrace in Hyde Park or the Garden of the Tuileries, it would form a new order ... not unworthy to stand side by side with the remains of Egyptian, Grecian, and Roman art.

This, the most harmonious of Uxmal's structures, is raised up on three man-made terraces, over 100 m long. An undulating mosaic unwinds along it with five stacked Chac masks on each corner, curving round the edges. A reptilian uncoiling from end to end incorporates thatched huts, step frets and human heads. As in the Nunnery and the Dovecot Group, there are 11 entrances leading back into 24 rooms, divided between a long central section and two side sections, linked by recessed arrow-head arches.

Above the main entrance, a figure in a feathered headdress represents Lord Chac the ruler, for whom it was built in the 10th century (unrelated to the divine Chac). Directly in front, but on the terrace below, stands a column and, behind that, a double-headed jaguar. A track, part of an 18-km raised causeway or *sacbe*, leads past a grass-covered pyramid, the **Casa de la Vieja**, which is one of the oldest buildings at Uxmal. It carries on to the **Temple of the Phalli**, where fragments of phallic stone sculptures, perhaps water spouts, litter the ground. The path continues into the thick, thorny scrub beyond, where several more ruins are watched over by birds such as road-runners, orioles, and the blue-crowned mot-mot with its long, naked tail.

THE REST OF THE SITE

Southwest of the Governor's Palace, the **Great Pyramid**'s only remaining temple of four is decorated with Chac masks and macaws (a sun symbol). To the west, **El Palomar**, so called for its latticed roof comb, like a dovecot, has three diminishing courts, leading up to the pyramid and its broad stairway.

To the west of the ball court, a path leads to the **Cemetery Group**, where skulls and crossbones decorate the retaining walls of a platform in the inner courtyard. This may have been a Maya stone equivalent of the *tzompantli* (skull rack), brought down by the Toltecs to display the skulls of sacrificed prisoners. Further north, the path leads back to a platform with eroded stelae and beyond that to the little excavated northern group.

WHERE TO STAY AND EAT (area code 992)

There are four hotels around the site, although most tourists return to Mérida for the night. The most established is the ****Hacienda Uxmal (tel 47142), originally built for archaeologists. Occasionally the elderly owner comes down from Mérida with her sisters and plays her long Yucatecan guitar in the gardens around the swimming pool, where iguanas bask in the sun. Three wings of elegant colonial rooms, with high ceilings and heavy wooden furniture, are set around the garden and pool. The restaurant, however, is over-priced and under-spiced, its fish a frozen disppointment. The excellently run ****Villas Arqueológicas (tel 47053) is right at the entrance to Uxmal—a haven after the heat of the ruins. It has everything from billiard tables to chronological Maya wall-charts. The library is filled with archaeological books, and the rooms are set around a courtyard and swimming pool.

The ****Misión Inn (1 km north, tel 47308) is an eyesore, scandalously granted planning permission within view of the site. Guests who want to take advantage of it should ask for the top floor. With a large garden and pool, it has a tranquil setting for a tour-group hotel. The ***Rancho Uxmal (on Highway 261, the Muna–Uxmal road, 5 minutes by car from the site) is the only cheaper hotel close to the site. The rooms are plain but comfortable, with showers, and the large palapa-roofed restaurant specializes in *poc chuc*. It advertises itself as a trailer park, providing hook-ups and camping space.

For cheaper accommodation, the town of Ticul (30 km east) has a simple hotel on the main square, the *Sierra Sosa, with fans and showers.

The Other Puuc Ruins

Kabah, 21 km south of Uxmal, is an acquired taste. On a wide elevated terrace, the **Palacio de los Mascarones** is festooned with an endless repetition of mesmeric masks of Chac, whose hooked nose was associated with lightning. In front of the palace are a repaired cistern and a small platform decorated with hieroglyphs around its lower edges. Over the road, the well-worn path opens up after 200 m at the foot of an unadorned free-standing arch, which marked the start of the raised causeway leading through the scrub-jungle to Uxmal.

At **Sayil**, 9 km south of Kabah (bear left after 5 km), a beautiful three-tiered **Palace** is mounted on a pyramidal base. The wide doorways are supported by pairs of thick, free-standing columns; over one, a diving figure is flanked by two reptiles. The lower floor is the least well preserved. The recessed upper floor is sectioned off by Chac masks and bamboo-shaped columns built into the wall. These columns were a common feature in Puuc architecture, representing a stylized version of the reeds which were used to construct retaining walls, knotted with fibres, on the traditional Maya thatched huts. This whimsical reference to the humble Maya hut on the facades of the grand palaces and temples kept power in perspective, never far from its origins.

Xlapak is 5 km due east of Sayil. Its principal building, given no more romantic or evocative a name than Structure One, is a classic Puuc temple, 20 m long and 12 wide, with nine rooms on a rectangular base. It was built in two stages: the east facade was literally stuck onto the earlier west facade, with no connecting doorway. Three-tiered Chac masks surmount the doors and corners.

The small site of **Labná**, 3 km to the east, comprises two groups of buildings linked by a raised causeway. On one corner of the palace, the first structure, a great, gaping jaw opens to reveal a human head. Along the causeway, to the left, a pyramidal mound known as the **Mirador** or Lookout rises up above the scrub. On the right is Labná's outstanding legacy: a **monumental arch**, 3 m high and 6 m wide. Unlike the free-standing arch at Kabah, this is sumptuously decorated on both sides. The front is beautifully stylized, carved with Maya huts set against a background of knotted reeds. The back is more sober.

The Caves of Loltún

From Labná, follow the road northeast for 15 km and then bear left at the signpost (5 km). The tourist bumph explains that the caves are 'artistically lighted to enhance their natural beauty': there is also a guide to enhance their natural history, with tall tales and lengthy explanations. Tours start at 09.00, 11.00, 12.30, 14.00 and 15.00, and last over an hour, winding through the 1.5 km of tunnels and huge cavities. By 500 BC, these caves were well-known to the Maya, who initially came for shelter, leaving behind drawings on the walls. They were also used during the 19th-century War of the Castes, as hiding places for fugitives.

The quickest way back to Mérida is via Highway 184, through Oxkutzcab (the great orange-growing centre of the Yucatán) and Ticul; bear north on Highway 261 at Muna.

South along the Colonial Route

For those who tire of ruins or want to slip off the beaten track, this route leads in a loop to the south, winding through Maya hamlets, past working and abandoned haciendas and the fortress-like monasteries of early Franciscan evangelists. The scene has changed little over the centuries. Thick thatched roofs protect the rough-cut stone walls of Maya huts and cottages, and the streets are often dusty and unpaved. All the women, and even the little girls, wear white embroidered shifts, the traditional *huipil*, and carry their washing or shopping nonchalantly on their heads as they walk gracefully back home.

Maya women

The villages in this region are dominated by the huge Moorish facades of abandoned Franciscan monasteries, topped by rounded cupolas, rising tall above the flat limestone. Haunting in their disrepair, they still emanate an aggrieved power, testifying to the bellicose faith of the Spanish, whose genuine, if self-serving, belief was that they conquered in the name of God. For those who can't get enough of ancient cities, Mayapán, an important late-Classic Chontal Maya city, sits to one side of the road, drowning in jungle, largely unexplored and unvisited.

GETTING AROUND
With time and patience this route can be done by local bus or by thumb, but it is strongly advisable to go by car. Take Highway 18 southeast to **Kanasin**, and continue to **Mama** and **Teabo**, before turning west to **Mani**. Then head south to **Oxkutzcab**, before returning north to **Ticul**. (Uxmal and the sites of Sayil, Xlapak and Labná are close by: see The Puuc Route.) From Ticul, Highway 184 leads northwest to **Muna**, from where main Highway 261 heads north to the capital. The whole route is an easy day's journey, by car.

Almost all the churches close between 12.00 and 16.00, although keys can always be found by asking for the sacristan (*sacristano*).

SOME MAYA
The following phrases, transcribed by ear and pronounced with an English accent, may or may not help, but will at least show willing.

Dios bootic tech (dee-os boutique tetch)	Thank you
Bix a be (beesh a bay)	How do you do
Dias	Good day
Patik bim (pat eek beem)	Excuse me (on leaving)
Man	Woman/Señora
Tat	Man/Señor

Phrases are normally used with a title: ie '*Bix a be, man*' or '*Dias, tat*'.

475

WHAT TO SEE

Kanasin, Acanceh and Tecoh

Southeast of Mérida on Highway 18, **Kanasin** is a bustling village with a small 16th-century church, more famed for **Susana International** (Calle 21), a café selling appetite-whetting *antojitos*, where Méridans crowd of a Sunday evening. The road continues past **San Antonio Tehuitz**, where a working hacienda turns henequen to hemp, and on to **Acanceh**. Here past and present converge in the main plaza. The remains of a once resplendent pyramid overlook a 16th-century church in a colonial square, where the trenchantly 20th-century market sells its wares. Some traces of pre-Hispanic frescoes remain, on a stuccoed palace next to the pyramid (similar to the Temple of the Dolls in Dzibilchaltún).

Follow signs from here for **Tecoh**, capital of the Chenes at the time of the conquest, which has a huge abandoned monastery. Ceremonial caves and *cenotes* have recently been discovered in the area, possibly linked with Mayapán which is some 11 km down the road.

Mayapán

This late post-Classic Maya site doesn't stand up to comparison with Uxmal or Palenque and is a pale copy of Chichén-Itzá. Today a sprawling maze of rubble mounds, it was once a byword for all things powerful. In AD 1194 three principal cities formed the League of Mayapán: Uxmal, Chichén-Itzá and Mayapán. The alliance was designed as much to quash rivalry between the three cities as to form a united front against outsiders. Exhausted by a series of wars, Chichén-Itzá subsequently bowed out of the political arena, which was then dominated by Mayapán, with the aid of Aztec mercenaries, until its fall in AD 1450.

Mayapán's rise to power is clothed in mystery. It is thought that Hunac Ceel, Lord of Mayapán, offered himself (or was thrown) into the sacred *cenote* at Chichén-Itzá. To the amazement of the crowds, he surfaced. Claiming to have conversed with the gods, he demanded sovereignty of the area. Doubtless other Machiavellian intrigues went on behind the scenes, but from about 1200 Mayapán emerged as the most powerful city of northern Yucatán. To ensure their loyalty, the chiefs of other cities were forced to reside at Mayapán, where they were closely watched. Surrounded by a thick wall, defended by a private army and with potential enemies kept in check, Hunac Ceel and his descendants retained power for 250 years, before resentment finally erupted and the city was set on fire.

Bishop Landa described the site of Mayapán thus:

> ... surrounded with a very broad stone wall ... leaving in it only two narrow gates. The wall was not very high and in the midst of this enclosure they built their temples, and the largest, which is like that of Chichén-Itzá, they called Kukulkán, and they built another of a round form, with four doors entirely different from all the others in the land ... in this enclosure they built houses for the lords only ...

In fact, archaeologists found twelve gates not two, but surprisingly few temples. They also found porticoed houses built for the merchant class, with kitchens and chapels, and even larders and cages for birds. Some had smaller houses attached, to accommodate servants. More urban than earlier Maya centres, Mayapán lacks any architectural distinction and the entire city was poorly built. It was highly derivative of Chichén-Itzá, even down to the *castillo* in its centre, a smaller copy of the *castillo* in Chichén. It would seem that its inhabitants were an irreligious lot, paying lip service with hastily constructed temples but really concerned with maintaining their empire by force.

Mama

The road continues to **Tekit**, where the 16th-century church has a Moorish facade, firmly stamped with the Spanish crown, and merlons. Inside is an impressive wooden *retablo*, of burnished red with gold filigree.

Mama is a further 7 km south. The village is dominated by a huge church and monastery. Inside the church is a capacious font for baptizing the heathen, hewn from one single piece of stone. In contrast, the fragile pulpit is decorated with delicately painted baskets of flowers, and the altar is flanked by two cane altarpieces, woven like basketwork. The flowing nave is surrounded by faded wooden *retablos* of the saints, painted by local craftsmen, and haloed by wonderful carved frames. The small paintings around the door were also the work of Mayan sculptors. In the large garden at the back of the church, a round cupola covers a well, known as a *noria*. The monks would have used a mule to draw up the water, to irrigate their gardens. By appropriating the local well, they forced the locals to come to the monastery for water, which enabled them to extract penances at the same time.

Teabo

The road from Mama to Teabo passes through **Chumayel**, notable mainly because the *Chilam Balam*, the priestly bible of the Maya (see Mani), was found there. In **Teabo**, tall painted houses exude an air of erstwhile prosperity, once the property of doctors and lawyers. The 17th-century Franciscan monastery is the finest of all the monasteries in the region, built a century later than the others, when aesthetics rather than defence was the primary concern. It has delicate porticoes outside, and a number of *retablos* and paintings within. The pulpit is covered in a fretwork of diamonds in squares, while the *retablo* above the altar bears the crossed-arm symbol of the Franciscans.

Mani

Some 12 km west of Teabo, Mani has one of the oldest convents in the area, built by the Franciscans in 1549, only two years after they arrived. Of all the churches on the route, this is the one to head for, as it is the best preserved.

The area was originally ruled by Tutul-Xiú, a powerful Maya leader who allied with the conquistador Francisco de Montejo, thereby enabling the Spanish to conquer the area. They were obviously impressed by his capital of Mani, the largest city they encountered in the Yucatán, which had risen to power after the fall of Mayapán. When the Franciscans established themselves soon after the conquest, they brought with them the notorious Bishop Diego de Landa. In 1562, before being returned to Spain for gross maltreatment of the Maya, de Landa conducted a public ceremony in the town, in which he burnt all the traces of the Maya culture that he could find. He thereby single-handedly destroyed the greatest collection of Maya documents ever assembled, whose substance archaeologists are still trying to piece together today. In an attempt to redress the damage, jaguar priests, the high priests of the Maya, subsequently wrote their own history in the five books of *Chilam Balam*, using Latin characters under the auspices of benign priests. The *Chronicle of Mani* is one of the most important of these books, detailing the main historical events of the city.

Mani's monastery looks distinctly fort-like, its thick smooth walls crowned with battlements. The simple interior is hung with outstanding *retablos*, depicting the benign qualities of the conquistadors in elaborate detail—the Franciscans were determined to thrust home the message that God was on the side of the Spanish conquest. The tiny museum of religious artefacts at the back contains two small *serafinas* or portable organs that the friars took with them. The murals in the cloisters have been recently restored. Outside, the open *noria* now fills the swimming pool for the incumbent padre. Under the arches next door, sinners were imprisoned on trumped-up charges, during the in-quisition conducted under the auspices of Diego de Landa.

Around the corner, a small restaurant, **El Principe Tutul-Xiú** offers a limited menu of regional dishes such as *poc chuc* (spicy pork) and *relleno negro* (stuffed turkey). Cheap.

Oxkutzcab

Oxkutzcab is the orchard of the Yucatán, and its big fruit and vegetable market engulfs most of its centre. The streets are weighed down with piles of enormous avocados, juicy mangoes and the psychedelic pink and green pitaya. Around the bustle, yellow tricycles swarm, waiting for passengers and bags to taxi around. These taxis cost next to nothing and are a quick way of seeing the centre.

The church peers over the market from behind iron railings, entered through a double Moorish arch. Its facade is carved with 17th-century symbols of the sun and moon, and an inscription dated 6091 (1609: it was put in upside down by masons unfamiliar with Western script). Inside, three naves, stripped bare, are dominated by an elaborate altar *retablo* which fills a whole wall. Over the painted wooden pulpit a fragile crown teeters, symbolic of Spain's nebulous hold.

Ticul

Shoe factory upon shoe factory line the streets of Ticul. Lest visitors should miss them, huge ceramic boots sit proudly under the 'Welcome to Ticul' signs in every direction. Even if you don't want to shop, it is worth stopping in the town to taste the home-cooking of **Los Almendros** (just off the plaza, on Calle Principal, tel 20021). This is the most famous and the first of three family-run restaurants (the others are in Mérida and Cancún). Fans whir in the dining room, with its red-beamed high ceiling and black and white tiled floor. Families flock in for lunch, usually either chicken or turkey. Try drinking *xtabentun*, a local drink made from the *xtabentun* flower, mixed with anise and honey.

Hacienda Yaxcopoil

(Open 08.00–sunset, Tue–Sat; 09.00–13.00, Sun; closed Mon; adm.)

Some 12 km beyond Muna on the Mérida road (Highway 180), the hacienda announces itself to passing traffic with a distinctive double Moorish arch outside the main house. The family left in the 1950s and the interior has been kept exactly as it was, as if they had merely left to go to Mérida for the day. The white tiled kitchen is filled with copper pans, the more formal dining room with French, English and Japanese china. Originally the hacienda's grounds extended to 9000 hectares. It has its own chapel, orchard and corral, as well as extensive outbuildings for storing and working the vital crop of henequen. A small shop sells local honey and upmarket souvenirs.

WHERE TO STAY
This whole route can be done in a day from Mérida or Uxmal. Alternatively, there are a couple of simple hotels in Ticul, including the *Sierra Sosa on the main square.

North to Dzibilchaltún and Progreso

North of Mérida is the Gulf coast. Just before the peninsula falls into the sea come the early Maya ruins of Dzibilchaltún and the happy-go-lucky port of Progreso, the largest town on the coast. The Yucatán beaches are not worth writing home about but do provide relief from the heat of Mérida. With the turquoise waters of the Caribbean only a few hours' drive away, 95 per cent of foreigners give this coast a miss. Yucatecans, however, prefer it for just that reason: it is thoroughly Mexican without any infiltration of dollars.

GETTING AROUND
Dzibilchaltún is 20 km north of Mérida. By car, follow the first sign to Universidad del Mayab off Highway 261 (a right turn after the golf club, 15 km from Mérida) but keep right at the second. The ruins are 5 km off the highway.

Progreso is 36 km north of Mérida, via Calle 60 and the dual carriageway Highway 261.

Progreso-bound buses leave Mérida from Calles 62 and 67, every 20 minutes until 20.00. Only four a day go direct to Dzibilchaltún (30 minutes). Local buses from Progreso make sporadic journeys along the coast (approximately every 90 minutes).

WHAT TO SEE

Dzibilchaltún
(Open 08.00–17.00; closed Mon.)
The Maya site of Dzibilchaltún has few visitors, despite its proximity to Mérida, and only one notable building. It was one of the longest continually inhabited sites—from 1500 BC to the time of the Spanish conquest, and also one of the largest—with an estimated population of over 50,000 and more than 8000 structures. Only a fraction of the whole has been uncovered. The **Cenote Xlacah**, with a maximum depth of 40 m, was dredged by a National Geographic team in 1958. They found over 6000 artefacts, including human skeletons, which implied that, like Chichén, it was used for sacrifices.

To the left of the *cenote* and the entrance, a towering Roman arch is all that remains of a Spanish church begun in 1591. To the left of the church, an uncovered temple has an L-shaped tomb. Here the 7th-century Stela 19, of a man holding a manikin sceptre (the symbol of office) in his right hand, was crudely slashed in half to bolster up a falling wall in a structure erected 70 years later.

A broad causeway formed the principal thoroughfare around which the other buildings were placed. Only the **Temple of the Seven Dolls** stood directly in the middle of it, still graced with nine large masks. Named after the deformed doll-like clay figures found there, it has the unusual addition of windows (two facing east, two west and one high up in the inner temple).

Progreso and the Yucatán Coast

At Progreso, beach houses line the broad stretch of sand. A road follows the coast eastwards for 79 km, passing only growing hamlets and ending at Dzilam de Bravo. To the west is the new resort of Yucalpetén and, 27 km further along, the deteriorating village of Sisal, formerly the centre of the henequen rope trade.

Under an hour's drive from Mérida, Progreso is easily accessible for weekends and day trips. It was once an important international port, the gateway for henequen exportation, with more shipping lines to New Orleans than to Veracruz. After the collapse of the henequen industry in the 1920s, Progreso declined. More recently, it has been rediscovered by cruise liners and merchant ships serving Mérida. Yucatán's limestone shelf sinks only gradually into the sea, and so a 6-km-long pier has had to be built into the Gulf, at mind-boggling expense, to give modern ships the depth they need.

WHERE TO STAY   (area code 993)

Summer weekends are packed in Progreso, but throughout the rest of the year there are always rooms available in a few modest boarding houses. The tourist office in Progreso (Calle 30, no 176, tel 50104) has a list of cottages for rent. The **Tropical Suites** (Av Malecón and Calle 70, tel 51263) has basic seaside rooms with modern bathrooms, and makes a big effort to be tidy. The **Real del Mar**, close by, is a similar family-run establishment.

A few km to the west in Yucalpetén is the *****Fiesta Inn (tel 50300, fax 50699), signposted from the Zócalo and the flagship of a rejuvenating Progreso. At this Marbella-inspired marina, expensive yachts line up like cars outside a motel. Right on the beach, it gets knocked for six by hurricanes (the hotel minibus once landed up in the dining room).

At the other end of the scale, 55 km east in Chabihau, is an unnamed camping hotel with hammock hooks and showers in the concrete-walled rooms. Dzilam also has a very modest place to stay.

EATING OUT

Although there are any number of fish restaurants in Progreso, the better ones are in the next-door village of **Chixulub**, where the patrons bring a selection of the daily catch to the table. This might include lobster, cod's roe, squid, bream or skate, and will be cooked exactly as you want it. **Los Tiburónes** and **El Moctezuma** are the two to go for. Moderate.

West to Celestún

West of Mérida, on a sandy strip of the Gulf coast, Celestún is the only village in a large natural park and bird sanctuary, famous for its flamingos. It lives in a haphazard way from the proceeds of fishing, bird-watchers and summer visitors. Despite the wide, inviting sandy beach, the flamingos and the cheap seafood cafés, its charm is, at best, tawdry.

GETTING AROUND
Celestún is an easy day-trip by bus from Mérida. Buses take 1½ hrs, leaving Mérida from Calles 50 and 67, every hour on the hour until 14.00 and every 2 hours until 22.00.

By car, it is not so easy. Take the dual carriageway (Highway 180) south to Umán, turn right down Calle 21 (just before the church) to **Oxlom** (with an overgrown hacienda) and continue straight through **Samahil** (a village of whitewashed walls with a salmon-pink church) and **Kinchil**. Finally, after Kinchil, there is a sign to Celestún, 49 km away on Highway 281. Sundays, July, August, Christmas and Easter are all busy times: mid-week is generally better.

FLAMINGOS
Flamingos are hounded in Celestún. From 08.00 to 16.00, boat loads leave from the bridge across the estuary to distract the desperately feeding birds (see Río Lagartos). On a Sunday, they will be made to fly and show their plumage hundreds of times. In addition, the boats churn up the estuary bed, destroying a great deal of their natural food. Unfortunately, until controls are introduced, nothing can be done to stop it. The estuary is also visited by some 230 different species of birds, of which the most easily seen are pelicans, herons, cormorants and egrets.

WHERE TO STAY AND EAT
(area code 992)

Three hotels and three posadas are strung along the beach front, as simple as can be, with a bathroom apiece, filled in the summer with extended families on holiday. The *****Gutiérrez** (Calle 12, 117, tel 246348), with white walls and pink framed windows, is right on the beach, with sand coming up to and over the front door. The **San Julio**, in the same street, is a second choice.

The restaurants are all beach-front shacks, open to the sea. The **Celestún** serves excellent fresh fish, from crab or shrimp omelettes to red snapper *a la veracruzana*. To try a bit of everything, order a plateful of *botanas*. Cheap.

Chichén-Itzá

If Palenque is the Mozart of the Maya and Uxmal the Beethoven, then Chichén-Itzá is the undoubted Wagner. Loud and bellicose, strident and proclamatory, it is the angry young man of pre-Hispanic Yucatán.

Close to the main Mérida–Caribbean road, 120 km from Mérida and 200 km from the coast, it is the most famous and the most visited of all Maya sites. It is over-run with tourists during the heat of the day, between 11.00 and 15.00, when distracting, scantily clad day trippers disclose more about the North American culture than the Maya.

Chichén-Itzá is jammed with visitors for the spring equinox. Book hotels weeks or months before, as nearby Pisté and Valladolid fill up fast. Otherwise, avoid the area completely: the phenomenon of the serpent uncoiling down the nine tiers of the Castillo is hidden from sight because of the crowd, and can be seen every night in a mock-up version in Cancún.

History

Founded in the 5th century, Chichén was an influential Maya city throughout the Classic era (AD 600–900). The mystic waters of its sacred *cenote* were said to hold answers from the gods and pilgrims from all over the peninsula came for advice. In the latter half of the 10th century, control of Chichén passed to the Itzá. The takeover was largely bellicose, as is illustrated by the murals in the Temple of the Jaguars, which show battle scenes between the Toltec-influenced Itzá and Maya warriors. The Itzá eased their ascendancy by the simple expedient of making a cult out of Quetzalcóatl, a universal Mesoamerican god already known to the Maya as Kukulkán, the God of the Arts and the Wind, who breathed life into the world. His image, in the form of a feathered serpent, adorns every aspect of Chichén's architecture.

This great epoch of expansion and theocratic militarism ended at the beginning of the 13th century when the ruler, Chac Xib Chac, snatched the bride of the neighbouring Lord of Izamal, just as she was preparing for her wedding. The resulting civil war saw the end of Chichén-Itzá: the remaining Itzá fled deep into the Petén jungle of Guatemala, where they were finally conquered by the Spanish in 1697.

THE TOLTEC CONNECTION

Chichén is a Mayan anomaly, because of its similarity to the Toltec capital of Tula in central Mexico. The shortest possible distance from Tula to Chichén is over 1000 km, yet no intermediary settlement so resembles Tula in architecture and imagery. (The contemporary equivalent might be for US astronauts to arrive at Mars to find that Mcdonalds already had a franchise).

Imported Toltec gods, principally Quetzalcóatl-Kukulkán, but also his great enemy, the War God Tezcatlipoca, took over from and merged with the Maya pantheon at the end of the 10th century. Theories abound as to how these cultural interchanges took place. Some suggest that the Maya took over Toltec sites in central Mexico, leaving behind their mural paintings at sites like Cacaxtla in Tlaxcala, and reimporting Toltec gods on their return to the Yucatán. A more popular theory is that Toltec influences were brought by the Itzá, who traded with both the Yucatán and central Mexico from their halfway lands in the lowlands of Tabasco. Whichever is correct, the symbolism if not the workmanship of Maya architecture was undoubtedly altered by Toltec influences.

Signs of the Toltecs range from depiction of sacrifices, ways of dressing and types of weapons to statues such as the Chac-Mool, the messenger of the gods. Most striking of all is the feathered serpent with a plumed head and a rattlesnake's tail—an extension and continuation of the Quetzalcóatl myth. He had been incorporated into the architecture of Teotihuacán long before he was rediscovered by the Toltecs in the 9th century. The Aztecs later believed him to be the only god to have taken a human form, while to the Maya he was the fountain of wisdom, a Solomon amongst gods.

To confuse the issue, supreme rulers often took on the name of Quetzalcóatl to add prestige to their rank. Here myth and fact merge. In about AD 970, at the Toltec capital of Tula, Topiltzin added the god's name to his own and became deified in the process. Topiltzin-Quetzalcóatl was expelled from Tula in about AD 980, after falling out with the military elite. Folklore maintains that he sailed to the east, vowing to return (Cortés made full use of this legend when he arrived from the east). Others claim that he sailed from Veracruz and landed in the Itzá region of Tabasco, from where he himself, or his Toltec followers, took over Chichén and its sacred *cenote*.

GETTING AROUND
Chichén-Itzá is on Highway 180, 120 km (2 hrs) east of Mérida and 200 km (3 hrs) west of Cancún. Buses between the two towns stop at the site every half-hour. Valladolid, the nearest town, is 20 minutes from Chichén on the Cancún bus. The main road is also an easy one to hitch along. Pisté, the village which services the site, is 2 km from the entrance.

TOURIST INFORMATION
The **visitor's centre** is open from 08.00 to 20.00 but the site closes at 17.00. A daily Sound and Light performance takes place in English at 21.00—so lurid and appalling that it is almost worth seeing. Guides can be hired from the centre, which also includes a small museum, bookshop, café, locker room, and cybernetics centre. The latter has a computer which can reproduce calendar dates in Maya hieroglyphics.

VISITING THE SITE
To make chronological sense, go first to the south group (to the right of the Castillo), built before the Itzá arrived. Return to the main plaza and skirt round the back of the Castillo to the central group, which includes the market and the Temple of a Thousand Columns. A path leads north from the plaza to the sacred *cenote*, a 10-minute walk. Finish by returning to the plaza, the consummation of Toltec Chichén-Itzá.

CASTILLO
This 24-m-high pyramid, the most important building in Chichén-Itzá, is slap bang in the middle of the great plaza, itself the size of several football pitches. On each face, 91 steps lead up to a temple on the top, the final step producing a total of 365, the number of days in a solar year. During the spring and autumn equinoxes (21 March and 21 September), Chichén is packed with people from all over the world who come to see the curious phenomenon of light and shadow falling down the nine tiers, simulating an undulating serpent, uncoiling down the side of the building to the sculptured-stone snake's head at the base of the stairway. This head and the snake-shaped columns supporting the entrance to the sanctuary are further examples of Toltec influences and their cult of the feathered serpent.

Built on nine tiers, the number associated with death and the underworld, the Castillo is similar to the funerary pyramids of Palenque. No tomb has been excavated but the intriguing possibility remains that possibly the great Topiltzin-Quetzalcóatl himself was buried here.

It was constructed over a smaller pyramid and temple, entered on the north side (with restricted opening times). Within is a Chac-Mool (a reclining figure holding up a shallow sacrificial bowl), and a jaguar throne, painted in bright red cinnabar with inlaid jade for the eyes and spots.

SOUTH GROUP
The oldest section of Chichén-Itzá is hidden in characteristic Yucatecan scrub jungle. A path leads down from the Castillo to a 10-m-tall pyramid on the right, known as the

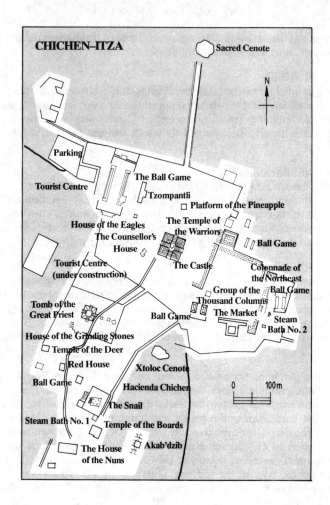

CHICHEN–ITZA

Sacred Cenote

N

Parking

Tourist Centre

The Ball Game

Tzompantli

Platform of the Pineapple

House of the Eagles

The Temple of
the Warriors

The Counsellor's
House

Ball Game

Tourist Centre
(under construction)

The Castle

Colonnade of
the Northeast

Group of the
Thousand Columns

Ball Game

Tomb of the
Great Priest

Ball Game

The Market

Steam
Bath No. 2

House of the Grinding Stones

Temple of the Deer

Red House

Xtoloc Cenote

Ball Game

Hacienda Chichen

0   100m

Steam Bath No. 1

The Snail

Temple of the Boards

Akab'dzib

The House
of the Nuns

Osario (ossuary) or the High Priest's Grave. At the end of the last century, seven tombs with skeletons intact were found here, together with offerings of jade, copper and gold. The temple is surmounted by columns sculpted into warrior figures. The next two structures on the right are the **Casa Colorada** (named after the faint traces of red paint on the interior walls) and, behind it, the ruined remains of the **Casa del Venado**. Both are small temples set on raised platforms.

The path opens up into a clearing with the striking **Caracol** on the left, described by an eminent archaeologist as a 'two-decker wedding cake on the square carton in which it came'. This cylindrical astronomical observatory is a highly complex structure. It is made up of concentric vaults which rise to an upper chamber by means of a spiral stairway. The narrow windows at its top may have been used to trace the movements of Venus.

At the far end of the clearing, the **Templo de las Monjas** (nunnery) with its annex and Iglesia (church) was named by the Spanish, who were stumbling to make sense of the abandoned, half-forgotten cities. This complex, about 38 m wide and 65 long, is in the Puuc style, with Chac masks and key-pattern decorations superimposed in various stages. At the entrance to the right of the main stairway, an older base can be distinguished beneath the present structure, discovered by a piece of rash dynamiting in the 1860s. On the small Iglesia to the left of the larger Templo de las Monjas, masks alternate between Chac and the four *bacabs* who held up the world at its four corners: an armadillo, a snail, a tortoise and a crab.

Beyond this, to the southwest of the temple, the **Chichén Viejo** group comprises some of the oldest of all structures, little restored and little visited. This group is a 20-minute walk down a rough path, past a group of thatched huts, and is best visited with a guide. Although the original structures predated any Toltec influence, some were repaired with Toltec additions, such as the Atlantean figures holding up the lintels.

THE NORTH GROUP

This group represents the height of Toltec influence at Chichén-Itzá. The path from the South Group leads back to the main plaza and the Castillo. To the east, behind the Castillo, the first set of ruins are the so-called market, once colonnaded, and a small ball court. Further to the east, a sweat bath was uncovered, complete with underground oven and drains. To the north, the **Templo de las Mil Columnas** encloses the **Templo de los Guerreros** within its 1000 columns. Representing armed warriors, these columns would have held up a perishable roof, as at Toltec Tula. The Temple of the Warriors, approached through the colonnade and up the narrow, steep stairway, enclosed a smaller temple named after Chac-Mool. The broad doorway is flanked by thick columns, with a plumed serpent at the base, and the four rattles of the snake at the top. In the first chamber, an enigmatic Chac-Mool holds an offering bowl on his belly, perhaps for sacrificial human hearts. The platform behind him, held up by mini-Atlanteans, may have been the ruler's throne. The walls were originally covered in frescoes of battle scenes between the darker Toltecs and the bound captive Maya.

Halfway across the plaza, in line with the northern side of the Castillo, a 300-m track leads back into the undergrowth, to the sacred **cenote**. This natural, deep well, long associated with sacrificial offerings to the gods, was dredged by Edward Thompson at the turn of the century. (He came to the Yucatán at the age of 25, as the American consul in Mérida.) He described the *cenote* as having:

> scattered carved and square stones in countless thousands and fallen columns by the hundreds ... Facades, though gray and haggard with age and seamed by time, sustain the claim that Chichén-Itzá is one of the world's greatest monuments of antiquity.

When dredging the *cenote*, he found the skeletons of children, men and fewer women. The very few victims who survived an hour or more in the well were pulled out. Their words then took on immmense significance, interpreted as messages from the gods and portents of the future. Out of the murky water came jade, amber, crystal and some Toltec gold discs, dating from the 13th century and inscribed with battle and sacrifice scenes.

To the west of the *cenote* path, back on the main plaza, the square platform with its four stairways is dedicated to **Venus**. The relief decorations symbolize a feathered monster with tiger claws and plumed serpents. Carved around the base of the next, small platform, eagles and jaguars, representing military elites, swallow human hearts as serpents uncoil down the four stairways. Behind, the long T-shaped **tzompantli** is carved with hallucinatory rows of over 500 skulls. Originally, the skulls of captured prisoners would have been displayed on a frame, a distinctly Toltec innovation. Against the east wall of the ball court, the small **Lower Temple of the Jaguars** was painted with an elaborate 12th-century procession mural. The upper temple looks out over the ball court from within two towering serpent columns with fanged heads and feathered tails. The door jambs have low-relief carvings of warriors with exposed genitals: a definite break with traditional Maya modesty. This too was painted with scenes of a long drawn-out siege.

The **Great Ball Court** is the largest yet discovered, measuring 146 m in length and 36 m in width. Halfway along the vertical walls, at a height of 8 m, stone rings are set into the masonry. The solid rubber ball had to pass through these, hit off the hips, elbows or knees of the players. The hoops are decorated with intertwining serpents, representing the sun which was thought to renew itself like the skin of the snake. Under these goals, carved panels (replicated on the two facing walls) depict the game in eye-popping detail. Each team comprised seven players. The leading member of the victorious team is shown decapitating his kneeling opponent. Six jets of blood spurt from the head, turning into fork-tongued serpents.

The Caves of Balankanche
(4 km east of Chichén-Itzá; open 09.00–17.00; tours in Spanish at 09.00, 10.00, 12.00, 14.00 and 16.00; tours in English at 11.00, 13.00 and 15.00; take a torch, as the lighting may be erratic.)
Both the Maya and the Toltecs used caves as a place of worship, believing them to be the gateway to the Underworld. In the dry Yucatán, they had a special significance as sources of water and therefore became associated with the Corn God and with Tlaloc, the Rain God. One key reason for Maya acceptance of the Toltecs in the 10th century was the similarity between the Toltec Tlaloc and the Maya Chac. Both of these rain gods represented four deities in one, each of which represented a compass point. Both gods would have been worshipped here by the nearby inhabitants of Chichén-Itzá. The tour follows long, winding, dank passageways, leading to sombre pools surrounded by votive offerings, as a voice of doom intones something unintelligible over the loudspeaker.

WHERE TO STAY
(area code 985)
There are three good hotels around the ruins. The ****Villas Arqueológicas (tel 62830) is a well-appointed rest and read-up hotel, providing French menus, a library with Maya tomes, a swimming pool, tennis and billiards. The ***Hacienda Chichén (open Nov–Easter; reservations through travel agents in Mérida) was bought by the US consul, Edward Thompson, for $75 at the turn of the century. There are 18 cottages, painted in the local mustard yellow as natural protection against mosquitoes. Large gardens surround the swimming pool. The ****Mayaland (tel 252122 in Mérida, fax 257022) would be utterly peaceful, set in gardens of tamed jungle and bougainvillea,

were it not for the tour groups. Accommodation is divided between palm-thatched cottages in the garden, with tiled bathrooms, or large rooms in the main building. The main entrance hall frames Chichén's Observatory in the distance, and the reception room the Castillo. The hotel organizes highly informative tours of the ruins, which leave at the sensible times of 07.00 and 15.45.

The village of **Pisté**, the closest to the ruins, is a 20-minute walk. The main street is lined with grocery stores, hotels, and restaurants serving inferior Yucatecan cooking. The ***Posada El Paso** (no phone) is a convenient cheap hotel with beds, showers and hammock hooks in modern rooms. The ***Pirámide Inn** (tel 5) organizes tours around Chichén-Itzá and further afield, including the 23 pyramids of Yaxuná, 25 km away. Four km along the Cancún road is the charming 20-room ****Dolores Alba** (for reservations, tel Mérida 213745 or write to Calle 63, no 464). It has a swimming pool, and is well stocked with English books. It also operates a taxi service to the ruins.

Northeast to Río Lagartos

East of Mérida is the Caribbean, the ultimate aim of nearly every tourist. Highway 180 leads east to Cancún, passing on the way the famous archaeological site of Chichén-Itzá and the colonial town of Valladolid (see East to Izamal and Valladolid). Off this road, to the northeast, is the Natural Park and Bird Sanctuary of Río Lagartos, famed for its flamingos.

GETTING AROUND

By Bus: Buses for Tizimín leave Mérida's terminal on Calle 69. A couple are 'direct' (which means they stop at every village on the way); eight a day go straight to Tizimín, without stops. From here there are regular connections to Río Lagartos. There are also eight buses a day from Valladolid.

By Car: There are two routes to Río Lagartos: via Motul or via Chichén-Itzá and Valladolid. Both pass through Tizimín. For speed, take the Motul road from Mérida's Av Yucatán and turn left at Tizimín for Río Lagartos.

WHAT TO SEE

The Road from Motul to Río Lagartos

The small town of **Motul**, 45 km northeast of Mérida, is unselfconsciously traditional, still preferring horses and carts to taxis. The market serves pithaya fruit drinks: the white flesh, dotted with countless tiny black seeds, is removed from its Schiaperelli-pink skin and crushed with fresh lime and mineral water to make a delicious drink.

The road passes through Yucatecan villages that are small, inconsequential and traditional, dominated by a towering church. They have nothing more than a weekly market, a single shop and a hall daubed with political posters woefully out of date. The language is still Maya, and festivals honour the Bee God. Women wear their long *huipiles* and the men work in henequen fields, coconut groves or citrus-fruit orchards. Mérida is still referred to by its pre-Hispanic name of Ti'ho and every village uses its Maya name.

Tizimín, Yucatán's second largest city, has little of interest bar two curiosities: a run-down zoo, opened by Queen Elizabeth II, and the largest disco in the state, Extravaganza. Between Tizimín and Río Lagartos (50 km), the road passes through cattle ranches and the tiny village of Kikil, where the tree-rooted ruins of a Franciscan church echo the one-time strength of the Catholic Church.

Río Lagartos

The only conceivable reason to visit Río Lagartos is to see its colonies of flamingos. The village itself is an unattractive sprawl with a single down-at-heel hotel. For a small fee, fishermen will ferry out the occasional visitor who wants to swim in the Gulf to the beaches at Punta Holchit.

Three-hour boat trips to see the flamingos leave from the boat rank outside the Hotel Nefertiti. The boatman cuts the engine and rows in amongst the birds. When cameras are ready and shutter speeds set, he obnoxiously throws a stone to set them soaring away—often to the enthusiastic applause of his passengers. In such an ecologically fragile area, tourism that leaves no mark on nature is actively encouraged, but is often hijacked by this sort of eco-terrorism.

Los Colorados Salt Mines

Two km before Río Lagartos, bear right (east) at the crossroads for Los Coloradas Salt Mines, 17 km to the right. First tarmac and then hard-packed sand, the road passes a haunting moonscape of great white salt pyramids. This important local industry has taken over many of the flamingos' nesting grounds and turned them into evaporation ponds. The pools of iridescent pink water are coloured by the algae *artemai*, which the flamingos feed on. These algae have been badly eroded by hurricanes and will take up to a decade to replenish themselves, making the flamingos lighter in colour. For the next few km, the white sands between the Gulf of Mexico and the Lagartos estuary are the summer home of hundreds of flamingos, together with herons, pelicans, snowy-white ibis, oyster catchers and yellow-breasted bee-catchers.

FLAMINGOS

The flamingos arrive in Río Lagartos in April, to court and make their nests. They lay their eggs in June, feeding their young by regurgitating their own food and so losing a great deal of body weight. In this weakened condition (which lasts till November), they should not be disturbed. In September they leave Río Lagartos for Celestún and other estuaries, where they eat their heads off on the widgeon grass. At the end of February they begin to preen their feathers, ready to move back to Río Lagartos and start courting again. On their long, treacherously twig-like legs, they look like chic turn-of-the-century French women, with a bustle behind and a proud neck, studiously avoiding what is underneath their aristocratically hooked noses.

WHERE TO STAY AND EAT   (area code 986)

In Río Lagartos, the **Nefertiti (Calle 14, 109, tel 14) is a white breeze-block establishment, right on the water, with warped wooden furniture and a damp mustiness. It has its own palapa restaurant on the waterfront. Restaurant Negritos specializes in *pan de cazón* (a tortilla sandwich filled with fish and tomato sauce). Cheap.

In **Tizimín**, the ****San Jorge** is in the main square (*'parque'*) and the *****San Carlos** (Calle 54, tel 32024) two blocks behind. Both are acceptable but not much more. On the corner of the laurel-lined square, the **Restaurant Tres Reyes** is the best in town, although it doesn't bestir itself much beyond sandwiches, roast chicken or eggs. Cheap.

East to Izamal and Valladolid

These two colonial towns are both worth visiting, east of Chichén-Itzá on the road to the Caribbean. Picturesque Izamal seems to belong to a different century, whilst Valladolid has a quiet provinciality and offers a good choice of hotels. Both are sufficiently far away from the hubbub of either Chichén or Cancún.

GETTING AROUND
By Bus: From Mérida (Calle 69/68 and 70, tel 249055), first-class buses to Valladolid leave at 06.15 and 16.30, while second-class go every hour from 05.00 to 21.00. For Izamal get dropped off either at Hoctún or at Kantunil and take a taxi. Alternatively, take a slower direct second-class bus.
By Car: Leave Mérida on eastbound Highway 180 (the road for Cancún and the Caribbean coast). At Hoctún (50 km) turn north (left) to Citlcúm and then right to Izamal (24 km from the main highway). For Valladolid either return to Highway 180 and continue eastwards, past Chichén-Itzá, or take a back road, via the villages of Sitilpech, Tunkas, Dzitas and Tinum.

Izamal

The village of Kimbila, beyond Hoctún, with its small primrose-coloured church, is a foretaste of things to come. The closer the road gets to Izamal, the more houses wear a pale saffron front with faded blue doors. Finally, every single house, petrol pump and

Outside the convent of Izamal

spire is swathed in yellow. This colour deters mosquitoes, and has become synonymous with Izamal.

Izamal itself got left behind at the turn of the century. Carriages, *calesas*, line up outside the monastery, not as a tourist attraction but to taxi people around—old women with shopping, young children with ices and those returning from a trip to the bright lights of Mérida. Whole families live in easy disarray amongst the colonial patios and arches, built by the Spanish.

Bishop Diego de Landa had his base here and, egoist that he was, determined to build himself a seat to rival that of St Peter's in Rome. At 80,000 square metres, his monastery's atrium alone is a worthy contender. This Franciscan monastery, of St Anthony de Padua, is the biggest in Mexico. All of the buildings are high off the ground, constructed over the ruins of the ceremonial pyramid of Popul Chac. Stones from surrounding temples were used for the foundations, and the stairways are those of the original Maya temple. In the entrance to the simple chapel are the faintest tracings of early wall paintings. In contrast, the surrounding monastery is propped up with flying buttresses. The prison cells inside are more reminiscent of a barracks than a place of prayer.

A statue of Diego de Landa was recently commissioned and put up in the plaza next to the monastery, a site reserved for heroes. Outraged, the citizens of Izamal demanded its removal. It now sits uncomfortably on the other side, a solitary island in the midst of traffic.

To the north of the monastery is the large pyramid of Kinich Kak-Mo where the heart of Zamna, ancient lord of the land, is buried. The rest of him was divided into equal parts and scattered amongst the surrounding four hills.

WHERE TO STAY AND EAT

The *Kabah (opposite the monastery, no telephone) is the only hotel in Izamal. Crumbling rooms with showers surround a flower-filled patio.

The town's best restaurant is the **Puerto de Manzanillo**, in a colonial house, near Hotel Kabul in the main park. Its eclectic menu includes Chinese, Yucatecan and European food such as *potage española* and *hígado a la italiana* (Italian liver), served with surprising aplomb.

Valladolid

The lovely colonial town of Valladolid is a relaxing place in which to spend the night, either before or after visiting the site of Chichén-Itzá. Remarkably free of groups, who are parked as close as possible to Chichén, or driven in and out by bus from Mérida or Cancún, it is also renowned as the gastronomic centre of the Yucatán.

Despite its distinctly colonial air, Valladolid has a long history of resistance, first against the intruding Spanish and later against the wealthy hacienda owners. The original Maya town of Zaci was finally conquered after a long struggle, by Montejo the Younger, and renamed Valladolid. It was too far from the bigger cities of Mérida and Campeche to attract much notice. Consequently, feeling defenceless, the Spanish formed a tight-knit group, which, like an Afrikaner ghetto, practised a rigid system of apartheid to keep anyone with a drop of Maya blood out of the township. When the Maya rose up in the War of the Castes in 1847 (see History, The Yucatán Peninsula), Valladolid was savagely attacked. It remained an outpost until the arrival of the railway in the 19th century. Later, during the Revolution, it was given another going-over. Today Maya women flood the market and the town appears to have forgotten its stormy past.

WHAT TO SEE

The **cathedral** in the main square hasn't had much luck. Originally built by the conquistadors, it fell to ruin and had to be completely rebuilt in the 18th century. In 1915, General Alvarado and his revolutionary forces came along and ransacked the interior. Today it has given up struggling, preferring a bland inoffensive style.

More interesting is the **Convent of Sisal**, southwest of the main square in Calle 41A (a continuation of Los 5 Calles from the main square). It was built for the Spanish, with salamonic columns and vaulted ceilings. The Maya were confined to a small open chapel, the remains of which can be seen to the west of the nave. Ask to see the wall paintings which were hidden away during the War of the Castes. In an opening in the wall, behind a *retablo*, they are a fragile record of early Franciscan frescoes.

Five km west of town, the subterranean pool of **Cenote Dzitnup** was a gateway to the Underworld, according to ancient Maya belief. Today bathers can swim under stalactites in glistening clear water.

WHERE TO STAY
(area code 985)

There are a number of good hotels in Valladolid. Try the ****María de la Luz** (Calle 39, on the main square, tel 62017), which is a perfectly comfortable plain hotel with a large café downstairs. The colonial *****Mesón del Marques** (Calle 39, also on the main square, tel 62073) is more upmarket—a mansion with a bedroom wing. The white-washed rooms have stone floors and wrought-iron bedsteads. Lavish breakfasts and lunches which run from buttered lobster to eggs and bacon are served outside in the colourful courtyard. Another good choice is the modern ****Zaci** (Calle 44/39 and 39, tel 62167), which has an always empty swimming pool and rooms with big tiled bathrooms and fans.

EATING OUT

Valladolid is famed for its local dishes. A good place to eat them in is **Casa de los Arcos** (Calle 39, east of the main square, tel 62467). Wooden tables are packed in amongst heavy stone arches, on a black and white tiled floor. It serves a cheap comida corrida, as well as *mariscos* (sea food), *sopa de lima* and a variety of turkey dishes. Both the María de la Luz and the Mesón del Marques have restaurants which will serve all-comers.

The State of Quintana Roo

The main attraction of Quintana Roo is its long stretch (860 km) of Caribbean coast. Of all the coasts in Mexico, this is the most beautiful, with calm, azure water, parched white sand beaches dotted with soft pink conch shells, and palm trees fringing the water line. The second-largest coral reef in the world (after the Barrier Reef in Australia) lies off the coast: it is the presence of coral which makes the water so clear and the beaches so white.

The tranquillity of once inaccessible shores now lures a continuous stream of holiday makers. They mainly stick to the north of the state, where these natural advantages have been exploited by resorts and massive tourist development, extolled in glossy, hyperbolic brochures. Far smaller resorts and deserted strips of sand can still be found further south. The state capital of Chetumal, in the southeast corner of Quintana Roo, is the point of departure for Belize.

Avoid Cancún and Isla Mujeres and stick to the smaller resorts. Best of all, try to go off-season (April–October) when much of it is empty. Sun seekers are scared off by the possibility of rain in the summer (it only lasts for an hour or so) and hurricanes in the early autumn (these are rare, and there is usually good warning).

The Caribbean delivered the first Spaniards to Quintana Roo, when Jerónimo de Aguilar and Gonzalo Guerrero were washed up off the shores of Cozumel after a shipwreck, a few years before Hernán Cortés arrived in 1519. The first mestizos were born here, to Guerrero and the daughter of the Maya chief Nachancan. Always rebellious and anxious to remain apart from the rest of Mexico, Quintana Roo did not become one of the federal states of Mexico until 1974.

GETTING AROUND
Highway 180 from Mérida and Valladolid hits the coast at Cancún. Long, straight Highway 307 runs south from Cancún to Chetumal. Buses thunder up and down it, sometimes passing at awkward hours and as often as not full. Should this be the case, the Yucatecans stick out a thumb, and Highway 307 is one of the fastest roads to hitch up and down in Mexico. Drivers may expect a small sum (half the price of the bus) in return for a lift.

Cancún

One of the wonders of the world, Cancún is a none too stately pleasure dome. The resort encircles the Laguna Nichupté, its hotels stretching along an 18-km thin finger of powdered sugar sand, lapped by the bluer-than-blue Caribbean. The site was chosen by computer and the result is a playground for weekending North Americans who come down for a bit of sea, sand and 24-hour hangover. In this fairyland of conspicuous consumption, English is universal, prices are in dollars, and the only Mexicans around are mute bellboys and sweating taxi drivers. Contestants line up for 'Sexy Silhouette' parades, chemists sell plastic sex dolls which 'take up to 250' over-weight pounds and vendors sell linguistically dextrous T-shirts with slogans like 'Too Mucking Fuch' which many find amusing on their twelfth margarita. For those who wished they'd gone to Florida it will be paradise; for those who hoped to find Mexico, it won't.

There are advantages, of course. The resort boasts a wide range of restaurants—Polynesian, Cajun, German, Japanese and Italian—all serving distinctly Mexican-tasting food. Endless water sports can be laid on—jet skiing, scuba diving, parasailing, snorkelling and windsurfing. As Cancún is the most expensive resort in Mexico, it is worth investigating cheaper package holidays, offered in abudance by numerous travel agents. Anyone turning up on spec will be fleeced within minutes.

GETTING AROUND
If you are stuck or determined, the airport (which has a tourist information booth) is south of town on the road to Tulum. The bus station is to the north in Av Tulum between Avs Uxmal and Chichén-Itzá. Taxis have a fixed tariff.

TOURIST INFORMATION
There are two tourist offices, one at the airport, and one opposite the Palacio Municipal in the centre. Head straight for either and get a copy of the free magazine, *Cancún Tips*, which is a fund of necessary information. Copies of this same magazine sit by the side of every bed in every hotel and are flung at people in the street.

WHERE TO STAY   (area code 988)
Cancún isn't a town for paupers. Europeans and Mexicans tend to congregate downtown, off the seafront, in hotels costing triple the amount charged by their equivalents elsewhere. Of these the ***Bonampak (Calle Bonampak 225, tel 40280), the ***Plaza Caribe (Tulum with Uxmal, tel 41377, tlx 73352) and the ***Plaza del Sol (Yaxchilán, tel 43888) are all good, well-run hotels.

At the top end of the scale, Cancún really knows how to pamper. The (GT) Sheraton Towers (at the end of the hotel zone, tel 31988, tlx 31450) runs a de luxe butler service: guests are greeted with a glass of champagne by the white-gloved major-domo who will be in charge of them for the rest of their stay. A glass-fronted lift floats them up to their room, where clothes will be pressed and shoes shined in the twinkling of an eye. The bathrooms are so well equipped, even running to hairdryers, that guests can hardly be persuaded to leave. All the rooms have individual terraces, where guests are served with their morning breakfast and their evening canapés and margaritas. For those who venture out, the hotel's large beach includes a fully equipped sports club. A stay at this hotel is a treat worth splashing out on.

Some other hotels run much the same service. Of these, the (GT) Camino Real (Punta Cancún, tel 30100, tlx 31730) is extremely well equipped, even providing a crèche. It has been decorated with imagination, in bold bright colours, with local wall coverings and ceramics. Huge tresses of henequen hang in the hallway and all the rooms have wide sofas splashed with cushions. On the other hand, it has to be said that all the bell boys are queuing for jobs at the *****Hyatt Regency (Playa Chac-Mool, tel 30966), which they rate the best hotel.

The rest of the hotels are along the seafront in Blvd Kukulcán. Beverly Hills meets post-modernism as hotel after hotel competes with architectural styles: a Fiesta Americana seems to resemble a federal correctional facility, its inmates daily tormented by lack of beach, and a towering Rajput palace with Muslim-style onion domes sits incongrously by its side.

EATING OUT
Although there are no finds in Cancún, most of the restaurants are of a fairly high standard and almost all specialize in seafood. Captain's Cove down beyond the Sheraton is a perennial favourite, serving huge plates of lobster, red snapper and langoustine. The Japanese Seryna (Plaza Flamingo, Hotel Zone, tel 32991) specializes in sushi, sashimi, shabu-shabu, tempura and yosenabe. Restaurant Los Almendros of

Mérida fame also has a branch in Cancún (Av Bonampak, tel 40807): this is the closest that you'll get in Cancún to indigenous Maya cooking.

Isla Mujeres

The tiny Island of Women lies off the coast opposite Cancún. Hourly boats make the 45-minute lurching trip from Puerto Juárez, just north of the resort. In the heady days when Cancún was no more than a byte on the computer, Isla Mujeres was a get-away-from-it-all hideaway, famed for its long, languorous and deserted beaches, and its dusty town where lone travellers set the world to rights, lounging in hammocks and watching the sun go down. The double blow of the crowded resort and Hurricane Gilbert, which devastated the island in the late 1980s, has been its death knell. The beaches are now filled with daytrippers from Cancún, come for a peaceful snorkel with boats full of companions. Leave the shanty town, where the ferry arrives, in search of something better and you'll soon be back, welcoming it like a long-lost friend, happy to spend the night in a cement box of a hotel where the plumbing only works intermittently. The island is small and it is hard to avoid anyone. A patch on the beach as far away as possible from the municipal sewage outlet is the best to hope for.

WHERE TO STAY AND EAT   (area code 988)
Isla Mujeres has jacked up its prices because of its proximity to Cancún. There are still a couple of recommendable hotels. Of these the ****Bel Mar (Hidalgo, above the Pizzeria Rolandi, tel 20429) is the nicest, with expensively rustic furniture and Maltese-cross-shaped windows. Rooms are stocked with a large selection of foreign-language books and there is a good café opposite for set breakfasts and food throughout the day. The ***Motel del Mar (Playa Nte, tel 20179) has big plain rooms and a restaurant, Bucho, offering a large selection of dishes, set in a small palm grove. Next door, Na-Balam (Calle Zacil Ha, Playa Nte, 20279) is much the same. In the centre of town, Rocamar has big ocean-facing rooms and feels like a family boarding house. For budget travellers, the Poc Na youth hostel (in the centre, tel 20090) is clean and basic, although even they charge extra for a mattress on a wooden bunk.

Ciro's Lobster House, on the north end of the island, off Hidalgo, is popular as much for its nightly screening of Hurricane Gilbert wreaking havoc with the island as for its food. Round the corner, a German-run café, Cafécito, serves good coffee, long fruit-drinks and crêpes.

Holbox Island

For anyone with camping equipment, Holbox is an ideal escape. This long thin island off the north coast of Quintana Roo has minimal services (one half-finished hotel and a couple of cafés) and almost no people. A buffer island between the Caribbean Sea and the waters of the Gulf, it is one of the best shell-collecting points in Mexico, although the crystal-clear waters of the Caribbean have lost out in the fight with the murkier, darker waters of the Gulf.

Three buses a day leave from Valladolid (2½ hrs) or Puerto Juárez for the ferry at Chiquilá. Try to get the earliest bus, as the last ferry leaves for the 1-hour journey to the island at 15.00 and there is no hotel in Chiquilá. The last ferry from Holbox to the mainland leaves at 14.00.

South of Cancún to Playa del Carmen

Arrow-straight Highway 307 marches south of Cancún, parallel to but rarely in sight of the coast. Rough tracks lead off at regular intervals, down to the occasional village, camping ground or resort hotel on the sea. Cancún is soon just a dark cloud on the horizon—one which everyone hopes won't come any closer.

The small fishing village of **Puerto Morelos** is 17 km south of Cancún (at km 328). It is linked to the island of Cozumel by car ferry (daily ex Mon) but is more popular for the reef in sight of the shore. The village was badly hit by Hurricane Gilbert: two hotels were flattened and only the modest ****Posada Amor** was left standing. The rooms are spartan but the restaurant is small and cosy. The village also has a grocer's shop and a kitchen-restaurant, where **Doña Zenaida** serves *sopa mixta* and the catch of the day.

Some 23 km further along, a large billboard announces ******Capitán Lafitte's** (from the US tel toll-free 1 (800) 538 6802 or write to TRR, PO Box 2664, Evergreen, Colorado 80439; locally tel Mérida 262622). The 27 bungalows on the beach provide an antidote to Cancún, with a turtle-nesting sanctuary rather than turtle on the menu. The complex is family-orientated, with a games room for ping-pong or billiards, books and videos. Fishing and snorkelling trips leave daily. Families return year after year and it has to be booked months ahead. ******Kaa'lum**, next door (same tel nos), advertises itself as a 'camptel', taking all the strain out of camping. Here there is no digging of holes for lavatories, nor hammering of thumbs into the ground leaving the tent-peg untouched. Guests are transported to and from the airport, housed in large tents, and provided with good home cooking.

The next turn-off is to **Xcalacoco** beach. Here two brothers who no longer talk to each other have set up rival camping grounds, both nearly always deserted. The thin, short brother has the land to the right of the barbed-wire fence, with a line of scruffy but hopeful *cabañas* about to fall into the turquoise waters. The large brother over the fence was left behind in the rush for dollars and has only three *cabañas* completed.

A few kms before Playa del Carmen, a sign points east to the ******Shangri-La Caribe**—another expensive way of returning to nature. The palm-thatched huts, suspiciously like an African kraal, are equipped with hanging beds, bathrooms and hammocks on the porches, facing an open beach. There is also a swimming pool, games room, diving shop and restaurant.

Playa del Carmen

Still, blissfully, a one-horse, one-telephone town, Playa del Carmen lulls its mostly European visitors to indolence with the slow lap of its waves. It's a simple paradise, fronting long white sands where the sea is so clear you can see dropped contact lenses 3 m below. There is little to do but lie by the shore: most package tourists fly direct to Cozumel or Cancún in search of brighter lights. Although there are now ominous signs of buildings going up to the south, it will take some time for these to interfere with the easy-going tempo of small-town life.

GETTING AROUND
By Bus and Car: Playa del Carmen is 66 km south of Cancún, on Highway 307, opposite the island of Cozumel.

The bus station is on the west corner of the square in Av Juárez, with first-class services to Mérida, Valladolid and Chichén-Itzá, and second-class to Cancún, Tulum and Chetumal. Tickets should be bought as far in advance as possible, as they go fast. **By Air or Ferry to Cozumel:** The mainland is linked to Cozumel by a 7-minute flight or by a 60-minute ferry. Flights leave every 2 hours from the airport south of the town. Tickets for the ferry or hydrofoil to Cozumel can be bought on the pier. The tricycles used as taxis in the town line up to meet people coming off the ferry with heavy baggage. **In Town:** Playa del Carmen stretches along the sea front and is only a couple of streets deep. Av Juárez, the main street, leads from Highway 307 to the square. Most of the hotels and restaurants are on Av Juárez and an unmarked road, Av Norte, which runs north.

TELEPHONING
Woe betide anyone needing to make a long-distance telephone call. The only telephone is in the Hotel Playa del Carmen on the main street. Queues can involve a wait of up to two hours, whilst Gretchen from Germany struggles to get through to her bank manager and Juan whispers sweet nothings to his intended in Jalisco.

WHAT TO DO
The beach begins as a village beach, well peopled and much used, but stretches endlessly to either side, deserted but for the odd fisherman. The Caribbean is seductively inviting, its deep aquamarine waters a bright swimming-pool blue which darkens at night under the light of smudged pink sunsets. There is little to do but begin with a long-drawn-out breakfast and then sling a hammock between two palms for the day.

Yax-ha Dive, on the north beach, provides some diversion, renting out scuba and snorkel equipment. The owner will take people out in his boat for the day, at a reasonable price which includes breakfast and, for lunch, the fish caught on the way. He is also a qualified scuba instructor. **Mopeds**, for forays out into the surrounding countryside, can be rented from Av Norte.

WHERE TO STAY
As there is only one telephone in town, reservations are impossible. Rooms are almost always available, except during the crowded December–January high season, when Playa del Carmen picks up overspill from Cozumel and Cancún. The town offers a choice between good, simple, traditional hotels, or palapa-thatched *cabañas*. The latter are much more fun than hotels, and also more practical for those planning a longer stay on the Caribbean. If you've never tried one, this is as good a place as any to begin.

The smartest hotel is the ******Molcas**, by the pier. The rooms are all modern colonial, leading off a large swimming pool. The hotel is well run, with friendly staff and a mostly Mexican clientele. In the main square, *****Jardín Tropical** (Av Benito Juárez) is run by an American, married to a Mexican doctor, who treats her guests like members of the family. Seven rooms straggle round a lush garden, each equipped with English books and with family photographs on the walls.

On the north end of the beach, Jorge Loria has built three delightful round houses, with whitewashed walls and palapa roofs, known as ***Yax-ha. Each has a kitchen and bathroom. For those who prefer the security of four square walls and a tiled roof, the ***Delfín (Av Norte), resplendently painted in pistachio green edged in strawberry pink, has good plain rooms. The nicest *cabañas* of all are **Nuevo Amanecer (5th with Av Norte). The whole site exudes a relaxed air of efficiency. Each of the 13 *cabañas* is scrupulously clean, with its own bathroom and hammocks slung outside. There is a jacuzzi round the back, beside a popular pool table. **Cabañas Bananas (Av Norte) are almost as good, with shuttered windows and palapa roofs. Each has a bathroom and a small kitchen, with a basic cooker and fridge.

EATING OUT
Playa del Carmen doesn't go in for fancy restaurants. Prices are much of a muchness and always clearly advertised.

Limónes Café serves some of the best breakfasts in Mexico—lashings of hot coffee, huge fruit *licuados*, granola, big flour tortillas (rarely seen in the south) and eggs served any way but best of all as omelettes filled with avocado and melon. Once replete, guests can loll about on sofas, with foreign-language books to read and unobtrusive music to write letters home to. Moderate. La Tarraya is a another popular café on the beach front, serving fresh fish, *guacamole* and *nachos* at reasonable prices. El Capitán, next to Nuevo Amanecer, looks like a fragile tree house, high on stilts above the street. Inside, fish is grilled above a wood-burning fire. Moderate. Cueva Parca on Av Norte is always full, renowned for its large plates of fish and lingering breakfasts. Cheap. For plain and simple Mexican food, try El Chino, up the road from Nuevo Amanacer. Cheap. There are plenty of other cafés to the north of the beach, of which Los Cocos and Blue Parrot Inn have the best seafood. Moderate.

Cozumel

The largest island off Mexico's Caribbean coast has become a diver's haunt. Jacques Cousteau filmed its reefs in the 1960s, putting it firmly on the international scuba-diving map, and ever since then, old-timers have returned year after year to plunge 50 metres into another world. As expensive as Cancún, it caters for a more sporting tourist, whose first thought is the water. Although much of the island has been claimed by hotels, there are still strips of deserted sea and sand to the northeast.

In 1519, when Hernán Cortés sailed over from Cuba on a voyage of discovery, his first port of call in Mexico was the island of Cozumel. Here he learnt of two shipwrecked Spaniards who lived in nearby Yucatán. One, Gonzalo Guerrero, had become thoroughly assimilated into native society, with a wife, three children and tattoos to prove it, but the second, Jerónimo de Aguilar, rushed to meet his countrymen. His knowledge of the Maya language and people proved indispensable in the conquest. The diseases brought by the Spanish galleons more or less wiped out the islanders. Too far from anywhere to be important, Cozumel was abandoned and rapidly became a base for

Dutch, French and particularly English pirates. Sanctioned by his monarch, the English pirate Wallace went on to found the colony of Belize, while his compatriot Henry Morgan became governor of Jamaica.

Much later the island was colonized by Wrigleys, who used the port of San Miguel as a storage and distribution point for their gum. Today Cozumel thrives on tourism. Many come over for just a day or two: daily cruise ships pull in to disgorge shop-happy trippers who re-embark in toppling sombreros, clutching phallic onyx statuettes.

GETTING AROUND

By Air: The airport is in the north of the island, connected to the centre by minibus. International flights come in from Houston, Chicago, Dallas and Miami, as well as domestic flights from Mexico City, Mérida and Cancún. Planes to Playa del Carmen, operated by AeroCozumel (tel 20928), leave every 2 hours, for a flight lasting 7 minutes.
By Ferry: Six daily ferries, and six slightly faster and more expensive hydrofoils, link the island with Playa del Carmen.

Anyone intending to continue to Mérida by bus from Playa del Carmen should try to book tickets in advance, as the buses are few and often full.
On the Island: San Miguel, the capital of the island, is a small, drab town built around a simple grid system, and is hard to get lost in. The main square is opposite the pier where the ferries arrive. The centre of the town is compact and the main street, Av Melgar, runs parallel to the sea.

The syndicate of local taxi drivers has a strong hold, and Cozumel has next to no public transport. To avoid taking expensive taxis outside town, rent bikes or mopeds from **Ruben's**, just south of the main plaza. Cars are also available, but at 53 km long by 14 km wide, the island may be too small to put them to good use.

TOURIST INFORMATION

A small booth on the pier supplies maps to passengers coming off the ferry. A less helpful office is in the main square (tel 20335). There is a long-distance **telephone** in Av 5 Calle 2 Nte.

WHAT TO SEE AND DO

There isn't much to do in Cozumel, outside of diving and snorkelling. An hour or so can be whiled away in the town **museum** (Av Melgar, north of the pier), where Cozumel's history is graphically displayed alongside dual Spanish and English explanations. Exhibits include some excellent recreations of the reefs, and even a copy of one of the old clapperboard houses which used to be commonplace on the island. The arts **cinema** attached shows international films with Spanish subtitles.

Shopping is expensive, even though Cozumel is a duty-free port. Almost none of the goods on sale are indigenous to the island. Away from the tourist stampede, on 5th Av Norte between 2 and 4, an enchanting old man weaves hammocks on a frame, taking up to 10 days on a double: he will sell them if asked.

Pre-Hispanic Sites

In pre-Hispanic days the island was much visited by women, come to venerate the temples of Ixchel, Goddess of the Moon, pregnancy and childbirth, and consort of

Itzamná, Lord of the Heavens. Ixchel was venerated from as far afield as El Salvador and most Maya women made this journey at least once in a lifetime, which accounts for the disproportionate number of temples built on the island. Today, there is little to see except many crumbling remains of foundations, as US air bases built during the Second World War swept away most traces. The site of San Gervaiso in the north was the commercial and administrative centre of the island. The best preserved temple is in the hamlet of **Cedral**, in the south. Here, in the middle of the jungle, a high Maya arch is surrounded by scarlet hibiscus flowers. The Spanish used it as a prison, and the smattering of locals ignore it.

Chankanaab Lagoon
On the road to the San Francisco beach, this laguna is filled with piercingly coloured fish. It used to be possible to swim in the lagoon, alongside startled and startling fish, but now it has been turned into a nature reserve to prevent oily bodies polluting its waters. It is still possible to snorkel in the sea nearby. The reserve also includes botanical gardens, where every conceivable variety of tropical plant can be found. ´

BEACHES
The most isolated beaches are to the northeast of the island (half an hour by moped), where mile upon mile of parched white sand fringes the languid blue of the Caribbean. Most of this area has been abandoned, because this is where the hurricanes rage. No one wants to build hotels here, and there is scarcely a palapa hut in sight. Although the undertow can be strong, for the most part the sea is shallow and within depth for half a kilometre.

At the southern tip of the island, a large white lighthouse, near the remains of a temple, overlooks good snorkelling beaches. From here, the road curls round to Playa San Francisco in the southwest, a crowded beach where hotels are going up thick and fast. The west coast between San Francisco and San Miguel holds few surprises: most of the beaches have been appropriated by hotels and dive clubs.

DIVING AND SNORKELLING
There are almost as many dive companies as hotels, and the talk around the bars of an evening is all 85-foot drop-offs, air-pressure gauges and two-tank night dives. Anyone down on his first trip will swear by his own instructor, equipment and boat. For more impartial advice, try to find someone on a second or third trip. Many recommend taking a couple of diving lessons at home and then coming to Cozumel to get certified in a group or package trip. However, starting from scratch or finding an instructor is never a problem. Finding the right boat is probably the most important aspect. Old-timers sneer at the cattle tubs which go out overloaded with divers, but beginners may find security in numbers and will also find them considerably cheaper.

Reefs
Cozumel's reefs are surrounded by crystal-clear waters. The eerie coral forms a silent world of heights and depths, where fish slip past in a gaudy profusion of colour. **Palancar** is 5 km long and has 70-m visibility. **Maracaibo** is more challenging because of its strong currents. **Paraiso** has the best coral. **Yocab** is shallow, frequented by

endless shoals of luminous tropical fish—electric yellow and blue grunts, striped spade-fish, yellow-tailed damselfish and the ominous flat-bellied stingrays.

Diving Instruction
Almost every hotel offers diving instruction and a diving package. The Stouffer Presidente Hotel (the smartest on the island) uses **Fantasia Divers** and lessons can be arranged from the hotel. One of the longest-established companies is **Discover Cozumel** (Calle 5 Sur, tel 20280). Alternatively, try **Tom and Dusty Hartdegen** (Calle 3, behind the Orbi department store, tel 21007). Their dive school is run by bilingual English/Spanish staff and provides equipment. **Pro Dive** has a glossy profile, selling knives, wetsuits and designer suncream. Californian prices accompany the Californian gear, but the school is tried and tested. There are plenty of others all along Av Melgar, in town and down the west coast.

Snorkelling
For those who find the deep sea claustrophobic, there is an equal number of snorkelling agencies. **Discover Cozumel** (Calle 5 Sur, tel 20280) rent diving and snorkelling equipment and have been running courses for 17 years.

Some agencies provide snorkelling equipment and lunch on board 14-m catamarans which sail off into the blue, returning at dusk. Beware of 'boom netting': passengers are expected to cling to a net thrown from the back of the boat, as they drift over the reefs. It is quite easy to break a toe jumping into it. Remember to take a T-shirt: the midday sun can scorch.

WHERE TO STAY   (area code 987)
Hotels are spread over three separate areas. The cheapest are in the centre of town, often including basic kitchen facilities. The older, well-established hotels are to the north, on the west coast of the island. The newest hotels are in the south, where scaffolding is going up all the time.

The Centre
The best bargain is the ****Flamingo** (Calle 6, half a block from the seafront, no tel). This is a new, clean hotel, whose prices may rise with its popularity. ***Pepita** (15 Av Sur 120, tel 20098) is well run by Don Pepe and good value for money. It has only 30 rooms and is often full even in low season. If so, ***Posada Letty**, run by the Vivas family, provides eight simple well-scrubbed rooms with slatted blinds, fans and showers.

Several more cheap hotels are in Calle Adolfonso Salis, which runs from the sea to the market, such as the ***Kary** and the ***Saolima**. ****Suites Elizabeth** (at 44, tel 20330, Box 70) are better value, with 14 big, light, spick-and-span rooms. Some of these are suites, equipped with a large fridge, sink, two-ring cooker, sitting room, TV and shower. Back on the shorefront, **Bahía** (Melgar and 3 Sur, tel 20209) is similar but smaller. In the main square, the central location of ****López** (tel 20108) and **Mesón San Miguel** (tel 20233) makes up for their mediocre rooms.

The North
The north has a scattering of smart hotels. Of these, *******Mayan Plaza** (Punta Norte) is a tall several-storeyed hotel which surprisingly has no phone (a wake-up call is a gentle

tap on the door). This is the furthest north of all the hotels, with good snorkelling from its beach outside. Next door and owned by the same family, *****Cabañas del Caribe (PO Box 9, tel 20072) is equally attractive, with its own beach and tropical gardens.

The South

The island's pride is the ******Stouffer Presidente (10 km south of town, tel 20322), which provides every conceivable service from laundry to water skiing. The rooms are minimal but extremely comfortable. The hotel faces its own, natural harbour, once used by pirates. Closer to town, ***Casa del Mar (km 4, PO box 129, tel 21665) is the most attractive of the diving hotels which line the coast, unpretentious and family-run. All the rooms have balconies, tiled in bold yellow, with indestructible floors for wet divers to pad in on. It has a couple of good restaurants and its own pool. Most of its guests are on pre-arranged diving packages. Closer still to town, the **La Perla (tel 21088) and the ***Galapago Inn (tel 20663) are both comfortable dive-orientated hotels.

EATING OUT

Outside of hotels, all the restaurants are in San Miguel. The Stouffer Presidente is a good choice for a special meal; otherwise, it's worth walking round town to see what is around. The restaurants cater mostly for North Americans, with overpriced hamburgers and pizzas, and they open and close with notorious frequency.

Perennially popular fish and steak houses, such as Carlos and Charlie's on the seafront, tend to be noisy, crowded and self-evident. Those which escape the crowds often have less to recommend them. Of these, La Misión (tel 21641), behind the main square, is worth a detour. Owned by a grandfatherly North American, it specializes in 'gourmet Mexican', particularly seafood. Delicious, brightly coloured platefuls never fail to tempt as they pass by on their way to other tables. With 30 tables under a long thin palapa roof, where fans whir incessantly, it is always busy but never too noisy. The owner discourages the 'cussin', swearin' crowd from Mexico City and the States'. Moderate. Also worthwhile, and part-American owned, Mickey's (10th Av) serves down-home Southern and traditional Yucatecan food, taking chicken from Mom's kitchen and wrapping it in the banana leaves of the traditional palapa-hut oven. It is popular with taxi drivers and tour guides, serving sandwiches and snacks as well. Cheap. The main square is surrounded by cafés for coffees and snacks.

Akumal

About 40 km south of Playa del Carmen, set in a beautiful bay lined with palms, Akumal is a tiny, rather exclusive resort with only three hotels and a couple of restaurants. It's the haunt of Parisians and New Yorkers, who come in on up-market diving tours. Even in high season, there is room for only 100 people and enough beach to lose them on. The water is calmer and less startlingly blue than elsewhere along the coast, sheltered by the reef which closes off the wide neck of the bay. Many visitors spend most of their time lying idly in bodyshaped plastic chairs, exchanging divers' tales and after-sun lotion. With no discos and no late-night restaurants or bars (and no telephones), people get up early and eat early, and the resort is asleep by 10 o'clock at night.

Two dive shops hire out equipment and run diving courses. There are lagoons and *cenotes* all around the resort. The best lagoon for snorkelling is a 20-minute walk north of the bay. The largest *cenote* is known as 'car-wash *cenote*', used by taxi drivers to rinse off the dust.

WHERE TO STAY AND EAT

The hotels have confusingly similar names. The ****Club Akumal Caribe Villas Maya, on the north beach, is a smart modern hotel with bungalows attached. Each of the latter have fridges and small cookers. The pastel-pink ****Akumal Caribe, on the south end of the beach, is the newest hotel, filled with tour groups from Europe. ****Aventuras Akumal on the northern point are *cabañas*, comprising a living room, two bedrooms, two bathrooms and a fridge.

Lol Ha restaurant stands head and shoulders above the rest—always full and always excellent, serving imaginative home cooking. Deadpan waiters prepare *camarones rancheros* (devilled shrimps) over a flame, one ingredient following another to produce a tantalizing sauce. The Zacil, the only other separate restaurant, doesn't attempt to compete, offering desultory service and bland plates of rice and fish. The big palapa-roofed restaurant of the Akumal Caribe Hotel tries a bit harder, with fresh vegetables and good squid, and alarmingly fast service. There is a bar on the beach and another small café, outside the entrance to the resort, which is cheaper and more Mexican, patronized by hotel staff. A small supermarket next door sells hot fresh *pan dulce* and other life lines.

South of Akumal to Tulum

Some 7 km south of Akumal, and 1 km off the road, Chemuyil's narrow stretch of alabaster sand has fallen victim to the Mexicans' unfortunate habit of coming to the beach armed with the kitchen sink, 16 relations, three mangy dogs, tortillas, Lilos and cans of drinks. Set around a beautiful lagoon, where the palm trees come right down to the shore, the beach has little to offer other than somewhere to string a hammock. One km south, the neighbouring beach of Xcacel is still one of the wonders of the Caribbean, with nothing to spoil it and nowhere to stay.

On the other hand, the lagoon of Xelha daily labours under the influx of Cancún tour buses. This ecological reserve, shaped like a leg of mutton, is full of rare and beautiful tropical marine life, offering a veritable kaleidoscope of angel fish, vast green parrot fish, lobster, barracuda, shoals of tuna, and fierce, flat, long-tailed stingray. Every afternoon, a horrifying film of sun-tan oil forms on the water, emanating from well-oiled snorkellers insensitive to the destruction they're bringing. The reserve is open from 08.00 to 17.00 but it is impossible to hire equipment before 09.00 when the first tour buses arrive and destroy both the peace and the ecosystem.

On the opposite side of the road, 500 m on, a turning to the right leads to the ruins of Xelha. Not much remains, other than a few temples, still with traces of frescoes, and a *cenote* surrounded by thick foliage. There are *cenotes* all along this stretch of the peninsula, many marked by rough and ready signposts nailed up along the road. One close to the ruins of Xelha is known as the *manatee cenote* for the rare, antediluvian sea mammal (*trichechus manatus*) which is supposed to live there.

Tulum

Once renowned as the only coastal Maya city, Tulum is one of the few remaining villages on the Caribbean coast which hasn't given in to the American dollar. There are, in fact, three Tulums: the ruins, the beach and the village. The village has a telephone exchange, a few grocery stores and a weekly market. Although the proximity of the ruins to the cultural vacuum of Cancún draws daily bus loads, once the archaeological site has closed at 17.00, the cicadas have stopped their insistent drilling, and the sand has resettled on the last tyre treads, blissfully little remains but peace and beach.

GETTING AROUND

Bus services are lousy all the way along the coast between Cancún and Chetumal. Buses travelling in either direction are usually full, and consequently don't bother to stop to take on extra passengers. The locals leave early or late. The backpackers merely look confused or disconsolate, while the foolhardy hitch (usually with other tourists) in the midday sun.

In Tulum: Modern Tulum is no more than a long, thin village straggling along the sides of Highway 307, trying to detain visitors with its endless speed bumps. A regular, inexpensive taxi service runs from the village to the ruins and on to the beach, picking up and dropping off passengers along its route. The ruins are 3 km south down a narrow coastal road. This road continues all the way south to Punta Allen, past the occasional group of beach huts and fishing camps, but few cars make the journey—in the rainy season, the road is often flooded (see Where to Stay).

VISITING THE RUINS

(Open 08.00–17.00.)

Tulum has an incomparable and perfectly defendable setting, perched on white lime-stone cliffs above the azure Caribbean. A stone wall encloses it on three sides. The fourth lies open to the sea, but is protected from the full force of the Caribbean by a reef, with only a couple of breaches along its length. An archaeologist, testing Tulum's defences, placed a lantern behind each of the two windows located high on the face of the Castillo. The two beams crossed to pinpoint a natural opening in the reef through which boats could pass.

Tulum is not the only Maya construction on the coast—they built lookouts all along it—but it is the only sizeable city. Neither is it monumental: its squat temples are far less impressive than those of inland Cobá, Chichén and Uxmal. It was, however, the first Maya settlement to be spied by the Spanish on reconnaissance trips along the coast in 1518, and the only one known to have been inhabited. The conqueror, Juan de Grijalva, compared the city to the splendours of Seville, and decided not to risk a landing. Tulum was spared until the 1530s, when a more ruthless conqueror, Montejo, squashed Maya resistance throughout the Yucatán.

Tulum is a small, late-Classic site, and many of its buildings show the slackening standards of Maya architects. Temples no longer soar, rather they remain rooted solidly to the ground. Strangely, many of the buildings have doors too low to enter, which implies that they were offertories or altars. Others were colourfully stuccoed both inside and out in once brilliant primary colours, outlined in black: the faded remains of these murals cling to the walls of those furthest from the sea air. The colours and the imagery imply that this far-off outpost was known to, and traded with the Aztecs at Tenochtitlán, who introduced some Aztec gods into the Maya iconography of Tulum.

The **Temple of the Descending God** is one of the most unusual structures, similar in some ways to buildings at Cobá, but unique to this stretch of Quintana Roo. Above the low doorway, a figure—the descending god—plunges headfirst towards the ground, the soles of his feet pointing towards the sky. It may represent an emblem of the setting sun falling into the sea, or an unknown god—possibly even the Bee God (honey still holds an important place in the rural economy).

Structure 16, more commonly known as the **Castillo**, is the largest of all the buildings, with excellent commanding views out over the Caribbean. As on so many of the temples, its walls slope outwards, as if it is digging its heels into the ground, resisting the pull of the sea. Just below and to the left of the castle is a small cove where many people swim in the clear waters of the Caribbean.

Sian Ka'an Biosphere Reserve

The whole area south of Tulum is now part of the 500,000-hectare Sian Ka'an Biosphere Reserve, home to some 350 species of birds and 30 known Maya sites. From May, the female green, loggerhead, hawksbill and leatherback turtles heave themselves onto deserted beaches to bury their eggs in the sand. The eggs take eight weeks to hatch, and the unprotected young then float out to sea in the surf. Up to 70 per cent, however, are eaten by seabirds before they reach the water.

WHERE TO STAY

The only hotels on the main road are the clean and responsible ***Nuevo (with cable television to catch US sport), the uninviting **El Crucero motel, at the turn-off to the ruins, and the **Maya. Young people prefer to be on the beach whilst the vast majority of tourists are day trippers from Cancún.

Beyond the ruins, along the road down to Boca Paila and Punta Allen, several camping grounds provide palapa-roofed huts, endless stretches of deliciously empty beach and not a great deal else. They are, however, a byword amongst travellers all over the country, considered the most perfect place to stay on the Caribbean, for next to nothing. The *cabañas* are primitive: communal showers emit weak dribbles, but the crystalline sea is within 50 m. **El Mirador** and **Santa Fe** are the closest to the ruins, and the cheapest of the lot. The Santa Fe has a small café, run by an Italophile who serves nerve-shatteringly strong coffee. **Don Armando's** is the next down the road, a 10-minute walk from the ruins. Knocked down by one hurricane and built back up to fight others, it is now supported by stone foundations, although the walls are still palm thatch. Its café serves freshly caught grilled fish (including, on occasion, barracuda) and *burritos* stuffed with avocado and cheese, presided over by the bear-like Don Armando himself. Five minutes further on, **El Paraiso** comprises a row of 10 modern rooms with double beds and showers, and a vast mushroom-shaped restaurant. It is certainly more comfortable than most *cabañas*, but has a reputation for being badly run and is usually ominously empty. Other groups of *cabañas* are further south, along the same coast road, including some run by a French Canadian: these are more than a walk from the ruins in the hot sun and are best reached by car.

The very best of these rustic beach huts are out on their own, 5 km south of the ruins, set around a small, sheltered bay. Run by Californians, the stone-walled, thatched-roof ***Sian Ka'an Osho Oasis *cabañas* are truly idyllic (Box 99, Tulum, Quintana Roo; no phone but space is usually available; in USA tel (415) 381 9861 and in Europe, tel Holland (20) 969 372). The beds are suspended from the roof, draped in mosquito nets, looking out over the sea. The Mexican cook prepares excellent vegetarian dishes, served as a buffet three times a day when starving lotus-eaters come in out of the sun. Possibilities abound for snorkelling, biking, boating and trips to *cenotes*. Although the establishment is linked to a distinctly Californian mystic (shown in photographs with his stretch limousine), there is absolutely no need to do anything more than lie languorously in a hammock under the palm trees.

EATING OUT
A number of small restaurants are scattered around the ruins. The best are **El Faisán y El Venado** (opposite El Crucero) and the vegetarian **Alexander's** on the far side of the main road. On the road south, just beyond the second speed bump, is a small café with no name apart from its 'pescado frito' and 'XX Equis' signs. Bob, the cook, is highly esteemed. In the south of the village, an excellent bakery faces Don Pancho's, selling Chihuahua cheeses and pots of honey. For those with a car or taxi, there is a good fish restaurant, south along the coast road (past Osho), called **Ana and José's**.

Cobá

Cobá seems to be fighting a losing battle against the jungle. The great distance between the groups of buildings, its isolation, damp, jungle-infested terrain and half-submerged ruins make it better suited to the intrepid rather than the casual tourist.

Rediscovered in 1891 by the eccentric and indefatigable Austrian archaeologist, Teobert Maler, this important Classic site is best known for the remains of many *sacbes* (causeways), raised above the boggy ground. Like a spider's web, the Maya equivalent of motorways made up a network of routes connecting Cobá with all parts of the peninsula. With no navigable waterways in the region, all transport had to be by foot, and the long, straight *sacbes* replaced rivers as the main trade routes. (Astonishingly, the highly civilized Maya never used either the beast of burden or the wheel, despite the fact that their children played with intricate wheeled toys.)

GETTING AROUND
Cobá is 42 km northwest of Tulum village, signposted from Highway 307. At the ruins themselves, a 2-km side road leads off to the site entrance. The main road continues on to Nuevo X-Cán and Highway 180, the cross-peninsular road linking Cancún to Mérida. Two inconvenient and erratic second-class buses leave Tulum early in the morning: hitching, or hiring a car or a taxi are all better options.

VISITING THE SITE

Cobá thrived between AD 550 and 950, and then sank back into the jungle. Propitiously surrounded by five lakes, it was one of the few sites in northern Yucatán to enjoy an adequate water supply. It was built on marshy ground in deep rain forest, and many of the finely detailed monuments have since been eroded by the damp. Conversely, these conditions are ideal for captivating electric blue, orange and yellow butterflies, and numerous bird species, including toucans, egrets, herons and mot-mots with their long, delicate tail feathers and mournful calls. The high jungle would also have sheltered spider monkeys, wild boar, deer, pheasant and ocellated turkeys (*Agriocharis ocellata*), now much diminished in numbers.

Guides can help to sort out temples from trees. Alternatively, a map at the entrance shows clearly marked tracks. Head first for **La Iglesia**, the so-called Church Pyramid. It was built in nine rounded tiers, attaining a height of 24 m, traversed by steps which become ever more narrow. Until recently, the local Maya prayed for good crops and hunting to Stela 11, at its base. Satellite buildings surround it—a ball court, palaces and a temple, superimposed as each generation attempted to outdo its predecessor. Now nature has outdone them all as vines strangle the masonry and trees root tenaciously in the rubble.

Two km to the northeast, the towering **Nohoch Mul** is the highest pyramid on the peninsula, at 42 m exceeding both Chichén's Castillo and Uxmal's Adivino. Two stairways lead up from the south side. The temple on the top was decorated with a simple stucco frieze: representations of the inverted Descending God, often identified as the Bee God, are carved into the niches above the doorways.

The stone monuments at the foot of this and other temples are vanity mirrors to each successive ruler. These larger-than-life profiles, exquisitely carved on the delicate limestone, are draped in feathered headdresses and all the regalia of office. No record remains of the anonymous craftsmen.

WHERE TO STAY

One of Club-Med's highly successful archaeological hacienda-style hotels is 5 minutes from the ruins—**Villa Arqueológica Cobá** (book through the Chichén Itzá Club-Med, tel 985 62830, or in the US tel (800) 528 3100). It has an excellent restaurant, library and pool. Two small and extremely basic hotels, the **Isabel** and **El Bocadito**, are on the road in to the site.

Chetumal

Chetumal, the capital of Quintana Roo, was built at the end of the 19th century, to keep English loggers out and to maintain a Mexican presence on the border. Lacking in charm, with dull houses and broad modern streets, it is not a place to linger in, although after the ruinous expenses of the resorts further north, it's no-nonsense prices make it a sensible stop before going further south to Central America. The border point for Belize and thence to Guatemala, it is already Central American in character, with easy-going people, used to a cosmopolitan mix of race and colour. Afro-Carribeans and pink-cheeked army majors from Belize, Central Americans and Mexicans from all over the republic come to take advantage of its duty-free status (which lasts until 1996). Hotel lobbies are thronged with eclectic gatherings: archaeologists on their way down to Guatemala, buying last-minute provisions before heading into the jungle, sophisticated French journalists rushing off special reports, laden Mexicans, bags bulging with purchases, and startled Belize Englishmen, defiantly Anglo-Saxon in the face of tropical languor.

GETTING AROUND

By Bus: The big modern bus station is on Av Insurgentes, north of the centre, with hourly services to Cancún, Campeche, Mérida and Belize. Combis for Bacalar leave from Av Colón (between Belize and Héroes) every 20 minutes (30 mins).

By Car: South of Tulum, Highway 307 heads inland to pass through Felipe Carillo Puerto, the junction for Valladolid and Mérida, and the site of the 'Talking Cross' (an important Mayan oracle which became a symbol for revolt in the 19th century: see History, The Yucatán Pensinsula). Some 243 km of long straight road cuts through interminable low-lying jungle, finally rejoining the coast at the port of Chetumal.

TOURIST INFORMATION

The **tourist office** is in the Palacio de Gobierno, on Héroes where it hits the waterfront. It is closed at weekends and between 14.00 and 18.00. The **Guatemalan consulate** is in Obregón 342 (tel 21365; open 09.00–14.00, Mon–Fri). Visas are necessary for Guatemala but not for Belize. Banks will change currency between 09.00 and 13.00: try Bancomer at Héroes 6 or Banamex between Obregón and Juárez.

WHAT TO SEE AND DO

The shops, particularly those in Héroes, the main street, attract frantic custom, and are filled with cut-price typewriters and cheap booze. A mix of Yucatecan *jaraña* and Belizean Caribbean music plays on discount music machines everywhere. In contrast to this commercial modernity, the town still retains many brightly painted wooden 'New Orleans' houses, often built on stilts, which have been declared of historic importance and so can't be pulled down. Look in 5 de Mayo and down by the waterfront.

Laguna Bacalar

North of Chetumal (36 km), the small town of Bacalar sits on the shore of Lake Bacalar, known as the Lake of Seven Colours for the different hues it takes on as the sun strikes it from different angles during the day. It still has clear warm waters and has become a favourite weekend spot, with a few small hotels. During the week, it is empty and wonderfully refreshing. Above the lake a squat fortress stands guard, built to repulse pirates. It now houses a few Maya remains, including the symbols of a phallic cult whose sodomistic overtones so horrified the Spanish that they attempted to destroy all traces. The fort was seized by the Maya during the War of the Castes and held until Quintana Roo was finally conquered by Díaz's forces in 1902.

Kohunlich

(See The State of Campeche for the ruins of Kohunlich, 65 km west of Chetumal, near the Quintana Roo–Campeche border.)

WHERE TO STAY   (area code 983)
There isn't a big choice in **Chetumal**. Its best hotel is the ****del Prado**, which is modern and comfortable, with cable television and a swimming pool. **Quintana Roo** (Obregón 193, east of Héroes) has big rooms with fans and bathrooms. The alternative, at the bottom end of the scale, is *El Dorado** (5 de Mayo with Blanco, tel 20315), which offers a bed with a fan and no more.

If time allows, it is worth going 36 km north to **Bacalar**. ****Rancho Encantado** (write in advance to the North American owners, PO Box 1644, Taos, New Mexico 87571, USA, tel 505 758 3065, or risk it and just turn up) is signed to the east off the main Chetumal–Cancún highway. Four enchanting log cabins are set in a large well-maintained garden. The sympathetic owners built them originally for visiting archaeologists and have a large library of books on the Maya and Mexico. The food is delicious and water skiing, windsurfing and walks can be laid on.

Around the lake itself, ***Las Lagunas** has comfortable rooms and a pool. There are also a few cheaper places nearby, for hammocks or tents.

EATING OUT
Chetumal has no unmissable restaurants. Ask what the regional dish is, and you'll be told 'rice an' beans', borrowed from English-speaking Belize. The rice is cooked in coconut milk and coconuts are used as much as possible—even fish is fried in its oil. In most restaurants, plates come piled high with rice, beans, fried chicken and bananas.

Machacados are refreshing drinks of crushed ice, fruit and milk. Try them in **Machacados** (Blvd Bahía with Vicente Guerrero).

Rocamar (Calz Veracruz with Blanco) is a decent Lebanese restaurant, patronized by the large Lebanese community. Moderate. The **Puente al Sol** (Blvd Bahía, on the seafront) has a palapa roof and specializes in seafood. It can also arrange boat trips for guests, out on the lagoon. Moderate. For good rice and beans, try **Dora María** (Obregón with Madero and Independencia: the entrance is all to easy to pass). Cheap. In the evening, foreigners and locals congregate in the street café of the Hotel del Prado for shots of tequila or coffee.

Outside Chetumal, on the road to Bacalar, the large, blue **Cenote Azul** has a pleasant restaurant serving fresh lobster and fish. Moderate. Six km north of Chetumal, palapa huts around the seafront village of **Calderitas** serve freshly fried fish, seafood cocktails and lashings of beer. Cheap.

The State of Campeche

The western third of the Yucatán peninsula, the state of Campeche makes its living from fertile farming lands and the large deposits of oil off its coast. It largely ignores and is ignored by tourists, who pass through on their way between Mérida and Palenque. The city of Campeche is a charming crumble of colonial architecture and there are plenty of lesser-known sites to visit around the state. Along the Gulf coast, between the city and Ciudad del Carmen in the south, deserted beaches are fringed with palm.

The state of Campeche was once peppered with important Maya centres, both religious and civic, such as Calakmul and Río Bec. The Spanish met strong resistance from the Itzá and Cocome tribes and the area was not conquered until 1540, when Villa San Francisco de Campeche was founded on top of the city of Ah Kin Pech. Campeche was not allowed to rest on its laurels for long. It was besieged by Dutch and English pirates on and off throughout the 17th century. In desperation, its citizens erected thick, 2.5-m defensive walls, which completely encircled the city by the end of the century. Campeche now shares with Cartagena de Indios in Columbia the honour of having more defensive walls than any other city in Latin America. The attempt to keep marauding bucaneers at bay was not always successful: on more than one occasion, this, the most important port in the Yucatán peninsula, was ravaged by pirates looting African slaves and precious woods, from their base in the nearby port of Ciudad del Carmen.

Campeche

The city of Campeche, the state capital, is Mérida's poor relation, with the air of a moderately distressed gentlewoman, clutching at the remains of her fading lace and unable to conceal gaping seams. Its colonial pedigree was forced into an alliance with brass when oil was discovered in the Gulf. Enclosed within the city walls are narrow, cobbled streets, tall town houses and small family-run shops which support the towns-people and the itinerant sailors, fishermen and farmers who visit this comparative metropolis. Formerly grand hotels, built during the boom years of the 1960s, now lack something of their former lustre, like ageing beauty queens. Crumbling buildings, once inhabited in solitary splendour by wealthy landowners, now echo to to the sounds of a number of families, their peeling facades appearing to have suffered yet another pirate attack.

GETTING AROUND
By Air: Campeche has a small airport, to the south of the city, with regular flights to Mexico City. These are often fully booked: the nearest alternatives are Mérida to the north, or Ciudad del Carmen to the south.
By Bus: The first-class bus station is a 30-minute walk to the east of the centre, on Av Gobernadores where it crosses Calle Chile. Hourly buses run to and from Mérida (2 hrs) and Villahermosa (6 hrs). There are three buses a day to Chetumal and two to Mexico City.
By Car: Highway 180 crosses Campeche, on its way from Mérida in the north of the peninsula to Ciudad del Carmen in the southwest. South of Campeche, at Champotón, Highway 261 branches south off 180, joining up with Highway 186, the main road from Chetumal to Villahermosa.
In Town: Town buses, marked 'Centro', connect the bus station on Gobernadores with the centre. Taxis are cheap.
Campeche was laid out on a grid pattern and all streets are numbered. Av Ruíz Cortínes runs along the sea front, north–south. Parallel to it, and the sea, are Av 16 de Septiembre and then Calles 8 to 18. Calles 65 to 51 run east–west. These streets comprise the old city, the most interesting part of Campeche, within the city walls. A fast road, the Circuito, encircles the city outside the walls.

TOURIST INFORMATION
The friendly tourist office is set in a cement bunker on the sea front (Av Ruíz Cortínez 16, tel 65593).

WHAT TO SEE

Plaza Principal
If you want to have your shoes shined, buy chewing gum, drink coffee, listen to the band or just sit and watch the world go by, head straight for the Plaza Principal (off Calle 10 between 57 and 55). Campechan dances are performed here every Thursday evening. Off the square sits the Yucatán's oldest cathedral, built in 1540, and a more exciting **archaeological museum** (Calle 8), filled with stelae from nearby sites. These eroded pictures, carved on worn limestone, are well presented, accompanied by helpful explanations and drawings.

Baluartes
Campeche is a paradise for naval historians, with enough cannons, blunderbusses and forts to last a lengthy visit. To find them, walk a circuit of the old walls, known as the **Circuito Baluartes**. En route, visit the Baluarte de San Carlos with its dungeon and scale models of the various fortifications, Baluarte de Santiago with its botanical garden, Baluarte de San Pedro with its exhibition of regional crafts, and Baluarte de San Miguel, on the outskirts of the city, with its archaeological museum filled with Maya artefacts.

Museo Regional
(Calle 59; open 09.00–20.00, Tues–Sat; 09.00–13.00, Sun; closed Mon.)
The russet- and mustard-coloured colonial facade of the museum dominates its narrow street. Inside are a variety of displays devoted to the history of the state, from the early settlers, the development of Maya kingdoms, the arrival of the Spanish, the perils of pirates and the power of the monasteries, and on through various revolts to the wealth of the 19th-century sugar-cane hacienda owners. It is well laid out and clearly labelled.

Casa de la Cultura
The Casa de la Cultura occupies an ex-Jesuit monastery with a mosaic facade, on Calle 10. Its right-hand bell tower has been converted into a lighthouse. It houses temporary exhibitions, usually from within the state.

SHOPPING
Campeche is famed for its Panama hats from nearby Becal, handmade in subterranean caves which maintain the right humidity. These are sold in the market, to the east of town and in many shops.

WHERE TO STAY
The hotels reflect Campeche itself. In the 1960s, the interiors of old colonial mansions were given a final injection to turn them into hotels, but since then time has failed to move them on and standards have fallen genteelly low.

In town, on the sea front, the ******Baluartes** (Ruíz Cortínes, tel 63911) is the oldest of the hotels built to accommodate the oil boom. Its rooms are furnished in an unappetizing mixture of brown carpets, custard-yellow curtains and tangy-orange bed covers. The friendly service is more than an apology. Next to it, the executive *****Presidente (Rúiz Cortínes, tel 62233) has a little more spark and its 119 rooms all have a sea view.

The **América (Calle 10, no 252, tel 64588) has black and white tiled floors, balconies with rocking chairs and basic clean rooms, each with its own bathroom. Further down the same street, **Posada del Angel (Calle 10, no 309, tel 67718) is functional, with dark claustrophobic rooms. The run-down but charming *Castlemar (Calle 61, no 2) prefers to offer its guests a chest of drawers with no shelves rather than not offer them anything at all. Its rooms provide a bare minimum of comfort, with bathrooms attached. The **Colonial (Calle 40, no 122) is small and friendly, set in a colonial building filled with 1930s furniture. The **López (Calle 12, tel 63344) grandiosly gives itself two stars, but even the taxi drivers warn against it. Looking like a jaunty ocean liner, it conceals dark dingy rooms behind banistered balconies, which could only be welcome as a last resort. More upmarket, the modern, Moorish-looking ***Alhambra (2 km out of town on the road to Ciudad del Carmen) has a cinema and swimming pool, and is much frequented by businessmen.

WHERE TO EAT
The place to eat in Campeche is the Miramar (Calle 8 and 61), renowned for its seafood and always packed. Old-fashioned waiters in white jackets bring plates of *botanas* and squid soup, grilled fish and *ceviche* (raw seafood cocktails). The Poquito restaurant in the Presidente hotel is another popular spot for coffees and snacks. A number of cafés and simple restaurants are set around the main square. Natura 2000 (Calle 12 with 59; open 08.00–16.30) provides refreshing fare—huge plates of fruit, yoghurt and granola, and set lunches which end with thick home-made mango ice cream.

Edzná

Out of the way, but well worth a visit, the site of Edzná has only recently received attention. Guatemalan refugees were set to work clearing the site in the 1980s, enabling archaeologists to move in and discover traces of far earlier civilizations than had previously been imagined. The remains of the city bear witness to its waxing and waning fortunes, providing an architectural record of each successive invader.

History
Recent discoveries in Edzná suggest it may have been inhabited from as early as 800 BC, although palapa-roofed structures dating from AD 250 provide the earliest indication of a permanent city. Between AD 300 and 450 the city seems to have been influenced by a number of regions, including the Puuc region to the north, Guatemala and Tikal in the Petén. By 450 it had assumed its own identity and acquired a huge population of 70,000, controlling the surrounding area and exacting tribute from other smaller cities, including nearby Campeche. By 650 it began to show the symptoms of a mysterious decline, caused possibly by the destruction of its own environment, by dynastic weakness or by

in-fighting. By 800, the degenerate Edzná was ripe for invasion by the powerful cities of the Río Bec and Chenes to the southeast. The conquerors sacked the city, destroying much of the Petén architecture and remoulding it in their own style, as a mark of cultural conquest.

GETTING AROUND

The site of Edzná is about 60 km east of Campeche, and is best reached by private transport. Take eastbound Highway 180 (the Mérida road) out of Campeche, and after about 28 km bear east on Highway 261. At Cayal (14 km), fork right for Edzná (a further 19 km).

A local bus leaves Campeche at 07.30 and returns at 11.00. Tours (including the hire of a guide and a car) are easier but more expensive.

A sleepy vendor sells fizzy drinks at the entrance, but it's advisable to take your own water. In addition, take plenty of insect repellent, as the site seems to attract the entire mosquito population of Campeche during the rainy season.

VISITING THE SITE

Considered a peripheral part of the Petén and contemporary with Tikal and Dzibilchaltún, Edzná also shows strong traces of the Chenes, who invaded the city. Characteristics of the Petén are buildings with terraces, acropoli, stuccoed decoration and elevated temples with little space inside. Although the city's name is spelt 'Edzná' on all the signposts, it was in fact known as 'Itzná', which suggests a later cultural influence from nearby Chichén-Itzá. A number of stelae were found buried to the south of the main Pyramid of the Five Niches, the last one dated AD 726. These would have been ripped down and buried by the conquering Chenes forces. They are now displayed at the entrance, beneath a palapa roof.

PYRAMID OF THE FIVE NICHES AND THE GRAND ACROPOLIS

The pyramid dominates the site from the east, showing a marked variety of architectural styles. A long central stairway leads up to a small temple with a distinctive roof comb. Every year, on 3 May (and again on 8 August), the sun hits the exact spot marked by a fading stela in the centre of the temple. The date marks the beginning of the Maya agricultural year and the phenomenon would have been watched from the terraces opposite. Each of the five levels of the pyramid can be reached from the main staircase. The sun's rays centre directly on the doorway of each of the chambers once a year, on dates which would have been linked with other festivals.

The temple's walls were once adorned with huge masks of gods and priests. The Chenes invaders altered this original Petén facade, covering it with worked stone and adding mouldings to each layer. The pillars on the bottom level are built up of piled stones, betraying a Río Bec influence which contrasts with the monolithic early Puuc columns of the fourth floor.

TEMPLE OF THE MASKS

Dating from between AD 300 and 600, the temple to the south of the Grand Acropolis is lined with stuccoed masks representing the Sun God. The cross-eyed squint was synonymous with great beauty in the Maya world, while the fringe of hair was a sign of deity, also worn by priests. The single tooth represented the regeneration of life, and the well-fed jowly face and protruding lips were other symbols of this all-important god. As if these signs weren't clear enough, a cross was added—the ultimate portent of a celestial being.

BALL COURT

In front of the Temple of the Masks is a narrow ball court, originally stuccoed, similar to the one in Tikal. Its two goal markers were torn down by the raiding Chenes: one was found to the north of the site.

THE TRIBUNE

Opposite the Acropolis, the Gran Tribune was used as an amphitheatre, directly overlooking the main temple. Its 15 tiers of steps served as hard seats, accommodating almost 5000 people for religious events.

PALACE OF THE KNIVES

To the northwest of the main temple, this palace owes its name to the number of offertory knives which were found inside. It is clearly divided into rooms, which probably

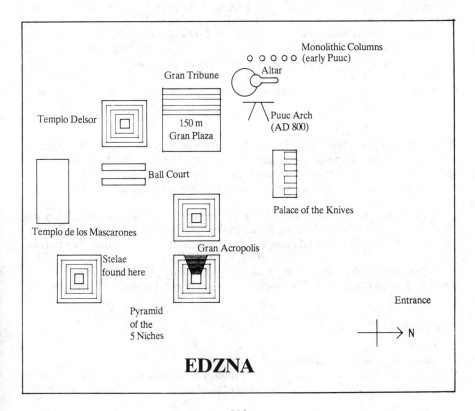

EDZNA

513

served as royal or priestly quarters. Each has a raised platform, on which its occupant would sleep under a palapa roof.

To the west of the palace, between it and the Tribune, there is an altar in the shape of a ball-court marker (like a baby's dummy). One of the original markers was buried underneath it, by Chene conquerors. Beside it remains a solitary Puuc arch. Signs of a *sacbe* or raised road have been found between the arch and the main temple: these would once have surrounded the whole city. There is also evidence of *choltúns*, or concrete tanks, in which water for the city would have been collected.

The Río Bec Sites on Highway 186

This east–west road cuts through one of the least inhabited parts of the Yucatán peninsula. The recently approved Calakmul Biosphere Reserve encompasses 60 known sites within its 730,000 hectares, stretching south of Highway 186 into the rain forest. These were hidden until gum gatherers stumbled over them in their endless search for gum from the sapodilla tree.

These late Classic sites (AD 700–900) are collectively named after their archaeological prototype at Río Bec, in which chambers are flanked by towers made to look like pyramids. The structures were not in themselves particularly large or monumental but were aggrandized by the later addition of roof combs (stylized, stucco-faced balconies), doorways in the shape of gaping mouths, and lavish ornamentation, repeated in a modified form in the better known Puuc sites of Uxmal, Kabah, Labná and Sayil. Situated in southern Campeche, on the border with Quintana Roo, they occupy the geographical boundary between the scrubland of the northern Yucatán and the rain-forest of the Petén to the south.

GETTING AROUND
The sites are on the first 100 km of Highway 186 between Chetumal and Francisco Escárcega, near the Campeche–Quintana Roo border. The long, straight road has little traffic and passes few villages. Buses are loath to stop at or pick up passengers from the ruins. Hire cars and tours are available in Chetumal (ask at the Hotel Continental or the Hotel del Prado).

All the sites described below can be visited in one (long) day, from Chetumal. They are all on Highway 186, except Kohunlich, just in the state of Quintana Roo, which is 9 km off the highway (65 km from Chetumal), down a little used side road from the village of Francisco Villa.

Visits to several other sites off the road, such as Calakmul, Hormiguero and Río Bec, require special organization. The tourist offices in either Chetumal or Campeche can give advice.

VISITING THE SITES
Kohunlich
(Open 08.00–1700; closed Mon.)
The Maya-sounding name is actually a derivation of the English 'Cahoon Ridge', named after a mahogany logger. It is superbly situated, looking out over palm, *ceiba* and *amate*

trees to the invisible borders of Belize and Guatemala. Palm trees crawl over the mounds, spreading their branches like peacock tails. President López-Portillo had an entire symphony orchestra flown in to play for him in these ruins.

Kohunlich is an early Classic site (AD 300–600) with one outstanding pyramid, the Temple of the Masks. The path from the car park leads in past the main plaza, made up of a quadrangle with two facing temples. Each one was adorned with several stelae on the upper platform but most have been removed. Both the plaza and the crucial reservoir (a large floor on the way to the Temple of the Masks) would have had smooth limestone floors to catch the rain water.

The path leads past the reservoir and a sacrificial altar stone to the 21-m-high **Temple of the Masks**. A flight of steep, narrow steps leads up to a double-chambered sanctuary at the top. When the archaeologist Victor Segovia began excavations in the early 1960s, it had already been looted by grave robbers and its contents have disappeared without trace. Four stucco masks, however, remain in place. (Originally, there were two on each of the three tiers.) Each mask is 2 m high and was originally painted black, red and white in celebration of the Maya Sun God, Kinich Ahau. The bottom right-hand mask shows an encircling serpent, coiling round from its forked tongue and eye in the top left-hand corner to its tail in the bottom left-hand corner. The eyes were incised with hieroglyphs, the ears pierced with nose pieces, the moustache tweaked into shape and the teeth filed down to a T. The temple itself would have been covered over with a plaster-like stucco and painted red (traces of which remain): the small, irregularly shaped bricks were never meant to be visible.

The Other Sites

Xpujil is 59 km west of Kohunlich, 100 m off the road, visible from the road by virtue of the spiky points of the three towers along the terrace. These towers were embellished with elevating roof combs and a false door like a gaping serpent's mouth, probably associated with Itzamná, the Creation God. Curiously, only the south tower has a stairway leading up to the roof; the other two certainly have steps, but the treads are too narrow to be used. The building they enclose, now in ruins, would have had several chambers.

Six km on and 600 m off to the right, **Becán** was once a great city, surrounded by a moat-like stream crossed by 2-m foot-bridges, which made it a well-fortified island. Although it is now dry, the moat is nevertheless one of the oldest defensive constructions in Mexico. Becán's temples are more varied than those in the other Río Bec sites, particularly the pyramid on the north side of the central plaza which would have enclosed several rooms. The main construction has two flat-topped pyramids, similar to Xpujil's. Paths lead further back into the scrub jungle, away from the main complex, passing mounds and ruins, half-buried, half-uncovered.

The third of this close-knit group, **Chicanná**, is 2 km further on and 700 m to the left. A simple three-doored temple in the small plaza is beautifully decorated with geometric stucco inlays. The central doorway is a great fanged mouth, its sabre teeth hanging over the entrance. Masks of Chac, the Rain God, hang on corners, mounted in tiers for effect.

Points of Communication

Escárcega

This dirty town has nothing to recommend it but is an unavoidable junction, at the crossroads of Highway 186 between Chetumal and Villahermosa, and Highway 261 from Campeche.

GETTING AROUND

Escárcega is a major changeover point between buses to the north and the west. The main bus station is on Highway 261, the main road to Campeche. First-class buses go in and out all the time, bound for Campeche (2 hrs), Mérida (4 hrs), Chetumal (4 hrs), Chiapas and Tabasco. The second-class bus station, for buses to Palenque (2 hrs), is on Justo Sierra and Calle 31. It's a quick taxi ride from one to the other but just too far to walk with any luggage.

WHERE TO STAY AND EAT

As first-class buses are often fully booked, it is quite easy to get caught for the night. A few hotels around the first-class bus station have been tailor-made for this eventuality. Of these, the **Akim-Pech** (off Highway 186, the road to Chetumal, 100 m from the first-class bus station) is the best, with clean rooms and hot showers. The spartan restaurant downstairs doesn't go in for anything fancy, relying on the usual selection of egg and bean dishes. The **María Isabel** (Av Justo Sierra 127, near the second-class bus station) is a good second best. Both bus stations have cafeterias and are surrounded by cafés selling *poc chuc* (spicy pork) and *pollo pibil* (chicken cooked in banana leaves).

Ciudad del Carmen

If domestic flights from Mérida and Campeche are booked up, Ciudad del Carmen is a good option. The airport, however, is the main lure of this beginning-to-sprawl oil and fishing port.

The drive from Campeche is in itself another attraction. Highway 180 runs for 212 km parallel to the coast, through green fields and fishing villages where the long poles used to punt the boats double as perches for flocks of pelicans. In August and September, octopus is the main catch and all the restaurants serve *pulpo* in a variety of forms. These villages were badly damaged in the 1988 hurricanes. Further south, long strips of deserted beach are set amidst Rousseau jungles of palms.

GETTING AROUND

Ciudad del Carmen is on an island, linked to the mainland state of Campeche by a series of long bridges and to next-door Tabasco by ferry.

The airport is to the east of town, with two daily flights to and from Mexico City. First-class buses connect the town with Mérida (5 hrs) via Campeche (3 hrs), Escárcega (2 hrs) and Villahermosa (3 hrs).

WHERE TO STAY

It's better to fly straight out of Ciudad del Carmen. *In extremis*, try **Zacarís** (Calle 24, no 701, tel 20121, just off the Zócalo), a standard Mexican family hotel. The **Isla del Carmen** (Calle 20A, no 9) is more up-market and nearer the airport.

GLOSSARY OF
ARCHITECTURAL TERMS

Adobe: mud brick dried in the sun.

Altar: table for celebration of Mass; in Mexico also used for *retablo* behind the table.

Apse: polygonal or curved recess at the altar end of the church, generally the east.

Atrium: the space in front of a church, usually enclosed or raised on a terrace.

Azulejo: painted glazed tiles popular in mudéjar work.

Baroque: a style of architecture common to the Western world during the 17th and 18th centuries, characterized by excessive ornamentation.

Bóveda: vault.

Capilla abierta: an open chapel. In 16th-century monasteries, these were often adjacent to the church and consecrated for Mass.

Caryatids: human female figures often used ornamentally on estípitic columns.

Churrigueresque: florid baroque style from Spain, erroneously named after a Spanish architect, a variation of which arrived in Mexico in the 18th century.

Convento: a Spanish word applied to both monasteries and convents, though more usually to the former in 16th-century Mexico.

Corbel: a stone or wooden bracket, usually built into a wall to support a beam or vault section.

Estípite: a pillar in the shape of an inverted obelisk, commonly used during the mid-18th century.

Mudéjar: ornamental, particularly geometric form, produced by Christians under Muslim rule in Spain.

Plateresque: heavily ornamented architectural and decorative style, combining late gothic and Renaissance with mudéjar features.

Retablo: carved or painted altarpiece. In Mexico, also used for small votive paintings.

Salamonic column: a column with a twisted shaft, often covered with grapes and vines.

Tezontle: reddish volcanic stone or pumice.

LANGUAGE

The official language of Mexico is Spanish, but without the affected lisped 's' of Spain. Mexican Spanish is generally easier to read and pronounce and more open to North American slang and expressions. In addition, another 30-odd languages are spoken in different regions by different peoples. Survivors from the days before the Spanish, 500 years ago, these resilient languages are most often heard at markets, in buses and in many of the mountain villages. In parts of Oaxaca, Chiapas, Michoacán and the Yucatán, there are still villages where only a very few people speak Spanish, although as the language of commerce it always wins over tradition eventually. When the Spanish first arrived, the Aztec language of Nahuatl was spoken throughout central Mexico. Many, many words that are now part and parcel of Mexican Spanish are, in fact, of Nahuatl origin. Many have achieved international currency, such as 'tomato', 'chocolate' and 'avocado'.

Spanish courses are provided by schools in many of the major cities. The University of Mexico (UNAM) in Mexico City (tel (5) 548 6500) offers several graded classes. So does a plethora of private language schools, especially in Cuernavaca, San Miguel de Allende and Oaxaca (see relevant sections). The state-sponsored fine arts institute, the Instituto Nacional de Bellas Artes (INBA), has 38 schools, including one in each state capital. These offer a wide range of courses, from painting and dancing to Italian and German, including Spanish classess wherever there are the numbers to justify it.

The BBC has an excellent book, tape and television course on Latin American Spanish, called *México Vivo* and set in Mexico City, which is undoubtedly the best self-teaching course available.

Pronunciation of Spanish in Mexico

Unlike the Spanish of Madrid, Mexicans pronounce the letters 'c' or 'z' before an 'e' or 'i' as 's'. (In Madrid, these are pronounced with a lisping 'th', as in 'thin'.)

The letter 'j' is pronounced 'h' in Mexico and not 'ch' (like 'loch') as in Spain.

In Mexico, 'll' is pronounced with the 'y' of 'yard', and not the 'lli' of 'billion'.

The letter 'x' can be pronounced in at least four different ways: 'h' as in México (*MEHEECO*); 'sh' as in Uxmal (*OOSHMAL*); 'ks' as in Necaxa (*NECAKSA*); or 's' as in Xochimilco (*SOCHIMEELCO*).

Other Consonants

b	–in the middle of a word, often pronounced as 'v'
g	–before 'e' or 'i', pronounced as a hard 'h'
h	–usually silent
ñ	–'ny' as in 'canyon'
q	–as 'k'
r	–usually rolled

Vowels

a	–short as in 'father'
e	–short as in 'set'
i	–long 'e' as in 'complete'
o	–long as in 'for'
u	–long as in 'flute'
ie	–both vowels pronounced separately
ue	–short 'e' (the 'u' is silent)
üe	–'we' as in 'dwell'

Stress is on the penultimate syllable if the word ends in a vowel, on the last syllable if the word ends in a consonant. Exceptions are marked with an accent (´).

519

Useful Words and Phrases

yes	*sí*
no	*no*
I don't know	*No sé*
I don't understand (Spanish)	*No entiendo (Español)*
Does someone here speak English?	*¿Hay alguien que hable inglés?*
Speak slowly	*Hable usted despacio*
Can you assist me?	*¿Puede usted ayudarme?*
help!	*¡Socorro!*
please	*por favor*
thank you (very much)	*(muchas) gracias*
you're welcome	*de nada*
It doesn't matter	*no importa*
all right	*está bien*
excuse me	*perdóneme*
be careful!	*¡Tenga cuidado!*
maybe	*quizás*
nothing	*nada*
It is urgent!	*¡Es urgente!*
How do you do?	*¿Cómo está usted?*
Well, and you?	*¿Bien, y usted?*
What is your name?	*¿Como se llama?*
hello	*¡Hola!*
goodbye	*Adiós/Hasta luego*
good morning	*Buenos días*
good afternoon	*Buenas tardes*
good evening	*Buenas noches*
What is that?	*¿Qué es eso?*
what	*qué*
who	*quién*
where	*dónde*
when	*cuándo*
why	*por qué*
how	*cómo*
how much	*cuánto*
how many	*cuántas*
I am lost	*Estoy perdido*
I am hungry	*Tengo hambre*
I am thirsty	*Tengo sed*
I am sorry	*Lo siento*
I am tired	*Estoy cansado*
I am sleepy	*Tengo sueño*
I am ill	*No me siento bien*
Leave me alone	*Déjeme en paz*
good	*bueno/buena*
bad	*malo/mala*
it's all the same	*es igual*
slow	*despacio*
fast	*rápido*
big	*grande*
small	*pequeño*

hot	*caliente*
cold	*frío*
up	*arriba*
down	*abajo*

SHOPPING/SIGHTSEEING

I would like...	*quisiera...*
where is/are...	*dónde está/están...*
how much is it?	*¿cuánto cuesta eso?*
open	*abierto*
closed	*cerrado*
cheap/expensive	*barato/caro*
bank	*banco*
beach	*playa*
bed	*cama*
church	*iglesia*
hospital	*hospital*
money	*dinero*
museum	*museo*
newspaper (foreign)	*periódico (extranjero)*
pharmacy	*farmacia*
police station	*comisaría*
policeman	*policía*
post office	*correos*
sea	*mar*
shop	*tienda*
telephone	*teléfono*
toilet/toilets	*servicios/baños*
men	*señores/hombres/ caballeros*
women	*señoras/damas*

TIME

what time is it?	*qué hora es?*
month	*mes*
week	*semana*
day	*día*
morning	*mañana*
afternoon	*tarde*
evening	*noche*
today	*hoy*
yesterday	*ayer*
soon	*pronto*
tomorrow	*mañana*
now	*ahora*
later	*despues*
early	*temprano*
late	*tarde*

DAYS

Monday	*lunes*
Tuesday	*martes*
Wednesday	*miércoles*
Thursday	*jueves*

Friday	viernes
Saturday	sábado
Sunday	domingo

NUMBERS

one	uno/una
two	dos
three	tres
four	cuatro
five	cinco
six	seis
seven	siete
eight	ocho
nine	nueve
ten	diez
eleven	once
twelve	doce
thirteen	trece
fourteen	catorce
fifteen	quince
sixteen	dieciséis
seventeen	diecisiete
eighteen	dieciocho
nineteen	diecinueve
twenty	veinte
twenty one	veintiuno
thirty	treinta
forty	cuarenta
fifty	cincuenta
sixty	sesenta
seventy	setenta
eighty	ochenta
ninety	noventa
one hundred	cien
one hundred and one	ciento uno
five hundred	quinientos
one thousand	mil

TRANSPORT

airport	aeropuerto
bus stop	parada
bus/coach	autobús/camión
railway station	estación de tren
train	tren
port	puerto
port station	terminal marítima o embarcadero
ship	buque/barco/embarcadero
automobile	coche
ticket	boleto
customs	aduana
seat	asiento

TRAVEL DIRECTIONS

I want to go to...	Deseo ir a...
How can I get to...?	¿Cómo puedo llegar a...?
Do you stop at...?	¿Para en...?
Where is...?	¿Dónde está...?
When is the next...?	¿Cuándo sale el próximo...?
From which stop does it leave?	¿De dónde sale?
How long does the trip take?	¿Cuánto tiempo dura el viaje?
How much is the fare?	¿Cuánto cuesta el boleto?
Good trip!	¡Buen viaje!
here	aquí
there	allí
close	cerca
far	lejos
full	lleno
left	izquierda
right	derecha
forward	hacia adelante
backward	para atrás
north	norte/septentrional
south	sud/sur/meridional
east	este/oriente
west	oeste/occidente
corner	esquina
square	plaza

DRIVING

rent	alquilar
car	coche
motorbike/moped	motocicleta/motoneta
bicycle	bicicleta
petrol	gasolina
garage	garaje
This doesn't work	Esto no funciona
mechanic	mecánico
map	mapa
Where is the road to?	¿Dónde está el camino a...?
Is the road good?	¿Es buena la carretera?
breakdown	avería
(international) Driver's licence	licencia (internacional)
driver	conductor, chofer
speed	velocidad
exit	salida
entrance	entrada
danger	peligro
no parking	estacionamento prohibido

narrow	*estrecha*	*huachinango*	red snapper
yield	*ceda el paso*	*langosta*	lobster
How far is it?	*¿Qué tan lejos está?*	*langostino*	giant prawns
Is there a mechanic	*¿Hay algún taller cerca?*	*lenguado*	sole
nearby?		*mariscos*	shellfish
Fill up with petrol	*Llene el tanque de*	*mejillones*	mussels
	gasolina	*mero*	halibut
Give me 20 litres	*Deme veinte litros*	*ostras*	oysters
My tyre has a	*Mi llanta se ponché*	*pez espada*	swordfish
puncture		*pulpo*	octopus
		raya	skate
		salmón	salmon

Menu and Restaurant Vocabulary

ENTREMESAS Y	HORS D'OEUVRES AND	*sardinas*	sardines
HUEVOS	EGGS	*trucha*	trout
alcachofas con mayonesa	artichokes with	*zarzuela*	fish stew
	mayonnaise		
ancas de rana	frog legs	*CARNES Y AVES*	MEAT AND FOWL
aceitunas	olives	*albóndigas*	meatballs
caldo	broth	*asado*	roast
entremeses variados	assorted hors d'oeuvres	*bistek*	beefsteak
huevos a la méxicana	scrambled eggs with	*cerdo*	pork
	chilli and tomato	*chorizo*	spiced sausage
huevos rancheros	baked eggs in tomato	*chuletas*	chops
	sauce	*conejo*	rabbit
gazpacho	cold soup	*corazón*	heart
huevos al plato	fried eggs	*cordero*	lamb
huevos revueltos	scrambled eggs	*faisán*	pheasant
sopa de arroz	rice soup	*filete*	fillet
sopa de espárragos	asparagus soup	*hígado*	liver
sopa de ajo	garlic soup	*jabalí*	wild boar
sopa de fideos	noodle soup	*jamón cocido*	baked ham
sopa de garbanzos	chick pea soup	*jamón serrano*	smoked ham
sopa de lentejas	lentil soup	*lechón*	suckling pig
sopa de verduras	vegetable soup	*lengua*	tongue
tortilla	flat, unleavened corn	*lomo*	pork loin
	or wheat pancake	*moronga*	blood sausage
tortilla española	Spanish omelette (with	*paloma*	pigeon
	potatoes)	*pancita*	tripe
		pato	duck
PESCADOS	FISH	*pavo*	turkey
anchoas	anchovies	*perdiz*	partridge
anguilas	eels	*pollo*	chicken
angulas	baby eels	*riñones*	kidneys
almejas	clams	*salchicha*	sausage
atún	tuna fish	*sesos*	brains
bacalao	codfish (usually dried)	*ternera*	beef
calamares (or	squid (*en su tinta*, in its		
chipirones)	own ink)		
camarones	prawns		
cangrejo	crab		
dorada	sea bass		
escabeche	pickled or marinated		
	fish		

*Note that *potajes, cocidos, guisadas, estofados, fabadas* and *cazuelas* are various kinds of stews.

VERDURAS	VEGETABLES
LEGUMBRES	
alcachofas	artichokes
apio	celery

arroz	rice	*queso*	cheese
berenjena	aubergine (eggplant)	*requesón*	soft white cheese
betabel	beetroots (beets)	*sandía*	watermelon
cebolla	onion	*tarta*	pie
champiñones	mushrooms	*toronja*	grapefruit
chícharos	green peas	*turrón*	nougat
col	cabbage	*uvas*	grapes
coliflor	cauliflower		
ejotes	French beans	BEBIDAS	BEVERAGES
endivias	endives	*agua mineral*	mineral water
ensalada	salad	*(Tehuacán) (sin/con*	(without/with fizz)
espárragos	asparagus	*gaz)*	
espinacas	spinach	*cerveza*	beer
garbanzos	chickpeas	*café (con leche)*	coffee (with milk)
hongos	Spanish mushrooms	*chocolate*	chocolate
lechuga	lettuce	*leche*	milk
lentejas	lentils	*licuado*	milkshake
papas	potatoes	*té (con limón)*	tea (with lemon)
papas fritas	fried potatoes	*vino (tinto, rosado,*	wine (red, rosé, white)
papas al horno	baked potatoes	*blanco)*	
pepino	cucumber		
pimento	pepper	OTHER WORDS	
poro	leeks	*aceite (de oliva)*	(olive) oil
zanahorias	carrots	*ajo*	garlic
		almuerzo/comida	lunch
		azúcar	sugar
FRUTAS Y POSTRES	FRUITS AND	*bocadillo*	sandwich
	DESSERTS	*cambio*	change
almendras	almonds	*carta*	menu
arroz con leche	rice pudding	*cena*	dinner
cerezas	cherries	*cuchara*	knife
chabacano	apricot	*cuchillo*	spoon
ciruelas	plums	*cuenta*	bill
ciruela pasa	prune	*desayuno*	breakfast
durazno	peach	*hielo*	ice
flan	custard (crême	*limón*	lemon
	caramel)	*mantequilla*	butter
flan con helado	flan with ice cream	*mermelada*	marmalade
frambuesas	raspberries	*mesa*	table
fresas (con crema)	strawberries (with	*mesero*	waiter
	cream)	*miel*	honey
galletas	biscuits (cookies),	*pan*	bread
	shortcake	*panecillo*	roll
helados	ice creams	*pastel de carne*	meat pie
higos	figs	*pimentón*	ground pepper
manzana	apple	*plata*	plate
melón	melon	*sal*	salt
naranja	orange	*salsa*	sauce
nieve	slush, iced squash	*servilleta*	napkin
pastel	cake	*taza*	cup
pasteles	pastries	*tenedor*	fork
pera	pear	*tostada*	toast
piña	pineapple	*vaso*	glass
plátano	banana	*vinagre*	vinegar

523

FURTHER READING

The books listed below (designed to weigh down already heavy suitcases) represent just a fraction of what is available. Copies can be bought in Mexico, or in specialized travel bookshops. The Canning Library in London's Belgrave Square also has every book listed.

Art
Kubler, George, *The Art and Architecture of Ancient America* (Pelican History of Art, 1962).
Heyden, Doris, and Gendrop, Paul, *Pre-Columbian Architecture of Meso-America* (Faber): a well-illustrated, in-depth study of the pre-Hispanic civilizations from an architectural standpoint.
Coe, Michael D, *The Maya* and *Mexico*; and Miller, Mary Ellen, *The Art of Mesoamerica* (Thames and Hudson): these concise companion volumes are written by Yale colleagues and together provide one of the best introductions to Mexico before the Spanish.
Sayer, Chloë, *Mexican Costume* (British Museum Publications, 1985) and *Arts and Crafts of Mexico* (Thames and Hudson): two excellent beginner's guides to the costumes, arts and crafts of Mexico.
Toussaint, Manuel, *Colonial Art in Mexico* (University of Texas Press, 1967).

Comment
Covarrubias, Miguel, *Mexico South* (Cassell): written and illustrated by the *Vanity Fair* caricaturist, muralist, painter and respected archaeologist, this book is a most sympathetic portrayal of the Isthmus of Tehuantepec, Oaxaca and Veracruz in the 1950s.
Riding, Alan, *Distant Neighbours* (Vintage): this book provides an indispensable insight into contemporary Mexico—it had the politicians steaming. Also published in Great Britain as *Inside the Volcano* (I B Tauris).
Paz, Octavio: the Nobel Prize-winning poet, author and man of letters is still the most revered writer in his country. The most outstanding of his many commentaries on Mexico is *The Labyrinth of Solitude* (Grove). His most recent study is *Sor Juana Inés de la Cruz* (Faber, 1989).
Lewis, Oscar, *The Children of Sánchez* and *Five Families*: first published in the 1940s, these two books are early studies in modern anthropology, based on the oral histories of an extended family in Mexico City and village life in Tepoztlán.
Franz, Carl, *The People's Guide to Mexico* (John Muir): endlessly reprinted and deserving of its near cult status, this anecdotal guide is indispensable for anyone planning longer visits to Mexico. Rest assured that whatever unforeseen eventuality may happen, it has already happened to Carl Franz and his friends.
Hatt, John, *The Tropical Traveller* (Penguin): an amusing guide to life in the Tropics, not specifically about Mexico, with invaluable advice on Anglo-Saxon survival in the heat and dust.
Kennedy, Diana, *The Cuisines of Mexico* (Harper and Row, 1986, and Lourdes Nichols, *Mexican Cookery* (Collins, 1984): the best of the many cookbooks.
Stephens, John Lloyd, *Incidents of Travel in Central America and the Yucatán* (Century): the North American Stephens and his English malaria-ridden companion, Frederick

Catherwood, were the first to bring the hidden ruins of southern Mexico to the eyes of the public; this book combines Stephens' phlegmatic text and Catherwood's romantic lithographs.

History

Meyer, Michael C, and Sherman, William L, *The Course of Mexican History* (OUP, 1987): for an extensive overview of Mexican history, from fossils to contemporary life, this fat book is the answer.

Gallenkamp, Charles, *Maya* (Penguin): a well-documented and very readable account of the Maya Empire.

Díaz, Bernal, *The True History of the Conquest of New Spain* (Penguin): this book by one of Cortés' companions stands as the Catholic-Spanish account of and justification for the conquest, written shortly after the event (partly as a redress for the disgraced Cortés). The sheer audacity of the original conquerors and the very human emotions of fear and wonder come across beautifully.

Reed, John, *Insurgent Mexico*: before Reed went on to greater fame and fortune with his *Ten Days that Shook the World* about the Russian Revolution, he wrote this account of living with Pancho Villa's troops throughout the 1910 Mexican Revolution.

Travel

The resounding clash and bang of the ordered Anglo-Saxon mind hitting the less obvious order of the Mexican has spawned a whole series of wonderfully funny, generally bad-tempered books on the country. Amongst the best are:

Bedford, Sybille, *A Visit to Don Otavio* (Eland): perhaps the best of the lot, this book written in the 1950s lyrically desribes Bedford's travels through the country, invariably accompanied by her friend, the nameless E.

Calderon de la Barca, Fanny, *Life in Mexico* (Century): the frank and amusing letters of the 19th-century Scottish wife of the first Spanish ambassador to be allowed into Mexico after independence.

Greene, Graham, *The Lawless Roads* and *The Power and the Glory* (various editions): the latter is the fictional outcome of the real journey Greene took, in excruciating discomfort, through southern Mexico when anticlerical feeling was at its height. He hated it and it hated him, and the clash created a travel classic.

Huxley, Aldous, *Beyond the Mexique Bay* (Grafton): in the few short chapters devoted to Mexico, Huxley extravagantly describes his horror of and fascination with the country.

Flandrau, Charles Macomb, *¡Viva Mexico!* (Eland); as relevant today as when it was first written in 1908—the author simply let Mexico wash over him and hilariously wrote down the results.

Fiction

After the great Octavio Paz, the most respected Mexican authors are Carlos Fuentes (*The Old Gringo, The Death of Artemio Cruz* and *Where the Air is Clear* amongst others), Jorge Ibargüengoitia (*Dead Girls*) and Juan Rulfo (*Pedro Paramo*). The best-known of all novels in English are Malcom Lowry's *Under the Volcano* about the last drunk day of a one-time British consul in Cuernavaca, and D H Lawrence's irritating *The Plumed Serpent* which tries to explain the Mexican mind on the strength of a few superficial weeks in the country.

Jack Kerouac made it to Mexico, and holed up with American GIs, in *Desolation Angels*, and Carlos Castaneda wrote a whole series of factional novels, known as the *Don Juan* series, on the search for inner truth through the use of peyote.

GENERAL INDEX

Note: Names of states are in **bold**. A list of abbreviations follows:

State	Abbreviation	Capital
Aguascalientes	Ags.	Aguascalientes
Baja California Norte	BCN	Mexicali
Baja California Sur	BCS	La Paz
Campeche	Camp.	Campeche
Coahuila	Coah.	Saltillo
Colima	Col.	Colima
Chiapas	Chis.	Tuxtla Gutiérrez
Chihuahua	Chih.	Chihuahua
Durango	Dgo.	Durango
Guanajuato	Gto.	Guanajuato
Guerrero	Gro.	Chilpancingo
Hidalgo	Hgo.	Pachuca
Jalisco	Jal.	Guadalajara
Mexico	Mex.	Toluca
Michoacán	Mich.	Morelia
Morelos	Mor.	Cuernavaca
Nayarit	Nay.	Tepic
Nuevo León	NL	Monterrey
Oaxaca	Oax.	Oaxaca
Puebla	Pue.	Puebla
Querétaro	Qro.	Querétaro
Quintana Roo	QR	Chetumal
San Luis Potosí	SLP	San Luis Potosí
Sinaloa	Sin.	Culiacán
Sonora	Son.	Hermosillo
Tabasco	Tab.	Villahermosa
Tamaulipas	Tamps.	Ciudad Victoria
Tlaxcala	Tlax.	Tlaxcala
Veracruz	Ver.	Jalapa
Yucatán	Yuc.	Mérida
Zacatecas	Zac.	Zacatecas

INDEX